CRIMINAL LAW CASES & MATERIALS

Peter Charleton

*B.A. (Mod) of the Dublin Circuit,
Barrister at Law, formerly lecturer
in law at Trinity College Dublin.*

**BUTTERWORTH IRELAND LTD
DUBLIN 1992**

Ireland	Butterworth Ireland Ltd, 26 Upper Ormond Quay, DUBLIN 7
Australia	Butterworths Pty Ltd, SYDNEY, MELBOURNE, BRISBANE, ADELAIDE, PERTH, CANBERRA and HOBART
Canada	Butterworths Canada Ltd, TORONTO and VANCOUVER
Malaysia	Malayan Law Journal Sdn Bhd, KUALA LUMPUR
New Zealand	Butterworths of New Zealand Ltd, WELLINGTON and AUCKLAND
Singapore	Reed Elsevier (Singapore) Pte Ltd
South Africa	Butterworth Publishers (Pty) Ltd, DURBAN
United Kingdom	Butterworths, a Division of Reed Elsevier (UK) Ltd, Halsbury House, 35 Chancery Lane, LONDON WC2A 1EL and 4 Hill Street, EDINBURGH EH2 3JZ
USA	MICHIE, CHARLOTTESVILLE and VIRGINIA

Published 1992
Reprinted 1995

A CIP Catalogue record for this book is available from the British Library.

ISBN 1 85475 169 7

© Butterworth Ireland Ltd
Cover by Dante Design, Dublin Ireland
Typeset by Phoenix Photosetting, Chatham, Kent
Printed and bound in Great Britain by Ashford Colour Press, Gosport, Hants

In memory of
Aengus Charleton, sc

PREFACE

The essential purpose of this book is to provide an introduction to the principles of criminal law as they apply in Ireland. A collection of cases, materials and statutes is of no assistance unless the student, or practitioner has, at the same time, a guide to the manner in which they should be interpreted. The narrative in this work is more extensive than that in source books from other jurisdictions because a basic text was necessarily incorporated.

In selecting these materials I have had to supplement the paucity of Irish decisions on many subjects. Cases from other common law jurisdictions have been included as indicating an approach which is consistent with the fundamental principles of Irish criminal law and which seem to me to be consistent with the manner in which it is applied in practice.

The approach of this work is, in essence, practical. This book is designed to be read from beginning to end, the reader thereby gaining a more detailed appreciation of the principles which underlie the materials which are included. In dealing with some problems in greater detail, I have been guided, in part, by the absence of any Irish treatment of that topic. Notwithstanding that, this source book can only succeed if, of itself, it is capable of rendering an explanation of criminal law and giving access to the most fundamental and appropriate materials to that task.

My thanks are due to the authors of and the holders of copyright in the various materials included. They have generously given permission to reproduce their work. My thanks are also due to Paddy McEntee SC who exercised a guiding hand at all stages in the production of this work. Maxwell Barrett, Eugene Smartt and Leonard Parker acted as my research assistants and were invaluable in their assistance. My friends and my family, I hope, realise the debt which I owe them. Embarrassment would result from an elaboration of that sentiment but it is, nonetheless, real. Fiona and Clare sustained this work from beginning to end. Professor John Larkin originally collaborated with me on this text. His return to Ulster forced his withdrawal but many of his suggestions were of real assistance. Kathleen Moylan prepared the text with commendable skill.

All of the trouble involved in the production of works on law, and criminal law in particular, would be greatly eased if the Oireachtas were to take seriously its function of law-making and reform. As a practitioner I can say that this derogation from duty by our politicians has led to chaos in the criminal courts. The idea of including extracts from the Model Penal Code and from other codes is to indicate that chaos could be replaced by order by the simple exercise of causing the law to be written down. I have tried to state the law as of September 1992.

Peter Charleton
Feast Day of St Thomas of Villanova

ACKNOWLEDGEMENTS

The publishers and author wish to thank the following for permission to reprint material from the sources indicated:

Archibold, John Frederick	*Criminal Pleading, Evidence and Practice*, Sweet and Maxwell, 26th ed
Carney, Paul	*Anachorisms of our Criminal Insanity Laws*, Irish Times, 13.01.90
Charleton, Peter	*Offences Against the Person*, Round Hall Press, 1992
Barnes, Eamonn	*Addresses to the Law Society* 16.11.91 and 04.05.88
Law Reform Commission	Report on Child Sexual Abuse, LRC 32 – 1990 Report on Rape, LRC 24 – 1988
McAleese, Mary	*Just What is Recklessness?* [1981] DULJ 29
McCutcheon, Paul	*Revision of the Larceny Act*, ICLJ 1991
O'Hanlon, Roderick	*Not Guilty Because of Insanity*, 1968 Irish Jurist (ns) III.61
Williams, Glanville	*Criminal Law: The General Part*, Sweet and Maxwell, 2nd ed, 1961

CONTENTS

Contents

Contents

Contents

TABLE OF CASES

(Paragraph numbers in **bold** indicate where a case or part of is set out.)

TABLE OF STATUTES

(References are to page numbers. Paragraph numbers in **bold** indicate where a section or part of is set out.)

Chapter 1

BASIC PRINCIPLES

Constructing liability

1.01 The foundation of criminal law is the idea that people should be punished by the State when they are to blame for conduct involving, or causing, certain grievous wrongs. Rationality demands that before stigmatising a citizen as a criminal, and possibly punishing him severely, he should be blameworthy in respect of that for which he stands accused. That blameworthiness is a consensus of the ideas of right-thinking citizens. In previous centuries the moral law, as interpreted by various religions, indicated the behaviour that was proscribed. In the present century a substratum of moral order is still clearly discernible in our law, particularly in those areas where human conduct has not been assisted or altered by technological advance. Thus it has always been a crime to deliberately kill someone or to sexually assault them. New methods lead to new mischief and often the law lags behind in describing as crimes what the people regard as grave social wrongs.

1.02 If the moral law had remained a vital source of law giving, old ideas could easily be adapted to outlaw newly invented or discovered wrongs. Since 1937 the judicial law-making power of common law, once the source of English law through the acceptance by centralised judges of local customary laws, has been frozen. The Constitution provides that the sole and exclusive power for making laws for the State is vested in the Oireachtas; Article 15.2. In consequence the judges are powerless to intervene by declaring a perceived common mischief to be a criminal offence. Unless conduct is proscribed no person can be charged with it before a criminal court. Nor can the law move backwards and declare criminal today that which was not criminal yesterday; Article 15.5.

1.03 Regrettably, the bulk of our laws were made during the reign of Queen Victoria (1837–1901) and have remained almost unaltered since that time. Little of the law was then written down as the prevailing view was that it was better to trust to the wisdom of judges, in interpreting their prior decisions, rather than stating the law in the form of an all embracing code. Sir

James Stephen proposed the complete codification of the criminal law but, partly due to the jealousy of others and to inertia, was unsuccessful in his effort.[1] Griffiths used this work as the basis of the Queensland Code which was enacted on 1 January 1901. It was subsequently copied in Western Australia and in Tasmania where it was improved by incorporating precedent charges into its text. These efforts reflected a desire to preserve the best features of the common law by writing them into a permanent form. Inevitably the Codes contain self-inconsistencies. Identification of these problems has usually been met by speedy reform in jurisdictions which have codified their criminal law; the will to make law was already manifest.

This jurisdiction has left undefined the most fundamental concepts of criminal liability. Nowhere is there to be found a statement by the Oireachtas on the foundation of criminal liability and the various mental elements of crime. Even proscribed conduct is often described in imprecise language. This work has been drawn from a multiplicity of sources in an attempt to construct basic ideas of criminal liability which the practice of criminal law in our courts would seem to indicate applies in Ireland. The remedy of codification cannot be expected from politicians who, despite the constitutional imperative demanding law-making of them, have almost entirely abrogated this responsibility, save where a particular topic either forces itself upon them or commends itself to their attention due to public interest. It can hardly have escaped the attention of our legislators that no major criminal fraud case has succeeded over the past ten years due to the unreformed state of our laws of evidence, and particularly the hearsay rule which remained unreformed until the Criminal Evidence Act of 1992. The protection of property, which informs the law as to stealing, has been subject to only one bungled reform since 1922 (see para **8.33**). Listing is futile; this work is not a polemic though it must justify the use it makes of external sources by pointing to the reason for turning to these.

The Australian code models are in themselves a sufficient guide to the direction of obvious reform. The most cohesive and far-reaching structure yet produced, the Model Penal Code of the American Law Institute, is referred to in this work to contrast the confusion of judge made law with the simplicity, certainty and ease of reference of a written text. Its merits are all too obvious.[2]

Basic elements

1.04 "An act does not make a man guilty of a crime, unless his mind be also guilty"; *Haughton v Smith*.[3] For example, a person lighting a cigarette in O'Connell Street is not guilty of murder or manslaughter if his match detonates a huge pocket of natural gas, recently leaked from a cracked pipeline, and results in the deaths of a number of passers-by. It could be otherwise if the actor had chosen to disregard warning signs against such conduct placed on gas excavations along the street. Consistently, we make an assessment of the blameworthiness of a citizen in causing harm by morally assessing his conduct in the circumstances. The gravity of the consequences can alter our view as to the wrong done. A simple error causing little harm is normally

---

1 *Digest of the Criminal Law* (5th ed, 1894).
2 See Wechsler *Challenge of a Model Penal Code* (1952) 65 Harvard Law Review 1057.
3 [1975] AC 476 at p 491 per Lord Hailsham.

regarded as trivial but the same error is abhorred if it results in great harm. Arguably, a person's conduct should only be judged according to his state of mind. People act, or omit to act, either according to decisions as to what they wish to do or by focusing their mind on the task in hand. So, it is really only the gravity of mental culpability which should determine our attitude to a crime or its consequent punishment. In reality that approach is not the one which people take. If, in the example given, the cigarette smoker were to cause no more than the explosion of a small pocket of gas which merely startled passers-by, no one would think of prosecuting him. His stupid conduct is coloured differently in the eyes of ordinary people by the fact that it caused death. In assessing what conduct is to be made criminal we look both at the wrong done inside the person (the mental element) and his conduct or its consequences (the external element).

1.05 In some circumstances apparently blameworthy conduct can become less culpable, or be extinguished entirely, if another element is taken into account. In our example of the gas explosion, the apparent culpability of ignoring warning signs seems less blameworthy if the actor lit the cigarette, not for himself, but for a gas worker who emerged, unlit cigarette in mouth, from one of the excavations and asked for a light. An enquiry as to whether the accused had a defence tends to complete the picture as to whether he is criminally liable (see chapter 4). Some factors merely lessen or mitigate the punishment due to a crime others are recognised as being so fundamental to the wrong as to extinguish it or transform it into a lesser crime. We will discuss this in due course.

1.06 To take another example; a man is found with a bloodied hand standing over the body of another who is recently deceased due to a fracture of the skull caused by a boulder which lies on the ground close by. To cause the death of another human being is the crime of homicide which, depending on the mental element which accompanies that external element, is either murder or manslaughter (see paras **5.12–5.14**). The conduct is therefore proscribed. There are several alternative sets of facts which may explain the man's actions. The accused merely came on the scene and is an innocent by-stander who is not responsible because he had "no hand act or part" in the killing; he is not blameworthy because he had nothing to do with the external elements. The accused was a steeplejack working on a church spire overhead when, due to an inexplicable fault, an apparently new and sound rope recently purchased from a reputable supplier snapped, causing a pile of rubble to kill the victim; the accused is not responsible because he did not cause the death of the victim with a coincident mental element of either intention or criminal negligence (see paras **5.47–5.50** and **5.55–5.64**). The accused deliberately struck the victim on the head but in the course of defending himself against a murderous attack with a flick-knife which was on the point of success; he is not responsible because he made lawful use of force in circumstances and in a degree which was reasonable (see paras **4.06–4.14**). The accused used a rock to defend himself against a friend who, due to jealousy over a girl, offered him a fight; this is certainly manslaughter and may be murder (see paras **5.12–5.14**). The accused decided to rob the deceased, a task made easier if the skull of the victim was bashed-in; this intentional infliction of serious harm is murder (see para **5.13**).

1.07   Criminal responsibility thus depends on:

(a)   a law making the specified act or omission criminal at the date when it is performed;

(b)   an act or omission by the accused covered by the definition of the offence;

(c)   a state of mind accompanying the act which is of sufficient gravity to come within the definition of the offence; and

(d)   the absence of a defence.

Proscribed conduct

1.08   The rule is that there must be a law outlawing the particular activity or conduct alleged against the accused.

1.09   *Constitution*

Article 15:

1.1   The National Parliament shall be called and known, and is in this Constitution generally referred to, as the Oireachtas.

1.2   The Oireachtas shall consist of the President and two Houses, viz: a House of Representatives to be called Dáil Éireann and a Senate to be called Seanad Éireann.

1.3   The Houses of the Oireachtas shall sit in or near the City of Dublin or in such other place as they may from time to time determine.

2.1   The sole and exclusive power of making laws for the State is hereby vested in the Oireachtas: no other legislative authority has power to make laws for the State.

2.2   Provision may however be made by law for the creation or recognition of subordinate legislatures and for the powers and functions of these legislatures.

4.1   The Oireachtas shall not enact any law which is in any respect repugnant to this Constitution or any provision thereof.

4.2   Every law enacted by the Oireachtas which is in any respect repugnant to this Constitution or to any provision thereof, shall, but to the extent only of such repugnancy, be invalid.

5   The Oireachtas shall not declare acts to be infringements of the law which were not so at the date of their commission.

Article 50:

1   Subject to this Constitution and to the extent to which they are not inconsistent therewith, the laws in force in Saorstát Éireann immediately prior to the date of the coming into operation of this Constitution shall continue to be of full force and effect until the same or any of them shall have been repealed or amended by enactment of the Oireachtas.

2   Laws enacted before, but expressed to come into force after, the coming into operation of this Constitution, shall, unless otherwise enacted by the Oireachtas, come into force in accordance with the terms thereof.

1.10   *Shaw v DPP*

[1962] AC 220; [1961] 2 All ER 446; [1961] 2 WLR 897;
(1961) 45 Cr App R 113
House of Lords, 1961

Facts: The accused published a book called "The Ladies' Directory", advertising the names and addresses of prostitutes and indicating special services they might provide together, in some cases, with an accompanying photograph. He was charged with, among other offences, a conspiracy to corrupt public morals and was convicted. It was not necessary for the prosecution to charge him with this offence as his activities also came within the definition of living on the earnings of prostitution contrary to s 30 of the Sexual Offences Act 1956 and publishing an obscene article contrary to s 2 of the Obscene Publications Act 1959. The House of Lords, however, took it as an opportunity to declare that the protection of certain public interests could require the judges to retain the legislative function.

Viscount Simonds: When Lord Mansfield, speaking long after the Star Chamber had been abolished, said [*R v Delaval* (1763) 3 Burr. 1434, 1438, 1439] that the Court of King's Bench was the *custos morum* of the people and had the superin-tendency of offences *contra bonos mores*, he was asserting, as I now assert, that there is in that Court a residual power, where no statute has yet intervened to supersede the common law, to superintend those offences which are prejudicial to the public welfare. Such occasions will be rare, for Parliament has not been slow to legislate when attention has been sufficiently aroused. But gaps remain and will always remain since no one can foresee every way in which the wickedness of man may disrupt the order of society.[4]

1.11   ***A-G (SPUC) v Open Door Counselling Limited***
[1988] IR 593; [1987] ILRM 477
High Court, 1986

This judgment is reproduced at para **2.47**.

1.12   ***The People (DPP) v MacEoin***
[1978] IR 27
Court of Criminal Appeal, 1978

This judgment is reproduced at para **4.155**.

What is remarkable about the *MacEoin* decision is that the Court of Criminal Appeal reversed the law inherited at independence and simply substituted a rule of their own which was not applied in any other common law jurisdiction. Such a change was, it is submitted, for the Oireachtas to make and it is consequently of no effect.

Conduct of the accused

1.13 The accused must act, or omit to act, or stand, by reason of his volun-tary conduct, in relation to a situation or event which the definition of the crime declares to be unlawful. Generally speaking, mere coincidence is insufficient; it is fundamental to the construction of criminal liability that the accused is placed in a situation where he is criminally liable by reason of his own voluntary act.

Modern jurisprudence has developed this concept into the defence of automatism; where the accused acts as a mere body, disengaged from, and not subject to, the control of the mind he is not criminally responsible (see paras **4.117–4.126**). The concept of voluntariness is fundamental to criminal liability. A person cannot be responsible for an act, an omission, or a situation which he has not contributed to by some voluntary action or omis-sion. Two exceptions can be pointed to but both have been heavily criticised.

---

4 Further see *Knuller v DPP* [1973] AC 435; *DPP v Bhagwan* [1972] AC 60; *DPP v Withers* [1975] AC 842; *Kamara v DPP* [1974] AC 104.

1.13 Basic principles

In *R v Larsonneur*[5], the accused was convicted under the Aliens Order 1920 on a charge that she "being an alien to whom leave to land in the United Kingdom had been refused was found in the United Kingdom". She had been expelled from Ireland and taken to that jurisdiction in the custody of the police. A different view was taken in *Finau v Department of Labour*[6] where it was held not to be an offence to fail to leave New Zealand where this was impossible because of pregnancy. As criminal law is in the process of developing a generally applicable defence of impossibility, and as the Constitution implies the standards of fundamental justice in the administration of law, the New Zealand decision is strongly to be preferred. Departing from the rule requiring a willed act by the accused, the law will ignore the absence of voluntary conduct if it has its origin in a state brought on by the voluntary consumption of alcohol or other drugs (see paras **4.81–4.96**). So in *R v Lipman*[7] the accused was convicted of manslaughter, notwithstanding that he killed the victim under the influence of drugs and believing he was strangling snakes in the underworld. The decision has been heavily criticised and could easily have been brought within an established principle by a finding that the accused had been guilty of criminal negligence by taking a mind-altering drug in physical proximity to another person.

1.14 It is possible to roughly categorise the typical situations on which criminal liability is constructed:

(1) The accused bears a relationship of physical control to an object which is either close at hand or in a place to which he can resort when he has need of it or is with a person subject to his control. Possession based offences are fundamental to the prohibition on the use of dangerous articles and have been resorted to because the proof of this kind of relationship is far easier than the proof of an ulterior intent to use the article in a dangerous way, or the proof that it was so used, or the proof that the accused had such an article in order to attempt a crime with it. Examples are to be found at paras **7.17–7.20** and possession generally is considered at paras **7.02–7.13**.

(2) The accused may be required to have struck at, or moved towards striking at, some other person. Those are assault-based offences. The majority of offences against the person are based on the concept that it is wrong to strike another person, or to put them in fear of being immediately struck (see paras **7.35–7.44**). Murder and manslaughter had their origin in this concept but are now analysed in terms of the result of the accused's conduct being death to the victim caused by a voluntary act of the accused, which, in the case of murder was intentional or which, in the case of manslaughter, was criminally negligent, was criminal and dangerous or was an assault. It is also a wrong to deprive someone of their liberty without justification (such as a sentence of imprisonment) but in early law this was usually accompanied by an assault (see paras **7.45–7.47**).

(3) Exceptionally, where the accused bears a relationship giving rise to a duty to protect the welfare of another, he may be liable for failing to act. Traditionally, such a relationship was based on a duty arising from a contract

---

5 (1933) 24 Cr App Rep 74.
6 [1984] 2 NZLR 396.
7 [1970] 1 QB 152.

(such as employment) or on ties of blood or family. The modern tendency is towards identifying duty to act by reference to all the circumstances affecting the relationship between the victim and the accused. This is further discussed in the context of manslaughter (see paras **5.61–5.63**). In general the criminal law does not enforce unselfish behaviour and it may not be an offence to watch someone drown even though the means of saving them are readily to hand at no consequence to oneself. Some minor offences proscribe a failure to act when requested by authority. Examples include failure to co-operate with Gardaí when exercising their statutory functions:

Criminal Justice Act 1984

13 Failure to surrender to bail

(1) If a person who has been released on bail in criminal proceedings fails to appear before a court in accordance with his recognisance, he shall be guilty of an offence and shall be liable on summary conviction to a fine not exceeding £1,000 or to imprisonment for a term not exceeding twelve months or to both.

18 Inferences from failure, refusal to account for objects, marks, etc

(1) Where –

　　(*a*) a person is arrested without warrant by a member of the Garda Síochána, and there is –

　　　　(i) on his person, or
　　　　(ii) in or on his clothing or footwear, or
　　　　(iii) otherwise in his possession, or
　　　　(iv) in any place in which he is at the time of his arrest

　　　　any object, substance or mark, or there is any mark on any such object, and the member reasonably believes that the presence of the object, substance or mark may be attributable to the participation of the person arrested in the commission of the offence in respect of which he was arrested, and

　　(*b*) the member informs the person arrested that he so believes, and requests him to account for the presence of the object, substance or mark, and

　　(*c*) the person fails or refuses to do so,

　　then if, in any proceedings against the person for the offence, evidence of the said matters is given, the court, in determining whether to send forward the accused for trial or whether there is a case to answer and the court (or, subject to the judge's directions, the jury) in determining whether the accused is guilty of the offence charged (or of any other offence of which he could lawfully be convicted on that charge) may draw such inferences from the failure or refusal as appear proper; and the failure or refusal may, on the basis of such inferences, be treated as, or as capable of amounting to, corroboration of any other evidence in relation to which the failure or refusal is material, but a person shall not be convicted of an offence solely on an inference drawn from such failure or refusal.

Road Traffic Act 1961

40 Production of driving licence on demand by member of Garda Síochána

(1) (*a*) A member of the Garda Síochána may demand, of a person driving in a public place a mechanically propelled vehicle or accompanying pursuant to regulations under this Act the holder of a provisional licence while such holder is driving in a public place a mechanically propelled vehicle, the pro-

duction of a driving licence then having effect and licensing him to drive the vehicle, and if such person refuses or fails to produce the licence there and then, he shall, unless within ten days after the date on which the production was demanded he produces such licence in person to a member of the Garda Síochána at a Garda Síochána station to be named by such person at the time at which the production was so demanded, be guilty of an offence.

(b) In a prosecution for an offence under this subsection it shall be presumed, until the contrary is shown by the defendant, that he did not, within ten days after the day on which the production was demanded, produce a driving licence in accordance with paragraph (a) of this subsection.

Road Traffic (Amendment) Act 1978

13   Obligation to provide specimen at Garda station (section 49)

(1) Where a person arrested under section 49(6) of the Principal Act or section 12(3) has been brought to a Garda station, a member of the Garda Síochána may at his discretion do either or both of the following –

(a) require the person to provide, by exhaling into an apparatus for indicating the concentration of alcohol in breath or blood, a specimen of his breath,

(b) require the person either to permit a designated registered medical practitioner to take from the person a specimen of his blood or, at the option of the person, to provide for the designated registered medical practitioner a specimen of the person's urine.

(2) A person who refuses or fails to comply forthwith with a requirement under subsection (1)(a) shall be guilty of an offence and liable on summary conviction to imprisonment for a term not exceeding six months or, at the discretion of the court, to a fine not exceeding £500, or to both.

(3) A person who, following a requirement under subsection (1)(b) –

(a) refuses or fails to comply with such a requirement, or

(b) refuses or fails to comply with a requirement of a designated registered medical practitioner in relation to the taking under this section of a specimen of blood or the provision under this section of a specimen of urine.

shall be guilty of an offence and liable on summary conviction to imprisonment for a term not exceeding six months or, at the discretion of the court, to a fine not exceeding £500, or to both.

In the circumstances of an arrest under s 30 of the Offences Against the State Act 1939, a person in custody commits a criminal offence for which the penalty is six months imprisonment, if he fails, on request by a Garda, to give an account of his movements or actions (s 52).

(4) It is inherent in the human personality, and in an ordered society, that people will be allowed to own goods. Often the State will limit this right by a form of personal wealth on inheritance tax but, apart from such powers, it is an offence for anyone to deprive another of their property. If it were otherwise commerce could not function and violence would flow from disputes based on the use of force to seize goods.

(5) Apart from a voluntary action the definition of the offence sometimes requires a further ulterior intent to perpetrate a particular consequence. For example in murder the accused must intend to kill or to cause serious injury by his actions; Criminal Justice Act 1964, s 4 (see para **5.06**). The most grievous assault is committed when the accused intends by his actions to

maim, disfigure or disable or to do some other grievous bodily harm to the victim; s 18 of the Offences Against the Person Act 1861 (see para **7.36**).

(6) The definition of inchoate offences involves a consideration of whether the conduct of the accused amounted to an attempt, a conspiracy, or incitement as well as the substantive offence to which these are related (see chapter 2).

(7) Persons who do not themselves perpetrate an offence, or who cannot be proved to have perpetrated an offence, are considered separately under the rules relating to aiding and abetting an offence (see chapter 3), and the rules imposing liability for a common design to commit an offence (see paras **3.24–3.25**). Exceptionally, in the case of a felony, it is a crime to aid another who has committed a felony with intent to further his escape (see paras **3.41– 3.49**).

(8) The constituent elements of an offence can be seen from an examination of the wording of the statutory or common law definitions. A set of examples are given in the final chapter of this work. Often those will fit within the foregoing principles but some less serious offences are based on the idea that careless conduct causing harm should be punished.

The mental element

1.15 Criminal law, originating as it did from the moral law, retains the principle that liability depends on the coincidence of a mental element appropriate to the offence together with the commission of the external elements of that offence. Different crimes call for different mental elements. Instead of the vast array of definitions which are necessary to cover all the possible permutations of socially harmful behaviour that necessarily make up the criminal calendar, the mental element of a crime is capable of being classified in the following categories:

(1) Intention (often expressed in the statutory form as requiring that the accused should act "knowingly").
(2) Recklessness.
(3) Criminal negligence.
(4) Negligence.
(5) Strict liability subject to a defence of reasonable mistake.
(6) Absolute liability.

1.16 Only the first two categories could truly be said to require mental states. These are the categories most often employed in serious crimes. Criminal negligence is limited to the commission of manslaughter but logically should be extended to situations where, apart from death, the accused causes serious physical harm to the victim. Crimes of negligence are essentially regulatory in nature. The final two classifications are concerned with the less serious crimes which are truly regulatory in nature; that classification itself is suggested by Canadian authorities.

Concurrence

1.17 The mental element and the external element must both concur in time in order that a crime be committed. It is insufficient, for example, to commit larceny, that the accused mistakenly takes a fur coat belonging to another person, believing it to be hers, but on arriving home and discovering her mistake, decides to keep it. Larceny requires that the accused intend to permanently deprive the owner of her goods (see paras **8.12, 8.16**). It would be otherwise if the definition of the offence were cast in terms of dishonestly handling another person's property: see the Larceny Act 1990. For offences which are defined in terms of a single act or omission the mental element must coincide at the point when the external element is committed. In many offences the external element is defined as a continuing state of affairs; in those circumstances it is enough that the mental element appropriate to the offence should be present while those circumstances continue; *Fagan v Metropolitan Police Commissioner*[8] (see para **5.48**). For example it is an offence to possess heroin. That offence is not committed if a packet of heroin is slipped unawares into a person's pocket. If the man later finds it, and keeps it, the offence of possession is committed (see para **7.15**). So also, the offence of handling is committed when the lady with the fur coat discovers her mistake and decides to profit from it by keeping it for herself.

1.18
R v Scott
[1967] VR 276
Supreme Court of Victoria, 1966

Facts: The accused escaped from a jail after he had been attacked by another prisoner and struck on the head with a piece of timber. He had no recollection of leaving the place. Not until two days after his leaving the jail, the accused said, was he aware that he had escaped. He was nonetheless convicted with an escape from lawful custody under Section 35 of the Jails Act (Victoria), 1958. This conviction was overturned.

Smith J: . . . The common law crime of escape has a recorded history of many centuries. It was the subject of modifying legislation as long ago as the reign of Edward I: see the statute of 23 Ed 1, *de frangentibus prisonam*. In *Staunford's Pleas of the Crown*, published in 1560, half a dozen pages were required to set out the detailed rules of law then applicable to the crime. Yet it has never, until now, so far as I have been able to discover, been suggested that the crime of escape could be committed by finding oneself at large and deciding to remain so. . . .
    . . . It is clear also, I consider, that the element of going at large out of an actual custody, which is essential to constitute an escape, must be a conscious act done by the prisoner with the intention of liberating himself from that custody. This conclusion is supported by the general principles of the common law; for it is a "cardinal rule" that "the intent and the act must both concur to constitute the crime": see *R v Reynhoudt* (1962), 107 CLR 381, at p 386; [1962] ALR 483, at p 484; and compare *Hardgrave v R* (1906), 4 CLR 232, at p 237; 13 ALR 206, at p 207. It is true that in the law of larceny this rule has not always prevailed. But I see no justification for introducing into the law of escape the artificialities of the law of larceny. Furthermore the conclusion stated is supported by precedents of indictments and informations for escape in which the word "wilfully" or the word "voluntarily" commonly appears: see, for example. *Burn's Justice of the Peace*, 29th ed, vol 2, at pp 346, 349: *Chitty, Criminal Law*, 2nd ed, vol 2, at pp 161, 171, 191–2, and vol 4, at p 78. It finds support, too, in the case of *R v Martin* (1811), Russ & Ry 196; 168 ER 757. . . .
    . . . For these reasons, I consider that there is no foundation for the view contended for on behalf of the Crown that the offence of escape is committed when a

8 [1969] 1 QB 439.

prisoner who has not been discharged or released according to law finds himself innocently at large and decides not to give himself up. . . .

Gillard J: . . . It is one of the fundamental principles of our criminal law that a person is not criminally responsible for an act which is done independently of the exercise of his will: see *R v Tolson* (1889), 23 QBD 168; [1886–90] All ER Rep 26; *Hardgrave v R* (1906), 4 CLR 232, at p 237; 13 ALR 206, at p 207. The legal problem raised by the alleged defence is a nice one. If his story were true, at the time the applicant was missing from the working party, his mind did not go with the act. The difficulty that arises from such a statement, however, is to give a proper and accurate meaning to the word "act". It has been accepted by eminent jurists both in the British Commonwealth and the United States, that those acts which carry legal liability must be willed movements or voluntary omissions: see *Salmond's Jurisprudence*, 7th ed, pp 381–2. "In legal understanding an *act* is an exertion of the will manifested externally. It implies a choice. A convenient distinction sets off acts, 'voluntary muscular motions' from events, those occurrences which take place independently of human will": *Roscoe Pound, Jurisprudence*, vol 4, pp 410 *et seq*. It has, accordingly been said that "no involuntary action, whatever effects it may produce, amounts to a crime by the law of England". See *Stephen's History of the Criminal Law*, vol 2, p 100; *Stephen's Commentaries*, 21st ed, vol 4, p 14; cf *Holmes, The Common Law*, p 54. According to the opinion of the jurists, the exercise of the will is essential to the *actus reus* of an offence, quite apart from the existence of the *mens rea*: see article by *J W C Turner* in *Modern Approach to Criminal Law*, pp 200 *et seq*; cf *Glanville Williams, Criminal Law*, pp 10–21. Whatever differences they may entertain as to the precise nature of an "act", the jurists would probably describe the movement of the applicant (if his story be true) from the prison working area to the Hume Highway (since it was done involuntarily) as an *event* but not an *act* of the applicant: *Roscoe Pound, Jurisprudence*, vol 4, pp 410 *et seq*. See also *Paton's Jurisprudence*, pp 273–6; cf *Kilbride v Lake*, [1962] NZLR 590, at p 593. But even it it can be considered as an *actus reus*, it is well established that there must be a *mens rea* to which the *actus reus* must be attributed. There must be a causal relationship between the two . . .

. . . Despite the rule established in *R v Riley* (1853), Dears 149; 169 ER 674; [1843–60] All ER Rep 675, in relation to larceny, the better opinion now appears to be that "the intent and the act must both concur to constitute a crime": per Lord Kenyon, CJ, in *Fowler v Padget* (1798), 7 TR 509, at p 514; 101 ER 1103, at p 1106; see *Hale PC*, vol 1, pp 229, 560; *Stephen's History of the Criminal Law of England*, vol 2, pp 97, 112; *Glanville Williams, Criminal Law*, p 494; *Russel on Crime*, 12th ed, p 54; *3 Current Legal Problems* (1950), at p 150; (1950), 66 LQR at p 202; cf *R v Flowers* (1886), 16 QBD 643, at p 646; *R v Harrison-Owen*, [1951] 2 All ER 726; [1951] WN 483; *Korp v Egg and Egg Pulp Marketing Board* [1964] VR 563, at p 566. . . .

. . . it appears to me that the story told by the applicant (if believed or even to raise a doubt in the jury's mind as to proof of the *actus reus*) could afford an answer to the charge as laid. To summarize my reasons, it would appear on the evidence given at the trial –

(a) that at all times material up to 2 May 1962 the applicant was a male person imprisoned at the Beechworth Training Prison by sentence of a court of competent jurisdiction;
(b) that during such imprisonment, he was in the custody of the governor of the training prison and under the control and supervision of the subordinates of the governor;
(c) that if his story is true, without any voluntary action on his part, the applicant on 2 May moved out of the imprisonment and was thereafter at large;
(d) that since his mind did not go with the act, his failure to return with the party to

the Beechworth Gaol did not, because of the involuntary nature of his departure, constitute an escape;

(*e*) that without committing any offence, from that stage he was then physically at large outside the custody, control and power of his keeper;

(*f*) that when he regained sufficient consciousness to exercise his volition and to form the relevant intention, he was then physically at large, with the consequence that he was not bound under any rule of law to return to the place of custody, and he was no longer lawfully imprisoned and in the lawful custody of the gaoler of the Beechworth gaol;

(*g*) that, accordingly, if the applicant's story be true, there was no causal relationship between the formation of an intention to go to Sydney and the act of withdrawing from the lawful custody of the gaoler. The two elements necessary to constitute the crime were never brought together. An unlawful action and an evil intention never concurred. No withdrawal in the relevant sense can be attributed to a guilty intention to bring about such withdrawal. . . .

Intention

1.19 The mental state is normally proved by an irresistible inference from the circumstances in which the accused committed the external elements of the crime. In all serious offences the elements of a crime have to be proved by the prosecution so that the jury are satisfied of the guilt of the accused beyond reasonable doubt. Because the accused is presumed by law to be innocent he bears no burden of proving his innocence. The exception to that occurs where the law presumes some fact or inference against him. Otherwise his role in a trial can be roughly stated as meeting a case by testing whether the prosecution evidence discloses a reasonable doubt. Often in a criminal trial there will be no contest as to the mental element but the issue will be as to whether the right person is before the court, in other words, was it the person in the dock who robbed the bank? The course of everyday events indicates that this approach is correct. If a person disguises himself and holds up a bank teller, managing to escape with £10,000, few people would seriously entertain an argument that he had no intention to deprive the bank permanently of its cash. In murder trials there is often a real contest, and this is sometimes the only issue, as to whether the accused intended to kill or to cause serious injury to his victim. This is the mental state required by s 4 of the Criminal Justice Act 1964. The course of human affairs is such that people, unless they are trained to pursue killing to earn money or in pursuit of a political ideal, do not usually kill unless they are driven to the extreme of passion. Intention is a simple word which, when it is used in the definition of a criminal offence, requires that a person be proved to have acted with the purpose of causing the harm or circumstance outlawed. In other words, that he meant to do what he did. The recent history of this concept in England has shown it to be far from easy to define in a context where human sympathy will tend to distort the meaning of the concept beyond its natural elasticity.

1.20 In the earliest of a series of cases decided by the House of Lords a Mrs Hyam had a relationship with a man who then moved in with another woman. She poured petrol through the letter box of that house and ignited it. She knew that there were people asleep there. Two children died in the fire. The jury, at her subsequent murder trial, were directed that the necessary intention for murder was present if Mrs Hyam foresaw death or grievous bodily harm as a highly probable result of her actions and that it was not necessary to prove that she wanted or aimed at that happening. The House of Lords agreed; *Hyam v DPP*[9]. In *R v Moloney*[10], the victim was killed by his apparently affectionate stepson in the course of a mad contest, with loaded shotguns, as to which of them was quicker on the draw. Following a taunt to pull the trigger, he did so and discharged the shotgun directly at the victim's head. The House of Lords disapproved a direction to the jury that the accused intended serious bodily harm if he foresaw that serious bodily harm would probably happen. Lord Bridge indicated that foresight of a consequence as being probable or likely was not to be taken as the equivalent of an intention but that juries might infer intention from such a state of mind. The meaning of intention was a matter for a jury to decide, thus leaving the law as to a vital component of many offences undefined. Lord Bridge went on to say that in cases where the accused had a purpose other than causing the prohibited harm, but where the result was an inevitable or likely consequence, the jury should be directed to consider whether the relevant forbidden result was a natural consequence of the accused's action and whether he foresaw it as such. If he did foresee it, it would be proper to infer that he had intended such a forbidden consequence. Lord Bridge was referring to 'oblique intention' where, for example, a person wishes merely to destroy an airplane in order to collect insurance monies but knows that the one hundred passengers and crew will not survive the bomb he intends to explode.

In *R v Hancock and Shankland*[11] two miners, during a major strike, pushed a concrete block off a bridge on top of a taxi identified as taking a strike-breaking miner to his work. It killed the taxi driver. The miners claimed they intended to push the block from the bridge onto a different lane of the motorway to the one in which the taxi was travelling; that they intended to frighten the working miner but not to hurt anyone. A direction in accordance with *Moloney* was given and the subsequent conviction was overturned by the House of Lords. That direction was wrong because it failed to refer to the probability of the consequence occurring, which was of vital importance. The greater the probability of a consequence the more likely it was foreseen and, consequently, intended. Foresight was not to be taken as equivalent to intention and even the highest degree of probability was only a factor to be considered by the jury in the light of all the evidence in order to decide if the accused acted with intent. In *R v Nedrick*[12], the Court of Appeal indicated that an accused would need to foresee a consequence as a virtual certainty, barring some unforeseen intervention, if the inference of intent was to be made. Where an accused realised that a consequence was for all practical purposes inevitable the inference that he intended such a result might be irresistible. *Smith and Hogan*[13] summarise the decisions thus:

(1) A result is intended when it is the actor's purpose.

9 [1975] AC 55.
10 [1985] AC 905.
11 [1986] AC 455.
12 [1986] 3 All ER.
13 See p 56.

(2) A court or a jury may also infer that a result is intended, though it is not desired, when:
   (*a*) the result is a virtually certain consequence of the act, and
   (*b*) the actor knows that it is a virtually certain consequence.[14]

1.21   *Charleton – Offences Against the Person (1992)*

One can only mean something to happen when one realises that one's conduct, or the consequences of one's conduct, involves its occurrence. Intent necessarily involves a conscious choice to bring about a particular state of affairs. If one consciously chooses not to bring about a state of affairs one cannot intend it. In all but the rarest circumstances choosing to do something will mean that one also actively desires it. That rare exception may occur where the desire of the accused is to bring about a result knowing, albeit with regret, that another consequence will, in the ordinary course of events, follow from it or necessarily involve it. That state of mind is nonetheless intent[15].

Probability and foresight are relevant to the decision as to whether intent exists but they do not, of themselves, amount to intent. It has never been an ingredient of intent that it must be possible for the accused to bring about the result that is his purpose. No matter how unlikely the success of the object which it is his purpose to achieve, once he is engaged on a course of conduct in order to bring about that particular result, he intends it. He will not normally engage in such conduct unless his object is achievable. It is a separate matter that an objective bystander will find it difficult or impossible to realise or infer from a person's conduct what his particular intent is. As a matter of practicality it follows that the less likely it is that the accused can achieve an object the less easily one can infer that he intends it.

A person cannot intend anything unless his mind activates him towards a purpose. That can only happen where there is foresight of what his purpose is, or what his purpose involves. Foresight causes differing mental states which vary almost infinitely from an inkling to a clear realisation as to a result or consequence. When the result or consequence is contemplated the mind may categorise what is foreseen from a possibility, through a probability, up to a certainty.

Intent is not recklessness; it is not the conscious taking of an unjustifiable risk. The line of distinction must not be blurred. It follows that although mental states may vary intent will involve a realisation that it is virtually certain or at least highly probable that a result will be achieved or a consequence will follow as a result of an action or an omission to act. Complete certainty is as difficult a state of mind to achieve in the commission of a crime as in other human endeavours; it is thus not necessary to form intent. A state of mind which can, in ordinary language, be categorised as risk-taking does not suffice. That state of mind is recklessness and will fall to be dealt with, as criminal negligence, within the ambit of the crime of manslaughter.

Intent is thus present where the purpose of the accused is to engage in conduct (which includes omissions), or to achieve a result, or when the accused acts in order to achieve some purpose which he knows, or of which is virtually certain, if he is successful, involves a result or consequence in the ordinary course of events.

The effect of s 4 of the Criminal Justice Act 1964 was stated in *The People (A-G) v Dwyer*[16] to be that an unlawful homicide was not murder unless the

---

14 For an interesting discussion of these cases see Norrie *Oblique Intention and Legal Politics* [1989] Crim LR 793.
15 *Mohan* [1976] QB 1, [1975] 2 All ER 193, [1975] 2 WLR 859, [1975] RTR 337, 60 Cr App R 272, [1975] Crim LR 283 CA; *Pearman* (1984) 80 Cr App R 259, [1984] Crim LR 675 CA; Smith & Hogan 288; *Williams* [1987] CLJ 417 at 423; (1989) 105 LQR 387 at 388.
16 [1972] IR 416, 420, 108 ILTR 17 SC.

necessary intent was established; the onus on establishing this beyond a reason-able doubt remains at all times on the prosecution, as also does the onus of proving beyond a reasonable doubt that the presumption that an accused person intended the natural and probable consequence of his action was not rebutted.

Definitional Analysis

The definition of intent approved by the Court of Criminal Appeal, in the context of intent to kill, in *The People (DPP) v Douglas & Hayes*[17] is that of Asquith LJ in *Cunliffe v Goodman*[18]:

> An "intention" to my mind connotes a state of affairs which the party "intending" – I will call him X – does more than merely contemplate: it connotes a state of affairs which, on the contrary, he decides, so far as in him lies, to bring about, and which, in point of probability he has a reasonable prospect of being able to bring about, by his own fruition[19].

There is no requirement in criminal law that the accused have a reasonable prospect of achieving his intention. Where a person shoots at another from a great distance, intending to kill him, and striving to ensure the accuracy of his aim for that purpose, it is not any the less his intent because the death of the victim is extremely unlikely. Nor is it any the less his intent, in the example given, that death resulted from exceptionally favourable wind conditions, or the missile striking a particularly vulnerable spot, or the absence of medical attention for hundreds of miles. However, it may be unlikely for a person to be engaged in conduct which cannot reasonably achieve a desired result. That is a question of evidence and proof by inference and has nothing to do with intent. Intent is a purpose peculiar to the individual mind of the accused.

In Canada the courts have colloquially construed intent as being an actual desire, end, purpose, aim, objective or design[20] without settling on a particular definition. In Victoria it has been held that the trial judge need not explain the meaning of intent to a jury where the prosecution case is simply that the accused acted with the purpose of bringing about the criminal wrong[21]. After much dithering the House of Lords have agreed that in a case of straightforward intent, as opposed to oblique intent (where the accused is trying to achieve an object knowing it involves another consequence or result) it should be left to the jury to apply this ordinary word without further assistance from the judge. In *Moloney*[22] Lord Bridge explained:

> The golden rule should be that when directing a jury on the mental element necessary in a crime of specific intent, the judge should avoid any elaboration or paraphrase of what is meant by intent, and leave it to the jury's good sense to decide whether the accused acted with the necessary intent, unless the judge is convinced that, on the facts and having regard to the way the case has been presented to the jury in evidence and argument, some further explanation or elaboration is strictly necessary to avoid misunderstanding[23].

---

17 [1985] ILRM 25 CCA.
18 [1950] 2 KB 237, [1950] 1 All ER 720 CA – later adopted by Hailsham LJ in *Hyam* (1975) AC 55 HL, other ref. fn 10.
19 Fn 2, 28.
20 Stuart 128.
21 Tait [1973] VR 151, 153 SC.
22 [1985] AC 905, [1985] 1 All ER 1025, [1985] 2 WLR 648, 81 Cr App R 93, [1985] Crim LR 378 HL. This point was not overruled in the cases which follow in the text. See further *DPP for NI v Lynch* [1975] AC 653, 690, Lord Simon [1975] 1 All ER 913, [1975] 2 WLR 641, 61 Cr App R 6, [1975] NI 35, [1975] Crim LR 707 HL.
23 AC at 926, All ER at 1036, WLR at 664, Cr App R at 106.

It is difficult to see sense in that view. The jury is entitled to have the defence and prosecution cases put to it. A proper jury charge requires an explanation of the burden and standard of proof and an elucidation of the elements of the crime but not, apparently, an explanation as to a subject the House of Lords itself has tackled with a singular lack of clarity[24]. A jury hearing an ordinary word in a legal context are likely to wonder as to its meaning. Their puzzlement may increase with the elaboration of so many other matters peripheral to what they are attempting to decide in a murder trial. It is submitted that even in a simple case of intention the jury are entitled to be instructed as to its meaning in law; a sufficient explanation is given if they are told that they must give the word its ordinary meaning of a purpose or objective. That exercise may be further elucidated by the judge contrasting conscious risk taking with intention. The standard of proof in a criminal trial is, similarly, often explained by comparing the criminal standard of proof beyond reasonable doubt with the civil standard of probability or likelihood.

Intention cannot exist where the accused purposely acts in order to ensure that the result or consequence charged does not happen. The fact that he does not succeed in stopping the result or consequence can be evidence, where it was extremely unlikely that he would be successful, that he intended it to happen, notwithstanding his protestations to the contrary. While the running of a substantial risk does not amount to intent it has been proposed that the classic example of the person who sets off a bomb in a crowded public street should inspire a broadening of the mental element in the crime of murder into a form of recklessness to correspond to "wicked" recklessness[25].

For example, a criminal leaves a time bomb in the foyer of a hotel and then telephones a warning, which is not acted upon, and thereby causes a number of horrific deaths. He knowingly takes a substantial risk of that occurrence. He can plead, and it may be correct, that he intended to cause damage to property and intended to avoid death or serious injury[26]. Similarly, the accused may have left a time bomb in a public place intending that it should go off when the place is likely to be deserted. In such a case the culpability of the accused may be thought to be higher because he has consciously initiated a substantial risk of death or serious injury and failed to take any step to ensure that the risk was kept to the minimum. Finally, the accused may plant a bomb where it is likely to kill or cause serious injury and express his defence in terms of a hope that no one would be injured. In each case it is a jury function to analyse the evidence, assisted by the presumption that the accused intended the natural and probable consequences of his action[27], in order to decide whether there was an intention to cause death or serious injury. If they are left in a state of reasonable doubt on the evidence, which may include the explanation by the accused that he did not intend to kill or cause serious injury[28], they must acquit.

The three examples given direct the mind towards the conclusion that in the third one the bomber intended to kill or cause serious injury. That is because, in

24 See Goff –*The Mental Element in the Crime of Murder* (1988) 104 LQR; Williams – *The Mens Rea for Murder: Leave it Alone* (1989) 105 LQR 387. For a similar view see Tait [1973] VR 151, 153–154 SC.
25 As in Scots Law: Gordon – *The Criminal Law of Scotland* (2nd ed, 1978); MacDonald – *Criminal Law* (5th ed); Scottish Law Reform Commission Report No. 80 (1983) paras 2.14–2.15. This view is held by Lord Goff, fn 8, 57.
26 See the facts of *McFeely* [1977] NI 149 which was decided on the basis of an analysis of the law as it stood after *Hyam* [1975] AC 55, [1974] 2 All ER 421, [1974] 2 WLR 607, 59 Cr App R 91 HL.
27 See para 2.23.
28 It has yet to be decided in this jurisdiction how far the self-serving statements of A are admissible or the extent to which they must be adduced by the prosecution. *Pearce* [1979] 69 Cr App R 365 CA.

the ordinary course of events, a bomb in a public place brings about that consequence. The considered object of the terrorist's intention is not distracted, as in the other examples, by a contrary purpose, such as damage to property, or a conscious attempt to divert that prospect.

Motive

1.22 Motive can be an item of evidence which assists the prosecution in proving the crime. Its absence can assist the accused in pointing to material which the jury may consider raises a reasonable doubt in his favour. Motive is never part of the mental element of a crime. It is the underlying impetus which may lead to the commission of the crime. For example, someone may wish to fake their death in order that their family may collect life insurance money. So they leave their clothes on a beach and assume a new identity, hoping the insurance company will believe that they have been drowned in a swimming accident.

1.23   *R v Lewis*
(1979) 47 CCC (2d) 24
Supreme Court of Canada, 1979

Facts: The accused was charged together with one Tatley with the murder of the latter's daughter and son-in-law. The murder was committed by Lewis posting to the victims a bomb in the form of a kettle rigged with dynamite which exploded on being plugged in. The issue on appeal to the Supreme Court of Canada was whether the trial judge should have admitted evidence that Tatley was angry that his daughter had married without his consent and whether the jury should have been instructed that Lewis had no motive for the bombing.

Dickson J: [The relevant principles are:]

   (1) As evidence, motive is always relevant and hence evidence of motive is admissible.
   (2) Motive is no part of the crime and is legally irrelevant to criminal responsibility. It is not an essential element of the prosecution's case as a matter of law.
   (3) Proved absence of motive is always an important fact in favour of the accused and ordinarily worthy of note in a charge to the jury.
   (4) Conversely, proved presence of motive may be an important factual ingredient in the Crown's case, notably on the issue of identity and intention, when the evidence is purely circumstantial.
   (5) Motive is therefore always a question of fact and evidence and the necessity of referring to motive in the charge to the jury falls within the general duty of the trial judge "to not only outline the theories of the prosecution and defence but to give the juries matters of evidence essential in arriving at a just conclusion."
   (6) Each case will turn on its own unique set of circumstances. The issue of motive is always a matter of degree.

The necessity of charging a jury on motive may be looked upon as a continuum at one end of which are cases where the evidence as to identity of the murderer is purely circumstantial and proof of motive on the part of the crown so essential that reference must be made to motive in charging the jury. The Crown's case against Tatley was such a situation. It was essential to establish motive and the trial judge properly referred to motive in charging the jury in relation to Tatley. At the other end of the continuum, and requiring a charge on motive, is the case where there is proved absence of motive and this may become of great significance as a matter in favour of the accused. Between these two end points in the continuum there are cases where the necessity to charge on motive depends upon the course of the trial and the nature and probative value of the evidence adduced. In these cases, a substantial discretion must be left to the trial judge. In *Imrich* (1974) 21 CCC (2d) 99, 6 OR 496, 39 CRNS 77, for example, the evidence of exclusive opportunity was such that motive receded into the background.

Knowledge

1.24 It is not correct to state that knowledge is the equivalent of intention. Knowledge, however, implies a highly culpable state of mind which is equivalent, in terms of its gravity, to intention. Offences which require knowledge can be seen from the definitions contained in the final chapter of this work, for example see paras **9.20, 9.25, 9.32**.

Other examples:

Criminal Law Amendment Act 1935

13 Offence of keeping a brothel

(1) In lieu of section 13 (repealed by this Act) of the Criminal Law Amendment Act 1885, it is hereby enacted that any person who –

(*a*) keeps or manages or acts or assists in the management of a brothel, or
(*b*) being the tenant, lessee, occupier, or person in charge of any premises, knowingly permits such premises or any part thereof to be used as a brothel or for the purposes of habitual prostitution, or
(*c*) being the lessor landlord of any premises or the agent of such lessor or landlord, lets such premises or any part thereof with the knowledge that such premises or some part thereof are or is to be used as a brothel, or is wilfully a party to the continued use of such premises or any part thereof as a brothel,

shall be guilty of a misdemeanour and shall be liable, in the case of a first conviction of such misdemeanour, to a fine not exceeding one hundred pounds or, at the discretion of the court, to imprisonment for any term not exceeding six months or to both such fine and such imprisonment and, in the case of a second or any subsequent conviction of such misdemeanour, to a fine not exceeding two hundred and fifty pounds or, at the discretion of the court, to penal servitude for any term not exceeding five years nor less than three years or imprisonment for any term not exceeding two years or to both such fine and such penal servitude or imprisonment.

Misuse of Drugs Act 1977
As amended by the Misuse of Drugs Act 1984

Section 19(1), see para **7.31**.

1.25   *Hanlon v Fleming*
[1981] IR 489
Supreme Court, 1981

Facts: This was an extradition case. A warrant was issued in England for the arrest of the accused charging him that he dishonestly received stolen goods, namely, nine electric detonators and four ounces of plastic gelatine, knowing or believing

4 0012922

the same to be stolen goods. This offence was proscribed by section 22(1) of the United Kingdom Theft Act 1968. Correspondence between the offence for which the accused is requested, and an offence in our jurisdiction must be proved if the accused is to be extradited. It is thus necessary to decide whether section 33(1) of the Larceny Act 1916 was equivalent. This provided: "Every person who receives any property knowing the same to have been stolen or obtained in any way whatsoever under circumstances which amount to felony or misdemeanour, shall be guilty of an offence . . .". The section has been subsequently replaced in the Larceny Act 1990 to require a less stringent external and mental element of handling stolen property "knowing or believing it to be stolen"; McCutcheon – Revision of the Larceny Code [1991] ICLJ 23. In the context of determining whether there was correspondence the Supreme Court discussed the meaning of knowledge.

Henchy J: . . . At common law it was a misdemeanour, punishable by fine and imprisonment, to receive goods knowing them to have been stolen; the indictment commonly charged an accused with receiving the stolen goods *well knowing* at the time when he received them that they had been feloniously stolen. The offence eventually became a statutory one and, with the replacement of the Larceny Act 1896, and the Larceny Act 1901, by the Act of 1916, the offence of receiving stolen property "knowing the same to have been stolen" became a felony deriving from s 33, sub-s 1, of the latter Act.

A series of judicial decisions, both in this country and in England, has firmly established that it is essential for a conviction for receiving stolen goods contrary to s 33, sub-s 1, of the Act of 1916 that an accused must, at the time of the receiving, have actually known the goods to have been stolen. Recklessness as to whether they were or were not stolen is not sufficient. Actual knowledge of the fact that they were stolen is of the essence of the offence. This is not the same as direct knowledge, such as an accused would have if he saw a looter smash a shop window and abstract goods which were displayed inside. Of course, the actual knowledge may be proved circumstantially. In giving the judgment of the Court of Criminal Appeal in *The People (Attorney General) v Berber*[29], Black J said at pp 411–412 of the report:

"The question of guilty knowledge is well dealt with in Wills on Circumstantial Evidence, 7th ed, p 103 in the following passage: 'It is not necessary that the receiver of stolen property should have obtained a guilty knowledge by direct information; it is sufficient if the circumstances under which it was received were such as must have satisfied any reasonable mind that it must have been dishonestly obtained.' The word 'must' deserves emphasis in both places where it occurs in this passage."

The judgment went on to say:

"The fact that a person has been so imprudent that he did not know that the property was stolen, when, if he had not been so imprudent, he would have known it, is a negation of guilty knowledge. It would be absurd to regard it as a proof of the very thing it negatives. To set up ordinary prudence as the test of guilty knowledge is to make imprudence a necessary badge of fraud, whereas a reasonable mind may often be satisfied that property was received under circumstances indicating a transaction that was casual or incautious, indiscreet or venturesome, or even rash, without being criminal."

In dealing with the arguments propounded in this case I am not entitled to analyse or interpret the Theft Act 1968. I must focus my attention on the words

29 [1944] IR 405.

"knowing or believing the same to be stolen goods" and first consider whether a conviction under s 33, sub-s 1, of the Act of 1916 which contained those words would be good. I am satisfied that it would not. Apart from the fact that it might be held bad for duplicity, it would indicate that the jury may have found the *mens rea* to be something less than actual knowledge that the goods had been stolen; that would be in the teeth of s 33, sub-s 1, of the Act of 1916 and the judicial decisions under it.

While knowledge and belief frequently coincide or overlap (for example, I both know and believe that this is the Supreme Court), there are many matters which one may believe to be correct without being able to say that one knows them to be correct. For example, I may believe that there is life in outer space, that evolution is the origin of species, that a particular person did a particular act, but I may have to admit that I do not know, or do not know with any substantial degree of certainty, that such beliefs are well founded. Without entering into the intricate logical, metaphysical and philosophical problems involved in a comparison of knowledge with belief, and keeping the matter on the plane of ordinary usage (which is, presumably, how it would be dealt with by both judge and jury), I would point to the commonly used expression "I believe it to be so, but I do not really know."

If a person were being tried for the offence of receiving goods "knowing or believing the same to be stolen goods," contrary to s 33, sub-s 1, of the Act of 1916, the judge when charging the jury, would not be entitled to tell them to ignore the words "or believing" in the indictment and in the issue paper; nor, if a conviction ensued, could they be ignored in the warrant. As appears from a consideration of the Criminal Justice (Administration) Act 1924, and the rules and forms annexed thereto, the fact of the matter is that the introduction into the indictment of the words "or believing" would invalidate the indictment and, thereby, a consequent conviction. The introduction of those words as an ingredient of the offence would amount to an unconstitutional amendment of s 33, sub-s 1, of the Act of 1916 for it would allow a dilution of relaxation of the *mens rea* required by that subsection.

Glanville Williams in his Textbook of Criminal Law says at p 87: "The word 'knowing' in a statute is very strong. To know that a fact exists is not the same as taking a chance whether it exists or not. The courts ought not to extend a *mens rea* word by forced construction. If, when Parliament says 'knowing' or 'knowingly,' it does not mean actual knowledge, it should be left to say as much by amending the statute." Therefore, I would hold that the words "or believing" in the description of the specified offence prevent the component elements of that offence, if set out in their entirety in an indictment for an offence in this State, from having exact correspondence with an offence contrary to s 33, sub-s 1, of the Act of 1916. I have reached that conclusion, as the authorities require, by confining my inquiry to a comparison of the factual components of the two offences that are said to correspond. But I am fortified in my conclusion by noting that if I were free to study the statutory evolution of s 22, sub-s 1, of the Theft Act 1968, and to give it a judicial interpretation, I would reach the same opinion.

Section 22, sub-s 1, of the Act of 1968 is the translation into statutory form of a recommendation that had been made in a report of the Criminal Law Revision Committee: see Theft and Related Offences – Cmnd 2977. That committee had been entrusted with the task of reforming the law relating to theft. In introducing the words "or believing" into the definition of handling stolen goods, the committee intended to extend the law as it is set out in s 33, sub-s 1, of the Act of 1916. In their report (Cmnd 2977, 64) they stated: "It is a serious defect of the present law that actual knowledge that the property was stolen must be proved. Often the prosecution cannot prove this. In many cases indeed guilty knowledge does not exist, although the circumstances of the transaction are such that the receiver ought to be guilty of an offence. The man who buys goods at a ridiculously low price from an unknown seller whom he meets in a public house may not *know* that the goods were stolen, and he may take the precaution of asking no questions. Yet it may be clear on the evidence that he believes that the goods were stolen. In such cases the prosecution may fail (rightly, as the law now stands) for want of proof of guilty knowledge."

That the change in the law intended by the committee (who drafted what is now s 22, sub-s 1) was actually effected is a conclusion that is supported by high judicial authority. For example, in *Reg v Smith*[30] Lord Hailsham of St Marylebone, LC (with whose speech in the House of Lords Lord Reid and Lord Salmon agreed) said at p 490 of the report:

"But, on consideration, I am sure that this would be a false construction, and that the expression 'believed' was inserted to guard against acquittals which had taken place under the former Larceny Act when it was necessary to prove knowledge that the goods were stolen and belief was not enough."

In referring to s 22, sub-s 1, of the Act of 1968 Viscount Dilhorne said at p 503 of the report:

"The word 'believing' was, I think, inserted to avoid the possibility of an accused being acquitted when there was ample evidence that he believed the goods stolen but no proof that he knew they were."

However, the fact that there is not total correspondence between the ingredients set out in the warrant and the ingredients necessary for an offence contrary to s 33, sub-s 1, of the Act of 1916 does not dispose of this ground of appeal. If the ingredients enumerated in the warrant were necessarily less in number than those required for an offence under the law of this State, there would be an absence of the correspondence of offences envisaged by s 47, sub-s 2, of the Extradition Act 1965: see *per* Ó Dálaigh CJ in *The State (Furlong) v Kelly*[31] at p 141 of the report. However, the ingredient expressed by the words "or believing" does not necessarily or invariably extend the scope of the offence specified in the warrant beyond the ingredients of an offence contrary to s 33, sub-s 1, of the Act of 1916. In essence, the only difference between the factual ingredients of the two offences in question is that the English offence allows "believing" as an alternative to "knowing." Therefore, if the Director of Public Prosecutions were to lay, *mutatis mutandis*, an indictment in the factual form set out in the warrant, but omitting the words "or believing," then, on the authority of the decision of this Court in *The State (Furlong) v Kelly*[32], he would be charging a corresponding offence for the purpose of s 47, sub-s 2, of the Act of 1965 as the Irish offence would not have "an additional essential ingredient" – to use the words of Ó Dálaigh CJ at p 141 of *Furlong*'s case[33]. On the contrary, the true position is that it is the English offence that has an additional alternative ingredient. Therefore, I am compelled by authority to reject this third ground of appeal.

Recklessness

1.26 Recklessness is a less culpable mental state than intent. Where a person intended the external element of a crime, recklessness, criminal negligence and negligence will also be incorporated in that state as they are lesser in terms of blameworthiness. The system does not work in the opposite direction; negligence or criminal negligence do not amount to reckless-

---

30 [1975] AC 476.
31 [1971] IR 132.
32 *Ibid.*
33 *Ibid.*

ness. Recklessness does not suffice for crimes of intent. Each is separately defined and distinct. In general, intent and recklessness are alternative mental elements for most offences. Examples are rape and assault (see paras **6.45–6.61** and paras **7.36–7.44** respectively). Where a statute specifies intent then that must be proven; an example is murder (see paras **5.03–5.21**). Where a statute specifies that an act is done maliciously, this requires proof that the accused either intended to do the particular kind of harm that in fact was done or was reckless as to whether such a kind of harm would occur or not (the accused foreseeing that the particular kind of harm might be done but going on to take the risk of it) and this word is not limited to, nor does it require, any ill-will towards the victim; *R v Cunningham*[34]. Recklessness can be simply defined as the conscious running of an unjustifiable risk.

1.27 The House of Lords in *R v Caldwell*[35] and in *R v Lawrence*[36] have reversed the traditional analysis of recklessness and replaced it with a test based on mere negligence. According to Lord Diplock, in those cases, recklessness involves the accused doing an act which creates an obvious and serious risk and giving no thought to the possibility of their being any risk or recognising that there was some risk involved, but nonetheless going on to do the act. Excluded from this definition is the person who considers whether there is a risk but then discounts it. The House of Lords appeared to see no difference between a person who foresees a risk that may be occasioned by his conduct and one who does not foresee such a risk. Indeed comments of the Law Lords indicated that they regarded them as equivalent moral states. Proceeding with an act in circumstances where an ordinary person would have foreseen that it was creating a risk of a consequence which is outlawed is equivalent to the civil standard for negligence; failing to exercise the standard of care appropriate to a reasonable person in the circumstances in question. In civil law damages are awarded where harm is caused by a failure to exercise reasonable care. Crime is much more serious. Conviction involves stigma and punishment. The imposition of a test of negligence for criminal liability removes the foundation of blameworthiness necessary to justify punishment for a culpable mental state. Obviously, it is far less wrong to genuinely fail to foresee a risk than to continue with conduct being aware of that risk. These decisions undermine the moral foundation of the criminal law and substitute standard ideas of the acceptable behaviour of notional ordinary people in the place of individual blame[37].

1.28 The definition of recklessness in Ireland does not conform to these standards. The accused must have foreseen the risk but have proceeded with his conduct nonetheless; *The People (DPP) v Murray*[38] (see para **1.31**). The Supreme Court in *Murray* did not indicate whether the foreseen risk must be serious. The Model Penal Code definition indicates such a test. It is submit-

---

34 [1957] 2 QB 396.
35 [1982] AC 341.
36 [1982] AC 516.
37 For an interesting discussion see Patient *Caldwell after Moloney – Another look at Caldwell Recklessness* (1987) SI JCL 82.
38 [1977] IR 360.

22

ted that the foreseen risk must be serious, or that the culpability in failing to exclude that risk must be high. The definition of criminal negligence, discussed in chapter 5, deliberately incorporates a definitional element of a high degree of risk. As criminal negligence is a lesser standard than reckless-ness that element of high risk must also apply. A contractor involved in the construction of a bridge who downgrades the quality of the steel structuring knowing of the danger to the stability of the bridge, is taking a serious risk. A person who has a faint suspicion that the woman with whom he is having sexual intercourse is not consenting to the act, can remove that suspicion by the simple expedient of an enquiry; to fail to do so involves a high degree of moral culpability and is so equivalent to taking a serious risk. A risk can also be justifiable, or unjustifiable, depending on the circumstances. Situations in which that would be a real issue in a criminal trial will be rare. For example, a contractor about to embark on the construction of a major tunnel project through a mountain will be aware that there are serious risks involved to the safety of his employees. It is not recklessness for him to proceed provided he takes every reasonable precaution to ensure that those dangers are kept to the absolute minimum. His task is justifiable and he has no moral culpability should an accident occur. Similarly a surgeon about to embark on an operation to save a patient's life may know that his procedure involves, in itself, a serious risk to the patient's survival. Failing to take that risk may mean that the patient will die in the normal course of events whereas if he is successful the patient's life may be extended for a long period. The risk is therefore justifiable, even though serious, and again moral culpability is absent.

1.29   *Mary McAleese – Just What is Recklessness?*
                        [1981] DULJ 29

Section 2 of the Criminal Law (Rape) Act 1981 creates for the first time a statutory definition of the offence of rape. . . .
. . . As stated in the Dáil, "The intention is not to change the law as to the meaning of rape but only to make it clear what constitutes the offence."[39]
. . . Can any definition of any offence ever be "clear" where "reckless" forms the basis of the requisite *mens rea*? (Just what is "recklessness"?) Does the requirement of "recklessness" mean the same thing in both the Irish and English jurisdictions? Does it mean that the prosecution must prove that the accused actually adverted his mind to the possibility that the victim was not consenting but persisted regardless, or need the prosecution merely prove that any reasonable man would have considered the possibility that she was not consenting? Does recklessness mean something different when it is applied to circumstances rather than conduct? This article attempts to answer some of those questions.
The public debate on the issue of rape was initiated primarily in both jurisdic-tions by the decision of the House of Lords in the case of *The DPP v Morgan*.[40] This decision that an honest but reasonable belief that the victim was consenting would negative the *mens rea* of rape caused a largely unjustified hue and cry, and indeed that principle was subsequently endorsed and adopted by the legislature of both jurisdictions.[41]

39 Per Minister for State at the Department of Justice, Sean Doherty, *Dail Reports*, 4.XI.80, p 1454.
40 [1975] 2 All ER 347.
41 In Ireland, see s 2(2) of Criminal Law (Rape) Act 1981.

In deciding what was or was not "recklessness", the court in *Morgan* seemed to be in no difficulty. Recklessness quite clearly meant the actual adversion of the mind to the possibility that the victim was not consenting – in other words, the test was purely subjective. . . .

. . . Continuing what one writer calls "its dismal record in criminal cases",[42] the House of Lords in two recent judgments has, it seems, decided that recklessness in the narrow sense ascribed to it above . . . (ie as involving a subjective test), is *not* the only sense in which the courts recognise it. Lord Diplock puts it thus in *R v Caldwell*[43].

"'Reckless' as used in the new statutory definition of the *mens rea* of these offences is an ordinary English word. It had not by 1971 become a term of legal art with some more limited esoteric meaning than that which it bore in ordinary speech – a meaning which surely includes not only deciding to ignore a risk of harmful consequences resulting from one's acts that one had recognised as existing, but also failing to give any thought to whether or not there is any such risk in circumstances where, if any thought were given to the matter it would be obvious that there was".

. . . It is submitted that the court in *Caldwell*'s case fell into the trap described so well by Jerome Hall:
"Recklessness, no less than intention, includes a distinctive state of awareness. To ascertain whether recklessness existed, we must determine the actor's knowledge of the facts and his estimate of his conduct with reference to the increase of risk. In the determination of these questions, the introduction of the 'reasonable man' is not a substitute for the defendant's awareness that his conduct increased the risk of harm any more than it is a substitute for the determination of intention, where that is material. It is a method used to determine those operative facts in the minds of normal persons. The method should not be confused with the fact to be determined . . . The confusion of the material mental state with the proof of its presence has been greatest in the case law on recklessness. This is the combined result of misinterpretation of the 'reasonable man' test and failure to recognise the distinctive subjective character of recklessness".[44]

. . . The scope of "recklessness" was debated at some length by the Supreme Court in *The People v Murray*[45] This is what each of the five judges had to say of "recklessness".
Walsh J said:

"Recklessness may be found either by applying a subjective test as where there has been conscious taking of an unjustified risk of which the accused actually knew, which imports foresight, or by applying an objective test as where there has been a conscious taking of an unjustified risk of which the accused did not actually know but of which he ought to have been aware".[46]

It is difficult to see the relevance or significance of the word "conscious" in the second half of that quotation. How can one be conscious of taking a risk the existence of which one is ignorant? In any event, Walsh J's analysis accords fully with that of the House of Lords in *Caldwell*.

42 J C Smith (1981) *Criminal Law Review*, 393 commentary on *R v Caldwell* cited below.
43 [1981] 2 All ER 961.
44 Jerome Hall: *General Principles of Criminal Law*, 2nd ed, p 120.
45 [1977] IR 360.
46 *Ibid* at p 386.

Henchy J, having decided at the outset that "the test of guilt for capital murder as well as murder must be a subjective one", went on:[47]

"The test of recklessness in this context[48] is well stated in the Model Penal Code – s 2.02(2)(c) – drawn up by the American Law Institute: 'A person acts recklessly with respect to a material element of an offence when he consciously disregards a substantial and unjustifiable risk that the material element exists or will result from his conduct.'"

Henchy J then quotes from early Glanville Williams (Criminal Law: The General Part, 2nd ed, p 152) in which the writer claims that a person who has given *no* thought to the existence of a probability and a possibility can be guilty of recklessness. But, and here Henchy J's judgment is ambiguous, Henchy J immediately says:

"I do not accept that *mens rea* as to the concomitant circumstances that the victim of the murder was a Garda acting in the course of his duty is proved if the mere unconsidered possibility of his being so existed".

Does Henchy J mean:

(*a*) that he rejects Williams' definition of recklessness as including negligence, ie an objective standard; or
(*b*) is he accepting Williams' formulation but saying that in relation to capital murder only recklessness in its "subjective" sense will suffice;
(*c*) is he accepting the Model Penal Code formula as being exhaustive of the definition of recklessness; or
(*d*) as merely an apt statement of the *kind* of recklessness applicable specifically to the offence of capital murder?

There is at least some substance in the belief that (*b*) and/or (*d*) is the correct conclusion, for Henchy J also said:

"Whether Marie Murray had the *required* recklessness is essentially a matter of fact to be inferred from the evidence."[49]

It could be plausibly argued that the word "required" is superfluous if "subjective recklessness" is all that there is to the entirety of "recklessness", but makes sense in the context of an assumption that there are different degrees of recklessness, not all of which may apply to a particular type of offence.

If that belief is correct (although it may not be), then Henchy J, like Walsh J, is in agreement with *Caldwell* to the extent that it defines the scope of recklessness as a concept in criminal law.

Griffin J, is more selective than Henchy J in his quotations from the pre-*Morgan* Glanville Williams,[50] confining them solely to remarks about subjective recklessness, and it is difficult to tell whether or not he accepts the existence of a wider ambit for recklessness, though he contends (without satisfactorily explaining why) that recklessness as to consequences is quite distinct from recklessness as to circumstances. (*Murrays'* case is concerned only with the latter). Later he summarises his view:

". . . there must be advertence on the part of the accused – recklessness involves foresight of the possibility and the taking of a risk".

47 *Ibid* at pp 402–405.
48 Ie in the context of deciding whether the accused knew or was reckless as to whether his victim was a Garda Síochána acting in the course of his duty.
49 At p 404; emphasis supplied.
50 At p 413.

However, the apparent clarity of that statement is obscured by two factors:

(a) the clear distinction Griffin J makes between recklessness as to consequence and recklessness as to circumstances, and (b) the confinement of his remarks only to subjective recklessness and silence on Williams' wider view of the term.

Kenny J introduces totally new terminology without actually clarifying the ambit of recklessness.

Parke J is brief and to the point:

"It seems clear on the authorities that it (ie *mens rea*) can be recklessness in the sense that it motivates conduct with a total disregard to the legal and other consequences which may follow". He then "expressly adopts the observations of Mr Justice Griffin on this subject".

So in summary of at least two of the five Supreme Court judges (Walsh J and Henchy J) appear to approve a broad notion of "recklessness", which accords with Lord Diplock's formulation in *Caldwell*, although it is impossible to say whether they would necessarily agree with the extent of its application to criminal offences as stated in *Caldwell*. The three remaining can be interpreted more or less as one pleases, but are probably best left uninterpreted until the issue is more specifically and coherently debated sometime in the future. Perhaps on that day the court might remember that there are other eminent writers in the field of criminal law besides Glanville Williams.

What then are the implications for the offence of rape in particular? There are several possibilities arising out of the dicta in *Murray*:

(1) Irish law recognises that recklessness means both subjective and objective recklessness, but s 2(1) of the Criminal Law (Rape) Act 1981 limits the *mens rea* of rape to subjective recklessness by implication,[51] or

(2) Irish law recognises recklessness as meaning only "subjective recklessness" where it is used as a test of *mens rea* in the criminal law, though it may have a wider meaning in common parlance, or

(3) "Recklessness" means what *Caldwell* says it means and the offence of rape is to be read accordingly.

It is submitted that the second possibility is the one which the legislature intended in the Criminal Law (Rape) Act 1981; it is in accord with the preponderance of legal thought on the ambit of recklessness; it establishes the highest degree of clarity and certainty; it simply makes profound legal and common sense; and it contains the ambit of criminal liability within justifiable limits. To hold otherwise leads inescapably to the conclusion that rape and indeed many other offences having recklessness as the test of *mens rea* can be committed by someone who was simply careless, who ought to have seen the risk but who in actual fact did not, ie by someone who was negligent. That view considerably widens the mesh of the net of the criminal law, if it is correct. Perhaps it is time we introduced some certainty into this area one way or the other. We need some standardisation of the definition of concepts basic to criminal liability, eg intention, negligence, and the one in question, recklessness. If the courts cannot do it, why not the legislature?

Subjectivism versus objectivism

1.30 The judgments of the Supreme Court in *The People (DPP) v Murray*[52] are an analysis of the elements of the offence of capital murder. However, notwithstanding the later abolition of the death penalty the

51 That implication is to be drawn from *DPP v Morgan*.
52 [1977] IR 360.

judgments are of fundamental importance as a source of the basic principle of criminal law in this jurisdiction. Prior to 1964 everyone convicted of murder had to be sentenced to death. The Criminal Justice Act, of that year, removed the death penalty for murder except in the specified cases set out in that section. Subsequently the death penalty has been abolished entirely by s 1 of the Criminal Justice Act 1990 and those categories of murder replaced by a minimum sentence that a person sentenced to life imprisonment must serve. A person found guilty of murder in 1963 would have been automatically sentenced to death. A person committing murder after the coming into force of the 1964 Act could only be sentenced to death if his victim fell within the categories to which that Act applied the death penalty. In constructing the elements of an offence the judges, particularly Walsh J, Henchy J, and Griffin J seemed concerned with four factors:

(1) Depending on the status of the victim the penalties immeasurably increased from life imprisonment to actual death.
(2) The form of the charge appropriate to capital murder, as opposed to ordinary murder, required a statement that the victim fell within the category which attracted the more severe penalty.
(3) Criminal law had always assumed that a legislature requires a mental element in respect of the commission of each of the external factors of the crime. In most ordinary crimes there is a single external element. An example is assault and a single mental element, of intention or recklessness, would suffice. For capital murder there were two external elements; the killing of a person and that person's status as a diplomat or Garda, etc. Consequently, a mental element was required in relation to both. As s 4 of the Act defined the mental element for murder as an intention to kill or cause serious injury, no dispute arose as to the mental state of the accused when killing the victim. Left at large, however, was the question of the status of the victim. Simply requiring that there be an external element unaccompanied by any knowledge or suspicion on the part of the accused that the victim was a Garda would cause the most severe sanction to be imposed simply on the basis of a chance occurrence. Fundamental requirements of blameworthiness indicated that before being culpable the accused should also have had awareness of the status (or occupation) of his victim. In deciding that the intention of the Oireachtas could not have been that the accused should know the victim was a Garda, and in indicating recklessness as the appropriate mental standard for this additional element, the Supreme Court firmly established the subjective state of mind of an individual accused as being fundamental to blame. The court indicated recklessness as a sufficient mental element for crime in the absence of an indication to the contrary in the text of legislation.
(4) The Supreme Court had no law making function but merely declared the elements of the offence from an analysis of the law as it stood in its historical context and gleaned the intention of the Oireachtas from the words they had used to create the offence, and from its context.

1.31   ***The People (DPP) v Noel and Marie Murray***
                                        [1977] IR 360
                                    Supreme Court, 1976

Facts: The accused, who were husband and wife, escaped in a motor car after an
armed bank robbery in which each of them had taken an active part. The driver of
a private car, who was passing the bank at the time of the escape, pursued the
robbers' car in his car until eventually the robbers' car stopped and the accused ran
away from it. The pursuer stopped his car and ran after and overtook the husband.
When the pursuer was about to seize the husband (who was then unarmed) the
wife shot and killed the pursuer. The pursuer was a policeman and a member of
the Garda Síochána who was not in uniform and who was not on duty at the start of
the chase. The accused were charged jointly in the Special Criminal Court on an
indictment containing 11 counts, of which the first charged them with the commission of capital murder. They were convicted on the first count and sentenced to
death by execution; they were also convicted on five other counts and sentenced to
terms of penal servitude. The accused appealed to the Court of Criminal Appeal
and from there to the Supreme Court.

Walsh J: Counsel for the prosecution have relied upon the submission that, as
murder is a common-law offence, it continues to be such unless some statute
clearly alters that position; and that there is a presumption or a canon of construction to the effect that, where it appears to alter or interfere with a rule of the
common law, a statute is to be construed strictly and that, in effect, it may alter the
common law only as little as can be clearly read from the statute. That submission,
even if it were correct, begs a number of important questions.

The guiding rule is that a court must give effect to the ordinary or, where
appropriate, the technical meaning of words in the general context of the statute.
The court must also determine the extent of general words with reference to their
context. If the words, given their ordinary meaning, produce a result which cannot
reasonably be supposed to have been the intention of the legislature, then the
court must apply them in any secondary meaning which they are capable of
bearing. In *Maunsell v Olins*[53] Lord Simon of Glaisdale says:

> ". . . in statutes dealing with ordinary people in their everyday lives, the
> language is presumed to be used in its primary ordinary sense, unless this
> stultifies the purpose of the statute, or otherwise produces some injustice,
> absurdity, anomaly or contradiction, in which case some secondary ordinary
> sense may be preferred, so as to obviate the injustice, absurdity, anomaly or
> contradiction, or fulfil the purpose of the statute: while, in statutes dealing with
> technical matters, words which are capable of both bearing an ordinary
> meaning and being terms of art in the technical matter of the legislation will
> presumptively bear their primary meaning as such terms of art (or, if they must
> necessarily be modified, some secondary meaning as terms of art)."

In *Black-Clawson International Ltd v Papierwerke Waldhof-Aschaffenburg
AG*[54]. Lord Reid deals with the effect of statutory changes in the common law, so
far as construction is concerned, in the following manner:

> "There is a presumption which can be stated in various ways. One is that in the
> absence of any clear indication to the contrary Parliament can be presumed not
> to have altered the common law further than was necessary to remedy the
> 'mischief.' Of course it may and quite often does go further. But the principle is

---

53 [1975] AC 373, 391.
54 [1975] AC 591, 614.

that if the enactment is ambiguous, that meaning which relates the scope of the Act to the mischief should be taken rather than a different or wider meaning which the contemporary situation did not call for."

So far as the construction of penal statutes is concerned – and the Act of 1964 is a statute of that class – they must be fairly construed according to the legislative intent as expressed in the enactment, and persons liable to a penalty should be entitled to the benefit of any genuine doubt or ambiguity as distinct from spurious doubts or ambiguities. Punishment should not be extended to cases which are not clearly embraced in the statutory provisions. In my view, these are the correct approaches to the problem of construction of the statute under consideration and I now propose to examine the statutory provisions with which this case is concerned.

The Act of 1964 was intended to alter, and quite clearly did alter, the provisions of the common law relating to the crime of murder. Section 4 of the Act abolished what was known as the doctrine of constructive malice and introduced a statutory definition of murder which distinguished murder from any other form of unlawful killing. As was pointed out by this Court in *The People (Attorney General) v Dwyer*[55], the effect of the provision was that unlawful homicide shall not be murder unless the necessary intent is established and that the onus of establishing this beyond reasonable doubt remains at all times upon the prosecution, as also does the onus of proving beyond reasonable doubt that the presumption that the accused person intended a natural and probable consequence of his conduct has not been rebutted. In effect, the section introduced a new definition of murder. One of the consequences of that change was that some homicides were transferred from the category of murder to that of manslaughter. The effect of the abolition of the doctrine of constructive malice was to make it impossible to have anyone convicted of murder on the basis of a test of malice which used as its criterion not what the accused contemplated but what the ordinary reasonable man would have contemplated as the probable result of the criminal act. So far as the facts of a case such as the present one are concerned, one of the immediate effects of s 4 of the Act was that a killing done in the course of or for the purpose of resisting a lawful arrest by a member of the Garda Síochána would no longer amount to murder unless the killing fulfilled the requirements as to the malice set out in s 4 of the Act. Prior to that, the law had been that the killing of a Civic Guard by someone using force while endeavouring to resist arrest, and for the purpose of resisting the arrest, was murder as the intent to oppose by force the Civic Guard was sufficient malice to establish the crime of murder. . . .

I think it is a fair inference, as counsel for the prosecution pointed out, that the Oireachtas bore in mind when enacting this legislation that our police force was an unarmed police force and had a special claim to whatever additional protection the law could give its members by providing the deterrent of the death penalty for violent criminals with whom members of the Garda Síochána often have to contend. The same or similar considerations probably existed with regard to the murder of prison officers in the course of their duty, as the type of criminal likely to be involved in such an affair would probably not be deterred by the threat of a prison sentence. . . .

It is to be noted that a person going to the aid of a member of the Garda Síochána in the course of his duty is not protected in the same way as the Guard himself. This, to my mind, indicates that what the Oireachtas had in mind was (a) that an assailant who contemplates killing a member of the Garda Síochána would be aware that his punishment would be quite different from that which he would incur by killing a private citizen, and (b) that if that is to have a deterrent effect, it will have it only if the assailant is aware that his prospective victim is a member of

55 [1972] IR 416, 420.

the Garda Síochána. I think it may be reasonably assumed that in the ordinary way an armed assailant is much more likely to succeed in frightening away a civilian without killing him than in frightening away a member of the Garda Síochána. The facts of the present tragic case illustrate this view in that, of all the persons who witnessed and were present at this armed robbery, the only person who gave chase to the armed robbers was the person who, though outwardly appearing to be a civilian, was in fact Garda Reynolds who was murdered in an attempt to apprehend the robbers. It is a fair inference that the robbers were prepared to kill, if necessary, in the course of the robbery and their flight from it and that, if in a confrontation with civilians and police the success of their flight depended upon killing someone, the victim was more likely to be a member of the police, even though the robbers were aware of his identity or because they were aware of his identity.

I think it is an inescapable inference that the Oireachtas intended that the offence of capital murder should be a separate and distinct offence from those categories of murder which one may describe as non-capital. The deterrent effect of the possibility of capital punishment as a protection for members of the Garda Síochána would come into play only if the assailant is in a position to weigh up the consequences of his action before murdering a member of the Garda Síochána. If, with the knowledge he has, the assailant nevertheless carries out the murder, in the vast majority of cases he would be committing a premeditated murder that is as well an offence against public order and the authority of the State and an offence that attracts a particular penalty not attached to other types of murder.

In my view, the whole context of the statute indicates the intention of the Oireachtas to create a new offence of capital murder. To my mind, the statutory requirement that it should be charged as such requires that it should be charged as a statutory offence in the indictment. One must also bear in mind that additional weight for the view that capital murder is a new offence is to be found in the statutory provision for the alternative verdict to it being a verdict of murder. The statute also provides that, for the purposes of an appeal against a conviction, capital murder shall be treated as a distinct offence from murder.

The Court of Criminal Appeal appears to have attached some importance to the provisions of sub-s 5 of s 3 of the Act of 1964 which provide that, subject to the special provisions set out in sub-ss 1–4 inclusive, "capital murder shall not be treated as a distinct offence from murder for any purpose." Counsel for the prosecution did not make any convincing submissions to this Court as to the meaning or possible effect of this sub-section. Coming where it does in the section and following the particular matters referred to in the first four sub-sections, I take it as being primarily directed, if not wholly directed, towards procedural matters. Although it is not necessary to decide the point here, it is possible that it captures such matters as are covered by s 4 of the Offences Against the Person Act 1861, which deals with conspiracy to murder, and s 9 of the same Act which deals with murder outside of the territory of the State, and s 16 of the same Act which deals with the sending of letters threatening to murder. I do not think, however, that it can be read as if it said that there was no such offence as capital murder, and that the expression "capital murder" is simply to be used in cases of murder where capital punishment may be imposed. If that had been the intention of the Oireachtas I think that the statute would have been worded in a very different way.

Having come to the conclusion that capital murder is a new offence, I now turn to the question of what must be proved by the prosecution in such a case. I respectfully agree with what was said in the judgment of the Court of Criminal Appeal dealing with this point when it said: "If capital murder is a new offence or a new variety of an existing offence, there would be a presumption at common law that it was the intention of the Oireachtas that an accused person was not guilty unless he had a *mens rea* in relation to all the ingredients of the offence. That would mean that no person could be convicted of the capital murder of a member of the Garda Síochána unless the prosecution established that the accused knew that the victim was a member of the Garda Síochána and was acting in the course of his duty. That presumption might be rebutted by the express or implied intention of the Oireachtas to be gathered from the language of the statute and the nature of the subject matter with which it dealt."

It has been submitted on behalf of the prosecution that, as the statute does not expressly require knowledge, such a requirement should not be read into the statute. Attention was drawn to the provisions of the Criminal Law Amendment Act 1935, where, in the case of unlawful carnal knowledge of a girl under the age of 17 or 15, it is not necessary to prove that the accused knew the girl was under age whereas, by contrast, the offence of having unlawful carnal knowledge of a woman who is an imbecile or an idiot does require the prosecution to prove knowledge of that fact on the part of the accused. The prosecution also drew attention to the fact that all the reported decisions in England in the cases dealing with assaults upon the police in the execution of their duty have decided that proof of knowledge that the victim was a policeman was not required. So far as this last matter is concerned the line of authority is based upon the doubtful authority of *R v Forbes*[56], the very facts of which are shrouded in uncertainty. It appears clear that the English courts were following this earlier decision and were prepared to abide by it, though no serious explanation has ever been given as to why it should be followed. It may well be that, because the offence is a comparatively minor one, it was decided to leave the early decision undisturbed. The same vew was taken in the Supreme Court of Victoria in Australia in *R v Galvin (No 1)*[57] but that case was overruled by the same court in *R v Galvin (No 2)*.[58] The matter came to the High Court of Australia in *R v Reynhoudt*[59] where a majority of the court took the view that in such an offence knowledge was not necessary, and preferred to follow the decision in *R v Forbes*.

For my own part, I prefer the reasoning of that eminent and world-famous jurist Chief Justice Dixon of the High Court of Australia who found himself in the minority in expressing the view which, in effect, coincides with the view expressed by the Court of Criminal Appeal in this present case on the question of knowledge – if capital murder be a separate offence. In a similar case of a charge of assaulting a police officer in the execution of his duty, the British Columbia Court of Appeal in *R v McLeod*[60] decided that knowledge that the person assaulted was a police officer was a necessary proof. So far as I am aware, there has never been any decision on this point by the High Court or the Supreme Court in Ireland, or by any of the superior courts prior to 1922. However, I do not think that anything of value is to be gained in this case by resorting to what was decided in the courts of other countries in cases which were not only trivial by comparison with the present one but were of a totally different kind, in that in no one of these cases was the offence charged one requiring a specific intent.

With regard to the submission made in relation to the requirements of the Criminal Law Amendment Act 1935, the position is somewhat different. There it is obviously the policy of the Act of 1935 to protect young girls. The Oireachtas thought it necessary to ensure this by imposing upon a male person who undertakes to have carnal knowledge of a young woman the risk of her turning out to be under the age of consent. It might well be impossible for the prosecution to prove in most cases that the accused had knowledge, and it is to be noted that the statute does not even envisage the accused successfully setting up a defence of lack of

56 (1865) 10 Cox CC 362.
57 [1961] VR 733.
58 [1961] VR 740.
59 (1962) 107 CLR 381.
60 (1954) 111 Can CC 106.

knowledge on his part even with the whole onus of proving that fact resting upon himself. The Oireachtas also apparently thought that an honest belief or an honest mistake with regard to age would not be consistent with the general policy of those statutory provisions, the object of which was to protect young girls from themselves as much as from men. The essential difference between that class of case and the present case is that in those cases the defendant is aware that he is dealing with a young woman, because the Act makes no distinction between one class or category of girl and another when they are under age. So far as capital murder of a member of the Garda Síochána is concerned, it is the occupation of the victim which is the decisive matter. Before the offence of capital murder was created it mattered not in the proof of the offence of murder whether the victim was a member of the Garda Síochána or not. If the protection afforded by the Act of 1935 to girls under the age of 17 were to be confined only to girls of a particular occupation, then the position would be quite different as obviously the intention of the Act would be quite different from that Act as it now stands. Therefore, I think there is no valid comparison to be made between the statutory provisions relating to capital murder and those relating to unlawful carnal knowledge of girls under the age of consent.

What is to be borne in mind, however, and it is a matter which it must be assumed the Oireachtas also had in mind, was the peculiar position always occupied by police officers as the victims of a homicide. The position was fully set out in the judgment of the former Court of Criminal Appeal in *The State v McMullen*[61] to which I have already referred. That was a case which turned upon the question of a trial judge's direction to a jury in a case where a Civic Guard had been shot and killed by an armed bank robber. The bank robber had fired deliberately at the Civic Guard but, because there was some suggestion that he did not have a deliberate intention to hit the Guard, it was submitted that the jury should have been free to find a verdict of manslaughter. The trial judge had expressly refused to put that issue to the jury. Chief Justice Kennedy stated what was the law on the subject of homicide in the course of forcibly resisting arrest by citing the following passages which appear at p 21 of the report. He said: "It [*the appeal*] raises a question which is the subject of authority, ancient and modern. 'The second kind of malice implied is, when a minister of justice, as a bailiff, constable, or watchman, etc, is killed in the execution of his office, in such a case, it is murder.' So says Hale (1 PC 457), and again: 'If a constable, or tithing-man, or watchman be in execution of his office, and be killed, it is murder; and in all cases of implied malice, or malice in law, the indictment need not be special, but general *ex malitia sua praecogitata interfecit et murdravit*, and the malice in law maintains the indictment' (1 PC 460), which proposition he rests on *Mackalley*'s case."[62] . . .

In the case before the Court of Criminal Appeal on that occasion the appellant was aware that the person pursuing him was a member of the Garda Síochána as the latter was actually in uniform and kept calling on the appellant to halt. The Chief Justice said: "It matters not that he did not – if, indeed, he did not – mean to hit him. It is murder according to the law, and the learned trial judge, O'Shaughnessy J, was absolutely right in so directing the jury." That case, as dealt with by Kennedy CJ, is an example of the type of malice which was abolished by s 4 of the Act of 1964, that is to say, that once the accused was resisting arrest and killed the police officer it was murder even if the accused did not mean to hit the officer at all. As was pointed out in the passage from Foster's Crown Cases quoted by the learned Chief Justice, the offence was "an outrage wilfully committed in defiance of the justice of the Kingdom." That clearly indicates that, before an accused

61 [1925] 2 IR 9.
62 (1611) 9 Co Rep 68.

could have been guilty of murder upon that form of malice, it had to be shown that the accused knew that the person he attacked was a policeman. Otherwise the necessary malice or *mens rea* was not established.

The Oireachtas, in enacting s 4 of the Act of 1964, repealed what had hitherto been the law, *viz*, that the killing of an officer or a member of the Garda Síochána done in the course of or for the purpose of resisting or preventing a lawful arrest was murder in the absence of any intent to kill or cause grevious bodily harm, even in the case where it was known to the assailant that his victim was a member of the Garda Síochána. I find this expressed legislative intention utterly irreconcilable with an intention which it is now sought to impute to the Oireachtas that a person can be guilty of the offence of capital murder by the fortuitous circumstance that his victim is, unknown to the murderer, a member of the Garda Síochána. Having regard to the content and the nature of the Act of 1964, such a meaning could not be read into it in the absence of clear and unambiguous wording to that effect. There is no such wording in the Act. The absence of a word such as "knowingly" in the reference to the offence in the statute does not raise any question of constructive knowledge; that is to say that, if the appellants did not know that their victim was a Civic Guard, they ought to have known it. The whole tenor of s 4 of the Act contradicts this. There is not evidence of any actual knowledge in the present case. The only evidence dealing with that topic is the statement of Marie Murray to the effect that she did not know the murdered man was a member of the Garda Síochána. It is well established that the mere non-belief of a denial does not prove the affirmative.

The question which now remains to be considered is whether there is any intermediate condition which might establish the necessary knowledge. During the course of the argument the question of the possibility of the necessary *mens rea* being established by recklessness was raised – largely as a result of a reference that was made to it in *R v McLeod*.[63] This possibility was rejected by counsel for the appellants but was adopted by counsel for the prosecution. Recklessness may be found either by applying a subjective test as where there has been conscious taking of an unjustified risk of which the accused actually knew, which imports foresight, or by applying an objective test as where there has been a conscious taking of an unjustified risk of which the accused did not actually know but of which he ought to have been aware. As applied to knowledge, subjective recklessness could amount to what might be termed "wilful blindness." If, for example, an armed bank robber is facing four men who are all in civilian attire and one of whom is to the actual knowledge of the robber a policeman but he does not know which one of the four it is, and if the robber then elects to shoot one or two of the men without actually knowing which is the policeman and kills the one who is the policeman, a question may well be raised as to whether or not this would provide the required degree of knowledge. However, that is not the case we are dealing with. The absence of the word "knowingly" or any similar word is not a decisive factor. There have been many decisions to show that that word merely says expressly what is normally implied. In this context objective recklessness is really constructive knowledge: and constructive knowledge has no place in our criminal law in establishing intent.

It is well established that, unless a statute either clearly or by necessary implication rules out *mens rea* as a constituent part of a crime, a court cannot find a person guilty of an offence against the criminal law unless he has a guilty mind. It has been pointed out earlier in this judgment that s 4 of the Act of 1964 makes murder an offence of specific intent. A person cannot be guilty of the capital murder of a Civic Guard in the course of his duty unless that person intends to murder a Civic Guard in the course of his duty, or intends to do serious injury to a

63 (1954) 111 Can CC 106.

Civic Guard in the course of his duty, and that injury causes the death of the Civic Guard. To intend to murder, or to cause serious injury to, a Civic Guard in the course of his duty is to have in mind a fixed purpose to reach that desired objective. Therefore, the state of mind of the accused person must have been not only that he foresaw but also willed the possible consequences of his conduct. There cannot be intention unless there is also foresight, and it is this subjective element of foresight which constitutes the necessary *mens rea*. Therefore, where a fact is unknown to the accused it cannot enter into his foresight and his conduct cannot be taken to be intentional with regard to it. It is well established that before an act can be murder it must be "aimed at someone" and must in addition be an act committed with the necessary statutory intention, the test of which is always subjective to the actual defendant.

The whole question of risk-taking has been the subject of much discussion and debate but it is, I think, accepted that a person who does not intend to kill and does not intend to cause serious injury but nevertheless does an act which exposes others to the risk of death or serious injury would not be guilty of murder when the *mens rea* required is an intent to kill or an intent to cause serious injury. Even if the specified and specific intent can be established not only when the particular purpose is to cause the event but also when the defendant has not substantial doubt that the event will result from his conduct, or when he foresees that the event will probably result from his conduct, the test is still based on actual foresight. Even on that basis, foresight of probable consequences must be distinguished from recklessness which imports a disregard of possible consequences. The essential difference between intention and foresight on the one hand and recklessness on the other is the difference between advertence and inadvertence as to the probable result. Some statutory offences are, by the terms of the statute, established by proving recklessness; but intention or specific intention can never be proved by recklessness, which is a lesser degree of criminal responsibility.

As Professor Glanville Williams points out at p 152 of the second edition of his Criminal Law (The General Part): "Either simple ignorance or mistake is sufficient to destroy the intentional nature of an act as to the unknown circumstance. Mistake will displace recklessness also." He goes on to express the view that simple ignorance is not enough to displace recklessness. At p 58 of the same work he describes recklessness as a branch of the law of negligence, that it is the kind of negligence where there is foresight of consequences. He goes on to confirm his view that recklessness is a kind of negligence by quoting at p 59 the formulation of the American Law Institute which is contained in the Model Penal Code, section 2.02(2)(c) (TD No 4 p 13). However, we are not here concerned with discussing the question of negligence but with intent and foresight.

It is of interest to note that this is no new concept and to recall the words of the British Royal Commission on Criminal Law in its 7th report (1834) at p 23 where it is stated:

"The degrees of likelihood or probability being in truth infinite, it is clear that no assigned degree of likelihood or probability that an injurious consequence will result from any act can serve as a test of criminal responsibility. Such a degree of likelihood or probability admits of no legal mode of ascertainment, and it would, if capable of being ascertained, afford no proper test of guilt, for it is not the precise degree of likelihood or probability in such cases, but the *knowledge or belief* that the thing is likely or probable which constitutes the *mens rea*, although the greater or less degree of probability may afford important evidence as to the real intention of the parties."

Over one hundred years later another British Royal Commission (the Royal Commission on Capital Punishment) formulated the principle in stating that persons ought not to be punished for the consequences of their acts which they did not intend or foresee. This is precisely the basis of the definition of murder laid down in s 4 of the Act of 1964. If the *actus reus* includes surrounding circumstances, it cannot be said to be intentional unless all its elements, including those circumstances, are known. This is how the matter is put succinctly, and in my view correctly, by Professor Glanville Williams at p 141 of the second edition of his Criminal Law (General Part). He goes on to set out the rule, as stated in generalized form by the American Law Institute, by quoting the following passage from their Model Penal Code:

> "When the law defining an offence prescribes the kind of culpability that is sufficient for the commission of an offence, without distinguishing among the material elements thereof, such provision shall apply to all the material elements of the offence, unless a contrary purpose plainly appears."

On the following page Professor Glanville Williams goes on to state:

> "It hardly needs to be said, by way of qualification of the foregoing, that an act is intentional as to a circumstance even though the actor does not positively know the circumstance to exist, *provided that he hopes that it exists.*" The italics are mine.

There is no evidence whatever that the latter consideration arises in the present case.

It is interesting to note the observations of Lord Diplock in *R v Mowatt*[64] where he points out at p 426 of the report that in s 18 of the Offences Against the Person Act 1861 (which requires specific intent to be established) the word "maliciously" adds nothing. He points out that the intent expressly required by that section is more specific than such element of foresight of consequences as is implicit in the word "maliciously," and that in directing a jury about an offence under that section the word "maliciously" is best ignored. In *R v Belfon*[65] the Court of Appeal in England quashed a conviction for wounding with intent to do grievous bodily harm under s 18 of the Act of 1861 because the judge directed the jury to the effect that specific intent was established if the defendant foresaw that serious injury was likely to result from his act and committed the act recklessly.

In the present case the appellants are undoubtedly guilty of murder but, in my view, the absence of the knowledge of the status of their victim means that the offence of capital murder has not been established. Whether the fact that the victim was a member of the Garda Síochána is to be described as an accompanying circumstance or a surrounding circumstance, it is part of the *actus reus* and for the reasons I have already given it cannot be said to be intentional unless the evidence at the trial did establish that the person who fired the shot (the appellant Marie Murray) knew that her victim was a member of the Garda Síochána. Indeed, the court of trial did not find that she did have that knowledge and, in my view, that fact alone is fatal to any submission that she can be said, under any circumstances, to have had the necessary knowledge.

Even if the appellant Marie Murray had been proved to have had the necessary knowledge and to have been guilty of capital murder, the position of the other appellant, Noel Murray, is that he could not be convicted of capital murder unless it was established that he had the same knowledge, or at least that it was part of a common design to murder a member of the Garda Síochána if it should prove necessary to execute successfully the robbery planned and undertaken and in the course of which the Guard was murdered.

This brings me to the final point but one which I believe to be fundamental to the verdict of capital murder and the conduct of the trial. Our criminal trials are conducted on the adversary or accusatorial system. An accused person is entitled

64 [1968] 1 QB 421.
65 [1976] 1 WLR 741.

as of right to know the case he has to meet so that he may be in a position to test it and, if necessary, to reply to it by calling evidence or otherwise. The prosecution in the present case was conducted on the basis of an incorrect interpretation of the law (*viz*, that capital murder was not a new offence) and so the evidence called and the submissions made took no account of the necessity to establish the *mens rea* on the part of the appellants necessary to establish the element of the offence which related to the status or occupation of the murdered man. The trial court misdirected itself in law on this fundamental point in ruling that capital murder was not a new offence and in ruling that the question of the degree of knowledge, if any, of the appellants of the status or occupation of their victim was not relevant to the proof of the offence of capital murder, and that it was not necessary for the prosecution to prove *mens rea* concerning that aspect of the case. In the result the trial court made no finding as to the state of knowledge or the state of mind of either of the appellants concerning this matter. This was a misdirection of law crucial to the charge of capital murder against the appellants.

The question of recklessness as a basis for the necessary *mens rea* was not raised at the trial or in the Court of Criminal Appeal; it was raised for the first time in this Court. Even if recklessness was sufficient to constitute the necessary *mens rea* – which, in my view, it is not – the prosecution cannot now seek in this Court to establish recklessness as constituting the necessary *mens rea*. In so doing, the prosecution is asking this Court to make findings of the primary facts necessary to establish subjective recklessness; that is to say, to make findings of fact of the actual state of mind of each of the appellants and of the actual knowledge or degree of advertence of each of them at the relevant times. It is obvious that such findings cannot be made by seeking to draw inferences by the application of objective standards even if the Criminal Justice Act 1964, did not (as it does) preclude such a course in the proof of murder. All the subjective elements have to be proved at the trial where the accused can meet them. This Court cannot be asked to uphold a conviction of capital murder by finding facts which not only were not found by the trial court but which the trial court did not even consider.

For the reasons I have given, I am of opinion that the conviction of capital murder in each case should be quashed and that a conviction in respect of the murder of Garda Reynolds should be substituted in each case, and that this Court should impose the mandatory[66] statutory penalty of penal servitude for life on each of the appellants.

Henchy J: . . . The Act of 1964 itself shows elsewhere that capital murder and murder *must* be treated as distinct in two crucial respects not dealt with in section 3. First, the penalty for capital murder is different, and s 5 (by amending ss 1, 2 and 3 of the Offences Against the Person Act 1861) ensures that the special statutory provisions dealing with conviction and sentence for murder shall henceforth apply only to capital murder. Secondly, and of more fundamental importance, the provisions of s 1 show that the two offences must be treated as substantively different, for there is an extra compound element in each of the four categories of capital murder which is not required for non-capital murder.

Take the particular capital murder charged in this case. Before the passing of the Act of 1964, the appellants could only have been charged with murder in respect of the killing of Garda Reynolds, and the count in the indictment would simply have charged that the appellants "murdered Michael Reynolds" – see the form given in the appendix to the Criminal Justice (Administration) Act 1924. That is how the alternative count of murder was formulated in the indictment in this case. However, the count of capital murder charged correctly that the appellants "murdered Michael Reynolds, he then being a member of An Garda Síochána,

66 See [1966] IR 361.

acting in the course of his duty." Looking at what the prosecution has to prove in each count to support a conviction, I find it impossible to say that capital murder is but common-law murder in a limited and retained form. On the contrary, I find it to be a new offence with a more limited application than common-law murder – the precise limited application depending on which of the four categories of capital murder set out in s 1, sub-s 1(*b*), of the Act of 1964 fits the facts of the case. In each of those four categories the proofs for a successful prosecution are more extensive and specific than those required for non-capital murder. The extra elements required produce an offence which in substance and gravity is radically different from common-law murder.

Since, as I have pointed out, capital murder and murder must be treated as distinct offences for the purpose of proof of guilt, of sentence and of consequence of sentence, the bar in s 3, sub-s 5, on treating capital murder as a distinct offence from murder for any purpose must be read as a prohibition against doing so for any *procedural* purpose. The legislature cannot have intended that the substantive and consequential differences between the two offences are to be ignored.

Capital murder, in my view, is a new offence, or type of offence, not simply in nomenclature but in the sum of its essential component elements. As to the particular type of capital murder charged in this case (the murder of a policeman acting in the course of his duty), it is an aggravated form of murder; it is aggravated by the fact that the person murdered was a policeman and was acting in the course of his duty, just as an assault on a peace officer in the execution of his duty, contrary to s 38 of the Offences Against the Person Act 1861, is not a simple assault but a particular kind of aggravated assault.

Finally, a test which marks out the existence of capital murder as an offence distinct from murder may be applied from the law of extradition. If an application were made in our Courts for the extradition of a person to, say, England to stand trial for what is now in our law classified as capital murder, and if the only type of murder our law recognized was non-capital murder, would the application succeed? The answer is "No." Capital murder would not, as is required by s 47, sub-s 2, of the Extradition Act 1965, "correspond with" murder because there are essential ingredients in the offence of capital murder which are not comprehended in the definition of murder.

A conclusion that, save for the purposes specified in s 3 of the Act of 1964, capital murder may not be treated as a distinct offence from murder for any purpose would produce illogical and unjust consequences beyond the possible intention or contemplation of those who framed or enacted the Act of 1964. It would mean, as counsel for the prosecution contends, that *mens rea* need not be proved as to the circumstances of the victim having been a member of the Garda Síochána acting in the course of his duty. If that were correct, then a person could be found guilty of capital murder not only if he did not know but also if he had no reason to know that his victim was a Garda, and even if he had been assured that his victim was not a Garda. If capital murder were to depend on the purely adventitious circumstance that the victim turned out to be a Garda acting in the course of his duty, and not on any moral culpability of the killer in that respect, the awesome distinction in penal severity between murder and capital murder would have no ethical or rational foundation. It would be repugnant to reason and fairness if the death penalty were to depend on the outcome of what, in effect, would have been a lottery as to the victim's occupation and activity. Fortunately, as I read the Act of 1964, that conclusion does not follow.

For the foregoing reasons I respectfully differ from the Special Criminal Court and the Court of Criminal Appeal. I hold that the Act of 1964 brought into existence capital murder as a new offence which is distinct from murder but which, for all procedural purposes except those permitted by s 3, is not to be deemed a distinct offence from murder.

The next matter to be considered is whether *mens rea* is required for all the elements of the new offence of capital murder created by the Act of 1964. The offence charged was essentially an assault, but a particular kind of compound or aggravated assault. What the prosecution had to prove (and which they did prove), as an *actus reus*, was that the appellant Marie Murray (and, through her, her husband) unlawfully killed Garda Reynolds when he was acting in the course of his duty. As is made clear by s 4, sub-s 1, of the Act of 1964, the *mens rea* for the offence of non-capital murder required proof that Marie Murray intended to kill or cause serious injury to her victim. The circumstances were such that the court of trial had no hesitation in finding that Marie Murray had that intention. That finding has not been questioned.

The further element in the *actus reus* of the offence of capital murder charged is that the victim of the killing was a Garda acting in the course of his duty. I have already rejected the submission that *mens rea* is not required for that element on the ground, as the submission went, that the offence is not made a new offence by the Act of 1964 and is but a version of common-law murder. In my judgment it is a new statutory offence. But, as such, does it involve *mens rea* for that further element?

The question is *res integra* under the Act of 1964, and such judicial decisions as throw light on the question arise in cases dealing with prosecutions under s 38 of the Offences Against the Person Act 1861 (or under analogous statutory provisions) charging an assault on a peace officer in the execution of his duty. Those decisions show a sharp cleavage of judicial opinion. A denial that the relevant statutory provision requires *mens rea* (in the form of intent or knowledge in relation to the fact that the victim of the assault was a member of the police acting in the execution of his duty) is to be found in a line of authorities running from *R v Forbes*[67] and including *R v Prince*[68]; *R v Maxwell*[69], *R v Mark*[70]; *Kenlin v Gardiner*[71], *R v Galvin (No 1)*[72] and *R v Reynhoudt*.[73] On the other hand, strong judicial opinion to the effect that *mens rea* in the form of either intent or knowledge is required for this element is to be found in *R v Galvin (No 2)*[74] which overruled *R v Galvin (No 1)*, in the dissenting judgments of Dixon CJ and Kitto J in *R v Reynhoudt*; and in the unanimous decision of the British Columbia Court of Appeal in *R v McLeod*.[75]

I do not propose to analyse the judicial reasoning of those decisions – for that, see Howard (79 LQR 247) and Zuckerman (88 LQR 246). I confine myself to saying that I find the reasoning leading to the conclusion that the element in question does not require *mens rea* to be of questionable origin, weak and unconvincing. It seems to stem from the idea that, because the section did not qualify the reference to a peace officer acting in the execution of his duty with words indicating a requirement of knowledge on the part of the accused of that fact, the offence should be held to be one of strict liability as to that fact. I believe that to be an incorrect method of interpreting a statutory provision imposing criminal liability. The correct rule of interpretation in such a case is that stated by Lord Reid at p 148 of the report of *Sweet v Parsley*[76]:

"Sometimes the words of the section which creates a particular offence make it clear that *mens rea* is required in one form or another. Such cases are quite frequent. But in a very large number of cases there is no clear indication either way. In such cases there has for centuries been a presumption that Parliament did not intend to make criminals of persons who were in no way blameworthy in

---

67 (1865) 10 Cox CC 362.
68 (1875) LR 2 CCR 154.
69 (1909) 2 Cr App R 26.
70 [1961] Crim LR 173.
71 [1967] 2 QB 510.
72 [1961] VR 733.
73 (1962) 107 CLR 381.
74 [1961] VR 740.
75 (1954) 111 Can CC 106.
76 [1970] AC 132.

what they did. That means that whenever a section is silent as to *mens rea* there is a presumption that, in order to give effect to the will of Parliament, we must read in words appropriate to require *mens rea*."

Admittedly Lord Reid was referring to a whole offence rather than to a constituent element of an offence, but the basis for the presumption is the same in both cases, ie, to avoid the unjust or oppressive application of the section to those who have not merited the guilt and punishment envisaged by the section, either because they are totally blameless or because their blameworthiness is only such as to attract guilt for a lesser offence.

I find an unrebutted presumption that Parliament, in enacting s 1 of the Criminal Justice Act 1964, and in creating the new offence of capital murder which is defined for the purpose of this case as "murder of a member of the Garda Síochána acting in the course of his duty," intended that the section should be read as requiring *mens rea* for all the elements of that definition. As I have indicated earlier, to hold otherwise would be to remove any logical or ethical basis for the distinction between murder and capital murder.

In those judgements which hold that *mens rea* is necessary in regard to the circumstances that the victim was a policeman acting in the course of his duty, the nature and extent of the required *mens rea* is expressed in varying ways. The majority judgment of the Supreme Court of Victoria (O'Bryan, Dean and Hudson JJ) in *R v Galvin (No 2)*[77] states at p 749 of the report:

"Knowledge may be excellent evidence of intention but it is not an essential element in the crime. The mental element in our opinion is the intention to do the *whole act* which is prohibited."

In the same case Barry J said at p 753 of the report:

"I consider that to be guilty of the offence of assaulting (or resisting or wilfully obstructing) a member of the police force in the due execution of his duty which s 40 creates, an accused person must have, at the time of the event, not only an intention to assault (or resist or wilfully obstruct) but also an intention to do so to a person who he is aware possesses at that time a particular character, ie that of a member of the police force, and who is engaged in a particular activity, ie the due execution of his duty."

The remaining judge, Sholl J, said at p 758 of the report:

"To hold it to be necessary for the Crown to prove actual knowledge by an accused that the person assaulted, resisted or obstructed is a police officer would create substantial difficulties in the enforcement of a useful section, and would, when many police officers, carry out important duties in plain clothes, substantially reduce the protection which the law, as always previously interpreted, has afforded them. For it would ordinarily be possible only to prove, at the very most (unless the accused knew the officer personally), that he may or must have had good reason to believe the person concerned to be an officer. But to hold further that the accused must actually know the officer to be engaged in the *due execution* of his duty would be to impose on the prosecution a burden which in many cases it would be impossible to discharge."

In *R v Reynhoudt*[78] Dixon CJ expressed his concept of the necessary *mens rea* as follows at pp 386–7 of the report:

"My conclusion is that to be guilty of the offence of assaulting a member of the police force in the due execution of his duty the intent of the supposed offender

77 [1961] VR 740.
78 (1962) 107 CLR 381.

must go to all the ingredients of the offence. I do not of course use the word intention to refer to the consequences of an act or the desire that a result shall ensue but simply to the commission of what I regard as a compound offence."

Kitto J was the other member of the High Court of Australia in that case who considered *mens rea* to be necessary in regard to the element in question, and he stated the requirement in these words at p 389 of the report:

"It does not mean that the Crown had to prove that the respondent *knew* that the person he was assaulting was a policeman in the due execution of his duty. Consistently with the decision [*under appeal*] the necessary intention might have existed though the respondent hoped, or even believed, that the person was not a policeman or was not at the time in the due execution of his duty, provided only that his intention extended to doing to that person what in fact he did to him even if the fact should be that he was a policeman in the execution of his duty. *Advertence to the possibility of his being such a policeman is, I think, required, but not knowledge.*" – (italics supplied).

In *R vMcLeod*[79], the only other case in which it was held that *mens rea* is necessary for this element. O'Halloran JA (with whose judgment the other two judges, Bird and Davey JJA, agreed) stated at p 113 of the report:

". . . even if there was a common assault upon an unknown person, it could not, in my judgment at least, be magnified into the aggravated and distinct offence of assaulting a Police Officer in the execution of his duty unless it was found as a fact by a jury or fact-finding Judge that the circumstances of the assault were foreseeably such that it would rationally have been directed against a Police Officer if he had been known as such."

It should be noted that the issue in that case was whether an acquittal had been correctly given where there was a finding of fact by the trial judge that the accused did not know, and had every reason for not knowing, that the person assaulted was a police officer. In upholding the acquittal, the British Columbia Court of Appeal in effect held that the accused's absence of knowledge negatived intent.

The preponderance of judicial opinion, therefore, is that, as to the assaulted person being a policeman acting in the course of his duty, the required *mens rea* is intention, not knowledge. I believe that to be the correct opinion. It accords with the *mens rea* or malice required for the act of non-capital murder, ie, an intention to cause death or serious injury. If the less serious intention of causing serious injury is proved, it is no defence to a charge of murder for the accused to say that he had no knowledge that death would occur. While the type of constructive malice or intention exemplified by *The State v McMullen*[80] is no longer recognized since the enactment of s 4 of the Criminal Justice Act 1964, the offence of murder is basically one of intention which need not encompass the resulting death.

Once the prosecution proved (as they clearly did) that the appellant Marie Murray murdered Michael Reynolds, it was necessary for a conviction on the capital offence to prove the further *mens rea* of intention (or recklessness, its alternative in the law of *mens rea* in this context) as would be required if the charge were one of assaulting a peace officer in the course of his duty. That, in my judgment, is the *mens rea* required for the element in the capital murder charge which referred to a member of the Garda Síochána acting in the course of his duty.

Has the necessary *mens rea* been proved for the capital murder charged? In considering whether the evidence in this case constituted the necessary *mens rea*, it must be said at the outset that there was no finding that when she fired the fatal shot the appellant Marie Murray intended to kill or cause serious injury to a

79 (1954) 111 Can CC 106.
80 [1925] 2 IR 9.

member of the Garda Síochána acting in the course of his duty. While the attack was clearly intentional, the evidence would not support a finding that it was intentional in that respect. Therefore, I proceed on the footing that when Marie Murray fired the shot she did not know that the victim was a member of the Irish police force.

What, then, was the state of her mind? Its importance is that the test of her guilt for capital murder as well as murder must be a subjective one. The court of trial was not entitled to judge her by what a reasonable person would have done in the circumstances, but it was entitled to evaluate what she did in the light of what she must have adverted to at the time.

It is common case that, in making the murder of a member of the Garda Síochána acting in the course of his duty a capital offence, the purpose of the legislature was to give an added protection to the members of an unarmed police force by making death the penalty for murdering one of its members on duty. I have rejected, as being irreconcilable with the legislative intent, the submission that guilt for this capital offence should follow regardless of the intent or knowledge of the killer as to his victim being a Garda. The legislature, not having expressed such a consequence in words, should not be taken to have intended that a person who murdered in circumstances when he could not possibly have thought that the victim was a member of the police force should suffer the death penalty.

On the other hand, it is no less difficult to credit the legislature in enacting the Criminal Justice Act 1964, with the intention that actual knowledge that the victim was a Garda acting in the course of his duty should be a necessary ingredient of the capital offence charged here. If that was the statutory intention, the deterrent of capital punishment was intended never to operate for the murder of a Garda in plain clothes, unless the murderer actually knew the victim to be a Garda acting in the course of his duty. This would largely remove the application of the legislation from a substantial section of the police force, the nature of whose duties – frequently very hazardous duties – requires them to operate out of uniform.

In my judgment, it is not proper to construe either s 38 of the Offences Against the Person Act 1861, or s 1 of the Criminal Justice Act 1964, in such a way as to make those sections hardly ever applicable to assaults on or murder of policemen in plain clothes. In the case of such an assault or murder, the required *mens rea* as to the victim's occupation and activity is a matter of intention or, in the alternative, recklessness. Just as a person who does not intend an assault may be held guilty of an assault if he has been reckless as to whether his physical activity would have that effect (*R v Venna*[81]), so a person may be found guilty of the capital murder of a Garda if it is shown (*a*) that he murdered the Garda and (*b*) that he was reckless as to whether his victim was a Garda acting in the course of his duty.

The test of recklessness in this context is well stated in the Model Penal Code – s 2.02(2)(*c*) – drawn up by the American Law Institute:

> "A person acts recklessly with respect to a material element of an offence when he consciously disregards a substantial and unjustifiable risk that the material element exists or will result from his conduct. The risk must be of such a nature and degree that, considering the nature and purpose of the actor's conduct and the circumstances known to him, its disregard involves culpability of high degree."

What is in issue on this aspect of the case is recklessness not as to the consequences of an act but as to a concomitant circumstance of an act. In dealing with whether simple ignorance will displace recklessness in that context, Professor Glanville Williams (Criminal Law: The General Part; 2nd ed, p 152) has written:

---

81 [1975] 3 WLR 737.

"A person who does not know for certain whether or not a fact exists may think that its existence is probable, or only possible; or he may have given no thought to the question of probability or possibility. The last will be particularly likely if he does not know the criminal law and so does not realise the relevance of the fact to his legal responsibility. The proposition to be maintained is that in each of these situations there is recklessness for legal purposes. Simple ignorance is not enough to displace recklessness. It is only where the actor's mind is filled with mistaken knowledge that the act is not reckless (though it may be negligent) as to that circumstance."

For the reasons I have given earlier in this judgment, I do not accept that *mens rea* as to the concomitant circumstance that the victim of the murder was a Garda acting in the course of duty is proved if the mere unconsidered possibility of his being so existed. In the present case, however, if it were held that the appellant Marie Murray must have adverted to the possibility that the man who was trying to apprehend her husband was a Garda, and that, regardless of that risk, she shot him, *mens rea* for capital murder would have been proved because she would have consciously disregarded a substantial and unjustifiable risk.

The court of trial, acting on the basis that neither intention nor recklessness was necessary for the capital murder charged, did not make a finding that Marie Murray had the required guilty mind which, in the circumstances, was recklessness. The court did not address its mind at all to the question. Therefore, it misdirected itself in law in holding her guilty of capital murder without finding that, in shooting Garda Reynolds, she was reckless as to whether he was a Garda acting in the course of his duty. Therefore, the verdict of guilty on that count cannot stand.

Whether Marie Murray had the required recklessness is essentially a matter of fact to be inferred from the evidence. In order to make a valid finding as to it, there should be a judicial consideration of all the relevant evidence. It is not a matter that can be determined at second hand, away from the courtroom where the witnesses were seen and heard, which is how this Court would be deciding the point when the only evidential material before it is the transcript of the evidence given at the trial. Were the Court to decide such a vital matter of fact on such secondary material, it would be ignoring the necessity of an oral hearing for the determination of facts in issue in a criminal case. I have already referred in outline to the evidence given at the trial which would be relevant to this issue of recklessness. I refrain from expressing any opinion which might be thought to prejudge that issue. I confine myself to holding that, in the case of the appellant Marie Murray, there should be a retrial on the count of capital murder, the verdict on which will depend primarily on whether she had the required recklessness. If she is found not guilty on that count, a verdict of guilty of murder would in the circumstances be correctly substituted under s 3, sub-s 2, of the Criminal Justice Act 1964.

As to the appellant Noel Murray, if the recklessness required for the capital murder charged is held to have been proved in the case of Marie Murray, that recklessness could not be imputed to Noel Murray. In the absence of evidence that a decision to shoot a would-be captor, even if there was a risk that he was a Garda, was an express or implied part of the common design, recklessness in this respect on the part of Marie Murray must be deemed to be personal to her and outside the scope of the common design. The activities of the parties to the bank robbery, particularly the carrying and use of loaded guns, amply support the inference that there was a common agreement to shoot to kill or to cause serious injury if necessary. It may, however, have been the case that it was part of the pre-arrangement that a shot would not be discharged at a Garda. At all events, it cannot be fairly inferred from the evidence that the discharge of a shot at a Garda was part of the pre-arranged scheme of things, and more particularly the discharge of a shot at a Garda in the circumstances in which Marie Murray shot Garda Reynolds. . . .

Griffin J: . . . In my opinion, on a proper construction of the Act of 1964, capital murder as defined by the Act is a new offence created by the Act and is not the offence of murder at common law. My reasons for so concluding can be shortly stated.

1. Capital murder is specifically defined by s 1, sub-s 1(*b*), of the Act of 1964 and contains elements not to be found in murder at common law.

2. The person accused must be charged with capital murder in the indictment – as was done in this case.

3. Prior to the passing of the Act of 1964, in the circumstances of this case, murder at common law would have been committed by any person killing Michael Reynolds with malice aforethought. All that the prosecution need have alleged in the indictment, and proved, was that he was killed by the accused. For the offence of capital murder, it must in addition be alleged and proved that he was a member of the Garda Síochána and was acting in the course of his duty. Indeed, the first count (capital murder) and the second count (murder) in the indictment in the present case clearly demonstrates this distinction.

4. Section 3 of the Act of 1964 is a section dealing exclusively with procedural matters. In my view, therefore, the provisions of sub-s 5 of s 3 must be limited to such matters and cannot be interpreted as being of general application. If this were not the case, one would expect to find the provisions of sub-s 5 in a separate section and to be expressed in somewhat different terms. Further, the Act itself treats capital murder as a distinct offence from murder for the purpose of punishment, and this is not one of the matters included in sub-ss 1–4 of section 3.

For these reasons, in my view, the contention of the prosecution that capital murder is not a new offence fails.

As the offence of capital murder is a new statutory offence, the further question that arises is the nature and extent of the *mens rea* required in the case of the murder of a member of the Garda Síochána acting in the course of his duty. As appears from the long title of the Act, one of the purposes of the Act was to amend the law as to malice in the case of murder, and this was done by the provisions of section 4. The effect of s 4 of the Act was to retain the doctrine of transferred malice (the intention to kill or seriously injure one person while killing another) and to abolish, for the purpose of murder, the doctrine of constructive malice. Thus, for example, a person whose intention was to injure (but only slightly) a member of the Garda Síochána, or to resist arrest, but whose act resulted in the death of the Garda, would no longer be guilty of murder as the intention now required is to kill or cause serious injury to the person killed.

The net question for decision in the present case is whether, where the intention to kill or seriously injure the person actually killed is proved, it is also necessary to prove that there was an intention to kill a member of the Garda Síochána, ie, that the accused *knew* that the victim was a member of the Garda Síochána. On the findings of the Special Criminal Court, it is not contested that Garda Reynolds was acting in the course of his duty when he was killed.

The contention of the prosecution is that, as the overriding intention of the Act was to give protection to members of the Garda Síochána and, in particular, to those in plain clothes whose duties brought them into the areas of greatest danger, the offence of capital murder has been committed once it is established (a) that the person who did the killing had the intention to kill or seriously injure the person actually killed, and (b) that the victim was a member of the Garda Síochána then acting in the course of his duty, whether the killer knew that he was such Garda or not – in other words, that the victim happened to be a member of the Garda Síochána who was then acting in the course of his duty – and that *mens rea* is not necessary in respect of those elements or ingredients of the offence. In support of this contention, counsel for the prosecution relied on a number of cases decided in England under s 38 of the Offences Against the Person Act 1861, and in Australia and Canada under statutory provisions similar to those contained in section 38. Section 38 of the Act of 1861 made it an offence (inter alia) to assault, resist, or wilfully obstruct any peace officer in the due execution of his duty. . . .

. . . I find it very difficult to accept that, once the intention to kill or seriously injure is proved, the Oireachtas intended that guilt under s 1 of the Act of 1964 should depend on the accidental or fortuitous event that the person killed happened to be a member of the Garda Síochána acting in the course of his duty. Nowadays, it is often necessary for members of a police force (including the Garda Síochána) to operate in plain clothes for the purpose of obtaining information leading to the discovery of crime. For the proper performance of their duties, these officers must not only not identify themselves as policemen but on the contrary must necessarily act as if they were not and, in appropriate cases, ensure as best they can that those with whom they come into contact believe that they are not. If in such circumstances two persons, one being a member of the Garda Síochána and the other being one of his associates who was not such member, were killed by assailants who believed, and had every reasonable ground for believing, that the victims were private citizens, can it be said that, because one of the victims turned out to be a member of the Garda Síochána, the killing of such member would warrant the death penalty whilst the killing of the private citizen would warrant penal servitude for life?

In the circumstances outlined, the moral responsibility of the assailants would have been the same, and there seems to be no basis in justice, reason, or expediency for imposing increased punishment on those whose victim was, fortuitously, a member of the Garda Síochána.

In my view, it could not have been, and was not, the intention of the Oireachtas, as expressed in the words of the statute, that such a result would be achieved. Accordingly, I would hold that *mens rea* is a necessary ingredient of all the elements which go to make up the offence of capital murder.

The question then arises as to the nature and extent of the *mens rea* which is necessary in respect of the aggravating elements of the new offence of capital murder before a conviction for capital murder can be sustained (instead of the lesser offence of murder) – ie, in this case the fact that the victim was a member of the Garda Síochána. If the specific intent required by s 4 of the Act of 1964 is also necessary in respect of the additional ingredients of the offence of capital murder, a convict for capital murder under s 1, sub-s 1(*b*)(i), of the Act of 1964 cannot stand in the absence of evidence that the accused knew that the victim was a member of the Garda Síochána. Therefore, it becomes necessary to consider what is the necessary *mens rea*.

At p 31 of his work on Criminal Law (General Part – 2nd ed) Professor Glanville Williams defines *mens rea* as referring to "the mental element necessary for the particular crime, and this mental element may be either *intention* to do the immediate act or bring about the consequence or (in some crimes) *recklessness* as to such act or consequence. In different and more precise language, *mens rea* means intention or recklessness as to the elements constituting the *actus reus*. These two concepts, intention and recklessness, hold the key to the understanding of a large part of criminal law. Some crimes require intention and nothing else will do, but most can be committed either intentionally or recklessly. Some crimes require particular kinds of intention or knowledge."

At p 56 he states: "Recklessness as a form of *mens rea* is some enlargement upon the requirement of intention, but not a considerable one. This, at least, is true for recklessness as to the consequence of conduct. There is, however, another application of the concept of recklessness, namely as to the existence of present facts, ie, the circumstances surrounding conduct. A person is said to be reckless as to a surrounding circumstance if he is aware of the possibility that such a circumstance exists and does an act regardless of it." It is this latter form of recklessness with which, if at all, we are concerned in these appeals. In dealing with this latter concept of recklessness he states at p 148: ". . . an act is not intentional as to a circumstance of which the actor is ignorant. A somewhat similar rule may be stated for recklessness: an act is not reckless as to a circumstance in respect of which the actor is mistaken. We have seen that the term 'recklessness,' as it has come to be used in juristic thinking, means emphatically a mental state. It has two distinct though related applications: recklessness as to consequence and recklessness as to circumstance. The first, which has already been considered (para 24), involves foresight of the possible consequence of conduct. The second involves knowledge of the circumstances, or of the possibility of the circumstances. It occurs where there are some circumstances, specified by law as part of the *actus reus*, which the actor does not positively know to be present in his own case, but which he consciously takes the risk of being present. . . . The element common to the two kinds of recklessness is the conscious taking of a risk. The presence or absence of the fact (the consequence or circumstance) is not part of the actor's purpose, but he chooses to ignore the possibility of the fact in order to pursue his purpose."

I accept these statements as correct statements of the law. Therefore, in an appropriate case, the necessary *mens rea* may exist not only where there is intention but where there is recklessness as to surrounding circumstances. In my view, recklessness on the part of an accused as to the existence of present facts will not be sufficient to support a conviction if a specific intent as to those facts is necessary. Applied to the present case, the relevant fact is membership of the Garda Síochána. A specific intent, ie, to kill or cause serious injury, is required by s 4 of the Act of 1964 and the contention of the appellants is that this specific intent must also be extended to the aggravating elements or ingredients of s 1, sub-s 1(*b*)(i), of the Act of 1964. Support for this contention is claimed to be obtained from the dictum of Dixon CJ in *Reynhoudt's* case[82], but it must be remembered that he was there construing a specific statutory provision.

In this case it has not been contested nor, indeed, could it be contested that one of the main purposes of the Act of 1964 is to protect the Garda Síochána which is an unarmed police force (and, in particular, to protect those Gardaí who are on duty in plain clothes) by retaining the death penalty in respect of the murder of a member acting in the course of his duty. The intention of the Oireachtas would appear to have been that the death penalty should act as a deterrent for those who are minded to kill a member of the force. Those members of the force who, by reason of their duties, are most vulnerable are the plain-clothes Gardaí and detectives. The Oireachtas must be taken to have known that the onus of proof is, and at all time remains, on the prosecution. If it is intended to extend the specific intent to the aggravated elements in s 1, sub-s 1(*b*)(i), of the Act (ie, membership of the Garda Síochána), the result would be that the murder of a plain-clothes Garda could never be capital murder unless it could be proved that he was personally known as such to the person committing the murder. I find it extremely difficult to accept that this was the intent of the Oireachtas in enacting the Act of 1964. The malice necessary in the case of murder is clearly spelled out in s 4 of the Act. If, as is submitted, the Oireachtas intended that the specific intent in s 4 should equally apply to the aggravated offence of the murder of a member of the Garda Síochána acting in the course of his duty, it seems to me that this should have been done in express terms by appropriate words either in s 4 or in s 1, sub-s 1(*b*)(i), of the Act.

As the concepts of "wilful blindness" and "recklessness" as to consequences" have been canvassed in this appeal, I should emphasise that the recklessness with which we are concerned (ie, recklessness as to surrounding circumstances – as to the existence of present facts) is quite distinct from the other two concepts

---

82 (1962) 107 CLR 381.

mentioned. "Wilful blindness" is equivalent to actual knowledge in the eyes of the law: see Devlin J in *Roper v Taylor's Central Garages (Exeter) Ltd.*[83] And where, in a statutory offence, knowledge is required either expressly or impliedly, a court can properly find wilful blindness *only* where it can almost be said that the accused actually knew – where he suspected the fact or realised its probability but refrained from obtaining the final confirmation because he wanted to be able to deny knowledge. This is frequently encountered in prosecutions for offences such as receiving goods knowing them to have been stolen. However, the doctrine has no relevance to the present case.

Again, the principles which apply to the concept of recklessness as to consequences are irrelevant to the facts of this case. The "natural and probable consequences" of firing a shot from close range is to kill or cause serious injury and, under s 4, sub-s 2, of the Act there is a presumption of intention. The Special Criminal Court has found as a fact that the killing was intentional, so no question of recklessness in that behalf can arise or be relevant.

In my opinion, therefore, on the correct construction of the Act of 1964 the specific intent required by s 4 does not extend to the aggravated ingredients of s 1, sub-s 1(*b*)(i), and knowledge that the person killed was a member of the Garda Síochána is not an ingredient of the offence of capital murder under that subsection. Therefore, there would be the necessary *mens rea* if there was recklessness as to this fact on the part of the person doing the killing. However, there must be *advertence* on the part of the accused – recklessness involves foresight of the possibility and the taking of a risk. It is of interest to note that in *R v Reynhoudt*[84] Kitto J, although discussing intention and not recklessness, appears to have taken the view that the recklessness under discussion in this judgment would amount to intention; at p 389 of the report he said:

> "It does not mean that the Crown had to prove that the respondent *knew* that the person he was assaulting was a policeman in the due execution of his duty. Consistently with the decision [*under appeal*] the necessary intention might have existed though the respondent hoped, or even believed, that the person was not a policeman or was not at the time in the due execution of his duty, provided only that his intention extended to doing to that person what in fact he did to him even if the fact should be that he was a policeman in the execution of his duty. Advertence to the possibility of his being such a policeman is, I think, required, but not knowledge."

In my opinion, therefore, the necessary *mens rea* as to the murder is the intent required by s 4 of the Act; the necessary *mens rea* as to the concomitant circumstances is recklessness. . . .

. . . First, as to the appellant Marie Murray, the *mens rea* required is not that she *ought* to have known that the possibility existed that the captor was a Garda (for that would be an objective test), but that she *must* necessarily have known that this possibility existed. Before there can be recklessness or her part there must be advertence to this possibility. All that is positively known of her state of mind is what appears in her statement, namely, that later that evening she heard on Radio Éireann that a Garda had been shot. Therefore, the case must be approached on the basis that there is no evidence that she *knew* that the victim was a member of the Garda Síochána. The state of a person's mind can only be gathered from the known facts and all the surrounding circumstances. Both appellants were highly intelligent – as was demonstrated by their submissions and arguments at the trial.

Taking into account the excited conversation in the car when the raiders knew they were being followed, all the circumstances of the chase, and the fact that a

---

83 [1951] 2 TLR 284.
84 (1962) 107 CLR 381.

lone pursuer was following four persons of whom one at least was armed, the Special Criminal Court *could* have considered that it is inconceivable that the possibility of the person following them being a Garda did not occur to the appellant Marie Murray. In my opinion, at the trial there was evidence on which it would have been open to the Special Criminal Court to hold (a) that in all the circumstances the appellant Marie Murray must have adverted to the fact that there was a risk that their pursuer was a member of the Garda Síochána, and (b) that, in shooting that person, who was holding her husband, she disregarded that risk. If the Special Criminal Court (as the fact-finding court) so found, it would follow as a matter of law that she would have had the necessary *mens rea* to support a conviction for capital murder.

In the case of the appellant Noel Murray – with due respect to the colleagues with whom I differ – I can see no logical or rational basis for differentiating between him and Marie Murray. They were engaged in a common design to rob the bank and Noel Murray, on the findings of the Special Criminal Court, was the person who appeared to be in charge of the operation. Each carried a loaded gun which was ready to fire, and his gun had the safety catch off. The only inference which can be drawn from these facts is that, if necessary, the guns would be used for the purpose of carrying out the robbery or enabling the participants to escape. Indeed, not only is that inference reasonable, but it is borne out by what the appellant Noel Murray said to the manager of the bank and Mrs Branigan when this appellant pointed the gun at Mrs Branigan's head and informed them that he would shoot if the alarm was raised. Each appellant was in possession of a gun to the knowledge of the other. Therefore, the law is clear. Where two or more persons combine to steal in circumstances such as the present, and agree (as they must inferentially have agreed in this case) to use force to effect the theft or to resist arrest, the use of force by one will implicate the other. The chase by Garda Reynolds commenced immediately outside the bank and continued right up to the time of the killing. At some time during the course of that chase, the appellant Noel Murray gave his gun (which was fully loaded and with a bullet in the breach and the safety catch off) to his wife. On the available evidence, he had precisely the same means of knowledge as his wife of the possibility of the person by whom they were being followed being a member of the Garda Síochána. I can see no reason for a court holding that, in shooting the person who had caught her husband for the purpose of enabling her husband to escape, the appellant Marie Murray was doing an act which could be interpreted as being beyond the scope of the common purpose or design. In my opinion, on the facts of this case, there was evidence on which it would be open to the court of trial to hold that the appellant Noel Murray could properly be convicted of the capital murder of Garda Reynolds.

For the foregoing reasons, as there was a misdirection in law at the trial, I would quash the conviction of capital murder in the case of each appellant and I would hold that a retrial on the count of capital murder should be directed in respect of each appellant.

In the course of these appeals the propriety of trying the appellants on counts other than the first three[85] (and the imposition of sentences in respect of those on which they were found guilty) was questioned. Whilst I agree that, in a trial for capital murder before a jury, it would be advisable, in the absence of some unusual special circumstances, to try the count of capital murder alone, in my view it is not improper to join such counts in the indictments, in particular where the trial is being conducted by three members of the Bench. Equally, once accused persons are convicted on counts other than capital murder, it is in my opinion not improper that they should be sentenced in respect of those counts. If sentences were not

85 [1977] IR 360 at p 361.

imposed on accused persons in respect of offences other than capital murder, it is easy to foresee circumstances in which considerable difficulties might be created; for example, if there was an appeal in respect of the conviction for capital murder and it was sustained, and if the trial judge died, was seriously ill, or retired in the meantime, there would be no means of sentencing the accused in respect of offences on which they had been found guilty.

In my opinion, there was nothing improper in joining the offences other than capital murder in the indictment, or in imposing sentences in respect of counts, other than capital murder, on which the appellants had been found guilty, and the convictions and sentences on those counts should stand.

Finally, as to the form of the certificate which should be granted by the Court of Criminal Appeal under s 29 of the Courts of Justice Act 1924, as re-enacted by s 48 of the Courts (Supplemental Provisions) Act 1961, while this question was not raised or argued in the appeals, my view is that the certificate should specify the point of law in respect of which the certificate is given by the Court of Criminal Appeal or by the Attorney General. Whether, or to what extent, this Court should allow any question other than that certified to be argued on such an appeal is a matter on which I would reserve my opinion for consideration if and when the matter arises in an appropriate case. . . .

Kenny J: . . . The prosecution have urged that s 3, sub-s 5, of the Act of 1964 shows that capital murder is not to be treated as an offence distinct from murder for any purpose and that this indicates that it is not a new offence. Sub-s 5 of s 3 appears as the last sub-section in a series of sub-sections dealing with procedural matters and, in my opinion, it is confined to these. Read in isolation and without reference to the context of the whole Act, its literal meaning leads to absurdities. If capital murder is not to be treated as an offence distinct from murder for any purpose, then penal servitude for life is the proper sentence for a person who is convicted of it. But this meaning contradicts s 1 of the Act of 1964 which, together with ss 1 and 2 of the Offences Against the Person Act 1861, makes the sentence of death obligatory in the case of conviction of capital murder. Further, if it is given this meaning, it would not be necessary for the prosecution to prove that the person murdered was a member of the Garda Síochána who was acting in the course of his duty. The prosecution would then be dispensed from proving one of the essential ingredients of the defined crime. In my opinion sub-s 5 of s 3 of the Act of 1964 has not the meaning contended for by the prosecution. When I take into consideration that the expression "capital murder" was unknown to our law before 1964, and that it is defined by the Act of 1964, I come to the conclusion that it is a new offence and is not to be equated with murder.

The next problem is whether the prosecution had to prove, in order to justify a verdict of capital murder, that the appellant Marie Murray knew or suspected that Garda Reynolds was a member of the Garda Síochána who was acting in the course of his duty, or that she was recklessly indifferent as to whether he was or not. It is a general rule of our law that the act itself is not criminal unless it is accompanied by a guilty mind. The Oireachtas may make acts crimes although the accused was not aware that he was committing an offence: these are usually called crimes of strict liability. But, to effect this, clear language must be used. In the absence of such an indication, the general rule is that the guilty mind or criminal intent involved proof that the appellant Marie Murray knew that Garda Reynolds was a member of the Garda Síochána acting in a course of his duty, or that she knew facts from which she could infer or advert to this or that she was recklessly indifferent as to whether he was a member of the Garda Síochána or not: *In re Borrowes*.[86]

---

86 [1900] 2 IR 593.

There was no evidence that Marie Murray knew that the Guard was a member of the Garda Síochána or that she knew anything from which she could infer that he was. In these circumstances she could not be held to have been recklessly indifferent as to whether he was. To prove that a person was recklessly indifferent, it must be established that there were facts which indicated to the person concerned the possibility that the forbidden consequences might occur. I do not think that the possibility that the deceased was a Guard occurred to Marie Murray. There was nothing to indicate to her that he was not a member of the public.

The prosecution have contended that, even if the offence under the Act of 1964 is a new one, they have not to prove that the appellant Marie Murray knew that the deceased was a member of the Garda Síochána acting in the course of his duty in order to sustain a conviction but that it is sufficient to establish that he was a member of the Garda Síochána acting in the course of his duty. They have relied upon English (and Australian) cases decided upon s 38 of the Offences Against the Person Act 1861 (and a similar section in Victoria) which so far as relevant reads: "Whosoever . . . shall assault, resist, or wilfully obstruct any peace officer, in the due execution of his duty, or any person acting in aid of such officer . . . shall be guilty of a misdemeanour . . ." These words seem to me to constitute an offence only if it is established that an accused assaulted a person whom he knew, or had reason to believe, was a police officer. . . .

. . . It is unnecessary in this Court to review the many arguments which appear in the numerous judgments on the interpretation of this seemingly simple but deceptive section. I have considered the many conflicting decisions on it and the application to it of one of the basic principles of our law – that, when the common law or a statute creates an offence, the guilty mind must be shown to have existed in relation to each ingredient of it. I find nothing in the decisions which induces me to alter the view which I have already expressed – that the section makes an assault on a police officer in the due execution of his duty an offence only when it is established that the accused assaulted a person whom the accused knew or had reason to believe was a police officer. I am fortified in this conclusion by what that great master of the common law Sir Owen Dixon CJ said in *R v Reynhoudt*[87] in the course of his dissenting judgment at pp 386–7 of the report:

> "My conclusion is that to be guilty of the offence of assaulting a member of the police force in the due execution of his duty the intent of the supposed offender must go to all the ingredients of the offence. I do not of course use the word intention to refer to the consequences of an act or the desire that a result shall ensure but simply to the commission of what I regard as a compound offence. The offence is an aggravated assault, aggravated by the fact that the person assaulted is a policeman and is in the execution of his duty. That is a compound offence and I think that the guilty mind should go to the elements of which it is composed."

The appellant Marie Murray was not guilty of capital murder as she did not know that Garda Reynolds was a member of the Garda Síochána and she did not know anything from which she could infer or advert to the fact that he was such a member, and as she was not recklessly indifferent as to whether he was or not. Therefore, I would substitute a verdict of murder against both appellants for the verdicts of guilty of capital murder pronounced by the Special Criminal Court and affirmed by the Court of Criminal Appeal.

Parker J: I agree with the conclusions reached in the judgment delivered by Mr Justice Henchy and in the judgment delivered by Mr Justice Griffin, save in so far as the latter relates to the appellant Noel Murray.

87 (1962) 107 CLR 381.

The facts and all the relevant authorities have been fully set out and considered in the judgments already delivered, and I will do no more than to refer briefly to such of them as I consider necessary for the purpose of this judgment.

I agree with all the judgments delivered in finding that capital murder is a new statutory offence and, therefore, it is not necessary for me to say more on this topic than to consider the consequences which appear to follow from such a finding. The definition of capital murder in s 1, sub-s 1(*b*)(i), of the Criminal Justice Act 1964, introduces ingredients which are not present in the crime of murder at common law and it is, in my opinion, a compound offence as described by Dixon CJ in *R v Reynhoudt*[88] at pp 386–7 of the report and, accordingly, *mens rea* must go to and be established in respect of each of the elements of which it is composed.

In applying this principle, it is essential to distinguish two different states of mind: knowledge and intention. The distinction is clearly drawn in the judgment of the majority of the Supreme Court of Victoria *R v Galvin (No 2)*[89] which contains the following passage at p 749 of the report:

"Knowledge may be excellent evidence of intention but it is not an essential element in the crime. The mental element in our opinion is the intention to do the *whole act* which is prohibited."

In the same case Barry J at p 753 and Sholl J at p 758 considered the matter in passages already quoted in full in the judgment of Mr Justice Henchy. The second sentence in the passage I have just quoted *supra* is expressly approved of by Dixon CJ in *R v Reynhoudt*[90], but it is to be noted that nowhere in the passage in which he considers the matter does the learned Chief Justice make use of the word "knowledge." The matter is put even more explicitly in the judgment of Kitto J in the same case in a passage from p 389 which has already been cited by Mr Justice Henchy and, therefore, I will only quote the final sentence:

"Advertence to the possibility of his being such a policeman is, I think, required, but not knowledge."

With the greatest respect I believe that failure to distinguish between knowledge and intention has been the cause of much judicial confusion. It appears to be the explanation of the extraordinary divergence of judicial opinion in the three Australian cases: *R v Galvin (No 1)*[91], *R v Galvin (No 2)*[92] and *R v Reynhoudt*.[93]

It may be that the prime cause of this confusion is a short and possibly not very carefully considered observation made by the Recorder of London to a jury in *R v Forbes*[94] as supported by an *obiter dictum* of Lord Alverstone LCJ in *R v Maxwell*.[95] I respectfully suggest that the cases based upon this passage, which continue in England up to *R v Mark*[96], are of doubtful authority; but I also consider that many of the judgments which reject these cases have erred in the other direction by failing to take into account that absence of knowledge does not necessarily mean absence of intention.

If knowledge alone were to be the test, a secondary problem immediately arises as to whether there can be such a thing as imputed knowledge in the context of such cases. No such problem arises if the test is the ascertainment of the intention

---

88 (1962) 107 CLR 381.
89 [1961] VR 740.
90 (1962) 107 CLR 381.
91 [1961] VR 733.
92 [1961] VR 740.
93 (1962) 107 CLR 381.
94 (1865) 10 Cox CC 362.
95 [1909] 2 Cr App R 26.
96 [1961] Crim LR 173.

of the accused person, and it is to be noted that s 4 of the Criminal Justice Act 1964, uses the word "intended" in both its sub-sections.

I am not overlooking the fact that the judgments of Dixon CJ and Kitto J to which I have referred are dissenting judgments on the facts of the case in which they were delivered but, apart altogether from the very great weight which must be attached in all common-law countries to the opinion of Sir Owen Dixon, I am of opinion that they correctly expressed the law which ought to be applied in this State.

Accordingly, I regret that I must respectfully dissent from the passage in the judgment of the Court of Criminal Appeal in this case which has been cited[97] with approval in the judgment of Mr Justice Walsh. I am in complete agreement with the passage in so far as it lays down that an accused person should not be guilty of capital murder unless he had a *mens rea* in relation to all the ingredients of the crime, but I differ from the conclusion which is drawn from that finding, *viz* – "That would mean that no person could be convicted of the capital murder of a member of the Garda Síochána unless the prosecution established that the accused *knew* that the victim was a member of the Garda Síochána and was acting in the course of his duty." The italics are mine.

If, as I believe to be the case, the true test of guilt is the intention of the accused, the prosecution must prove that intention in the sense that it has been for many centuries comprehended in the expression *mens rea*. *Mens rea* may manifest itself in different ways and to different degrees in connection with the *actus reus* with which it must be associated. "Sometimes it is negligence, sometimes malice, sometimes guilty knowledge . . ." – per Cave J in *Chisholm v Doulton*.[98] It also seems clear on the authorities that it can be recklessness in the sense that it motivates conduct with a total disregard to the legal or other consequences which may follow: see *In re Borrowes*[99]; *R v McLeod*.[1] Therefore, I share the view expressed by Mr Justice Henchy, Mr Justice Griffin, and Mr Justice Kenny that recklessness can constitute the necessary element of *mens rea*. I expressly adopt the observations of Mr Justice Griffin on this subject.

The question of whether the appellant Marie Murray had or had not such *mens rea* was not considered by the Special Criminal Court because that court misdirected itself in law by finding that capital murder was not a new statutory offence and, therefore, it did not direct its mind to the degree of *mens rea* required for such new offence. It is not a question which should be decided by an appellate court depending only on the transcript of the evidence given before the court of trial. However, before directing a new trial, this Court must be satisfied that there was evidence upon which such an issue could properly be decided. The evidence on this part of the case has been fully examined and considered in the judgments of Mr Justice Henchy and Mr Justice Griffin and I entirely agree with the conclusion which they have reached in respect of the appellant Marie Murray. Accordingly, I would quash her conviction on the charge of capital murder and order a retrial on this charge.

I am not satisfied that the same considerations apply to the appellant Noel Murray. Of course, it is possible that during the pursuit he may have thought or even believed that the pursuer was a Garda, but there is no evidence whatsoever of this. Furthermore, this appellant had no gun and, therefore, was never faced with the decision of whether to fire or not to fire. Finally, it appears from the evidence that at the time when the shot was fired this appellant was in the grip of Garda Reynolds so that he had neither the opportunity nor the means of either assisting

---

97 [1977] IR 360 at p 381.
98 (1889) 22 QBD 736, 741.
99 [1900] 2 IR 593.
 1 (1954) 111 Can CC 106.

or preventing his wife in the commission of the actual murder. Intention is a personal mental state and it cannot, by implication, be transferred from one individual to another. Accordingly, I would allow the appeal of Noel Murray against his conviction for capital murder and substitute therefore a conviction of murder.

However, I must make clear that nothing which I have said in this connection is to be construed as meaning or implying that in such a case of capital murder only those who directly cause the death of a Garda can be convicted. I leave over for further consideration cases in which a number of persons have joined together in the carrying out of an unlawful purpose during the course of which a Garda is murdered in the execution of his duty, and in which not only the actual killer or killers may be found to have had the necessary *mens rea* but in which one or more of the other or others of them, not immediately implicated in or even present at the killing, may nevertheless have formed an equally guilty intention. . . .

All modern common law systems reject a criminal law which imposes blame on the basis of what a reasonable man would have known, intended or suspected in the situation under analysis. In England, the high point of this objective doctrine came with *DPP v Smith*[2]. The House of Lords' decision imposed liability on the basis that it was irrelevant what an actual accused contemplated, the real test being stated to be what the ordinary reasonable man or woman would, in all the circumstances of the case, have contemplated as the natural and probable result of their action. The decision was greeted with a storm of protest which caused it to be rejected in all common law countries. It never applied in Ireland. In *Murray* the Supreme Court definitely and clearly rejected any such notion. Further, in *The People (DPP) v MacEoin*[3] the Court of Criminal Appeal adopted an entirely subjective test for provocation, based on the effect of the victim's actions on an individual accused, as opposed to their effect on a reasonable individual (see para **4.155**). It should also be noted in this regard, that the presumption in s 4 of the Criminal Justice Act 1964 is expressly stated to be rebuttable (see para **5.06**).

Criminal negligence

1.32 The concept of criminal negligence is fully considered in the context of manslaughter (see paras **5.55–5.57**). Essentially, where the mental element of a crime is cast in terms of criminal negligence the prosecution are relieved from the burden of proving that an individual accused was aware that his conduct might result in the harm constituting the external element of the offence. The general effect of the decisions on criminal negligence has been that the degree of carelessness required to fulfil the definition is such that almost no normal person would ever be unaware of the danger which they are creating. Criminal negligence applies only in the case of manslaughter. As was mentioned in the introduction to this chapter, an act of criminal negligence will go unnoticed and unpunished unless death results to another. Where arguably lesser forms of damage are caused to others, such as serious or permanent injury, an accused will be guilty of a crime only on the application of the higher standard of recklessness which, as we have seen, requires an advertent fault. A reform of the law making culpable those

2 [1961] AC 290.
3 [1978] IR 27.

who cause serious harm to others, through criminal negligence, is overdue. There is no good reason why a person who carelessly drops a brick on someone's head is guilty of manslaughter if he dies, but is guilty of nothing if the victim lives on with brain damage. Notwithstanding the obvious culpability of the accused's actions he can only be found guilty of an assault if the prosecution can prove an intent to attack the victim or recklessness as to the consequences of his action.

Negligence

1.33 Negligence consists of a failure by an accused person to exercise that degree of care in the conduct of his affairs, where they affect others, which would be exercised by a reasonable or ordinary person performing the task in question. Some statutes create simple offences of negligence. These are mostly summary offences which are usually dealt with in a trial before a judge, without a jury, in the District Court.

1.34 Prior to the reforms introduced by the Road Traffic Act 1961, situations where death was caused in road traffic accidents could only be dealt with by charging manslaughter. Where serious injury was caused there was no offence designed to deter and punish even those offenders who had behaved in a criminally culpable fashion. Two new offences were created by ss 53 and 52 of the Road Traffic Act 1961, and later amended by s 51 of the Road Traffic Act 1968. These were the offences of dangerous driving and careless driving. Section 52 indicates that careless driving is an offence and s 53 indicates that dangerous driving is an offence. There is clearly, therefore, a qualative difference in the character of the negligence which will suffice for a conviction for careless driving, but not for one of dangerous driving.

The mode of prosecution of an offence under s 53 will depend on the result of the dangerous driving. If death or serious bodily harm is caused to another, then trial is by way of indictment, i.e. with a jury. Otherwise, it is a summary trial. Because no advertent mental element is required in relation to the driving of the accused person there is equally no requirement of an advertent mental element in relation to the consequence of death or serious injury. This new offence has been criticised as unfair to an accused person on the grounds that it adds punishment for dangerous driving (which is a summary offence) not because of any additional gravity in the defendant's negligence but because of the result of that negligence. Consequences may be out of proportion to fault. In answer to that criticism the following passage from Stephen's "*History of Criminal Law*"[4] sets out the philosophy of distinguishing punishment by results:

> "If two people are guilty of the very same act of negligence and if one of them causes thereby a railway accident involving death or mutilation of many persons whereas the other does no injury to anyone, it seems to me that it would be rather pedantic than rational to say that each had committed the same offence, but the one had the bad luck to cause a horrible misfortune and to attract public attention to it and the other the good fortune to do no harm. Both certainly deserve punishment but it gratifies public feeling to chose out for punishment the one who,

4 Volume 3, p 311, (1883).

actually, has caused great harm, and the effect in the way of preventing a repetition of the offence is much the same as if both were punished."

1.35   *Road Traffic Act 1961*
                   as amended by the Road Traffic Act 1968 and
                      the Road Traffic (Amendment) Act 1984

52(1) A person shall not drive a vehicle in a public place without due care and attention.

(2) Any person who contravenes subsection (1) of this section shall be guilty of an offence and shall be liable on summary conviction to a fine not exceeding three hundred and fifty pounds or, at the discretion of the court, to imprisonment for any term not exceeding three months or to both such fine and such imprisonment.

53(1) A person shall not drive a vehicle in a public place in a manner (including speed) which, having regard to all the circumstances of the case (including the condition of the vehicle, the nature, condition and use of the place and the amount of traffic which then actually is or might reasonably be expected then to be therein) is dangerous to the public.

(2) A person who contravenes subsection (1) of this section shall be guilty of an offence and

(*a*) in case the contravention causes death or serious bodily harm to another person, he shall be liable on conviction on indictment to penal servitude for any term not exceeding five years or, at the discretion of the court, to a fine not exceeding three thousand pounds or to both such penal servitude and such fine, and

(*b*) in any other case, he shall be liable on summary conviction to a fine not exceeding one thousand pounds or, at the discretion of the court, to imprisonment for any term not exceeding six months or to both such fine and such imprisonment.

(3) In a prosecution for an offence under this section, it shall not be a defence to prove that the speed at which the accused person was driving was not in excess of the ordinary, general built-up area or special speed limit applying in relation to the vehicle.

(4) Where, when a person is tried on indictment or summarily for an offence under this section, the jury, or, in the case of a summary trial, the District Court, is of opinion that he was not guilty of an offence under this section but was guilty of an offence under s 52 of this Act, the jury or court may find him guilty of an offence under s 52 of this Act and he may be sentenced accordingly.

(5) A person liable to be charged with an offence under this section shall not, by reference to the same occurrence, be liable to be charged with an offence under s 35 of the Offences Against the Person Act 1861.

(6) Where a member of the Garda Síochána is of opinion that a person has committed an offence under this section he may arrest the person without warrant.

1.36   *Offences Against the Person Act 1861*

35 Whosoever, having the charge of any carriage or vehicle, shall by wanton or furious driving or racing, or other wilful misconduct, or by wilful neglect, do or cause to be done any bodily harm to any person whatsoever, shall be guilty of a misdemeanour . . . [and shall be liable to imprisonment for a term not exceeding two years].

1.37 The following standard direction on the meaning of dangerous driving was given by O'Briain J: ". . . driving in a manner which a reasonably prudent man, having regard to all the circumstances, would clearly recognise as involving a direct and serious risk of harm to the public."[5] Neylon J used to explain to juries that "dangerous driving" was an ordinary expression which was best approached by, firstly, deciding what facts had been proved by the prosecution and then considering whether, if the jury had been witnesses to such driving, they would have regarded it as dangerous.

The essence of negligence is a failure to act as a reasonable person would and it is not surprising that in clarifying the elements of the offence of dangerous driving that the courts have required that the accused person should be at fault.

1.38   *R v Gosney*
[1971] 2 QB 674; [1971] 3 All ER 220; [1971] 3 WLR 343
(1971) 55 Cr App R 502
Court of Appeal England, 1971

Facts: The accused was found driving her car in the wrong direction up a dual-carriageway against oncoming traffic. She sought to adduce evidence that this circumstance had been caused by a deceptive road layout which might reasonably have caused a competent and careful driver to be put in the same situation. In other words that the objectively dangerous situation had not been caused by her own inattention. The Court of Appeal ruled that the fault element in dangerous driving required a consideration of the circumstances which led to the driver being in a situation where he could be adjudged as driving dangerously. That consideration required that there be fault on the part of the driver in addition to the objective circumstances. This fault element essentially consists of inattention which is a species of negligence.

Megaw LJ: In order to justify a conviction there must be, not only a situation which, viewed objectively, was dangerous, but there must also have been some "fault" on the part of the driver, causing that situation. Fault certainly does not necessarily involve deliberate misconduct or recklessness or intention to drive in a manner inconsistent with the proper standard of driving. Nor does fault necessarily involve moral blame. Thus there is fault if an inexperienced or a naturally poor driver, while straining every nerve to do the right thing, falls below the standard of a competent and careful driver. Fault involves failure; a falling below the care or skill of a competent and experienced driver, in relation to the manner of driving and to the relevant circumstances of the case. A fault in that sense, even though it might be slight, even though it be a momentary lapse, even though normally no danger would have arisen from it, is sufficient. The fault need not be the sole cause of the dangerous situation. It is enough if it is, looked at sensibly, a cause. Such fault will often be sufficiently proved as an inference from the very facts of the situation. But if the driver seeks to avoid that inference by proving some special fact, relevant to the question of fault in this sense, he may not be precluded from seeking so to do.

Strict responsibility

1.39 It is possible to analyse crimes of strict liability as removing any mental element from the definition of an offence. The prosecution would simply have to prove the responsibility of the accused in relation to the

5 Reported (1963) 97 ILT 219 and referring back to and varying slightly the definition given earlier and reported at (1962) 96 ILT 123. Referred to as *The People (AG) v Quinlan* in R Pierse *Road Traffic Law in the Republic of Ireland* Butterworths (1989) p 157.

physical circumstances which constitute the offence. Smith and Hogan suggest, however, that offences of <u>strict liability</u> do not constitute offences of <u>absolute liability</u>. They argue that there is nothing in the general law indicating that general defences of infancy, insanity, duress, automatism or necessity should not be applied[6]. Further they indicate that the case of *R v Prince*[7] (see para **6.32**), should not exclude some ~~other~~ <u>mistake</u> <u>apart</u> from age. This case is usually taken as an authority for the proposition that where an offence is alleged involving sexual misconduct with a girl below the age of consent that knowledge as to her age, or a reasonable mistake placing her age above that limit is not a defence. Other mistakes can be involved. For example, Smith and Hogan would agree in cases of abduction, a mistake that the girl was a boy, or in cases of unlawful sexual intercourse, that the accused was married to the victim, should cancel criminal liability.[8] The manner in which offences of strict liability have operated in this jurisdiction can be seen from the cases which follow.

1.40   ***M'adam v Dublin United Tramways Company Limited***
[1929] IR 327
Case stated to the High Court from the District Court, 1929

Facts: The defendants were charged with an offence under the Dublin Carriage Act, 1853 of overloading a tram. There was a conductor on this tram and the company introduced evidence of letters written by them to their conductors essentially urging compliance with the law. Four questions were asked of the High Court by the District Justice. One, was the evidence that the tram company had asked their conductors to comply with the law admissible. Two, whether the prohibition was absolute and so take the offence outside the rule that a principal is not criminally responsible for the acts of his servants. Three, whether the District Justice was correct in refusing to convict the defendant company. Four, whether he was entitled to convict and fine the conductor of the tram but not the defendant company.

Sullivan P: . . . Now, the offences charged against the defendants are offences against the by-laws and regulations made by the Commissioner of Police under the Dublin Carriage Act 1853, s 50. The particular regulation which was infringed provides that: "No passenger shall be permitted to travel on the platform, or on any part of such stage carriage, except in or on the place or places set apart and specified in the licence for conveying passengers, and no stage carriage shall contain at any one time any greater number of inside or outside passengers than the number of same respectively specified in the licence."
    I am of opinion that the prohibitions contained in that regulation are absolute. The object of the regulation is to protect the public against the danger that may result from the over-loading of an omnibus, and that object could be achieved only by absolutely prohibiting the carriage in any omnibus of more than a limited number of passengers, and by penalising the owner for any breach of such prohibition, irrespective of his knowledge of such breach.
    It was argued on behalf of the defendants that, in order to establish the offence charged, it was necessary for the prosecutor to prove that the defendants had *mens rea*, a knowledge of the facts rendering the act unlawful. If, as I hold, the prohibitions imposed by the regulation are absolute, the defendant company

---

6 Smith and Hogan at pp 111–112.
7 (1875) LR 2 CCR 154.
8 Smith and Hogan at p 41.

would be liable, irrespective of knowledge on their part that such prohibitions have not been observed. They would be answerable for the acts of their servant, the bus conductor, in the course of his employment in permitting the overloading of the omnibus on the occasion in question. The conductor undoubtedly knew that such overloading was wrongful, but, in my opinion, that consideration is immaterial in the present case.

In *Sherras v De Rutzen*[9] Wright J in his judgment, at p 921, says: "There is a presumption that *mens rea*, an evil intention, or a knowledge of the wrongfulness of the act, is an essential ingredient in every offence; but that presumption is liable to be displaced either by the words of the statute creating the offence, or by the subject-matter with which it deals, and both must be considered." And, having mentioned certain exceptions to the general rule, he proceeds: "Apart from isolated and extreme cases of this kind, the principal classes of exceptions may perhaps be reduced to three. One is a class of acts which, in the language of Lush J in *Davies v Harvey*[10], are not criminal in any real sense, but are acts which in the public interest are prohibited under a penalty." In *Toppin v Marcas*[11], Palles CB, having quoted that passage from the judgment of Wright J, says: "It is not necessary here to rely upon this judgment further than to say that where an act, not in any real sense criminal, is in the public interest prohibited under a penalty, the innocent nature of the act is at least an element to assist the Court in determining whether or not *mens rea* is an essential ingredient."

The acts in this case are not in any real sense criminal, but in the public interest they are prohibited under a penalty. Having regard to that fact, and to the terms of the regulation and the object it had in view, I am of opinion that *mens rea* is not an essential ingredient in the offences charged against the defendants.

One further question is raised in the case stated. It appears that at the hearing the District Justice admitted in evidence on behalf of the defendants two notices issued by the defendants to their conductors, dated respectively the 25th February 1927, and the 7th September 1928, cautioning the conductors not to allow buses to be overloaded. As I have come to the conclusion that *mens rea* is not an ingredient in the offence charged, these notices were not admissible as evidence negativing the guilt of the accused; though the District Justice might take them into account in determining the penalty which he would impose.

The questions submitted to us should; in my opinion, be answered as follows: (1) No; save in mitigation of penalty. (2) Yes. (3) No. (4) No.

Hanna J delivered a concurring judgment.

1.41   ***Duncan v Gleeson***
[1969] IR 116
Case stated to the High Court from the District Court, 1969

Facts: The defendant was charged with the offence of permitting intoxicating liquor to be consumed on licensed premises during prohibited hours, contrary to s 2 of the Intoxicating Liquor Act 1927, and other offences under the same Act.

Pringle J: The only question upon which the opinion of the High Court is sought is whether, on the facts found by him, the District Justice was bound to convict the defendant in respect of complaints (v) and (vi) in the summons: that is to say, that the defendant permitted intoxicating liquor to be consumed on the premises and permitted persons to be on licensed premises at a prohibited time. The only facts found by the District Justice were that persons consumed intoxicating liquor

9 [1895] 1 QB 918.
10 LR 9 QB 433.
11 [1908] 2 IR 428.

during prohibited hours and that persons were on the premises during prohibited hours. There is no finding of fact that the defendant either permitted intoxicating liquor to be consumed or permitted persons to be on the premises during prohibited hours. The explanation of this is that the submission on behalf of the complainant was that there was an absolute liability on the defendant to have his premises cleared at the expiration of the "ten minutes" concession allowed by s 7 of the Intoxicating Liquor Act 1962.

The word "permit" is used in a number of places in the Intoxicating Liquor code, extending as far back as the Refreshment Houses (Ireland) Act 1860, and the legal effect to be given to it has been considered in several cases. In the case of *Attorney General v Carrol*[12] Mr Justice Hanna said at p 7 of the report: "Now, under these circumstances did the publican in law 'permit' the consumption of the stout by the guests of the lodger? I think he did 'permit' it within the meaning of the Act. My reasons are as follows: from the publican's point of view, short of sharing in the stout himself, I do not see how he could have done anything more in fact to permit, suffer, or allow the act. He was aware of all the circumstances in connection with the consumption of the drink, and suffered these persons to carry on their drinking in his presence – himself being one of the party – without protest, or prevention, or making any reasonable effort to carry out his duty under the Act." Again at p 10 of the report he said: "I am satisfied that the publican 'permits' in law the consumption of intoxicating liquor on his premises, if he does not take reasonable steps to prevent it. Here there was neither protest, nor any attempt at prevention, but acquiescence and full knowledge." That case was followed by Maguire P in *Attorney General v Egan*[13]; and Davitt P, in the case of *Attorney General v James Greeney* and *Attorney General v Charles Strong* (mentioned in para 8 of the Case Stated), clearly took the view that it was open to the publican to make the defence that he had taken all reasonable steps to clear the premises.

In regard to the offence of permitting persons to be on licensed premises during prohibited hours, this was first made an offence by s 29 of the Intoxicating Liquor Act 1962, and it must be assumed that the legislature, in using the word "permit" in that section, was aware of the construction put on that word in *Attorney General v Carroll*[14] and in *Attorney General v Egan*, and that it was not intended to create an absolute liability on the publican. The main argument advanced on behalf of the complainant before me was that s 7 of the Act of 1962, which provided for the "ten minute" concession, had the effect of imposing on the publican an absolute liability after the expiry of that period of ten minutes. I cannot see anything in s 7 of the Act of 1962 to warrant such a construction. If the legislature had intended such a result, it could easily have said so by providing that on the expiry of the ten minutes there would be an offence by the publican if drink was consumed on the premises, or if persons were on the premises. Instead of doing so, s 7 and s 29 of the Act of 1962 continue to use the word "permit".

In my opinion, the onus remains on the prosecution to prove that the defendant permitted drink to be consumed, or persons to be on, the premises after the permitted hours and the ten minutes allowed by s 7 of the Act of 1962; and that if the court is satisfied that the defendant took all reasonable steps to clear the premises, on the expiry of the permitted hours and during the ten minute extension, the charges should be dismissed. I think that the statement of the law by Judge McGivern in *McHale v Cole*[15] was correct and I agree with his remarks as to the duty of publicans. I express no view in the present case whether, on the facts proved, the defendant did, or did not, take reasonable steps to clear the premises. This is a matter for decision by the District Justice. The question asked in the Case stated will be answered in the negative.

12 [1943] LR 357.
13 [1943] LR 357.
14 [1932] LR 1.
15 (1965) 100 ILTR 83.

1.42 Manslaughter is the only offence of criminal negligence. Offences of negligence and of strict liability are always created by statute; they were unknown to the common law. Offences of simple negligence are easily identifiable from the terms of the statute. However, the identification of offences of strict liability has been the subject of debate. Essentially it is presumed that for each external element of an offence there is a corresponding mental element; *The People (DPP) v Murray*.[16] To find that an offence is one of strict liability it is necessary to consider both the wording of the statute creating the offence and the subject matter with which it deals; *Toppin v Marcus*.[17] The subject matter should deal with social evil and the manner in which the offence works must be such that putting the defendant under strict liability assists in the enforcement of the law. There must be something that he can do, directly or indirectly, by supervision or inspection, by improvement of his business methods or by exhorting those whom he may be expected to influence or control, which will promote the observance of the law. In the absence of an ability to influence or control, the law would be imposing liability on a blameless person; *Lim Chin Aik v R*.[18] The traditional criminal offences are excluded from strict liability. Instead, the legislation must deal with the matter of economic or social resolution; *Brown v Green*[19]. Brennan J of the High Court of Australia has quoted with approval in *He Kaw Teh v R*[20], the five propositions enunciated by Lord Scarman in *Gammon Limited v A-G of Hong Kong*[21] with a reservation as to the fourth, that it "seems to be too categorical an approach to what is, after all, a question of statutory interpretation". These five propositions are:

(1) There is a presumption of law that *mens rea* is required before a person can be held guilty of a criminal offence;

(2) The presumption is particularly strong where the offence is "truly criminal" in character;

(3) The presumption applies to statutory offences, and can be displaced only if this is clearly, or by necessary implication, the effect of the statute;

(4) The only situation in which the presumption can be displaced is where the statute is concerned with an issue of social concern, and public safety is such an issue;

(5) Even where a statute is concerned with such an issue, the presumption of *mens rea* stands unless it can also be shown that the creation of strict liability will be effective to promote the objects of the statute by encouraging greater vigilance to prevent the commission of the prohibited act.

Alternative approach

1.43 In Australia and New Zealand the courts have adopted an in-between solution to the problems posed by strict liability. Clearly, it can be unfair to

16 [1977] IR 360.
17 [1908] 2 IR 483.
18 [1963] AC 150 at p 174.
19 (1951) 84 CLR 285 at p 294.
20 (1985) 157 CLR 523 at p 566.
21 [1985] 1 AC 1 at p 14.

impose liability for an offence simply on the basis that it occurred. This is so especially where the accused, as a corporation or employer, is held liable for a breach of some social regulation by an employee. The solution arrived at, distinguishes between offences requiring a mental element and those of strict responsibility, by allowing the accused to indicate in the latter that the offence occurred due to a mistake based on reasonable grounds; *Cameron v Holt*[22], *R v Ewart*[23]. Offences of strict liability are therefore based on objective negligence with a burden of proof on the accused to prove that the care he has taken was reasonable in the circumstances. On that criterion the Dublin United Tramways Company would have been acquitted.

The Courts of Canada differ from other common law jurisdictions in dividing those 'social regulation' offences into crimes of strict liability and absolute liability. The reasoning is attractive to a legal system based on fault and incorporating justice as the ultimate test of the fairness of a law; *McGee v A-G*[24].

The Canadian solution

1.44   *R v City of Sault Ste Marie*
(1978) 85 DLR (3d) 161; 40 CCC (2d) 353
Supreme Court of Canada, 1978

Facts: The case concerned a contract between the City of Sault Ste Marie and the Cherokee Company to dispose of its garbage. The Cherokee Company pursued this task by a land-fill method in which the compacted refuse was covered by sand or gravel. This resulted in a large mound which sloped steeply towards a stream which flowed into a river. Seepage caused pollution and the Cherokee Company was convicted of discharging, causing to be discharged or permitting to be discharged deleterious materials contrary to Section 32(1) of the Ontario Water Resources Act RSO [1970] c 332. The issue before the Supreme Court of Canada was whether the city was guilty of a similar charge.

Dickson J: *The mens rea point*

The distinction between the true criminal offence and the public welfare offence is one of prime importance. Where the offence is criminal, the Crown must establish a mental element, namely, that the accused who committed the prohibited act did so intentionally or recklessly, with knowledge of the facts constituting the offence, or with wilful blindness toward them. Mere negligence is excluded from the concept of the mental element required for conviction. Within the context of a criminal prosecution a person who fails to make such inquiries as a reasonable and prudent person would make, or who fails to know facts he should have known, is innocent in the eyes of the law.

In sharp contrast, "absolute liability" entails conviction on proof merely that the defendant committed the prohibited act constituting the *actus reus* of the offence. There is no relevant mental element. It is no defence that the accused was entirely without fault. He may be morally innocent in every sense, yet be branded as a malefactor and punished as such.

Public welfare offences obviously lie in a field of conflicting values. It is essential for society to maintain, through effective enforcement, high standards of public health and safety. Potential victims of those who carry on latently pernicious

22 (1980) 142 CLR 342, (1979) 54 ALJ 202.
23 (1905) 25 NZLR 709.
24 [1974] IR 284.

activities have a strong claim to consideration. On the other hand, there is a generally held revulsion against punishment of the morally innocent.

Public welfare offences evolved in mid-19th century Britain (*R v Woodrow* (1846), 15 M & W 404, 153 ER 907, and *R v Stephens* (1866), LR 1 QB 702) as a means of doing away with the requirement of *mens rea* for petty police offences. The concept was a judicial creation, founded on expediency. That concept is now firmly embedded in the concrete of Anglo-American and Canadian jurisprudence, its importance heightened by the ever-increasing complexities of modern society.

Various arguments are advanced in justification of absolute liability in public welfare offences. Two predominate. Firstly, it is argued that the protection of social interests requires a high standard of care and attention on the part of those who follow certain pursuits and such persons are more likely to be stimulated to maintain those standards if they know that ignorance or mistake will not excuse them. The removal of any possible loophole acts, it is said, as an incentive to take precautionary measures beyond what would otherwise be taken, in order that mistakes and mishaps be avoided. The second main argument is one based on administrative efficiency. Having regard to both the difficulty of proving mental culpability and the number of petty cases which daily come before the Courts, proof of fault is just too great a burden in time and money to place upon the prosecution. To require proof of each person's individual intent would allow almost every violator to escape. This, together with the glut of work entailed in proving *mens rea* in every case would clutter the docket and impede adequate enforcement as virtually to nullify the regulatory statutes. In short, absolute liability, it is contended, is the most efficient and effective way of ensuring compliance with minor regulatory legislation and the social ends to be achieved are of such importance as to override the unfortunate by-product of punishing those who may be free of moral turpitude. In further justification, it is urged that slight penalties are usually imposed and that conviction for breach of public welfare offence does not carry the stigma associated with conviction for a criminal offence.

Arguments of a greater force are advanced against absolute liability. The most telling is that it violates fundamental principles of penal liability. It also rests upon assumptions which have not been, and cannot be, empirically established. There is no evidence that a higher standard of care results from absolute liability. If a person is already taking every reasonable precautionary measure, is he likely to take additional measures, knowing that however much care he takes, it will not serve as a defence in the event of breach? If he has exercised care and skill, will conviction have a deterrent effect upon him or others? Will the injustice of conviction lead to cynicism and disrepect for the law, on his part and on the part of others? These are among the questions asked. The argument that no stigma attaches does not withstand analysis, for the accused will have suffered loss of time, legal costs, exposure to the processes of the criminal law at trial and, however one may downplay it, the opprobrium of conviction. It is not sufficient to say that the public interest is engaged and, therefore, liability may be imposed without fault. In serious crimes, the public interest is involved and *mens rea* must be proven. The administrative argument has little force. In sentencing, evidence of due diligence is admissible and therefore the evidence might just as well be heard when considering guilt. Additionally, it may be noted that s 198 of the *Alberta Highway Traffic Act* RSA 1970 c 169, provides that upon a person being charged with an offence under this Act, if the Judge trying the case is of the opinion that the offence (a) was committed wholly by accident or misadventure and without negligence, and (b) could not by the exercise of reasonable care or precaution have been avoided, the Judge may dismiss the case. See also s 230(2) [am 1976 c 62 s 48] of the Manitoba *Highway Traffic Act* RSM 1970 c H60, which has a similar effect. In these instances at least, the Legislature has indicated that administrative efficiency does not foreclose inquiry as to fault. It is also worthy of note that historically the penalty for breach of statutes enacted for the regulation of individual conduct in the interests of health and safety was minor, $20 or $25; today, it may amount to thousands of dollars and entail the possibility of imprisonment for a second conviction. The present case is an example.

Public welfare offences involve a shift of emphasis from the protection of individual interests to the protection of public and social interests: see F B Sayre, "Public Welfare Offenses", 33 *Columbia Law Rev* 55 (1933); Hall, *General Principles of Criminal Law* (1947), c 13, p 427; R M Perkins, "Civil Offense", 100 *U of Pa L Rev* 832 (1952); Jobson, "Far From Clear", 18 *Crim L Q* 294 (1975–76). The unfortunate tendency in many past cases has been to see the choice as between two stark alternatives: (i) full *mens rea*; or (ii) absolute liability. In respect of public welfare offences (within which category pollution offences fall) where full *mens rea* is not required, absolute liability has often been imposed. English jurisprudence has consistently maintained this dichotomy: see "Criminal Law, Evidence and Procedure", 11 Hals, 14th ed, pp 20–2, para 18. There has, however, been an attempt in Australia, in many Canadian Courts, and indeed in England, to seek a middle position, fulfilling the goals of public welfare offences while still not punishing the entirely blameless. There is an increasing and impressive stream of authority which holds that where an offence does not require full *mens rea*, it is nevertheless a good defence for the defendant to prove that he was not negligent.

Dr Glanville Williams has written: "There is a half-way house between *mens rea* and strict responsibility which has not yet been properly utilized, and that is responsibility for negligence" (*Criminal Law: General Part*, 2nd ed (1961), p 262. Morris and Howard, in *Studies in Criminal Law* (1964), p 200, suggest that strict responsibility might with advantage be replaced by a doctrine of responsibility for negligence strengthened by a shift in the burden of proof. The defendant would be allowed to exculpate himself by proving affirmatively that he was not negligent. Professor Howard ("Strict Responsibility in the High Court of Australia", 76 LQR 547 (1960)) offers the comment that English law of strict responsibility in minor statutory offences is distinguished only by its irrationality, and then has this to say in support of the position taken by the Australian High Court, at p 548.

> Over a period of nearly sixty years since its inception the High Court has adhered with consistency to the principle that there should be no criminal responsibility without fault, however minor the offence. It has done so by utilizing the very half-way house to which Dr Williams refers, responsibility for negligence.

In his work, "Public Welfare Offenses", at p 78, Professor Sayre suggests that if the penalty is really slight involving, for instance, a maximum fine of $25, particularly if adequate enforcement depends upon wholesale prosecution, or if the social danger arising from violation is serious, the doctrine of basing liability upon mere activity rather than fault, is sound. He continues, however, at p 79:

> On the other hand, some public welfare offenses involve a possible penalty of imprisonment, or heavy fine. In such cases it would seem sounder policy to maintain the orthodox requirement of a guilty mind but to shift the burden of proof to the shoulders of the defendant to establish his lack of a guilty intent if he can. For public welfare offences defendants may be convicted by proof of the mere act of violation; but, if the offence involves a possible prison penalty, the defendant should not be denied the right of bringing forward affirmative evidence to prove that the violation was the result of no fault on his part.

and at p 82:

> It is fundamentally unsound to convict a defendant for a crime involving a substantial term of imprisonment without giving him the opportunity to prove

that his action was due to an honest and reasonable mistake of fact or that he acted without guilty intent. If the public danger is widespread and serious, the practical situation can be met by shifting to the shoulders of the defendant the burden of proving a lack of guilty intent.

The doctrine proceeds on the assumption that the defendant could have avoided the *prima facie* offence through the exercise of reasonable care and he is given the opportunity of establishing, if he can, that he did in fact exercise such care.

The case which gave the lead in this branch of the law is the Australian case of *Proudman v Dayman* (1941), 67 CLR 536, where Dixon, J, said, at p 540.

It is one thing to deny that a necessary ingredient of the offence is positive knowledge of the fact that the driver holds no subsisting licence. It is another to say that an honest belief founded on reasonable grounds that he is licensed cannot exculpate a person who permits him to drive. As a general rule an honest and reasonable belief in a state of facts which, if they existed, would make the defendant's act innocent affords an excuse for doing what would otherwise be an offence.

This case, and several others like it, speak of the defence as being that of reasonable mistake of fact. The reason is that the offences in question have generally turned on the possession by a person or place of an unlawful status, and the accused's defence was that he reasonably did not know of this status: eg, permitting an unlicensed person to drive, or lacking a valid licence oneself, or being the owner of property in a dangerous condition. In such cases, negligence consists of unreasonable failure to know the facts which constitute the offence. It is clear, however, that in principle the defence is that all reasonable care was taken. In other circumstances, the issue will be whether the accused's behaviour was negligent in bringing about the forbidden event when he knew the relevant facts. Once the defence of reasonable mistake of fact is accepted, there is no barrier to acceptance of the other constituent part of a defence of due diligence.

The principle which has found acceptance in Australia since *Proudman v Dayman*, supra, has a place also in the jurisprudence of New Zealand: see *The Queen v Strawbridge*, [1970] NZLR 909; *The King v Ewart* (1905), 25 NZLR 709.

In the House of Lords case of *Sweet v Parsley*, [1970] AC 132, Lord Reid noted the difficulty presented by the simplistic choice between *mens rea* in the full sense and an absolute offence. He looked approvingly at attempts to find a middle ground. Lord Pearce, in the same case, referred to the "sensible half-way house" which he thought the Courts should take in some so-called absolute offences. The difficulty, as Lord Pearce saw it, lay in the opinion of Viscount Sankey, LC, in *Woolmington v Director of Public Prosecutions*, [1935] AC 462, if the full width of that opinion were maintained. Lord Diplock, however, took a different and, in my opinion, a preferable view, at p 164:

Woolmington's case did not decide anything so irrational as that the prosecution must call evidence to prove the absence of any mistaken belief by the accused in the existence of facts which, if true, would make the act innocent, any more than it decided that the prosecution must call evidence to prove the absence of any claim of right in a charge of larceny. The jury is entitled to presume that the accused acted with knowledge of the facts, unless there is some evidence to the contrary originating from the accused who alone can know on what belief he acted and on what ground the belief, if mistaken, was held.

In *Woolmington*'s case the question was whether the trial Judge was correct in directing the jury that the accused was required to prove his innocence. Viscount Sankey, LC, referred to the strength of the presumption of innocence in a criminal case and then made the statement, universally accepted in this country, that there is no burden on the prisoner to prove his innocence; it is sufficient for him to raise a doubt as to his guilt. I do not understand the case as standing for anything more than that. It is to be noted that the case is concerned with criminal offences in the true sense; it is not concerned with public welfare offences. It is somewhat ironic that *Woolmington*'s case, which embodies a principle for the benefit of the accused, should be used to justify the rejection of a defence of reasonable care for public welfare offences and the retention of absolute liability, which affords the accused no defence at all. There is nothing in *Woolmington*'s case, as I comprehend it, which stands in the way of adoption, in respect of regulatory offences, of a defence of due care, with burden of proof resting on the accused to establish the defence on the balance of probabilities. . . .

. . . It is interesting to note the recommendations made by the Law Reform Commission to the Minister of Justice (*Our Criminal Law*) in March, 1976. The Commission advises (p 32) that (i) every offence outside the *Criminal Code* be recognized as admitting of a defence of due diligence; (ii) in the case of any such offence for which intent or recklessness is not specifically required the onus of proof should lie on the defendant to establish such defence; (iii) the defendant would have to prove this on the preponderance or balance of probabilities. The recommendation endorsed a working paper (*Meaning of Guilt: Strict Liability*, June 20, 1974), in which it was stated that negligence should be the minimum standard of liability in regulatory offences, that such offences were (p 32):

. . . to promote higher standards of care in business, trade and industry, higher standards of honesty in commerce and advertising, higher standards of respect for the . . . environment and [therefore] the . . . offence is basically and typically an offence of negligence;

that an accused should never be convicted of a regulatory offence if he establishes that he acted with due diligence, that is, that he was not negligent. In the working paper, the Commission further stated (p 33), ". . . let us recognize the regulatory offence for what it is – an offence of negligence – and frame the law to ensure that guilt depends upon lack of reasonable care". The view is expressed that in regulatory law, to make the defendant disprove negligence – prove due diligence – would be both justifiable and desirable.

In an interesting article on the matter now under discussion, "Far From Clear", *supra*, Professor Jobson refers to a series of recent cases, arising principally under s 32(1) of the *Ontario Water Resources Act*, the section at issue in the present proceedings, which [at p 297] "openly acknowledged a defence based on lack of fault or neglect: these cases require proof of the *actus reus* but then permit the accused to show that he was without fault or had no opportunity to prevent the harm." The paramount case in the series *R v Industrial Tankers Ltd*, [1968] 4 CCC 81, [1968] 2 OR 142, 10 Crim LQ 346, in which Judge Sprague, relying upon *R v Hawinda Taverns Ltd* (1955), 112 CCC 361, and *R v Bruin Hotel Co Ltd* (1954), 109 CCC 174, 19 CR 107, 12 WWR (NS) 387, held that the Crown did not need to prove that the accused had *mens rea*, but it did have to show that the accused had the power and authority to prevent the pollution, and could have prevented it, but did not do so. Liability rests upon control and the opportunity to prevent, ie, that the accused could have and should have prevented the pollution. In *Industrial Tankers*, the burden was placed on the Crown to prove lack of reasonable care. To that extent *Industrial Tankers* and s 32(1) cases which followed it, such as *R v Sheridan* (1972), 10 CCC (2d) 545, [1973] 2 OR 192, differ from other authorities on s 32(1) which would place upon the accused the burden of showing as a defence that he did not have control or otherwise could not have prevented the impairment: see *R v Cherokee Disposals & Construction Ltd* (1973), 13 CCC (2d) 87, [1973] 3 OR 599; *R v Liquid Cargo Lines Ltd* (1974), 18 CCC (2d) 428, and *R v North Canadian Enterprises Ltd* (1974), 20 CCC (2d) 242.

The element of control, particularly by those in charge of business activities which may endanger the public, is vital to promote the observance of regulations designed to avoid that danger. This control may be exercised by "supervision or inspection, by improvement of his business methods or by exhorting those whom he may be expected to influence or control": Lord Evershed in *Lim Chin Aik v The Queen*, [1963] AC 160 at p 174. The purpose, Dean Roscoe Pound has said (*Spirit of the Common Law* (1906)), is to "put pressure upon the thoughtless and inefficient to do their whole duty in the interest of public health or safety or morale". As Devlin, J, noted in *Reynolds v GH Austin & Sons Ltd*, [1951] 2 KB 135 at p 149: "a man may be made responsible for the acts of his servants, or even for defects in his business arrangements, because it can fairly be said that by such sanctions citizens are induced to keep themselves and their organizations up to the mark". Devlin, J, added, however: "if a man is punished because of an act done by another, whom he cannot reasonably be expected to influence or control, the law is engaged, not in punishing thoughtlessness or inefficiency, and thereby promoting the welfare of the community, but in pouncing on the most convenient victim". . . .

It may be suggested that the introduction of a defence based on due diligence and the shifting of the burden of proof might better be implemented by legislative act. In answer, it should be recalled that the concept of absolute liability and the creation of a jural category of public welfare offences are both the product of the judiciary and not of the legislature. The development to date of this defence, in the numerous decisions I have referred to, of Courts in this country as well as in Australia and New Zealand, has also been the work of judges. The present case offers the opportunity of consolidating and clarifying the doctrine.

The correct approach, in my opinion, is to relieve the Crown of the burden of proving *mens rea*, having regard to *Pierce Fisheries* and to the virtual impossibility in most regulatory cases of proving wrongful intention. In a normal case, the accused alone will have knowledge of what he has done to avoid the breach and it is not improper to expect him to come forward with the evidence of due diligence. This is particularly so when it is alleged, for example, that pollution was caused by the activities of a large and complex corporation. Equally, there is nothing wrong with rejecting absolute liability and admitting the defence of reasonable care.

In this doctrine it is not up to the prosecution to prove negligence. Instead, it is open to the defendant to prove that all due care has been taken. This burden falls upon the defendant as he is the only one who will generally have the means of proof. This would not seem unfair as the alternative is absolute liability which denies an accused any defence whatsoever. While the prosecution must prove beyond a reasonable doubt that the defendant committed the prohibited act, the defendant must only establish on the balance of probabilities that he has a defence of reasonable care.

I conclude, for the reasons which I have sought to express, that there are compelling grounds for the recognition of three categories of offences rather than the traditional two:

(1) Offences in which *mens rea*, consisting of some positive state of mind such as intent, knowledge, or recklessness, must be proved by the prosecution either as an inference from the nature of the act committed, or by additional evidence.

(2) Offences in which there is no necessity for the prosecution to prove the existence of *mens rea*; the doing of the prohibited act *prima facie* imports the offence, leaving it open to the accused to avoid liability by proving that he took all reasonable care. This involves consideration of what a reasonable man would have done in the circumstances. The defence will be available if the accused reasonably believed in a mistaken set of facts which, if true, would render the act or omission innocent, or if he took all reasonable steps to avoid the particular event. These offences may properly be called offences of strict liability. Mr Justice Estey so referred to them in *Hickey*'s case.

(3) Offences of absolute liability where it is not open to the accused to exculpate himself by showing that he was free of fault.

Offences which are criminal in the true sense fall in the first category. Public welfare offences would, *prima facie*, be in the second category. They are not subject to the presumption of full *mens rea*. An offence of this type would fall in the first category only if such words as "wilfully", "with intent", "knowingly", or "intentionally" are contained in the statutory provision creating the offence. On the other hand, the principle that punishment should in general not be inflicted on those without fault applies. Offences of absolute liability would be those in respect of which the legislature had made it clear that guilt would follow proof merely of the proscribed act. The over-all regulatory pattern adopted by the legislature, the subject-matter of the legislation, the importance of the penalty, and the precision of the language used will be primary considerations in determining whether the offence falls into the third category. . . .

The decision of the court was that there was no clear legislative intention that liability was absolute. Consequently the offence was one of strict liability and the City could raise a defence of due diligence based on efforts to prevent pollution which were reasonable in the circumstances. At a subsequent trial the defence failed and the City was eventually fined $1,000. In the *Motor Vehicle Reference* case[25] this classification was raised to that of a constitutional imperative.

Proof of Guilt

1.45 It is impossible to separate criminal law from the rules of evidence which set the standard of proof to be achieved, before guilt can be proved, and the means which may be adopted to that end.

A person is presumed to be innocent until the jury finds him guilty; *Harvey v Ocean Accident and Guarantee Corporation*[26]. It is only where each element of the crime is proved against the accused, beyond reasonable doubt, that he may be found guilty; *The People (A-G) v Oglesby*[27]. The accused does not normally bear the burden of proving any fact. He need not, in the absence of a special provision, give evidence in his own defence. He may simply test the evidence, through counsel, by cross-examination and may call on the judge at the end of the prosecution's case to rule that there is insufficient material on which a reasonable jury, properly instructed, could find him guilty. This is called an application for a direction. It may be acceded to in practice, in cases where there is a gap in the evidence tendered on behalf of the prosecution or where some vital link in the chain of proof is missing. It can also arise in cases where an apparent link in the chain of proof is so tenuous that it would clearly be perverse for a jury, properly directed as to the onus of proof which rests upon the prosecution, to act upon it; *The People (DPP) v O'Shea (No 2)*[28]. In raising a defence the accused is not bound to give evidence but may merely point to some weakness in the prosecution case which may be sufficient for the jury to say that there is a reasonable doubt. Except in the case of insanity, where the accused has the

25 (1985) 48 CR (3d) 289.
26 [1905] 2 IR 1.
27 [1966] IR 162.
28 [1983] ILRM 592.

burden of proving this defence as a matter of probability (see para **4.106**), the accused can only be found guilty if the prosecution are able to disprove the material which supports a defence, beyond any reasonable doubt; *The People (A-G) v Quinn*[29] (see para **4.04**).

1.46 The accused must be found guilty where the elements of an offence have been proved against him beyond reasonable doubt. It is for the jury to find the facts of a case after an appropriate direction as to the law by the trial judge. Finding that the accused has, or has not, been proven guilty is a matter for the jury alone. A reasonable doubt is the kind of doubt which may affect the mind of a person in the conduct of important affairs; *Walters v R*[30]. In enunciating that standard, it is appropriate that the trial judge should contrast the degree of proof in a criminal case with that in a civil case, where a jury need only be satisfied before finding in favour of a plaintiff or defendant, that a version of events is the more probable; *The People (A-G) v Byrne*[31]. Achieving such a standard requires that the prosecution should be able to present evidence from which the inference of the accused's guilt is inescapable. They may do this either by presenting direct evidence as to his guilt or by presenting circumstantial evidence. Direct evidence would indicate that the accused is guilty from testimony available to the prosecution. For example, in a burglary case, the accused may be caught inside a house collecting together jewellery in a bag. The obvious inference is that he intended to steal. Where the proof is by circumstantial evidence it must be consistent with the guilt of the accused and must be inconsistent with any other rational hypothesis consistent with innocence; *The People (A-G) v McMahon*[32], *R v McGreevy*[33]. For example, an accused is alleged to have assisted in a kidnapping. At the time when ransom demands are made he is spotted by different policemen in the vicinity of the five different call boxes from which the ransom demands are made at around the same time. Of course, his presence there maybe a mere coincidence. He may present evidence indicating that a series of personal errands took him along the same route used by the real kidnapper and at the same precise time as him. Extraordinary coincidences rarely occur in sequence and juries are rarely taken-in by such stories. As a matter of practice juries seem most often to be motivated to acquit where the Gardaí are shown to have been, apparently, less than fully professional or honest. Such an acquittal may occur notwithstanding that the accused is, apparently, obviously guilty.

1.47 Apart from the warning that they may only convict if satisfied of the accused's guilt beyond reasonable doubt, certain other circumstances require an additional caution by the trial judge to the jury. For example, where a case depends wholly or substantially on visual identification evidence the jury must be warned that there is a danger in acting on that evidence even where it is apparently strong; *The People (A-G) v Casey*

29 [1965] IR 366.
30 [1969] 2 AC 26.
31 [1974] IR 1 at p 9.
32 [1946] IR 267.
33 [1972] NI 125.

(No 2)[34]. More recently, the practice of bringing witnesses to informally identify suspects, (usually in a court or outside a labour exchange) without holding an identification parade, has been subjected to exclusion at the discretion of the trial judge; *The People (DPP) v O'Reilly*[35]. In cases involving sexual offences, the jury used to be warned that it was dangerous to convict on the uncorroborated testimony of the victim. The Criminal Law (Rape) (Amendment) Act 1990 made this warning discretionary (see para **6.72**).

1.48 Essentially, a case is only ever proved against an accused person through the application by the jury of their common experience of life and of the state of mind with which people act in individual sets of circumstances. A person is presumed to intend the natural and probable consequences of his action. This is a proposition of ordinary good sense. A man is usually able to foresee what the natural consequences of his act are and so it is reasonable, in general, to infer that he did foresee them and intend them. This is an inference which may be drawn but it is not one which must be drawn if, on all the facts of the case, it is not the correct inference; *Hosegood v Hosegood*[36]. One returns to the example of the burglar in the house; no one who acts in the way outlined, in the absence of a severe psychiatric problem, could be intending to do anything other than steal the jewellery. If there is an alternative explanation and it is not supported on the facts of the prosecution case then the accused must establish it either by cross-examination or by giving evidence.

The accused may attack a prosecution case by seeking to have evidence excluded. If the accused can manage to have cogent evidence of his guilt excluded from the consideration of the jury he will stand a better chance of acquittal. Hearsay evidence cannot, in general, be produced against an accused. This position has been modified with respect to documentary evidence, and in certain sexual cases, by the Criminal Evidence Act 1992. Often an accused will have made a statement to the Gardaí. An admission by the accused can only be accepted in evidence if it is proved by the prosecution not to have been the result of any hope of advantage or fear of prejudice excited or held out by a person in authority, or of oppressive conduct[37]. Even where a confession is proved to have been voluntary it may be excluded if it was taken in breach of the Judge's rules; *The People (DPP) v Farrell*[38], *The People (DPP) v Cummins*[39]. An accused may also call for the exclusion of evidence against him on the grounds that it has been obtained in conscious and deliberate violation of his constitutional rights, or that the trial judge should, in the exercise of his discretion, exclude evidence obtained by an illegality. Finally, evidence which has a prejudicial effect which outweighs its probative value may be excluded on the grounds that a jury in

34 [1963] IR 33.
35 [1991] ILRM 10.
36 (1950) 56 TLR (PT 1) 735.
37 See generally *The People (AG) v Galvin* [1964] IR 325, CCA and Ryan & Magee *The Irish Criminal Process* at pp 121–135.
38 [1978] IR 13, 1 Frewen 558, CCA.
39 [1972] IR 312, SC.

hearing this evidence may unfairly jump to the conclusion that the accused is guilty as a result of being prejudice against him, as opposed to having the case proved; *The People (A-G) v Kirwan*[40] and Cole *Irish Cases on Evidence*[41].

It is outside the scope of this work to discuss the technical rules of evidence but it can be seen from the foregoing sketch that these are inextricably linked to the success or failure of a prosecution case. Sometimes these rules lack justification. They have grown up piecemeal and are not based on any fundamental premise. It is submitted that the fundamental purpose of a criminal trial should be to search for the truth. There are instances where the rules of evidence stand in the way of that search but in only one instance has the prosecution sought to challenge the common law rules of evidence on the ground that it is inconsistent with the Constitution; *The People (DPP) v JT*[42].

Presumptions

1.49 In exceptional circumstances the prosecution have been assisted by the legislature in discharging the burden of proof by provisions which require that a mental state should be inferred on the proof of certain external factors.

1.50 *The Criminal Justice Act 1964*

4 This section is quoted at para **5.06**.

1.51 *Misuse of Drugs Act 1977*

15(1) Any person who has in his possession, whether lawfully or not, a controlled drug for the purpose of selling or otherwise supplying it to another in contravention of regulations under section 5 of this Act, shall be guilty of an offence. (2) Subject to section 29(3) of this Act, in any proceedings for an offence under subsection (1) of this section, where it is proved that a person was in possession of a controlled drug and the court, having regard to the quantity of the controlled drug which the person possessed or to such other matter as the court considers relevant, is satisfied that it is reasonable to assume that the controlled drug was not intended for the immediate personal use of the person, he shall be presumed, until the court is satisfied to the contrary, to have been in possession of a controlled drug for the purpose of selling or otherwise supplying it to another in contravention of regulations under s 5 of this Act.

29(3) In any proceedings for an offence under section 15 of this Act a defendant may rebut the presumption raised by subsection (2) of that section by showing that at the time of the alleged offence he was by virtue of regulations made under section 4 of this Act lawfully in possession of the controlled drug to which the proceedings relate.

1.52 *Explosive Substances Act 1883*

4(1) Any person who makes or knowingly has in his possession or under his control any explosive substance, under such circumstances as to give rise to a reasonable suspicion that he is not making it or does not have it in his possession or

40 [1943] IR 279.
41 (1982) Chapter 2.
42 (1989) 3 Frewen 181.

under his control for a lawful object, shall, unless he can show that he made it or had it in his possession or under his control for a lawful object, be guilty of felony and, on conviction, shall be liable to penal servitude for a term not exceeding fourteen years, or to imprisonment for a term not exceeding two years with or without hard labour, and the explosive substance shall be forfeited.
(2) In any proceeding against any person for a crime under this section, such person and his wife, or husband, as the case may be, may, if such person thinks fit, be called, sworn, examined, and cross-examined as an ordinary witness in the case.

1.53 Traditionally it has been assumed that where a burden of proof is placed on the accused he must do more than raise a reasonable doubt and proceed to establish, on the balance of probability, the negative of the fact presumed against him; *R v Carr-Briant*[43], *Jayasena v R*[44], Williams *Evidential Burdens on the Defence*[45]. It may be fairer, and in accordance with constitutional standards of justice, to simply place on the accused a burden of raising a reasonable doubt by his own direct testimony, thus subjecting him to cross-examination; Charleton – *Offences Against the Person*[46].

Constructing criminal liability

1.54 In considering the revision of an old offence, or in creating a new offence, the elements must be examined in terms of what the prosecution needs to prove in terms of the external element of the offence, before considering what is a fair mental element. Often, a presumption as to a mental state, or a presumption that a particular fact may be inferred from the existence of another fact, may be of assistance. The construction of liability must depend on the principle that an offence should not be cast in terms which makes it reasonably possible that an innocent person might be convicted. However, laws which have been found to work incorrectly require revision. If persons who are obviously guilty of conduct which is gravely harmful to the fabric of society continually escape from the offence designed to punish their behaviour, then the law no longer works. Its revision must be considered and part of that task may involve the substitution of a less onerous mental element or the creation of a presumption which will assist the prosecution in its task. Section 4 of the Criminal Law (Amendment) Act 1935 has long been redundant because of the complications which are incorporated in the definition of the offence. The purpose of the law was to make it an offence for a person to have sexual intercourse with a woman who was mentally handicapped. Section 4 provides:

"Any person who, in circumstances which do not amount to rape, unlawfully and carnally knows or attempts to have unlawful carnal knowledge of any woman or girl who is an idiot, or an imbecile or is feeble-minded shall, if the circumstances prove that such person knew at the time of such knowledge or attempt that such woman or girl was then an idiot or an imbecile or feeble-minded (as the case may be), be guilty of a misdemeanour and shall be liable on conviction thereof to imprisonment for any term not exceeding two years".

43 [1943] KB 607.
44 [1970] AC 618.
45 (1977) 127 NLJ 182.
46 (1992) Chapter 9.

The task of the Law Reform Commission was to isolate the difficulties inherent in proof of this offence and to suggest a just alternative.

1.55   *Sexual Offences Against the Mentally Handicapped*
Law Reform Commission Report 1990
LRC 33 – 1990

Criticisms of the Present Law

18. There was unanimous agreement with our initial view that the language of s 4 is both offensive and out of date. This alone would justify the repeal of the section and its replacement by appropriately worded legislation. The categorisation of the persons who should be protected by legislation of this nature is, however, a question of considerable difficulty to which we shall return in our final chapter.

19. As noted, s 4 applies only to unlawful "carnal knowledge" of a woman or girl, ie vaginal sexual intercourse, or an attempt to have such unlawful carnal knowledge. It is accordingly not a crime to commit other acts of a sexual nature, such as cunnilingus or fellatio, with a woman or girl, no matter how severely mentally handicapped. We do not know why the present law is confined to vaginal sexual intercourse: it may be that it was considered that the law should only protect mentally handicapped women against the risk of pregnancy. If, however, the law has a broader justification, ie the protection of the mentally handicapped and mentally ill against sexual exploitation, then quite clearly such acts should be also unlawful. Moreover, if the law relating to homosexual acts between consenting adults is altered as a result of the judgment of the European Court of Human Rights in *Norris*, it might be thought that it should continue to be an offence for a man to have anal intercourse or commit what are at present described as acts of "gross indecency" with a man coming within the proposed definition of mental handicap or mental illness.

20. Clearly a major difficulty in the practical operation of s 4 is that in the typical case the principal (frequently indeed the only) evidence against the accused is that of the complainant herself. This immediately creates a dilemma: if the complainant can satisfy the judge that she is capable of giving sworn evidence in that she understands the nature and consequences of the oath, a doubt may arise as to whether she is "feeble minded", an "imbecile" or an "idiot" within the meaning of s 4. If, on the other hand, she is adjudged incompetent to give evidence because of her mental state, the prosecution collapses at the outset.

These difficulties were illustrated in two recent cases. In the first, *DPP v JS*, medical evidence classified the prosecutrix as being moderately mentally handicapped according to a scale graded in terms of mild, moderate and severe. The accused was charged with having unlawful carnal knowledge of a feeble minded woman contrary to s 4. When her deposition was taken in the District Court, she manifested an ability to carry on a fairly normal conversation on matters related to her every day household life. At the trial in the Circuit Court, however, she could not answer questions as to the nature of the oath or the nature of a lie. She made no response when asked by the judge what the moral and legal consequences of telling a lie were. In the result, she could not be sworn and, as there was no independent evidence of sexual intercourse, a *nolle prosequi* was entered. In the second case, *DPP v MW*, the prosecutix was again classified as moderately mentally handicapped but was normal in appearance and could converse on a similarly limited range of topics, albeit with a speech defect. She alleged that non-consensual intercourse took place in a car and accordingly there were two counts on the indictment, the first of rape and the second under s 4. The rape trial came on first and the judge ruled that she was competent to take the oath.

However, because her evidence as to consent was contradictory, the judge directed an acquittal. Upon the trial of the s 4 charge, her preliminary answers were less satisfactory than on the first occasion and a different judge declined to have her sworn. There being no other evidence, the State was compelled to enter a *nolle prosequi*. A member of the Bar with considerable experience in this field has remarked that these two cases:

> "highlight the fact that the legal regime designed to protect the mentally subnormal against sexual exploitation is totally inadequate and urgently needs reform."

21. There is a further feature of the offence created by s 4 which does not appear to have arisen for discussion in any recent Irish cases, but which should be borne in mind if that section is being replaced. The general principle of the criminal law is that, in the case of more serious crime, it is not sufficient to prove the commission of the act prohibited by the law: it must also be established that the accused possessed the mental state required for the particular crime in question. In the case of the offences under consideration, this necessity to prove *mens rea* is spelled out in the section. The prosecution must, accordingly, prove that the accused was aware that she was so impaired. This is in contrast to the offences created by the same statute of having sexual intercourse with girls beneath a defined age, where in Ireland it is necessary to do no more than prove the commission of the act and it is not even a defence for the accused to prove that he was reasonably mistaken as to the age of the girl. While the absence of a defence of reasonable mistake to the latter offences would be regarded by many as unduly draconian, there is undoubtedly an argument to be made that, in the case of the offences under consideration, the prosecution should not be required to establish knowledge on the part of the accused as to the complainant's mental condition, which can be extremely difficult: it should be sufficient, on this view, to prove the commission of the prohibited act, leaving the burden on the accused to establish by way of defence that he was not actually aware, or could not reasonably have been aware, of the complainant's mental condition. . . .

The Burden of Proof and Mens Rea

34. We have pointed out that under the present law the prosecution must prove that the accused knew at the time of the alleged offence that the woman was then suffering from the relevant mental condition. Our consultations have fully confirmed the provisional view we had formed, ie that this is an unnecessary obstacle to the prosecution of such offences and is not reasonably required in the interests of justice to the accused. The fact that the offence created by s 7 of the English Sexual Offences Act 1956 is one of strict liability does not appear to have given rise to any unease among commentators in that jurisdiction. Instead, criticism has tended to focus on the issue as to whether the criminal law has any role in this area. We accordingly *recommend that in prosecutions for the offences referred to in the preceding paragraphs, it should be presumed until the contrary is shown that, where the complainant was suffering from the relevant degree of mental handicap or mental illness at the time of the alleged offence, the accused was aware of that fact. It should also be provided that a person is not guilty of the offence if at the time the offence is alleged to have been committed, he did not know, and had no reason to suspect, that the complainant was suffering from mental handicap or mental illness as defined.*

35. It is possible that a sexual relationship between two people suffering from mental handicap or mental illness could result in the conviction of either or both, since it might not be possible for one of the participants to establish that he or she was unaware of the relevant degree of handicap or illness of the other. *A fortiori*, the general defence of insanity under the criminal law would not be available to

that participant. This would be clearly contrary to the underlying principles which, in our view, should inform the proposed legislation.

We accordingly *recommended that no act of vaginal sexual intercourse, or anal penetration or other proscribed sexual activity should constitute an offence where both participants are suffering from mental handicap or mental illness as defined, unless the acts in question constitute a criminal offence by virtue of some other provision of the law.*

36. We are also satisfied, and recommend, *that there should continue to be higher penalties where the relevant offences are committed by persons in charge of, or employed in, mental institutions or where the accused person had the care or charge of the other participant. The definition of "mental institution", in the Mental Treatment Act 1945 should be expanded so as to include residential centres and community based residences.*

1.56   ***Prosecuting Fraud in a Common Law Jurisdiction***
Address by Eamonn M Barnes, Director of Public Prosecutions,
to the Law Society Seminar on
Saturday 16th November 1991 on
Criminal law in the 1990s, A European Perspective

I am often amazed by the lack of appreciation of the artificial and restrictive nature of the procedures utilised for the investigation and prosecution of crime in this country which I regularly find among mature and experienced lawyers, whose practices do not require them to appear in the criminal courts. The situation sometimes seems little better among legislators. cabinet ministers and former cabinet ministers who have gone on the air and into print to express their "amazement" or "concern" regarding the absence of prosecutions in cases about which they professed to have a detailed knowledge. Assuming such professions to be well founded on fact, one would be driven to the conclusion that their knowledge and understanding of the relevant substantive criminal law and criminal procedure were less than perfect. Oireachtas members are from time to time moved on behalf of aggrieved constituents to write to me in protest or enquiry as to why a particular prosecution was not brought, in circumstances in which even a superficial knowledge of the facts of the case and an elementary understanding of the criminal justice system would have stayed their pens. And while there is no doubt that members of the public, whether personally affected by the particular matter or not, are regularly and rightly aggrieved by the spectacle of a perceived wrongdoer escaping not alone conviction but even accusation, they invariably identify the wrong target for their dissatisfaction, not appreciating that it is the system itself which is to blame rather than those seeking to operate it.

The result of this general lack of appreciation of the fundamental deficiencies of our system is that the three most important potential sources of the impetus for fundamental review of it are not sufficiently aware that there is a serious problem which needs to be addressed and solved. They are the general public, the generators of that public opinion which inspires legislative change, the legal profession, which in this specialised area can inform public opinion and influence the nature of necessary changes in law and procedure, and the legislators who possess the power to frame and effect such changes. Added to this lack of awareness is a built-in, often subconscious or instinctive, resistance to change among the legal profession and the legislators, particularly if that change amounts to any more than slight navigational adjustments of direction. Any suggestion of a total re-appraisal of our legal system sends a frisson of apprehension down the spine of lawyer and legislator alike. Any hint that any of the sacred cows with which our legal landscape is littered might come under critical scrutiny induces gasps of horror. And if there is the slightest possibility, however unwarranted by the particular proposal, that the dreaded words "erosion of our civil liberties" might at any stage be uttered, the game is up. But however great the obstacles to reform I believe it to be critically important now that members of the public, who so frequently complain about what they perceive to be non-enforcement of the criminal law against wrongdoers, or about what is to them the inexplicable outcome of a criminal prosecution, will know and fully understand the real reason for their grievances. Obviously that would be a good thing in itself, but in addition, a clear knowledge and perception of the nature and the limitations of their system of criminal justice would enable the general public to make informed choices as to whether or not that is the system which they want to have, as to whether or not the price paid for it in frustrated or failed prosecutions is too high, and as to what changes they would wish to see effected in it. Above all, they would appreciate that changes are possible, that they could have a choice and that there are indeed several other ways of ordering the affairs of the nation in this area.

This paper is primarily about our criminal procedure rather than our corpus of criminal law. It is set in the context of fraud, but my observations regarding our system of criminal procedure are equally applicable to all areas of the criminal law. The only difference between fraud and the other areas is that the difficulties encountered are greatly exacerbated in fraud cases. This is so because the nature of fraud, particularly of corporate fraud on the grand scale, with obscure and complex financial transactions involving a multiplicity of companies persons and accounts within and without the jurisdiction, makes the truth much more difficult to ascertain. Ascertaining and establishing the truth is or at least ought to be the primary concern of any criminal justice system. Accusation, conviction and imposition of punishment can safely be considered only when the full facts of the matter have been clearly and reliably established. This task is exceedingly difficult under our system. I do not wish to express any value judgement on any of the high profile fraud prosecutions brought in recent years in the United Kingdom and the United States, but I can say that had the events in question taken place in Ireland, there could not have been prosecutions, still less convictions in relation to them. This is a most serious situation if, as some believe, serious fraud is widespread and undetected here. It remains serious even if it is not widespread, because the very absence of an effective criminal justice system to deter it will soon create the problem.

It is, I believe, necessary that the sequence of investigation, accusation and adjudication be not alone preserved but that the three processes be conducted totally independently of one another. I propose to make some observations on each of those three processes and on how they might be altered with profit to the country as a whole. In doing so, I suggest that we should be less sensitive than we are to constructive criticism of legal institutions and systems of justice and that neither should be regarded as immune from scrutiny and change. There has been in the past what I think was a dangerous resentment of any such criticism or scrutiny. Legal principles which on analysis prove to be less than fundamental or of less than universal application have long been thought sacrosanct and untouchable. The legal system itself was thought to be the product of centuries of objective, almost infallible, legislative and judicial wisdom. Indeed the whole system of precedent, with its endless concern for minute parsing and analysis of judicial dicta often from another century and sometimes nearly from another world, is derived from this notion. The historical reality was rather different. Statute law has been a patchwork affair designed to meet the crisis of the moment. Great reforming statutes based on coherent general principles are few and far between. Judges down through the centuries have done the best they could with the material supplied, inventing rules, offences and safeguards to meet the needs of the case before them. Many of them were splendid, some heroic. But my point is that we should not regard the result, such as the enormous and intricate edifice known as the law of evidence or old enumerations of the essential ingredients of a particular offence, as being immutable for all time. We need not be perpetually spancelled by our history. Of the three processes to which I have referred, that of investigation of crime is arguably the most important. Certainly in the absence of a thorough and successful investigation the other two processes will be frustrated. In some other jurisdictions, that is in most inquisitorial systems of criminal justice, the three processes overlap and are intertwined. In particular, the investigation of crime is often conducted and always controlled by the judiciary.

While the final adjudication is made by a tribunal separate from and independent of the judge or judges involved in the investigation, vital decisions and conclusions will have been made and arrived at by the letter which will largely determine or at least influence the ultimate adjudication. The public prosecutor, in many jurisdictions himself a member of the magistrature, moves in and out of the investigative process at various stages. The essential feature of the system is that in cases of any substance, a judicial examination of the matter will be initiated and proceed without any accusation and often without any identified suspect.

Under our accusatorial system, with the current rigid separation of the prosecutorial and judicial functions, this is not possible, a fact that gives rise to a great deal of the public frustration to which I have referred. I have often been asked why in a particular case I did not summon a suspect to court, put him in the box and question him. Of course quite apart from the thorny question of the right to silence to which I will make reference later, such a procedure is simply not possible here. Under our system, before any criminal court procedure can start, there must first be an accusation, commonly referred to as a charge. Before there can be an accusation, there must be a credible prima facie case against the proposed accused. In other words the investigation has to be over and all relevant evidence obtained before the court procedure can be initiated. The courts function is to adjudicate, not to investigate. There can be no fishing expeditions in the judicial domain here. This often is of critical importance when it comes to investigating and prosecuting fraud. As I have stated, I firmly support the separation of the processes of investigation, prosecution and adjudication and the total independence of each. I would not favour the mélange of all three which one encounters in some jurisdictions, though it works well and no doubt suits well the traditions and jurisprudence of the countries in which it operates. But having a cordon sanitaire between the investigation and the final adjudication on the issue of guilt or innocence does not of course mean that another member of the judiciary, particularly one wholly unconnected with the adjudicating court, could not participate in the investigation of the suspected or alleged offence. Whether or not such participation would be necessary or desirable depends on the answers to the various questions which arise under the heading – what powers can properly and safely be entrusted to the police acting on their own and without hands on judicial supervision and control?

An interested and inquisitive Martian would I think be amazed at the paucity of such powers currently entrusted to the police in Ireland. A Garda can arrest a person without court sanction, ie a judge's warrant, on reasonable suspicion that the arrested person has committed a felony or an offence made so arrestable by statute. There are many serious statutory and common law offences not so arrestable. As a general rule, the arrest must be effected for the purpose of bringing the person before a court to be charged as soon as is practicable, i.e. the Garda must have had enough evidence to charge him before he arrested him, and "reasonable suspicion" has to be construed accordingly. With three exceptions, he cannot be arrested for any other purpose, such as for questioning. Two of these exceptions are of limited application and have no relevance to prosecutions for fraud. The third is where a person is suspected of having committed an arrestable offence for which he could be sentenced to five years imprisonment or to a more severe punishment. Under Section 4 of the Criminal Justice Act 1984, he can be detained for up to 12 hours, which can in certain circumstances be interrupted by up to 8 hours for undisturbed rest. I might mention at this juncture that some of the more important offences in the fraud area are not arrestable offences. A person guilty of, for instance, conspiracy to defraud or fraudulent conversion or falsification of accounts cannot be arrested and detained under this or any other provision of the law irrespective of how many millions he may have misappropriated. It is however no doubt comforting to know that he could be so arrested and detained if caught shoplifting or stealing your wallet. The more sophisticated up-market criminal will leave himself open to detention for up to 12 hours only if he is careless enough to commit an arrestable offence such as forgery or larceny. Few of them are so careless. When the Gardaí adopt the only course then open to them and seek an interview with the suspect, their request is almost invariably refused.

By European standards, these are exceedingly restricted powers of police detention. Other police powers normally regarded as essential for the detection and solution of crimes of fraud, and indeed other crimes, such as powers of entry, search and seizure, are even more restricted and in practice are often non-existent. But even if the police, or indeed any other judicial or non-judicial state authority, had unlimited powers of detention and of entry search and seizure, it would in my view achieve relatively little in the detection and solution of serious fraud in the absence of at least some modification of the right to remain silent and to refuse to co-operate with the efforts of the State's authorities to ascertain the truth of the matter. I believe that an objective examination and review of that right is now seriously overdue. In addressing it now I propose first to examine the right itself and to express my personal views as to how it should be changed, and then to consider the question of who should exercise any additional powers of interrogation which might be conferred and what safeguards would need to be established.

This is not the place to trace the origins and historical development of the right to remain silent. By a process of forensic transmogrification it has now become, or at least has come to be widely regarded as being, an essential and inalienable right without which the entire edifice of our civil liberties would collapse. It is invariably portrayed as the last defence of the vulnerable and lonely man pitted against the mighty apparatus of the State. It is of course nothing of the sort. It is availed of regularly, resolutely and routinely by the successful practitioner of large-scale fraud, by the hardened general criminal and by the terrorist, the amateur, the once-off or first-time offender, will usually not avail of his rights and will blurt out the truth, sometimes because he is genuinely ashamed of what he had done. In general the right to remain silent protects only the very type of wrong-doer which society would wish to see convicted and punished. It is of no value at all to the innocent. Proven miscarriages of justice are put forward as reasons for the preservation of the right to silence. This is patent and I believe dangerous nonsense. The right to remain silent existed in all such cases and proved to be no safeguard for the unfortunate persons wrongly accused and convicted. Had it not existed, had it been replaced by a system of investigation such as I propose for consideration in this paper, I believe that these miscarriages of justice could not have taken place. As has often been said, if a person is innocent he is most likely to have his innocence vindicated under an inquisitorial system, and if he is guilty he stands a much better chance of being acquitted under an accusatorial system. I do not of course want to pass judgement on anyone involved in such apparent miscarriages of justice. The essential point about them is, however, that if untrue confessions were wrongfully extracted from detainees, as appears to have been the case on many occasions this century, it was done despite the existence of a fully established and well publicised legal right to remain silent.

I shall deal later with the question of what measures might be considered necessary so as to guard against the ever present danger of an untrue confession if the right to remain silent were to be changed or modified. I wish first to consider whether that right, which includes the right not to incriminate oneself, is somehow inherent in mankind or is in some way sacred and inviolable. The question of the standing in our legal system of this right is of course a most important question which has relevance across the entire sweep of the criminal law. It has such a special and particular relevance to the area of fraud, however, that it may well be thought to merit separate consideration for the purposes of that area alone. As I mention later, the exigencies of other particular areas of criminal activities have already resulted in an erosion or modification of the right in those areas.

The right has to be considered on two levels. There is first the right of a person, not suspected of having committed the offence being investigated but who is believed to have information relating to its commission, not to co-operate in the investigation. Subject to the offences of misprision of treason and felony, and to certain obligations now imposed in very restricted areas by a very few statutes, there is no legal obligation on him to co-operate. Apart from special situations such as information incriminating a spouse or perhaps a member of one's family, it is difficult to defend this right in principle or to raise any reasoned objection to the proposition that a person, reasonably believed to possess information relating to the commission of a crime, should be obliged under pain of penal sanction to divulge that information to the public body charged with investigating the offence. In Ireland there is of course the traditional distaste for informers, but that is scarcely a reason in 1991 to relieve citizens of what should be regarded as their basic civic duty. Persons seeking to inhibit crime by detecting investigating and prosecuting offences should not be regarded in a "them against us" way by the population whose basic civil rights to bodily integrity and security of possessions are being protected.

I move on to the more contentious level of the right to silence of the person who is suspected of involvement in the commission of the crime. Again, it is difficult to identify the principle which would suggest that he should be immune from having to answer questions in relation to it. The question has not, I believe, been seriously and sufficiently addressed at any level, academic, judicial or legislative, in these islands or for the most part in any common law jurisdiction. The topic provokes a knee-jerk reaction of irritation and prejudice. It has for a century and more been hopelessly obscured by the big lie, bigger even than the one that commences "*Dulce et decorum est*", which says that under an accusatorial system you are innocent until proven guilty whereas under an inquisitorial system you are guilty until you prove yourself innocent. Two centuries ago the right was elevated to the level of legal revelation or theology by being enshrined in the constitution of the United States of America. The right has been defended on the basis of fairness and equality, suggesting the image of a lonely suspect against whom is arrayed the awesome panoply of the State's powers. Whatever validity this point may have had in the past, it can have little now having regard to the ready and free availability to him of the best legal advice. The real objection to interference with the right to remain silent, it seems to me, is essentially a sporting one, the feeling that it simply is not done to oblige a person to incriminate himself, not gentlemanly, not cricket. It is a point of view which reflects a wider attitude towards the criminal process, which sees a criminal trial, not as a procedure for ascertaining truth, but as a context or a sort of game in which the stronger team will and should win. Legal anecdotes reflect this attitude, in which particularly golden oratory or a brilliant forensic trick wins the day. Truth tends to get sidelined. The contest is the thing, in which one side wins and the other loses. Now this seems to me to be a somewhat inadequate approach to the important business of inhibiting serious crime and to serious questions such as the right to remain silent. If a person is innocent, he has nothing to fear from co-operation with the investigation. If he is guilty and the crime was fraud, he will often, very often, be the only one who knows what was done and how. In terms of equality between him and the investigator, the reality is that he holds all the aces. It is ultimately for society, through the legislature, to decide whether or not he should be immune from the obligation to answer questions about the fraudulent activity which is being investigated.

A decision to modify or even abolish the right would not be as revolutionary as it might at first appear to be. Persons suspected of the offence of driving while under the influence of an intoxicant are already obliged, under pain of severe penalty, to provide evidence which may well result in their conviction for that offence. Under Section 107 of the Road Traffic Act 1961 a person is obliged, under pain of imprisonment, to give information which may incriminate himself, or indeed another, of an offence under that Act. There are several other examples in our law, confined to specific areas of activity, of compulsory self-incrimination. Most notably, in the area of corporate fraud, the barricade has already and recently been breached to a very significant degree. Inspectors appointed under Sections 8 or 14 of the Companies Act 1990 to investigate the affairs or membership of a company are given very wide powers to compel, *inter alia*, answers to questions which, by virtue of Section 18, may be used in evidence against him. Most people would, I firmly believe, think it very odd indeed that a person suspected of involvement in a purely summary offence under the Road Traffic Acts is obliged to furnish the evidence, or an essential part of it, which will lead to his conviction, but that a person believed to be responsible for a major fraud, involving perhaps ruin and desolation for many innocent and helpless victims, is not obliged to co-operate in the investigation even to the extent of explaining matters in a complex web of affairs which are peculiarly within his knowledge. Unless and until he is so obliged, the chances of bringing him to criminal account in Ireland must be regarded as slight indeed.

Things however have improved and are improving. Part II of the Companies Act 1990 may prove to be a potent weapon in the fight against corporate fraud, though it, particularly Section 18, has yet to be tested in the courts. Some at least of the difficulties created by the rule against hearsay may be eliminated by draft legislation about to be introduced [now the Criminal Evidence Bill 1992]. Again it is not generally appreciated that in our system documents, with few exceptions, do not prove either themselves or the authenticity or truth of their contents, however reliable their provenance. It should be clearly understood that what, in the accounts and records, is patent fraud to an accountant is not necessarily proven fraud to a court and is certainly not fraud which can be brought home to a particular person. Before accountant and judge can coincide in judgement, there will clearly have to be some form of inquisition. It is in this context, and this context only, that I propose the modification of the right to silence.

In the United Kingdom, where 25 years ago the problems arising from the rule against hearsay were largely solved insofar as they related to documentary evidence, the difficulties in ascertaining the truth and punishing the guilty in cases of serious fraud were addressed in the Criminal Justice Act of 1987. Obviously I cannot examine in this paper all the provisions of that statute. It provided however for the modification, in cases of serious fraud, of the right to remain silent, subject to the proviso that in general information given could not be used against the giver. This provision was enacted on the principle of getting the evidence of the sprat to enable the salmon to be caught. It would be an enormous advance on what we have got at present which, apart from Section 18 of the Companies Act, is nothing. But I suggest that, at least in the highly secretive world of fraud, we should be courageous and provide simply that nobody, be they sprat or salmon, should be excused from disclosing the truth in cases in which so many innocent people can be so badly hurt. To do otherwise seems to me to amount to formulating a prescription for wholesale dishonesty.

The question now arises, if such disclosure is to become compulsory, as to who should exercise the necessary powers of investigation and interrogation and how they should be exercised. I believe that questioning of any suspect, in fraud or any other type of case, should be totally open to scrutiny, as the proceedings of our courts are required to be. If all the necessary safeguards, such as the presence of a lawyer of choice and in default of choice of some totally independent observer, and the video recording of all remarks and statements sought to be introduced as evidence against the person making them were required by law, I see no reason why the investigation of fraud, like the investigation of all other offences, could not be left where it now is, in the competent hands of the Garda Síochána. If, however, the consensus is that such matters as authority to enter, search and seize, and to compel answers to questions, are best transacted under the supervision of an independent judiciary, I see no objection, in principle or as a matter of practicality, to that being arranged, provided that the judge involved in the investigation plays no part either in the decision to prosecute or in the ultimate decision to convict or acquit. For the criminal justice system to be effective in the area of fraud, it seems clear to me that accusation has to be preceded by an adequate investigation, something which in most cases cannot happen at present. Whether that investigation takes the form of a judicial inquiry or inquisition or of a police investigation with adequate powers to get at the truth is a matter for consideration. Thereafter I see no reason why the present accusatorial and adversarial procedures could not continue to be utilised.

It would be wrong and misleading to conclude this paper without again adverting to the fact that, had we the most efficient and infallible fact finding system in the world, we could still not prosecute in many cases of undoubted fraud simply because there is no criminal offence which fits the facts. Again progress has been made. Dishonest activities in the area of company law and practice such as insider dealing now attract criminal sanctions. But the general law of dishonesty, however adequate or inadequate it may have been in 1861 or 1916, is hopelessly out of date in 1991. And it has to be said again, there is no criminal offence of fraud. There are only specific offences of dishonesty which sadly do not at all fit into the computer age. In short, Madam Chairman, Ladies and Gentlemen, I believe that in the area of fraud we need a new corpus of both criminal law and criminal procedure which will not alone see us through the 1990s but will see some of you well into the 21st century.

1.57   *Address by Eamonn Barnes, Director of Public Prosecutions to The Incorporated Law Society*
4th May 1988, Killarney

. . . From the prosecutor's point of view, and I suggest from that of the citizen also, the criminal law is in urgent need both of modernisation and of codification. A very great deal of the day to day commerce of my office is concerned with imprecise and ancient common law concepts and offences, some described in Norman French or Elizabethan English by Messrs. Coke, Hale and Blackstone, or else with overly precise definitions and delineations by that extraordinary animal, the mid 19th century legislative draughtsman. It is difficult to fathom what he might have been trying to achieve as he conjured up a hundred different circumstances in which the same basic offence could be committed. 1861 as we all know was one of the vintage years in the Mother of Parliaments. Luckily there have not been too many such years. Among the allegedly reforming and consolidating measures inflicted upon us in that year and with which we still have to struggle daily were a Larceny Act, a Forgery Act, an Accessories and Abettors Act, an Offences Against the Person Act and a Malicious Damage Act. . . . while with experience a criminal lawyer can find his way with reasonable confidence through the jungle, the criminal law remains an impenetrable mystery to the average citizen. And this should not be so, particularly when one of the fundamental propositions on which we operate is that *ignorantia juris neminem excusat* (ignorance of the law is not a defence). The law, especially the criminal law, should be clear and accessible to all if all are liable for breaches of it. The scourge of legislative amendments, of amendments of amendments, of substitutions, insertions and deletions and of cross-reference definitions has made the task of ascertaining the current status of some offence and penalty sections a nightmare. When I was called to the Bar, this was still, in most cases, a relatively simple exercise. Now there are not enough fingers on one's hands to keep open the various pages to be consulted. I believe and there is a pressing need for codification of the criminal law. Apart from the obvious advantages to both citizen and practitioner, codification, and the simplification which should accompany it, would make a substantial contribution to the effectiveness of the criminal process and therefore to the deterrent effect of law enforcement.

Code options

1.58 *Model Penal Code*

2.02 General requirements of culpability

(1) *Minimum requirements of culpability* Except as provided in section 2.05, a person is not guilty of an offence unless he acted purposely, knowingly, recklessly or negligently, as the law may require, with respect to each material element of the offence.

(2) *Kinds of culpability defined*

(a) *Purposely*
A person acts purposely with respect to a material element of an offence when:

(i) if the element involves the nature of his conduct or a result thereof, it is his conscious object to engage in conduct of that nature or to cause such a result; and
(ii) if the element involves the attendant circumstances, he is aware of the existence of such circumstances or he believes or hopes that they exist.

(b) *Knowingly*
A person acts knowingly with respect to a material element of an offence when:

(i) if the element involves the nature of his conduct or the attendant circumstances, he is aware that his conduct is of that nature or that such circumstances exist; and
(ii) if the element involves a result of his conduct, he is aware that it is practically certain that his conduct will cause such a result.

(c) *Recklessly*
A person acts recklessly with respect to a material element of an offence when he consciously disregards a substantial and unjustifiable risk that the material element exists or will result from his conduct. The risk must be of such a nature and degree that, considering the nature and purpose of the actor's conduct and the circumstances known to him, its disregard involves a gross deviation from the standard of conduct that a law-abiding person would observe in the actor's situation.

(d) *Negligently*
A person acts negligently with respect to a material element of an offence when he should be aware of a substantial and unjustifiable risk that the material element exists or will result from his conduct. The risk must be of such a nature and degree that the actor's failure to perceive it, considering the nature and purpose of his conduct and the circumstances known to him, involves a gross deviation from the standard of care that a reasonable person would observe in the actor's situation.

(3) *Culpability required unless otherwise provided* When the culpability suffi-

cient to establish a material element of an offence is not prescribed by law, such element is established if a person acts purposely, knowingly or recklessly with respect thereto.

(4) *Prescribed culpability requirement applies to all material elements* When the law defining an offence prescribes the kind of culpability that is sufficient for the commission of an offence, without distinguishing among the material elements thereof, such provision shall apply to all the material elements of the offence, unless a contrary purpose plainly appears.

(5) *Substitutes for negligence, recklessness and knowledge* When the law provides that negligence suffices to establish an element of an offence, such element also is established if a person acts purposely, knowingly or recklessly. When recklessness suffices to establish an element, such element also is established if a person acts purposely or knowingly. When acting knowingly suffices to establish an element, such element also is established if a person acts purposely.

(6) *Requirement of purpose satisfied if purpose is conditional* When a particular purpose is an element of an offence, the element is established although such purpose is conditional, unless the condition negatives the harm or evil sought to be prevented by the law defining the offence.

(7) *Requirement of knowledge satisfied by knowledge of high probability* When knowledge of the existe.ce of a particular fact is an element of an offence, such knowledge is established if a person is aware of a high probability of its existence, unless he actually believes that it does not exist.

(8) *Requirement of wilfulness satisfied by acting knowingly* A requirement that an offence be committed wilfully is satisfied if a person acts knowingly with respect to the material elements of the offence, unless a purpose to impose further requirements appears.

(9) *Culpability as to illegality of conduct* Neither knowledge nor recklessness or negligence as to whether conduct constitutes an offence or as to the existence, meaning or application of the law determining the elements of an offence is an element of such offence, unless the definition of the offence or the Code so provides.

(10) *Culpability as determinant of grade of offence* When the grade or degree of an offence depends on whether the offence is committed purposely, knowingly, recklessly or negligently, its grade or degree shall be the lowest for which the determinative kind of culpability is established with respect to any material element of the offence.

2.03 Causal relationship between conduct and result; Divergence between result designed or contemplated and actual result or between probable and actual result.

(1) Conduct is the cause of a result when:

   (a) it is an antecedent but for which the result in question would not have occurred; and
   (b) the relationship between the conduct and result satisfies any additional causal requirements imposed by the Code or by the law defining the offence.

(2) When purposely or knowingly causing a particular result is an element of an offence, the element is not established if the actual result is not within the purpose or the contemplation of the actor unless:

   (a) the actual result differs from that designed or contemplated, as the case may be, only in the respect that a different person or different property is injured or affected or that the injury or harm designed or contemplated would have been more serious or more extensive than that caused; or

(b) the actual result involves the same kind of injury or harm as that designed or contemplated and is not too remote or accidental in its occurrence to have a [just] bearing on the actor's liability or on the gravity of his offence.

(3) When recklessly or negligently causing a particular result is an element of an offence, the element is not established if the actual result is not within the risk of which the actor is aware or, in the case of negligence, of which he should be aware unless:

(a) the actual result differs from the probable result only in the respect that a different person or different property is injured or affected or that the probable injury or harm would have been more serious or more extensive than that caused; or

(b) the actual result involves the same kind of injury or harm as the probable result and is not too remote or accidental in its occurrence to have a [just] bearing on the actor's liability or on the gravity of his offence.

(4) When causing a particular result is a material element of an offence for which absolute liability is imposed by law, the element is not established unless the actual result is a probable consequence of the actor's conduct.

2.05 When culpability requirements are inapplicable to violations and to offences defined by other statutes; effect of absolute liability in reducing grade of offence to violation.

(1) The requirements of culpability prescribed by sections 2.01 and 2.02 do not apply to:

(a) offences that constitute violations, unless the requirement involved is included in the definition of the offence or the court determines that it application is consistent with effective enforcement of the law defining the offence; or

(b) offences defined by statutes other than the Code, insofar as a legislative purpose to impose absolute liability for such offences or with respect to any material element thereof plainly appears.

(2) Notwithstanding any other provision of existing law and unless a subsequent statute otherwise provides:

(a) when absolute liability is imposed with respect to any material element of an offence defined by a statute other than the Code and a conviction is based upon such liability, the offence constitutes a violation; and

(b) although absolute liability is imposed by law with respect to one or more of the material elements of an offence defined by a statutes other than the Code, the culpable commission of the offence may be charged and proved, in which event negligence with respect to such elements constitutes sufficient culpability and the classification of the offence and the sentence that may be imposed therefor upon conviction are determined by Section 1.04 and Article 6 of the Code.

Further materials

1.59 Turner *Russell on Crime* (12th ed, 1964) chapters 2 and 3.
Charleton *Offences Against the Person* (1992) chapters 1 and 2.
Smith and Hogan *Criminal Law* (6th ed, 1988) chapters 4,5, 6 and 7.
Radzinowick and Turner *The Modern Approach to Criminal Law* (1948) entire work.
Clarkson *Understanding Criminal Law* (1987).

Stuart and Delisle *Learning Canadian Criminal Law* (1st ed, 1982) chapters 1, 2, 3, 4, 6 and 12.
Canadian Criminal Code (Pocket ed, published by Carswell).
Stuart *Canadian Criminal Law: A Treatise* (entire work).
Howard *Australian Criminal Law* (entire work) (5th ed, 1991).
Brett, Walker and Williams *Criminal Law Text and Cases* (6th ed, 1989) chapters 1 and 2.

Chapter 2

INCHOATE OFFENCES

2.01 There are three inchoate offences: attempt, conspiracy and incitement.

Attempt

2.02 The law as to attempts arose from the determination of the Star Chamber to eradicate the practice of duelling. Where a fatality occurred the victor was treated as guilty of manslaughter or of murder. Because many duels did not result in a fatality and seeking, from policy reasons, to punish seconds and those who helped in the preparations for the duel, it became necessary to extend the law of homicide. This originated the idea of a preparatory crime from which the modern concepts of attempt, conspiracy and incitement evolved.

All criminal attempts, conspiracies and incitements are misdemeanours at common law. Some earlier cases are capable of analysis on the basis that any act done with intent to commit a crime was in itself an offence; *R v Fuller & Robinson*[1], *Dugdale v R*[2]. The modern law on attempt springs from the judgment of the Court for Crown Cases reserved in *R v Eagleton* in 1855.

2.03   *R v Eagleton*
(1855) Dears CC 376, 515;169 ER 766, 826; [1843–60] All ER 363;
1 Jur NS 940; 3 WR 1145; 6 Cox CC 559;
Court for Crown Cases Reserved England, 1855

Facts: The accused had an agreement with the local Poor Law Authority to supply bread at a standard weight to poor people holding the appropriate vouchers. Eagleton was entitled to a credit of 2d for each such loaf on presenting the vouchers to the authority. After his account had been credited, but before payment had been made, it was discovered that the loaves he had supplied to the poor were under the standard weight agreed. He was charged with attempting to

1 (1816) Russ & Ry 308.
2 (1853) 1 E & B 435.

obtain money by false pretences. The jury found as a fact that Eagleton had intended to represent that the loaves had achieved the standard weight.

Parke B: . . . the mere intention to commit a misdemeanour is not criminal. Some act is required; and we do not think that all acts towards committing a misdemeanour are indictable. Acts remotely leading towards the commission of the offence are not to be considered as attempts to commit it, but acts immediately connected with it are; and if in this case, after the credit with the relieving officer for the fraudulent over-charge, any further step on the part of the defendant had been necessary to obtain payment, as the making out a further account, or producing the vouchers to the Board, we should have thought that the obtaining credit in account with the relieving officer would not have been sufficiently proximate to the obtaining the money. But on the statement in this case, no other act on the part of the defendant would have been required. It was the last act depending on himself towards the payment of the money and therefore it ought to be considered as an attempt . . .

Mental Element

2.04   It is impossible in law to attempt a crime without intending that it be committed. The mental element of an attempt therefore requires that the accused act with the purpose of accomplishing that which he is alleged to be attempting. The crime of murder involves the death of the victim. By definition, murder requires that the accused act with the mental element of intending to kill or to cause serious injury to the victim; s 4 of the Criminal Justice Act 1964 (see para **5.06**). Since the crime of murder requires that the victim die, the accused, to be acting purposively, must do more than intend to cause serious injury – that would be the mental element for the crime of assault with intent to commit grievous bodily harm – he must intend to kill.

2.05   *The People (DPP) v Douglas & Hayes*
[1985] ILRM 25
Court of Criminal Appeal, 1984

McWilliams J: On 11 March 1983 the appellants were convicted in the Special Criminal Court of shooting with intent to commit murder contrary to s 14 of the Offences against the Person Act 1861. They were also convicted of robbery, possession of firearms with intent to endanger life and using firearms for the purpose of resisting arrest, but this appeal only relates to the conviction on the charge of shooting with intent to commit murder.

It was argued on behalf of the appellants that it was necessary for the prosecution to establish an intention on their part to commit murder and it was submitted that passages in the judgment of the Special Criminal Court show that that court did not consider the matter on a proper basis. It was submitted that the court placed reliance on the following propositions, that is to say: (1) if someone had actually been killed, the appellants would have been guilty of murder and, therefore, were guilty of an intent to murder; (2) that it was sufficient to establish an intent to murder to show that it must have been apparent to the appellants that the natural consequence of the shooting would be to cause the death or serious personal injury of one or more of the guards; (3) that an act done with reckless disregard of the risk of killing is done with intent to murder; (4) that it is not necessary to establish an intent to kill that that should be the desired outcome of what was done but that it is sufficient if it is a likely outcome; and (5) that the act was done with reckless disregard of that outcome.

The complete passage of the judgment on which this submission is based is as follows:

The evidence shows that fire was opened on the Garda Renault car before it had stopped and three shots struck the front part of the car, shots any one of which, two of which at least with a slight variation of aim, might have killed the driver of the car. We are satisfied that those who fired these shots would have been guilty of the crime of murder had any member of the Gardai who were in the car been in fact killed. There is no doubt in our mind that these were aimed shots. The charge of shooting with intent to commit murder is satisfied when the shots were fired with that intent because it must have been apparent that the natural consequence of the shooting would be to cause death or serious personal injury to one or more of the guards in the car and secondly, the person who fired the shots did so with reckless disregard of the risk of killing a guard and in the legal sense, he had the intent to commit murder. It is not necessary to constitute the intent to kill that that should be the desired outcome of what was done. It is sufficient if it is a likely outcome and that the act is done with reckless disregard of that outcome.

Section 14 of the 1861 Act provides as follows:

Whosoever . . . shall shoot at any person . . . with intent . . . to commit murder, shall whether any bodily injury be effected or not, be guilty of a felony . . .'

Section 4 of the Criminal Justice Act 1964, provides as follows:

(1) Where a person kills another unlawfully the killing shall not be murder unless the accused person intended to kill, or cause injury to, some person, whether the person actually killed or not.
(2) The accused person shall be presumed to have intended the natural and probable consequences of his conduct; but this presumption may be rebutted.

In each case intent is a necessary constituent of the offence, but s 14 provides that there must be intent to commit murder whereas s 4 provides that it is sufficient if there is an intent to cause serious injury.

This leads to an anomalous situation which has been discussed in a number of English cases, in that where a person shoots at another intending to cause only serious injury to that person and that other person dies the offence of murder has been committed, whereas, if that other person does not die, the offence of shooting with intent to commit murder has not been committed: see *Rex v Whybrow* (1951) 35 Cr App R 141; *Reg v Mohan* [1976] QB 1.

Anomalous or not, the words of s 14 "shoot at any person . . . with intent . . . to commit murder" specifically require proof of an intent to commit murder and no other intent is sufficient. The Scottish case of *Cawthorne v HM Advocate* 1968 JC 32 was cited on behalf of the Director of Public Prosecutions as an authority to the contrary but, although some observations in the judgments appear to support the argument that it should be sufficient for the prosecution to prove that the offence of murder would have been committed had one of the guards died, it is to be noted that the prosecution in *Cawthorne's* case was for a common law offence of attempting to murder four people and not for an offence under s 14 of the 1861 Act, which declares the offence to be that of shooting with intent to murder, which in that context, means intent to kill. Without some knowledge of Scots law it is not possible to obtain assistance from this case, and in the opinion of this Court it was irrelevant to the issues in this case that the court of trial was satisfied that those who fired the shots would have been guilty of murder had any guard been killed.

Unless an accused has actually expressed an intent, his intent can only be ascertained from a consideration of his actions and the surrounding circumstances, and a general principle with regard to establishing intention has regularly been stated as being that every man is taken to intend the natural and probable consequences of his own acts: see *Archbold* 28th ed (1931) p 634 and 32nd ed (1949) p 346; although it is noted that his form of words has been altered in the 41st ed where it is stated at p 995 that in law a man intends the consequences of his voluntary act when he foresees that it will probably happen, whether he desires it or not.

Byrne J in *Reg v Smith* [1961] AC 290 explained the application of this principle in this way. He said at p 300:

> The law on this point as it stands today is that this presumption of intention means this: that, as a man is usually able to foresee the natural consequences of his acts, so it is, as a rule, reasonable to infer that he did foresee them and intend them. But, while that is an inference which may be drawn, and on the facts in certain circumstances must inevitably be drawn, yet if on all the facts of the particular case it is not the correct inference, then it should not be drawn.

At p 301 he said:

> . . . the essence of the matter remains that whilst the accused may be presumed to have intended the natural consequences of his act, the question is: "Did he actually intend them?"

And at p 302 he said:

> The final question for the jury must always be whether on the facts as a whole an actual intent to do grievous bodily harm was established, remembering, of course, that intent and desire are different things and that once it is proved that an accused man knows that a result is certain the fact that he does not desire that result is irrelevant.

The judgment of Byrne J in the Court of Criminal Appeal was reversed in the House of Lords, the judgment of the House of Lords being delivered by Viscount Kilmuir LC who made the following observations at p 327:

> The unlawful voluntary act must clearly be aimed at someone in order to eliminate cases of negligence or of careless or dangerous driving. Once, however, the jury are satisfied as to that, it matters not what the accused in fact contemplated as the probable result or whether he ever contemplated at all . . . the sole question is whether the unlawful and voluntary act was of such a kind that grievous bodily harm was the natural and probable result.

The policeman in that case having died, it was a case of murder. Later, however, in the case of *Reg v Hyam* [1975] AC 55, the House of Lords as then constituted criticised the judgment of Viscount Kilmuir to the extent of overruling it, although in considering this case it has to be borne in mind that the English Criminal Justice Act 1967, had been passed in the interval. Lord Hailsham LC at p 74 adopted an interpretation of "intention", given by Asquith LJ in the case of *Cunliffe v Goodman* [1950] 2 KB 237, in the following terms:

> An "intention" to my mind connotes a state of affairs which the party "intending" – I will call him X – does more than merely contemplate: it connotes a state of affairs which, on the contrary, he decides, so far as in him lies, to bring about, and which, in point of possibility, he has a reasonable prospect of being able to bring about, by his own act of volition.

In *Reg v Belfon* [1976] 1 WLR 741 Wien J said at p 749:

> There is certainly no authority that recklessness can constitute an intent to do grievous bodily harm. Adding the concept of recklessness to foresight not only does not assist but will inevitably confuse a jury. Foresight and recklessness are evidence from which intent may be inferred but they cannot be equated either separately or in conjunction with intent to do grievous bodily harm.

There seems to be no reason why these observations should not apply equally to intent to murder. In the circumstances of any particular case evidence of the fact that a reasonable man would have foreseen that the natural and probable consequence of the acts of an accused was to cause death and evidence of the fact that the accused was reckless as to whether his acts would cause death or not is evidence from which an inference of intent to cause death may or should be drawn, but the court must consider whether either or both of these facts do establish beyond a reasonable doubt an actual intention to cause death.

The judgment in the present case suggests that the court of trial was or may have been influenced by the fact that the offence of murder would have been committed had one of the guards died. As already stated, it is the opinion of this Court that such a consideration is not relevant to a charge under s 14 of the 1861 Act. The judgment also suggests that the court was or may have been influenced by the fact that it must have been apparent to the accused that the natural consequence of the shooting would be to cause personal injury. Again, it is the opinion of this Court that an intention to cause serious personal injury only, if that were the correct inference to be drawn, would not be sufficient to support a conviction on a charge under this section. Although it may be accepted that it is not necessary to constitute an intent to kill that that should be the desired outcome of what was done, a reckless disregard of the likely outcome of the acts performed is not of itself proof of intent to kill but is only one of the facts to be considered in deciding whether the correct inference is that the accused had an actual intent to kill. Again, the judgment suggests that the court did not consider or may not have considered whether reckless disregard of the outcome of his acts by the accused did in fact lead to the inference that he had an intent to kill.

Although the evidence might properly have supported an inference of an intent to murder on the part of the accused, the form of the judgment indicates that the decision was or may have been based on one or more of the considerations which have been discussed above rather than on a consideration of whether the evidence established an actual intent to commit murder. Accordingly this Court considers that the conviction on the first count should be quashed.

2.06   A distinction is drawn between an intention as to the consequence of a crime and an intention as regards its circumstances. The accused must intend the consequence of a crime, such as death in murder, but he need not necessarily intend its surrounding circumstances. The classic example is attempted rape. The accused must intend to have sexual intercourse with a woman but the definition of the crime contained in s 2 of the Criminal Law (Rape) Act 1981 requires that he act with knowledge or with recklessness that she does not consent (see para **6.53**). In *R v Khan and Others*[3] the Court of Appeal in England defined the elements of the crime of attempted rape in terms requiring an intent to have sexual intercourse with recklessness as to the circumstances of the victim not consenting.

2.07   *R v Khan and Others*
[1990] 2 All ER 783; [1990] 1 WLR 813;
(1990) 91 Cr App R 29; [1990] Crim LR 519;
Court of Appeal England, 1990

Russell LJ: In our judgment an acceptable analysis of the offence of rape is as follows: (1) the intention of the offender is to have sexual intercourse with a woman; (2) the offence is committed, but only if, the circumstances are that (a) the woman does not consent *and* (b) the defendant knows she is not consenting or is reckless as to whether she consents.

3 [1990] 2 All ER 783.

Precisely the same analysis can be made of the offence of attempted rape: (1) the intention of the offender is to have sexual intercourse with a woman; (2) the offence is committed if, but only if, the circumstances are that (a) the woman does not consent *and* (b) the defendant knows that she is not consenting or is reckless as to whether she consents.

The only difference between the two offences is that in rape sexual intercourse takes place whereas in attempted rape it does not, although there has to be some act which is more than preparatory to sexual intercourse. Considered in that way, the intent of the defendant is precisely the same in rape and in attempted rape and the *mens rea* is identical, namely an intention to have intercourse plus a knowledge of or recklessness as to the woman's absence of consent. No question of attempting to achieve a reckless state of mind arises; the attempt relates to the physical activity; the mental state of the defendant is the same. A man does not recklessly have sexual intercourse, nor does he recklessly attempt it. Recklessness in rape and attempted rape arises not in relation to the physical act of the accused but only in his state of mind when engaged in the activity of having or attempting to have sexual intercourse.

If this is the true analysis, as we believe it is, the attempt does not require any different intention on the part of the accused from that for the full offence of rape. We believe this to be a desirable result which in the instant case did not require the jury to be burdened with different directions as to the accused's state of mind, dependent on whether the individual achieved or failed to achieve sexual intercourse.

We recognise, of course, that our reasoning cannot apply to all offences and all attempts. Where, for example as in causing death by reckless driving or reckless arson, no state of mind other than recklessness is involved in the offence, there can be no attempt to commit it.

In our judgment, however, the words "with intent to commit an offence" to be found in s 1 of the 1981 Act mean, when applied to rape, "with intent to have sexual intercourse with a woman in circumstances where she does not consent and the defendant knows or could not care less about her absence of consent". The only "intent", giving that word its natural and ordinary meaning, of the rapist is to have sexual intercourse. He commits the offence because of the circumstances in which he manifests that intent, ie when the woman is not consenting and he either knows it or could not care less about the absence of consent.

Accordingly, we take the view that in relation to the four appellants the judge was right to give the directions that he did when inviting the jury to consider the charges of attempted rape.

2.08 As we saw in chapter 1, crimes are capable of commission by a mental state other than intention. Most are capable of commission by recklessness. Manslaughter can be committed by criminal negligence and other crimes can be committed by negligence or by simply causing the external element of the offence to occur. One theory holds that the mental element required for an attempt should merely mirror that required for the completed crime. This view has not been accepted in England; *R v Mohan*[4]. Howard justifies this view on the basis that the requirement for a more blameworthy state of mind than the completed offence is balanced by the fact that the accused need not have done so much, or indeed any, harm in order to be convicted.

4 [1976] QB 1.

Theories of Attempt

2.09 Before considering the Irish cases on attempt, some mention should be made of the theories prevalent in attempting to intellectualise the point at which an intention becomes manifest in a criminally punishable external act.

In general, the law requires that a citizen manifest his intention to commit a crime by some overt act. Were it otherwise a man would be punishable on the basis of his bad thoughts. Hence, the law of conspiracy requires that at least two persons agree to commit an unlawful act, the law of incitement requires that the accused engage in persuasion of another to commit a crime, and the law of attempts demands that the accused do something more than merely prepare to commit a crime at some future time.

2.10 In America the theory of probable desistance indicates that conduct will amount to an attempt if it would have resulted, in the ordinary and natural course of events, in the completion of the crime if there had been no interruption from an outside source[5]. Holmes J authored the dangerous proximity doctrine under which the act done must come pretty near to accomplishing the result before the law will notice it; *Commonwealth v Kennedy*[6].

2.11 Sir John Salmond contended that:

"An act done with intent to commit a crime is not a criminal attempt unless it is of such a nature as to be in itself sufficient evidence of the criminal intent with which it is done. A criminal attempt is an act which shows criminal intent on the face of it. The case must be one in which *res ipsa loquitur;*" *R v Barker*[7].

He went on to defend this approach in his text book on jurisprudence; *Salmond on Jurisprudence*[8]. This test was finally abolished in New Zealand by legislation in 1961. Unfortunately this test placed the external element within constricted boundaries and confused the proof of intent, which is necessary to a conviction, with the external act from which it may, or may not be inferred.

2.12 The last act doctrine was superficially attractive. It required the accused to have done the last act prior to the completion of the offence. If applied logically it would often produce strange results. Someone points a loaded gun at the victim but does not pull the trigger. That would not be the "last act" which the accused could do. It would be if he pulled the trigger and the bullet missed its target.

2.13 Similar to the American doctrine of dangerous proximity was the test invented by Sir James Stephen. This test required the accused to do some act which formed part of a series of acts which would constitute the actual commission of a crime if it had not been interrupted[9]. The test lacks precision in defining the point at which the series of acts begins and places human actions on a par with physical happenings as if, in the preparations to

5 Wechsler, Jones & Korn *The Treatment of Inchoate Crimes in the Model Penal Code of the American Law Institute*. (1961) 61 Columbia LR 571.
6 (1897) 170 MASS 18.
7 (1924) 43 NZLR 865, at p 874.
8 (7th ed 1924) at p 404.
9 *A Digest of Criminal Law* (9th ed, 1950) article 29.

commit a crime, a point of no return is reached beyond which reversal is impossible.

2.14 Perhaps most satisfactory is a test simply requiring that the act of the accused should not be remote from the crime and leaving the test of proximity to commonsense judgment; *Deutsch v R*[10].

2.15   ***The People (Attorney-General) v England***
1 Frewen 81
Court of Criminal Appeal, 1947

Facts: The accused was convicted of attempting to procure the commission, by a young man of 18 years, of an act of gross indecency with another man. The young man was employed at a nursery garden in Dublin where the accused had become acquainted with him. One evening he accosted him on an evening walk and reminisced over his sexual exploits and described the attractions of a vice den known to him in Dublin. He immediately enquired as to whether there was any secluded spot nearby to which they would both go and, on receiving a positive answer, offered the young man ten shillings to accompany him there.

Gavin Duffy P: . . . This Court has had to consider carefully whether the curious evidence disclosed an attempt in law to procure K to commit the crime specified in the indictment, and in particular whether on the evidence the language used was near enough to the criminal procurement of K to be an attempt in law. The extreme difficulty of attaining precision in the conception of an attempt at crime has baffled many a court and this is one of the rare offences that has defied scientific definition in exact language. The prosecution asks the Court to go very far indeed. Hitherto there seems to have been no reported case of a conviction for an attempt to commit a crime grounded solely upon words, setting before one who did not know the attractions and facilities of and for that crime at a particular place, where the words, making no appointment to co-operate, did not amount to a deliberate effort to induce the person addressed to commit the crime and that person could not, for all his newly acquired knowledge, perpetrate the crime depicted without further aid from the talker or tempter. There are numberless ways in which a man may describe the attractive facility for crime to another in lurid terms without incurring a charge of attempting to turn the hearer into a criminal; everyone has come across instances both in literature and on the screen. And something more beyond description is reasonably required by the law for an attempt to procure the commission of a crime.

A long argument seems to have been necessary in England a century and a half ago in *R v Higgins*, 2 East 5, to obtain a clear decision that it is a misdemeanour at common law to solicit and incite a servant to steal his master's goods, though no one could question that ruling today, provided, since the offence is verbal, that there be no reasonable doubt about the tenor of the words of solicitation and incitement, whereof no record in writing can be produced. Here it is doubtful whether the words used, described by a gardening labourer as an invitation but not reproduced, really amounted to solicitation or incitement; certainly one would hesitate to say that they did on the rather tenuous testimony of K. But, whatever K may have meant to convey by the the word "invited", there is another and a very serious difficulty, for we have seen that there are good grounds for believing that K received at most only an inchoate invitation. It has been settled law for at least ninety years that an attempt to commit a misdemeanour is not an indictable attempt unless it is an act directly approximating to the commission of an offence; I am

10 (1986) 52 CR (3d) 305.

quoting the law laid down by Baron Parke in *Reg v Roberts* (1855) Dears 539, 551. Accordingly in a recent English case the writing of a very obscene letter, designed, apparently without making any express appointment, to find out whether the addressee was the kind of person to lend himself to criminal practices, was held to fall short of an attempt to procure the commission of an act of gross indecency by the recipient with the writer. (*R v Woods*, 22 Cr App Rep 41). The nexus of proximity between the attempt and the contemplated offence cannot be disregarded, because it is indispensable to constitute the crime alleged here against the appellant; and, in the opinion of this Court, the conversation to which K deposed as to the flat, whether it be read with or without the subsequent proposal already the subject of a prosecution, was not, in fact, near enough to the actual criminal procurement of K to constitute in law the attempt to procure charged in the indictment.

This Court further holds, in the words of article 74 of the Draft Criminal Code of 1879, the very distinguished work of Mr Justice Stephen and his colleagues, that "the question whether an act done or omitted with intent to commit an offence is or is not only preparation for the commission of that offence, and too remote to constitute an attempt to commit it, is question of law". Therefore, as in *R v Woods (supra)*, the learned trial Judge ought to have directed the jury that the language attributed to the appellant did not in the circumstances of this case constitute in law an attempt to procure the commission of the crime set out in the indictment.

The order of this Court allows the appeal and quashes the conviction of the appellant and the sentence passed upon him thereon.

The Proximity Theory

2.16   In *The People (Attorney-General) v Thornton*[11] the Court of Criminal Appeal held that a jury should be informed by the trial judge that a mere desire to commit a crime, or a desire followed by an intention to do so, is not sufficient to constitute an attempt. In that case the prosecution evidence was of a conversation alleged to have taken place between the accused and a medical doctor. The doctor was treating a girl whom the accused had made pregnant. He asked the doctor whether he would prescribe to this girl a drug to interfere with pregnancy. His request was refused and he asked the doctor "wasn't there some drug named ergot".

2.17   *The People (Attorney-General) v Sullivan*
[1964] IR 169
Supreme Court, 1963

Facts: Mary Sullivan was a mid-wife who was contracted to provide her services to pregnant women in accordance with the terms of the South Cork Board of Public Assistance. She was paid a basic salary but where she attended more than 25 cases she became entitled to an additional allowance in respect of every such case beyond 25. Mary Sullivan prepared forms in respect of fictitious patients. No evidence was presented as to the number of patients she attended in the relevant year. There was thus no evidence that she would exceed her 25 cases and become entitled to the extra allowance. Obviously, however, every fictional case would help her towards that goal. A case was stated to the High Court, and that decision was appealed to the Supreme Court.

Teevan J [High Court]:   A dishonest midwife can further a fraudulent claim for fictitious cases with a view to obtaining individual fees either by fabricating cases

11 [1952] IR 91.

after she has already attended twenty-five patients or by including fictitious cases to make up the twenty-five fixed salary limit. The result will be precisely the same. Indeed, it might well appear to an astute cheat that the latter method is more likely to escape detection. It is said, however, that in the latter instance the twenty-five might not be reached and if, in fact, it should not be, the fraudulent scheme or intention is frustrated, could never have succeeded and no attempt could be charged. Counsel contend that the evidence here establishes no more than an intention to commit the crime, or preparations for it.

I think this is fallacious.

In *The People (Attorney General) v Thornton*[12] Haugh J, delivering the judgment of the Court of Criminal Appeal, says, at p 93, of the attempt to commit a crime, that it "consists of an act done by the accused with a specific intent to commit a particular crime; that it must go beyond mere preparation and must be a direct movement towards the commission after the preparations have been made; that some such act is required and if it only remotely leads to the commission of the offence and is not immediately connected therewith, it cannot be considered as an attempted to commit an offence."

In applying the definition, the determining question is; Was the act forming the factual basis for the charge a step in mere preparation for the commission of a crime or was it a step in the commission of the intended crime? It will satisfy the second clause of the question I put, even if it be only one of a necessary series of steps to complete the originally intended crime. Thus, the mere asking for the drug in *Thornton's* case[13], its intended use being criminal, would have constituted the criminal attempt, although its administration at a later time would have been necessary to fulfil the original criminal design.

Nor is the possibility of a successful completion of the criminal plan an essential ingredient of this form of offence. It is sufficient if the accused supposed or expected his plan to be effective. In *Rex v White*[14] the prisoner had been convicted of attempting to murder his mother by poison. The victim had been found dead on a sofa. Beside her was a wine glass, the contents of which were found, on analysis, to contain potassium cyanide, which, on a jury's finding, must have been put into the liquid in the glass by the prisoner with the intention of poisoning his mother. But it was also established at the trial that the deceased had not died from poisoning; no trace of potassium cyanide was found in her stomach; the probable cause of death was heart failure due to fright, or some other external cause. Further, the amount of potassium cyanide found in the glass, even if she had taken the whole, was insufficient to cause her death. But there was evidence to show that the prisoner knew the deadly character of the substance and supposed that a very small quantity would be lethal. Yet the Court of Criminal Appeal held that the appellant had been rightly convicted of attempted murder.

It may be of assistance to the learned District Justice to quote the following from Mr Justice Bray, in delivering the judgment of the Court (at p 129):—

"The next point made was that if he [the appellant] put it [the poison] there with that intent there was no attempt at murder; that the jury must have acted upon a suggestion of the learned Judge in his summing up that was one, the first or some later, of a series of doses which he intended to administer and so cause her death by slow poisoning; and that if they did act on that suggestion there was no attempt at murder, because the act of which he was guilty, namely, the putting of poison in the wine glass, was a completed act and could not be and was not intended by the appellant to have the effect of killing her at once. It *could not kill unless it were followed by other acts which he might never have done*. There

12 [1952] IR 91.
13 [1952] IR 91.
14 [1910] 2 KB 124.

seems no doubt that the learned judge in effect did tell the jury that if this was a case of slow poisoning the appellant would be guilty of the attempt to murder. We are of opinion that this direction was right, and that the completion . . . of *one of a series of acts intended by a man to result in killing* is an attempt to murder even although this completed act would not, unless followed by other acts, results in killing. It might be the *beginning of the attempt*, but would none the less be an attempt. While saying this we must say also that we do not think it likely the jury acted on this suggestion, because there was nothing to show that the administration of small doses of cyanide of potassium *would* have a cumulative effect; we think it much more likely, having regard to the statement made by the prisonor . . . that the appellant supposed he had put sufficient poison in the glass to kill her. This, of course, would be an attempt to murder." (The italics are mine).

For present purposes the importance lies in the earlier part of the foregoing – that based on the theory of possible intention to effect the murderous design by the cumulative effect of a series of small doses none of which alone would be lethal. In my opinion each fictitious case put in by the respondent was analogous to the individual doses of poison in cases of attempted murder by slow poisoning. In the one case the design could be frustrated by the intervention of some circumstance cutting off the criminal's access to the intended victim, or, as happened in the case cited, the victim's death from some other cause. In the other by, let us say, failure to exceed an aggregate of twenty-five cases by the end of the contract year, or the premature discovery of the fraudulent scheme. In *White's* case[15] the prisoner's criminal design could not have succeeded in its purpose even if carried out to its final detail; yet he was held rightly convicted of the attempt.

Of the many authorities cited, I need refer only to the following which on their facts most resemble the present case.

In *Reg v Rigby*[16] the prisoner was a collier. His employers' system for ascertaining the amount of wages earned by their workman was to issue to each a number of tallies, each tally marked with a number corresponding with that marked against the workman's name in the employers' books. In each tub of coal got by a workman he placed one of his tallies and the tubs with the tallies in them were then sent to the canal and the tubs emptied; the tallies were all put in one tub and sent back to the pit mouth when they were removed by the tally-man and hung on the tally-board over the number on that board corresponding with the number on the tally and as showing the amount of work for which each man was entitled to be paid. The tallies were then counted by the book-keeper and that number was booked to the credit of the workman.

The prisoner was seen to place three extra tallies in the tally tub as it was about to start back from the canal for the pit mouth where, according to the practice they would have been placed on his number on the tally board and credited to him. The extra tallies were however extracted from the tub by the employee who had seen the prisoner put them in the tub and who immediately informed the employers. They did not reach the tally-board and accordingly the prisoner could not have been credited with wages for the spurious tallies.

It was held that the prisoner had been rightly convicted of an attempt to obtain money by false pretences.

In *Reg v Cheeseman*[17] the prisoner had achieved no more than the substitution of a false weight on the scale weighing the meat in the delivery of which he was assisting, when the trick was discovered. He also failed to upset his conviction. It

15 [1910] 2 KB 124.
16 7 Cox CC 507.
17 9 Cox CC 100.

appears to me that the present defendant's action if carried out before completion of twenty-five cases is very similar to a case of false weights or measures.

In *Reg v Hensler*[18] the false pretence was made by letter but could not have deceived the addressee because of prior knowledge. Again conviction was upheld, Kelly CB saying, at p 573:—

"This is an attempt by the prisoner to obtain money by false pretences which might have been so obtained. The money was not so obtained because the prosecutor remembered something which had been told him previously. In my opinion, as soon as even the letter was put into the post the offence was committed."

In the present cases, there can be no doubt that when the claims for £4 4s 0d. were submitted to the Corporation on the prescribed forms the offences of attempting to obtain money by false pretences were complete. Claims were lodged in respect of the pretended attendances on Mrs Mohally and Mrs Murphy. As in *Hensler's* case they *might* have resulted in payment of excess fees if the limit of twenty-five should later be exceeded.

No claim was lodged in the case of Mrs Dunlea and at first sight I was much inclined to the learned District Justice's view in that case. While *Hensler's* case[19] puts the charges in regard to Mrs Mohally and Mrs Murphy beyond doubt, consideration of all the authorities cited removed doubt from the Dunlea case. As I have said, there is no distinction in principle between what the defendant did in the Dunlea case and the use of false weights or measures in transactions relating to measurable commodities.

As soon as the defendant completed an act the result of which could lead the Corporation officers to believe that she had attended Mrs Dunlea and should be credited with that attendance, the offence was committed, even if some further act or acts (ie, further maternity cases) were necessary to complete a series and so lead to fee-producing credits. The defendant caused a false application by the patient to be lodged with the Medical Officer, nominating her as midwife, and lodged her own false acceptance of the case.

While it does not seem to have reached the stage of certification by the City Medical Officer, as in the Murphy and Mohally cases, in my opinion the facts disclose an attempt in the Dunlea case also.

The offence of attempt to commit a crime has been frequently defined in decided cases. Its definition does not give rise to any difficulty and, as is quite clear, caused none to the learned District Justice. The difficulty lies, to use the words of Lord Reading CJ in *Rex v Robinson*[20], in the application of that principle to the facts of the particular case. In some cases it is a difficult matter to determine whether an act is immediately or remotely connected with the offence of which it is alleged to be an attempt. In other cases the question is easier of solution, as for instance in *Reg v Button*[21]. There upon the evidence there was a false pretence made directly to the race authorities with the intent to make them part with the prize, and one which, but for the fact of the fraud being discovered, would necessarily have had that effect. In the present case, the real difficulty lies in the fact that there is no evidence of any act done by the appellant in the nature of a false pretence which ever reached the minds of the underwriters, though they were the persons who were to be induced to part with the money. The evidence falls short of any communication of such pretence to the underwriters or to any agent of theirs.

18 11 Cox CC 570.
19 *Ibid*.
20 [1915] 2 KB 342 at p 348.
21 [1900] 2 QB 597.

In the respondent's case the pretence went beyond the stage of mere preparation. It was communicated by the respondent to the appropriate Corporation officer.

I feel that the learned District Justice gave undue consideration to the prospect or chances of fruition of the pretences. Paragraph 3 of the Case reveals the factual basis of the respondent's contention, as accepted by the learned District Justice: ". . . a claim for payment did not arise until the respondent had attended twenty-five cases." Failure of the design to commit the intended crime must necessarily be a feature of every case of attempted crime.

If what I have just quoted from para 3 of the Case alone should justify an acquittal it follows that success of the criminal plan but for premature discovery or unexpected frustration would be an essential proof in cases of attempted crime. That this is erroneous is clear from the authorities cited but can be demonstrated within the framework of the present case. Thus if, at the time of presentation of her false documents, the respondent had already attended twenty-five genuine cases, she would be guilty; while if she presented her false documents earlier her guilt or innocence would depend on the chance whether or not subsequent calls on her services should bring her year's aggregate to more than twenty-five cases. As I have already said, it must not be overlooked that failure of the design to commit the intended crime must necessarily be a feature of every case of criminal attempt. Guilt or innocence is not determined by the nature of that failure, or its cause.

The respondent's counsel relied strongly – and the learned District Justice based his decision – on *Hope v Brown*[22]. That case is not a binding authority in this country but on the facts I would respectfully follow it. It is in line with the earlier authorities. The false tickets had been prepared but as yet no act had been done to connect them to the goods. The position at the stage of interception by the enforcement officers might be equated to the stage in the present case where the respondent had the false form of application and acceptance of the supposed case written out but had not yet commenced the act of presenting them to the Corporation. Even if she had had the application signed, while another offence may be thus committed, I should think although it is unecessary so to decide, the present charges would not lie. Once the first step of presentation to the Corporation was taken, however, even if that be but the simple act of putting the false documents in the post (if postal delivery had been resorted to) the defendant had thereby attempted the intended crime and is amenable to the charges laid.

I was at first inclined to the view that the Dunlea case went no further than intention and preparation and that without the actual claim fell short of an indictable attempt. I have come away from that view for I think the Corporation becomes liable for the fees for cases over the twenty-five on completion of the individual cases by the midwife, rather than on presentation of the claims for the fees or the prescribed form.

One statement in *Hope v Brown*[23] may have unduly impressed the learned District Justice. The Lord Chief Justice in the course of his judgment said, at p 252:—

"In all these cases where it has been held that there has been an attempt; the Court has always found that the crime would have been committed but for the intervention of someone."

A strictly literal interpretation of that statement, which indeed was unnecessary to the judgment, would seem to obliterate such cases as *Rex v White*[24]. What his Lordship no doubt intended by the word, "crime," was criminal project. The

22 [1954] 1 WLR 250.
23 [1954] 1 WLR 252.
24 [1910] 2 KB 124.

intended crime in *White's* case was murder; the criminal act, poisoning the victim's liquor. Contrary to the criminal's supposition the amount of poison introduced could not have killed. The criminal enterprise would have been completed but the crime *(murder)* could not have been consummated.

. . . Taken literally, however, 'I can see that the passage to which I refer may well have stimulated the over-emphasis of the learned District Justice on the fact that, so far as the proofs went, the respondent would not have been paid fees for any of the three cases. In so far as the *dictum* might be taken to mean that likelihood of a successful issue of the criminal enterprise, as of the time the attempt is charged, is, in law, material to the question of chargeable attempt, I respectfully disagree with it.

Walsh J (O Dalaigh CJ agreeing) [Supreme Court]: . . . The next question to be considered is whether the presentation of these forms should be regarded merely as a preparation for the commission of offences or whether they constituted acts sufficiently proximate to amount to attempts to commit the substantive offences. There are many cases dealing with this subject, some of which were cited during the argument in this Court, and it is clear from all of these cases that mere preparation for the crime is not enough. This has been stated in various forms, as, for example, "acts remotely leading towards the commission of the offence are not to be considered as attempts to commit it, but acts immediately connected with it are": *R v Eagleton*[25], which is one of the cases cited in this Court. That quotation is, of course, a statement in the negative form of what is referred to as "the proximity rule." The cases provided many examples of acts which were considered sufficiently proximate and those which were considered not sufficient to constitute an attempt, but they do not formulate any exhaustive test.

The evidence in this case did not disclose whether or not the accused had already attended twenty-five cases for which she was entitled to credit before the cases referred to in the charges. For the purpose of this appeal, therefore, the case must proceed on the assumption most favourable to the accused, namely, that she had not attended twenty-five cases and that these cases were the first and second cases respectively in the current contract year. On that basis it was clear that she was not entitled to be paid for either of those two cases but that she would be entitled to have them credited to her, assuming they were cases which she had attended personally or for which she had provided another midwife in accordance with the terms of her agreement already referred to. If these two cases were cases for which she was not entitled to be so credited they would nevertheless be credited to her, unless detected, and have the effect of making necessary only twenty-three other cases for which she would be entitled to be credited to enable her to enter the category of fee-paying cases. That would depend on her doing another twenty-three cases within the current contract year and of course there was no certainty of that. Even, however, if that should have proved impossible in the event, it is, I think not a matter material to the discussion of this point because it has been well established in various cases that the ultimate impossibility of achieving or carrying out the crime attempt is not a defence to a charge of an attempt. It might also be suggested that even assuming that she had the criminal intent she might have changed her mind and not gone ahead with the plan some time before the twenty-sixth case was reached. That again, in my opinion, is not a consideration to be taken into account in examining this charge, and indeed there is authority for holding that even if there were evidence that she had in fact changed her mind it would not amount to a defence because the offence charged is that of having the intent at the time the act constituting the attempt is carried out. That cannot be answered by evidence of a subsequent abandonment of the intent. Every false report made during the first twenty-five cases and not detected would

25 Dears CC 515, at p 537.

amount to a case credited to the person making the report and would bring that person a step nearer to actual payment of fees. If twenty-five false reports were made one might say that the twenty-fifth was a good deal closer than the first, but in my view each one is distinguishable from the other and, while the effect of all of them may be cumulative in the sense that they were all aimed at the same object and the more there were the quicker the object would have been attained, it cannot be said that number twenty-five is more proximate than number one. Each one is a complete act in itself, and is in itself in a position to cause the fee to be paid if there is a sufficient number of other cases to the credit of the accused. In that event each such false report would in itself be sufficient to achieve the desired result. For example, if the false report was the twenty-sixth one, no further act would be necessary to enable the person 'claiming' to be paid the money and thus commit the substantive offence. Instead, if the first "claim" be the false one, no further criminal or illegal act would be necessary to achieve a similar payment because the first fraudulent report could be followed by twenty-five which could be perfectly truthful. If the first fraudulent report were to be followed by twenty-five other fraudulent ones it would, in my view, be fallacious to suggest that all the following reports save the first one were necessary links in the chain of causation and that therefore at least the first twenty-five of all the fraudulent reports must be regarded merely as preparations and that only the last one would constitute the actual attempt. In *R v White*[26] the English Court of Criminal Appeal decided that an act is proximate if it is the first of a series of similar acts intended to result cumulatively in the crime. That was a case where the appellant had been found guilty of an attempt to murder because he had put into the wine glass of another person a quantity of cyanide which was not in itself sufficient to cause death. The following passage appears in the judgment, at p 129:

> "The next point made was that if he put it there with that intent there was no attempt at murder; that the jury must have acted upon a suggestion of the learned judge in his summing up that this was one, the first or some later, of a series of doses which he intended to administer and so cause her death by slow poisoning; and that if they did act on that suggestion there was no attempt at murder, because the act of which he was guilty, namely, the putting the poison in the wine glass, was a completed act and could not be and was not intended by the appellant to have the effect of killing her at once. It could not kill unless it were followed by other acts which he might never have done. There seems no doubt that the learned judge in effect did tell the jury that if this was a case of slow poisoning the appellant would be guilty of the attempt to murder. We are of opinion that this direction was right, and that the completion or attempted completion of one of a series of acts intended by a man to result in killing is an attempt to murder even although this completed act would not, unless followed by the other acts, result in killing."

In my view each false "claim" put in, whether it be the first or the twenty-sixth, would, in law, be an act sufficiently proximate to constitute an attempt to commit the substantive offence of obtaining by false pretences a sum of £4 4s 0d, the fee for each case.

Voluntary Desistance

2.18   A strong argument has been made in favour of applying a defence of voluntary desistance similar to that applying to accessories to crime[27]. In Canada abandonment is not a defence in itself but may be used as evidence

26 [1910] 2 KB 124.
27 Smith *Withdrawal from Criminal Liability for Complicity and Inchoate Offences* (1983) 12 Anglo-Amer L Rev 200.

to support the view that the accused did not intend to complete the crime that he apparently embarked on. In Victoria it has been held that the fact that the accused desisted of his own volition affords no answer to the charge; *R v Page*[28].

2.19   *R v Franklind*
                                (1985) 23 CCC (3d) 385
                              Ontario Court of Appeal, 1985

Facts: the accused gave a lift to a hitch-hiker. He attempted to have intercourse with her but claimed that he had desisted from his efforts as soon as she began to cry.

Dubin J: In light of the evidence, the critical issue for the jury to consider on the charge of attempted rape was whether the appellant intended to have intercourse without the consent of the complainant. It was his intent which was pivotal. In Adams, *Criminal Law and Practice in New Zealand*, 2nd ed (1971), the following proposition is stated at p 272:

> The intent to commit rape is essential . . . *and the Crown must prove, as part of its case, that the accused intended rape*, ie, intercourse either *without consent* or with consent obtained in one or other of the ways described in s 1218(1)(*b*) to (*e*). A mere intent to have intercourse will not suffice. (Emphasis added.)

This point is also referred to in *Russell on Crime*, 12th ed (1964), p 718, as follows:

> Upon an indictment for an assault with intent to commit a rape, Patteson J, in summoning up, said: "In order to find the prisoner guilty of an assault with *intent to commit a rape*, you must be satisfied that the prisoner, when he laid hold of the prosecutrix, not only desired to gratify his passions upon her person but that he intended to do so at all events, and notwithstanding any resistance on her part." (Emphasis added.)

Furthermore, as has already been noted, the appellant never alleged that he believed the complainant actually consented to intercourse although at one stage he thought that she would. It was because she did not consent that he desisted. If he had not and had made penetration, he would have been guilty of rape on his own evidence. Thus, the instruction to the jury that "if the accused honestly believed that the plaintiff was consenting to the act of sexual intercourse, even though she was not, he is entitled to be acquitted" did not address the real issue.

In my respectful opinion, the failure of the trial judge to instruct the jury that on the charge of attempted rape, the Crown had to prove beyond a reasonable doubt that when the appellant attempted to have intercourse with the complainant he intended to do so without her consent, constituted non-direction amounting to misdirection.

Furthermore, in the circumstances of this case the appellant's desistance was relevant to the critical issue as to whether the appellant intended to have intercourse without the consent of the complainant.

In the case of *R v Lankford*, [1959] Crim LR 209, the accused was charged with attempted rape. The following excerpts from the report of the case at pp 209–10 are, I think, on point:

28 [1933] VLR 351.

At the trial it was proved (and admitted by the defence) that L had knocked down with his hand an old lady of seventy-eight years of age, had knelt over her and taken out his person. Somebody passing heard the old lady shout, came to the scene and at that time L got up and ran off. The defence was that L, when he was kneeling over the old lady, had a change of heart and was already getting up to go away when the other person came up. The recorder, summing up to the jury, said *inter alia*: "Whether he desisted or not, is is still an attempt to rape her." L appealed to the Court of Criminal Appeal against his conviction upon the main grounds of misdirection . . .

Held . . . The real point of the case, as it seemed to this court, was that the prisoner's defence was never put to the jury. It was only right to say, without laying down what constituted attempted rape, that there were, in this case, acts which, taken by themselves, would have entitled the jury to come to the conclusion that there was an attempted rape. But L's defence was that, having done the acts, he had a change of heart and desisted and, so far from putting this defence, the recorder said, in effect, that even if L's case were true there was nevertheless an attempt. This court could not agree with that view of the position. *In deciding whether an attempt had been committed in any case all the facts must be put before the jury. In some cases it would be open to the jury to find that a voluntary change of heart at some point in the proceedings enabled them to say that there had been no attempt; in other cases a point might be reached where, even if a man voluntarily desisted, he had already been guilty of the attempt.* (Emphasis added.)

The trial judge, in my opinion, erred in failing to instruct the jury that the appellant's desistance was relevant to the issue of the appellant's intent.

Because the trial judge failed to instruct the jury that the Crown had to prove beyond a reasonable doubt that when the appellant attempted to have intercourse with the complainant he intended to do so without her consent, and that the appellant's desistance was relevant to the issue of the appellant's intent, the real defence was never placed before the jury. As a result the verdict cannot stand.

Merger

2.20 Attempt implies failure. It would, however, be strange if an accused had to be acquitted in the event of an uncertainty as to whether he had succeeded or not. It can be argued that for a person who has committed a crime to be liable for both the substantive offence and the attempt would render him open to punishment twice-over for the same wrong. This problem is not uncommon and arises every day in the courts. An accused may be convicted of burglary but at the same time might be guilty of carrying house-breaking implements and of larceny. The prosecution deals with this sensibly by accepting a plea of guilty only on one offence. A person found guilty of several concurrent offences receives a sentence commensurate with the actual wrong he has done. A complete absurdity arises where an accused is entitled to defend himself on a charge of one crime on the basis that he has committed another; see for example s 4 of the Criminal Law Amendment Act 1935 (see para **6.14**)[29].

2.21 At common law there is a doctrine of merger; where the same facts constitute both a felony and a misdemeanour, the misdemeanour mergers in the commission of the felony and ceases to have a separate legal existence.

29 See also Howard *The Successful Attempt* (1961) 24 MLR 166.

2.22 In Australia it has been accepted by the Victorian Full Court that merger is still part of the common law; *R v Welker*[30]. In England a Divisional Court has held that there was no separate doctrine of the merger of an attempt in the full offence but that it was restricted to the merger of misdemeanours in felonies; *Webley v Buxton*[31]. It has been persuasively argued that this latter doctrine never existed at all[32].

2.23 Uncertainty could be removed from the law if each time a new offence was created the legislation specified a separate offence of attempt.

At common law all attempts to commit a crime are, in themselves, common law misdemeanours. In the case of summary offences this can mean that an attempt, being a misdemeanour, would carry a higher unlimited penalty than the substantive offence. The tradition has been not to exceed the penalty for the substantive offence but in a grave case this can be departed from; *The People (Attorney-General) v Giles*[33].

Jurisdiction

2.24 Jurisdiction of the criminal courts is territorial; *R v Sanders*[34]. If a person abroad initiates an offence, part of the essential elements of which take place within Ireland, he is amenable to our jurisdiction. There is an attempt triable in Ireland despite all of the acts done by the accused being perpetrated abroad if those acts have an effect here; *DPP v Stonehouse*[35]. On another view, it is immaterial that no effect occurs within the jurisdiction provided what the accused does is an act sufficiently proximate to the commission of an offence in Ireland. Similarly, an extra-territorial conspiracy to commit a criminal offence in Ireland is triable here despite the fact that no overt act in furtherance of the conspiracy took place within the jurisdiction. This rule applies whether it is a conspiracy under statute or common law; *R v Sansom and Others*[36].

2.25   ***Ellis v O'Dea and Governor of Portlaoise Prison***
[1991] ILRM 365
Supreme Court, 1990

Facts: The appellant was challenging an extradition order issued on foot of two warrants from the United Kingdom. The first alleged that the appellant conspired with others to cause an explosion likely to endanger life or cause serious injury to property in the UK. The second warrant alleged possession of explosives with intent to endanger life or cause serious injury to property in the UK.

The alleged offences were contrary to s 3(1)(*a*) and s 3(1)(*b*) of the Explosive Substances Act 1883 and s 7 of the (UK) Criminal Jurisdiction Act 1975. The corresponding Irish offences were identified as offences contrary to s 3 of the Explosive Substances Act 1883 as amended by s 4 of the Criminal Law (Jurisdiction) Act 1976.

---

30 [1962] VR 244.
31 [1977] QB 481.
32 Glazebrook *The Merging of Misdemeanours*, (1962) 78 LQR.
33 [1974] IR 422.
34 [1984] 1 NZLR 636.
35 [1978] AC 55.
36 [1991] 2 All ER 145.

Having examined both statutory provisions, the court held that it was "clear that a corresponding offence would appear to exist". However, on the basis of his assertion of never having been in the United Kingdom during the period alleged in the warrants, the appellant argued that, notwithstanding this similarity, there was no doctrine of extra-territorial jurisdiction in Irish law and therefore no corresponding Irish offences. The court firmly rejected this argument.

Finlay CJ (Griffin, Hederman and O'Flaherty JJ concurring): . . . A consideration of the terms of the warrants and of the English Act of 1975 and the Irish Act of 1976 make it clear that a corresponding offence would appear to exist. Counsel for the appellant, however, urges upon the court that there is no truly corresponding offence, by virtue of the following contention. An affidavit of English law filed on behalf of the defendant in these proceedings sets out two relevant principles of the common law applicable to criminal cases in England which are:

(a) That a person who conspires with another or others and is at that time situated outside the jurisdiction of the United Kingdom courts, is amenable to trial in those courts if one of his co-conspirators does an act within the United Kingdom in furtherance of the criminal conspiracy.

(b) Where two or more persons are engaged in a joint venture constituting a criminal offence, each is responsible for the acts of the others and accordingly any one of the persons so engaged is amenable to trial in the courts of the United Kingdom if one of his accomplices does an act in furtherance of the crime within the United Kingdom.

Thus, in the particular example, it is suggested as a matter of English law that a person outside the United Kingdom, who has never entered the United Kingdom, is capable of being in control of an explosive substance within the United Kingdom if his accomplice in the crime of possessing and controlling it for the purpose of causing an explosion is with the explosives in the United Kingdom.

It was submitted that neither of these two principles applies in Irish law, and that, therefore, notwithstanding the close similarity between the terms of the English and Irish statute creating the offences involved in this case, there is no corresponding offence to that contained in Irish law. I am satisfied that this submission must fail because it is a fundamental principle of the Irish common law, applicable to the criminal jurisdiction of the Irish courts, that a person entering into a conspiracy outside Ireland in futherance of which an overt act is done in Ireland is amenable to trial in the courts of Ireland. I am equally satisfied that a person who, though located outside Ireland, does an act which either in itself or by reason of the conduct of an accomplice has the effect of completing a criminal offence in Ireland, is amenable to the Irish courts.

Th broad reason underlying these two principles is, of course, that the criminal law must take cognisance of any crime committed within the State and must make persons, if charged before it, amenable for that crime, irrespective of where they were located at the time of its commission. It would be the very negation of an adequate criminal jurisdiction and an absurdity if a person joining in a criminal act being either a conspiracy or a joint venture could escape responsibility by reason of the fact that he has committed no overt act within the jurisdiction.

I have no doubt, therefore, that the learned district justice was correct in holding that the offences charged in the warrants corresponded to the offences inserted in the Explosive Substances Act 1883 by the Criminal Law (Jurisdiction) Act 1976.

Procedure

2.26 In general, at common law, a person charged with the commission of a felony could be found guilty of a misdemeanour where the misdemeanour is contained within the felony. The law on attempts is cast in statutory form.

9 . . . if on the trial of any person charged with any felony or misdemeanour it shall appear to the jury upon the evidence that the defendant did not complete the offence charged, but that he was guilty only of an attempt to commit the same, such person shall not by reason thereof be entitled to be acquitted, but the jury shall be at liberty to return as their verdict that the defendant is not guilty of the felony or misdemeanour charged, but is guilty of an attempt to commit the same, and thereupon such person shall be liable to be punished in the same manner as if he had been convicted upon an indictment for attempting to commit the particular felony or misdemeanour charged in the said indictment; and no person so tried as herein lastly mentioned shall be liable to be afterwards prosecuted for an attempt to commit the felony or misdemeanour for which he was so tried.

Impossibility

2.28 The defence of impossibility is peculiar to the inchoate offences of attempt, conspiracy and incitement. In England, incitement and common law conspiracy are still governed by common law rules but statutory conspiracy and attempt are now reformed through the Criminal Law Act 1977 and the Criminal Attempts Act 1981[37].

All the authorities agree that where the accused attempts, or conspires with another, to perpetrate a situation which does not amount to a crime at law, he cannot be guilty of any offence. An example is *R v Taaffe*[38] where the accused imported cannabis resin into the United Kingdom, which he mistakenly believed to be currency. As currency is not subject to any restriction on importation and, under the Customs and Excise Management Act 1979, the accused is to be judged on the facts as he believes them to be, he successfully appealed his conviction. It is possible to argue that where the objective of the accused is impossible nothing he does can ever be proximate to a substantive crime. That argument has not been identified as the basis of the defence of impossibility as it applies to inchoate crimes. An appreciation of the senselessness of convicting persons who do something that could never lead to a crime seems, instead, to inform the law.

2.29 In *Haughton v Smith*[39] the House of Lords decided that impossibility was a general defence at common law, the only exception to which was that the accused may be convicted where the impossibility results from the failure or inadequacy of the means adopted, or to be used, to commit the offence. In so deciding the House of Lords over-ruled *R v Ring*[40] which held that it was not an answer to a charge of attempted larceny that the subject-matter of the proposed theft was not available to be stolen. The reality is, however, that a pick-pocket who puts his hand in a bag or a pocket and finds it empty (or in circumstances where the prosecution are not able to prove there was anything to steal in that place) is targeting the person and not the pocket and would just as easily try another pocket to fulfil his purpose; *DPP v Nock &*

---

37 See *R v Shivpuri* [1987] AC 1.
38 [1984] AC 539.
39 [1975] AC 476.
40 (1892) 61 LJMC 166.

Alsford[41]. The decision in *Haughton v Smith* has been criticised[42].
  The rules laid down are:
(1) Acts which are not crimes can never become crimes due to the belief of the accused. This is the *R v Taaffe*[43] situation.
(2) Where the objective of the offence does not exist the accused cannot be guilty in relation to it. Thus no one can attempt to steal from an empty safe but they would be guilty of burglary if they entered a building as a trespasser with intent to steal[44].
(3) Where the victim of the offence is non-existent a crime cannot be committed in relation to him. So, A1 cannot incite A2 to murder an already dead victim. An example of this category would be the accused plunging a knife into the heart of a corpse intending to kill a person already dead.
(4) It is impossible to commit an offence in relation to a subject matter which does not have the quality necessary to found the charge. The classic example is *Haughton v Smith*[45] where the accused were charged with receiving stolen corned beef. This beef had been intercepted and thus recovered by the police, but the accused were allowed to attend a later rendezvous with the lorry carrying the consignment. The idea of the police was to catch the "bigger fish". At that later stage the goods were in police control and so no longer technically stolen goods under English law.
(5) Equally, the victim of the offence may lack a quality essential to the definition of the offence. So the accused may have sexual intercourse with a woman believing her to be mentally defective when she is of sound mind.

2.30 The accused may be guilty where the objective he is intent on achieving would be a crime, if he was successful, but it either fails or cannot be achieved because he uses means inadequate to accomplish his purpose. Examples include an attempt to break into a house using a glass cutter which merely scratches the window, an attempt to obtain by false pretences which does not deceive, shooting the victim with a dart smeared with an ineffective poison or using a spoiled explosive in an attempt to wreck a building.

2.31 In *DPP v Nock & Alsford*[46] the House of Lords applied these principles to conspiracy and later the Court of Appeal in *R v Fitzmaurice*[47] applied them to incitement.

2.32 It is impossible to attempt to commit certain crimes such as perjury, riot, libel, and the offering of bad money[48]. Many of these situations are covered by offences of possession. Indeed these possession based crimes, in many instances, replace the law of attempts in controlling the mischief which

---

41 [1978] 2 All ER 654 per Lord Diplock.
42 Ribeiro – *Criminal Liability for Attempting the Impossible: Lady Luck and the Villains*. (1974) 4 Hong Kong LJ 109.
43 [1984] AC 539.
44 Section 23A of the Larceny Act 1916 as inserted by s 6 of the Criminal Law (Jurisdiction) Act 1976.
45 [1975] AC 476.
46 [1978] 2 All ER 654.
47 [1983] QB 1083.
48 Stephen – *A History of the Criminal Law of England* (1883) Vol 11 p 227.

is almost always clearly in the mind of a person who has control of an explosive, a drug or an offensive weapon, see chapter 7. The rationale behind such tight regulation is obvious and the necessity to create a separate category of possession offences is that the circumstances of possession will rarely be sufficient to allow for proof of criminal intent or an act proximate to the commission of another crime[49].

An Alternative View

2.33   ***Britten v Alpogut***
                              (1987) 11 Crim LJ 182
                         Supreme Court of Victoria, 1986

Facts: The defendant was charged with attempting to import a prohibited substance into Australia contrary to s 233B of the Customs Act, 1901. The defendant believed that he was importing and intended to import a prohibited substance (cannabis) but the substance he believed to be cannabis and which he imported was something else altogether, which was not a prohibited import within s 233B of the Customs Act, 1901.

Murphy J: . . . It will be seen that in the law of attempt the emphasis lies on the criminal intent of the actor, rather than on the patent criminality of the act which he performed. The act itself may be innocuous.

The intention which the Crown must prove is an intention to bring about each element of the crime alleged to be attempted, and it must be proven that this intention is accompanied side by side by an act sufficiently proximate to the offence attempted to take it out of the class of mere preparatory acts.

The latter consideration has been developed in many subsequent cases and is not a matter of any moment in the present case.

If a charge of attempting to commit a crime is to lie, it is of course usual (though perhaps not necessary cf *Webley v Buxton* [1977] 2 QB 481) that the crime attempted fails, for one reason or another. That the crime attempted fails also assists to emphasise that the law, in punishing criminal attempts, is really punishing the person concerned for his criminal intention, so as to deter or neutralise dangerous individuals, and does not punish to deter dangerous acts as such: cf *US Model Penal Code*.

This is so even though: "The mere intent to commit a misdemeanour is not criminal – some act is required": see *R v Eagleton* (1855) Dears CC 515 at 538, *per* Baron Parke. Thus John Austin wrote, in *Lectures in Jurisprudence*, 1861 p 120, "where a criminal intent is evidenced by an attempt, the party is punished in respect of the criminal intention". See also J W C Turner, *Attempts to Commit Crime* (1933) 5 *Camb LJ* 230 at p 235; *Russell on Crime*, 10th ed, p 1784; P J Fitzgerald, *Criminal Law Punishment*, 1962, pp 97–8.

The English Law Commission in its report on *Criminal Law: Attempt and Impossibility in Relation to Attempt Conspiracy and Incitement* (Report No 102 (1980)), p 6 reported that "the main jurisdiction for the retention of inchoate offence is the need to permit the law to impose criminal sanctions in certain cases where a crime has been contemplated but not in fact committed".

But this view was expressed after the decision in *Haughton v Smith* [1975] AC 476.

In my opinion, it can be said that before *Haughton v Smith* the law of attempt punished a manifest criminal intention to commit a crime which was not accomplished.

---

49 Charleton – *Offences Against the Person* (1992), chapters 9, 10 and 11.

For some inexplicable reason the law of attempt became involved with the question whether or not the crime attempted could have been in fact accomplished by the accused.

It was thought by some that the accused could not be convicted of an attempt to commit a particular crime, when on the facts of the case it would not have been possible for the accused to commit the crime in question.

Immediately, there was a confusion demonstrated between a relevant step in the commission of a possible crime and a relevant step in the commission of an intended crime, but one not capable of being accomplished.

Courts began to ignore the importance of the intention of the accused and tended to concentrate on the question whether what was done was a step towards a crime, which if uninterrupted, would have been committed: cf *R v Percy Dalton (London) Ltd* (1949) 33 Cr App R 102 at 110.

It was at this stage that the embryo of the heresy in *Haughton v Smith* was conceived.

Courts spoke of attempts as interruptions in the commission of acts which, if not interrupted, would have amounted to the crime intended. Clearly, if accompanied by the necessary and vital intent, such acts, if performed sufficiently proximately, would amount to an attempt. But the emphasis in thinking wrongly changed from the element of subjective intent, to the element of objective doing of a forward or proximate act in the actual commission of the crime itself.

It tended to be forgotten that the crime of attempt derives its criminality from the conduct intended or sought to be done: cf *Gillies Criminal Law*, 1985, p 519.

However, the submission on behalf of the Crown in this case is that in 1910 when s 233 was first introduced into the *Customs Act* 1901 (cf *Beckwith v R* (1976) 135 CLR 569 at 578–80, *per* Mason J.) the common law of attempt was that anyone who, believing that a certain state of facts exists, does an act the doing of which would, if that state of facts existed, be an attempt to commit an offence, attempts to commit the offence, although its commission in the manner proposed was by reason of the actual state of affairs impossible.

Mr Weinberg of counsel for the applicant took this statement from the 1879 *Draft Criminal Code*, s 74. He also relied in support of it upon *R v Brown* (1889) 24 QB 357; *R v Ring* (1892) 17 Cox CC 491; *McMillan v Reeves* (1945) 62 WN (NSW) 126; *O'Sullivan v Peters* [1951] SASR 54; *Haas v R* [1964] Tas SR 1; *R v Perera* [1907] VLR 240; *Stephens v Abrahams* (1902) 27 VLR 753.

It should however be noted that in the *Draft Code* appended by the Criminal Code Bill Commission to their report, this passage coming after the definition of an attempt bears an asterisk, which in the margin attracts the comment by the Commissioners:

> This declares the law differently from *R v Collins* L & C 471 where it was held that a person who put his hand into the pocket of another in order to steal, was not guilty of an attempt to steal, because it happened that that pocket was empty.

In the body of their report the Commissioners state as to his proposed section, "This alters the law from what it has been held to be". The Commissioners were Lord Blackburn, Barry J, Lush J and Sir James Fiztjames Stephen QC.

It was shortly after that report that *R v Brown* and *R v Ring* were decided.

In *R v Brown* (1890) 24 QBD 357 at 359. Lord Colerdige CJ, Pollock B, Field, Manistry, Cave, Day and Granham JJ stated bluntly that *R v Collins* "is no longer law". Nor was *R v Dodd* (unreported) which "proceeded upon the same view that a person could not be convicted of an attempt to commit an offence which he could not actually commit. Some of the judges, I know, yielded with great reluctance to the authority of *R v Collins*, and thought that decision was wrong".

Then again in another Crown case reserved, *R v Ring* (1892) 17 Cox CC 491 before Lord Coleridge CJ, Hawkins, Wills, Lawrence and Wright JJ, the prisoners were charged with an attempt to steal from the person of a person unknown. Apparently, it is assumed that they were unable to find the pocket of the dress of their victim. They were convicted at Quarter Sessions and the case was stated, following the Deputy Chairman's ruling that *R v Collins* had been overruled by *R v Brown*. Lord Coleridge said, at 149: "The case was stated to ascertain whether or not *R v Collins* is good law. That case was overruled by the decision in *R v Brown*, a case decided by five judges [The reporter notes that this should be seven, although the reporter includes Charles J instead of Day J] and since this case will also be decided by five judges, one of whom was one of the judges who decided *R v Brown* the learned judge who stated the case will have the satisfaction of knowing that now nine judges hold that *R v Collins* is bad law". The number of judges should of course have been eleven, all, I think, recognised to be judges of great experience in the criminal law.

It has been submitted that as the crime of attempting to import into Australia any prohibited imports to which the section (s 233B(1)(*b*) of the *Customs Act* 1901) applies, is a statutory offence, the only possible attempt of which the accused could have been guilty would be an attempt to do that which is forbidden by the legislature.

But if the word "attempt" is used in s 233B(1)(*b*) in its common law sense, as I believe that it is, then it is to beg the question to say that it is only if the goods imported or sought to be imported, are in fact prohibited imports that an "attempt" within the meaning of the subsection can be committed.

For if the evil intent of the actor can make a sufficiently proximate though objectively innocent act criminal, so as to amount to an attempt, it would seem irrelevant to have to go on to see whether the attempt could or would have succeeded. At common law, if the intent was to commit a recognised and not an imagined crime, and the act done was not merely preparatory but sufficiently proximate, then at that stage an attempt to commit the recognised crime has been committed, and it seems to me it is not necessary to go further.

It follows, in my view, that to prove the statutory crime created by s 233B(1)(*b*) of the *Customs Act*, of attempting to import prohibited imports into Australia, the Crown must prove that the accused at all material times intended to import something which was as a matter of law a prohibited import and known by him to be so, and that pursuant to this intention he did an act or acts (including omissions) not merely preparatory but sufficiently proximate to be intended commission of the crime.

It is my opinion, sitting in this Court, that we ought to say that we are unable to accept the law as to criminal attempts set forth in *Haughton v Smith*, and that we should affirm the general body of the law on this subject as it stood preceding *R v Percy Dalton (London) Ltd* (1949) 33 Cr App R 102.

This would be, in my opinion, to affirm the reasoning apparent in our own Full Court in decisions preceding *Haughton v Smith* (for example, *R v Perera* [1907] VLR 240) and to accord with the revised general reasoning of the House of Lords in *R v Shivpuri* [1986] 2 All ER 334, [1986] 2 WLR 988.

It would also be to recognise that at common law a criminal attempt is committed if it is proven that the accused had at all material times the guilty intent to commit a recognised crime and it is proven that at the same time he did an act or acts (which in appropriate circumstances would include omissions) which are seen to be sufficiently proximate to the commission of the said crime and are not seen to be merely preparatory to it. The "objective innocence" or otherwise of those acts is irrelevant.

Impossibility is also irrelevant, unless it be that the so-called crime intended is not a crime known to the law, in which case a criminal attempt to commit it cannot be made.

Code Options

2.34 *Model Penal Code*

Article 5. Inchoate crimes

5.01 Criminal Attempt.

(1) *Definition of Attempt.* A person is guilty of an attempt to commit a crime if, acting with the kind of culpability otherwise required for commission of the crime, he:

> (*a*) purposely engages in conduct that would constitute the crime if the attendant circumstances were as he believes them to be; or
>
> (*b*) when causing a particular result is an element of the crime, does or omits to do anything with the purpose of causing or with the belief that it will cause such result without further conduct on his part; or
>
> (*c*) purposely does or omits to do anything that, under the circumstances as he believes them to be, is an act or omission constituting a substantial step in a course of conduct planned to culminate in his commission of the crime.

(2) *Conduct That May Be Held Substantial Step Under Subsection (1)(c).* Conduct shall not be held to constitute a substantial step under subsection (1)(*c*) of this section unless it is strongly corroborative of the actor's criminal purpose. Without negativing the sufficiency of other conduct, the following, if strongly corroborative of the actor's criminal purpose, shall not be held insufficient as a matter of law:

> (*a*) lying in wait, searching for or following the contemplated victim of the crime;
>
> (*b*) enticing or seeking to entice the contemplated victim of the crime to go to the place contemplated for its commission;
>
> (*c*) reconnoitering the place contemplated for the commission of the crime;
>
> (*d*) unlawful entry of a structure, vehicle or enclosure in which it is contemplated that the crime will be committed;
>
> (*e*) possession of materials to be employed in the commission of the crime, that are specially designed for such unlawful use or that can serve no lawful purpose of the actor under the circumstances;
>
> (*f*) possession, collection or fabrication of materials to be employed in the commission of the crime, at or near the place contemplated for its commission, if such possession, collection or fabrication serves no lawful purpose of the actor under the circumstances;
>
> (*g*) soliciting an innocent agent to engage in conduct constituting an element of the crime.

(3) *Conduct Designed to Aid Another in Commission of a Crime.* A person who engages in conduct designed to aid another to commit a crime that would establish his complicity under section 2.06 if the crime were committed by such other person, is guilty of an attempt to commit the crime, although the crime is not committed or attempted by such other person.

(4) *Renunciation of Criminal Purpose.* When the actor's conduct would otherwise constitute an attempt under subsection (1)(*b*) or (1)(*c*) of this section, it is an affirmative defense that he abandoned his effort to commit the crime or otherwise prevented its commission, under circumstances manifesting a complete and voluntary renunciation of his criminal purpose. The establishment of such defence does not, however, affect the liability of an accomplice who did not join in such abandonment or prevention.

Within the meaning of this Article, renunciation of criminal purpose is not voluntary if it is motivated, in whole or in part, by circumstances, not present or apparent at the inception of the actor's course of conduct, that increase the probability of detection or apprehension or that make more difficult the accomplishment of the criminal purpose. Renunciation is not complete if it is motivated by a decision to postpone the criminal conduct until a more advantageous time or to transfer the criminal effort to another but similar objective or victim.

2.35   ***Canadian Criminal Code***

24(1) Every one who, having an intent to commit an offence, does or omits to do anything for the purpose of carrying out the intention is guilty of an attempt to commit the offence whether or not it was possible under the circumstances to commit the offence.

(2) The question of whether an act or omission by a person who has an intent to commit an offence is or is not mere preparation to commit the offence, and too remote to constitute an attempt to commit the offence, is a question of law.

463 Except where otherwise expressly provided by law the following provisions apply in respect of persons who attempt to commit or are accessories after the fact to the commission of offences:

(a) every one who attempts to commit or is an accessory after the fact to the commission of an indictable offence for which, on conviction, an accused is liable to be sentenced to death or imprisonment for life is guilty of an indictable offence and liable to imprisonment for a term not exceeding 14 years;

(b) every one who attempts to commit or is an accessory after the fact to the commission of an indictable offence for which, on conviction, an accused is liable to imprisonment for 14 years or less is guilty of an indictable offence and liable to imprisonment for a term that is one-half of the longest term to which a person who is guilty of that offence is liable;

(c) every one who attempts to commit or is an accessory after the fact to the commission of an offence punishable on summary conviction is guilty of an offence punishable on summary conviction;

(d) every one who attempts to commit or is an accessory after the fact to the commission of an offence for which the offender may be prosecuted by indictment or for which he is punishable on summary conviction

(i) is guilty of an indictable offence and liable to imprisonment for a term not exceeding a term that is one-half of the longest term to which a person who is guilty of that offence is liable or

(ii) is guilty of an offence punishable on summary conviction.

Note: Similar provisions as to sentence apply in respect of counselling and conspiracy in ss 464 and 465.

660 Where the complete commission of an offence charged is not proved but the evidence establishes an attempt to commit the offence, the accused may be convicted of the attempt.

661(1) Where an attempt to commit an offence is charged but the evidence establishes the commission of the complete offence, the accused is not entitled to be acquitted, but the jury may convict him of the attempt unless the judge presiding at the trial, in his discretion, discharges the jury from giving a verdict and directs that the accused be indicted for the complete offence.

(2) An accused who is convicted under this section is not liable to be tried again for the offence that he was charged with attempting to commit.

Further Materials

2.36 Stuart *The Actus Reus in Attempts* [1970] Crim LR 505.
Williams *Salmond on Jurisprudence* (10th ed, 1974).
Glazebrook *Should we have a Law of Attempted Crime* (1969) 85 LQR.
Williams *Police Control of Intending Criminals* [1955] Crim LR 626.
Anon *Merger of Felonies in Misdemeanours* (1876) 10 ILTSJ 350.
Anon *Attempt* (1967) 101 ILTSJ 243.
Anon *Inchoate Crimes – Attempt* (1968) 102 ILTSJ 364.
Binchy *Criminal Liability for Attempting Non-Criminal Acts* (1972) 106 ILTSJ 1/11/17/27.
Williams *The Lords and Impossible Attempts, or Quis Custodiet Ipsos Custodes?* (1986) 45 CAMBLR 33.
Williams *Wrong Turnings on the Law of Attempts* [1991] Crim LR 416.
Smith *Proximity in Attempt – Lord Lane's "Mid Way Course"* [1991] Crim LR 576.

Conspiracy

2.37 The law of conspiracy is distinguished from the law of attempt by failing to make any requirement that the accused act in a manner proximate to the commission of a crime. In this respect it should be easier to prove than attempt. Practical reality indicates that it is not. It is an indictable misdemeanour at common law for two or more persons to agree to commit an unlawful act. A lawful act achieved by unlawful means is within that definition. The essence of the crime is the agreement; it is complete upon the parties entering into same. The reality of the struggle faced by the prosecution in proving any case beyond reasonable doubt requires in practice, though not in law, that the conspirators exhibit their shared intention to effect an unlawful purpose by overt acts and declarations. What the conspirators have agreed must be proven by what they have done and said while the conspiracy was in progress. In order to secure a conviction those acts and statements must be proximate to the crime in order to be inconsistent with any other rational explanation than the existence of the agreement charged. That is the manner of proof by which a conspiracy prosecution usually succeeds. Consequently, the standard of proof required in a conspiracy prosecution differs little from that in attempt. Absence of any rule of proximity at least allows the courts to avoid the desperate confusion which has sometimes arisen in the effort to define that concept in concrete fact or example. In the absence of overt behaviour a confession to conspiracy will suffice for a conviction.

Nature of Conspiracy

2.38 A conspiracy is an agreement to do an unlawful act. Principles of contract law have no applicability to the understanding or the concept of agreement in the law of conspiracy. People do not have to sit down together and draw up a definite plan executed in predefined terms in order to enter into a conspiracy. A conscious understanding of a common design is sufficient; *R v Orton*[50]. This essentially means that the parties are pursuing the

50 [1922] VLR 469 at 673.

same unlawful purpose in combination. A slight rearrangement of words changes the thrust of the definition and Don Stuart suggests that the law can be captured "by saying that there must be a firm decision as to a joint venture"[51].

2.39   *R v Controni & Papalia*
                                        (1979) 45 CCC (2d) 1
                                   Supreme Court of Canada, 1979

> Dickson J (for the majority): The word "conspire" derives from two Latin words, "con" and "spirare", meaning "to breathe together". To conspire is to agree. The essence of criminal conspiracy is proof of agreement. On a charge of conspiracy the agreement itself is the gist of the offence: *Paradis v The King* (1933), 61 CCC 184 at p 186, [1934] 2 DLR 88 at p 90, [1934] SCR 154 at p 168. The actus reus is the fact of agreement: *Director of Public Prosecutions v Nock*, [1978] 3 WLR 57 at p 66 (HL). The agreement reached by the co-conspirators may contemplate a number of acts or offences. Any number of persons may be privy to it. Additional persons may join the ongoing scheme while others may drop out. So long as there is a continuing overall, dominant plan there may be changes in methods of operation, personnel, or victims, without bringing the conspiracy to an end. The important inquiry is not as to the acts done in pursuance of the agreement, but whether there was, in fact, a common agreement to which the acts are referable and to which all of the alleged offenders were privy. In *R v Meyrick and Ribuffi* (1929), 21 Cr App R 94 at p 102 (CCA), the question asked was whether "the acts of the accused were done in pursuance of a criminal purpose held in common between them", and in 11 Hals, 4th ed., at p 44 it is said: "It is not enough that two or more persons pursued the same unlawful object at the same time or in the same place, it is necessary to show a meeting of minds, consensus to effect an unlawful purpose." There must be evidence beyond reasonable doubt that the alleged conspirators acted in concert in pursuit of a common goal.

2.40 The law essentially attempts to distinguish a coincidence of actions from an agreement. Clearly, persons who are not in combination with one another, but are coincidentally working towards a shared goal are not fulfilling an agreement. There has been no understanding, or meeting of minds, between them that they should combine to effect a particular purpose either unlawful in itself, or by unlawful means. What is done to prove a conspiracy is to show that the way in which the parties behaved was consistent only with the pursuit of a common object and indicates co-ordination of effort by an arrangement beforehand. It is equally a conspiracy for A and B, or for A alone, to commence an unlawful enterprise and then to be joined in their actions by C. In such circumstances C has entered into the understanding which moves towards a common purpose; that is a conspiracy.

2.41 In such spirit the law has recognised "wheel conspiracies" where a number of accused persons act through a middle man knowing that they are part of a larger design; *US v Bruno*[52]. In a "chain conspiracy" the conspirators are acting in a line linked up to each other by their understanding with the person interacting immediately with them, but conscious of their part in a larger design leading ultimately to the unlawful purpose. These types

---

51 Canadian Criminal Law (2nd ed 1987) 571.
52 (1939) 105 F 2d 921.

merely illustrate methods and do not substitute for the basic law requiring an overall design common to the parties, although it can be uncertain in the detail to be used to accomplish it. There must not be wrapped up in one conspiracy charge what is, in fact, two or more conspiracies; *R v Ardalan*[53].

2.42   ***R v Meyrick & Ribuffi***
(1929) 21 Cr App R 94
Court of Criminal Appeal England, 1929

Facts: This case concerned corruption of the police in Soho. Following an investigation it was found that Sergeant Goddard had been bribed by a number of night-club operators, including the accused, to enable them to avoid complying with licensing laws. The "wheel conspiracy" theory was upheld by the court.

Lord Hewart LCJ: These appellants, Mrs Meyrick and Luigi Ribuffi, were convicted at the Central Criminal Court, together with one George Goddard, of conspiracy and of corruption, contrary to the first section of the Prevention of Corruption Act 1906. Each of them was sentenced to 15 months' imprisonment with hard labour, and each of them now appeals against that conviction.

The argument upon the appeal has taken up a considerable amount of time, but not too much time, and the Court is indebted to all the learned counsel for all the care and the thoroughness with which the appeal has been presented.

The first count of the indictment alleged that Goddard and these two appellants on diverse days between the 1st October, 1924, and the 24th November, 1928, in the County of London, conspired together, and with one Anna Gadda, and other persons unknown, to contravene the provisions of the Licensing Acts by the unlawful sale of intoxicating liquors, and to effect a public mischief by obstructing the Metropolitan Police in the execution of their public duty, and by corrupting officers of that force and contriving to secure that they should make to their superior officers false and misleading reports upon matters referred to them in the course of their official duty for investigation, and thereby to prevent the due administration of the law, and to defeat and pervert the course of justice. Each of these appellants was found guilty upon that count.

The third count charged that the appellant, Ribuffi, between the 9th November, 1925, and the 26th April, 1926, did corruptly give to an agent, that is, George Goddard, a gift or consideration, to wit £260, as an inducement or reward for doing or forbearing to do certain acts in relation to his principal's affairs or business, for for showing or forbearing to show favour or disfavour to the said Ribuffi in relation to his principal's affairs or business. The acts or forbearances in relation to the principal's affairs and business were referred to in the previous count, namely, reporting favourably, or forbearing to report truly and honestly, upon the conduct of a certain club.

Finally, so far as this appeal is concerned, in the fifth count of the indictment Mrs Meyrick was charged for that between the 21st July, 1925, and the 2nd December, 1927, in the County of London, she did corruptly give to an agent, namely, Goddard, a gift or consideration, to wit £155 as an inducement or reward for doing or forbearing to do certain acts in relation to his principal's affairs or business, or for showing or forbearing to show favour or disfavour to Mrs Meyrick in relation to his principal's affairs or business.

Upon the third count, Ribuffi was found guilty. Upon the fifth count, Mrs Meyrick was found guilty. In other words, each of these appellants was found guilty upon the count charging conspiracy, and also upon a count charging the corrupt giving of an inducment or reward within the meaning of the Prevention of Corruption Act.

Now it was urged, and it is urged, on behalf of each of these appellants that they ought to have been separately tried; that there was no evidence of the conspiracy alleged in the indictment; that the making of that charge of conspiracy had the effect of letting in injurious evidence improperly; and finally that the learned Judge misdirected the jury.

Upon analysis those four objections appear to resolve themselves into one. They are an objection to the conspiracy count, and to the mode in which it was dealt with, and the effects which it produced at the trial.

Sir Henry Maddocks has laid before the Court with great ability, I need hardly say, the effect of the law with regard to conspiracy. It is, no doubt, a difficult branch of the law, difficult in itself, and sometimes even more difficult in its application to particular facts or allegations. There is no substantial contest between the appellants and the prosecution upon the question what the law is. The real contest is on the way in which it was applied and ought to be applied to matters such as are disclosed in this prosecution. I will refer to two passages only in the mass of authorities of which the Court has been very properly reminded during the past three days. In the first place, in *Mulcahy's* case, reported in 3 English and Irish Appeals, p 306, at p 317, Mr Justice Willes, delivering the opinion of the Judges to whom questions had been put, said this: "A conspiracy consists not merely in the intention of two or more, but in the agreement of two or more to do an unlawful act, or to do a lawful act by unlawful means. So long as such a design rests in intention only, it is not indictable. When two agree to carry it into effect, the very plot is an act in itself, and the act of each of the parties, promise against promise, *actus contra actum*, capable of being enforced, if lawful, is punishable if for a criminal object or for the use of criminal means. And so far as proof goes, conspiracy, as Grose, J, said in *Rex v Brissac*, is generally 'matter of inference deduced from certain criminal acts of the parties accused, done in pursuance of an apparent criminal purpose in common between them.'" The other passage to which I wish to refer is in the well-known charge of Mr. Justice FitzGerald in the case of *Queen v Parnell and Others* reported in 14 Cox, Criminal Cases, at p 515. Mr Justice FitzGerald, having cited the words of Mr Justice Grose which I have just read, said: "It may be that the alleged conspirators have never seen each other, and have never corresponded. One may have never heard the name of the other, and yet by the law they may be parties to the same common criminal agreement. Thus, in some of the Fenian cases tried in this country, it frequently happened that one of the conspirators was in America, the other in this country; that they had never seen each other, but that there were acts on both sides which led the jury to the inference, and they drew it, that they were engaged in accomplishing the same common object, and when they had arrived at this conclusion, the acts of one became evidence against the other"; and the learned Judge proceeded further to illustrate that proposition.

It has not been seriously disputed that the law relating to conspiracy is as it is stated to be in those passages. But it is said, first of all, and somewhat faintly, that this indictment itself is open to objection, and objection upon a particular ground. I say "somewhat faintly" because no application was made at the commencement of the trial to quash the first count in this indictment. But the criticism was undoubtedly made at more than one point in the trial at the Central Criminal Court that the first count might be regarded as alleging more than one conspiracy, or, alternatively, if it alleged one conspiracy, one conspiracy to effect two separate and distinct objects. That argument was presented, and presented more than once, before the learned Judge, and he dealt with it, and he held that upon the true construction of this count the conspiracy which was alleged was one conspiracy. In the words of the learned counsel for the prosecution it was "one big conspiracy revolving round the figure of Goddard," and when at a later stage the learned Judge came to deal with the matter again, he used these words (I am quoting from p 328 of the transcript) "In my opinion this count charges a conspiracy to do an unlawful thing, that is to say, in substance to effect public mischief by corrupting the police force." That may be stated quite generally to be the object of this conspiracy in this indictment. But further, it is objected that there was, at any rate, confusion, and confusion not removed by sufficient direction on the nature of the conspiracy which this count alleged. That criticism seems to us to fail. It is quite obvious from various parts of this voluminous transcript that great stress was laid, and naturally laid, by learned counsel for each of these appellants upon the contention that there was no evidence that either of them knew each other, or had met each other, or had consulted together. The learned Judge says, for example, at p 539: "All the observations which have been made to you," that is to the jury, "of there being no evidence that Ribuffi and Mrs Meyrick ever met or ever consulted together, or ever spoke to each other, are all beside the point altogether." It is argued that the jury were left under the impression that there might be various conspiracies and that it would suffice if they found the accused individually guilty of some one or other conspiracy. That seems to be an inaccurate criticism. It has been suggested that a clear distinction is to be drawn between two things which it is said are sharply opposed – on the one hand, a series of individual conspiracies between Goddard and one other person in each case, and, on the other hand, a general conspiracy to which the parties were Goddard and all the other persons. It is argued that those two things are mutually exclusive. No doubt in particular circumstances they might be mutually exclusive, but once it is conceded, as it must be conceded, that in order that persons may conspire together it is not necessary that there should be direct communication between each and all, one has to look at the circumstances to see whether this criticism of mutual exclusion is satisfactory. How precisely here is the case for the prosecution put? It is not suggested that Mrs Meyrick was in direct communication with Ribuffi, but it is more than suggested – nay, the jury are asked to find as a fact upon the evidence – that Mrs Meyrick was in communication with Goddard, and that Ribuffi was in communication with Goddard, and not for a purpose individual and special in the one case to Mrs Meyrick, or in the other case to Ribuffi, but for a common design – a design common to all of them – a common design, namely, that stated by the learned Judge in the words I have just mentioned.

It seems to us that it was clearly put to the jury that in order to find these persons, or any of them, guilty of the conspiracy charged in the first count of this indictment, it was necessary that the prosecution should establish, not indeed that the individuals were in direct communication with each other, or directly consulting together, but that they entered into an agreement with a common design. Such agreements may be made in various ways. There may be one person, to adopt the metaphor of counsel, round whom the rest revolve. The metaphor is the metaphor of the centre of a circle and the circumference. There may be a conspiracy of another kind, wehre the metaphor would be rather that of a chain; A communicates with B, B with C, C with D, and so on to the end of the list of conspirators. What has to be ascertained is always the same matter: is it true to say, in the words already quoted, that the acts of the accused were done in pursuance of a criminal purpose held in common between them? Now, if that is the true view, it seems to us that that view was made plain to the jury. No doubt this first count in the indictment is not quite happily expressed. It might well have been expressed otherwise. But once it appears that the true meaning of that count is what the learned Judge described it as being – a construction, one may observe, accepted by both of the learned counsel for the appellants – then the matter becomes plain.

Various criticisms have been made upon particular passages in the summing-up. They come back, really, to the same criticism, that the jury were not sufficiently directed, or, even in one passage, were actually misdirected upon the law of conspiracy in relation to this indictment. In the opinion of the Court that criticism fails. It really depends upon a misuse of the passage in which the learned judge is dwelling upon the lack of necessity to prove that the various conspirators actually met or consulted together, or spoke to each other. The essential ingredient of conspiracy, conspiracy that is to say, for one common design, was, it seems to us, made quite clear.

Now, if that is so, various consequences follow. The further crticism that this indictment could not fairly be made to comprehend a charge of conspiracy fails.

The attention of the Court has been directed to a well-known passage in which judicial remark was made upon the unfairness that flows from the inclusion of a count for conspiracy in an indictment in which there ought to be no such count. The unfairness in such a case is, of course, manifest. But the criticism has no relation at all to a case where the circumstances are such as to call for the inclusion of a count for conspiracy, and to call for it in the public interest for the due administration of justice. No doubt, if one may follow an illustration which was suggested, if two persons are about to be charged with the substantive crime of larceny, and the evidence is that they did in fact steal something, unfairness might arise if they were charged with a conspiracy to commit that crime. But that criticism does not apply to the present indictment. What is alleged here is something far more than the individual acts referred to, for example, in counts three and five. What is referred to here is a conspiracy not only between Ribuffi and Mrs Meyrick and Goddard, but also between them and other persons – a widespread conspiracy for the accomplishment of a purpose going beyond the giving or receiving of a bribe. The object of the conspiracy was to secure the results which the bribes were intended to secure. The object of the conspiracy was not to bribe; the bribe was a means to the end. The end of the conspiracy was of a more far-reaching character than the individual act. Finally, it is said that here there was no evidence upon which this conspiracy could properly be found to exist. In our opinion the evidence was ample. It is not necessary to review the whole of the circumstances, but here was a comparatively small geographical area where there was a police sergeant of a particular position, charged with the performance of particular duties. The evidence clearly made it apparent to the mind of the jury that considerable sums of money reached that sergeant – money which had been in the banks of the other persons charged; and there was further evidence to show that the money not only reached Goddard, but passed on to subordinates also.

In our opinion, therefore, the arguments which have been addressed to us, powerful as they are, fail. Here, as it seems to us, this count was sustained by sufficient evidence. The law was made clear to the members of the jury. The count was properly included in the indictment, and there is no ground whatever for suggesting that there has been anything in the nature of a miscarriage of justice.

Remarks have been made on the proviso to section 4 of the Criminal Appeal Act. In our opinion, those questions do not arise. There is no question here of the kind which is referred to in that proviso.

In these circumstances, and for these reasons, it appears to us that these appeals, and both of them fail, and ought to be dismissed.

2.43 The case was distinguished in *R v Griffiths*[54] where, on facts differing in only unconvincing detail from *Meyrick* and *Ribuffi*, the court indicated that the evidence disclosed a number of different conspiracies instead of one overall conspiracy[55]. It is important to note that the "wheel" and "chain" conspiracy theories tend to indicate a mental element of an intention to effect an unlawful act but recklessness as to the extent of involvement of others. The law as to the mental element remains uncertain. An intent to enter into a joint venture incorporating an unlawful element coupled with either wilful blindness or recklessness as to the role or identity of other participants is, it is submitted, sufficient.

Unlawful Element

2.44 It would greatly simplify the law in relation to conspiracy if it were declared by statute that only an agreement to commit a criminal offence

54 [1966] 1 QB 589.
55 Similarly see *MacDonald* (1963) 10CCC (2d) 488 and *Kotteakos v US* (1946) 328 US 750.

could amount to a conspiracy. That is not the case; the law is left at large, the definition of the element of unlawfulness being decided as cases arise and in accordance with prevailing judicial views. In the past the crime of conspiracy was used against the trade union movement and statutory intervention was needed in the form s 3 of the Conspiracy and Protection of Property Act 1875 as amended by the Trade Disputes Act 1906, to end judicial activism.

2.45   *R v Parnell & Others*
                              (1881) 14 Cox 508
                              High Court, 1881

Facts: Charles Stewart Parnell and others were charged with various counts of soliciting tenants to refuse to pay their rent by using the unlawful means of "boycotting" those who did not join in this policy. Fitzgerald J, in his charge to the jury, indicated to them that a conspiracy was an agreement between two or more persons to do that which was unlawful and that it was unlawful to agree to accomplish an injury to a third person, or body of persons. In requisitions to the judge counsel for the accused indicated that such a proposition was so vague and broad as to leave a discretion in the hands of the judges to declare it to be a crime to combine to do almost anything which they regard as morally wrong or politically or socially dangerous. The trial was before Fitzgerald and Barry JJ and the latter upheld the form of direction given by his brother judge.

Barry J: . . . It would seem that two extreme opinions were put forward as to the law on this point, and that is not a matter of surprise when politics became more or less involved in the legal controversy. The one proposition was that an act perfectly innocent in itself, if it be carried out by perfectly innocent means, might, if two or more persons combined to carry it out, become criminal. The other was the proposition I understand Mr Macdonogh to put forward now as his contention in this case, namely, that there could be no indictable conspiracy unless the thing to be done or the means by which the thing was to be done were in themselves criminal; that would constitute a crime and be the subject-matter of an indictment for a prosecution. Now, as to the first of these propositions, I do not think it necessary to discuss it further (I do not think it has any application to this case) than to say I should be very slow to adopt such a view of the law. I think there must be necessarily in the law of conspiracy considerable vagueness and uncertainty, which in many respects is contrary to our law, and I agree with Mr Macdonogh that it should be administered with very great care, and not extended beyond the limits it has gone; therefore, if I had to pronounce a definite opinion I should be clearly of opinion that a combination to do an act innocent in itself by innocent means does not constitute an indictable conspiracy. As regards the second proposition, however, which has been so often mooted, namely, that the thing to be done must be criminal, or the means to be used must be criminal. With reference to that I am not prepared to adopt that view of the law, because I think the weight of modern authority is against it. I shall not refer any further to the cases cited by my brother Fitzgerald, and again referred to by Mr Macdonogh; but I shall now read this very lucid exposition of the law of conspiracy laid down by that most distinguished commission, a commission deserving, in the sense in which Mr Macdonogh would put it, a greater amount of popular confidence than the decision of a mere court of lawyers, and presided over by so distinguished a man as the late Lord Chief Justice Cockburn: "The law protecting the relation of master and servant, employer and employed, from interference by third parties is supplemented by the common law relating to conspiracy. This law becomes applicable not only where two or more persons combine to do any act which is in itself an offence, and would be criminal if done by any one of them, but also in many instances in which the act which is the purpose of the conspiracy, if done by one, would not be criminal; as for instance, where several, with the malicious intention to injure, combine to violate a private right, the violation of which by a single individual, though not criminal, would be wrongful, and would give a right of civil action to the party aggrieved. We are directed to consider whether it is desirable to limit or define this law either generally or as affecting the relation of masters and workmen." He then goes on to say, "Conspiracy may be divided into three classes: first, where the end to be accomplished would be a crime in each of the conspiring parties, a class which offers no difficulty. Secondly, where the purpose of the conspiracy is lawful, but the means to be resorted to are criminal as where the conspiracy is to support a cause believed to be just by perjured evidence. Here the proximate or immediate intention of the parties being to commit a crime, the conspiracy is to do something criminal, and here again the case is consequently free from difficulty. The third and last case is where a malicious design to do an injury, the purpose is to effect a wrong, though not such a wrong as when perpetrated by a single individual, would amount to an offence under the criminal law. Thus an attempt to destroy a man's credit, and effect his ruin by spreading reports of his insolvency would be a wrongful act which would entitle the party whose credit was thus attacked to bring an action as for a civil wrong, but it would not be an indictable offence. If it be asked on what principle a combination of several to effect the like wrongful purpose becomes an offence, the answer is, upon the same principle that any other civil wrong, when it assumes a more aggravated and formidable character, is constituted an offence, and becomes transferred from the domain of the civil to that of the criminal law. All offences, it need hardly be observed, are either in their nature offences against the community, or are primarily offences against individuals. As regards the latter case, every offence against person or property, or other individual rights involves a civil wrong, which would have entitled the person injured to civil redress were it not that owing to the aggravated nature of the wrong and the general insecurity to society which would ensue from such acts, if allowed to go unpunished, the State steps in, and merging the wrong done to the party immediately interested in the larger wrong done to the community, converts the wrong done by the infraction of individual right into a crime, and subjects the wrong doer to punishment to prevent as far as possible the recurrence of the offence. Thus the dividing line between private wrongs, as entitling the party injured to civil remedies, and private wrongs thus converted into public wrongs, in other words into offences and crimes, is to be found in the more aggravated and formidable character which the violation of individual rights under given circumstances assumes. It is upon this principle that the law of conspiracy, by which the violation of private right, which if done by one, would only be the subject of civil remedy, when done by several is constituted a crime, can be vindicated as necessary and just. It is obvious that a wrongful violation of another man's right committed by many assumes a far more formidable and offensive character than when committed by a single individual. The party assailed may be able by recourse to the ordinary civil remedies to defend himself against the attacks of one. It becomes a very different thing when he has to defend himself against many combined to do him injury. To take the case put by way of illustration, that of false representations made to ruin a man's business by raising a belief of his insolvency, such an attempt made by one might be met and repelled. It would obviously assume very different proportions, and a far more formidable character if made by a number of persons confederated together for the purpose, and who should simultaneously and in a variety of directions take measures to effect the common purpose. A variety of other instances, illustrative of the principle, might be put. The law has therefore, and it seems to us wisely and justly established that a combination of persons to commit a wrongful act with a view to injure another, shall be an offence, though the act if done by one would amount to no more than a civil wrong. We see no reason to question the propriety of the law as thus established, nor have we any reason to believe that in its general application it operates otherwise than beneficially." It seems to me that that is an extremely lucid and able exposition of the law coming from a most authoritative source. If that law be erroneous as there laid down, if it should be found objectionable on public or political grounds, it is for the Legislature to interfere. At present I do not think this Court has authority to interfere.

Fitzgerald J: I would only add to what my learned brother has said, as the objections were very much an appeal from what I have said, I entirely concur in what he has said.

2.46 It is possible to isolate the categories of unlawful conduct which the courts have, traditionally, acted on as sufficient to found a criminal conspiracy.

These would appear to be:

(1) An agreement involving the commission of a crime; *R v Porter*[56].

(2) An agreement involving the commission of a summary offence; *R v Blamires Transport Services Limited*[57].

(3) An agreement to defraud; *Scott v Metropolitan Police Commissioner*[58]. An example is *R v Cooke*[59] where stewards employed by British Rail sold their own refreshments on trains instead of the company fare. A conspiracy to defraud may extend to the making of devices which only serve the purpose of defrauding others; *R v Hollinshead*[60]

(4) An agreement to pervert the course of justice. This may simply reflect the substantive common law offence of perverting or attempting to pervert the course of justice; *R v Andrews*[61].

(5) An agreement to effect a public mischief has been held by the House of Lords not to amount to a conspiracy; *DPP v Withers*[62]. In *R v Boston*[63] the High Court of Australia held that acceptance of money by a member of the New South Wales legislative assembly in return for the use of his influence to procure the purchase of land by the government was such a public mischief as to make an agreement to that end a conspiracy; *R v Howes*[64].

(6) An agreement to commit a tort is sufficient according to the House of Lords; *Kamara v DPP*[65].

(7) More problematic is the acceptance as a criminal offence of a conspiracy to corrupt public morals and a conspiracy to outrage public decency; *Shaw v DPP*[66]; *Knuller v DPP*[67].

(8) There are no recent examples of the successful use of breach of contract as the unlawful element in criminal conspiracy.

(9) There seems to be decisive rejection of the idea that an immoral act suffices as the unlawful element in conspiracy.

56 [1980] NI 18.
57 [1964] 1 QB 278.
58 [1975] AC 819.
59 [1986] AC 909.
60 [1985] AC 975.
61 [1973] QB 422.
62 [1975] AC 842.
63 (1923) 33 CLR 386.
64 See also *R v Howes* (1971) 2 SASR 293.
65 [1974] AC 104.
66 [1962] AC 220.
67 [1973] AC 435.

2.47   ***A-G (SPUC) v Open Door Counselling Limited***
[1988] IR 593; [1987] ILRM 477
High Court, 1986

Facts: The defendants advised pregnant women from a clinic in Dublin in relation
to their options on being pregnant. Abortion was one of the options open for
discussion in the course of this counselling. The defendants admitted that if a
pregnant woman wished to consider the abortion option further they would
arrange to refer her to a medical clinic in Great Britain for that purpose. The 8th
Amendment to the Constitution guaranteed the right to life of the unborn in the
following form in Article 40.3.3: "The State acknowledges the right to life of the
unborn and, with due regard to the equal right to life of the mother, guarantees in
its laws to respect, and, as far as practicable, by its laws to defend and vindicate
that right." The trial judge granted a declaration that the activities of the defendants were unlawful having regard to the provisions of this Article of the Constitution.

Hamilton P: . . . It is submitted on behalf of the Attorney General that the
admitted activities of the defendants, their servants or agents amount to a conspiracy to corrupt public morals. It was decided by the House of Lords in *Shaw v
Director of Public Prosecutions* [1962] AC 220 that conspiracy to corrupt public
morals is a common law misdemeanour and is indictable at common law.
    In the course of his judgment in *Knuller v Director of Public Prosecutions* [1973]
AC 45 Lord Morris stated at p 459 of the report that:

'[I]n the case of *Shaw v Director of Public Prosecutions*, it was clearly
recognised and affirmed that a conspiracy to corrupt public morals is a common
law misdemeanour which is indictable at common law."
    It is submitted on behalf of the defendants:

(1) that the Attorney General is not entitled to such a declaration, and
(2) that the admitted activities of the defendants cannot amount to a conspi-
    racy to corrupt public morals because what they are doing is engaging in
    non-directive counselling, referring and assisting pregnant women for
    further advice and dependent on that advice a termination of pregnancy
    which would not be a crime in the jurisdiction in which it is carried out if
    the requirements of section 1, sub-s 1 of the Abortion Act 1967, were
    complied with.

    It is submitted that the termination of a pregnancy is lawful in England and
Wales if the requirements of this Act are complied with and that it is unreasonable
and cannot be the law that they are guilty of an offence namely conspiracy to
corrupt public morals if they merely put pregnant woman, who have sought their
counselling and assistance, in touch with medical clinics in which the pregnancy
may be terminated in accordance with law.
    In *Knuller v Director of Public Prosecutions* [1973] AC 435 the House of Lords
considered a point of law which had been certified by the Court of Appeal as being
of general public importance. As appears from the judgment of Lord Morris at
p 459 of the report, the point of law was:

"Whether an agreement by two or more persons to insert advertisements in a
magazine, whereby adult male advertisers seek replies from other adult males
who are prepared to consent to commit homosexual acts with them in private, is
capable of amounting to the offence of conspiracy to corrupt public morals."
Having recited this point of law, he went on to say at p 460 that:

"It was contended on behalf of the appellants that, in view of the provisions of
s 1, sub-s 1 of the Sexual Offences Act 1967, no offence had in the present case
been committed. By that sub-section it is provided as follows:

'Notwithstanding any statutory or common law provision, but subject to the provisions of the next following section, a homosexual act in private shall not be an offence provided that the parties consent thereto and have attained the age of 21 years.'

It was submitted that where Parliament has altered the law so that certain sexual conduct which was formerly illegal becomes under certain circumstances no longer an offence there can be no commission of the offence of conspiring to corrupt public morals by the insertion of advertisements which only have in view such sexual conduct under the specified circumstances . . . In considering the submission which is made I propose to leave out of account any question whether some of the advertisements might be regarded as having been addressed to or might have been responded to by persons under the age of twenty-one years. The submission which is made is, I think, fallacious. What s 1 of the 1967 Act does is to provide that certain acts which previously were criminal offences should no longer be criminal offences. But that does not mean that it is not open to a jury to say that to assist or to encourage persons to take part in such acts may be to corrupt them. If by agreement it was arranged to insert advertisements by married people proclaiming themselves to be such and to be desirous of meeting someone of the opposite sex with a view to clandestine sexual association, would it be justification to say that adultery is not of itself a criminal offence? A person who, as a result of perusing the Ladies Directory, decided to resort to a prostitute was committing no legal offence; but it was open to a jury to hold that those who conspired to insert the advertisements did so with the intention of corrupting the morals of those who read the advertisements. So in the present case it was open to the jury to hold that there was an intention to corrupt; it was for the jury to decide whether the advertisements would induce readers of them to meet those who inserted the advertisements and to meet them for the purpose of the contemplated sexual practice; it was for the jury to decide whether readers would be or might be encouraged to indulge in such practices; it was for the jury to decide whether those conspiring together to insert the advertisements had the intent to debauch and corrupt the morals of the readers."

In the course of his judgment in the same case, Lord Reid stated at p 457 of the report that:

"I can now turn to the appellants' second argument. They say that homosexual acts between adult males in private are now lawful so it is unreasonable and cannot be the law that other persons are guilty of an offence if they merely put in touch with one another two males who wish to indulge in such acts. But there is a material difference between merely exempting certain conduct from criminal penalties and making it lawful in the full sense. Prostitution and gaming afford examples of this difference. So we must examine the provisions of the Sexual Offences Act 1967, to see just how far it altered the old law. It enacts subject to limitation that a homosexual act in private shall not be an offence but it goes no farther than that. Section 4 shows that procuring is still a serious offence and it would seem that some of the facts in this case might have supported a charge under that section.

I find nothing in the Act to indicate that Parliament thought or intended to lay down that indulgence in these practices is not corrupting. I read the Act as saying that, even though it may be corrupting, if people chose to corrupt themselves in this way that is their affair and the law will not interfere. But no licence is given to others to encourage the practice. So if one accepts *Shaw's* case as rightly decided it must be left to each jury to decide in the circumstances of each case whether people were likely to be corrupted."

This case is clear authority for the proposition that the offence of conspiracy to corrupt public morals may be committed even when the agreement between two or more persons is to assist in the commission of a lawful act.

The question which I have to consider is whether the admitted activities of the defendants, their servants or agents in counselling and referring pregnant women within the jurisdiction of this Honourable Court, to travel abroad to obtain an abortion or to obtain further advice on abortion within that foreign jurisdiction amounts to a conspiracy to corrupt public morals contrary to the common law.

While I am dealing with the defendants together, I am doing so for convenience sake as their admitted activities are similar and were I to deal with them separately, it could lead to unnecessary repetition. I do not consider that they conspire together to engage in their admitted activities and do not approach the consideration of this question on the basis that they did so.

At this stage, I should also make it clear that I consider that the two defendants are reputable organisations providing many and needed services to women, that their employees are skilled and concerned people and well-motivated with regard to the counselling and other services which they provide and consider necessary.

This is illustrated by the manner in which they have met this case; they have avoided unpleasant controversy by openly admitting the activities in which they are engaged and contend that such activities are lawful.

Consequently, a finding that such activities or conduct is liable to corrupt public morals is one not lightly to be reached.

Lord Simon of Glaisdale said at p 491 of the same case:

"The words 'corrupt public morals' suggest conduct which a jury might find to be destructive of the very fabric of society."

The fabric of our society is woven from the threads of the law and the Constitution and respect therefor is an essential component of our society.

As stated by the former Chief Justice in the course of his judgment in *Norris v The Attorney General* [1984] IR 36 at p 64 of the report:

"The preamble to the Constitution proudly asserts the existence of God in the Most Holy Trinity and recites that the people of Ireland humbly acknowledge their obligations to 'our Divine Lord, Jesus Christ'. It cannot be doubted that the people, so asserting and acknowledging their obligations to our Divine Lord, Jesus Christ, were proclaiming a deep religious conviction and faith and an intention to adopt a Constitution consistent with that conviction and faith and with Christian beliefs."

This is a view which which I respectfully agree.

Article 6, s 1 of the Constitution provides that:

"All powers of government, legislative, executive and judicial, derive, under God, from the people, whose right is to designate the rulers of the State and, in final appeal, to decide all questions of national policy, according to the requirements of the common good."

As late as 1983, the people enacted the Eighth Amendment to the Constitution. Consequently, there can be no doubt but that abortion, which is an interference with and destruction of the right to life of the unborn, is contrary to national policy, publc morality, contrary to law, both common law and statute law, to the fundamental right of the unborn and contrary to that right to life as acknowledged by the Eighth Amendment to the Constitution.

Both defendants, their servants or agents, know that a significant number of the pregnant women who sought their counselling and who were referred to a medical clinic in Great Britain would be contemplating an abortion. The action of the defendants in referring them to such clinics, after they had satisfied themselves that the said clinics operated at the highest standard, could amount to an assent to the pregnant women obtaining an abortion, if the conditions set forth in s 1, sub-s 1 of the Abortion Act 1967, were complied with and the abortion was legal, to the provision of assistance and encouragement to procure an abortion and an agreement with the pregnant woman to procure an abortion.

Such an agreement could constitute a conspiracy to corrupt public morals as the defendants' services are available to the public and well advertised. In a prosecution alleging a conspiracy to corrupt public morals, it would however be a matter for a jury to decide whether the activities of the defendants amounted to a conspiracy to corrupt public morals and whether in fact public morals were corrupted.

The declaration sought by the plaintiff is that the defendants, their servants or agents are engaged in a criminal conspiracy to corrupt public morals and this court should, as stated by Mr Justice Woolf in *Attorney General v Able* [1984] QB 795 at p 808 of the report – "should bear in mind the danger of usurping the jurisdiction of the criminal courts."

He further stated at p 808 that:

> "[I]t would only be proper to grant a declaration if it is clearly established that there is no risk of it treating conduct as criminal which is not clearly in contravention of the criminal law."

As already stated, conspiracy to corrupt public morals is a common law misdemeanour which is indictable at common law.

Article 38, s 1 of the Constitution provides that:

> "No person shall be tried on any criminal charge save in due course of law."

Indictable offences are tried by a judge and jury.

When a case turns on public morals or standards, the question is for the jury though of course the judge rules whether there is evidence upon which they can find the case proved.

Lord Reid stated in *Knuller v Director of Public Prosecutions* [1973] AC 435 at p 457 that:

> "[I]t must be left to each jury to decide in the circumstances of each case whether people were likely to be corrupted."

That being so, I am not satisfied that there is no risk in my treating conduct as criminal when a jury might consider otherwise. Consequently, the plaintiff is not entitled to this declaration.

The judgment was appealed to the Supreme Court which did not deal with this issue.

2.48   *R v Cahill & Others*
                              (1978) 22 ALR 361
                      Court of Appeal New South Wales, 1978

Facts: Three Australian women agreed to marry three immigrants in order to diminish the chance of their being deported from Australia. The first marriage took place but the other two were stopped by the police. The plan was to proceed with the ceremonies but not to consummate the marriages which were later to be dissolved. Nonetheless, such amounted to a valid and effective marriage and involved no deception or misrepresentation. A complete discretion vested in the Minister for Immigration and Ethnic Affairs under the Migration Act 1985 to deport or allow the men to stay in Australia. The men and women involved were charged with a conspiracy to prevent the enforcement of a law of the Commonwealth. The prosecution argument was that the general law of conspiracy was applicable and that if the jury found that the agreement between the accused contemplated conduct so offensive to public morality that it could be said to be unlawful then they were entitled to convict because of that unlawful means. The trial judge stated a case.

Street CJ: It has always been permissible in many fields so to order one's affairs as to avoid attracting the operation of a law, whether it be a law of the Commonwealth or a law of the State. Equally, it has always been permissible to bring about circumstances which will create a climate favourable to the person concerned in respect of a statutory discretion which might be exercised for or against his interests. It is not necessary to canvass the many areas where such planning and action is both commonplace and legitimate, but the revenue field comes at once to mind. For these reasons I would regard the present convictions as unfounded.

The Crown contends, however, that the decision of the Court of Criminal Appeal in *R v Corak* (unreported, 24 November 1967) is a sufficient basis to sustain the present convictions. The appellant in that case had been charged with a conspiracy in similar terms to that charged against the present appellants. The agreement proved by the Crown in that case was "to bring into existence a series of marriages, which can only be called shams, to prevent the Act being applied to" a number of prohibited Chinese immigrants. It was held that the evidence called in support of the Crown case could in law establish a conspiracy to prevent the enforcement of the *Immigration Act* and the appeal against the conviction was dismissed.

There were many points of similarity between the Crown case against the present appellants and the Crown case against the appellant in *R v Corak*. There were also, however, points of distinction inasmuch as misleading statements had been made to immigration officials in connection with the marriages and some of them were in fact bigamous. In the course of the reasons of the Court of Criminal Appeal the nature of the Crown case was stated as: ". . . his Honour dealt with the question of arranging lawful marriages, and says that it is not the matter of the charge here but it is the question of telling lies about it, misleading the officers and so forth".

I should like to reserve for further consideration, if the point should ever arise, whether active misrepresentations in a context similar to the present facts should lead to a conviction of an offence charged in the terms of the present indictment. The question does not arise in this case as there is here no suggestion of any active misrepresentation. *R v Corak* is accordingly to be distinguished.

I have thus far stated my reasons that have led me to the conclusion that the present convictions cannot stand. The matter comes before this court, however, in the form of a stated case. The specific question set down in the stated case for determination by this court is whether the ruling set out in para 4(b) of the stated case was erroneous in point of law. The ruling as recorded in para 4(b) is in the following terms:

4 On such application I held that: . . .
(b) That there was evidence fit to go to the jury as to whether the agreement between the accused contemplated conduct so offensive to public morality that it could be said to be unlawful and if the jury did so find it to be unlawful the jury would be entitled to convict the accused on the first count of the indictment in that they had conspired together to achieve an unlawful object by lawful means.

As Judge Thorley has specifically submitted to this court a question touching upon the morality of the agreement, I should briefly indicate my views upon that aspect. In so doing, however, it is neither necessary nor desirable to undertake a wide ranging analysis of this aspect.

There was much attention directed during the course of evidence and in submissions both to the trial judge and to this court on appeal to the relevance of the fact that the sole purpose of the marriage was to enhance the prospect of the male appellants enjoying a favourable exercise by the Minister of his discretion in relation to the ordering of their deportation. It was open to the jury on the evidence to conclude that there was no common intention to consummate the marriages and that although each respective couple would share a household for a limited period, with some attendant financial advantage to the female appellants, the marriages would be dissolved by divorce once the male appellants were assured of their prospects of remaining in Australia. The Crown's contention was summarised in the summing-up as being that the conduct of the appellants "would have been morally repugnant to the community; that is, the institution of marriage was not designed for that purpose and you would stamp your disapproval of that conduct by finding that it was an unlawful agreement to involve themselves in that form of action".

I fail to see what justification there is for the criminal law thus seeking to lift what might be described, borrowing from another field, as the bridal veil. The law prescribes in considerable detail the formal requirements which must be met in order to achieve the change of status consequent upon two persons marrying. The law regulates the marriage relationship in well recognised aspects both during its currency as well as in making provision for its termination. Active misrepresentations regarding a marriage, or for that matter active misrepresentations regarding anything else, are capable of giving rise in appropriate circumstances to criminal as well as civil liability. But there were present here no active misrepresentations. The Crown's case involved an assertion that, over and above the relevant statutory provisions, the criminal law has a legitimate concern with what was described as the purpose for which the institution of marriage was designed. This postulates some recognition of a moral significance of the institution of marriage superadded to its legally prescribed significance. The moral repugnancy suggested in this case is that the intentions of the appellants involved a repudiation of this moral significance.

I do not for one moment disregard, or minimise the importance within the community of, the teachings of the various churches and other groups in connection with the moral significance of the marriage relationship. The moral fibre of our society is dependent to no small extent upon the codes of conduct and personal standards required of their adherents by the great religions. But these religious or moral requirements are matters of individual conscience, varying, as they do, from church to church and from group to group. We do not, in Australia have an established church, as there is an England. The contribution made to the common law by the Ecclesiastical Courts in England and the history of the jurisdictional struggles between those courts and the Royal Courts where questions in religion or morality arose were discussed in *R v Knuller (Publishing, Printing and Promotions) Ltd* [1973] AC 435. The extent to which common law doctrines in this field may have been affected by the *Act of Settlement* and the existence in England of an established church raises questions of extreme difficulty and I do not intend to stray into this field. It is, however, clear that religious precepts do not in this country affect the application of the ordinary criminal law unless and until such precepts and expression through a validly made law of the Commonwealth or the State. Freedom of religion means not merely freedom of the individual to choose which religion he or she will embrace or to reject religion in its entirety. It imports, also, the necessity to take care lest religious precepts enter into the administration, in particular, of the criminal law. The criminal courts are secular, and it is only by giving full significance to this that the criminal law can operate fairly across all members of the community, no matter what may be the particular religious persuasion, if any, of each individual Australian. The concomitants of what is described as the institution of marriage vary from one religion to another, and it is not only impermissible, but dangerous, when administering the criminal law, to travel beyond the strict letter of the statute law governing the marriage relationship. If it were otherwise the outcome of a criminal trial could be affected by the varying religious convictions of the persons who happen to constitute the jury. In

R v Bailey [1956] NI 15 at 22, Lord MacDermott CJ voiced a warning in respect of another aspect of the law of criminal conspiracy which is apposite in relation to a conspiracy such as the Crown seeks to establish in this case. His Lordship said that to recognise as indictable crimes all acts or attempts which tended to the prejudice of the community would bring about the result that: ". . . not only would one wide field of the criminal law lose all claim to certainty, but the guilt or innocence of persons charged within it could, to an unwholesome degree, depend upon the personal views or prejudices of those constituting the tribunal appointed for their trial."

It was not, in my view, open to the Crown in the present case to invite the jury to convict these appellants upon an opinion that the actual or contemplated marriages, although perfectly valid and effective at law, and although not associated with any deceptions or misrepresentations, were morally repugnant.

Quite apart from matters of religious teaching, it is known that marriages are at times contracted for reasons falling short of the more generally recognised purposes of entering into that relationship. In England in bygone days there were instances of celibate marriages being contracted for the purpose of affecting rights of inheritance of titles. The same situation exists both here and elsewhere in relation to marriages affecting rights of property succession. At times marriages were or are entered into in connection with legitimation of existing or imminent issues of a since-terminated intimate relationship. The purposes and motives, equally as the hopes and anticipations, affecting two peope when they enter into a marriage, are susceptible of too wide a variation to render it possible for the criminal law to classify some as offending and the others as according with what is meaninglessly described as "community expectation" in so far as this may travel beyond the specifically prescribed concomitants of a marriage.

I consider that, for the reasons I have indicated earlier in this judgment, the appellants are entitled to have orders made in their favour of the terms proposed by Reynolds JA. Even if the Crown were able to surmount this difficulty, I would remain of the view that the charges against the present appellants were ill-founded in that, in answer to the specific question asked, I do not regard the agreement between the accused as contemplating conduct so offensive to public morality that it could be said to be unlawful.

Concurring judgments were delivered by Reynolds and Mahoney JJ.

Mental Element

2.49   It is difficult to envisage a conspiracy where the parties do not intend both to agree and to carry-out the object of their agreement. Such is the mental element suggested for conspiracy by *R v Stuart*[68], relying on *R v O'Brien*[69]. Similar arguments can be advanced here, in line with those on the law of attempt, that intention is required in respect of offences capable of being committed by recklessness, or those of strict or absolute responsibility. The question has lacked rigorous analysis and as we have seen, the courts, by relying on "chain" and "wheel" conspiracies, would seem to have indicated a kind of mental element which is less than intent in relation to the role or identity of the other participants.

In *R v Porter* the mental element was briefly discussed in the context of an accused charged with various conspiracies in relation to the possession of explosives and firearms and of making available to terrorists material which

68 Canadian Criminal Law (2nd edn 1987) p 578.
69 (1954) 110 CCC 1.

would be likely to be useful in carrying out acts of terrorism. The accused made a statement indicating that he had picked up a parcel at the behest of a member of the UVF.

2.50   *R v Porter*
                                      [1980] NI 18
                         Court of Appeal Northern Ireland, 1980

Lowry LCJ: . . . The offence of conspiracy was complete at the end of the telephone call, and that is the time at which one must judge the existence of consensus and the state of the appellant's mind and knowledge, but the fact that the parcel in which the appellant later took such a close interest contained, among other things, two pistols should not be overlooked.

In further considering what is meant by knowledge, one may refer to the statement of Lord Reid in *Southern Cement Ltd v Cooper* [1974] AC 623 where he said (at p 638G):

> "In many branches of the law, civil and criminal, it is now well established that a man who deliberately shuts his eyes to the truth will not be heard to say that he did not know."

In *Davies, Turner & Co Ltd v Brodie* [1954] 3 All ER 283 Lord Goddard CJ said (at p 286B):

> "I only repeat what I said with the assent of the other members of the Court in *Johnson v Youden* [1950] 1 All ER at p 302 that:
>
> > 'A person cannot be convicted of aiding and abetting the commission of an offence if he does not know of the essential matters which would constitute the offence.'
>
> If a person shuts his eyes to the obvious or, perhaps, refrains from making any inquiry where a reasonably sensible man would make inquiry, I think the court can find that he was aiding and abetting."

I might also refer to my comment in *R v Maxwell* [1978] NI 42 at 54C:

> "*Johnson v Youden* is merely one example of many cases in which the distinction is between knowledge and ignorance of facts which constitute a criminal offence."

It is unnecessary on the facts of the present case, to decide how far the "blank cheque" principle discussed in *Maxwell's* case might extend in the field of conspiracy, because the learned trial judge made no attempt to saddle the appellant with any responsibility in relation to the explosives found in the parcel which was taken to Drumbo. It is enough to say that he was proved, to the satisfaction of the tribunal of fact, to have sufficient knowledge of the essential matters of the offences that he was accused in counts 1 and 4 of conspiring to commit.

Merger

2.51 There seems to be no authorities to support the idea that where a conspiracy is fulfilled by the achievement of its object it is subsumed in the substantive offence. The arguments against such a principle are even stronger than on the law of attempt. The objective of conspiracy is to bring within the criminal net those concerned in the perpetration of a crime, but who have sought to limit their vulnerability by furthering their purpose through the hands of others. It is a singularly unattractive argument that persons who have behaved in a manner consistent only with an intention of furthering an unlawful act should escape liability because of the success of those with whom they acted in fulfilling that objective.

Advantage to the Prosecution

2.52 It is a rule of the law of evidence that the actions and statements of a conspirator done or made in pursuance of the conspiracy are admissible against his co-conspirators. This is an exception to the general rule that an act or statement by an accused is only admissible against a co-accused if done or said in his presence. The rule would appear to work to the advantage of the prosecution. Joinder of a conspiracy count, where two or more accused are being charged with the substantive offence, would appear therefore to operate gravely to the prejudice of the accused. Traditionally, the courts have indicated that the prosecution should first establish a *prima facie* case of conspiracy and identify the conspirators, after which evidence of acts and declarations of each in the course of its execution are admissible against all; *Krulewitch v US*[70]. In *The People (A-G) v Keane*[71], the Court of Criminal Appeal indicated that charges of conspiracy ought not, in practice, to be laid when the substantive offence can be proved.

In a recent case concerning extradition, *Ellis v O'Dea and D J Sheils*[72] Walsh J not only reiterated this view but went on to question the constitutionality of the special rules of evidence which apply to conspiracy trials:

> One of the charges laid in the present case is that of conspiracy. It is accompanied by a charge relating to the substantiative offence. For many years judicial authorities have condemned the joinder of a conspiracy charge when there is a charge for the substantive offence. Whatever justification may exist in certain cases for preferring a charge of an inchoate crime, such as that it may prevent substantive crime from being committed, it is difficult to see what, if any, justification can exist in justice for adding as a count where the substantive offence is charged. To adopt it as a policy is, to say the least, very dubious. Because of the wide ambit and the elasticity of the offence it can operate most oppressively. Naturally the advantage to the prosecutor of such a charge is that it widens the evidence which may be introduced and permits the introduction of evidence which would be totally inadmissible against the accused person tried on the substantive charge, whether he was tried with another person or alone. The special rules of evidence which apply to conspiracy have, in the light of experience, demonstrated that it is not always desirable in the interest of justice to have such a charge. It can, for example, result in wholly innocent persons being convicted on the untrue "admissions" of a co-accused. Thus, if the courts of this country should at some future time decide that these special rules of evidence were such as to fall foul of the constitutional guarantees of fair procedures it is obvious that no court here could extradite a person from the protection of this jurisdiction to another where such protection would not be enjoyed.

Inconsistent Verdict

2.53 Where A and B are charged with conspiring with C the acquittal of C is not necessarily determinative of the non-involvement of A and B. The

70 (1949) 336 US 440, 453.
71 (1975) 1 Frewen 392.
72 [1989] IR 530 at p 538.

conviction of a conspirator, whether tried together with, or separately from, an alleged co-conspirator, may stand notwithstanding that the latter is or may be acquitted, unless in all the circumstances of the case his conviction is inconsistent with the acquittal of the other person. Such a determination focuses upon the justice of the case rather than the technical obscurities with which the subject can be confounded; *R v Darby*[73] following *DPP v Shannon*[74]. The rule is necessary because a jury may accept a case proven against conspirator A or B but have a reasonable doubt in relation to conspirator C.

Code Options

2.54 *Model Penal Code*

Section 5.03 Criminal conspiracy

(1) *Definition of Conspiracy.* A person is guilty of conspiracy with another person or persons to commit a crime if with the purpose of promoting or facilitating its commission he:

(a) agrees with such other person or persons that they or one or more of them will engage in conduct that constitutes such crime or an attempt or solicitation to commit such crime; or

(b) agrees to aid such other person or persons in the planning or commission of such crime or of an attempt or solicitation to commit such crime.

(2) *Scope of Conspiratorial Relationship.* If a person guilty of conspiracy, as defined by subsection (1) of this section, knows that a person with whom he conspires to commit a crime has conspired with another person or persons to commit the same crime, he is guilty of conspiring with such other person or persons, whether or not he knows their identity, to commit such crime.

(3) *Conspiracy with Multiple Criminal Objectives.* If a person conspires to commit a number of crimes, he is guilty of only one conspiracy so long as such multiple crimes are the object of the same agreement or continuous conspiratorial relationship.

(4) *Joinder and Venue in Conspiracy Prosecutions.*

(a) Subject to the provisions of paragraph (b) of this subsection, two or more persons charged with criminal conspiracy may be prosecuted jointly if:

(i) they are charged with conspiring with another; or

(ii) the conspiracies alleged, whether they have the same or different parties, are so related that they constitute different aspects of a scheme of organized criminal conduct.

(b) In any joint prosecution under paragraph (a) of this subsection:

(i) no defendant shall be charged with a conspiracy in any county [parish or district] other than one in which he entered into such conspiracy or in which an overt act pursuant to such conspiracy was done by him or by a person with whom he conspired; and

(ii) neither the liability of any defendant nor the admissibility against him of evidence or acts or declarations of another shall be enlarged by such joinder; and

73 (1982) 40 LAR 594.
74 [1975] AC 717.

(iii) the court shall order a severance or take a special verdict as to any defendant who so requests, if it deems it necessary or appropriate to promote the fair determination of his guilt or innocence, and shall take any other proper measures to protect the fairness of the trial.

(5) *Overt Act.* No person may be convicted of conspiracy to commit a crime, other than a felony of the first or second degree, unless an overt act in pursuance of such conspiracy is alleged and proved to have been done by him or by a person with whom he conspired.

(6) *Renunciation of Criminal Purpose.* It is an affirmative defense that the actor, after conspiring to commit a crime, thwarted the success of the conspiracy, under circumstances manifesting a complete and voluntary renunciation of his criminal purpose.

(7) *Duration of Conspiracy.* For the purposes of section 1.06(4):

(a) conspiracy is a continuing course of conduct that terminates when the crime or crimes that are its object are committed or the agreement that they be committed is abandoned by the defendant and by those with whom he conspired; and

(b) such abandonment is presumed if neither the defendant nor anyone with whom he conspired does any overt act in pursuance of the conspiracy during the applicable period of limitation; and

(c) if an individual abandons the agreement, the conspiracy is terminated as to him only if and when he advises those with whom he conspired of his abandonment or he informs the law enforcement authorities of the existence of the conspiracy and of his participation therein.

Further Materials

2.55 Goode *Criminal Conspiracy in Canada* (1975).
Law Commission (UK) Report No 76: *Criminal Law: Report on Conspiracy and Criminal Law Reform* (H.C. 176) 1976.
Criminal Law Act 1977 (United Kingdom) discussed by Smith [1977] Crim LR 598, 638.
Hunt *Evidentary Rules Peculiar to Conspiracy Cases* (1974) 16 CLQ 307.
Dennis *The Rationale of Criminal Conspiracy* (1977) 93 LQR 39.
Wechsler, Jones & Korn *The Treatment of Inchoate Crimes in the Model Penal Code of the American Law Institute: Criminal Conspiracy* (1961) 61 Columbia LR 657.
Orchard *"Agreement" in Criminal Conspiracy* [1974] Crim LR 297–335.
Lanham – *Complicity, Concert and Conspiracy* (1980) 4 Crim LJ 276.

Incitement

2.56 It is a common law misdemeanour to incite another to commit a crime. This may be done by persuasion or by intimidation. The essence of the crime lies in the mere incitement: it is not necessary that the person approached proceed to commit the crime; *The People (A-G) v Capaldi*[75]. If that person proceeds to commit the offence then the accused will be guilty as a party to the crime[76].

---

75 (1949) 1 Frewen 95.
76 See chapter 3.

2.57 The accused must intend to bring about the criminal result in question and he must know of all the circumstances of the act incited which constitutes the elements of the crime; *R v Whybrow*[77]. In addition the accused must believe that the person possesses the necessary mental element to commit the crime in question. In other words, the accused must be inciting his agent to commit a crime and not simply to cause the external elements of a crime without its accompanying mental element; *R v Curr*[78]. Equally, the person incited must be one who is capable of committing the crime and not, for example, in the category of persons which the crime is designed to protect by declaring them to be victims; *R v Whitehouse*[79].

2.58 *The Prohibition of Incitement to Hatred Act 1989*

1 Interpretation

(1) In this Act—

"broadcast" means the transmission, relaying or distribution by wireless telegraphy or by any other means or by wireless telegraphy in conjunction with any other means of communications, sounds, signs, visual images or signals, intended for direct reception by the general public whether such communications, sounds, signs, visual images or signals are actually received or not;

"distribute" means distribute to the public or a section of the public and cognate words shall be construed accordingly;

"hatred" means hatred against a group of persons in the State or elsewhere on account of their race, colour, nationality, religion, ethnic or national origins, membership of the travelling community or sexual orientation;

"publish" means publish to the public or a section of the public and cognate words shall be construed accordingly;

"recording" means any record from which visual images or sounds may, by any means, be reproduced, and references to the distribution, showing or playing of a recording are to its distribution, showing or playing to the public or a section of the public and "distribute", "show" and "play", and cognate words, in relation to a recording, shall be construed accordingly;

"written material" includes any sign or other visual representation.

(2) In this Act—

(*a*) a reference to any enactment shall, unless the context otherwise requires, be construed as a reference to that enactment as amended or extended by any subsequent enactment,

(*b*) a reference to a section is a reference to a section of this Act unless it is indicated that reference to some other enactment is intended.

(*c*) a reference to a subsection or paragraph is a reference to the subsection or paragraph of the provision in which the reference occurs unless it is indicated that reference to some other provision is intended.

2 Actions likely to stir up hatred

(1) It shall be an offence for a person—

(*a*) to publish or distribute written material,

(*b*) to use words, behave or display written material—

---

77 (1951) 35 Cr App R 141.
78 [1968] 2 QB 944.
79 (1977) 65 Cr App R 33.

(i) in any place other than inside a private residence, or
(ii) inside a private residence so that the words, behaviour or material are heard or seen by persons outside the residence,

or

(c) to distribute, show or play a recording of visual images or sounds,

if the written material, words, behaviour, visual images or sounds, as the case may be, are threatening, abusive or insulting and are intended or, having regard to all the circumstances, are likely to stir up hatred.

(2) (a) In proceedings for an offence under *subsection (1),* if the accused person is not shown to have intended to stir up hatred, it shall be a defence for him to prove that he was not aware of the content of the material or recording concerned and did not suspect, and had no reason to suspect, that the material or recording was threatening, abusive or insulting.

(b) In proceedings for an offence under *subsection (1)(b),* it shall be a defence for the accused person—

(i) to prove that he was inside a private residence at the relevant time and had no reason to believe that the words, behaviour or material concerned would be heard or seen by a person outside the residence, or

(ii) if he is not shown to have intended to stir up hatred, to prove that he did not intend the words, behaviour or material concerned to be, and was not aware that they might be, threatening, abusive or insulting.

(3) In this section "private residence" means any structure (including a tent, caravan, vehicle, vessel or other temporary or moveable structure) or part of such a structure used as a dwelling but does not include any part not so used or any part of which a public meeting is being held; and in this definition "public meeting" means a meeting at which the public are entitled to be present, on payment or otherwise and as of right or by virtue of an express or implied permission.

3 Broadcasts likely to stir up hatred

(1) If an item involving threatening, abusive or insulting visual images or sounds is broadcast, each of the persons mentioned in *subsection (2)* is guilty of an offence if he intends thereby to stir up hatred or, having regard to all the circumstances, hatred is likely to be stirred up thereby.

(2) The persons referred to in *subsection (1)* are:

(a) the person providing the broadcasting service concerned,
(b) any person by whom the item concerned is produced or directed, and
(c) any person whose words or behaviour in the item concerned are threatening, abusive or insulting.

(3) In proceedings against a person referred to in *paragraph (a)* or *(b)* of *subsection (2)* for an offence under this section, if the person is not shown to have intended to stir up hatred, it is a defence for him to prove—

(a) that he did not know and had no reason to suspect that the item concerned would involve the material to which the offence relates, or
(b) in a case other than one to which *paragraph (a)* relates, that, having regard to the circumstances in which the item was broadcast, it was not reasonably practicable for him to secure the removal of the material aforesaid.

(4) In proceedings against a person referred to in *subsection (2)(b)* for an offence under this section, it is a defence for the person to prove that he did not know and had no reason to suspect—

(a) that the item would be broadcast, or

(*b*) that the circumstances in which the item would be broadcast would be such that hatred would be likely to be stirred up.

(5) In proceedings against a person referred to in *subsection (2)(c)* for an offence under this section, it is a defence for the person to prove that he did not know and had no reason to suspect—

(*a*) that an item involving the use of the material to which the offence relates would be broadcast, or

(*b*) that the circumstances in which such an item would be broadcast would be such that hatred would be likely to be stirred up.

(6) In proceedings for an offence under this section, it is a defence for the person charged to prove that he did not know, and had no reason to suspect, that the material to which the offence relates was threatening, abusive or insulting.

(7) In any proceedings for an offence under this section alleged to have been committed in respect of an item—

(*a*) a script on which the item was based shall be evidence of what was included in the item and of the manner in which the item or any part of it was performed, and

(*b*) if such a script is given in evidence on behalf of any party to the proceedings, then, except in so far as the contrary is shown, whether by evidence given on behalf of the same or any other party, the item shall be taken to have been performed in accordance with that script.

(8) (*a*) If a member of the Garda Síochána not below the rank of a superintendent has reasonable grounds for suspecting—

(i) that an offence under this section has been committed by a person in respect of an item included in a broadcast, or

(ii) that an item is to be so included and that an offence under this section is likely to be committed by a person in respect of the item,

he may make an order in writing under this section authorising any member of the Garda Síochána—

(I) at any time or times within one month from the date of the making of the order, on production if so requested of a copy of the order, to require any person named in the order to produce, if such a thing exists—

(A) a script on which the item aforesaid was or, as the case may be, will be based, or

(B) a recording of any matter which was or, as the case may be, will be included in the item,

and

(II) if the script or recording is produced to him, to require the person to afford him an opportunity of causing a copy thereof to be made.

(*b*) An order under this subsection shall be signed by the person by whom it is made, shall name the person to whom it is directed and shall describe the item to which it relates in a manner sufficient to enable the item to be identified.

(*c*) Any person who without reasonable excuse fails or refuses to comply with a requirement made pursuant to an order under *paragraph (a)* shall be guilty of an offence.

(*d*) Where, in the case of an item based on a script, a copy of a script on which the item was based has been made by or on behalf of a member of the Garda Síochána by virtue of an order under this subsection relating to the item, *subsection* (7) shall apply in relation to that copy as it applies in relation to a script on which the item was based; and a document purporting to be a copy of the script and to be signed by the member shall be deemed, for the purposes of this section, to be such a copy and to be so signed unless the contrary is shown.

(*e*) Nothing done under this subsection or in pursuance of an order under this subsection or the use of a script or recording such as aforesaid or a copy thereof exclusively for the purposes of the enforcement of this section shall constitute—

    (i) an infringement of the copyright of any work, sound recording, cinematograph film or television or sound broadcast, or

    (ii) an offence under any of the provisions of the Performers' Protection Act, 1968.

(9) In this section "script", in relation to an item, means the text of the item (whether expressed in words or in musical or other notation) together with any directions for its performance, whether contained in a single document or not.

4 Preparation and possession of material likely to stir up hatred

(1) It shall be an offence for a person—

(*a*) to prepare or be in possession of any written material with a view to its being distributed, displayed, broadcast or otherwise published, in the State or elsewhere, whether by himself or another, or

(*b*) to make or be in possession of a recording of sounds or visual images with a view to its being distributed, shown, played, broadcast or otherwise published, in the State or elsewhere, whether by himself or another,

if the material or recording is threatening, abusive or insulting and is intended or, having regard to all the circumstances, including such distribution, display, broadcasting, showing, playing or other publication thereof as the person has, or it may reasonably be inferred that he has, in view, is likely to stir up hatred.

(2) In proceedings for an offence under this section, if the accused person is not shown to have intended to stir up hatred, it shall be a defence for him to prove that he was not aware of the content of the material or recording concerned and did not suspect, and had no reason to suspect, that the material or recording was threatening, abusive or insulting.

(3) In proceedings for an offence under this section, where it is proved that the accused person was in possession of material or a recording such as is referred to in *subsection (1)* and it is reasonable to assume that the material or recording was not intended for the personal use of the person, he shall be presumed, until the contrary is proved, to have been in possession of the material or recording in contravention of *subsection (1)*.

5 Savings for reports of proceedings in Houses of Oireachtas or judicial proceedings

(*a*) a fair and accurate report of proceedings in either House of the Oireachtas or a committee of the Oireachtas or of either such House or an official report or publication of the Oireachtas or either such House or such a committee, or

(*b*) a fair and accurate report of proceedings publicly heard before a court, or a tribunal exercising functions or powers of a judicial nature, where the report is publisehd contemporaneously with the proceedings or, if it is not a reasonably practicable or would be unlawful to publish a report of them contemporaneously, as soon as publication is reasonably practicable and lawful.

6 Penalties

A person guilty of an offence under *section 2, 3* or *4* shall be liable—

(*a*) on summary conviction, to a fine not exceeding £1,000 or to imprisonment for a term not exceeding 6 months or to both, or

(*b*) on conviction on indictment, to a fine not exceeding £10,000 or to imprisonment for a term not exceeding 2 years or to both.

7 Offences by bodies corporate

(1) Where an offence under this Act has been committed by a body corporate and is proved to have been committed with the consent or connivance of or to be attributable to any neglect on the part of a person being a director, manager, secretary or other similar officer of the body corporate, or a person who was purporting to act in any such capacity, that person as well as the body corporate shall be guilty of an offence and shall be liable to be proceeded against and punished as if he were guilty of the first-mentioned offence.

(2) Where the affairs of a body corporate are managed by its members, *subsection (1)* shall apply in relation to the acts and defaults of a member in connection with his functions of management as if he were a director of the body corporate.

8 Certain proceedings only by or with consent of Director of Public Prosecutions

Where a person is charged with an offence under *section 2, 3* or *4*, no further proceedings in the matter (other than any remand in custody or on bail) shall be taken except by or with the consent of the Director of Public Prosecutions.

9 Search and seizure

(1)(*a*) If a justice of the District Court or a Peace Commissioner is satisfied on the worn information of a member of the Garda Síochána not below the rank of sergeant that there are reasonable grounds for suspecting that material or a recording the possession of which would be in contravention of *section 4* or a script or recording referred to in *section 3(8)* is in or at any premises or other place, he may issue a warrant under his hand authorising any member of the Garda Síochána, accompanied by any other members of the Garda Síochána, at any time or times within one month from the date of the issue of the warrant, on production if so requested of the warrant, to enter, if need be by force, and search the premises or other place specified in the warrant and—

(i) to seize any such recording, material or script as aforesaid found there, and

(ii) to require any person found there to give him his name and address.

(*b*) A justice of the District Court or a Peace Commissioner shall not issue a warrant under *paragraph (a)* in relation to a script or recording referred to in *section 3(8)* unless he is satisfied by information on oath—

(i) that a requirement specified in *subparagraph (1)* of *section 3(8)(a)* was made in relation to it and was not complied with,

(ii) that the requirement specified in *subparagraph (II)* of *section 3(8)(a)* was made in relation to it and was not complied with, or

(iii) that, in all the circumstances, it is necessary to issue the warrant notwithstanding that a requirement specified in the said *subparagraph (I)* or that specified in the said *subparagraph (II)* was not made in relation to it.

(2) A person who—

(*a*) obstructs or interferes with a member of the Garda Síochána acting under the authority of a warrant under this section, or

(*b*) is found in or at the premises or other place specified in the warrant by a member of the Garda Síochána acting as aforesaid and who fails or refuses to give the member his name and address when required by the member to do so or gives him a name or address that is false or misleading,

shall be guilty of an offence and shall be liable on summary conviction—

(i) if the offence is under *paragraph (a)*, to a fine not exceeding £1,000 or to imprisonment for a term not exceeding 6 months or to both, or

(ii) if the offence is under *paragraph (b)*, to a fine not exceeding £500.

(3) In this section "premises" includes a vehicle, vessel, aircraft or hovercraft or an installation in the territorial seas or in a designated area (within the meaning of the Continental Shelf Act, 1968) or a tent, caravan or other temporary or moveable structure; and a vessel or hovercraft or such an installation as aforesaid may be treated, for the purposes of the jurisdiction of a justice of the District Court under this section, as being in any place in the State.

10 Powers of arrest

(1) If a member of the Garda Síochána reasonably suspects that a person has committed an offence under *section 2(1)(b)*, he may arrest him without warrant.

(2) If a member of the Garda Síochána reasonably suspects that a person has committed an offence under this Act (other than an offence under *section 2(1)(b)* or *9(2)(b))*, he may require him to give him his name and address and, if the person fails or refuses to do so or gives a name or address that the member reasonably suspects to be false or misleading, the member may arrest him without warrant.

(3) A member of the Garda Síochána acting under the authority of a warrant under *section 9* may arrest without warrant a person whom the member reasonably suspects of having committed an offence under *subsection (2)(b)* of that section.

11 Forfeiture

(1) The court by or before which a person is convicted of an offence under *section 2, 3 or 4* may order any written material or recording shown to the satisfaction of the court to relate to the offence to be forfeited and either destroyed or otherwise disposed of in such manner as the court may determine.

(2) A court shall not order written material or a recording to be forfeited under this section if a person claiming to be the owner of it or otherwise interested in it applies to be heard by the court, unless an opportunity has been given to him to show cause why the order should not be made.

(3) An order under this section shall not take effect until the ordinary time for instituting an appeal against the conviction or order concerned has expired or, where such an appeal is instituted, until it or any further appeal is finally decided or abandoned or the ordinary time for instituting any further appeal has expired.

12 Short title and commencement

(1) This Act may be cited as the Prohibition of Incitement to Hatred Act, 1989.

(2) This Act shall come into operation one month after the date of its passing.

2.59   ***The People (A-G) v Sabatino Capaldi***
(1949) 1 Frewen 95
Court of Criminal Appeal, 1949

Facts: The facts appear in the judgment of the court below.

Black J: This appeal, as eventually presented to the Court, resolves itself into a very net single question, namely, whether certain words and conduct imputed to the appellant, and not denied by him, amounted to an incitement to the commission of the crime of bringing about an abortion.

The conduct and words in question were as follows:

The appellant, referring to a girl who had been brought by him to a doctor and was found to be pregnant, asked the doctor "to do something for her". The doctor, understanding that he was being requested to bring about an abortion, at once said to the appellant "do you realize what you are asking me to do, you are asking me to perform an illegal operation". To this the appellant replied "Yes. Would you operate; there is ample money to meet your fees". Thereupon, the doctor, in his own words, showed the appellant to the door.

Mr Casey for the appellant contended that the conduct and words in question did not amount to an incitement in law, but only to an expression of a desire, and further that in any event the trial judge did not properly instruct the jury as to the nature of an incitement or adequately explain to them the distinction between a mere expression of a desire and an incitement in the legal sense of that word. He relied for this upon several authorities, but most of all, we think, upon *R v Landow* 29 TLR 375. In that case the appellant had been convicted of an attempt to procure his wife to become an inmate of a brothel. The conviction was quashed on the ground that the Recorder had failed to explain to the jury the difference between an attempt and an intention or a mere idle threat. The accused then had certainly indicated a desire that his wife should do what he was accused of attempting to procure her to do, and the Court recognised that the mere indication of his desire would not be sufficient. This was, of course, no new view of the law. It had been laid down as far back as the year 1801 in *R v Higgins* 2 East 5 where Le Blanc J said "It is contended that the offence charged is no misdemeanour because it amounts only to a bare wish or desire of the mind to do an illegal act. If that were so, I agree that it would be indictable". He added, however, "But this is a charge of an act done, namely, an actual solicitation of a servant to rob his masters, and not merely a wish or desire that he should do so".

Mr Casey contended in the present case that the alleged incitement must involve what he called "an effort to overcome the reluctant mind". He did not refer to any authority for this particular proposition. But the Court is of opinion that a person may truly incite another to commit a crime by the action of stirring up enmity in his mind against another, or by offering him some pecuniary or other inducement. Such action would be an incitement if, but for it, it would not have occurred to the party incited to commit the crime, whether he had any particular reluctance to commit it or not.

In this case, however, if the uncontradicted evidence of Dr Nightingale is accepted, as the verdict of the jury indicates that it must have been, the doctor was distinctly reluctant to comply with the appellant's request. His conduct showed this and she made it quite plain to the appellant by the conversation already referred to. That was a very plain and specific request, to the doctor to bring about an abortion and an offer to him of a pecuniary inducement to comply with the request, coupled with an assurance that an ample inducement was available. *R v Woods* 22 Cr App R 41 was conversant *(sic)* with an alleged attempt to commit an act of indecency which did not go beyond the stage of preparation. A request to bring about a specific abortion for a promised reward is a very different thing.

It is equally different from what was relied upon in *The People (Attorney General) v England* – in which case a certified copy of the judgment of the Court of Criminal Appeal delivered by the President of the High Court was supplied to us. Then, it was sought to treat the mere extolling of an immoral haunt to one K as an attempt to procure the doing of an immoral act which it was alleged the accused subsequently asked to have done. The learned President held that, at most, this description of the immoral haunt could not be more than what he called "an inchoate invitation". There was nothing inchoate about the invitation in the present case to bring about an abortion nor about the inducement held out to comply with that invitation. In *The King v Bentley* [1923] 1 KB 403 the charge was incitement by the appellant to procure the commission of an act of indecency. He had telephoned to one Williams to ask if he could have two unnamed boys at 10/- each that evening for an indecent purpose. Hewart CJ said "Here the appellant offered money to Williams to procure boys for that purpose. That is to say, if the jury accepted that evidence, he incited Williams to procure the boys for that purpose." In that case there was no evidence, so far as the Report shows, that the accused made any effort to overcome the mind of a reluctant person, or as to whether Williams was reluctant or not.

Next as to the contention that the trial judge did not properly explain the difference between a mere desire and an incitement, the learned Judge said "Incitement is holding up to a person encouragement to commit a crime. The doctor said 'do you realise you are asking me to perform an illegal operation?' He said 'yes, there is ample funds'. You will have to consider and use your judgment whether those words were only an expression of a desire."

This Court thinks that the jury must have understood this to mean that the mere expression of a desire would not suffice to justify a conviction and also that the Judge's description of an incitement must have prevented any such misunderstanding on the part of the jury as has been suggested.

Further, even if the trial Judge's explanation were to be regarded as inadequate or as leaving something to be desired, the Court is of opinion that, on the evidence in this case, if the jury accepted it, they must, in the words of Channell J in *Rex v Landow* 29 TLR 375 necessarily have taken the view they did take. That was not the position in *Rex v Landow*, but the Court made it clear that if it had been, there would have been no miscarriage of justice, and it would not have quashed the conviction, notwithstanding the failure of the trial Judge adequately to explain the difference between an attempt and a mere idle threat or the mere expression of a desire.

In this case the Court is of opinion that the jury, without any further explanation than that given them by the trial Judge, must in the words of Channell J in *Rex v Landow* necessarily have taken the view that the appellant was doing something essentially different from giving vent to a mere desire, and was in fact seriously and specifically seeking to employ Dr Nightingale to perform an illegal operation upon an indicated female for reward. Accordingly the application for leave to appeal will be refused.

2.60   *Martin v Police*
                              [1967] NZLR 396
                     Court of Appeal New Zealand, 1967

Hardy Boys J: It must always be a matter of evidence or of necessary inference whether the particular alleged "counselling was uttered *in vacuo*, so to speak or with the knowledge that it may, and an intention that it should, be acted upon".

Code Options

2.61   *Model Penal Code*

5.02   Criminal Solicitation

(1) *Definition of Solicitation.* A person is guilty of solicitation to commit a crime if with the purpose of promoting or facilitating its commission he commands, encourages or requests another person to engage in specific conduct

that would constitute such crime or an attempt to commit such crime or would establish his complicity in its commission or attempted commission.

(2) *Uncommunicated Solicitation.* It is immaterial under subsection (1) of this Section that the actor fails to communicate with the person he solicits to commit a crime if his conduct was designed to effect such communication.

(3) *Renunciation of Criminal Purpose.* It is an affirmative defense that the actor, after soliciting another person to commit a crime, persuaded him not to do so or otherwise prevented the commission of the crime, under circumstances manifesting a complete and voluntary renunciation of his criminal purpose.

Further Materials

2.62 Law Commission (U.K.) Working Paper No. 50 *Codification of the Criminal Law: General Principles Inchoate Offences Conspiracy Attempt and Incitement.*
Buxton *The Working Paper on Inchoate Offences (1) Incitement and Attempt* [1973] Crim LR 656.
Dickey *Prosecution Under the Race Relations Act, 1965, s 6 (Incitement to Racial Hatred)* [1968] Crim LR 489.

Chapter 3

PARTIES TO OFFENCES

Introduction

3.01 Criminal liability for committing an offence is not limited solely to the actual perpetrator. The policy of the law requires that those who knowingly assist in the commission of an offence, whether mentally, by encouraging it, or physically, by supplying the means for its commission, will equally be guilty of that crime. A commonplace example is where A and B set out to rob a bank using C's car for that purpose. All the parties will be equally guilty of the crime of robbery, even though A was the only person who entered the bank. B waited outside in the get-away car and C remained at home knowing that his car was to be used for this purpose. This is often referred to as the doctrine of common design. It is described in ordinary language as offenders being "in cahoots" with one another.

3.02 Complicity in a crime depends on the degree of knowledge of those who assist it. Often the live issue in the trial of an accused on a charge of complicity is whether he knew, or was reckless as to the offence that was perpetrated in his absence. In the example given no difficulty is encountered. The bank robbery will, necessarily, involve actual or threatened violence. So where A punches a bank teller in the face in order to seize money both B and C will be guilty of an assault. A slight change in the facts of the example illustrates a legal difficulty which may only be resolved by reference to fundamental principles. Where A, to the knowledge of B and C, carries a loaded weapon into the bank and encounters a heroic customer who resists him and is then killed by him, specialised rules are required to deal with the liability of B and C. Tentatively, it is possible to state the following as a solution which appears to be consistent with a constitutional requirement of moral blameworthiness commensurate with the crime charged: where the mental element of the crime is recklessness, if those who assist the principal consciously take an unjustifiable risk that a further or ancillary crime may be committed, they are as guilty of the crime as the principal; but where the mental element of the crime is intent, those who assist the principal must expressly, or tacitly, accept that this further or ancillary crime will be committed, if it is necessary, before they can be found guilty of

141

its commission. Shortly stated, this would require secondary participation to be tested on a subjective basis. In our example A and C would normally contemplate that B may have to drive in a criminally negligent fashion in order to escape arrest. If, during the course of such driving, another road-user is killed then all participants will be guilty of manslaughter under the rules as to criminal negligence further explored at paras **5.55–5.56**. But for B and C to be guilty of the murder of the customer who resists, however, they must participate in the crime with the knowledge that A is carrying a deadly weapon and accept that, if it is necessary to effect the purpose of robbing the bank, A may have to kill or cause serious injury to anyone who gets in the way. As in all crimes the existence of such a mental state may be inferred from the facts or it may later be admitted by one or other of them. Such crimes usually involve a conspiracy but an admission after its completion is only admissible against the party who makes it.

3.03 A person can be convicted as an accessory after the fact notwithstanding the acquittal of the principal in a prior separate trial unless, in all the circumstances, the conviction is inconsistent with the acquittal of the other person. Inconsistency depends on the state of the evidence and not on the state of the record; *R v Breen*[1].

3.04 These rules are explored in the cases which follow. Criminal procedure is strictly outside the scope of this work but in this instance it is so integral to the working of the law as to require a knowledge of it.

Legislation

3.05 This jurisdiction retains a distinction between a felony and a misdemeanour. At common law all parties to a misdemeanour are principals for procedural purposes. One cannot be an accessory after the fact to a misdemeanour. It is possible to be an accessory after the fact to a felony. Participants in a felony have their own distinctive nomenclature. The person who commits the crime is referred to as the principal in the first degree, the person who is present and assists him is called the principal in the second degree and the person who counsels or procures the crime is called an accessory before the fact. All of these distinctions have now been abolished in England; *Attorney-General's Reference (No 1 of 1975)*[2].

3.06   *Accessories and Abettors Act 1861*

Accessories before the Fact may be tried and punished as Principals

1 Whosoever shall become an Accessory before the Fact to any Felony, whether the same be a Felony at Common Law or by virtue of any Act passed or to be passed, may be indicted, tried, convicted, and punished in all respects as if he were a principal Felon.

1 (1990) 47 A Crim R 298.
2 [1975] 2 All ER 684.

Accessories before the Fact may be indicted as such, or substantive Felons

2 Whosoever shall counsel, procure, or command any other Person to commit any Felony, whether the same be a Felony at Common Law or by virtue of any Act passed or to be passed, shall be guilty of Felony, and may be indicted and convicted either as an Accessory before the Fact to the principal Felony, together with the principal Felon, or after the Conviction of the principal Felon, or may be indicted and convicted of a substantive Felon whether the principal Felon shall or shall not have been previously convicted, or shall or shall not be amenable to Justice, and may thereupon be punished in the same Manner as any Accessory before the Fact to the same Felony, if convicted as an Accessory, may be punished.

Accessories after the Fact may be indicted as such, or as substantive Felons

3 Whosoever shall become an Accessory after the Fact to any Felony, whether the same be a Felony at Common Law or by virtue of any Act passed or to be passed, may be indicted and convicted either as an Accessory after the Fact to the principal Felony, together with the principal Felon, or after the Conviction of the principal Felon, or may be indicted and convicted of a substantive Felony whether the principal Felon shall or shall not have been previously convicted, or shall or shall not be amenable to Justice, and may thereupon be punished in like Manner as any Accessory after the Fact to the same Felony, if convicted as an Accessory, may be punished.

Punishment of Accessories after the Fact

4 Every Accessory after the Fact to any Felony (except where it is otherwise specially enacted), whether the same be a Felony at Common Law or by virtue of any Act passed or to be passed, shall be liable, at the Discretion of the Court, to be imprisoned in the Common Gaol or House of Correction for any Term not exceeding Two Years, with or without Hard Labour, and it shall be lawful for the Court, if it shall think fit, to require the Offender to enter into his own Recognizances and to find Sureties, both or either, for keeping the Peace, in addition to such Punishment: Provided that no Person shall be imprisoned under this Clause for not finding Sureties for any Period exceeding One Year.

Prosecution of Accessory after Principal has been convicted, but not attainted

5 If any principal Offencer shall be in anywise convicted of any Felony, it shall be lawful to proceed against any Accessory, either before or after the Fact, in the same Manner as if such principal Felon had been attained thereof, notwithstanding such principal Felon shall die, or be pardoned, or otherwise delivered before Attainder; and every such Accessory shall upon Conviction suffer the same Punishment as he would have suffered if the Principal had been attainted.

Several Accessories may be included in the same Indictment although principal Felon not included

6 Any Number of Accessories at different Times to any Felony, and any Number of Receivers at different Times of Property stolen at One Time, may be charged with substantive Felonies in the same Indictment, and may be tried together, notwithstanding the principal Felon shall not be included in the same Indictment, or shall not be in Custody or amenable to Justice.

Trial of Accessories

7 Where any Felony shall have been wholly committed within *England* or *Ireland*, the Offence of any Person who shall be an Accessory either before or after the Fact to any such Felony may be dealt with, inquired of, tried, determined, and punished by any Court which shall have Jurisdiction to try the principal Felony, or any Felonies committed in any County or Place in which the Act by reason whereof such Person shall have become such Accessory shall have been committed; and in every other Case the Offence of any Person who shall be an Accessory either before or after the Fact to any Felony may be dealt with, inquired of, tried, determined and punished by any Court which shall have Jurisdiction to try the principal Felony or any Felonies committed in any County or Place in which such Person shall be apprehended or be in Custody, whether the principal Felony shall have been committed on the Sea or on the Land, or begun on the Sea and completed on the Land, or begun on the Land and completed on the Sea, and whether within Her Majesty's Dominions or without, or partly within Her Majesty's Dominions and partly without; provided that no Person who shall be once duly tried either as an Accessory before or after the Fact, or for a substantive Felony under the Provisions herein-before contained, shall be liable to be afterwards prosecuted for the same Offence.

Abettors in Misdemeanours

8 As to Abettors in Misdemeanours:

Whosoever shall aid, abet, counsel, or procure the Commission of any Misdemeanour, whether the same be a Misdemeanour at Common Law or by virtue of any Act passed or to be passed, shall be liable to be tried, indicted, and punished as a principal Offender.

As to Offences committed within the Jurisdiction of the Admiralty

9 As to other Matters:

Where any Person shall, within the Jurisdiction of the Admiralty of *England* or *Ireland*, become an Accessory to any Felony, whether the same be a Felony at Common Law or by virtue of any Act passed or to be passed, and whether such Felony shall be committed within that Jurisdiction or elsewhere, or shall be begun within that Jurisdiction and completed elsewhere, or shall be begun elsewhere and completed with that Jurisdiction, the Offence of such Person shall be Felony; and in any Indictment for any such Offence the Venue in the Margin shall be the same as if the Offence had been committed in the County or Place in which such Person shall be indicted, and his Offence shall be averred to have been committed "on the High Seas;" provided that nothing herein contained shall alter or affect any of the Laws relating to the Government of Her Majesty's Land or Naval Forces.

Act not to extend to Scotland

10 Nothing in this Act contained shall extend to *Scotland*, except as herein-before otherwise expressly provided.

Commencement of Act

11 This Act shall commence and take effect on the First Day of *November* One thousand eight hundred and sixty-one.

3.07 *Petty Sessions (Ireland) Act 1851*

Aiders and Abettors in the Commission of Offences to be punishable on Summary Conviction as Principals

22 . . . every Person who shall aid, abet, counsel, or procure the Commission of any Offence which is or shall be punishable on Summary Conviction, shall be liable to be proceeded against and convicted for the same, either together with the principal Offender or before or after his Conviction, and shall be liable, on Conviction, to the same Forfeiture and Punishment to which such principal

Offender shall be by Law liable (except where the Age of such Aider or Abettor shall exceed Fourteen Years, in which Case he shall be liable to the same Forfeiture and Punishment to which any principal Offender whose Age shall exceed Fourteen Years shall be liable), and may be proceeded against and convicted either in the Country where such principal Offender may be convicted, or in that in which such Offence of aiding, abetting, counselling, or procuring may have been committed.

3.08   *Criminal Justice Administration Act 1914*

43(7) So much of section twenty two of the Petty Sessions (Ireland) Act,1851 as relates to the liability of persons aiding, abetting, counselling, or procuring the commission of offences punishable on summary conviction shall, as amended by any subsequent enactment, extend to the police district of Dublin Metropolis; and every person who aids, abets, counsels, or procures the commission of any such offence may be proceeded against and convicted in that district in any case where the principal offender may be convicted in that district, or where the offence of aiding, abetting, counselling, or procuring was committed in that district.

3.09   *Explosive Substances Act 1883*

Punishment of accessories

5 Any person who within or (being a subject of Her Majesty) without Her Majesty's dominions by the supply of or solicitation for money, the providing of premises, the supply of materials, or in any manner whatsoever, procures, counsels, aids, abets or is accessory to, the commission of any crime under this Act, shall be guilty of felony, and shall be liable to be tried and punished for that crime, as if he had been guilty as a principal.

3.10   See further, s 4 of the Piracy Act 1837; s 2 of the Treason Act 1939; s 56 of the Malicious Damage Act 1861; s 11 of the Forgery Act 1913; s 67 of the Offences Against the Persons Act 1861. For an application of these provisions see *Dawson v Glynn*[3] and *Bradley v McGivern*[4].

3.11   Notwithstanding the clear terms of the provisions quoted, there is authority that the accused is entitled to know whether he has been charged as a principal offender or with complicity in some other way; *Ministry of Food v O'Rourke*[5]; *DPP for Northern Ireland v Maxwell*[6]. In this jurisdiction the proposition that an accused is entitled to know the nature of the charge against him can be supported on constitutional grounds; *The State (Healy) v Donoghue*[7]. In all serious cases the nature of the charge is easily found from the witness statements and list of charges that must be supplied to an accused in a criminal trial before a jury; Criminal Procedure Act 1967.

The minimum conduct for participation

3.12   This branch of the law focuses upon participation and not on causation. One can participate in a crime without necessarily causing it. If A and B come on the scene of a gang rape and do nothing except watch, they are behaving reprehensibly but they are not participating in the crime. If they

3 [1945] IR 489.
4 [1963] NI 11.
5 [1951] NI 97.
6 [1978] NI 59.
7 [1976] IR 325.

yell and shout encouragement at the perpetrators they become part of the crime being inflicted on the victim. It is probably not a necessary element of participation that the actual perpetrators hear them and are encouraged by them; it is essential only that they intend to participate in the crime and do, on an objective view, participate by some overt act. Mere intention is insufficient; the law does not punish a person because of what they think. If a causative factor is necessary it would be easy for a jury to find that A and B, by their activity, discouraged the victim from resisting or were ready to stop her escaping. Smith and Hogan see differences depending on whether A is charged with procuring, abetting, counselling or aiding the offence[8].

3.13   In *R v Dunlop and Sylvester* the two accused were charged with raping a girl. She testified that they physically had intercourse with her against her will. However, the trial judge also left the case to the jury on the basis that, if they had not had intercourse with her, they stood by and watched a rape.

3.14   ***Dunlop and Sylvester v R***
                     (1979) 99 DLR (3d) 301
                 Supreme Court of Canada, 1979

Dickson J: . . . Mere presence at the scene of a crime is not sufficient to ground culpability. Something more is needed: encouragement of the principal offender; an act which facilitates the commission of the offence, such as keeping watch or enticing the victim away, or an act which tends to prevent or hinder interference with accomplishment of the criminal act, such as preventing the intended victim from escaping or being ready to assist the prime culprit. Thus, in an early work, *Foster's Crown Law*, p 350, we read:

> . . . in order to render a person an accomplice and a principal in a felony, he must be aiding and abetting at the fact, or ready to afford assistance if necessary, and therefore if A happeneth to be present at a murder, for instance, and taketh no part in it, nor endeavoureth to prevent it, nor apprehendeth the murderer, nor levyeth hue and cry after him, this strange behaviour of his, though highly criminal, will not of itself render him either principal or accessory.

The leading case of *R v Coney* (1882), 8 QBD 534, decided that non-accidental presence at the scene of the crime was not conclusive of aiding and abetting. The accused were present at a prize fight, then illegal, though taking no part in the management of the fight. It did not appear that the accused said or did anything. The Chairman of the Quarter Sessions directed the jury that, prize fights being illegal, all persons who went to a fight to see the combatants strike each other, and being present when they did so, were guilty of assault unless they were casually passing by. If they stayed at the place, they encouraged it by their presence although they did not say or do anything. Eight of the 11 judges hearing the case reserved were of the opinion that the direction was not correct. Two passages from the judgment of Cave J, at p 539 bear repeating:

> Now it is a general rule in the case of principals in the second degree that there must be participation in the act, and that, although a man is present whilst a felony is being committed, if he takes no part in it, and does not act in concert with those who commit it, he will not be a principal in the second degree merely because he does not endeavour to prevent the felony, or apprehend the felon.

and [at p 540]:

8 Criminal Law (6th ed 1988) at p 134.

Where presence may be entirely accidental, it is not even evidence of aiding and abetting. Where presence is *prima facie* not accidental it is evidence, but no more than evidence, for the jury.

Hawkins J, in a well-known passage had this to say, (pp 557–8):

In my opinion, to constitute an aider and abettor some active steps must be taken by word, or action, with the intent to instigate the principal, or principals. Encouragement does not of necessity amount to aiding and abetting, it may be intentional or unintentional, a man may unwittingly encourage another in fact by his presence, by misinterpreted words or gestures, or by his silence, on non-interference, or he may encourage intentionally by expressions, gestures, or actions intended to signify approval. In the latter case he aids and abets, in the former he does not. It is no criminal offence to stand by, as a mere passive spectator of a crime, even of a murder. Non-interference to prevent a crime is not itself a crime. But the fact that a person was voluntarily and purposely present witnessing the commission of a crime, and offered no opposition to it, though he might reasonably be expected to prevent and had the power to do so, or at least to express his dissent, might under some circumstances, afford cogent evidence upon which a jury would be justified in finding that he wilfully encouraged and so aided and abetted. But it would be purely a question for the jury whether he did so or not. So if any number of persons arranged that a criminal offence shall take place, and it takes place accordingly, the mere presence of any of those who so arranged it would afford abundant evidence for the consideration of a jury of an aiding and abetting.

In this Court the question of aiding and abetting was canvassed in *Preston v The King* (1949), 93 CCC 81, [1949] SCR 156, 7 CR 72. The appellant and another were accused of having set fire to a school. Mr Justice Estey delivered the majority judgment in this Court, in the course of which he stated (p 149) that in order to find the appellant guilty of aiding, abetting, counselling or procuring, it was only necessary to show that he understood what was taking place and by some act on his part encouraged or assisted in the attainment thereof. Later he said (p 160) that mere presence does not constitute aiding and abetting, but presence under certain circumstances may itself be evidence thereof. He proceeded to review the evidence and concluded, p 85 CCC, p 161 SCR:

If the appellant's explanation was not believed by the jury there was *evidence in addition to his mere presence* upon which they might well conclude that he was guilty of aiding, abetting, counelling or procuring. (Emphasis added.)

Two Canadian cases make the distinction between presence with prior knowledge, and accidental presence. In *R v Dick* (1947), 87 CCC 101, [1947] 2 DLR 213, 2CR 417 (Ont CA), the accused was charged with the murder of her husband. According to her own statement, she met her husband and Bohozuk, a friend, and they went with her in a borrowed car, her husband in the front seat and Bohozuk in the back. The two men began to quarrel, both were drinking; Bohozuk pulled a gun and shot Mr Dick. It was not a happy marriage, nor were Mr Dick and Bohozuk on best of terms. There was some surrounding evidence casting doubt upon the non-involvement of the accused. As Chief Justice Robertson noted, she did not admit that there was any design, nor that she knew Bohozuk intended to shoot Dick, nor even that she knew Bohozuk had a weapon with him. Yet the trial Judge gave only general directions on aiding and abetting to the jury. Robertson CJQ, concluded at p 116 CCC, pp 432–3 CR:

Now, while it may be that a jury might infer from the evidence a good deal that is not expressly admitted, it is not at all certain that this jury did infer that the appellant knew more than she admits knowing of Bohozuk's then present purpose. This jury should have been instructed that if they found that the appellant was no more than passively acquiescent at the time of the shooting, and that she had no reason to expect that there would be any shooting until it actually occurred, then s 69 did not apply.

In the result, a new trial was ordered.

In *R v Hoggan* [1966] 3 CCC 1, 47 CR 256, 53 WWR 641 (Alta SC, AD), the charge was that the accused aided and abetted in wilfully attempting to defeat the course of justice by attempting to dissuade a witness from giving evidence. Johnson JA, concluded at p 5 CCC, p 260 CR:

> There are two things that must be proved before an accused can be convicted of being a party by aiding and abetting. It must first be proved that he had knowledge that the principal intended to commit the offence and that the accused aided and abetted him. Where there is no knowledge that an offence is to be committed, the presence of an accused at the scene of the crime cannot be a circumstance which would be evidence of aiding and abetting.

The basis for Johnson JA's approach to aiding and abetting is found in *Preston* and *Coney*, both of which he cites.

The case of *R v Salajko*, [1970] 1 CCC 352, [1970] 1 OR 824, 9 CRNS 145 (Ont CA), is like the instant case in many respects. A girl was raped by 15 young men in a lonely field. Three were charged. Two of these were identified as having had intercourse with the girl. She admitted, however, that the third accused, Salajko, though seen to be near the girl with his pants down while she was being raped by others, did not have intercourse with her. The Crown placed its case against him on s 21(1)(*b*) and (*c*) of the *Criminal Code*. One might be forgiven for thinking that it was open to the jury to infer encouragement by conduct, but the Ontario Court of Appeal thought otherwise. Chief Justice Gale, delivering the judgment of the Court, stated that in the absence of evidence to suggest something in the way of aiding, or counselling, or encouraging on the part of the accused with respect to that which was being done by the others, there was simply no evidence upon which a jury could properly arrive at a verdict of guilty against the particular accused. The learned Chief Justice also found error in the trial Judge's charge which seemed to indicate that a person could abet another in the commission of an offence if, knowingly, he stood by while the offence was being committed.

Finally, there are the cases of *R v Black* [1970] 4 CCC 251, 10 CRNS 17, 72 WWR 407, and *R v Clarkson*, [1971] 3 All ER 344. The victim in *Black's* case was conveyed to a clubhouse where he was subjected to various sordid indignities. Many of the accused took an active part in torturing the victim while others stood around laughing and yelling. The British Columbia Court of Appeal confirmed the convictions, being of the view that the spectators furnished encouragement to the perpetrators of the outrages and their mere presence in the circumstances of the case ensured against the escape of the victim. There was thus something more than "mere presence", as in *R v Conney, supra*. Most important, the trial Judge directed the jury in language drawn from the judgment of Hawkins, J, in *Coney* and reviewed the evidence relating to the presence of the accused in clear terms.

In contrast to *R v Black* is the case of *R v Clarkson*, a decision of the Court Martial Appeal Court. A girl was raped in a room in a barracks in Germany by a number of soldiers. Another group of soldiers clustered outside the door and later "piled in" to the room. They remained there for a considerable time while the girl was raped. There was no evidence that the appellants had done any physical act, or uttered any word which involved direct physical participation or verbal encouragement. There was no evidence that they touched the girl, or did anything to prevent others from assisting her or to prevent her from escaping. The Appeal Court held that it was not enough that the presence of the accused, in fact, gave encouragement. "It must be proved that the accused intended to give encouragement; that he *wilfully* encouraged" (p 347). There must be, the Court held, an intention to encourage and encouragement in fact. The convictions were quashed.

The case at bar

In the case at bar I have great difficulty in finding any evidence of anything more than mere presence and passive acquiescence. Presence at the commission of an offence can be evidence of aiding and abetting if accompanied by other factors, such as prior knowledge of the principal offender's intention to commit the offence or attendance for the purpose of encouragement. There was no evidence that while the crime was being committed either of the accused rendered aid, assistance or encouragement to the rape of Brenda Ross. There was no evidence of any positive act or omission to facilitate the unlawful purpose. One can infer that the two accused knew that a party was to be held, and that their presence at the dump was not accidental or in the nature of casual passersby, but that is not sufficient. A person cannot properly be convicted of aiding or abetting in the commission of acts which he does not know may be or are intended: *per* Viscount Dilhorne in *Director of Public Prosecutions for Northern Ireland v Maxwell* [1978] 3 All ER 1140 at p 1144 (HL). One must be able to infer that the accused had prior knowledge that an offence of the type committed was planned, *ie*, that their presence was with knowledge of the intended rape. On this issue, the Crown elicited no evidence.

. . . The error, unfortunately, was compounded when the jury, which had retired at 3:15 pm, returned at 5:10 with the following question:

> If the accused were aware of a rape taking place in their presence and did nothing to prevent or persuade the discontinuance of the act, are they considered as an accomplice to the act under law?

That question should have been answered in one word – "No".

A person is not guilty merely because he is present at the scene of a crime and does nothing to prevent it: Smith & Hogan, *Criminal Law* 4th ed (1978), p 117. If there is no evidence of encouragement by him, a man's presence at the scene of the crime will not suffice to render him liable as aider and abettor. A person who, aware of a rape taking place in his presence, looks on and does nothing is not, as a matter of law, an accomplice. The classic cases is the hardened urbanite who stands around in a subway station when an individual is murdered.

Participation by passenger

3.15   Participation in manslaughter has been found in respect of a passenger in a car, where the car was stolen, and driven with criminal negligence by the driver.

3.16   *R v Baldessare*
                          29 Cox CC 193; 22 Cr App R 70
                        Court of Criminal Appeal England, 1932

Hewart LCJ: The appellant appeals on two grounds, first, that there was no evidence on which the jury could properly convict him of manslaughter, and secondly, as he alleges, that there was misdirection in the summing up of the learned judge. With reference to a considerable part of the case, there was no real dispute. [After stating the facts, His Lordship continued:] It is undoubtedly a cardinal fact in the case that the jury thought fit to acquit both the appellant and Chapman on the charge of stealing the car. The question, therefore, was whether, nevertheless, the two men were associated together in the driving of the car so that, when death resulted form the collision, each was guilty of manslaughter. With regard to the summing up, we are all of opinion that this was an excellent summing up: it stated the law clearly and fairly, and if there was any error in it, the error was in favour of the appellant. After that perfectly fair summing-up, the jury came to the conclusion that the appellant was guilty of manslaughter: in other words, they came to the conclusion that the appellant and Chapman were acting together and joined in responsibility, not merely for the taking away of the car from the owner's possession, but also for the driving of it in the way in which it was in fact driven.

The only question for this Court is whether there was any evidence on which the jury could properly find that conformity of purpose and action. The matter was very carfully argued before us, and we have very carefully considered it, and our conclusion is that we are not prepared to say that there was not evidence on which the jury were entitled to arrive at their verdict. Here was a clandestine ride commonly called a "joy-ride" on a dark night in February, without proper lights, and the two men had taken the car for a purpose, which the jury have found was not felonious, but which had as its object a "joy-ride" without the knowledge and assent of the owner. Looking at these facts, and at the actual speed of the car and its movements before and after the collission, we think that the jury were entitled to find that both the appellant and Chapman were responsible for the way in which the car was being driven at the moment of collision.

This appeal, therefore, fails, but, leave to appeal having been granted, the sentence will run from the date of conviction.

3.17 See further *R v Russell*[9].

Victims

3.18 Where the law is designed to protect a particular class of persons, for example, girls who are under the age of consent to sexual intercourse, the law will penalise the principle offender, but the victim cannot participate in a crime despite the fact of consent; *R v Whitehouse*[10]; *R v Halligan*[11]. Certain well-defined exceptions have been made by statute; see for example s 2 of the Punishment of Incest Act 1908.

Strict liability

3.19 Where the principal offender is committing an offence of strict liability the other party, to participate in the crime, must have a knowledge of the facts which constitute the crime, but not necessarily knowledge that the facts amount to a crime; *R v Giogianni*[12]; *R v Woolworth & Co*[13]; *R v Leeu You-Kwong*[14].

What degree of knowledge constitutes participation?

3.20 The law does not draw fine distinctions between the crime which an accused contemplated participating in and that actually committed. Nor does it draw a distinction between an accessory before the fact and a principal in the second degree. It is only where the principal offender commits a crime of an entirely different character from that which the accused contemplated, that the accused will thereby be rendered a non participant; *The People (DPP) v Madden*[15].

9 [1933] CLR 59.
10 [1977] QB 868.
11 [1973] 2 NZLR 158.
12 (1985) 59 ALJR 461.
13 (1974) 46 DLR (3rd) 354.
14 [1985] LRC (Crim) 604.
15 [1977] IR 337 at p 341.

3.21 *R v Maxwell*

[1978] NI; [1978] 3 All ER 1140; [1978] 1 WLR 1350 HL;
[1978] Crim LR 40; (1978) 68 Cr App R 128;
[1978] Crim LR 422 CA (NI)
Court of Criminal Appeal Northern Ireland
House of Lords, 1978

Facts: Maxwell was convicted of unlawfully and maliciously doing an act with intent to cause an explosion likely to endanger life, contrary to section 3(*a*) of the Explosive Substances Act 1883 and possession of a bomb with intent, contrary to section 3(*b*) of that Act. On the 21st January 1976 he was interviewed by officers of the Royal Ulster Constabulary and admitted that he had used his own car to guide another car, containing four men, to a bar owned by a Roman Catholic. He was a member of the "Ulster Volunteer Force" and stated that after the death of his father he had been told by his "officer commanding" that he would not be used for any further military actions but would be doing welfare work such as collecting money for loyalist prisoners. When Maxwell had led the other car to the bar one of the other men jumped out and pushed a "pipe bomb" into the hallway. The bar was packed but no one was injured because the owner's son courageously diffused it. Maxwell described this action as "a job". This was a commonly used euphemism for paramilitary terrorist activities. It was argued at his appeal that as he did not know the precise nature of "the job", he could not be an accessory before the fact or an abettor. This argument was rejected in the Northern Ireland Court of Appeal and that judgment was upheld by the House of Lords.

Lowry LCJ [Court of Criminal Appeal]: The burden of counsel's submission was that, in order to be guilty as an aider and abettor, an accused must be shown to have known the type of crime to be committed and the kind of means of offence being carried to the scene: as he was not shown to have that knowledge, it was argued, he could not be said to have been an aider and abettor and accordingly he could not be said to have been an accessory either to the placing of the bomb or to its possession by the occupants of the Cortina car.

The five inferences in the learned trial judge's judgment were not seriously challenged in this court by Mr Kennedy. Indeed he expressly accepted, when it was put to him in the course of the argument, –

1. That the appellant facilitated – that is, made possible – an attack (though he later expressed a preference for the expression "hostile visit") on Crosskeys, although he did not know, as Mr Kennedy submitted, what form the attack would take; and

2. that it was a reasonable inference from the evidence that the appellant knew he was participating in a military type job.

Of course, it is necessary to examine the facts to see whether these concessions were justified, since, although Mr Kennedy is a very experienced advocate, it is the duty of this court to see for itself whether it is satisfied with an inference, even in the form of a concession, to the detriment of the appellant. When, however, one examines the appellant's statements, both oral and written, it appears to us that the learned trial judge's inferences and counsel's concessions were (with one possible exception to which I shall refer) not only justified but inevitable. whatever the appellant may have known earlier, as soon as he got to Dunadry, he knew there was a job on. The only sort of job suggested in argument as an alternative to a military, or hostile, job seems to have been a welfare task, which the appellant described as collecting money and doing tote cards for loyalist prisoners, but was any such task entailed in guiding another car, containing three or four men, on a hostile visit (to use words of Mr Kennedy's own choice) over several miles of roads at night to a public house? Such a suggestion has only to be made for its unreality to be demonstrated. Therefore we consider that the learned trial judge's inferences, and Mr Kennedy's concessions in this court, were reasonable.

The only question is whether it follows from the evidence that it was of necessity clear in the mind of the appellant, when he was briefed, that the object was an attack on the Crosskeys Inn; it is possible (although these were not suggested by Detective-Superintendent Hylands to be typical of UVF activities in the area) that the appellant could have contemplated a robbery or a shooting at the Inn as one of the alternatives. The facts proved could also, it seems, support the conclusion that, so far as the accused was concerned, the Inn might simply have been a landmark or rendezvous for the purpose of an attack on a person or premises in the vicinity. The behaviour of the sports car which Mr Stinson saw tended to show that it was the Inn itself which interested the driver, but, although the judge thought that this was probably the appellant's car, he was (because of Mr Stinson's description of the roof) not satisfied of this beyond reasonable doubt.

One can at least be sure beyond reasonable doubt that a UVF-type attack must have been in the mind of the appellant and that a bombing attack on the Inn must have been one of the likeliest jobs to occur to him when he was briefed for the mission. This is, in our view, a crucial point so far as the requirement of guilty knowledge and intent is concerned.

With reference to the particulars in counts 1 and 2 we must remember that the appellant was convicted for being an accomplice and not regarded by the judge as a principal. At common law, of course, and under Section 8 of the Accessories and Abettors Act 1861 he was liable to be "tried, indicted and punished as a principal offender." This section now applies to all offences: see section 1 of the Criminal Law Act (Northern Ireland) 1967. Section 5 of the Act of 1883 is to the same effect. But what had to be proved beyond reasonable doubt against the appellant was that he intentionally assisted in the placing of the bomb by the principals and in the principals' having possession of the explosives, not that he himself personally placed the bomb or had possesion of the explosives.

I shall, like the learned authors of *Smith and Hogan* (3rd ed, Chap 8, use the terms "abettor" and "counsellor" to cover aiding and abetting on the one hand and counselling and procuring on the other. An abettor is one who is present assisting or encouraging the principal at the time of the offence while a counsellor is one who before the commission of the crime conspires to commit it, advises its commission or knowingly gives assistance to one or more of the principals. It is enough to prove an accused to be an abettor or a counsellor without showing which. Abetting and counselling are by origin common law offences and a guilty mind is a necessary ingredient. The Crown must prove that an accused participated before or during the commission of the crime, assisted the principal and intended to assist him. The *mens rea* required goes to intent only and does not depend on desire or motive *NCB v Gamble* [1959] 1 QB 11, 23; *R v Lynch* [1975] NI 35, 55–37.

The classic statement of Lord Goddard CJ in *Johnson v Youden* [1950] 1 KB 544, 546 was cited and approved in *Churchill v Walton* [1967] 2 AC 224, 236:

"Before a person can be convicted of aiding and abetting the commission of an offence he must at least know the essential matters which constitute that offence. He need not actually know that an offence has been committed because he may not know that the facts constitute an offence and ignorance of the law is not a defence. If a person knows all the facts and is assisting another person to do certain things, and it turns out that the doing of those things constitutes an offence, the person who is assisting is guilty of aiding and abetting that offence, because to allow him to say 'I knew of all those facts but I did not know that an offence was committed' would be allowing him to set up ignorance of the law as a defence. The reason why, in our opinion, the justices were right in dismissing the information against the first two defendants is that they found, and found on good grounds, that they did not know of the matters which in fact constituted the offence; and, as they did not know of those matters, it follows that they cannot be guilty of aiding and abetting the commission of the offence."

The question for the purpose of this case is therefore what is meant by the requirement that the alleged counsellor or abettor "must at least know the essential matters which constitute that offence."

Johnson v Youden is merely one example of many cases in which the distinction is between knowledge and ignorance of facts which constitute a criminal offence. There are a few cases, however, where the contrast is between knowledge of facts constituting a particular crime and knowledge of a less detailed kind which nevertheless is enough to show that the accused (1) know that something criminal was afoot, and (2) intended to facilitate its commission.

R v Bullock [1955] 1 WLR 1 is such a case. It was concerned with two counts of breaking and entering at different times and places, the common link between which was the use of a car which had been hired by the accused. His defence was an alibi and at the trial the Crown case proceeded on the basis of an allegation that the accused was present at the commission of each crime. The judge charged the jury on the same basis, but, after they had retired to consider their verdict, they returned and asked what was the law if the accused knew that his car was being used for an unlawful purpose. The trial judge directed them that, if the accused was not present but the car was, to his knowledge, being driven by the thief or thieves, he would be an accessory before the fact. The Court of Criminal Appeal upheld the conviction.

Remarkably enough, when one considers the course of the trial, the accused could hardly be said to have been convicted "secundum allegata et probata," but what we are now concerned with is the principle stated in the judgment of the Court of Criminal Appeal by Devlin J. Counsel for the appellant in *Bullock*'s case sought to rely on *R v Lomas* 9 Cr App R 220, where the headnote (misleadingly, as the court held) included a statement to the effect that there must be some particular crime in view. Devlin J said at page 4:

"Mr Lawton has cited and relied upon *Rex v Lomas*. The headnote to that case reads: 'Mere knowledge that the principal intends to commit crime does not constitute an accessory before the fact: there must be some particular crime in view.' The first part of that headnote, that is, 'Mere knowledge that the principal intends to commit crime does not constitute an accessory before the fact' is unexceptionable as far as it goes: mere knowledge is not of itself enough, there must be something further. But in the circumstances of this case, once it was plain that the appellant had hired the car and had control of it, it was equally plain, if he knew that it was being used, that he must also have permitted it to be used. He must formally or informally have lent it for that purpose, and that is certainly enough."

R v Bainbridge [1960] 1 QB 129 is the case where the Stoke Newington Branch of the Midland Bank was broken into and oxyacetylene equipment was used in the crime. The arguments of counsel in the Court of Criminal Appeal illustrate many of the points which were taken in the case before us. The learned trial judge had directed the jury that the prosecution had to prove that the defendant knew that a felony of the type committed was intended and with that knowledge did something to help the felons commit the crime, but that they need not prove that he knew what premises were to be broken into. The Court held this direction to be correct and Lord Parker CJ said:

"Mr Simpson, who has argued this case very well, contends that that direction is wrong. As he puts it, in order that a man should be convicted of being accessory before the fact, it must be shown that at the time he bought the equipment in a case such as this he knew that a particular crime was going to be committed, and by a particular crime. Mr Simpson means that the premises in this case which were going to be broken into were known to the appellant and contemplated by him, and not only the premises in question but the date when the breaking was going to occur; in other words, that he must know that on a particular date the Stoke Newington branch of the Midland Bank is intended to be broken into.

The court fully appreciates that it is not enough that it should be shown that a man knows that some illegal venture is intended. To take this case, it would not be enough if he knew – he says he only suspected – that the equipment was going to be used to dispose of stolen property. That would not be enough. Equally, this court is quite satisfied that it is unnecessary that knowledge of the particular crime which was in fact committed, should be shown to his knowledge to have been intended, and by 'particular crime' I am using the words in the same way in which Mr Simpson used them, namely, on a particular date and particular premises.

It is not altogether easy to lay down a precise form of words which will cover every case that can be contemplated but, having considered the cases and the law, this court is quite clear that the direction of judge Aarvold in this case cannot be criticised. Indeed, it might well have been made with the passage in Foster's *Crown Cases* (3rd ed (1809 at p 369) in mind, because there the author says: 'If the principal totally and substantially varieth, if being solicited to commit a felony of one kind he willfully and knowingly committeth a felony of another, he will stand single in that offence, and the person soliciting will not be involved in his guilt. For on his part it was no more than a fruitless ineffectual temptation,' the converse, of course bieng that if the principal does not totally and substantially vary the advice or the help and does not wilfully and knowingly commit a different form of felony altogether, the man who has advised or helped, aided or abetted, will be guilty as an accessory before the fact.

Judge Aarvold in this case, in the passage to which I have referred, makes it clear that there must be not merely suspicion but knowledge that a crime of the type in question was intended, and that the equipment was bought with that in view. In his refence to the felony of the type intended it was, as he stated, the felony of breaking and entering premises and the stealing of property from those premises. The court can see nothing wrong in that direction."

Mr Kennedy would seek to say that, if *R v Bainbridge* is to be followed, its operation should be confined to the type of case where the accused knows that an attack by means of explosives is intended but perhaps does not know the target or the place or the precise date of the intended operation. Counsel would argue on the same principle that it was necessary that the appellant should at least be proved to have known that there were explosives of some kind in the Cortina, even if he did not know their precise nature. There are analogous cases concerning the possession of forbidden drugs where their existence but not their precise nature is known to the accused: *R v Warner* [1969] 2 AC 256, 289. I digress for a moment to point out that firearms and ammunition are, by virtue of section 9 of the 1883 Act, "explosive substances".

Clearly, in *R v Bainbridge* the Court of Criminal Appeal considered that the knowledge of the appellant was sufficient to satisfy the test propounded in *Johnson v Youden* which was cited in that case in argument for the appellant. Before leaving *Bainbridge* we would refer to the argument of Crown counsel in that case who said (at p 131):

"The word 'contemplated' is perhaps the most appropriate to use; a man is accessory before the fact if he gives assistance beforehand to the principal for the purpose of the principal carrying out the offence which he then contemplates. It need not be an offence against a particular contemplated subject."

Lord Pearce in *Thambiah v R* (1967) AC 37 said (at p 46):

"Nice problems may arise when preparations abetting one kind of crime are followed by the execution of a crime of another kind or when the abetting preparations are merely for some criminal but indefinite purpose. The only two cases on abetting to which their Lordships were referred do not help. In *Reg v Bullock* (explaining *Rex v Lomas*) a person who hired cars which were used in two burglaries was held guilty as an accessory. But the point there in issue was how far there had been any sufficient direction of the jury on the facts of that case. The case contains little guidance on the question how much particularity of intention must be shown in proving the charge of abetting. This is a matter which must clearly be affected by the extent and degree of the abettor's activities and their proximity to the actual crime."

It is just such a problem that we now have to decide. What then is the real principle? A clue may be provided by the words of Lord Goddard CJ in *Thomas v Lindop* [1950] 1 All ER 966, 968:

"More than once this court has pointed out that it is impossible to convict persons of aiding and abetting the commission of an offence unless they know the fact which must be proved to show that an offence has been committed. We pointed out that in *Ackroyd's Air Travel Ltd v Director of Public Prosecutions*, and Avory J, and Shearman J, said it in no uncertain terms in *Bowker v Premier Drug Co*. It is, of course, not necessary to show that the person knew that it was an offence, because he cannot plead ignorance of the law, but where anyone is charged with aiding and abetting a person to commit an offence, it must, at least, be shown that he knew what that person was doing. A person who does not know of the acts which another person is doing cannot be charged with aiding and abetting him because he does not know that he is doing acts which amount to an offence."

The emphasis here it not placed, as in *Johnson v Youden*, on knowing "the essential facts which constitute the offence" but on knowing "the facts which must be proved to show that an offence has been committed" and on knowing that the principal "is doing acts which amount to an offence".

Once the "particular crime" theory of guilty knowledge is rejected in favour of the *Bainbridge* principle, the question arises how far that principle goes. In a practical sense the question is whether the principle applies to the facts proved in this case.

Suppose the intending principal offender (whom I shall call "the principal") tells the intended accomplice (whom I shall call "the accomplice") that he means to shoot A or else leave a bomb at A's house and the accomplice agrees to drive the principal to A's house and keep watch while there, it seems clear that the accomplice would be guilty of aiding and abetting whichever crime the principal committed, because he would know that one of two crimes was to be committed, he would have assisted the principal and he would have intended to assist him. Again, let us suppose that the principal tells the accomplice that the intention is to murder A at one house but, if he cannot be found or the house is guarded, the alternative plan is to go to B's house and leave a bomb there or thirdly to rob a particular bank (or indeed murder somebody, or bomb somebody's house or rob any bank as to which see *Bainbridge*) and requests the accomplice to make a reconnaissance of a number of places and report on the best way of gaining access to the target. The accomplice agrees and makes all the reconnaissances and reports, and the principal then, without further communication, selects a target and commits the crime. It seems clear that, whichever crime the principal commits, all the ingredients of the accomplice's guilt are present. In each of these examples the accomplice knows exactly what is contemplated and the only thing he does not know is to which particular crime he will become an accessory when it is committed. His guilt springs from the fact that he contemplated the commission of one (or more) of a number of crimes by the principle and he intentionally lends his assistance in order that such a crime will be committed. In other words, he knows that the principal is committing or is about to commit one of a number of specifically illegal acts and with that knowledge he helps him to do so.

The situation has something in common with that of two persons who agree to rob a bank on the understanding, either express or implied from conduct (such as the carrying of a loaded gun by one person with the knowledge of the other), that violence *may* be resorted to. The accomplice knows, not that the principal *will* shoot the cashier, but that he may do so and, if the principal does shoot him, the accomplice will be guilty of murder. A different case is where the accomplice has only offence A in contemplation and the principal commits offence B. Here the accomplice, although normally culpable (and perhaps guilty of conspiring to commit offence A), is not guilty of aiding and abetting offence B. The principle with which we are dealing does not seem to us to provide a warrant, on the basis of combating lawlessness generally, for convicting an alleged accomplice of *any* offence which, helped by his preliminary acts, a principal may commit. The relevant crime must be within the contemplation of the accomplice and only exceptionally would evidence be found to support the allegation that the accomplice had given the principal a completely blank cheque.

Interesting hypothetical problems can be posed if, for example, one person supplies to another house-breaking implements or weapons which are used – and perhaps used repeatedly – by the person supplied or by a third person, either immediately or months or years later. Such questions must, we think, be solved by asking whether the crime actually committed is fairly described as the crime or one of a number of crimes within the contemplation of the accomplice. They are typical of the kind of problem which may be encountered in the application of any principle of the common law which, while requiring to be soundly based, can only proceed from one instance to another. But those questions do not arise in the present case.

The facts found here show that the appellant, as a member of an organisation which habitually perpetrates sectarian acts of violence with firearms and explosives, must, as soon as he was briefed for his role, have contemplated the bombing of the Crosskeys Inn as not the only possibility but one of the most obvious possibilities among the jobs which the principals were likely to be undertaking and in the commission of which he was intentionally assisting. He was therefore in just the same situation, so far as guilty knowledge is concerned, as a man who had been given a list of jobs and told that one of them would be carried out. And so he is guilty of the offence alleged against him in Count 1.

So far as Count 2 is concerned, the situation of the appellant and the reasoning which governs it are precisely analogous to the situation and reasoning in relation to Count 1. He must have known that materials of offence were, with the knowledge of the principals (or one or more of them), in their possession and control with the intention alleged in the indictment and that an explosive substance was one of the most obviously likely of those materials. And the appellant was intentionally assisting the principals to commit the substantive crime charged under section 3(*b*). Therefore he is guilty on Count 2 also.

Accordingly, the appeal against conviction will be dismissed on both counts.

Lord Scarman [House of Lords]: . . . The guilt of an accessory springs, according to the court's formulation:

> "from the fact that he contemplates the commission of one (or more) of a number of crimes by the principal and he intentionally lends his assistance in order that such a crime will be committed"; *per* Sir Robert Lowry CJ, post, p 1374G. "The relevant crime," the Lord Chief Justice continues, at p 1735A, B, "must be within the contemplation of the accomplice, and only exceptionally would evidence be found to support the allegation that the accomplice had given the principal a completely blank cheque."

The principle thus formulated has great merit. It directs attention to the state of mind of the accused – not what he ought to have in contemplation, but what he did have: it avoids definition and classification, while ensuring that a man will not be convicted of aiding and abetting any offence his principal may commit, but only one which is within his contemplation. He may have in contemplation only one offence, or several: and the several which he contemplates he may see as alternatives. An accessory who leaves it to his principal to choose is liable, provided always the choice is made from the range of offences from which the accessory contemplates the choice will be made. Although the court's formulation of the principle goes further than the earlier cases, it is a sound development of the law and in no way inconsistent with them. I accept it as good judge-made law in a field where there is no statute to offer guidance.

Upon the facts as found by the trial judge (there was no jury because of the Northern Ireland (Emergency Provisions) Act 1973), the appellant knew he was guidng a party of men to the Crosskeys Inn on a UVF military-style "job," ie an attack by bomb, incendiary device or bullet on persons or property. He did not know the particular type of offence intended, but he must have appreciated that it was very likely that those whom he was assisted intended a bomb attack on the inn.

If the appellant contemplated, as he clearly did, a bomb attack as likely, he must also have contemplated the possibility that the man in the car, which he was leading to the inn, had an explosive substance with them. Though he did not know whether they had it with them or not, he must have believed it very likely that they did. In the particular circumstances of this case, the inference that the two offences of possessing the explosive and using it with intent to cause injury or damage were within the appellant's contemplation is fully justified upon the evidence. The appellant was rightly convicted, and I would dismiss his appeal.

3.22   ***The People (DPP) v Michael Egan***
[1989] IR 681
Court of Criminal Appeal, 1989

Costello J: On the 27th of July 1983 in a very successful armed robbery there was stolen from premises in Harold's Cross, Dublin a large quantity of jewellery valued at over £1.3 million. On the 14th of February 1985 Michael Egan, the applicant before this Court, was arrested and detained under Section 30 of the Offences Against the State Act 1939 in connection with the robbery. On the following day he made a written statement whilst in custody. He was then charged with robbery and receiving stolen goods. The only evidence implicating him in the crimes with which he was charged was his written statement. In the course of that statement the applicant said:

"I am self employed and supply and fit aluminium windows for a living. I have a large workshop at the back of the house where I make up the windows. I remember Sunday evening the 24th of July 1983. I received a 'phone call at my home from a male caller requesting permission from me to leave a van in my workshop the following morning. He said he was a friend of an acquaintance of mine. I now know that name of this man who was on the 'phone on that occasion, but I don't want to say it. He told me there was a small stroke coming off and that he would want me to be at my garage door at the back lane at 9 o'clock on Wednesday morning the 27th July of 1983, to open up the door to allow the van to come in. The Wednesday morning after leaving my children to school I came back to the house. I went into the garage at 8.50 am. I opened the door a bit and at 9 o'clock on the dot the van came up the lane and I opened the door full. It was a blue Hiace van. There was at least for or five masked men in the van. The van was reversed into the garage and inside they all got out. As far as I know they all had what looked like .38 revolvers in their hands. When I saw this I got frightened and realized that this stroke was an armed robbery, which if I had known I would not wish to have any part in it".

The statement then went on to describe how one member of the gang had pointed a revolver at the applicant's head and warned him to keep his mouth shut; and it further described what subsequently occurred. The applicant stated that he had learned on the 1.30 news that there had been a big jewellery robbery at O'Connors Jewellery Harold's Cross in the morning and that he "figured" immediately that the gang in his garage was responsible for the robbery. He stated that he thought of ringing the police but was too scared to do so. Later he went into the workshop. He saw three men there and he saw a large amount of jewellery, rings, necklaces and bracelets and gold welding rods. He estimated there were 14 sacks of jewellery. He described how later the men who were in his workshop left and how he found a bag in the workshop which had a large amount of gold rings in it which he kept and disposed of subsequently in the way described in the statement.

The jury found the applicant guilty of robbery and not guilty of receiving stolen goods (having been directed by the trial Judge to treat the two counts as alternatives). He was then sentenced to seven years' imprisonment. The application for leave to appeal is against both the conviction and sentence.

A person may aid and abet the commission of a crime in a number of ways. If he does so at the scene of the crime he will be regarded at common law as an accessory *at* the fact and is frequently referred to as an "aider and abettor". But a person may aid and abet the commission of a crime and not be present when it is committed. He will then at common law be an accessory *before* the fact but he also may be referred to as someone who has "aided and abetted" a crime. Thus, in the *People v Madden* ([1977] IR 336) four accused were charged with the crime of murder as accessories before the fact and were referred to throughout the judgment of the Court of Criminal Appeal as having been charged with aiding and abetting the commission of the crime even though it is clear that there was no evidence they were present when the victim of the murder was killed. It was therefore correct for the learned trial Judge in this case to refer, as he did in his charge to the jury, to the allegation against the accused as being an allegation that he had aided and abetted the burglary on the 27th of July 1983 by his agreement to hide the van in his workshop premises. It should also be pointed out that Section 35 of the Larceny Act 1916 expressly provides that any person who knowingly and wilfully aids, abets, procures or commands the commission of an offence punishable under the Act is liable to be dealt with, indicted, tried and punished as a principal offender.

Although it was admitted that the accused's statement is evidence that he assisted in the commission of a crime, it was submitted on his behalf that the prosecution had failed to adduce evidence from which it could be inferred beyond a reasonable doubt that the applicant had that degree of knowledge of the crime which was in fact committed on the 27th of July 1983 which the law requires to constitute a person an accessory before the fact of that crime. It was urged

(1) that all the applicant knew was that a "small stroke" was to be carried out;
(2) that the applicant's statement established that he was appalled when he learned that the goods which were in the van had been stolen in an armed robbery and that
(3) even though it must be conceded that the statement established that the applicant was aware that goods were to be stolen and that he was being asked to hide them the prosecution had failed to establish that he knew that he was aiding in the crime of robbery and that this is a fundmentally different crime to the crime which he believed he was assisting.

The law on the point raised in this submission was expounded in *Madden's* case to which reference has already been made. In that case a man called Laurence White was shot and killed on the public road in the City of Cork late at night. His assailant escaped in a stolen motor car. It was later found abandoned. In it were found a book of parking discs and some spent discs bearing the fingerprints of two of the accused. The spent discs had been used in Cork on the morning of the murder. Four persons were accused of the murder. All four were convicted by the Special Criminal Court and all four appealed. There was no evidence that any of the accused were present when the deceased had been shot; the case against each of the accused was that he had been an accessory before the fact of murder.

It was pointed out in the judgment of the Court of Criminal Appeal that to sustain the conviction of any one of the accused as an accessory before the fact for aiding and abetting in the commission of the crime of murder the prosecution had to prove that the acts of aiding and abetting attributed to the accused were done in the knowledge of the intended commission, and assisted in the commission, of the actions carrying the *mens rea* of the offence committed by the principal (p 340). The judgment went on:

"In relation to the charge of aiding and abetting it is clear from the cited judgments in *Bainbridge*'s case and *Gamble*'s case that motives and desires are irrelevant, and that mere evidence of common association is insufficient. The kernel of the matter is the establishing of an activity on the part of the accused from which his intention may be inferred and the effect of which is to assist the principal in the commission of the crime proved to have been committed by the principal, or the commission of a crime of a similar nature known to the accused to be the intention of the principal when assisting him" (p 341).

Two of the appellants succeeded before the Court of Criminal Appeal, one (Madden) because the Court concluded that the appellant's statement (which was the only evidence against him) was inadmissible, the other (Lynch) because no admissible evidence had been adduced of any activity on his part in the preparation or commission of a crime of violence or of the murder of Laurence White. The Court upheld the conviction as accessories before the fact of the two other applicants.

In relation to the case of David O'Donnell the evidence against him was that in the white Cortina car used in the course of the murder there was found two parking discs indicating a user on two occasions on the day of the murder each of which contained O'Donnell's fingerprints. There was also found a book of unused parking discs which contained his fingerprints. Whilst in custody O'Donnell denied using parking discs and having then been informed of the finding of his fingerprints on the discs he stated, after caution, that he could not give any explanation for that fact. This failure or refusal to give an explanation took place after it had been made clear to him that an allegation was being made against him that he had parked the car on the morning of the 10th of June as part of the preparation for the murder of Laurence White. The Court concluded that it had been established as a reasonable inference that a necessary part of the preparation for the murder would be the availability of the stolen white Cortina car during the earlier part of the day and that a necessary ingredient of its availability was that it should be so parked as not to attract attention from Gardai or traffic wardens; that the trial Court was entitled to conclude that the denials of O'Donnell of the use of parking discs or of parking the car were false, and that having been made aware that the suspicion against him was involvement in murder the conduct of the accused was not reasonably consistent with any explanation other than that he was, at the time he parked the car, aware of the general nature of the purpose for which it was intended to be used. His application for leave to appeal accordingly failed.

The evidence against the fourth applicant, Bernard Lynch, was different. He made a statement (which the Court held had been properly admitted in evidence at the trial) which consisted in an admission to stealing the white Cortina car in Limerick four days before the morning and an account of how he had driven it to

Cork on the 8th of June, put false number plates on it, and how he had met the person who had asked him to steal it in Cork. His statement went on to give an account of driving with two persons to show them where he had parked the white Cortina car and an admission that in the course of the journey his two companions were talking of the feasibility of "getting" Larry White (the victim of the later killing). He said in his statement:

"I presumed that the car was going to be used to do something to the Whites. I thought they might be going to kidnap, wound, or beat up either one or other of them. I gathered there was going to be something of consequence and serious as the White Brothers had been troublesome to our movement Official Sinn Fein in Cork during the past three to four years".

The statement went on to describe how he had attempted to wipe the parking discs which were in the Cortina so as to clean them of fingerprints.

The Court concluded that after the knowledge which the accused had acquired as to the purpose for which the car was required the accused took active steps to assist in implementing that purpose by showing his two companions where the white Cortina was parked and by wiping the parking discs, and that the accused's statement was only consistent with his knowledge that the crime which was to be committed was one which would cause serious injury to one of the Whites. As a person who takes an active step in the preparation for the carrying out of a crime likely to cause serious injury to another is guilty of murder in the event of that other person being killed, the Court concluded that Lynch's conviction should stand.

Applying the principles established both in *Madden's* case and *Maxwell's* case the Court has reached the following conclusions:

(a) the prosecution was able to establish in this case that the applicant knew

    (i)   that a crime was to be committed,

    (ii)   that the crime involved the theft of goods,

    (iii)   that with this knowledge he assisted the commission of the crime which was actually perpetrated by the principal offender when he agreed to make his workshop available so that the goods to be stolen could safely be hidden after the theft.

(b) The law of theft in this country creates a number of different offences, depending on the circumstances in which goods are stolen. If a principal offender steals goods from another person he is guilty of a felony punishable with a maximum sentence of 14 years (Section 14 of the Larceny Act 1916); if he steals them and uses force whilst doing so he is guilty of the felony of robbery which is punishable with a maximum sentence of life imprisonment (Section 23 of the 1916 Act); if he steals goods having entered a building as a trespasser he is guilty of the felony of burglary which is punishable with a sentence of imprisonment for a maximum period of 14 years (Section 23(a) of the 1916 Act). When goods are stolen it is not, in the opinion of this Court, necessary for the prosecution to establish that a person who has aided the principal offender before the crime was committed knew either the means which were to be employed by the principal offender, or the place from which the goods were to be stolen or the time at which the theft was to take place or the nature of the goods to be stolen. It will suffice if the prosecution is able to show that the accused who gave assistance to a principal offender before the crime was committed knew the nature of the crime intended, namely the theft of goods.

It follows, therefore, that it was open to the Jury to conclude that the applicant was an accessory before the fact of the crime committed by the princpal offender and that the conviction of the applicant cannot be set aside. It also follows that the sentence was one which could properly be imposed by the learned trial Judge. As no challenge to the severity of this sentence had been advanced it follows that the conviction and sentence must stand.

Innocent agency

3.23 The accused cannot be convicted of being a party to an offence which has not taken place. It would seem to follow that where the principal offender has a defence to a crime then those who assist him should also be acquitted. However, a person could use a six-year old child, a madman or a dog to commit an offence. To meet this situation the courts have evolved the doctrine of innocent agency. This treats the legally innocent perpetrators of a crime in the same way as if they were merely instruments of the accused; *R v Cogan & Leak*[16]. Thus one may be guilty of murder if one has entered into a common design with a madman to kill another, provided the madman has sufficient sense to be capable of making that arrangement, or where one unleashes the madman on the victim knowing that death or serious injury will be the result of that action; *R v Matusevich*[17]. In *R v Howe*[18] the House of Lords held that there was no rule of law whereby an accessory could not be convicted of a more serious crime than the principal.

The doctrine of common design

3.24 A convenient statement of the doctrine of common design is to be found in *R v Anderson & Morris*.

3.25 *R v Anderson & Morris*
[1966] 2 QB 110; [1966] 2 All ER 644; [1966] 2 WLR 1195;
(1966) 50 Cr App R 216
Court of Criminal Appeal, 1966

Parker CJ: . . . where two persons embark on a joint enterprise each is liable for the acts done in pursuance of that joint enterprise and that includes liability for unusual consequences if they arise from the execution of the joint enterprise but (and this is the crux of the matter) that, if one of the adventurers goes beyond what has been tacitly agreed as part of the common enterprise his co-adventurer is not liable for the consequences of that unauthorised act.

3.26 The prosecution does not have to prove an express agreement; that may be inferred from the evidence; *The People (DPP) v Pringle McCann & O'Shea*[19]. At the start of this chapter the view was expressed that participation is not judged in accordance with objective rules but on the basis of subjective knowledge. It follows that for an accused to be found guilty of complicity in a crime of intent he must embark on the main crime, aware that

16 [1976] QB 217.
17 (1977) 15 ALR 117.
18 [1987] AC 417.
19 (1981) 2 Frewen 57.

the further crime may be committed, and must be willing that such further crime should be committed if it is necessary to the overall criminal purpose. This may be readily inferred if loaded firearms were used to carry out a robbery or, as in *R v McClafferty*, (below,) where a group of criminals set out to murder their victim in the bosom of his own family.

3.27   The Canadian Criminal Code contained an objective element as to what the accused "ought to have known" but this has been subject to constitutional scrutiny, as will be seen below. Murder by recklessness still remains in Australia; *R v Crabbe*[20]; *R v Zecevic*[21]. In this jurisdiction one must intend to kill or cause serious injury to be guilty of murder; s 4 of the Criminal Justice Act 1964.

3.28   If the accused embarks on a criminal enterprise knowing that it may be necessary to cause serious injury to a person, that is evidence that, if necessary, he intended such injury to be inflicted, and if death results, that intention will render him guilty of murder.

3.29   *R v McClafferty*
                            [1981] NI 1
                Crown Court Northern Ireland, 1980

Facts: The accused was charged with the murder of a prison officer and his wife at their home. In a statement the accused said that he drove a car containing two gunmen to the prison officer's home knowing that they intended to kill him, but the accused said that he did not know that they intended to kill the prison officer's wife.

Hutton J: On the first count the accused is charged with the murder of Mr Patrick Mackin on a date unknown between 2 February 1979 and 5 February 1979. On the second count the accused is charged with the murder of Mrs Violet Mackin on a date unknown between 2 February and 5 February 1979.

The Crown case against the accused on the first two counts consists of two parts. First, the Crown has sought to prove that between 2 and 5 February 1979 Mr Mackin, who was a retired prison officer, and his wife, Mrs Mackin, were murdered by a gunman at their home at 568 Oldpark Road. Secondly the Crown has sought to prove, in reliance upon oral statements and a written statement, which the Crown say were made by the accused, and also in reliance upon writing and drawing on a map, which the Crown say were made by the accused at about 7.00 pm or shortly after it on Saturday, 3 February 1979, that the accused drove the gunman, who murdered Mr and Mrs Mackin, and an accomplice through Etna Drive up to the Oldpark Road, knowing that the gunman was intending to kill a prison officer; that he stopped the car at a point on the Oldpark Road to let the gunman and accomplice out of the car; that he then turned the car and waited with the enging running for the gunman and accomplice to return; that the gunman and accomplice returned to the car in a few minutes and got into it, and that the accused then drove them back to Etna Drive. The Crown would therefore say the accused was guilty of the murders of Mr and Mrs Mackin as an aider and abettor.

As regards the first part of the Crown case, I find the following facts which have been proved beyond a reasonable doubt.

(1) Mr Mackin was a retired prison officer, having retired in November 1978 after

20 (1958) ALR 417.
21 (1987) 61 ALJ 375.

27 years service. Both Mr and Mrs Mackin were alive and well in their home at 568 Oldpark Road on Saturday, 3 February 1979 at 6.35 pm when they were visited there by their niece, Miss Eileen McCullough, who had a cup of tea with them and left at 6.35 pm.

(2) On Sunday, 4 February 1979 at about 9.25 am Mr and Mrs Mackin were found lying dead on the floor of the back downstairs living room in 568 Oldpark Road by their son, Mr Alan Mackin. Mr Mackin had been killed by two bullets fired into his chest. In addition a third bullet had struck him in the left arm and shoulder. Mrs Mackin had been killed by one bullet fired into her chest. The three bullets which had struck Mr Mackin and the one which had struck Mrs Mackin had all been fired from the same revolver, a Smith and Wesson .38 revolver. When Mr Alan Mackin arrived at the house about 9.25 am on 4 February, the front door was closed and the back door was open.

I therefore find it proved beyond a reasonable doubt that Mr and Mrs Mackin were murdered in their home at 568 Oldpark Road between 6.35 pm on 3 February 1979 and 9.25 am on 4 February 1979 by a person who killed them with shots fired from a single revolver.

The second part of the Crown case is based upon the oral statements and the written statement which the Crown say were actually made by the accused to the police during an interview from 8.10 pm on 5 February to 12.30 am on 6 February 1979 and upon the writing and drawing which the Crown say the accused made on the map during that interview.

I have already ruled that the oral statements and the written statement and the map are admissible in evidence and they have been given and put in evidence.

The police evidence is that in the two oral statements the accused gave an account (the second account being rather more detailed than the first one) of how he drove two men up the Oldpark Road to do a "screw", waited for them and then drove them back. The police evidence was that after the two oral accounts the accused drew on a map the route which he took from the Star Club in Balholme Drive to the Oldpark Road and wrote in on the map, in his own hand, where he picked up the two men, where he stopped the car on the Oldpark Road and where he turned the car.

The police evidence is that the accused then made a written statement which he signed at the end of each page and that he then wrote the certificate in his own hand at the end of the statement which he also signed.

The statement was as follows:

"I Gerard McClafferty wish to make a statement. I want someone to write down what I say. I have been told that I need not say anything unless I wish to do so and that whatever I say may be given in evidence.

G. McClafferty

I want to tell you that I joined the Provisional IRA last year. I think it was during the month of January after me and my wife separated. I was approached by a man in Ardoyne. I can't say who he was. I agreed to join. Some weeks after this I saw this same man. He told me that I was in. I was not asked to do anything until last Saturday night. I was in the Star Social Club, Balholme Drive, with my father and his mate. I don't know his name. We were upstairs in the lounge standing at the bar. The doorman, Peter Delaney, came to me and told me that I was wanted at the door. He is the same man who told me about my wife wanting me on the phone at 6.30 pm. I told you about that this morning. I went downstairs to the front door. There was a fellow standing at the door. He called me by my nickname Jona. He says 'There is a car sitting over there'. He says 'Go over and get into it, you're driving'. This car was parked up the cribby facing down the street towards Brompton Park. This would have been about 7 pm or shortly after. I walked across the street and got into the car. It was quite dark but I could see the car was a red colour. I don't know what make it was. I don't know much about cars. I was told by the man at the door that the keys were on the front seat. When I got into the car I saw the keys lying on the driver's seat. I did not know how to start the car. I got the key into the ignition but could not start it. I called the fellow over. He told me to press the button on the dash and it started. He told me to press the same button to stop the car. The fellow then disappeared. I did not know who he was. Before he left he told me that I was to pick two fellows up at the entry at the bottom of Etna Drive. I drove round to the entry via Brompton Park. I stopped the car at the entry. Two fellows came out of the entry and got into the back seat. One of them told me to drive up towards Oldpark and that they would tell me where to stop. I drove up Etna Drive and along Alliance Avenue and turned left up the Oldpark Road. On the way up the Oldpark Road I asked where was I supposed to stop and what was the score. They told me they were going to do a screw. I knew that what they meant by a screw, they were referring to a prison warden. I was told to stop near a garage on the left side of the road. The two boys got out and I saw them go up the side of a house. They appeared to go up a sort of an entry at the side. The house was on the same side of the road as we were on. I kept the engine going and drove up the road a bit. I turned round and drove back down and parked on the opposite side of the road. I kept the engine revving to keep the car going. After a few minutes the two fellows came out and got into the car. I drove off down the road towards the Ardoyne. On the way back down the two boys in the back were arguing and seemed to be panicking. I heard something said about a woman but I didn't know anything until the next morning about the woman being shot. I had a brave few drinks on me and things were a wee bit hazy. I drove back down Alliance Avenue and down Etna Drive. The two boys got out at the bottom of Etna Drive at the same spot where I picked them up. I drove the car back to the Star Social Club and parked it in the same place. I stopped the car by pressing the button, leaving the keys in the ignition. I walked straight home. The next morning at about 11 am when I got up out of bed my father told me about a prison officer and his wife being shot up the Oldpark.

G. McClafferty

I have read above statement and I have been told that I can correct, alter or add anything I wish. This statement is true. I have made it of my own free will.

G. McClafferty."

(The Judge then set out the reasons why he held that the written statement was a statement made by the accused and that the account contained in the written statement of the part played by the accused in driving two men up the Oldpark Road and back again was true. The judgment then continued):

In the statement the accused said, "On the way up the Oldpark Road I asked where was I supposed to stop and what was the score. They told me they were going to do a screw. I knew that what they meant by a screw, they were referring to a prison warden". I have no doubt that the accused knew that the words "do a screw" meant killing a prison officer.

Therefore the accused is guilty as an aider and abettor of the murder of Mr Mackin because he drove the two men up the Oldpark Road and let them out of the car and then turned the car and waited for them and on their return drove them away from the scene, knowing that their intention was to kill a prison officer; and I am satisfied that Mr Mackin was shot dead by one of the two men whom the accused drove up the Oldpark Road.

Accordingly I find the accused guilty under count 1.

In the second count the accused is charged with the murder of Mrs Violet Mackin, the wife of Mr Patrick Mackin, the retired prison officer. I have already found that Mr and Mrs Mackin were murdered in their home at 568 Oldpark Road by a gunman who killed them with shots fired from a .38 revolver. Mr Mackin had been struck by three bullets and Mrs Mackin by one.

I am satisfied that the killings of Mr and Mrs Mackin took place at the same time when they were together in the back living room of their home.

In part of his written statement the accused said:

"I drove round to the entry via Brompton Park. I stopped the car at the entry. Two fellows came out of the entry and got into the back seat. One of them told me to drive up towards Oldpark and that they would tell me where to stop. I drove up Etna Drive and along Alliance Avenue and turned left up the Oldpark Road on the way up the Oldpark Road I asked where was I supposed to stop and what was the score. They told me they were going to do a screw. I knew what they meant by a screw, they were referring to a prison warden. I was told to stop near a garage on the left side of the road. The two boys got out and I saw them go up the side of a house. They appeared to go up a sort of an entry at the side. The house was on the same side of the road as we were on. I kept the engine going and drove up the road a bit. I turned round and drove back down and parked on the opposite side of the road. I kept the engine revving to keep the car going. After a few minutes the two fellows came out and got into the car. I drove off down the road towards the Ardoyne. On the way back down the two boys in the back were arguing and seemed to be panicking. I heard something said about a woman but I didn't know anything until the next morning about the woman being shot."

I am satisfied from that statement that the accused drove the gunman and an accomplice to the Oldpark Road and let them out of the car, knowing that they were going to kill a prison officer, and then waited in the car for the gunman and accomplice to come back and on their return drove them away from the scene. I am satisfied that Mrs Mackin was shot dead by one of the two men whom the accused drove up the Oldpark Road. But, whilst I am satisfied that the accused knew that the gunman and the accomplice were going to kill a prison officer, there is no evidence that the accused was told that they were also going to kill the prison officer's wife. I have already found the accused guilty of the murder of Mr Mackin as an aider and abettor, and the Crown case is that the accused is also guilty as an aider and abettor of the murder of Mrs Mackin because he drove the gunman and accomplice up the Oldpark Road knowing that they were going to commit a murder.

The principle of law which determines whether the act of one party to a joint criminal enterprise involves another party in criminal liability has been stated in decisions of the English Court of Criminal Appeal in *R v Smith* (referred to in *R v Beatty* (1963) 48 Cr App R 6) and *R v Anderson*, [1966] 2 QB 110.

These cases were appeals against convictions for manslaughter, there being no joint enterprise to kill or cause grievous bodily harm, but I consider that the general principle stated in those cases applies also to a case where the purpose of the joint enterprise is to kill A and one of the adventurers also kills B. In *R v Smith* (1963) 48 Cr App R at page 9 Slade J, delivering the judgment of the court, said:

"The grounds of appeal in this case, although worded in different ways, really, as I understand them, amount to the same thing: that is, that the use of a knife by Atkinson in this case was a departure, that is to say, assuming against Smith, as must be assumed in the light of the jury's verdict, that he was a party to some concerted action being taken against the barman, he certainly was not a party to the use upon the barman of as knife which resulted in the barman's death. It is significant, as I have shown by reading Smith's own statement, that he knew that Atkinson carried a knife. Indeed I think he knew that one of the other men carried a cut-throat razor. It must have been clearly within the contemplation of a man like Smith who, to use one expression, had almost gone berserk himself to have left the public house only to get bricks to tear up the joint, that if the bartender did his duty to quell the disturbance and picked up the night stick, anyone who knew that he had a knife in his possession, like Atkinson, might use it on the barman, as Atkinson did. By no stretch of imagination, in the opinion of this court, can that be said to be outside the scope of the concerted action in this case. In a case of this kind it is difficult to imagine what would have been outside the scope of the concerted action, possibly the use of a loaded revolver, the presence of which was unknown to the other parties; but that is not this case, and I am expressing no opinion about that. The court is satisfied that anything which is within the ambit of the concerted arrangement is the responsibility of each party who chooses to enter into the criminal purpose."

And in *R v Anderson* the Court of Criminal Appeal approved the following principle formulated by Mr Geoffrey Lane, QC (as he then was), the judgment of the court, delivered by Lord Parker, LCJ, stated at page 118:

"He would put the principle of law to be invoked in this form; that where two persons embark on a joint enterprise, each is liable for the acts done in pursuance of that joint enterprise, that that includes liability for unusual consequences if they arise from the execution of the agreed joint enterprise; but (and this is the crux of the matter) that if one of the adventurers goes beyond what has been tacitly agreed as part of the common enterprise, his co-adventurer is not liable for the consequences of that unauthorised act. Finally, he says it is for the jury in every case to decide whether what was done was part of the joint enterprise, or went beyond it and was in fact an act unauthorised by that joint enterprise.

In support of that, he refers to a number of authorities to which the court finds it unnecessary to refer in detail, which in the opinion of this court shows that at any rate for the last 130 or 140 years that has been the true position."

I regard it as an inference of overwhelming strength that the killing of Mrs Mackin arose from the execution of the enterprise of killing her husband and that she was killed, it may be in a panic, by the gunman because he thought that she would go to the defence or assistance of her husband, or would attack him or (if she were left alive) would raise the alarm or give the police a description of his facial appearance or of his build and clothing.

Mr Nicholson QC submitted, in effect, that it was at least possible (and that the possibility therefore raised a reasonable doubt) that Mrs Mackin was killed for a reason which did not arise from the execution of the enterprise of killing her husband, such as that the gunman had a separate grudge against her or had a liking for killing. I do not accept that submission. I consider that it goes beyond the bounds of reality to conceive that the killing of Mrs Mackin did not arise from the execution of the enterprise of killing her husband and that she was killed for a purpose unconnected with the killing of her husband. I am satisfied that the killing of Mrs Macking cannot be viewed as "an overwhelming supervening event which is of such a character that it will relegate into a matter of history matters which could otherwise be looked upon as causative factors", to respectfully adopt the words of Lord Parker in *R v Anderson* at page 223, which words were applied as an appropriate test to determine the liability of a joint adventure in *R v Reid* (1975) 62 CR App R 109.

Therefore I find the accused guilty of the murder of Mrs Mackin under the principles stated in *R v Smith* and *R v Anderson*.

In addition, I consider that the accused is guilty of the murder of Mrs Mackin under the principle formulated by the English Court of Criminal Appeal in *R v Bainbridge* [1960] 1 QB 129 which was approved by the House of Lords in *R v Maxwell* [1978] NI 42. In *R v Bainbridge* at 133 Lord Parker LCJ stated:

"Mr Simpson, who has argued this case very well, contends that that direction is wrong. As he puts it, in order that a man should be convicted of being accessory before the fact, it must be shown that at the time he bought the equipment in a case such as this he knew that a particular crime was going to be committed, and by a particular crime Mr Simpson means that the premises in this case which were going to be broken into were known to the appellant and contemplated by him, and not only the premises in question but the date when the breaking was going to occur; in other words, that he must know that on a particular date the Stoke Newington branch of the Midland Bank is intended to be broken into.

The court fully appreciates that it is not enough that it should be shown that a man knows that some illegal venture is intended. To take this case, it would not be enough if he knew – he says he only suspected – that the equipment was going to be used to dispose of stolen property. That would not be enough. Equally, this court is quite satisfied that it is unnecessary that knowledge of the particular crime which was in fact committed should be shown to his knowledge to have been intended, and by 'particular crime' I am using the words in the same way in which Mr Simpson used them, namely, on a particular date and particular premises.

It is not altogether easy to lay down a precise form of words which will cover every case that can be contemplated but, having considered the cases and the law this court is quite clear that the direction of Judge Aarvold in this case cannot be criticised, indeed, it might well have been made with the passage in *Foster's Crown Cases* (3rd ed. (1809) at p 369) in mind, because there the author says 'If the principal totally and substantially varieth, if being solicited to commit a felony of one kind he wilfully and knowingly committeth a felony of another, he will stand single in that offence, and the person soliciting will not be involved in his guilt. For on his part it was no more than a fruitless ineffectual temptation,' the converse, of course, being that if the principal does not totally and substantially vary the advice or the help and does not wilfully and knowingly commit a different form of felony altogether, the man who has advised or helped, aided or abetted, will be guilty as an accessory before the fact.

Judge Aarvold in this case, in the passage to which I have referred, makes it clear that there must be not merely suspicion but knowledge that a crime of the type in question was intended, and that the equipment was bought with that in view. In his reference to the felony of the type intended it was, as he stated, the felony of breaking and entering premises and the stealing of property from those premises. The court can see nothing wrong in that direction."

The Crown submitted that the accused in the present case was guilty under the principle laid down in *R v Maxwell* itself. However, in *Maxwell* at page 70F Lord Scarman observed that the decision of the Court of Criminal Appeal in that case extended the *Bainbridge* principle and he stated:

"Counsel for the appellant submits that, if *Reg v Bainbridge* is to be followed, there is no evidence in the present case that the appellant knew the particular type of crime intended, i.e. doing an act with intent to cause an explosion of the nature likely to endanger life or cause serious injury to property. Counsel is really submitting that, if his client's conviction be upheld on either of the two counts with which his appeal is concerned, (count 1, doing an act with intent to cause an explosion, and count 2, possession of an explosive substance with intent), your Lordships will be extending the law beyond the decision in *Bainbridge*, and that, even if that decision be good law, such extension is unjustifiable. I think *Bainbridge* was correcly decided. But I agree with counsel for the appellant that in the instant case the Court of Criminal Appeal in Northern Ireland has gone further than the Court of Appeal for England and Wales found it necessary to go in *Bainbridge*. It is not possible in the present case to declare that it is proved, beyond reasonable doubt, that the appellant knew a bomb attack upon the inn was intended by those whom he was assisting. It is not established, therefore, that he knew the particular type of crime intended. The court, however, refused to limit criminal responsibility by reference to knowledge by the accused of the type of class of crime intended by those whom he assisted. Instead, the court has formulated a principle which avoids the uncertainties and ambiguities of classification. The guilt of an accessory springs, according to the court's formulation;

'from the fact that he contemplates the commission of one (or more) of a number of crimes by the principal and he intentionally lends his assistance in order that such a crime will be committed',: per Sir Robert Lowry CJ. 'The relevant crime', the Lord Chief Justice continues, 'must be within the contemplation of the accomplice, and only exceptionally would evidence be found to support the allegation that the accomplice had given the principal a completely blank cheque.'"

In my judgment the accused in this case is guilty under the *Bainbridge* principle and it is unnecessary for the Crown to invoke the extended principle formulated in the *Maxwell* case. In *R v Bainbridge* the Stoke Newington branch of the Midland Bank had been broken into by cutting the bars of a window, and the doors of the strong room and of a safe inside the strong room. The evidence established that the appellant had bought cutting equipment on behalf of one or more men knowing that it was going to be used for the purposes of breaking and entering premises. The appeal was argued on the basis that it was not proved that the appellant knew that the cutting equipment was going to be used to break and enter the Stoke Newington Branch of the Midland Bank. The conviction of the appellant was upheld on the ground stated by Lord Parker that:

"it is unnecessary that knowledge of the particular crime which was in fact committed should be shown to his knowledge to have been intended,"

and that it is sufficient to show:

"knowledge that a crime of the type in question was intended".

Therefore I consider that if, on the night when the thieves broke into the Midland Bank in Stoke Newington using the cutting equipment, they had also on that night used the cutting equipment to break into the Stoke Newington branch of Barclays Bank, Bainbridge would also have been guilty as an accessory before the fact to the second breaking and entering. Similarly I consider that if the thieves had told Bainbridge that they required the cutting equipment to break into the Stoke Newington Branch of the Midland Bank and he had supplied the equipment to them with that knowledge and on the night, after breaking into the Midland Bank in Stoke Newington, the thieves had also broken into the branch of Barclays Bank in Stoke Newington, Bainbridge also would have been guilty in respect of the second breaking and entering.

In the instant case the accused drove the two men up the Oldpark Road knowing that it was their intention to commit the crime of murder, the particular crime intended being the murder of a prison officer. At the same time as the men murdered the prison officer they murdered his wife. Therefore I consider that the accused is guilty of the murder of the wife because he had knowledge that "a crime of the type in question was intended".

For the accused to argue that he is not guilty of the murder of the wife because he did not know that the men would kill the wife, is to put forward the argument, advanced in the *Bainbridge* case and rejected by the Court in that case, that the Crown must show that the accused knew that a particular crime (in this case the killing of a particular person) was going to be committed. Therefore under the *Bainbridge* principle I find the accused guilty as an aider and abettor of the murder of Mrs Mackin.

3.30   *R v Calderwood & Moore*
                          [1983] NI 361; 92 Cr App R 131
                          Crown Court Northern Ireland, 1983

Hutton J: In his written statement Calderwood said that he fired one shot at the man after the front seat passenger had fired at him and the man had fallen and was lying on the ground. I am satisfied that a bullet from each of two revolvers struck the body of Paul Anthony Blake, and therefore I am satisfied that the bullet fired by Calderwood struck the body.

Mr Donaldson did not dispute that those facts made Calderwood a principal in the second degree because he was present at the scene of the attack aiding and abetting the front seat passenger, but Mr Donaldson submitted that it was not proved beyond a reasonable doubt that Calderwood was a principal in the first degree. He submitted that on the evidence, including the evidence of the State pathologist, it was reasonably possible that Mr Blake was already dead when Calderwood's bullet struck him, and that firing into a dead body could not make the firer a principal in the first degree because an essential ingredient of murder is the act of killing, and that firing into a dead body could not make the firer a principal in the first degree even although the firing was in the course of a joint attack on the victim and the victim had been killed instantaneously a moment before a bullet fired by the accused's confederate. On the evidence the front seat passenger fired at least two shots before Calderwood fired, and I think it is reasonably possible on the evidence that Mr Blake was killed almost instantaneously by one of the shots fired by the front seat passenger so that he was already dead when Calderwood's shot struck his body. But even if this were the factual position, in my judgment Calderwood was still a principal in the first degree to the murder. I consider that where two or more men attack another and death results, the attackers are all guilty of the homicide as principals in the first degree, even although it is not possible to say which of the accused inflicted the actual wound or blow which caused the death or even although only one fatal wound or blow was inflicted. In *R v Macklin* (1838) 2 Lewin CC 225; 168 ER 1136:

". . . a body of persons had assembled together, and were committing a riot. The constables interfering for the purpose of dispersing the crowd and apprehending the offenders, resistance was made to them by the mob, and one of the constables was beaten severely by the mob. The different prisoners all took part in the violence used, some by beating him with sticks, some by throwing stones, and others by striking him with their fists. Of this aggregate violence the constable afterwards died."

Baron Alderson ruled:

". . . it is a principle of law, that if several persons act together in pursuance of a common intent, every act done in furtherance of such intent by each of them is, in law, done by all."

In *R v Salmon* (1880) 6 QBD 79 where three men fired at a target in a field and one of the shots fired by them struck and killed a boy, although it was not known which of the three fired the shot, all three were held guilty of manslaughter. No doubt in *R v Salmon* the convictions could be explained on the basis that the one accused who actually shot the boy was guilty as a principal in the first degree and the other two accused were present aiding and abetting him and were thus guilty as principals in the second degree, but it appears that the eminent court which decided *R v Salmon* held that all three accused were guilty of manslaughter as principals in the first degree and did not think it necessary to uphold the convictions on the ground that two of the accused were principals in the second degree. Thus Crown counsel at page 82 submitted:

"The prisoner who fired the fatal shot was guilty of such wicked or culpable negligence as amounts to manslaughter; the other two were joint actors with him."

Lord Coleridge CJ stated:

"It was manslaughter in him who killed the boy. The death resulted from the action of all three and they are all liable."

And Stephen J stated at page 83:

"Firing a rifle under circumstances such as in the present case was a highly dangerous act and all are responsible for they unite to fire at the spot in question and they all omit to take any precautions whatever to prevent damage."

In *R v Evans and Gardiner (no 1)* [1976] VR 517 at 519 Lush J stated:

"I point out that in many cases of which *R v Lowry and King No 2* and *Harding's* case and *Lynch's* case and indeed the present are examples it has not been necessary for the jury to distinguish between principals in the first degree acting in concert and principals in the second degree. Of the cases that I have mentioned *Lynch's* case is perhaps that in which the classification of the accused man as an aider and abettor was most obvious. In the present case either classification of Evans' role is open and no doubt juries can be instructed on the distinction between acting in concert and aiding and abetting and instructed to treat duress as a defence in the latter and not in the former. This necessity would have the disadvantage of adding still another complication to a jury trial."

The defence of duress as discussed in this judgment is reproduced at para **4.48**.

3.31   ***R v Hyde & Others***
[1990] 3 All ER 892; [1990] 3 WLR 1115;
(1991) 92 Cr App R 131; [1991] Crim LR 133
Court of Appeal England, 1990

Facts: The three appellants kicked and punched a man outside a public house. The victim died from a kick to the head. The appellants were charged with murder. At their trial the prosecution alleged that the appellants had carried out a joint attack on the victim and were equally responsible for his death, even though it was impossible to say which of the three had inflicted the fatal blow or blows, and that either their intention had been to cause serious injury or each knew that such was the intention of the others when he took part. All three appellants gave evidence denying that there had been any joint enterprise or any intent to do serious harm to the victim. The appellants submitted that since the jury could not be sure whose act caused the death none of them should be convicted of murder. The judge directed the jury that if all three appellants intended to do grievous bodily harm to the victim then all three were guilty of murder; if they did not so intend but one of them decided to do it, then if either of the others could be shown to have had the same intention, inasmuch as he foresaw the real possibility that that might be the result of the fight which he was putting in train, then he too shared the responsibility. The jury convicted all three of murder. They appealed against their conviction on the ground that the jury had not been properly directed on joint enterprise.

Lord Lane CJ: Before us the primary ground advanced by counsel was the contention that the judge misdirected the jury on the law of joint enterprise. The passages in the summing up of which complaint is made are these:

"As I say ordinarily speaking if he does something which is beyond the scope of the agreement, that is as you might say the end of the agreement. But, what if the others anticipated that he might do some such thing? and here we have to apply common sense. Fights do get out of hand and escalate. A man who starts by punching may get excited and decide to kick. If there was a tacit agreement to punch and kick, a man who is kicking may decide to give a kick like that which was allegedly given by Collins and which has been described as a place kick or a penalty kick, a description which if the basic facts are right is not a bad description of the kick. If either of the other two, and you have to consider the case of each of them separately, foresaw and contemplated a real possibility that one of his fellows might in the excitement of the moment go beyond the actual plan and intend to do and do grievous bodily harm, then you have to consider whether that man, the one who had the foresight, did not in truth intend that result himself."

The judge then went on to explain to the jury the distinction which may, in some cases, exist between what a man desires should happen and what a man intends should happen. He explained to the jury that foresight that something will happen is not necessarily the same as an intention that it should happen, though it may be powerful evidence of such intention. The judge concluded this part of his summing up with the following words:

"We may summarise it shortly by saying that if all three intended to do grievous bodily harm, then that is that, they are all guilty of murder. If they did not but one of them decided to do it, then if either of the others can be shown to have had the same intention, inasmuch as he foresaw the real possibility that that might be the result of the fight which he was putting in train, then he too shares in the responsibility as in common sense he must."

The specific complaints as set out in the notice of appeal are as follows. (1) The judge, in the circumstances of the case, erred in directing the jury on foreseeability, such a direction being unnecessary and confusing. (2) Alternatively, the judge erred in directing the jury that the defendant's foresight of the state of mind of another defendant was a relevant consideration in determining whether the defendant having that foresight had the intention to do grievous bodily harm. (3) Alternatively, the judge's direction on foreseeability did not sufficiently distinguish between foreseeability and intention and/or did not sufficiently underline the necessity for the prosecution to prove the specific intent required for the offence of murder.

The judgment of this court in *R v Slack* [1989] 3 All ER 90, [1989] QB 775 was not delivered until some four months after the conclusion of the hearing of the instant case. Consequently the judge here did not have before him the distinction which we endeavoured to draw in *R v Slack* between the mental element required to be proved vis-à-vis the secondary party (hereinafter called "B") and that required in the case of the principal party, the actual killer (hereinafter called "A"). In the passages we have cited from the summing up of which complaint is made, the judge was endeavouring to apply the principles which were, prior to *R v Slack*, thought to apply to cases of joint enterprise.

The question is whether the directions in the present case were sufficient to comply with the law as it now stands.

There are, broadly speaking, two main types of joint enterprise cases where death results to the victim. The first is where the primary object of the participants is to do some kind of physical injury to the victim. The second is where the primary object is not to cause physical injury to any victim but, for example, to commit burglary. The victim is assaulted and killed as a (possibly unwelcome) incident of the burglary. The latter type of case may pose more complicated questions than the former, but the principle in each is the same. A must be proved to have intended to kill or to do serious bodily harm at the time he killed. As was pointed out in *R v Slack* [1989] 3 All ER 90 at 94, [1989] QB 775 at 781, B, to be guilty, must be proved to have lent himself to a criminal enterprise involving the infliction of serious harm or death, or to have had an express or tacit understanding with A that such harm or death should, if necessary, be inflicted.

We were there endeavouring, respectfully, to follow the principles enunciated by Sir Robin Cooke in *Chang Wing-siu v R* [1984] 3 All ER 877 at 880–881 [1985] AC 168 at 175:

> "The case must depend rather on the wider principle whereby a secondary party is criminally liable for acts by the primary offender of a type which the former foresees but does not necessarily intend. That there is such a principle is not in doubt. It turns on contemplation or, putting the same idea in other words, authorisation, which may be express but is more usually implied. It meets the case of a crime foreseen as a possible incident of the common unlawful enterprise. The criminal culpability lies in participating in the venture with that foresight."

It has been pointed out by Professor Smith, in his commentary on *R v Wakely* [1990] Crim LR 119 at 120–121, that in the judgments in *R v Slack* [1989] 3 All ER 90, [1989] QB 775 and also in *R v Wakely* itself, to both of which I was a party, insufficient attention was paid by the court to the distinction between on the one hand tacit agreement by B that A should use violence, and on the other hand a realisation by B that A, the principal party, may use violence despite B's refusal to authorise or agree to its use. Indeed in *R v Wakely* we went so far as to say:

> "The suggestion that a mere foresight of the real or definite possibility of violence being used as is sufficient to constitute the mental element of murder is *prima facie*, academically speaking at least, not sufficient."

On reconsideration, that passage is not in accordance with the principles set out by Sir Robin Cooke which we were endeavouring to follow and was wrong, or at least misleading. If B realises (without agreeing to such conduct being used) that A may kill or intentionally inflict serious injury, but nevertheless continues to participate with A in the venture, that will amount to a sufficient mental element for B to be guilty of murder if A, with the requisite intent, kills in the course of the venture. As Professor Smith points out, B has in those circumstances lent himself to the enterprise and by so doing he has given assistance and encouragement to A in carrying out an enterprise which B realises may involve murder.

That being the case it seems to us that the judge was correct when he directed the jury in the terms of those passages of the summing up which we have already quoted. It may be that a simple direction on the basis of *R v Anderson and Morris* [1966] 2 All ER 644, [1966] 2 QB 110 would, in the circumstances of this case, have been enough, but the direction given was sufficiently clear and the outcome scarcely surprising. That ground of appeal, which was in the forefront of the arguments of each of the appellants, therefore fails.

[The courts then considered certain subsidiary grounds of appeal against conviction and continued:] We do not consider that any of the grounds of appeal are substantiated so far as conviction is concerned, and the appeals against conviction are accordingly dismissed.

[The court then considered the appeals against sentence and held that in the light of the conviction for murder there was no necessity to impose any separate sentence in respect of the offence of assault occasioning actual bodily harm and that therefore the sentence of four year's imprisonment would be quashed.]
Appeal against conviction for murder dismissed. Sentences varied.

Recent judicial decisions on intention, which have culminated in *R v Nedrick* (see para **5.45**) have also caused a re-examination of the state of mind required of a secondary party when the principal does something which comes outside the express agreement between the parties.

3.32 While endeavouring to follow the principles laid down by the Privy Council in the case of *Chan Wing-siu v R*[22] the Court of Appeal has failed, in a number of recent cases (*R v Ward*[23]; *R v Slack*[24]; *R v Wakeley & Others*[25], to distinguish between foresight (or contemplation that the principal may act in the manner charged) and agreement or understanding that he may do so. In *R v Hyde*[26], Lord Lane CJ said that:

"If B realises (without agreeing to such conduct being used) that A may kill or intentionally inflict serious injury, but nevertheless continues to participate with A in the venture, that will amount to a sufficient mental element for B to be guilty of murder if A, with the requisite intent, kills in the course of the venture". B being the secondary part and A being the principal.

A constitutional analysis

3.33 In *R v Logan*[27] the Supreme Court of Canada indicated that the constitutional principle of fundamental justice required that an accused charged with murder could only be convicted on proof of his own wrongdoing which, in this context, was analysed by reference to what he foresaw and not what he ought to have foreseen[28].

Abandonment

3.34 An accused may withdraw from complicity in the commission of a crime. His withdrawal must be clear and unequivocal and it must also be timely.

3.35   ***R v Jensen and Ward***
                                      [1980] VR 1904
                           Supreme Court of Victoria, 1980

Young CJ, McInerney and Newton JJ: . . . (5)(a) As to acting in concert, the law says that if two or more persons reach an understanding or arrangement that a criminal act or acts will be committed by them or by one or some of them, and if while that understanding or arrangement is still afoot and has not been called off, a crime is committed by one or more of them of a kind which falls within the scope of the understanding or arrangement, and if they are all present at the scene of that crime, then they are all equally guilty of that crime, regardless of what part each played in its commission. In such a case they are said to have been acting in concert in the commission of the crime. For people to be acting in concert in the commission of crime, their assent to the understanding or arrangement between them need not be expressed by them in words; their actions may be sufficient to convey the message between them that their minds are at one as to what they shall do. The understanding or arrangement need not be of long standing; it may be reached only just before the doing of the act or acts constituting the crime. In deciding whether any understanding or arrangement existed, a jury may draw inferences from all the surrounding circumstances established by the evidence, including the conduct of the persons in question before and after the crime. For the purpose of

22 [1985] AC 168.
23 (JD) (1987 85 Cr App R 71.
24 [1989] 3 All ER 90.
25 [1990] Crim LR 119.
26 [1954] Crim LR 540.
27 (1990) 58 CCC (3d) 391.
28 Further see *R v JTL* (1990) 59 CCC (3d) 1; *R v Rodney* (1990) 58 CCC (3d) 408; *R v Kirkness* (1990) 60 CCC (3d).

these rules as to acting in concert a person is present at the scene of the crime even if he remains some distance away, provided that he is there for some purpose designed to facilitate or encourage the actual commission of the crime; for example to assist in the escape of the person or persons who perform the act or acts which constitute the crime. Although the understanding or arrangement must not have been called off before the commission of the crime, the mere fact that one or more parties to it feel qualms or wish that they had not got themselves involved or wish that it were possible to stop the criminal act or acts agreed upon, will not amount to a calling off of the understanding or arrangement once it has been made. In order to call it off so far as concerns himself, a party must communicate his withdrawal to the other parties, or at all events take some other positive step, such as informing the police. (We may here refer to *R v Lowery and King (No 2)* [1972] VR 560; *R v Ryan and Walker* [1966] VR 553, at pp 567–7; *R v Adams* [1932] VR 222; *R v Murray* [1924] VLR 374; *R v Dunn, supra: R v Kalinowski* (1930), 31 SR (NSW) 377; *R v Surridge* (1942), 42 SR (NSW) 278; *R v McDonald* (1963), 80 WN (NSW) 1716: *Davies v DPP* [1954] AC 378, esp at p 401; [1954] 1 All ER 507; *R v Anderson and Morris* [1966] 2 QB 110; [1966] 2 All ER 644; *R v Lovesey; R v Peterson* [1970] 1 QB 352; [1969] 2 All ER 1077; *R v Richards* [1974] QB 776; [1974] 3 All ER 696; *Archbold* 36th ed., paras 4124–4126; Smith and Hogan, *Criminal Law*, 1st ed, pp 68–72, 75–78, and 82–83; Howard, *Australian Criminal Law*, 1st ed, pp 221–31; and s 323 of the *Crimes Act* 1958.)

3.36   ***R v Whitehouse***
                      (1940) 55 BCR 420
          British Columbia Court of Appeal, 1940

Facts: The accused was charged with murder. The accused, who was alleged to have struck the blow which killed the victim was aided in the commission of the crime by two youths who performed part of the tasks assigned to them, but quitted the scene almost immediately before the victim was struck. The question arose as to whether the two youths were accomplices or whether they had abandoned the common unlawful object.

Sloan JA: . . . I would not attempt to define too closely what must be done in criminal matters involving participation in a common unlawful purpose to break the chain of causation and responsibility. That must depend upon the circumstances of each case but it seems to me that one essential element ought to be established in a case of this kind: where practicable and reasonable there must be timely communication of the intention to abandon the common purpose from those who wish to dissociate themselves from the contemplated crime to those who desire to continue in it. What is "timely communication" must be determined by the facts of each case but where practicable and reasonable it ought to be such communication, verbal or otherwise, that will serve unequivocal notice upon the other party to the common unlawful cause that if he proceeds upon it he does so without the further aid and assistance of those who withdraw.

3.37 This statement was adopted by the English Court of Appeal in *R v Becerra & Cooper*[29]. It will be seen that the defence of withdrawal is dependent on the facts of each particular case. Withdrawal may be verbal in the early stages of a criminal enterprise; it may involve countermanding permission to use a vehicle or withdrawing from confederacy in a plan to commit a crime. Where more positive steps have to be taken withdrawal

29 (1975) 62 Cr AppR 212, see further *R v Wheatfield* [1984] Crim LR 97.

may only be valid where it counteracts the help given. This could be fulfilled by reporting the proposed crime to the authorities. At the more extreme stages of a criminal enterprise a withdrawal may only be effective where the accused takes positive action to thwart the plan by, for example, attempting to protect a potential victim from a murderous attack.

Code options

3.38 *Model Penal Code*

206 (6) Unless otherwise provided by this Code or by the law of defining the offence, a person is not an accomplice in an offence committed by another person if . . .

(c) he terminates his complicity prior to the commission of the offence and

(i) wholly deprives it of effectiveness in the commission of the offence; or

(ii) gives timely warning to the law enforcement authorities or otherwise makes proper efforts to prevent the commission of the offence.

3.39 *Canadian Criminal Code*

21(1) Everyone is a party to an offence who:

(a) actually commits it,

(b) does or omits to do anything for the purpose of aiding any person to commit it, or

(c) abets any person in committing it.

(2) Where two or more persons form an intention in common to carry out an unlawful purpose and to assist each other and any one of them, in carrying out the common purpose, commits an offence, each of them, who knew or ought to have known that the commission of the offence would be a probable consequence of carrying out the common purpose is a party to that offence.

22(1) Where a person counsels another person to be a party to an offence and that other person is afterwards a party to that offence, the person who counselled is a party to that offence, notwithstanding that the offence was committed in a way different from that which was counselled.

(2) Everyone who counsels another person to be a party to an offence is a party to every offence that the other commits in consequence of the counselling that the person who counselled knew or ought to have known was likely to be committed in consequence of the counselling.

(3) For the purpose of this Act, "counsel" includes procure, solicit or incite.

23(1) An accessory after the fact to an offence is one who, knowing that a person has been a party to the offence, receives comforts or assists that person for the purpose of enabling that person to escape.

(2) No married person whose spouse has been a party to an offence is an accessory after the fact to that offence by receiving, comforting or assisting the spouse for the purpose of enabling the spouse to escape.

23.1 For greater certainty, sections 21 to 23 apply in respect of an accused notwithstanding the fact that the person whom the accused aids or abets, counsels or procures or receives, comforts or assists cannot be convicted of the offence.

3.40 *United Kingdom Draft Criminal Code*

29: Parties to Offences:

A person may be guilty of an offence as a principal or as an accessory.

30: Principals:
(1) A person is guilty of an offence as a principal if, with the fault required for the offence, he: (a) does the act or acts specified for the offence; or (b) does at least one such act, any other such acts being done by another.
(2) For the purposes of subsection (1), a person does an act not only when he does it himself but also when: (a) an act of another is attributed to him under section 33 [vicarious liability], (b) he does an act by an innocent agent, that is, by one whom he procures, assists or encourages to do it and who is not guilty of the offence because: (i) he is under 10 years of age; or (ii) he is suffering from mental disorder; or (iii) he does the act without the fault required for the offence; or (iv) he has a defence.
(3) A person is not guilty of an offence as a principal by reason of an act that he does by an innocent agent if: (a) the offence can be committed only by a person complying with a particular description which does not apply to him; or (b) the offence is defined in terms implying that this act must be done by the offender personally;
and a person who is not guilty of an offence as a principal by virtue only of this subsection is guilty of that offence as an accessory.
31: Accessories
(1) A person is guilty of an offence as an accessory – (a) where the offence is committed by a principal, if he procures, assists or encourages the commission of the offence and does so with the fault specified in subsection (4); or (b) if section 30(3) or section 35(1) [liability of officer of corporation] applies.
(2) In determining whether a person is guilty of an offence as an accessory it is immaterial that the principal is unaware of that person's act of procurement or assistance.
(3) For the purposes of this section, encouragement includes encouragement arising from a failure by a person to take reasonable steps to exercise any authority he has to control the relevant acts of the principal in order to prevent the commission of the offence.
(4) A person has the fault referred to in subsection (1)(a) if he – (a) intends that what he does shall, or is aware that it will or may, cause, assist or encourage the principal to do an act of the kind he does and in the circumstances specified for the offence; and (b) where a result is an element of the offence in respect of that element, at fault in the way required for liability as a principal.
(5) For the purposes of subsection (4), and subject to subsection (6), it is immaterial that the accessory does not know the particulars of the offence committed by the principal.
(6) Notwithstanding section 28(1) [transferred fault], a person who assists or encourages a principal in pursuance of an agreement between them that an offence shall be committed in relation to a particular person or thing is not guilty as an accessory to an offence intentionally committed by the principal in relation to some other person or thing.
(7) A person is not guilty of an offence as an accessory by reason of anything he does – (a) with the purpose of preventing the commission of the offence or of nullifying its effects; or (b) only because he believes that he is under a legal obligation to do it.
(8) Where the purpose of an enactment creating an offence is the protection of a class of persons no member of that class who is a victim of such an offence can be guilty of that offence as an accessory.
(9) A person who has procured, assisted or encouraged the commission of an offence is not guilty as an accessory if after his act and before the commission of the offence he took all reasonable steps to prevent it.

Other modes of participation

3.41 An accessory after the fact is one who, knowing a felony has been committed by another, receives comforts or assists the felon in order to hinder his apprehension, trial or punishment[30].

3.42 The offence of misprision of a felony consists in concealing or procuring concealment of a felony known to have been committed. It is the duty of all citizens to disclose to the proper authorities all material facts as the commission of a felony which the citizen has definite knowledge. Failure to perform this duty on reasonable opportunity is an offence; *R v Sykes*[31]. A person may take active steps to conceal a felony and this too amounts to misprision; *R v King*[32]. A privilege against disclosure or self-incrimination will excuse the reporting of a felony; *R v Sykes*.

3.43 The offence of compounding a felony was described by Coke as follows:

"Where the owner not only knows of the felony, but taketh of the thief his goods again, or amends for the same to favour or maintain him, that is, not to prosecute him, to the intent that he may escape".

The common law offence was originally called "theftbote", which referred to an agreement between a thief and his victim that the stolen property would be returned in exchange for an undertaking not to co-operate in the prosecution. A modern definition is provided by the Model Penal Code.

3.44   *Model Penal Code*

242.5 A person commits a misdemeanour if he accepts or agrees to accept any pecuniary benefit in consideration of refraining from reporting to law enforcement authorities the commission or suspected commission of any offence or information relating to an offence. It is an affirmative defence to prosecution under this section that the pecuniary benefit did not exceed an amount which the actor believed to be due as restitution or indemnification for harm caused by the offence[33].

See also s 3 of the Larceny (Advertisements) Act 1870, *Miriams v Our Dogs Publishing Company Limited*[34], ss 5(3) and 34 the Larceny Act 1916.

3.45 The development of receiving stolen goods as an independent crime betokens the general fate of liability for being an "accessory after the fact". Harbouring a criminal and facilitating escape are independent wrongs, injuring the social interest in law enforcement rather than compounding the wrongs represented by the antecedent felony. As perjury is a crime independent of the crime whose prosecution might be defeated by perjurious testimony, harbouring a felon or covering up a crime is an independent assault on the administration of justice.

The category of "accessories after the fact" is being rapidly replaced in the

---

30 See, for example, *The State v Nama* 1987 LRC (Crim) 328; *R v Lamp* [1968] Crim LR 33.
31 [1962] AC 528.
32 (1965) 49 Cr App R 140.
33 See 3 Co Inst 34.
34 [1901] 2 KB 564.

United States, as well as in other jurisdictions, by specially legislated offences of obstructing justice.

3.46 *Model Penal Code*

242.3 A person commits an offence if, with purpose to hinder the apprehension, prosecution, conviction or punishment of another for crime, he:

(1) harbours or conceals the other; or

(2) provides or aids in providing a weapon, transportation, disguise or other means or avoiding apprehension or effecting escape; or

(3) conceals or destroys evidence of the crime, or tampers with a witness, informant, document or other source of information, regardless of its admissibility in evidence; or

(4) warns the other of impending discovery or apprehension, except that this paragraph does not apply to a warning given in connection with an effort to bring another into compliance with law; or

(5) volunteers false information to a law enforcement officer.

The offence is a felony of the third degree if the conduct which the actor knows has been charged or is liable to be charged against the person aided would constitute a felony of the first or second degree. Otherwise it is a misdemeanour.

242.4 A person commits an offence if he purposely aids another to accomplish an unlawful object of a crime, as by safeguarding the proceeds thereof or converting the proceeds into negotiable funds. The offence is a felony of the third degree if the principal offence was a felony of the first or second degree. Otherwise it is a misdemeanour.

Reform

3.47 In the U.K. the whole of the law relating to accessories after the fact was repealed by the Criminal Law Act 1967 and is replaced by s 4 of that Act.

3.48 *United Kingdom Criminal Law Act 1967*

4(1) Where a person has committed an arrestable offence, any other person who, knowing or believing him to be guilty of the offence or of some other arrestable offence, does without lawful authority or reasonable excuse any act with intent to impede his apprehension or prosecution shall be guilty of an offence.

(2) If on the trial of an indictment for an arrestable offence the jury are satisfied that the offence charged (or some other offence of which the accused might on that charge be found guilty) was committed, but find the accused not guilty of it, they may find him guilty of any offence under subsection (1) above of which they are satisfied that he is guilty in relation to the offence charged (or that other offence).

(3) A person committing an offence under subsection (1) above with intent to impede another person's apprehension of prosecution shall on conviction on indictment be liable to imprisonment according to the gravity of the other person's offence, as follows:

(a) if that offence is one for which the sentence is fixed by law, he shall be liable to imprisonment for not more than ten years;

(b) if it is one for which a person (not previously convicted) may be sentenced to imprisonment for a term of fourteen years, he shall be liable to imprisonment for not more than seven years;

(c) if it is not one included above but is one for which a person (not previously convicted) may be sentenced to imprisonment for a term of ten years, he shall be liable to imprisonment for not more than five years;

(d) in any other case, he shall be liable to imprisonment for not more than three years.

3.49 The effect of the House of Lords decision in *R v Courtie*[35] is that the section creates four offences, punishable with 10, 7, 5 and 3 years imprisonment, respectively.

Further materials

3.50 Gilles *The Law of Criminal Complicity* (The Law Book Company, Sydney, 1980).

Finlay *Criminal Liability for Complicity in Abortions Committed outside Ireland* (1980) XV (ns) Ir Jur 88.

Charleton *The Scope of the Doctrine of Common Design* (1985) ILT 199.

Hogan *Victims as Parties to a Crime* [1962] Crim LR 683.

Williams *Victims as Parties to a Crime* A Further Comment [1964] Crim LR 686.

Linham *Accomplices and Withdrawal* (1981) 97 LQR 575.

Smith *Withdrawal from Complicity and Inchoate Offences* (1983) 12 Anglo-Amer L Rev 200.

The Accused – Motion Picture, Paramount, 1988.

Criminal Law, Essays in Honour of J. C. Smith, (Butterworth, 1987).

Robinson *Imputed Criminal liability* (1984) 93 TLJ 609.

Kadish *Complicity, Cause and Blame: A Study in the Interpretation of Doctrine* (1985) 73 Cal. LR 324.

Buxton *Complicity in the Criminal Code* (1969) 85 LQR 252.

Williams *"Which of You Did It?"* (1989) 52 MLR 179.

Giles *Complicity – The Problems of Joint Enterprise* [1990] Crim LR 383.

Smith *Complicity and Causation* [1986] Crim LR 663.

Williams *Complicity, Purpose and the Draft Code – 1 and 2* [1990] Crim LR 4 and 98.

Sullivan *Intent, Purpose and Complicity* [1988] Crim LR 641.

Dennis *Intention and Complicity: A Reply* [1988] Crim LR 649.

Perkins *Parties to Crime* (1941) 89 U Pa L Rev 581.

Sayre *Criminal Responsibility for Acts of Another* (1930) 43 Harv. LR 689.

Howard *Misprisions, Compoundings and Compromises* [1959] Crim LR 750 and 822.

---

35 [1984] AC 463.

Chapter 4

THE DEFENCES

Introduction

4.01 The behaviour of a person may fit precisely within the definition of a crime yet he may be blameless, or have his culpability reduced to a lesser crime, by reason of some further circumstance which amounts to a defence at law. The most obvious example is where a person is approached by an intending mugger and, on being threatened, punches him in the face. Because the action of the person was inspired by the need for self-defence, and as no more force was used than was reasonable in the circumstances, he is entitled to be acquitted on a charge of assault.

4.02 The defences have their historical origin in the theories of justification and excuse for criminal action. These concepts are now rarely used. Conceptually they are of no benefit in discussing the modern approach to this subject. The common law does not have a self-consistent theoretical basis on which the defences rest. As with so much else in criminal law, the defences, in part, were formulated at a time when the accused could not give evidence on his own behalf and where, in consequence, the jury judged his actions, in the absence of his own testimony, by comparing what he had done with the behaviour of a hypothetical reasonable man. In consequence, the defences were, with the exception of insanity, rooted in the concept that they should not succeed in extinguishing criminal liability unless the accused had behaved in an objectively reasonable manner. No modern judicial theoretician has sought to support the partial retention of objective criteria in some of the defences on the basis that it is necessary to support social cohesion by ensuring that citizens are tried according to those accepted standards of behaviour which are held by the bulk of right-thinking people.

In contrast to the subjective approach to criminal liability which we have noted in the context of the mental element of crime, the defences retain strong objective elements. In self-defence the behaviour of the accused must be both objectively and subjectively reasonable; justified in terms of the force used by the actual or threatened attack, and invoked by the necessity of the occasion and not from motives of private revenge. Duress may successfully be pleaded only where the threat against the accused was objectively grave. Necessity contains objective elements requiring that the action arise from a need to divert a greater harm with no alternative course of action being reasonably open. Entrapment seems rooted in public policy considerations which are, in essence, objective. In contrast, provocation, which applies only as a defence to murder and which is only partial in its effect by reducing liability to manslaughter, seems to be entirely subjective. The origin of this entirely subjective rule and its validity are, however, extremely dubious. Mistake as a defence has not been subjected to analysis by an Irish court, but the most recent trends from other common law jurisdictions are towards accepting a genuine mistake as sufficient without requiring that it be objectively reasonable.

The materials which follow should be considered from the viewpoint of the historical origins of objective criteria. Their validity should also be examined by considering whether it is just to impose on a person standards of reasonableness in conduct which ensure a uniform set of criteria for extinguishing criminal liability. The alternative is, as in the case of provocation, that each person should be judged only by the standard of what was in their own mind at the time when the crime was committed, as opposed to what a reasonable man would have thought or felt at that time. The problem with adopting entirely subjective standards (as in provocation) is that the result will be an increase in the number of acquittals. Experience in the courts would indicate that the entirely subjective test for provocation has yielded that result. Of itself, that does not necessarily prove that the result is wrong. In the case of insanity the courts have been burdened by too easy a resort to the defence.

The problem may be simply stated. The prosecution must prove its case beyond reasonable doubt. As we shall see, where the accused raises material from which a jury may find an action to have been in the context of a defence, the burden is on the prosecution of disproving that material. A burden of proof set so high, coupled with a subjective standard of behaviour when pleading a defence, may result in wholesale acquittals because of the inability of the prosecution to disprove something so personal to the accused as the state of his own mind. If an entirely subjective theoretical basis to the defences is adopted, it may have to be coupled with a requirement that the accused prove the defence himself by clearly establishing material from which it may reasonably be inferred. That may be a way of imposing objective criteria in another guise.

Burden of Proof

4.03   The prosecution must prove its case beyond reasonable doubt. This requires the State, where a defence is pleaded, to disprove the existence of material supporting a denial of liability, or a defence, beyond reasonable doubt. So if the accused says he killed the victim because of a vicious attack, the prosecution must prove either that the attack did not occur, or was not of the gravity alleged or that the accused armed himself in anticipation of an attack (instead of seeking Garda protection) because he wanted to kill the deceased. This process of disproving doubt is done by cross-examining the accused and his witnesses or, sometimes, by calling further evidence in rebuttal. The rule that the prosecution must disprove a defence applies to all the defences with the exception of insanity. There the accused must clearly prove that he is insane.

4.04   *The People (A-G) v Quinn*
                                          [1965] IR 366
                                    Supreme Court, 1964

This was a case where self-defence was raised as an issue. The remarks following
constitute the correct approach, in our law, to the burden of proof on the prosecution and on the defence, with respect to proving material from which a denial or
defence can be made.

Walsh J: When the evidence in a case, whether it be the evidence offered by the
prosecution or by the defence, discloses a possible defence of self-defence the
onus remains throughout upon the prosecution to establish that the accused is
guilty of the offence charged. The onus is never upon the accused to raise a doubt
in the minds of the jury. In such case the burden rests on the prosecution to
negative the possible defence of self-defence which has arisen and if, having
considered the whole of the evidence, the jury is either convinced of the innocence
of the prisoner or left in doubt whether or not he was acting in necessary
self-defence they must acquit. Before the possible defence can be left to the jury as
an issue there must be some evidence from which the jury would be entitled to find
that issue in favour of the appellant. If the evidence for the prosecution does not
disclose this possible defence then the necessary evidence will fall to be given by
the defence. In such a case, however, where it falls to the defence to give the
necessary evidence it must be made clear to the jury that there is a distinction, fine
though it may appear, between adducing the evidence and the burden of proof and
that there is no onus whatever upon the accused to establish any degree of doubt in
their minds. In directing the jury on the question of the onus of proof it can only be
misleading to a jury to refer to "establishing" the defence "in such a way as to raise
a doubt". No defence has to be "established" in any case apart from insanity. In a
case where there is evidence, whether it be disclosed in the prosecution case or in
the defence case, which is sufficient to leave the issue of self-defence to the jury the
only question the jury has to consider is whether they are satisfied beyond
reasonable doubt that the accused killed the deceased (if it be a case of homicide)
and whether the jury is satisfied beyond reasonable doubt that the prosecution has
negatived the issue of self-defence. If the jury is not satisfied beyond reasonable
doubt on both of these matters the accused must be acquitted.

Consent

4.05   The absence of consent is an element of some crimes. As such the
proof of the absence of consent is an external element which must be proved,
as with every other element, beyond reasonable doubt by the prosecution.
Rape and indecent assault require that the victim did not consent to the
sexual activity of which she complains. Usually, the only issue at a trial on
these offences is whether the victim consented or not. We will consider this
further in the context of sexual offences in chapter 6.

Consent is also a defence to a charge of assault. However, a victim cannot
consent to an act which has as its purpose, or which will have the effect of
probably causing to him or her bodily harm: *R v Cooney*[1]; *R v Donovan*[2]. In
R v K[3], the Court of Appeal of Saskatchewan held that violent and dangerous

1 (1882) 8 QBD 534.
2 [1934] 2 FB 498.
3 [1989] 44 CCC (3d) 480.

conduct is excluded from the scope of an implied consent, even where there is express consent, because in law an assault cannot be consented to where actual bodily harm is intended. In *R v Brown and Others*[4], a number of men of homosexual inclination were charged with various forms of assault, including assault occasioning actual bodily harm. They were involved in a ring which engaged in masochistic acts of consensual mutilation. On the 20th December 1990 Judge Rant sentenced the men to average terms of around 4 years imprisonment each. With this can be contrasted the decision in *Attorney-General's Reference (No 6 of 1981)*[5] where two youths had met in a public street and decided to fight. It was held that it was not in the public interest that people should try to cause, or should cause each other actual bodily harm for no good reason. Applying these principles the Court of Appeal[6] indicated that satisfying a sado-masochistic libido did not come within the category of good reason, nor could the injuries inflicted be described as merely transient or trifling and in consequence the question of consent was immaterial.

The facts in *Brown* were particularly strong for although there was no permanent injury done to any of the willing victims, no infliction of any wounds, no evidence of any medical attention being sought and no complaint to the police, who discovered the activities by chance, the acts themselves were extreme. They involved the use of branding, the application of a blow lamp, a cat-o'nine-tails and genital torture using various implements.

The application of these principles has not been entirely consistent in other common law courts. In *Lergesner v Carroll*[7] the Queensland Court of Appeal indicated that consent was inapplicable where the force applied did not cause grievous bodily harm or wounding.

Lawful Use of Force

4.06   A person may use reasonable force in order to defend either himself or others against an attack, or to defend his property, to effect a lawful arrest, or to prevent the commission of a grave crime; *R v McKay*[8]. Force may lawfully be used only where it is necessary in the context of the occasion justifying it. For example, where a citizen might peacefully effect an arrest on a shop-lifter, or other felon, he is not justified in disabling the arrestee by shooting him in the legs. An unnecessary use of force is a crime because it constitutes an assault; *The People (A-G) v Keatley*[9].

4 Reported in *The Independent* 11 December – 14 December 1990.
5 [1981] QB 715.
6 See *The Independent* 20 February 1992.
7 (1989) 49 A Crim R 51.
8 [1957] VR 560.
9 [1954] IR 12.

4.07   ***The People (A-G) v Keatley***
                                        [1954] IR 12
                            Court of Criminal Appeal, 1953

Facts: It had been thought that the right of self-defence was limited to the accused person or to the defence of those with whom the accused person was closely related. This principle was denied by the Court in the context of a general discussion of the principles of self-defence.

Maguire CJ: The applicant was convicted of the manslaughter of one Edward Byrne. The incident occurred during the course of a game of pitch-and-toss in which the applicant and his brother, Peter Keatley, and Edward Byrne, were, with others, engaged. A dispute arose between the deceased and Peter Keatley and led to what was described by one witness as "a bit of an argument" and by other witnesses as "a tussle" between them. According to the account of two of the witnesses, the deceased pushed Peter Keatley against some piece of machinery that was on the spot and then struck him. Thereupon, the applicant, who was either standing behind the deceased or came from behind him, struck the deceased. This blow had the effect of causing the deceased to fall to the ground and, on examination, he was found to be dead. The medical evidence made it more probable that the immediate cause of death was his head striking a stone or other object embedded in the ground rather than the blow struck by the applicant. The skull of the deceased had been fractured, and there was a punctured wound on the side of his head. The whole incident was described by two of the witnesses as being a matter of seconds. All the witnesses who had seen the dispute between the deceased and Peter Keatley had not regarded it as very serious. The only witness who was asked about the force of the blow which the applicant struck the deceased said it was "not a very powerful blow at all . . . a box but not a very powerful one."

One witness said that, after the deceased struck Peter Keatley, the applicant rushed in and struck the deceased. Another accepted the suggestion that the applicant came to save his brother and ventured the opinion that the applicant "may have thought there was a bigger row going to develop and he came for that reason." The applicant did not give evidence but, in a statement which was put in evidence, he said that they – the deceased and his brother – were both standing beside him at the time and he went to take his brother's part. The brother, Peter Keatley, was younger than the deceased and, apparently, inferior to him in strength and physique. There was evidence that he had at least one of his hands in his pocket and offered little or no resistance to the attack by the deceased.

In these circumstances, it is clear that the applicant had no intention of killing the deceased. It is equally clear that the death of the deceased could not be held to be the natural and probable consequence of the blow struck by the applicant, so that no homicidal intention could be imputed to him. The death was, accordingly, unintended both in fact and in law, and criminal responsibility only arises if it was caused by an unlawful act. The blow struck by the applicant was, at least, a contributing cause of death, and a conviction for manslaughter could be sustainable if that blow was unlawful.

The fundamental question, therefore, was whether this blow was lawful or unlawful. The trial judge regarded it and described it as an assault and, very early in his charge, he told the jury that the case started with an unlawful act whereby the accused attacked the person of Edward Byrne. Inasmuch as every blow that is struck is not necessarily unlawful, and a so-called "assault" that proves to have been justifiable or excusable cannot strictly be called unlawful, this was a misdirection. It may have given the jury the impression that they had no question of fact to decide as to the lawfulness or otherwise of the use of force by the accused. This misconception could have been corrected later in the charge when the trial judge explained to the jury the nature of the defence as he conceived it but, in the event, his explanation could hardly have had this effect. This was because the defence which he explained, and which he left to the jury to decide, was a defence which would have been appropriate to the case of an intentional homicide but was not appropriate to the circumstances actually in question. It was that the killing would have been lawful if the blow had been struck by the accused in defending his brother from some felony involving violence or from some forcible and atrocious crime directed against the brother. He stated to the jury that the principle of self-defence did not extend to misdemeanours of any kind and that an assault was a misdemeanour. This must have only confirmed, rather than removed, the misconception he had already created in the minds of the jury. It was a further misdirection in the circumstances of the case.

In the Court's view the evidence was such as to leave open a reasonable possibility that the use of force by the accused was not unlawful. It would have been open to the jury to hold, on the evidence, that this force had been used in the necessary defence of his brother from an assault and that no more force had been used than was necessary; and, if they had taken the view that this was a reasonably possible interpretation of the incident, the accused was entitled to an acquittal.

On the other hand, in order to convict him, they would have required to have been satisfied that this was not the case and that the accused unnecessarily used force or used more force than was necessary or that he was merely acting in a spirit of revenge or retaliation or with a desire to fight. It is impossible to say that, on the evidence, they could not have been so satisfied. The Court is of opinion that it was a defect of the trial and of the charge that these matters were never explained to the jury and the case was left to them on a completely inappropriate and incorrect basis.

In the view of this Court, the correct legal position, applicable to the circumstances of this case, is set out in the following passage from Russell on Crime (10th ed, 1950) at p 763:

> "The use of force is lawful for the necessary defence of self or others or of property: but the justification is limited by the necessity of the occasion and the use of unnecessary force is an assault."

The limitations of this doctrine are futher illustrated in this passage on the following page: "If one man strikes another a blow, or does that which amounts to an assault on him, that other has a right to defend himself, and to strike a blow in his defence without waiting until he is struck, but he has no right to revenge himself; and if when all danger is past he strikes a blow not necessary for his defence, he commits an assault and battery."

It will be noted that the first passage cited is not limited to the defence of oneself but expressly extends to the "necessary defence of others." In the older textbooks, the right of defence is suggested to be limited to persons in a special relationship to the person charged, such as the wife, child or master; but, even if this were still the case, there seems to be no good reason why the relationship of brothers should not be included. If – as seems probable – the underlying principle is the right, if not the duty, to prevent a breach of the peace or the commission of an unlawful act, the question of any special relationship between the parties seems irrelevant. It is, perhaps, a recognition of this that has led to the modern view that any such distinction is anomalous. The true position seems to the Court to be correctly stated thus in Salmond on Torts (10th ed, 1945), at p 334: "It may be safely assumed, however, that at the present day all such distinctions are obsolete, and that every man has the right of defending any man by reasonable force against unlawful force." There is, of course, implicit in this statement the requirements to be deduced from the passage already cited from Russell on Crime that the use of force is necessary and that no more force than is necessary is used. These two matters are eminently questions of fact to be decided, in a criminal trial, by the jury. As already indicated in the present case, the jury could never have appreciated what their function was in this respect nor could they have considered or decided these fundamental questions.

In the Court's view, accordingly, there was misdirection of the jury and an unsatisfactory trial. Leave to appeal will be granted and the hearing of this application for leave to appeal will be treated as the hearing of the appeal. The conviction must be quashed and a new trial ordered.

Many matters were raised by the notice of application for leave to appeal, and argued on the hearing of the application, which, in view of the foregoing decision, it is not necessary now to decide. The Court feels, however, that mention should be made of two of these matters. One is that expressions were used by the trial judge in his charge which tended to suggest that some onus of proof or of giving evidence lay on the accused. The other is that the jury were not instructed as to the onus of proof which lay on the prosecution until they were recalled to Court in response to a requisition by counsel for the defence, and even then his direction to the jury contained unfortunate and possibly misleading references to the accused not having given evidence and to the shifting of the onus of proof. These matters constitute a serious criticism of the charge and might well have been a ground for holding, apart from the question already decided, that the trial was unsatisfactory.

Reasonableness

4.08 Only reasonable force may be used, where the use of that force is lawful and the degree of force must be reasonable in the circumstances. A measure of latitude, almost equivalent to an independent subjective test, is applied to those who are attacked. A person is entitled to use that force which a reasonable person would consider necessary in the circumstances faced by the accused; *The People (A-G) v Dwyer*[10] (see para **4.24**). Small errors in the degree of responsive action are discounted. The law considers that a measure of latitude, in judging what is reasonable, is appropriate where a person may have little time to think or assess his response to an attack. Holmes J in *Brown v US*[11], commented "Detached reflection cannot be demanded in the presence of an uplifted knife"[12].

Motive and preparation

4.09 An injury inflicted from motives of revenge can never amount to self-defence; *The People (A-G) v Commane*[13]. No one is entitled to carry on a fight when the necessity of defence has ceased. Nor is a person entitled, in anticipation of a fight breaking out, to carry a knife with the intention of killing his victim; *The People (A-G) v O'Brien*[14].

4.10 While the accused is limited to using such force as is reasonably necessary in the circumstances, he is not obliged to wait until a blow is struck. A person may act in defence where an attack is reasonably anticipated and no alternative course of action, to the use of force, is reasonably open; *R v Lane*[15]. Older authorities concentrated on the obligation of the accused to retreat from the attack as far as possible, or to take all

10 [1972] IR 416.
11 (1921) 256 US 335 at p 343.
12 See further *R v Robinson* [1984] 4 NIJB per McDermott J at p 19 of the judgment.
13 (1975) 1 Frewen 400.
14 (1969) 1 Frewen 343.
15 (1983) 8 A Crim R 182.

other available steps before resorting to the use of force. These tests have now been abandoned as independent criteria and, instead, are viewed as items of evidential significance for the jury in deciding whether or not the resort to force was, in all the circumstances, a reasonable one; *R v Julien*[16]. It follows that where someone immediately resorts to violence, or fails to take alternative courses of action, it may be inferred that the use of force was not reasonably necessary or that the accused was acting from some improper motive, such as revenge.

4.11   Self-defence normally contemplates a sudden attack on an unarmed person who has to defend himself with whatever weapon he has available. Sometimes a person will allege that he fled in order to find a suitable weapon. Acts of deliberate preparation in anticipation of an attack are not necessarily inconsistent with self-defence; it would be absurd if one could use a weapon in self-defence but not retain that weapon in reasonable anticipation of a vicious attack. If the weapon is a firearm, an explosive or an offensive weapon, various statutory prohibitions on the possession of these weapons may be infringed; e.g. the Firearms and Offensive Weapons Act 1990. Some acts of anticipatory self-defence may be so extreme that public policy will exclude their exercise. Thus, it has been held that a person cannot take action to exclude the police from an area of a city; *Devlin v Armstrong*[17].

4.12   *R v Fegan*
                                      [1972] NI 80
                          Court of Appeal Northern Ireland, 1971

Facts: The accused had married a person from a differing Christian denomination. In consequence the couple had been subjected to threats of extreme violence from racists and bigots. He sought to justify the possession of a firearm and ammunition on the basis of the anticipated necessity to defend his family.

McDermott LCJ: Where, as here, a firearm is possessed without certificate, permit or other authority as required by the Act of 1969, the possession is unlawful and will usually constitute an offence. But does that mean that a firearm so possessed cannot at the same time be possessed for a lawful object? The absence of a certificate, permit or other authority may well be evidence relevant to the question of the existence or non-existence of a lawful object, but we do not think such absence of authority is in law necessarily incompatible with the firearm concerned being possessed for a lawful object. A, for example, borrows a shot-gun to shoot birds despoiling his orchard. He has no certificate or other authority for possessing the gun and his possession is unlawful. To say that his object cannot be lawful is to confuse possession and purpose and we have not been referred to and are not aware of any decision supporting such a proposition. A firearm in lawful possession may undoubtedly be possessed for an unlawful object and there seems no good reason why the converse should not be equally true. Mr Staunton, for the Crown, conceded that a firearm held without certificate, permit or other authority might yet, in law, be possessed for a lawful object and the court regards this concession as well founded.

Possession of a firearm for the purpose of protecting the possessor or his wife or family from acts of violence, *may* be possession for a lawful object. But the

16 [1969] 2 All ER 856.
17 [1971] NI 13.

lawfulness of such a purpose cannot be founded on a mere fancy, or on some aggressive motive. The threatened danger must be reasonably and genuinely anticipated, must appear reasonably imminent, and must be of a nature which could not reasonably be met by more specific means. A lawful object in this particular field therefore falls within a strictly limited category and cannot be such as to justify going beyond what the law may allow in meeting the situation of danger which the possessor of the firearm reasonably and genuinely apprehends. One does not, for example, possess a firearm for a lawful object if the true purpose is merely to stop threats or insults or the like.

It was for the jury to consider the appellant's state of mind and to what extent the evidence led on his behalf was reliable. Having done this, it was open to the jury to conclude that the appellant genuinely and reasonably feared for the life and safety of himself or his family and held the pistol for use if necessary as a protection against this danger. On the evidence one cannot say what the jury, if sufficiently directed, would have done, but the court is of opinion that they could have come to these conclusions. They might well have been satisfied that the appellant's apprehensions went beyond threats and insults and occasional beatings and that he was reasonable and genuine in his fears that much worse might soon befall his family and himself. If the jury took his view and accepted the appellant's evidence as to why he armed himself they would, in the opinion of this court, have had grounds for a finding that his possession was for a lawful object. The appeal will therefore be allowed to this extent.

4.13 Once the circumstances whereby the accused reasonably feared an attack have ceased, his justification for holding a weapon is extinguished and he must surrender it.

4.14 *Attorney General's Reference Number 2 of 1983*
[1984] QB 456; [1984] 1 All ER 988; [1984] 2 WLR 465;
(1984) 78 Cr App R 183; [1984] Crim LR 289
Court of Appeal England, 1984

Lane CJ: . . . In our judgment a defendant is not left in the paradoxical position of being able to justify acts carried out in self-defence but not acts immediately preparatory to it. There is no warrant for the submission on behalf of the Attorney General that acts of self-defence will only avail a defendant when they have been done spontaneously. There is no question of a person in danger of attack "writing his own immunity" for violent future acts of his. He is not confined for his remedy to calling in the police or boarding-up his premises.

He may still arm himself for his own protection, if the exigency arises, although in so doing he may commit other offences. That he may be guilty of other offences will avoid the risk of anarchy contemplated by the Reference. It is also to be noted that although a person may "make" a petrol bomb with a lawful object, nevertheless, if he remains in possession of it after the threat has passed which made his object lawful, it may cease to be so.

The reduction effect

4.15 Where a person is charged with murder, a genuine, but unreasonable use of force operates to reduce guilt to manslaughter; *The People (A-G) v Dwyer*[18] (see para **4.24**). There is no formal doctrine whereby an excess in the amount of force used, or the behaviour of the victim, reduces a charge of

18 [1972] IR 417.

assault from one of its more serious categories, to a lesser charge. For example, a charge of assault occasioning actual bodily harm is not reduced to a charge of common assault because the accused mistakenly, but genuinely, believed that he had to use a knife. In practice these circumstances are urged by the defence in mitigation of sentence and, on pleas of guilty to less serious offences being offered by the defence, the prosecution will sometimes reduce the seriousness of the charge on the same basis.

4.16 The principles of self-defence adopted by the Court of Criminal Appeal in *The People (A-G) v Keatley*[19] (see para **4.07**) involve two elements; a necessity for the use of force and a necessary proportion between the degree of force used, or threatened, and the reply by the accused. It may be that the accused makes a genuine, though unreasonable, mistake by believing himself to be under attack. In England it has now been decided that in such circumstances the accused is entitled to be judged on the facts as he believed them to be, whether that belief was reasonable or not; *Beckford v R*[20]. It has also been argued in England that the accused should be relieved of liability where he makes a genuine, though unreasonable mistake, in the amount of force he uses in self-defence. The acceptance of that principle would clearly undermine the basis of the defence and it has not so far been accepted in any common law jurisdiction; *R v O'Grady*[21]. Both objective elements of necessity to use force and proportion in its use are fundamental to the judgments of the Supreme Court in *The People (A-G) v Dwyer*[22] (see para **4.24**).

4.17
Palmer v R
[1971] AC 814; [1971] 2 WLR 831; [1971] 1 All ER 1077;
(1971) 55 Cr App R 223
Privy Council, 1971

Facts: This case concerned two defendants who were each separately convicted in Jamaica of murder and sentenced to death. The only question raised for determination was whether, in cases of murder, where an issue of self-defence was left to the jury, it was in all cases obligatory to direct the jury that, if they found that the defendant while intending to defend himself had used more force than was necessary in the circumstances, they should return a verdict of guilty of manslaughter.

Lord Morris: . . . In their Lordships' view the defence of self-defence is one which can be and will be readily understood by any jury. It is a straightforward conception. It involves no abstruse legal thought. It requires no set words by way of explanation. No formula need be employed in reference to it. Only common sense is needed for its understanding. It is both good law and good sense that a man who is attacked may defend himself. It is both good law and good sense that he may do, but may only do, what is reasonably necessary. But everything will depend upon the particular facts and circumstances. Of these a jury can decide. It may in some cases be only sensible and clearly possible to take some simple avoiding action. Some attacks may be serious and dangerous. Others may not be. If there is some

19 [1954] IR 12.
20 [1988] AC 130.
21 [1987] QB 995.
22 [1972] IR 417.

relatively minor attack it would not be common sense to permit some action of retaliation which was wholly out of proportion to the necessities of the situation. If an attack is serious so that it puts someone in immediate peril then immediate defensive action may be necessary. If the moment is one of crisis for someone in imminent danger he may have to avert the danger by some instant reaction. If the attack is all over and no sort of peril remains then the employment of force may be by way of revenge or punishment or by way of paying off an old score or may be pure aggression. There may no longer be any link with a necessity of defence. Of all of these matters the good sense of a jury will be the arbiter. There are no prescribed words which must be employed in or adopted in summing-up. All that is needed is a clear exposition, in relation to the particular facts of the case, of the conception of necessary self-defence. If there has been no attack then clearly there will have been no need for defence. If there has been an attack so that defence is reasonably necessary it will be recognised that a person defending himself cannot weigh to a nicety the exact measure of his necessary defensive action. If a jury thought that in a moment of unexpected anguish a person attacked had only done what he honestly and instinctively thought was necessary that would be most potent evidence that only reasonable defensive action had been taken. A jury will be told that the defence of self-defence, where the evidence makes its raising possible, will only fail if the prosecution show beyond doubt that what the accused did was not by way of self-defence.

The appeals were dismissed.

4.18   *R v McKay*
                              [1957] VR 560
                     Supreme Court of Victoria, 1957

Facts: After a series of robberies the accused, a farmer, shot and killed a thief fleeing from his property. He argued that he had committed manslaughter not murder.

Lowe J: . . . (1) Homicide is lawful if it is committed in reasonable self-defence of the person committing it, or of his wife or children, or of his property, or in order to prevent the commission of a forcible and atrocious crime. Whether the position is the same in the case of all felonies is, I think, not clear, but we need not determine the question here.
(2) Reasonable self-defence is not limited to cases in which the life of the person committing homicide is endangered or grave injury to his person is threatened. It is also available where there is a reasonable apprehension of such danger or grave injuries. There is such a reasonable apprehension if the person believes on reasonable grounds that such danger exists.
(3) The homicide in order to be justified must be necessary, and the jury are to enquire as to the necessity of the killing.
(4) There must be no malice coloured under the pretence of necessity.
(5) Wherever a person who kills another acts in truth on malice and takes occasion from the appearance of necessity to execute his own private revenge he is guilty of murder.
(6) Motive is to be distinguished from intention. If the killing is held justifiable, motive is irrelevant but evidence of motive is to be considered in determining whether the killing is justified.
(7) If the occasion warrants action in self-defence or for the prevention of felony or the apprehension of the felon, but the person taking action acts beyond the necessity of the occasion and kills the offender, the crime is manslaughter – not murder.

4.19   Older statements of the law which justify a killing in terms of the defence of property, or the apprehension of a felon, are unlikely to be followed when tested in modern situations. Ordinarily, it can hardly be justified that a man kill another in defence of his property. In some circumstances a man struggling to resist arrest on a technical felony is better let go than seriously injured. If the law is to develop justly, in accordance with the fundamental principles of the Constitution, a general test of the use of force in situations other than self-defence will involve a public policy decision as to the circumstances under which force may be used. A general test of reasonableness, made up of proportionality between the object to be achieved and the force used, and a regard to the necessity of the occasion on which it was so used, will determine what degree of force may be used in such situations. In that regard the law could look to the developing jurisprudence in the area of necessity and the decision of Hanna J in *Lynch v Fitzgerald*[23], later approved by the Supreme Court, which endorses this view;

"... the armed forces can fire upon an unlawful or riotous assembly only where such a course is necessary as a last resort to preserve life. Force is threatened and it can be repelled by force. It goes back to the common law principle that it is lawful to use only a reasonable degree of force for the protection of oneself or any other person against the unlawful use of force, and that such repelling force is not reasonable if it is either greater than is requisite for the purpose or disproportionate to the evil to be prevented".

Code options

4.20   *Model penal code*

Section 3.04   Use of Force in Self-Protection

(1) *Use of Force Justifiable for Protection of the Person.*   Subject to the provisions of of this section and of section 3.09, the use of force upon or toward another person is justifiable when the actor believes that such force is immediately necessary for the purpose of protecting himself against the use of unlawful force by such other person on the present occasion.

(2) *Limitations on Justifying Necessity for Use of Force.*

(*a*) The use of force is not justifiable under this section:

(i) to resist an arrest that the actor knows is being made by a peace officer, although the arrest is unlawful; or

(ii) to resist force used by the occupier or possessor of property or by another person on his behalf, where the actor knows that the person using the force is doing so under a claim of right to protect the property, except that this limitation shall not apply if:

(A) the actor is a public officer acting in the performance of his duties or a person lawfully assisting him therein or a person making or assisting in a lawful arrest; or

(B) the actor has been unlawfully dispossessed of the property and is making a re-entry or recaption justified by section 3.06; or

(C) the actor believes that such force is necessary to protect himself against death or serious bodily injury.

23 [1938] IR 382 per Hanna J at p 405.

(*b*) The use of deadly force is not justifiable under this section unless the actor believes that such force is necessary to protect himself against death, serious bodily injury, kidnapping or sexual intercourse compelled by force or threat; nor is it justifiable if:

(i) the actor, with the purpose of causing death or serious bodily injury, provoked the use of force against himself in the same encounter; or

(ii) the actor knows that he can avoid the necessity of using such force with complete safety by retreating or by surrendering possession of a thing to a person asserting a claim of right thereto or by complying with a demand that he abstain from any action that he has no duty to take, except that:

(A) the actor is not obliged to retreat from his dwelling or place of work, unless he has the initial aggressor or is assailed in his place of work by other person whose place of work the actor knows it to be; and

(B) a public officer justified in using force in the performance of his duties or a person justified in using force in his assistance or a person justified in using force in making an arrest or preventing an escape is not obliged to desist from efforts to perform such duty, effect such arrest or prevent such escape because of resistance or threatened resistance by or on behalf of the person against whom such action is directed.

(*c*) Except as required by paragraphs (*a*) and (*b*) of this subsection, a person employing protective force may estimate the necessity thereof under the circumstances as he believes them to be when the force is used, without reteating, surrendering possession, doing any other act that he has no legal duty to do or abstaining from any lawful action.

Section 3.05 Use of Force for the Protection of Other Persons

(1) Subject to the provisions of this section and of section 3.09, the use of force upon or toward the person of another is justifiable to protect a third person when:

(*a*) the actor would be justified under section 3.04 in using such force to protect himself against the injury he believes to be threatened to the person whom he seeks to protect; and

(*b*) under the circumstances as the actor believes them to be, the person whom he seeks to protect would be justified in using such protective force; and

(*c*) the actor believes that his intervention is necessary for the protection of such other person.

(2) Notwithstanding subsection (1) of this section:

(*a*) when the actor would be obliged under section 3.04 to retreat, to surrender the possession of a thing or to comply with a demand before using force in self-protection, he is not obliged to do so before using force for the protection of another person, unless he knows that he can thereby secure the complete safety of such other person; and

(*b*) when the person whom the actor seeks to protect would be obliged under section 3.04 to retreat, to surrender the possession of a thing or to comply with a demand if he knew that he could obtain complete safety by so doing, the actor is obliged to try to cause him to do so before using force in his protection if the actor knows that he can obtain complete safety in that way; and

(*c*) neither the actor nor the person whom he seeks to protect is obliged to retreat when in the other's dwelling or place of work to any greater extent than in his own.

4.21   **Canadian Criminal Code**

"17".   See para **4.51**.

Further materials

4.22 Elliott *Necessity, Duress and Self-Defence* [1989] Crim LR 611.
Williams *The Theory of Excuses* [1982] Crim LR 732.
Reville *Self-Defence: Courting Sober but Unreasonable Mistakes of Fact*
[1988] 52 JCL 84.

Excessive self-defence

4.23 Excessive self-defence, applying only on a charge of murder and
operating to reduce the verdict to manslaughter, was formulated in its
modern context by the Supreme Court of Victoria in *R v McKay*[24]. A
chicken farmer had been subjected to persistent thefts of his property and,
as a result, had shot and killed a thief in an attempt to arrest him. The
principles enunciated by the Court are set out at para **4.18**. The High Court
of Australia later accepted the principle in *R v Viro*[25] on an application of the
blameworthiness principle. Stephen J reasoned that the moral culpability of
a person who kills another while defending himself, but who fails in a plea of
self-defence only because the force which he believed to be necessary
exceeded that which was reasonably necessary, fell short of the moral
culpability associated with murder. An attempt in that case to clarify the
law, restated it in so complex a fashion that judges did not usually try to
select the relevant principle or to restate the High Court judgment in
comprehensible language. This resulted in apparently unjustified acquittals
caused by confusion. The High Court abandoned the defence completely in
R v Zecevic[26]. There has been no challenge to the acceptance of the principle
in Ireland and the principles on which it is based were enunciated by the
Supreme Court with exemplary clarity and simplicity.

4.24   ***The People (A-G) v Dwyer***
                                        [1972] IR 416
                                    Supreme Court, 1972

Facts: The accused had been abusive to the parents of one of the two people who
later died. In consequence a fight began outside a chip shop. Dwyer had given
evidence at his trial that he believed that Philip Ney, with whose murder he was
charged, or one of his cohorts, had possession of some implement with which he
had been hit on the head. In consequence he claimed he was in fear for his life. The
prosecution clearly established at the trial that Dwyer had used a knife to kill
Philip Ney. The circumstances were not such as to suggest that the actions of the
accused were proportionate to the necessity of the occasion. The jury were
directed by the trial judge that the defence of self-defence could only succeed if the
force used by Dwyer was objectively proportionate to the necessity of the occasion
brought on by Philip Ney or those assisting him. In such a context the belief of

24 [1957] VR 560.
25 (1978) 141 CLR 88.
26 (1987) 71 ALR 641.

Dwyer that he was in fear for his life, if accepted by the jury (if the jury had a reasonable doubt in his favour in that regard) was therefore irrelevant.

Walsh J: Following the dismissal by the Court of Criminal Appeal of the appellant's appeal against his conviction for murder, the Attorney General granted a certificate to the appellant enabling him to take this appeal to the Supreme Court. The point of law stated in the certificate is as follows: "Where a person, subjected to a violent and felonious attack, endeavours, by way of self-defence, to prevent the consummation of that attack by force, but, in doing so, exercises more force than is necessary but no more than he honestly believes to be necessary in the circumstances, whether such person is guilty of manslaughter and not murder."

Section 4, subs-s 1, of the Criminal Justice Act 1964, provides that: "Where a person kills another unlawfully the killing shall not be murder unless the accused person intended to kill, or cause serious injury to, some person, whether the person actually killed or not."

. . . It is important to know that the effect of the provision is that unlawful homicide shall not be murder unless the necessary intent is established.

A homicide is not unlawful if it is committed in the execution or advancement of justice, or in reasonable self-defence of person or property, or in order to prevent the commission of an atrocious crime, or by misadventure. In the case of such self-defence, the homicide is justifiable and is therefore not unlawful.

. . . In the present case the prosecution set out to establish that the appellant had the intention to kill or to cause serious injury. For the purpose of testing the question posed in the certificate, I must assume that it deals with the question of voluntary homicide, namely, that it was the intention of the accused to kill or to cause serious injury but that he did so by way of self-defence but went beyond what a reasonable man would consider necessary in the circumstances.

[If an accused person in such a situation only does what he honestly believes to be necessary in the circumstances, even though that involves the use of a degree of force greater than a reasonable man would have considered necessary in those circumstances, the accused has been guilty of an error of judgment in a difficult situation which was not caused by himself.] Should he then be convicted of murder? In such a situation it is not contended that he should go free, as if it were a case of what I have described as full self-defence. If a person uses more force than he knows to be reasonably necessary, then he is guilty of murder. This presupposes a situation where he is justified in using some degree of force short of killing or causing serious injury. In the case of full self-defence the accused intends to kill or intends to cause serious injury but he does not commit any offence because the homicide is a lawful one. Therefore, his intention was to commit a lawful homicide or lawfully to inflict serious injury. Under our statute a person who kills another unlawfully as a result of an intention to do so is guilty of murder. Full self defence permits such a degree of force, up to and including the infliction of death, as may be regarded as being reasonably necessary.

Our statutory provision makes it clear that the intention is personal and that it is not to be measured solely by objective standards. In my opinion, therefore, when the evidence in a case discloses a question of self-defence and where it is sought by the prosecution to show that the accused used excessive force, that is to say more than would be regarded as objectively reasonable, the prosecution must establish that the accused knew that he was using more force than was reasonably necessary. Therefore, it follows that if the accused honestly believed that the force he did use was necessary, then he is not guilty of murder. The onus, of course, is upon the prosecution to prove beyond reasonable doubt that he knew that the force was excessive or that he did not believe that it was necessary. If the prosecution does not do so, it has failed to establish the necessary malice. If, however, at the same time it does establish that the force used was more than was reasonably necessary it has established that the killing was unlawful as being without justification and not having been by misadventure. In those circumstances the accused in such a case would be guilty of manslaughter.

Butler J: . . . In dealing with the plea of self-defence, the trial judge directed the jury that if the appellant, though acting in self-defence, killed through using more force than was reasonably necessary in the circumstances the verdict should be "guilty of murder". In the light of this direction the verdict of guilty of murder may mean either than the jury rejected the contention that the appellant acted in self-defence or it may mean that, while accepting that he acted in self-defence, they were of opinion that he used more force than was reasonably necessary in the circumstances . . .

. . . At common law, murder is the unlawful killing of a human being with malice aforethought . . .

. . . A person is entitled to protect himself from unlawful attack. If in doing so he uses no more force than is reasonably necessary, he is acting lawfully and commits no crime even though he kill his assailant. If he uses more force than may objectively be considered necessary, his act is unlawful and, if he kills, the killing is unlawful. His intention, however, falls to be tested subjectively and it would appear logical to conclude that, if his intention in doing the unlawful act was primarily to defend himself, he should not be held to have the necessary intention to kill or cause serious injury. The result of this view would be that the killing, though unlawful, would be manslaughter only . . .

4.25   See also *The People (AG) v Commane*[27].

Scope of the defence

4.26   For an accused to successfully plead that the force he used was lawful, three conditions must be fulfilled:

(1) The situation in which the force was used must amount to one in which the law allows it.

(2) The use of force must be necessary.

(3) There must be a proportion between the force used, or threatened, by the victim and the reply by the accused. The judgments in *The People (A-G) v Dwyer*[28] (see para **4.24**) only deal with the third situation. It may emerge that a victim is killed in a situation in which, objectively, the accused was not entitled to use force at all. Examples are given subsequently. In those circumstances it has been urged that the law would benefit by the *Dwyer* principles being applied whatever the nature of the genuine mistake made by the accused.

4.27   *Charleton – Offences Against the Person (1992)*

There appears to be no reason of logic or policy why a defence which applies to an honest mistake as to the amount of force necessary in self-defence, should not apply equally where the accused honestly uses force in a situation in which, if his belief was correct, he would legally have been entitled to so act. Where, for example, the accused kills a member of his family in his own home at night, believing, perhaps through a combination of fear of raiders due to a spate of

27 (1975) 1 Frewen 400.
28 [1972] IR 416.

violent burglaries and bad light, that there was a dangerous intruder in the house, there is no reason in principle why his culpability should be considered by a different rule than that in *Dwyer*. To result in a complete acquittal the defence of lawful use of force requires that, objectively and subjectively, a situation existed where force might be used and that the actual force used was limited to the necessity of the occasion. Where, on either leg of the test, the accused acts illegally, on an objective test, but honestly believes either that there existed facts which entitled him to use force, or that the necessity existed to use the degree of force he actually used, he would lack culpability judged by his own state of mind. The law still accepts the objective test in regulating the use of force and the accused would therefore be guilty, but only because of that criterion. To apply the reasoning of Walsh J in *Dwyer*, to the example given, the accused clearly intended to kill or cause serious injury but under the influence of a belief that such force was appropriate in the circumstances. Applying the reasoning of Butler J in *Dwyer*, to the example given, the intention of the accused was primarily to defend himself and his family and not to kill or cause serious injury. On the *Howe* test the accused lacks the moral culpability ordinarily associated with murder.

It is possible to question the necessity for a conviction at all in these circumstances since the accused, on the basis of his own perceptions, is free of guilt. Objective standards continue to apply but may be particularly unfortunate in their operation where, as in murder, a mandatory life sentence must be imposed. Since the failure to make such inquiry as a reasonable person would or the failure to give to a situation the degree of attention and foresight which allows society to attain a "true social order" is avoidable and therefore culpable, a conviction for unlawful killing appears appropriate. Degrees of guilt vary by ability, experience and the state of emotion into which a situation may have precipitated a person. It is therefore arguable that the flexible sentence applicable to manslaughter is appropriate.

The half-way defence should apply where the accused unlawfully used force believing himself to be in a situation where it could legally have been used. Such a development has not been sanctioned by any decision at common law . . . if this argument is accepted the rule as to self-defence may be simply stated: where the accused kills the victim intending to kill or cause serious injury but an issue as to self-defence is raised then—

(1)   the accused is entitled to be acquitted where both objectively and subjectively, the situation was one where he was entitled to resort to the use of force and the amount of force used was no more than was reasonably necessary;

(2)   the accused is guilty of murder where, on a subjective test, he had no honest belief that the situation was one where he was entitled to resort to the use of force, or where he had no honest belief that the amount of force he in fact used was more than was reasonably necessary;

(3)   the accused is not guilty of murder but guilty of manslaughter where, tested objectively, the situation was one where he was not entitled to resort to the use of force, or where, tested objectively, the amount of force he in fact used was more than was reasonably necessary, but, in either case, on a subjective test he honestly believed the situation was one where he was entitled to resort to force or that the amount of force he in fact used was more than was reasonably necessary;

(4)   where the accused is subjected to an attack he may also be provoked into an uncontrolled state where he kills, which may entitle him, apart from the above stated rules, to the defence of provocation.

Further materials

4.28   Doran *The Doctrine of Excessive Defence: Developments Past and Potential* (1985) NILQ 314.

Manson *Excessive Force in the Supreme Court of Canada* 29 CR (3d) 364.
O'Brien *Excessive Self-Defence: A Need for Legislation* (1983) 25 CLQ 441.
Douglas *The Demise of Excessive Self-Defence Manslaughter in Australia*
(1988) 12 Crim LJ 28.

Duress

4.29 The defence of duress contains strong objective elements. Necessity,
which could also be called duress of circumstances, shares some of these
elements. The full application of these principles to charges of murder may
lead to injustice and it has been argued that in such circumstances the *Dwyer*
solution (see para **4.24**) should apply[29].

4.30 In contrast to the defence of necessity, the defence of duress has long
been accepted as exculpating the accused; *R v M'Growther*[30]. It is often
difficult to distinguish the two defences. There is no difference in the
blameworthiness of a person who commits a crime because circumstances of
nature leave him no reasonable alternative and a person who acts under the
direction of a criminal godfather threatening dire consequences unless his
will is obeyed. The defence of necessity has, however, been distrusted for
fear that it would excuse a usurpation of authority. Duress as a defence has
similarly been limited due to an apprehension that it would be used by
criminal gangs to secure acquittal for their members who could plead fear of
the consequences of disobedience.

4.31 The parameters of the defence are fixed by a consideration of the
following factors:
(1) The nature of the threats against the accused.
(2) Whether the accused's reaction to these threats was in common with
self-defence, proportionate to the harm offered to him.
(3) Whether the accused in acting under duress is required to behave as a
reasonable person.

4.32 Since 1933 *Whelan*'s case has governed the law in this country. The
clarity and conciseness of the judgment of Murnaghan J are reflected in the
fact that it has been cited with approval in a large number of cases where the
defence of duress has arisen for consideration in other common law
countries.

4.33   ***The People (A-G) v Whelan***
[1934] IR 518
Court of Criminal Appeal, 1933

Facts: The defendant was charged with having received a sum of money, the
property of a bank, knowing the same to have been stolen. He admitted the crime,
but stated in evidence that he acted under violent threats.

---

29 Morris and Howard *Studies in Criminal Law* (Oxford) Clarendon Press, 1964 141–144; *R v
McCafferty* [1974] 1 NSWLR 89; *R v McConnell* [1977] 1 NSWLR 714.
30 (1946) Fost 13.

Murnaghan J: This appeal involves a question of principle in the administration of the criminal law and its solution is not unattended with difficulties.

The appellant, Peter Whelan, was tried at the Dublin Circuit Court upon a charge of having, with others, conspired to steal a quantity of silver coin while in course of transit upon the Great Northern Railway; and also upon a charge of having with several others been guilty of receiving stolen goods contrary to sect 33, sub-sect 1, of the Larceny Act, 1916.

The evidence against the appellant was that of one, Farnan, who pleaded guilty to having been the thief; and the jury, having regard to the judge's warning, found Whelan not guilty of the charge of conspiracy to steal. The evidence of Farnan as to the receiving by Whelan was not denied by the latter, but Whelan himself gave evidence and alleged that in receiving the stolen goods he acted under violent threats on the part of Farnan. It is not necessary to review the evidence owing to the finding made by the jury. The jury did not find a general verdict either of guilty or not guilty, but, in answer to a question placed by direction of the Circuit Judge on the issue paper, viz: "In receiving the money did Peter Whelan act under threat of immediate death or serious violence?" the jury returned the answer: "Yes."

The Circuit Judge formed the opinion that this finding in law amounted to a conviction, but that he should give full effect to the jury's finding in the admeasurement of the punishment, and he passed a suspensory sentence. From this conviction Peter Whelan has appealed, and he contends that he is entitled, on the finding of the jury, to an acquittal upon the charge of receiving stolen goods.

The authorities to be found in the books on the point so raised are few in number and, indeed, show some discrepancy. Counsel for the accused sought to evade the burden of arguing that, as a general principle of law, such coercion as was found by the jury freed from culpability, and he strove rather to say that it was for the judge in the particular case to say whether the charge was one to which a defence of this kind was applicable. He contended that by leaving the question to the jury the judge had ruled in effect that an answer favourable to the accused amounted to an acquittal. It is, however, clear that the learned Circuit Judge did not rule in this manner as he treated the jury's finding as a conviction. The Court therefore has to determine whether, in so interpreting the finding, the Circuit Judge was correct in law. Counsel for the accused has accordingly made a very full argument based upon the authorities to the effect that, in all crimes save murder, duress *per minas* of the nature present in this case amounted to a justification.

All the elements producing culpability concur in this conviction except the free exercise of will, and the point is accordingly narrowed down to the consideration whether there was such an absence of will as to absolve from guilt.

For the prosecution it was contended that actual physical force which left the accused no choice of will was sufficient to absolve from guilt but that anything short of such force was merely matter for mitigation of punishment.

In the case of treason, according to Hale, immediate fear of death was a justification: Hale: "Pleas of the Crown," Vol 1 p 50 in which place he cites *Oldcastle's* case in the year 1419. This rule was recognised also in *R v Gordon*[31]. In *MacGrowther's* case[32] in the year 1746, the distinction is drawn between threats directed against the person and threats upon property. Lee CJ said (at p 14): "The only force that doth excuse is a force upon *the person*, and present fear of death; and this force and fear must continue all the time the party remains with the rebels. It is incumbent on every man, who makes force his defence, to show an actual force, and that he quitted the service as soon as he could." We were also referred

31 1 East PO 71.
32 Fost 13.

to the opinion of Lord Mansfield in *R v Stratton*[33], where he refers with approval to the ruling in the case of treason and appears to base this ruling upon a general principle to be extended to other classes of crime. In *R v Crutchley*[34], which dealt with a charge under 7 & 8 Geo 4, c 30, sect 4, of breaking a threshing machine. Patteson J evidently considered that if the prisoner was forced by a mob under threats to his person to do the act complained of he was entitled to an acquittal. On the other hand in *R v Tyler*[35], Denman CJ appears to state as a general principle his view to be that the apprehension of personal danager does not furnish any excuse for assisting in doing an act which is illegal. *R v Dudley and Stephens*[36] does not afford any assistance on the point now before the Court save that the difficulty of formulating a rule of universal application is fully recognised.

Notwithstanding his long experience of the criminal law Sir FitzJames Stephen states that he never personally came across a case in which duress *per minas* was pleaded as a defence; neither have counsel been able to discover any reported case on the subject in more recent years. The matter before the Court must therefore be approached from the standpoint of general principle. It seems to us that threats of immediate death or serious personal violence so great as to overbear the ordinary power of human resistance should be accepted as a justification for acts which would otherwise be criminal. The application of this general rule must however be subject to certain limitations. The commission of murder is a crime so heinous that murder should not be committed even for the price of life and in such a case the strongest duress would not be any justification.

We have not to determine what class of crime other than murder should be placed in the same category. We are, however, satisfied that any such consideration does not apply in the case of receiving. Where the excuse of duress is applicable it must further be clearly shown that the overpowering of the will was operative at the time the crime was actually committed, and, if there were reasonable opportunity for the will to reassert itself, no justification can be found in antecedent threats.

In the case before the Court we consider that the finding of the jury was meant to imply that the coercion was present when the act, otherwise criminal, was committed, and we are of opinion that the conviction must be quashed and a verdict of acquittal entered.

4.34 A note on the course of the trial from which this case is an appeal, appears under the title of *The People (A-G) v Farnan and Others*[37].

4.35

R v Hurley and Murray
[1967] VR 526
Supreme Court of Victoria, 1967

Smith J: . . . I consider that the following affirmative proposition as may be stated. Where an accused has been required to do the act charged against him (1) under a threat that death or grievous bodily harm will be inflicted unlawfully upon a human being if the accused fails to do the act and (2) the circumstances were such that a person of ordinary firmness would have been likely to yield to the threat in the way that the accused did and (3) the threat was present and continuing, imminent and impending . . . and (4) the accused reasonably apprehended that the threat would be carried out and (5) he was induced thereby to commit the crime charged and (6) that crime was not murder, nor any other crime so heinous

---

33 21 How St Tr 1015, 1229, 1230.
34 5 C & P 133.
35 8 C & P 616.
36 14 QBD 273.
37 (1933) 67 ILTR 208.

as to be excepted from the doctrine and (7) the accused did not, by fault on his part when free from the duress, expose himself to its application and (8) he had no means, with safety to himself, of preventing the execution of the threat, then the accused, in such circumstances at least, has a defence of duress.

Basis of the defence

4.36 From the point of view of principle it is clear that, in common with the defence of necessity, a person acting under duress does not lack any necessary mental element of the crime. Instead, in the words of Murnaghan J, what is absent is "the free exercise of will" (see para **4.33**). It is the lack of blame to be ascribed to a person acting under duress, coupled with the policy consideration that society should allow the choice of a lesser evil when no other choice is available, that underpins the rationale for this defence. All the members of the House of Lords in *DPP for Northern Ireland v Lynch*[38] analysed as intentional the deeds of a person acting under duress. Lord Morris classified such an act as unwilling yet intentional[39], Lord Wilbeforce considered the defence to be a superimposed excuse on other elements[40], Lord Simon held that the will of the accused was deflected and not destroyed[41], Lord Kilbrandon considered the choice made by the accused to be morally less culpable[42] and Lord Edmund-Davies classified the defence as a plea in confession and avoidance[43].

Objective aspect

4.37 Murnaghan J in *The People (AG) v Whelan*[44] (see para **4.33**) speaks of "the ordinary power of human resistance". The Court of Criminal Appeal in *The People (DPP) v MacEoin*[45] abandoned the objective test in provocation and did so for policy reasons (see para **4.155**). An extension of that reasoning can be argued as applying to duress. The difference between the two defences is, however, that provocation as a defence is a concession to human frailty; where a person acts in the throes of passion to the extent that he is no longer master of his actions. To limit the defence of provocation to circumstances where a hypothetical, ordinary or reasonable man would act as the accused did, is often to exclude the defence from those who may deserve its protection. Duress, on the other hand, involves a rational choice between two evils. The threat made to the accused must be of a grave order of magnitude to excuse the commission of a crime. The law might fail to fulfil its objective of ordering society if petty excuses for criminal action were allowed. Section 24 of the New Zealand Crimes Act 1961 incorporates a subjective test in the defence of compulsion. This, in practice, is applied restrictively; *R v Raroa*[46]. Section 17 of the Canadian Criminal Code (see

38 [1975] AC 653.
39 *Ibid* at p 670.
40 *Ibid* at p 679.
41 *Ibid* at p 695.
42 *Ibid* at p 703.
43 *Ibid* at p 710.
44 [1934] IR 518.
45 [1978] IR 27.
46 [1987] 2 NZLR 486.

para **4.51**) requires a belief on the part of the accused that the threats will be carried out. It appears that the best view on the objective elements of this test, is that reasonableness should only be relevant in assessing the genuineness of the defence evidence. In other words, consideration of what was likely to have occurred can be used to test whether the accused may be telling the truth in claiming that he acted under duress; a test explicitly stated in s 2 of the Criminal Law (Rape) Act 1981 but general to the entire criminal law.

4.38 In England, duress is now expressly based, by the House of Lords, on objective standards. This requires the threat to be "of such a degree of violence that 'a person of reasonable firmness' with the characteristics and in the situation of the defendant, could not have been expected to resist"; *R v Howe*[47]. This is the modified objective test adopted by the House of Lords in *R v Camplin*[48]. This is further discussed under the heading of provocation. Similarly, a *Camplin* type test was approved by the South Australian Full Court in *R v Balazoff*[49]. The Court stated the test as been objective. They referred to "the person of ordinary firmness of mind, faced with the same threat, against whom the accused is to be judged is a person of the same age and sex and background and other personal characteristics (except perhaps strength of mind) as the appellant".

4.39 The common law does not allow the defence to be operative save where the threat is of death or serious injury of some kind. Most criminal codes retain this feature. Text writers have pointed out that in some circumstances a threat of loss of fortune or reputation ought to suffice where the harm done by the accused is less than that threatened against him. Paragraph 3.02 of the Model Penal Code (see **Code options** below) might, in respect of some minor crimes, recognise the defence as simply one of a choice of evils.

4.40 Clearly, the defence is not open if the threat has ceased to operate when the crime is committed by the accused. The prosecution will often argue that the defence can have no application where the accused could have sought police help to neutralise the threat.

4.41   *R v Hudson and Taylor*
          [1971] 2 QB 202; [1971] 2 All ER 244; [1971] 2 WLR 1047;
                           (1972) 56 Cr App R 1
                       Court of Appeal England, 1971

Facts: The accused were two young women who were called to testify against a man called Wright on a charge of wounding. In giving evidence they failed to identify Wright and positively stated that they did not know him. He was acquitted. When subsequently tried for perjury they admitted that their evidence had been false but pleaded duress. One of the women had been approached by a man called Farrell, who had a reputation for violence, who threatened to "cut her up". In giving evidence at the trial of Wright, both of them saw the man who had

47 [1987] AC 417 at p 426.
48 [1978] AC 705.
49 (1986) 130 LSJS 20.

threatened them in the public gallery. At their trial their defence was disallowed because of the immediate availability of the judge and the police and they were convicted.

Lord Widgery CJ: . . . it is clearly established that duress provides a defence in all offences including perjury (except possibly treason or murder as a principal) if the will of the accused has been overborne by threats of death or serious personal injury so that the commission of the alleged offence was no longer the voluntary act of the accused.

This appeal raises two main questions; first, as to the nature of the necessary threat and, in particular, whether it must be "present and immediate"; secondly, as to the extent to which a right to plead duress may be lost if the accused has failed to take steps to remove the threat as, for example, by seeking police protection.

It is essential to the defence of duress that the threat shall be effective at the moment when the crime is committed. The threat must be a "present" threat in the sense that it is effective to neutralise the will of the accused at that time . . . a threat of future violence may be so remote as to be insufficient to overpower the will at that moment when the offence was committed, or the accused may have elected to commit the offence in order to rid himself of a threat hanging over him and not because he was driven to act by immediate and unavoidable pressure. In none of these cases is the defence of duress available because a person cannot justify the commission of a crime merely to secure his own piece of mind. When, however, there is no opportunity for delaying tactics, and the person threatened must make up his mind whether he is to commit the criminal act or not, the existence at that moment of a threat sufficient to destroy his will ought to provide him with a defence even though the threatened injury may not follow instantly, but after an interval. This principle is illustrated by *Subramaniam v Public Prosecutor* [1956] 1 WLR 965, when the appellant was charged in Malaya with unlawful possession of ammunition and was held by the Privy Council to have a defence of duress, fit to go to the jury, on his plea that he had been compelled by terrorists to accept the ammunition and feared for his safety if the terrorists returned.

In the present case the threats of Farrell were likely to be no less compelling, because their execution could not be effected in the court room, if they could be carried out in the streets of Salford the same night. In so far, therefore, as the recorder ruled as a matter of law that the threats were not sufficiently present and immediate to support the defence of duress we think that he was in error. He should have left the jury to decide whether the threats had overborne the will of the appellants at the time when they gave the false evidence.

[Counsel for the Crown] however contends that the recorder's ruling can be supported on another ground, namely, that the appellants should have taken steps to neutralise the threats by seeking police protection either when they came to court to give evidence, or beforehand. He submits on grounds of public policy that an accused should not be able to plead duress if he had the opportunity to ask for protection from the police before committing the offence and failed to do so. The argument does not distinguish cases in which the police would be able to provide effective protection, from those when they would not, and it would, in effect, restrict the defence of duress to cases where the person threatened had been kept in custody by the maker of the threats, or where the time interval between the making of the threats and the commission of the offence had made recourse to the police impossible. We recognise the need to keep the defence of duress within reasonable bounds but cannot accept so severe a restriction upon it. The duty, of the person threatened, to take steps to remove the threat does not seem to have arisen in an English case but, in a full review of the defence of duress in the Supreme Court of Victoria a condition of raising the defence was said to be that the accused 'had no means, with safety to himself, of preventing the execution of the threat'.

In the opinion of this Court it is always open to the Crown to prove that the accused failed to avail himself of some opportunity which was reasonably open to him to render the threat ineffective, and that upon this being established the threat in question can no longer be relied upon by the defence. In deciding whether such an opportunity was reasonably open to the accused the jury should have regard to his age and circumstances, and to any risks to him which may be involved in the course of action relied upon.

The appeals were allowed and the convictions quashed.

Inapplicable to murder

4.42   The judgment in *The People (A-G) v Whelan*[50] (see para **4.33**) makes it clear that duress cannot be a defence to the crime of murder. It leaves open the question whether other offences of a heinous nature are also to be excluded from its operation. It is doubtful if, at common law, treason is also excluded; *R v Purdy*[51]. Many criminal codes also exclude other offences, for example, s 17 of the Canadian Criminal Code quoted at para **4.51**.

4.43   There are degrees of participation in any crime. One can aid a murder by supplying a weapon, abet a murder by cutting off an avenue of escape from the victim or knowingly shelter the perpetrator of murder afterwards. It is yet to be decided in this jurisdiction whether any or all of these acts are excusable on the basis of duress.

In *DPP for Northern Ireland v Lynch*[52] the House of Lords ordered a retrial where Lynch claimed, on a charge of aiding and abetting the murder of a police constable, that he acted under duress from the IRA. The House held that the defence was open to Lynch. Subsequently, he was retried but his evidence was disbelieved. He later died on hunger strike in the Maze Prison in 1981.

The Privy Council in *Abbott v R*[53] confirmed that the defence was not open to a person who played an active part in the killing. Subsequently, the House of Lords in *R v Howe*[54] over-ruled *Lynch* and excluded the defence on a charge of aiding and abetting murder. In New Zealand the courts do not appear to exclude the defence where a person is an accessory after the fact to murder; *R v Raroa*[55]. In *R v Gotts*[56], the House of Lords confirmed that duress was not available as a defence to a person charged with attempted murder.

4.44   It should be emphasised that if a person is to be convicted of murder he must genuinely have an intention to kill or cause serious injury. The House of Lords in *R v Howe*[57] canvassed some bizarre possibilities as to when the defence of duress ought to be excluded. Certain statements by the Law Lords in that case seem to include, in the categories of persons aiding

50 [1934] IR 518.
51 (1946) 10 JCL 182.
52 [1975] AC 653.
53 [1977] AC 755.
54 [1987] AC 417.
55 [1987] 2 NZLR 486.
56 [1992] 1 All ER 832.
57 [1987] AC 417.

and abetting murder, those who involuntarily participate by, for example, being hijacked and drive a get-away car to the scene of a crime. In *R v Paquete*[58] the Supreme Court of Canada ordered an acquittal of a person forced at gun-point to drive two acquaintances to the scene of a robbery where a by-stander was later killed. Martland J in the course of his judgment stated:

"A person whose actions have been dictated by a fear of death or grievous bodily injury cannot be said to have formed a genuine common intention to carry out an unlawful purpose with the person who has threatened him with those consequences if he fails to co-operate".

In *The People (AG) v Whelan*[59] the accused was acquitted on a charge of conspiracy to steal by reason of duress. In some circumstances, therefore, it is possible to argue the defence as removing entirely the element of mental culpability for a particular crime. In *Paquete* the accused did not intend to carry out the unlawful purpose, in *Whelan* he did not intend to enter into an agreement to commit a crime.

4.45 A possible compromise in the case of murder would be to apply a half-way house doctrine similar to that applied in *The People (AG) v Dwyer*[60], (see para **4.24**). This compromise was adopted in New South Wales in *R v McCafferty*[61], but was later over-ruled in *R v McConnell*[62].

Joining a violent organisation

4.46 In *R v Fitzpatrick*[63] the Court of Criminal Appeal in Northern Ireland held that the defence of duress was unavailable to a person who voluntarily joined an organisation of violent criminals. In *R v Calderwood and Moore*[64] this principle was extended to a situation where the accused was reckless in joining an organisation which he should have realised was violent and liable to subject him to duress. The principle in *Fitzpatrick* has been accepted in the English Court of Appeal in *R v Sharp*[65]. The unavailability of the defence will depend on the knowledge which the accused had of the organisation he joined, and in particular its propensity to violence; *R v Shepherd*[66].

4.47 If the accused is compelled under duress to join a violent organisation and is later coerced into committing a crime, the defence must, on principle, remain open to him. His failure to contact the police may be a matter of evidence indicating that his participation was voluntary. It does not appear to be just to exclude the defence from someone who, realising his wrongdoing in joining a violent organisation, makes every possible effort to leave it. Where such a person is unsuccessful in his efforts to leave an organisation but is forced to commit a crime, the law ought to develop a principle similar

58 [1977] 2 SCR 189.
59 [1934] IR 518.
60 [1972] IR 416.
61 [1974] 1 NSWLR 89.
62 [1977] 1 NSWLR 714.
63 [1977] NI 20.
64 [1983] NI 361.
65 [1988] QB 853.
66 (1987) 86 Cr App R 47.

to that of withdrawal from a common design. In that context the defence of withdrawal has been characterised by the Supreme Court of Victoria in *R v Jensens*[67] as follows:

"The mere fact that one or more parties to [an offence] feels qualms or wished they had not got themselves involved or wished that it were possible to stop the criminal act or acts agreed upon, will not amount to a calling-off of the agreement or arrangement once it has been made. In order to call it off so far as concerns himself, a party must communicate his withdrawal to the other parties, or at all events take some positive step, such as informing the police".

4.48   ***R v Calderwood and Moore***
                             [1983] NI 361
                   Crown Court Northern Ireland, 1983

Facts: On the night of the 27th March 1981 Paul Anthony Blake was shot dead in the Ardoyne District of Belfast. This was a Roman Catholic area. He was struck by three bullets each of which had been fired from a separate ·455 revolver. On 4th June 1982 the accused Calderwood made oral admissions and a written statement to interviewing police officers. He said that he had been a member of the Ulster Defence Association in the Shankill area since 1976. On the night in question he met two men who were his "officers" in the UDA and heard them discuss the theft of a motor car. He was instructed by the more senior man to accompany the other. They went to a spot where they waited until the person instructed to steal the car had arrived. All three then went to a nearby house where revolvers were produced. Calderwood indicated in his statement that he then knew that they were going to shoot someone "but there was nothing I could do about it as I was heart-feared of this officer". They got into the stolen car and drove to the Ardoyne area. The car stopped and the officer got out and he talked to a man on the footpath. Apparently after ascertaining this person's religion the officer then stepped back and fired two or three shots at the man's face. The man fell back and the officer got into the car and shouted at Calderwood to shoot. Calderwood then aimed at the man's legs and fired one shot. Calderwood's shot did not endanger life but passed through part of the leg and through his left flank and lower ribs. The next day the murder was discussed at UDA headquarters. The murders were praised and Calderwood was given some money and told to get himself a drink.

On the 7th June 1982 the accused Moore made oral admissions and a written statement to interviewing police officers. He said that he had been compelled to join the UDA in 1978. He described that he had been approached by a man and told to steal a car. He went to the rendezvous point where two persons with guns got into the car. They stopped the person on the footpath, shot him and then the car returned to the Shankill. Moore said that he was very scared at the time. The next morning he said he met the person who ordered him to get the car and was given some money. Moore indicated that since the murder he had been in hiding from the organisation until he was arrested.

Hutton J: . . . Following the decision in *Abbott v The Queen* I hold that the defence of duress is not open to him.

There is a further and separate ground on which I consider that the defence of duress is not open to Calderwood. Calderwood commenced his written statement by saying:

"I have been a member of the Ulster Defence Association on the Shankill Road since about 1976. I belong to 'C' Company. I have already told you all about the things which the organisation has been involved in since I joined."

67 [1980] VR 194.

And Calderwood then went on to recount how the criminal events of the evening of 27 March 1981 were initiated by two of his so-called "officers" in the UDA. Therefore I consider that, in accordance with the decision of the Court of Appeal in *R v Fitzpatrick* [1977] NI 20, Calderwood cannot rely on the defence of duress. In *R v Fitzpatrick* it was held:

"If a person by joining an illegal organisation or a similar group of men with criminal objectives and coercive methods voluntarily exposes and submits himself to illegal compulsion he cannot rely on the duress to which he has voluntarily exposed himself as an excuse either in respect of the crimes he commits against his will or in respect of his continuing but unwilling association with those capable of exercising upon him the duress which he calls in aid."

At page 33 in delivering the judgment of the Court Lowry LCJ stated:

"This court is satisfied that there are circumstances in which persons who associated with violent criminals and voluntarily expose themselves to the risk of compulsion to commit criminal acts cannot according to common law avail themselves of the defence of duress. We are further satisfied that, wherever the line should be drawn, this appellant falls on the side of it where the defence is not available to him.

The learned trial judge summarised at page 6 of his judgment the facts to which he applied the principle of non-availability of duress. While adopting his reasoning, we guard ourselves against the use of any expression which might tend to confine the application of that principle to illegal, in the narrow sense of proscribed, organisations. A person may become associated with a sinister group of men with criminal objectives and coercive methods of ensuring that their lawless enterprises are carried out and thereby voluntarily expose himself to illegal compulsion, whether or not the group is or becomes a proscribed organisation.

Nor indeed, so far as the facts are concerned, do we consider that the evidence of the nature and activities of the relevant organisation has necessarily to be the same formal and precise character as it apparently was in this case."

The Ulster Defence Association is not a proscribed organisation but I am satisfied beyond a reasonable doubt, and hereafter in this judgment when I state that I am satisfied, I mean that I am satisfied beyond a reasonable doubt, that the branch of the UDA on the Shankill Road to which the accused belonged was "a sinister group of men with criminal objectives and coercive methods of ensuring that their lawless enterprises were carried out."

In his evidence the accused Moore raised the defence of duress. In the course of his evidence the accused stated that in 1978 he was caught by the police in the back of a stolen car and that he told the police the name of the person who had been the driver of the car. This person was a member of the UDA and because he had given this information to the police the UDA classed him as an informer and told him that he would be shot unless he joined the UDA. He was never formally sworn into the UDA but he was told that he would have to attend meetings and pay dues. He attended three or four UDA meetings but then ceased to attend UDA meetings. He stated that he was beaten up on two or three occasions because he did not attend the meetings. The above was the account given by the accused in evidence.

In addition the accused stated in evidence that in February 1979 he was shot once in the right thigh as a punishment shooting. I am satisfied that the accused was shot in the right thigh in February 1979. The accused showed the Court the bullet wounds in his right thigh and police witness accepted that Moore had suffered a punishment shooting in the leg in February 1979.

In his evidence the accused stated that the UDA had inflicted the punishment shooting on him because in a fight at a club he had struck a 'bouncer' who held a rank in the UDA and he was punished by the UDA for having struck him.

The view of a police officer expressed in the course of his evidence was that he was punished for a different reason, but the police officer's view appeared to be based on hearsay and I therefore do not take account of the reason suggested by the police officer for the shooting. However, having observed the accused in the witness box giving the reason why he was subjected to the punishment shooting and having considered the account which he gave, I state that I do not believe his account that he was shot for striking a "bouncer" and I am satisfied that this explanation for the shooting was untrue, but as I have stated, I am satisfied that he was subjected to a punishment shooting in the leg by the UDA or by some other "Loyalist" paramilitary organisation.

In my judgment it is clear that as the driver of the car (as was the accused in *DPP v Lynch*) Moore was a principal in the second degree, but I consider that his defence of duress fails for two separate reasons, which I now state:

1. Whilst I have considerable doubt whether the accused's account of how he became a member of the UDA was true I think there is a reasonable possibility that the account was true. Therefore the Crown cannot contend, in reliance on the decision in *R v Fitzpatrick*, that the defence of duress is not open to the accused on the ground that he voluntarily joined the UDA. But I consider that the principle of the decision in *Fitzpatrick*'s case has a wider application and prevents the accused from relying on duress even if (as I think is a reasonable possibility) he joined the UDA under threats. In *R v Fitzpatrick* at page 33 Lowry LCJ stated:

> "This court is safisfied that there are circumstances in which persons who associate with violent criminals and voluntarily expose themselves to the risk of compulsion to commit criminal acts cannot according to the common law avail themselves of the defence of duress . . . A person may become associated with a sinister group of men with criminal objectives and coercive methods of ensuring that their lawless enterprises are carried out and thereby voluntarily expose himself to illegal compulsion, whether or not the group is or becomes a proscribed organisation."

And in *Lynch's* case at page 670 Lord Morris stated:

> ". . . duress must never be allowed to be the easy answer . . . of those who readily could have avoided the dominance of threats."

Therefore I consider that the *Fitzpatrick* principle applies not only to a man who voluntarily joins a sinister group of men with criminal objectives and coercive methods of ensuring that their lawless enterprises are carried out but applies also to a man who voluntarily associates himself with such a group of men and thereby exposes himself to the risk of compulsion to join the group and therefore to the subsequent risk of compulsion to commit criminal acts on their behalf.

Having regard to the evidence given by the accused in chief and on cross-examination I am satisfied that at the time when he joined the UDA the accused was a thief and knowingly associated with members of the UDA such as Frederick Truesdale and the man who was the driver of the stolen car in the back of which the accused was caught, which members were aware, to his knowledge, that he was a thief and I consider that that association by him left him very vulnerable to the sort of pressure which he described as bringing about his joining the UDA. Therefore I consider that the defence of duress is not open to him.

4.49 The judge also ruled, in this case, on a defence application that evidence should be given by a consultant psychiatrist as to the susceptibility of the accused, Calderwood, to duress. The judge ruled that evidence could be given as to the intelligence quotient of the accused but that evidence on his susceptibility to duress was inadmissible. This ruling followed the traditional principle of the law of evidence that expert testimony is only admissible in respect of matters which are outside the competence and experience of the tribunal of fact.

Code options

4.50 *Model penal code*

2.09 Duress

(1) It is an affirmative defence that the actor engaged in the conduct charged to constitute an offence because he was coerced to do so by the use of, or a threat to use, unlawful force against his person or the person of another, that a person of reasonable firmness in his situation would have been unable to resist.

(2) The defence provided by this section is unavailable if the actor recklessly placed himself in a situation in which it was probable that he would be subjected to duress. The defence is also unavailable if he was negligent in placing himself in such a situation, whenever negligence suffices to establish culpability for the offence charged.

(3) It is not a defence that a woman acted on the command of her husband, unless she acted under such coercion as would establish a defence under this section. [The presumption that a woman acting in the presence of her husband is coerced is abolished.]

(4) When the conduct of the actor would otherwise be justifiable under section 3.02, this section does not preclude such defence.

4.51 *Canadian Criminal Code*

17: A person who commits an offence under compulsion by threats of immediate death or bodily harm from a person who is present when the offence is committed is excused from committing the offence if the person believes that the threats will be carried out and if the person is not party to a conspiracy or association whereby the person is subject to compulsion, but this section does not apply where the offence that is committed is high treason or treason, murder, piracy, attempted murder, sexual assault, sexual assault with a weapon, threats to a third party of causing bodily harm, aggravated sexual assault, forcible abduction, hostage taking, robbery, assault with a weapon or causing bodily harm, aggravated assault, unlawfully causing bodily harm, arson or an offence under sections 280 to 283 (Abduction and Detention of Young Persons).

Further materials

4.52 Denis *Duress, Murder and Criminal Responsibility* (1980) 96 LQR 208.
Stephen *History of the English Criminal Law*, Volume 2 p 107 et seq.
Glazebrook *Committing Murder under Duress – Again* (1976) 35 Camb LJ 206.
Elliot *Necessity, Duress and Self-Defence* [1989] Crim LR 611.
Smith *Must Heroes Behave Heroically?* [1989] Crim LR 622.
Aristotle *Nichomanchean Ethics*, chapter 3.

Marital coercion

4.53 At common law it was presumed that where a wife committed a crime in the presence of her husband she had acted under his immediate coercion[68].

4.54   *The State (DPP) v Walsh and Conneely*
[1981] IR 412
Supreme Court, 1981

Facts: This case arose out of *The People (DPP) v Murray* [1977] IR 360 [see para **1.31**]. The Murrays were sentenced to death by the Special Criminal Court. Two days later a newspaper published a report containing the views of the accused in this case who had stated that the Special Criminal Court had no judicial independence and that, in trying the Murrays, it had "so abused the rules of evidence as to make the court akin to a sentencing tribunal". Walsh and Conneely were tried for contempt. They appealed to the Supreme Court seeking trial by judge and jury. The issue of marital coercion was introduced in an affidavit showing fresh evidence in support of the second accused.

Henchy J: . . . This fresh evidence shows that, as honorary secretary of the Dublin Central Branch of the Association for Legal Justice, she had been asked by the appellant Walsh to draft a statement for publication in the Dublin newspapers, that she proceeded to draft the statement and that her husband helped her extensively with the drafting of it, and that the sentence in the statement which accused the judges of so abusing the rules of evidence as to make the court akin to a sentencing tribunal was inserted in the statement at her husband's suggestion. On the basis of that degree of co-operation, the strange submission has been put forward on behalf of the appellant Conneely that, because of coercion on her husband's part, it is he, and not she, who could be found guilty of contempt.

For a number of reasons, this submission is in my view lacking in persuasiveness. In the first place, it is to be noted that this offence of contempt was committed not in composing the statement but in causing it to be published in a newspaper. Whatever part the husband of the appellant Conneely may have taken in the composition of the statement, it is clear that he took no part in the dissemination of it. Her affidavit goes no further than to state that he was present when she was telephoning the statement to the newspaper. His physical presence is all that can be relied on as constituting the coercion which is said by her counsel to exculpate her.

There was undoubtedly a common-law defence of coercion available to a wife in regard to certain offences if the act in question was done by her in the presence of her husband. In an effort to compensate the wife for her inferior status, and in particular to make up for her inability to plead benefit of clergy, as her husband could, the law concocted the fiction of a prima facie presumption that the act done by her in the presence of her husband was done under his coercion. But, be it noted, it was only a *prima facie* presumption. The authorities are agreed in saying that the presumption could be rebutted by evidence that the wife was the instigator of the act, or was the more active party. The so-called coercion was recognized only when there was no evidence of initiative by the wife: see Smith and Hogan on Criminal Law (3rd ed at p 168). Here the presumption is plainly rebutted. On the appellant Conneely's own evidence on affidavit, as between her husband and herself, she was the prime mover in the commission of the *actus reus*. It was she,

---

68 Pages 21 to 24 of the 26th edition (1922) of Archbold's *Criminal Pleading Evidence and Practice* make hilarious reading.

and she alone, who telephoned the statement to the newspaper. To do so was a duty committed to her (as honorary secretary of the Dublin Central Branch of the Association for Legal Justice) by the appellant Walsh as chairman of that branch. Her husband merely happened to be present when she did so. His mere physical presence in the room could no more provide a defence for her than it could form the basis of a conviction of him. It would be contrary to both reason and judicial authority to hold that in those circumstances the appellant Conneely could be acquitted of contempt simply because her husband was present when she telephoned the offending statement to the newspaper.

That is how I would dispose of this point if the presumption of coercion of a wife by the physical presence of her husband were applicable. But, in my judgment, that doctrine is no longer extant in this State. The idea that, where a wife performs a criminal act, there should be a *prima facie* presumption that the mere physical presence of her husband when she did it overbore her will, stultified her volitional powers, and drove her into criminal conduct which she would have avoided but for his presence, presupposes a disparity in status and capacity between husband and wife which runs counter to the normal relations between a married couple in modern times. The conditions of legal inferiority which attached at common law to the status of a married woman and which gave rise to this presumption have been swept away by legislation and by judicial decisions. Nowadays, to exculpate a wife for an *actus reus* because it was done when her husband was present is no more justifiable than if she were granted immunity from guilt because the act was done in the presence of her father, her brother or any other relative or friend. Any other conclusion would be repugnant to the degree of freedom and equality to which a wife is entitled in modern society and which has been extensively recognized in the statutes and judicial decisions of this State.

In particular, I would hold that the presumption relied on is inconsistent with the Constitution and was therefore, by virtue of Article 50, not given validity in the legal system after the Constitution came into force. A legal rule that presumes, even on a *prima facie* and rebuttable basis, that a wife has been coerced by the physical presence of her husband into committing an act prohibited by the criminal law, particularly when a similar presumption does not operate in favour of a husband for acts committed in the presence of his wife, is repugnant to the concept of equality before the law guaranteed by the first sentence of Article 40, s 1, and could not, under the second sentence of that Article, be justified as a discrimination based on any difference of capacity or of social function as between husband and wife. Therefore, the presumption contended for must be rejected as being a form of unconstitutional discrimination.

Necessity

4.55 Circumstances can arise where it may be necessary to break the criminal law in order to fulfil a human duty or to avoid an evil greater than that which the law is designed to prevent. Suppose a person is walking along the street and sees a baby choking on its bottle in a locked car. In the circumstances it would be normal and praiseworthy to intervene by breaking open the car door and rescuing the baby. If Mountjoy Jail were to catch fire a prisoner who immediately left without permission, reasonably believing that the alternative consequence was to die or be seriously injured, would not be blameworthy by normal rational standards.

4.56 Necessity, as a defence, is capable of being used in such a way as to overthrow the criminal law. Judicial fears have been expressed that the

4.56 *The Defences*

defence will give rise to anarchy[69]. As in duress, a person subjected to necessity chooses to break the criminal law. In duress his will is overborne by that of another party but, in necessity, circumstances alone will usually be to blame. In duress, therefore, some person will be to blame for the breach of the criminal law (the person who forced the accused to commit the crime). In necessity only the accused is identifiable as a potential wrong-doer. It may be that human society feels the need to blame some person for an obvious breach of its criminal law and that the early acceptance of the defence of duress and the reluctance to allow necessity as a defence is explicable from this fact alone.

Constitutional aspect

4.57 Acceptance of the defence is now becoming generalised. The House of Lords have never explicitly rejected the defence. The Court of Appeal has accepted a defence of duress of circumstances, which amounts to the same thing as necessity; *R v Denton*[70], *R v Conway*[71]. Lord Hailsham in *R v Howe*[72] indicated that there was no obvious distinction between duress and necessity as potential defences;

> ". . . duress is only that species of the genus of necessity which is caused by wrongful threats. I cannot see that there is any way in which a person of ordinary fortitude can be excused from the one type of pressure on his will rather than the other." Necessity has been accepted as a defence in Victoria in the case of *R v Dixon-Jenkins*[73] and in Canada by the Supreme Court in *R v Perka*[74].

4.58 It is submitted that the defence must be accepted in Irish criminal law. If a conviction were to result to a person accused in either of the examples given, the choking baby or the burning prison, the great mass of right-thinking people would consider that an injustice had been perpetrated. Justice is the foundation of the Constitution. The courts cannot, therefore, countenance unjust convictions being recorded; *McGee v A-G*[75]. It is only by recourse to institutions of arbitration that an ordered society makes justice available. Criminal litigation proceeds by applying rules, indicating whether behaviour is criminal, to the individual cases which come before the courts. The courts will not hear hypothetical cases and the defence of necessity has yet to be pleaded before our courts. Basic principle remains a sure guide in the absence of authority. Article 40.3 of the Constitution guarantees absolutely that the State will respect the personal rights of the citizen. These rights are generally interpreted as being based on justice. While justice is an elusive concept, the instinctive reaction to the examples quoted must be against a conviction in those circumstances. If the Oireachtas were to apply its mind to the problem, the defence of necessity might be circumscribed by particular limitations. In the absence of defined

69 See particularly the remarks of Lord Denning and Edmund Davies in *Southwark London Borough Council v Williams* [1971] Ch 734.
70 (1987) 85 Cr App R 246.
71 [1988] 3 All ER 1025.
72 [1987] AC 417 at p 429.
73 (1985) 14A Crim R 372.
74 (1984) 42 Cr (3d) 113.
75 [1974] IR 284 at 318.

parameters, each individual case will come to be tried on its own individual set of facts. From these, principles may emerge. The purpose of the Constitution is to found a true social order based on the observance of prudence, justice and charity. Limitations to the defence of necessity can be drawn from this fundamental precept.

Where the accused has negligently created the circumstances which gave rise to the need for the criminal law to be broken it may not be unfair that he should be convicted. Equally, where the accused has involved himself in a course of criminal conduct during which the need to break the law has arisen, it may be fair to disallow him from relying on circumstances created by his prior fault. There are persuasive analogies with self-induced provocation and duress arising from the accused's voluntary association with a violent organisation; see paras **4.46–4.48** and *R v Meuckon*[76].

History

4.59 The best known historical case is *R v Dudley and Stephens*[77]. This concerned the English ship Mignonette which foundered in mid-ocean 1,600 miles from the Cape of Good Hope. Four persons, including the accused, set to sea in an open boat with very little food and no water. After eleven days their food was exhausted. Eight days subsequently, the two accused suggested to their comrade that the cabin boy should be killed and eaten to save the rest. The following day lots were drawn but the cabin boy was not included and the dissentient refused to participate. The following day the two accused killed the cabin boy and all three lived on his body and blood for four days. When they were rescued they were close to death. The custom at the time, when such occurrences were not unknown, was for all of the sailors to draw lots. Apparently, in this case, the prosecution was only initiated because this observance had not been followed. In the circumstances the defence of necessity was rejected. Lord Coleridge added an interesting footnote to this judgment:

> "My brother Grove has furnished me with the following suggestion, too late to be embodied in the judgment but well worth preserving: If the two accused men were justified in killing Parker, then if not rescued in time, two of the three survivors would be justified in killing the third, and of the two who remained the stronger would be justified in killing the weaker, so that three men might be justifiably killed to give the fourth a chance of surviving."

4.60 In *R v Howe*[78] the House of Lords upheld the decision in *Dudley and Stephens* indicating that necessity could not be pleaded in answer to a charge of murder.

4.61   *US v Holmes*
                        (1842) Federal Case No 15383; 26 Fed Cas 360
                                    Federal Court, 1842

Facts: As a result of a shipwreck the passengers and crew took to a long boat which leaked so badly that it began to sink. Sixteen passengers were thrown overboard

76 (1990) 57 CCC (3d) 193.
77 (1884) 14 QBD 273.
78 [1987] AC 417.

but the crew, including a cook, remained on board. The accused was charged with manslaughter and convicted. The legal reasoning on which the charge to the jury was based, seemed to proceed on the basis that necessity was a defence. In the particular case the parameters were exceeded by the crew members saving more of their comrades than was necessary to man the boat and by the unfair selection procedures for those who were to perish. The custom of casting lots tends to imply a form of consent among those participating.

Baldwin CJ: But in addition, if the source of danger had been obvious and destruction ascertained to be certainly about to arrive, though at a future time there should be consultation, and some mode of selection fixed by which those in equal relations may have equal chance for their life. By what mode, then, should selection be made? The question is not without difficulty; nor do we know of any rule ascribed either by statute, by common law or even by speculative writers on the law of nature. In fact no rule of general application can be prescribed for contingencies which are wholly unforseen. There is however, one condition of extremity for which all writers have prescribed the same rules. When the ship is in no danger of sinking but all sustenance is exhausted, and the sacrifice of one person is necessary to appease the hunger of others, the selection is by lot. This mode is resorted to as the fairest mode and, in some sort, as an appeal to God, for selection of the victim . . . For ourselves, we can conceive of no mode so consonant both to humanity and to justice; and the occasion, we think, must be peculiar which will dispense with its exercise. If, indeed, the peril is instant and over-whelming leaving no chance or means, and no moment for deliberation, then, of course there is no power to consult, to cast lots, or in any such way to decide; but even where the final disaster is thus sudden, if it had been foreseen as certainly about to arrive, if no new cause of danger have arisen to bring on the closing catastrophe, if time had existed to cast lots, and to select the victims, then as we have said, sortition should be adopted. In no other than this or some like way are those having equal rights put upon equal footing, and in no other way is it possible to guard against partiality and oppression, violence and conflict . . .

Limitation on the defence

4.62   The courts which have accepted the defence of necessity require limitations based on:

(1) a real and pressing danger to the accused, or possibly someone close to him;
(2) an inescapable necessity to commit the criminal offence with which he is charged;
(3) proportionality between the harm to be avoided and that done by the breach of the criminal law; and
(4) that the accused should not have brought about the situation giving rise to the defence by his own criminal or negligent conduct.

4.63   *R v Loughnan*
[1981] VR 443
Supreme Court of Victoria, 1979

Facts: The accused escaped from prison together with three other inmates. His story was that he had secreted a gun and some bullets in a stool. Through another prisoner this had found its way into the cell of a fellow inmate called Regan. Following a search of Regan's cell the gun was found which resulted in that prisoner being sent to the punishment division. This led other prisoners to believe that the accused had set Regan up and was therefore working for prison officers as an informer. He asked to be moved to the punishment division in order to demonstrate that this was false. Loughnan claimed that he had been insulted and threatened and told, on the day of his escape, that he would be killed that night. He therefore joined in an existing escape plan without prior arrangement. The trial judge ruled that there was no sufficient evidence to be left to the jury on the question of necessity and, on appeal, the Supreme Court of Victoria agreed that the facts of the case did not give rise to the defence of necessity on the principles which they stated in their judgment.

Young CJ and King J: . . . There does not appear to be any reported case which is binding upon us in which a defence of necessity has *eo nomine* been accepted. There are, however, statements going back very many years by writers of distinction to some of which we shall refer, which recognise the defence. There is also a sharp controversy between academic writers: see Glanville Williams *Criminal Law: The General Part*, (2nd ed, 1961), p 724, para 231 where it is confidently submitted that the defence is recognised in English law and, on the other hand, P R Glazebrook, "The Necessity Plea in English Criminal Law", [1972] *Camb LJ* 87 where an opposing view is taken.

In this case we have come to the conclusion that the application should fail because even if there be a defence of necessity available to a prisoner who escapes from lawful custody we do not think that the facts adduced justified the leaving of the defence to the jury. If there be no such defence recognised by the law, of course, *cadit quaestio*. However since we are of the opinion that a prisoner who escapes may in certain circumstances raise a defence of necessity, we think it is necessary or at any rate desirable that we should state briefly the foundation for the conclusion which we have reached.

We do not find it difficult to accept a general proposition to the effect that the law in some cases does recognise a defence of necessity. The difficulty is to describe the elements of the defence and there is a great danger in attempting to describe those elements in general terms, that is to say, in terms applicable to crimes in general or to a particular class of crimes. In *Halsbury's Law of England*, 4th ed, vol 11, p 26, para 26, it is said that there is no general rule giving rise to a defence of necessity but this may be intended as no more than a cautious statement of the position. On the other hand, "there is authority for saying that in case of great and imminent danger, in order to preserve life, the law will permit an encroachment on private property", *per* Lord Denning MR in *Southwark LBC v Williams* [1971] Ch 734 at 743, where his Lordship cited *Mouse's* case (1608), 12 Co Rep 63. Lord Denning also said that "the doctrine so enunciated must, however, be carefully circumscribed. Else necessity would open the door to many an excuse".

In *R v Davidson* [1969] VR 667 at 670, Menhennitt J quoted Sir James Fitzjames Stephen's view as follows: "The principle of necessity is stated by Stephen in his *Digest of the Criminal Law* (1st ed, ch 3, art 43; 9th ed, ch 2, art 11) in the following terms: 'An act which would otherwise be a crime may in some cases be excused if the person accused can show that it was done only in order to avoid consequences which could not otherwise be avoided, and which, if they had followed, would have inflicted upon him or upon others whom he was bound to protect inevitable and irreparable evil, that no more was done than was reasonably necessary for that purpose, and that the evil inflicted by it was not disproportionate to the evil avoided. The extent of this principle is unascertained'".

Menhennitt J went on to point out at the same page that the concept of necessity finds its place in various branches of the criminal law: see the authorities which are there cited. There is also much reference to the question in academic writings not all of which are readily available here, but we mention some of those that we have consulted in addition to those already mentioned: Gardner, "The Defence of Necessity and the Right to Escape from Prison" 49 *SCLR* 110; Davies, "Law of

Abortion and Necessity" (1939) 2 *Mod LR* 126; Edwards, "Compulsion, Coercion and Criminal Responsibility" (1951) 14 *Mod LR* 297.

It will be seen from the statement by Sir James Fitzjames Stephen that there are three elements involved in the defence of necessity. First, the criminal act or acts must have been done only in order to avoid certain consequences which would have inflicted irreparable evil upon the accused or upon others whom he was bound to protect. The limits of this element are at present ill defined and where those limits should lie is a matter of debate. But we need not discuss this element further because the irreparable evil relied upon in the present case was a threat of death and if the law recognises the defence of necessity in any case it must surely do so where the consequence to be avoided was the death of the accused. We prefer to reserve for consideration if it should arise what other consequence might be sufficient to justify the defence: cf *People v Lovercamp* (1975) 43 California Appeals 3d 823, in which the consequence to be avoided was forcible homosexual activity.

The other two elements involved, which were identified by Menhennitt J in *R v Davidson, supra*, at 671 can for convenience be given the labels, immediate peril and proportion, although the expression of what is embodied in those two elements will necessarily vary from one type of situation to another.

The element of imminent peril means that the accused must honestly believe on reasonable grounds that he was placed in a situation of imminent peril. As Edmund Davies LJ (as he then was) pointed out in *Southwark LBC v Williams, supra*, at 746, all the cases in which a plea of necessity had succeeded are cases which deal with an urgent situation of imminent peril. Thus if there is an interval of time between the threat and its expected execution it will be very rarely if ever that a defence of necessity can succeed.

The element of proportion simply means that the acts done to avoid the imminent peril must not be out of proportion to the peril to be avoided. Put in another way, the test is: would a reasonable man in the position of the accused have considered that he had any alternative to doing what he did to avoid the peril? The two tests of imminent peril and proportion we have adapted from the tests propounded by Smith J in *R v McKay* [1957] VR 500 at 572–3, where they are referred to as necessity and proportion. It will be seen that in the application of the defence of necessity to a given situation these two elements may become interwoven. A person who receives a threat that he will be killed on a future day cannot seek out the person making the threat and kill him and escape liability on the ground that the killing was necessary in order to avoid his own death unless no other way of avoiding the danger was open to him. In such a case the accused will not be held to have had reasonable grounds for believing that it was necessary for him to do as he did in order to avoid the peril feared and it would also be held that his killing was in the circumstances out of proportion to the threat made to him.

A further example may be taken from *R v Kitson* (1955) 39 Cr App R 66 where a passenger awoke in a car to find that the driver had left and the car was moving. He managed to steer the car for some 300 yards on to a grass verge although he himself was intoxicated. Upon being charged with driving whilst under the influence of drink the defence of necessity was apparently not raised. If it had been, it might have succeeded. It might have been held that the accused was in a situation of imminent peril and that he had no reasonable alternative to doing what he did to avoid the peril. But if having placed himself in the driver's seat the accused had decided to drive himself home his actions would clearly have gone beyond what was reasonably necessary to avoid the imminent peril.

The well-known defence of self-defence, if not capable of being brought within the general description of a defence of necessity, is at least analogous to it, but in comparing the kind of necessity which requires self defence with the necessity which requires escape from prison there is, of course, an essential difference in that in the former the accused will always or almost always attack the person threatening him whereas in a case where a prisoner pleads necessity as a justification for escaping, the criminal act which he commits is not directed to the person making the threat. But we do not see any reason why the same two elements should not be involved. First, an urgent situation of imminent peril must exist in which the accused must honestly believe on reasonable grounds that it is necessary for him to do the acts which are alleged to constitute the offence in order to avoid the threatened danger. Secondly, those acts must not be disproportionate to the threatened danger. In other words, if a prisoner were confined in a small country gaol and were placed in a position where he honestly believed on reasonable grounds that to preserve his own life he had to escape from the place where he was confined, he might be allowed with impunity to escape to the outside world. But if he were confined in a large metropolitan prison containing many divisions a similar threat might only be held to justify escape from the particular division in which he was confined. In such a case the accused might not of course be charged with escaping from lawful custody but no doubt he might be open to a charge of some lesser offence.

We shall not attempt to fit the decision in the well-known case of *R v Dudley and Stephens* (1884) 14 QBD 273 into the views here expressed. That case has been elaborately considered and discussed by Glanville Williams, *op cit*, pp 741–5, para 237. It is sufficient to say that the decision does not require us to hold that a defence of necessity can never excuse a charge of escaping from lawful custody.

A question was raised during the argument whether a defence of necessity can be raised to a statutory offence such as that with which the applicant was charged. The offence of escaping from prison is created by s 132(1) of the *Community Welfare Service Act* 1970 which reads:

132. (1) Every prisoner who escapes or attempts to escape:

(*a*) from a prison or police gaol; or
(*b*) from the custody of a member of the police force or a prison officer in whose legal custody he is or is deemed to be:

shall be guilty of an indictable offence.
Penalty: Imprisonment for five years.

The section does not attach the word "unlawfully" to the word "escapes" but in our opinion the failure to do so does not exclude the possibility that a lawful justification or excuse may provide an answer to a charge under it. Many indictable offences are created without the use of the word "unlawfully" or some word of similar effect and yet the law has allowed the absence of *mens rea* or some unlawful justification or excuse to be raised by way of defence. In Victoria indictable offences are generally created without an attempt to set out in the statute all the elements of the offence and where what would otherwise be a defence is to be excluded, it is expressly so enacted; see, eg, *Crimes Act* s 49 (consent no defence to a charge of carnal knowledge of a female under the age of 16 years). See generally Glazebrook, "The Necessity Pleas in English Criminal Law" [1972] *Camb LJ* 87 at pp 93 *et seq*. We therefore think that a defence of necessity is open to a person accused of escaping from prison contrary to s 132(1) of the *Community Welfare Services Act*.

Before turning to consider whether the present applicant raised a *prima facie* case of necessity, we should notice *People v Lovercamp, supra*, to which Mr Sharp referred us. That was a decision of the Court of Appeal of California in a case in which a defendant to a charge of escape sought to show that two female prisoners, who had been subjected to demands for lesbian activities of which they had complained many times to the authorities, escaped from prison in fear of their lives. The trial court rejected their evidence but the Court of Appeal held that they should have been allowed to raise a defence of necessity. The judgment of the court included the following summary: ". . . we hold that the proper rule is that a limited defence of necessity is available if the following conditions exist:

(1) The prisoner is faced with a specific threat of death, forcible sexual attack or substantial bodily injury in the immediate future;

(2) There is no time for a complaint to the authorities or there exists a history of futile complaints which make any result from such complaints illusory;

(3) There is no time or opportunity to resort to the courts;

(4) There is no evidence of force or violence used towards prison personnel or other 'innocent' persons in the escape; and

(5) The prisoner immediately reports to the proper authorities when he has attained a position of safety from the immediate threat".

All that we need say about that decision, which is not of course binding upon us, is that the first proposition states in substance what we understand to be one of the elements of the defence in our law, although we have earlier reserved for future consideration the exact limits of the consequences for the avoidance of which the defence may be raised. The remaining propositions deal essentially with matters which may have evidentiary significance. We could not accept them as propositions of law applicable in this State. In particular the fifth proposition does not appear to us to be based upon principle or authority although evidence of whether or not a prisoner who escapes does voluntarily report to the authorities as soon as possible after attaining his freedom may have a considerable evidentiary significance, in particular upon the question whether the acts of the accused are proportionate to the danger to be avoided.

Crockett J: . . . In some commentaries there may be detected a suggestion that the defence can apply only when the circumstances which necessitate the choice between two evils arises from physical forces of nature (storms, fire etc.) and not from other human beings. The maintenance of any such supposed dichotomy is, in my judgment, insupportable in principle, and ought not, therefore, be regarded as relevant to any assessment as to the availability of the defence . . .

(1) The harm to be justified must have been committed under pressure either physical forces or exerted by some human agencies so that an 'urgent situation of imminent peril' has been created

(2) The accused must have acted with the intention of avoiding greater harm so as to have made possible 'the preservation of at least an equal value'

(3) There was open to the accused no alternative, other than that adopted by him, to avoid the greater harm, or 'to conserve the value'.

Other examples

4.64 In *R v Bourne*[79] MacNaghten J, as trial judge, ruled that it was a defence to a charge of abortion that the pregnancy was terminated for the purpose of preserving the life of the mother. The doctor was required to decide, on reasonable grounds, that the continuation of the pregnancy would make the woman a mental or physical wreck. The construction of the statute, s 58 of the Offences Against the Person Act 1861 was imported from the later Infant Life (Preservation) Act 1929. In *R v Davidson*[80], the Supreme Court of Victoria referred to but did not follow *Bourne*'s case in deciding that abortion could be lawful. By analogy with the defences of prevention of a felony, arrest of a felon and self-defence they held that a defence of necessity arose where the accused honestly believed on reasonable grounds that what he did was necessary, provided that there was a proportion between what was done and the danger to be averted. A similar

79 [1939] 1 KB 687.
80 [1969] VR 667.

decision was reached in New South Wales; *R v Wald*[81] and see also *R v Salika*[82]. The Supreme Court seemed to have moved towards a limited defence of necessity in *AG v X*[83] (see para **5.33**).

4.65 In Canada a majority of the Supreme Court had, as early as 1976, accepted that the defence of necessity existed. The formulation of the defence was as set out in Kenny's *Outlines of Criminal Law*[84]; *Morgentaler v R*[85]. In that case the Supreme Court held that insufficient evidence of the defence had been raised by the accused to allow it to be left for the consideration of the jury. On a second trial the accused was again acquitted of an abortion charge notwithstanding that the trial judge had not left the defence of necessity for the consideration of the jury. On the third jury trial on an abortion charge the accused was again acquitted despite a restrictive formulation of the defence of necessity. On the fourth trial the accused was charged with conspiracy to carry out abortions and the defence of necessity was left to the jury who acquitted the accused.

4.66 The defence of necessity is unlikely to succeed in an abortion charge in this country unless it is based on a need to preserve the life, and not merely the health or sanity, of the mother; Article 40.3.3 of the Constitution, see *A-G v X* (Supreme Court)[86].

4.67 In Canada Dr Morgentaler was again acquitted for performing an abortion when he alleged that it was impossible to obtain a timely decision from the appropriate statutory committee who authorised legal abortions; *R v Morgentaler*[87]. Further examples are to be had from that jurisdiction. In *R v Fry*[88] the accused was acquitted of exceeding the speed limit because the alternative was to allow a tail-gating car to crash into the rear of his vehicle. In *R v Pootlas*[89] the accused was forced to continue fishing, after the time for legal fishing had elapsed, because his boat was caught in a storm and the only alternative was to jettison the catch and tackle. In *R v Morris*[90] the defence succeeded where the accused had grabbed his wife around the neck, and therefore assaulted her, when she had been attempting to jump out of the car. In *R v Salvador*[91] the Nova Scotia Court of Appeal expressed grave reservations as to whether the defence of necessity had any application where the accused had brought about the situation requiring its exercise through his own fault. In that case a yacht carrying marijuana to the United States ran into difficulties at sea and sailed into Canadian waters for safe anchorage and repair. Jettisoning the huge quantity of cannabis could also

81 (1971) 2 NSW DCR 25.
82 [1973] VR 272.
83 [1992] ILRM 401.
84 19th edition (1966) at p 73.
85 (1975) 20 CCC (2d) 449, 53 DLR (3d) 161, [1976] ISCR 616.
86 [1992] ILRM 401.
87 (1976) 33 CRNS 244.
88 (1977) 36 CCC (2d) 396.
89 (1977) 1 CR (3d) 378.
90 (1981) 61 CCC (2d) 163.
91 (1981) 59 CCC (2d) 521.

have overcome the difficulties experienced by the yacht. In *Perka v R*[92] the Supreme Court of Canada rejected the notion of prior fault as a bar to the defence in similar circumstances of drug smuggling. The reasoning of the court is less than convincing, in this regard, concentrating as it does on the distinction which the court resurrected between defences which excuse and defences which justify.

Code options

4.68 *Model Penal Code*

Justification Generally: Choice of Evils.

3.02 (1) Conduct that the actor believes to be necessary to avoid a harm or evil to himself or to another is justifiable, provided that:

(a) the harm or evil sought to be avoided by such conduct is greater than that sought to be prevented by the law defining the offence charged; and

(b) neither the Code nor other law defining the offence provides exceptions or defences dealing with the specific situation involved; and

(c) a legislative purpose to exclude the justification claimed does not otherwise appear.

(2) When the actor was reckless or negligent in bringing about the situation requiring a choice of harms or evils or in appraising the necessity for his conduct, the justification afforded by this section is unavailable in a prosecution for any offence for which recklessness or negligence, as the case may be, suffices to establish culpability.

Further materials

4.69 Stephen *Homicide by Necessity* (1885) 1 LQR 51.
Williams *Necessity* [1978] Crim LR 128.
Huxley *Proposals and Counter Proposals on the Defence of Necessity* [1978] Crim LR 141.
Leigh *Necessity and the Case of Dr. Morgentaler* [1978] Crim LR 151.
Wasik *A Case of Necessity?* [1984] Crim LR 544.
Elliott *Necessity, Duress and Self-Defence* [1989] Crim LR 611.

Entrapment

4.70 Supposing A wishes to commit a bank robbery. He needs a driver for the getaway car and decides that B is the man for the job. On being approached B is initially reluctant. A then spends the best part of a fortnight working several hours a day in order to persuade B to join the illegal enterprise. His efforts include calling B up in the middle of the night, meeting him "by accident" at every possible opportunity and bursting into tears at B's persistent refusals. Eventually B succumbs. In the circumstances there can be no doubt that when B commits the robbery he has fulfilled all the necessary conditions for the external and mental elements of the offence. He intends to rob the bank, he knows what he is doing and his

92 (1984) 42 CR (3d) 113.

actions are the voluntary product of a rational mind. That analysis does not change if A is a Garda, acting under instructions, with the brief of entrapping B into committing an offence. The Garda may justify his actions by saying that he suspected B to be involved in this kind of criminal activity over several years; he was determined to catch a person whom he considered to be a notorious criminal. Police behaviour of this type is known as entrapment. Entrapment was defined by Laskin CJC in *R v Kirzner*[93] ". . . where the police have gone beyond mere solicitation or mere decoy work and have actively organised a scheme of ensnarement, of entrapment, in order to prosecute the person so caught".

4.71 The decided cases in the United States and in Canada make it clear that the defence of entrapment does not arise merely because an opportunity was provided to a person to commit a crime to which he was previously disposed. Entrapment only arises where a person who is not disposed to commit a crime is inveigled into that disposition and later commits it as a result of the persuasion of the agents of the State.

4.72 The rationale behind the defence of entrapment must be the maintenance of civilised standards of investigation by the agents of the State. It is not the function of the Courts to allow the prosecution of a previously blameless person who has had criminal intentions implanted into his mind by agents of the State.

4.73   ***Sherman v US***
                          (1958) 356 US 369
                  Supreme Court United States, 1958

Facts: Sherman was an addict who was attending a drug treatment programme at a clinic. Also attending the course was one Kalchinian. Instead of being an addict he was a government agent. Over the course of several conversations Kalchinian told Sherman of his extreme need for "a fix". He deliberately insured, on several occasions, that his path crossed with that of Sherman and used these "accidental meetings" to ask Sherman to buy heroin for him. After several refusals, and with apparent reluctance, Sherman purchased heroin for Kalchinian. When the heroin was passed narcotic agents observed the transaction and arrested Sherman.

Warren CJ: . . . The function of law enforcement is the prevention of crime and the apprehension of criminals. Manifestly, that function does not include the manufacturing of crime. Criminal activity is such that stealth and strategy are necessary weapons in the arsenal of a police officer. However, "a different question is presented when the criminal design originates with the officials of the Government, and they implant in the mind or an innocent person the disposition to commit the alleged offence and induce its commission in order that they may prosecute". [*US v Sorrells* 287 US 435 at 442 (1932)]. Then stealth and strategy become as objectionable police methods as the coerced confession and the unlawful search. Congress could not have intended that its statutes were to be enforced by tempting innocent persons into violations.

Frankfurter J: . . . The crucial question, not easy of answer, to which the Court must direct itself is whether the police conduct revealed in the particular case falls below standards, to which common feelings respond, for the proper use of governmental power . . .

93 [1982] 2 SCR.

Furthermore, a test that looks to the character and pre-disposition of the defendant rather than the conduct of the police loses sight of the underlying reason for the defence of entrapment. No matter what the defendant's past record and present inclinations to criminality, or the depths to which he has sunk in the estimation of society, certain police conduct to ensnare him into further crime is not to be tolerated by an advanced society . . .

This test shifts attention from the record and pre-disposition of the particular defendant to the conduct of the police and the likelihood, objectively considered, that it would entrap only those ready and willing to commit crime.

4.74 The issue which remains for decision in the United States is as to whether the defence should be based on a pre-disposition of the accused (the subjective approach) or on a test as to whether the entrapping conduct would have caused a reasonable person to commit the offence (the objective approach). The approach of Warren CJ, for the majority, is clearly based on the lack of pre-disposition by the accused to commit the offence when a favourable opportunity arises. The objective approach is enunciated in the judgment of Frankfurter J. Subsequently the United States Supreme Court in *Russell v US*[94] and *Hampton v US*[95] have, by a majority, adopted the subjective approach.

Approaches

4.75 There are four possible ways of dealing with entrapment.

(1) It can be used as a factor in mitigating sentence. This is accepted frequently by the courts where an accused alleges that he was inveigled into a crime by a co-accused. It is also the approach taken in England, the House of Lords having squarely rejected entrapment as a substantiative defence; *R v Sang*[96].

(2) Entrapment involves the Gardaí in the commission of a criminal offence. There is, therefore, a discretion to exclude illegally obtained evidence on balancing the public interest in the detection and punishment of crime against the competing public interest that individuals should not be subjected to illegal methods of investigation; *The People (AG) v O'Brien*[97]. It is also possible to argue that entrapment involves a breach of the accused's constitutional rights. That approach has not yet been adopted in the United States where the defence is recognised as a substantive one.

(3) Entrapment can be regarded as an offence against justice which the courts should not countenance by allowing the prosecution to proceed with the case on which it is based. This approach was adopted by four of the nine members of the Canadian Supreme Court in *Amato v R*[98]. This approach focuses on the activity of the police which requires the court to stay the proceedings if it is sufficiently outrageous. It does not take account of the prior disposition of the accused towards the commission of the crime. In *R v Jewitt*[99] the Supreme Court of Canada indicated that the courts had inherent

94 (1973) 411 US 423.
95 96 (1976) 425 US 484.
96 1980 AC 402.
97 [1965] IR 142.
98 (1982) 140 DLR (3d) 405.
99 (1985) 47 CR (3d) 193.

jurisdiction to control this process but that this power would be used sparingly and only in the clearest of cases. More recently in *R v Mack*[1] the Supreme Court have tended to look at whether the police were involved in a genuine investigation of a suspected offender or were simply testing at random[2]. In this jurisdiction the courts have yet to exercise a power to stay a criminal case on the grounds of an abuse of process. The power is there to be exercised, in the appropriate circumstances. O Dálaigh CJ in *The State (Quinn) v Ryan*[3] stated:

". . . It was not the intention of the Constitution in guaranteeing the fundamental rights of the citizen that these rights should be set at nought or circumvented. The intention was that rights of substance were being assured to the individual and that the courts were the custodians of these rights. As a necessary corollary it follows that no one can with impunity set these rights at nought or circumvent them, and that the courts' powers in this regard are as ample as the defence of the Constitution requires".

The power spoken of by O Dálaigh CJ was that of imprisonment for contempt of court. The inherent power of the courts to stay proceedings which are an abuse of its process is widely exercised in civil cases; *Barry v Buckley*[4]. In *The State (Trimbole) v The Governor of Mountjoy Prison*[5] a majority of the Supreme Court held that the courts had ample jurisdiction under the Constitution to prevent an abuse of process. This amplitude arose from the extended nature of constitutional rights to create appropriate remedies to ensure that those rights were vindicated.

(4) Entrapment can be recognised as a substantive defence. This is the position in the United States. The burden of proof is no different to that which applies generally in criminal law. This is discussed at the start of this chapter.

4.76   *The Dental Board v O'Callaghan*
[1969] IR 181
High Court, 1969

Facts: The Dental Board suspected that O'Callaghan, who was a dental technician, was in fact practising as a dentist. An investigator on behalf of the Board visited O'Callaghan and asked him to repair a set of upper dentures. These were deliberately ill-fitting and missing some teeth. O'Callaghan did so. The District Justice dismissed the subsequent prosecution of O'Callaghan on the basis that the investigator was an accomplice to the purported offence and that consequently he could not act on his evidence. On a case stated to the High Court a subsidiary question was that of the admissibility of the evidence of an agent- provocateur.

Butler J: . . . There is no rule of law to the effect that the uncorroborated evidence of an accomplice must be rejected. The rule is that the tribunal of fact, be it District Justice or jury, must clearly bear in mind and be warned that it is dangerous to convict upon the evidence of an accomplice unless it is corroborated; but that having borne that in mind and having given due weight to the warning, if the evidence is nonetheless so clearly acceptable that the tribunal is satisfied

1 [1988] 2 SCR 903.
2 See further *R v Kenyon* (1990) 61 CCC 3d 358 and *R v Meuckon* (1990) 57 CCC (3d) 193.
3 [1965] IR 70 at 122.
4 [1981] IR 306.
5 [1985] IR 550.

beyond doubt of the guilt of the accused to the extent that the danger which is generally inherent in acting on the evidence of an accomplice is not present in the case, then the tribunal may act upon the evidence and convict.

Counsel for the Board has submitted that on the facts in this case the actions of Mr Derivan did not in any event make him an accomplice. I must, however, for the purpose of this case stated, except the view of the learned District Justice that Mr Derivan was an accomplice. The fundamental reason for not acting on the evidence of an accomplice is that it may be untrue and that, to guard against this possibility, it should be corroborated. The danger is that in order to minimise or excuse his role in a crime or to obtain more favourable treatment, an accomplice may fabricate evidence to implicate the accused. In other words, that for reasons of self-interest an accomplice may lie. The question as to whether the evidence of a spy or agent provocateur, if his actions amount to those of an accomplice, requires to be corroborated has not been decided in Ireland in any reported case. Counsel for the Board has referred to *Rex v Mullins*[6] and to *R v Bickley*[7] which, together with *R v Heuser*[8], have been followed in the recent case of *Sneddon v Stevenson*[9]. In this last case, after referring to those cases, Lord Parker CJ says at p 1056 of the report: "It seems to me that on a true reading of those cases it can be stated that though a police officer acting as a spy may be said in a general sense to be an accomplice in the offence, yet if he is merely partaking in the offence for the purpose of getting evidence, he is not an accomplice who requires to be corroborated." And Waller J says at p 1058 of the report:

". . . it seems to me that where a police officer is engaged in obtaining evidence and is thereby, perhaps, participating in the offence, the circumstances are entirely different from that of the true accomplice, being somebody who was intending to carry out an important part of the offence. The reason why the latter ought to be corroborated is that he may have a number of mixed motives when he comes to give evidence, for example, that he will be treated more leniently or something of that sort, and it is for that kind of reason that the court has always thought it necessary to give a warning that corroboration should be looked for. In the case of the police officer, those considerations do not apply at all, and it seems to me that, even if he may be participating, that is why no warning about corroboration is required in the case of his evidence."

It appears to me that the principle stated in these decisions is correct and that the reasons which have led to the requirement as to corroboration in the case of a true accomplice do not apply in the case of a person acting in the course of his duty for the purpose of obtaining evidence of an illegal transaction.

Counsel for the respondent has submitted that, even accepting the correctness of the English decisions, the principle ought not to be extended to persons other than police officers. I do not think it can be so limited. Undoubtedly the principle must be applied with discretion and should not be extended to persons acting for merely private as opposed to public interest, but where a witness is employed by an official body to secure evidence of the commission of an offence which it is the duty of that body to investigate with a view to prosecution. I think his evidence is not to be treated as the evidence of an accomplice which needs corroboration. In the present case the Board is a body established by statute to regulate and control an important professional service. The Oireachtas has thought fit to make it an offence for an unqualified person to provide dental treatment and has empowered the Board to prosecute such offence. Clearly it is also charged with the duty of

6 (1848) 3 Cox CC 526.
7 (1909) 2 Cr App R 53.
8 (1910) 6 Cr App R 76.
9 [1967] 1 WLR 1051.

prevention and detection and I cannot see why its agents in that regard should be treated any differently from police officers who are likewise engaged in the detection and prosecution of other crimes.

Counsel for the respondent has also referred to *certain strictures* which have been levelled by the courts in England against police officers being parties to offences as agents provocateurs and in particular to the observation of Lord Goddard in *Brannan v Peek*[10]. However, as was pointed out by Lord Parker CJ, again in *Sneddon v Stevenson*[11] at p 1056 of the report, the methods used by the police for obtaining evidence in the former case were not a ground for quashing the conviction. Lord Goddard himself in the later case of *Browning v J W H Watson (Rochester) Ltd*[12] decided that the magistrates should act on the evidence of agents provocateurs (in that case officials of the Ministry of Transport) establishing an offence, but that they might mark their disapproval of the methods used when considering the question of penalty. He said at p 1177 of the report: "No court in England has ever liked action by what are generally called agents provocateurs, resulting in the imposition of criminal liability. We are often told that unless such action is allowed breaches of the law cannot be detected. But Parliament can if it sees fit, make provisions to meet that state of affairs. We must hold that . . . an offence was committed. We need only remind the justices that it is possible for them to grant an absolute discharge, and it is not even necessary for them when doing so to order payment of costs."

In the present case I have been told by counsel that the Board dislikes using methods such as those employed by Mr Derivan but that the private and clandestine nature of these transactions makes it difficult otherwise to obtain sufficient evidence to secure a conviction. This I can appreciate. No doubt action of this sort is distasteful and it is proper for the courts to ensure that it is only used where it is necessary. Where, however, as in this case, it is genuinely thought by those in authority that it is necessary having regard to the nature of the offence and the circumstances of its commission, the evidence thus obtained should be accepted and evaluated on its own merits without requiring as a matter of law that it should be corroborated.

The question in the case stated will be answered "No" and the case will be remitted to the District Justice to enter continuances.

4.77   *Drugs and the Law*
Paper presented by Superintendent John McGroarty to the
Forensic Science Symposium on Drugs and Crime
June 14, 1986

The scrutiny of drug-crime statistics as contained in the annual Garda Crime Reports for 1979/80 reveal a remarkable phenomenon, i.e., a dramatic increase in the arrival of heroin as shown by seizures and a sudden upward spiral in the crime statistics recorded over the same period.

This trend was to be maintained in succeeding years and led one to the conclusion that a strong causal relationship existed between heroin addicts and crime. After more than a decade of operational experience, I am convinced that all persons addicted to illicit drugs are criminogenic but the extent to which this is true depends, in my view, upon the substance being abused. Worthy of note in this context is the fact that high levels of drug abuse and crime play leapfrog in certain areas of Dublin where both problems are frequently described as being endemic in their nature and epidemic in their proportions.

10 [1948] 1 KB 68, 72.
11 [1967] 1 WLR 1051.
12 [1953] 1 WLR 1172.

There is considerable disagreement as to whether drug abuse precedes criminality or the reverse and there is much research data available to support either view. Research in the USA indicates that most drug addicts had criminal records before becoming involved in drug abuse. What is not known and which may be much more difficult to show is to what extent one behaviour initiates another. As regards the extent to which crime statistics can be influenced by a heroin problem, one survey in the USA shows that the amount of crime against property committed by heroin addicts can be set between 25% and 50% of all property offences.

A further finding in the Inciardi Report issued in the USA in 1978 demonstrated that the deterrent effect on heroin addicts by arrest and conviction was minimal. Another study carried out in Baltimore has revealed that heroin addicts commit crime on an average 360 days per year in order to get money to feed their habit. When one savours these findings, one will have little difficulty in understanding why heroin is regarded internationally as being the drug which causes the most damage to the fabric of society. Heroin has been known to wreck havoc in whole communities because it has after all, a capacity to enslave people beyond any other known power . . .

In confronting the nation's problems, the Gardaí have not shirked their responsibilities and have adapted the forces, manpower and expertise in ever changing ways in an effort to contain the corroding acid of modernity in the form of the creeping cancer of heroin addiction.

Many beneficial advances were made, e.g., a recent investigation by Dublin Drug Squad personnel involving the use of a detective to infiltrate a non-national heroin trafficking group operating in Dublin's south side. The defence had lodged objection to the infiltration technique as being unacceptable. However, the judge found it quite acceptable and so did the jury who convicted the trafficker upon whom a six year sentence was imposed. Much progress has been made in recent years but there can be absolutely no relaxation of effort on our part because the level of drug abuse is unacceptably high and must be reduced through the relentless pursuit of a three-pronged attack inclusive of Education, Law Enforcement and Rehabilitation programmes.

Code options

4.78   *Model penal code*

Entrapment
2.13 (1) A public law enforcement official or a person acting in co-operation with such an official perpetrates an entrapment if for the purpose of obtaining evidence of the commission of an offence, he induces or encourages another person to engage in conduct constituting such offence by either:

(a) Making knowingly false representations designed to induce the belief that such conduct is not prohibited; or
(b) employing methods of persuasion or inducement which create a substantial risk that such an offence will be committed by persons other than those who are ready to commit it.

(2) . . . a person prosecuted for an offence shall be acquitted if he proves by a preponderance of evidence that his conduct occurred in response to an entrapment. The issue of entrapment shall be tried by the court in the absence of the jury.

4.79   *The Ouimet Report*
                        Reform of the Criminal Code, Canada

1. That a person is not guilty of an offence if his conduct is instigated by a law enforcement officer or agent of a law enforcement officer, for the purpose of obtaining evidence for the prosecution of such person, if such person did not have a pre-existing intention to commit the offence.

2. Conduct amounting to an offence shall be deemed not to have been instigated where the defendant had a pre-existing intention to commit the offence when the opportunity arose and the conduct which is alleged to have induced the defendant to commit the offence did not go beyond affording him an opportunity to commit it.

3. The defence that the offence has been instigated by a law enforcement officer or his agent should not apply to the commission of those offences which involve the infliction of bodily harm or which endanger life.

Further Materials

4.80 Park *The Entrapment Controversy* (1976) 60 Min L Rev 163.
UK Law Commission Report No 83 *Defences of General Application* (1977, HC 556) at pp 44–53.
Ashworth *Entrapment* [1978] Crim LR 137.
Choo *A defence of Entrapment* (1990) 53 MLR 453.

Intoxication

4.81 Intoxication is not, as such, a defence to a criminal charge. A person who is intoxicated and who kills another may, as a result of his intoxication, not intend to kill that person. In those circumstances he lacks the mental element of the crime of murder. A person may begin to play with a loaded revolver when so intoxicated that he does not know what he is doing and during the course of this activity, he may wound somebody. He may be entitled to plead that his action was not voluntary and that, therefore, he is guilty of no crime. As we have seen in chapter 1, all crimes require that the accused should have, by his voluntary action, brought about the external element of the offence. In the last example, the law in England and in Canada has traditionally barred an intoxicated person from pleading that his action was involuntary. Logically, this may be justified on the basis that a person who is aware of his propensity to act in a violent or foolish fashion may, by the act of intoxicating himself into a state of senselessness, be either criminally negligent or reckless. However, the law has proceeded not from reasons of principle, but from reasons of policy.

4.82 The policy basis of the law in England has been that the purpose of the criminal law is to protect the people from unprovoked violence. An acceptance of the argument that intoxication excuses from criminal liability, would leave citizens legally unprotected from unprovoked violence for the unmeritorious reason that the voluntary taking of drink or drugs obliterated the capacity of the perpetrator to know what he was doing or what were its consequences; per Lord Simon in *DPP v Majewski*[13]. An example of this approach is *R v Lipman*[14]. Both the accused and the victim had ingested a quantity of the powerful hallucinogenic drug LSD. The accused took "a trip" in which he believed that he was being attacked by snakes in the

13 [1977] AC 443 at 476.
14 [1970] 1 QB 152.

underworld. He responded to what his mind told him by stuffing a sheet into the victim's mouth, thus suffocating her. The jury convicted him both on the basis of criminally negligent manslaughter and criminal and dangerous act manslaughter. On appeal the Court of Appeal ignored the negligent aspect of his conduct but upheld the conviction on the basis that he had been guilty of an unlawful assault. The court held that manslaughter was a crime of "general intent". In the circumstances a self-induced intoxication which obliterated the voluntary element was not a defence.

4.83   *C S Kenny – Outlines of Criminal Law*
                            11th Edition 1922

Drunkenness is ordinarily no excuse for the commission of a criminal act; even though it has produced for the time great aberration of mind. For, unlike insanity, it has been produced voluntarily; and to produce it was wrong, both morally and legally[15]. Accordingly the law will not allow one wrong act to be an excuse for another[16]. Hence the gross negligence[17] which has caused a fatal collision is punishable, not only in a sober driver but also in a drunken one. And if a man, when excited by liquor, stabs the old friend whom he never quarrelled with when sober, or steals the picture which never attracted him before, it is no defence to say that "it was the drink that did it." Indeed the older law (4 Coke 125a) regarded intoxication as even aggravating[18] the guilt of any crimes whose predisposing cause it was; but modern judges, whilst still holding that it cannot excuse that guilt, admit that it may mitigate the punishment[19].

Moreover, though drunkenness is thus no excuse for a guilty state of mind, it often affords a defence for an *actus reus* by being evidence that no guilty state of mind existed. For intoxication may cause – even on grounds slighter than could reasonably lead a sober person to the same erroneous conclusion – a mistake of fact, such as is incompatible[20] with *mens rea*. The drunken man fancies some one else's umbrella to be his own; or supposes an innocent gesture to be an assault, and hits back in supposed self-defence. Cf p 518 infra.

An authoritative declaration of the law as to intoxication was given in 1920 by the concurrence of eight law lords in *Beard's* case (LR [1920] AC 479). This judgment settles (1) that, as we have already seen, "Drunkenness . . . merely establishing that the man's mind was so affected by drink that he more readily gave way to some violent passion" forms no excuse. But (2) "if actual insanity in fact supervenes, [even] as the result of alcoholic excess, it furnishes as complete an answer to a criminal charge as insanity induced by any other cause . . . Insanity, even though temporary, is an answer." Yet (3) in cases of mere intoxication the test for exemption is more stringent than in case of insanity; a judge should not ask

---

15 Until 1872 it was a criminal offence, under 4 Jac I c 5, s 2; and even now a conspiracy to produce it would be indictable, and a contract for it would be void.

16 But actual insanity, even when produced by drunken habits (as in some cases of *delirium tremens*), exempts from criminal responsibility just as effectually as if it had not originated in misconduct (*Reg v Davis*, 14 Cox 563). And intoxication itself, in those rare cases where it is innocent – as companions – has the full exemptive effect of insanity. This exemption has been extended in Ireland and the United States even to the case of a person who, in consequence of fatigue or sleeplessness, becomes intoxicated by taking his accustomed small quantity of alcohol, which usually he takes with impunity (*Reg v Mary R*, see Kerr on Inebriety, ch XXII).

17 Cf 16 Cox, at p 309 (surgeon's negligence).

18 Though not on the principle of Lord Cockburn's convivial Scottish judge who argued, "If he remains so bad even when drunk what must he be when sober?"

19 1 Cr App R 181, 255; 25 TLR 76.

20 CS Kenny *Outlines of Criminal Law* at p 65.

the jury "the question 'whether the prisoner knew that he was doing wrong' in a defence of drunkenness where insanity is not pleaded." Still (4) evidence of such a drunkenness as "renders the accused incapable of forming the specific intent, essential to constitute the crime, should be taken into consideration, with the other facts proved, in order to determine whether or not he had this intent." In such a case the drunkenness, if incompatible with the indispensable mental element of the crime, "negatives the commission of that crime." Thus a drunken man's inability to form an intention to kill, or to do grievous bodily harm, at the time of committing a homicide, may reduce his offence from murder to manslaughter. The judgment adds that this principle is not "an exceptional rule applicable only to cases in which it is necessary to prove a specific intent; . . . for, speaking generally a person cannot be convicted of crime unless the *mens* was *rea*." A man's drunkenness may preclude him, not merely from forming one of these specific intentions, but from forming any intent at all.

Drunkenness thus may show that an apparent burglar had no intention of stealing[21]; or that an apparent suicide jumped into the water when "so drunk as not to know what he was about[22]." The more complex the intent required by the definition of the particular crime, the more likely is drunkenness to be useful in disproving the presence of some element requisite to it; as by showing that wounds were inflicted with no "intent to do grievous bodily harm," or that a false pretence was made with no "intent to defraud."

Let us finally note that the question "Was he drunk?" is often[23] answered too definitely as if there existed some single standard of sobriety. Intoxication, it should always be remembered, is a question of degree, ranging from mere exhilaration down to unconsciousness. The man may be too drunk to do this act properly, yet sober enough to do some other[24].

Majewski Approach

4.84 The leading authority in England is *DPP v Majewski*[25]. The accused took part in a fight in a public house. He attacked the owner and customers. On the police being called he attacked the officer who arrested him, an officer in the police car when he was being driven to the station and, the next day, attacked a police inspector in his cell. He was charged with several counts of assault occasioning actual bodily harm. His defence was that the offences had been committed while he was intoxicated from alcohol and drugs and that he had not intended to assault anyone. The trial judge directed the jury on the basis of the formulation in *R v Beard*[26], and told them to ignore intoxication in reaching their verdict. A point of law of general public importance was stated by the Court of Appeal for the consideration of the House of Lords: Whether a defendant may properly be convicted of assault notwithstanding that, by reason of his self-induced intoxication, he did not intend to do the act alleged to constitute the assault.

---

21 *The State v Bell*, 29 Stiles 316 (KSC 55).
22 *Reg v Moore*, 3 C and K 319.
23 Especially often when it is (not the excuse but) part of the offence.
24 We may add that an accused man may sometimes be helped towards acquittal by the fact of his having been drunk even on some occasion *subsequent* to the date of the crime in question. For it may afford an innocent explanation of conduct that otherwise would suggest a consciousness of guilt; as where, on being arrested, he has made untrue statements or has refused to make any statement at all.
25 [1977] AC 443.
26 [1920] AC 479.

4.84 *The Defences*

The House of Lords answered the question in the affirmative. Lord Salmon[27] stated that logic in human affairs was an uncertain guide and a very dangerous master and indicated that although the rule adopted by the House of Lords was illogical it was acceptable because the alternative was imperiling the safety of the public peace.

4.85 The distinction adopted by the House of Lords was between crimes of basic intent and crimes of specific intent. An attempt to commit a crime is a crime of specific intent even though the crime attempted, for example assault, may be committed by recklessness. The distinction moves towards obscurity. It could best be dealt with by statutory intervention.

4.86   ***DPP v Morgan***
[1976] AC 182; [1975] 2 All ER 347; [1975] 2 WLR 913;
(1975) 61 Cr App R 136
House of Lords, 1975

> Lord Simon: By "crimes of basic intent" I mean those crimes whose definition expresses (or, more often, implies) a *mens rea* which does not go beyond the *actus reus*. The *actus reus* generally consists of an act and some consequence. The consequence may be very closely connected with the act or more remotely connected with it; but with a crime of basic intent the *mens rea* does not extend beyond the act and its consequence, however remote, as defined in the *actus reus*. I take assault as an example of a crime of basic intent where the consequence is very closely connected with the act. The *actus reus* of assault is an act which causes another person to apprehend immediate and unlawful violence. The *mens rea* corresponds exactly . . . On the other hand there are crimes of ulterior intent – "ulterior" because the *mens rea* goes beyond contemplation of the *actus reus*. For example, in the crime of wounding with intent to cause grievous bodily harm, the *actus reus* is the wounding. The prosecution must prove a corresponding *mens rea* (as with unlawful wounding), but the prosecution must go further: it must show that the accused foresaw that serious physical injury would probably be a consequence of his act, or would possibly be so, that being a purpose of his act.

4.87 In *R v Leary*[28] the Supreme Court of Canada, by a majority, upheld the decision in *Majewski*. The court conceded the illogicality of the rule but attached greater weight to the social policy considerations that favoured a harsh regime for drunken offenders.

The question is not whether the accused was incapable of forming the intent but whether or not he formed such an intent; *R v Sheehan*[29], *R v Hart*[30].

Alternative Approach

4.88 The alternative approach is to regard intoxication as an element which may remove the mental element of either intent, recklessness or voluntary participation in criminal activity, absolutely.

27 *Ibid* at p 483/84.
28 (1977) 33 CCC (2d) 473.
29 (1975) 2 All ER 960.
30 [1986] 2 NZLR 408.

4.89   ***R v O'Connor***
                         (1979) 29 ALR 449
                   High Court of Australia, 1979

Facts: The accused was observed stealing from a police car. The officer in charge was alerted. When he reached the car O'Connor had removed a map holder and a knife. He was challenged as to why he had taken the map holder. He made no response and ran away. The officer caught up with him to arrest him. During the course of this arrest O'Connor opened up the blade of the knife he had taken from the car and, in an apparent endeavour to resist arrest, stabbed the constable. During the course of this he said "I don't know anything, I wasn't there". At his trial he gave evidence that he had been taking a particular drug and drinking alcohol during the day of the occurrence. He had no recollection of his encounter with the officer but only of placing his foot in an open door of a white car. According to medical evidence the drug was hallucinatory and in association with alcohol could have rendered O'Connor incapable of reasoning or of forming an intent to steal or wound.

Barwick CJ: . . . It is now appropriate to return to express the result of the decision of their Lordships in *Majewski's* case.
   The House in substance decided that on the trial of an accused for a criminal offence which does not require that the proscribed act should be done to attain or to attempt to attain a specified result beyond the immediate consequence of the physical act involved, evidence as to the effect which self-induced intoxication has produced on the relationship of the accused's will or intent to the activity of his body is irrelevant and therefore inadmissible, if tendered solely to raise a doubt as to the voluntariness of, or as to the presence of intention to do, the physical act involved in the crime charged. Although, as I have said, not formally involved in the question certified by the Court of Appeal, in my opinion, the reasoning favoured by their Lordships extends to all the consequences of the self-induced intoxication by any means and is not limited to those which affect only the presence of an intent to do the physical act involved in the charge. The effect of intoxication, as I have said, may be so extensive as to render the acts of the accused involuntary or it may preclude the formation of an intent to do that physical act. In substance, therefore, the decision in *Majewski's* case is that in the case of such a charge the act of the accused is to be incontestably presumed to have been voluntary and to have been done with an intent to do the physical act involved in the crime charged. Evidence to call in question either position is irrelevant and inadmissible if the accused's condition resulted from his own acts.
   The decision was in part built upon acceptance of the dichotomy of crimes into crimes of "specific" intent and crimes of "basic" intent. Although all of their Lordships did not specifically define the former, I think that they used the notion of a crime of specific intent in the sense in which I have used it in my summary of the substance of their decision. The purposive nature of the proscribed act is the indication of a crime of specific intent: hence the description I have used of what is involved in a crime of specific intent and by contrast what is not involved in a crime of so-called basic intent. My description is in line, I think, with Lord Simon's definition of specific intent. Having made this distinction, ie between crimes of basic intent and crimes of specific intent, their Lordships sought, as it seems to me, to bring their decision within the symmetry of the basic principles of criminal responsibility by treating the wantonness of becoming intoxicated as a form of recklessness or of wickedness of mind which satisfied the requirement of *mens rea*: see [1977] AC 443, *per* the Lord Chancellor at 474 and 475 of the report and Lord Simon at 479 of the report.
   . . . . But the description "basic intent" has been used to distinguish the intent required in a crime in which the *actus reus* does not require the physical act

involved in the charge to have been done to achieve a stated purpose from the intent required in crimes which do so require. The latter are then styled crimes of "specific intent".

With great respect to those who have favoured this technology in a classification of crimes, it is to my mind not only inappropriate but it obscures more than it reveals. The purpose with which a proscribed act must be done in order to be relevantly criminal is, in my opinion, part of the description of the *actus reus*; cf Lord Simon in *Morgan's* case at 216. Assault to resist arrest specifies, in my opinion, the *actus reus*. Although described in terms of intent it connotes the purposive quality of the proscribed act. It does not refer, in my opinion, to the *mens rea*, or intention to commit the act in question, though of course if, for example, an accused intends to assault a constable in order to resist arrest, it can scarcely be said that he did not intend the physical act necessary to carry out that purpose. None the less, the purpose of resisting arrest is, in my opinion, part of the *actus reus*. In other words, the suggested basis for classification of crimes is not, in my opinion, on the footing of a distinction based on the nature and extent of the relevant *mens rea* but, rather, it is a distinction founded on the description of the *actus reus*.

The description "specific intent" gained its currency from Stephen J's judgment in *Tolson's* case. As an expression calling attention to the elements of the *actus reus* it has no doubt its uses. As the intent or *mens rea* is related to the content of the *actus reus*, the transferance of the purpose of the *actus reus* to the *mens rea* is tempting, but it is preferable, in my opinion, not to effect that transference. In my respectful opinion, the distinction between basic and specific intent is unhelpful as a basis for distinction of crimes by reference to *mens rea*.

It is to my mind exceedingly strange that a person incapable of forming any intent may be found guilty of an offence which requires only an intent to do the physical act involved but may not be found guilty of doing an act to attain a specific result. If the cases to which Lord Birkenhead referred represented a movement in the common law, an amelioration in favour of the accused, there is no reason, it seems to me, why the movement had to stop at the point reached by these cases. That, it seems to me, is how the matter struck Lord Birkenhead and those who agreed with him: and, in my view, that is precisely the sense in which he expressed himself. Such cases were not exceptions from but examples of fundamental rules.

Thus, if the evidence of intoxication is sufficient to raise a doubt as to voluntariness or as to the presence of requisite intent, I can see no logical ground for determining its admissibility upon a distinction between a crime which specifies only the immediate result of the proscribed act and a crime which in addition requires a further result dependent on purpose.

But it is in substance held that the voluntary taking or administration of alcohol or other drugs producing an intoxicated stated so infects that situation that what is done in that state must incontestably be accounted to be voluntary or, at the lowest, as having been done with the requisite intent. The view, that of Lord Elwyn-Jones to which their Lordships subscribed, is that to become intoxicated by your own act, is to supply an element of recklessness to the performance of any criminally proscribed act performed during that state: and thus to satisfy the reuqirement of *mens rea*. But this, in my respectful opinion, is a novel use of the word "reckless" and, in my opinion, a use heretofore not thought acceptable. If to take alcohol or drugs with at least the risk of becoming intoxicated is in one sense a reckless thing to do, yet that variety of recklessness can scarce be carried forward and attributed as a substitute for actual intent to do the proscribed act. The recklessness which may on occasion satisfy the requirement of *mens rea* involves an awareness of possible consequences of doing the act, ie the proscribed act charged, and at least a decision to disregard them and to act without caring for appreciated consequences. The recklessness or wantonness of the person taking alcohol or other drug with at least the chance of becoming intoxicated is surely of a quite different order. Further, it is, in my opinion, in a legal sense remote from the performance of the act charged. It is quite unlike the intent formed in *Gallagher's* case which was not remote from the act charged but in truth directly connected to it because of the intent formed before intoxication. To find an analogy in the field of reckless to what occurred in *Gallagher's* case, it would be necessary to find an appreciation before intoxication of the risks of acts of a criminal kind during intoxication and a decision before intoxication to take those risks or at least a conceived indifference to the possibility of their turning into reality. For my part, I am unable to accept that the voluntary nature of the taking of the alcohol or other drug, whether or not it be an act of a wanton or reckless kind, supplies the *mens rea* for the commission of a crime which in the case supposed may have been done involuntary or without the requisite intent.

Then it is said that the protection of the community from violence, being a purpose of the criminal law, requires the conclusion to which the House came in *Majewski's* case. It may readily be granted that the frequency with which intoxicated persons act violently poses a distinct threat to our social order and, indeed at times to personal safety. Further, the use of drugs to produce intoxicated situations has become rife. It has added a new dimension to the possibility of violent and unsocial conduct on the part of those who have become intoxicated. That the society needs protection against violence by such persons can readily be conceded. But so it does in relation to armed robbery and, indeed, to housebreaking which is not infrequently accompanied by violence to the person. So it does in relation to many crimes of so-called specific intent. The question, it seems to me, which is posed for this court is whether it is consonant with the common law to make such an exception in the case of self-induced intoxiction as has been held to be the case by the House of Lords. Does the situation created by the use of drugs arising or which may arise from what I might call intoxicated violence warrant a radical departure from those principles of the common law evolved over a period of time, but particularly elucidated in the last 50 or so years? These principles have been established bearing in mind and not disregarding the need of the society for protection from violent and unsocial behaviour. These principles, on the one hand, provide the society with a protection against violent and unsocial conduct, whilst on the other hand, maintain a just balance between the Crown and the citizen who is charged with having broken the criminal law. That *Majewski's* case is a departure from such principles can scarce be gainsaid. It seems to me to be completely inconsistent with the principles of the common law that a man should be conclusively presumed to have an intent which, in fact, he does not have, or to have done an act which, in truth, he did not do.

I can readily understand that a person who has taken alcohol or another drug to such an extent that he is intoxicated thereby to the point where he has no will to act or no capacity to form an intent to do an act is blameworthy and that his act of having ingested or administered the alcohol or other drug ought to be visited with severe consequences. The offence of being drunk and disorderly is not maintained these days in all systems of the common law. In any case it has not carried a sufficient penalty properly to express the public opprobrium which should attach to one who, by the taking of alcohol or the use of drugs, has become intoxicated to the point where he is the vehicle for unsocial and violent behaviour. But, though blameworthy for becoming intoxicated, I can see no ground for presuming his acts to be voluntary and relevantly intentional. For what is blameworthy there should be an appropriate criminal offence. But it is not for the judges to create an offence appropriate in the circumstances: cf *Knuller (Publishing, Printing & Promotions) Ltd v DPP* [1973] AC 435 at 457–8, 464–5 and 490. It must be for the Parliament.

In my opinion, evidence of the state of the body and mind of an accused tendered to assist in raising a doubt as to the voluntary character of the physical act involved in the crime charged is admissible on the trial of an accused for any criminal offence, whether an offence at common law or by statute. Further, in my opinion, such evidence tendered to raise a doubt as to the actual intention with which the physical act involved in the crime charged, if done, was done is admissible on the trial of an accused for any offence, whether at common law or by statute, with the exception of such statutory offences as do not require the existence of an actual intent, the so-called absolute offences.

In my opinion, the Court of Criminal Appeal was justified in not accepting *Majewski's* case.

Stephen J: . . . after anxious consideration and free of the constraints which the unvaried practice of many years in England must necessarily impose upon any English tribunal, I find myself unpersuaded that for Australia the criminal law should be as their Lordships state it.

Considerations turning upon a concern for public order, coupled with forecasts of public outcry are, for me, answered by the experience of my own community in Victoria, which has, for some time now, lived with precisely that view of the law which is denied by *Majewski*. Since at least some time prior to 1964 some, perhaps many, Victorian judges have acted as did Monahan J in *R v Keogh* [1964] VR 400. There his Honour, founding himself upon what was, in fact, his own long experience as counsel in criminal cases in Victoria, upon his own experience on the Bench and upon his knowledge of the practice of other judges of his court, said that he held "firmly to the view that a state of automatism, even that which has been brought about by drunkenness, precludes the forming of the guilty intent which is the fundamental concept in criminal wrong-doing".

To this may be added references to *R v Haywood* [1971] VR 755, to *R v Bugg* [1978] VR 251, especially to its addendum at 252, and to what was said by Starke and by Gray JJ in their judgments delivered to the Full Court in the case now under appeal. Starke J said: "In this State in my own experience, until *Majewski's* case, intoxication has always been left to juries as evidence relevant to the issues of both general and specific intent", and Gray J was "satisfied that for many years self-induced intoxication has been left for the jury's consideration in relation to all questions of intent".

I am aware of no evidence suggesting that the incidence of crime committed under the influence of intoxication has been affected by this long-standing approach of Victorian judges, that Victoria stands in this respect in any worse position than do those jurisdictions where the *Majewski* principle prevails, including, as I understand it, most jurisdictions in the United States. Neither am I aware of any public outcry on the question.

The view that intoxication in itself furnishes the necessary element of a guilty mind, whether by way of recklessness or otherwise, thereby satisfying not only basic principles of law but also more generalised notions of abstract justice, in my view presents considerable difficulties. Recent academic writings on the topic abound with criticism of it and those interested in the topic will therefore already be familiar with the nature of the debate, upon which I have no occasion to enter in any detail. It is enough that I should state, quite shortly, my reasons for this view which I have formed.

To convict an accused, who was at the time intoxicated, of such serious crimes as manslaughter, rape, malicious wounding or assaults of varying degrees of gravity, none of which are, it seems, crimes of "specific intent", may in some cases offend no general notions of what is fair and just. What may be called the "Dutch courage" cases provide instances. So too, no doubt, do those cases in which an accused, while not contemplating any particular crime or, for that matter, any particular victim, well knows from past experience that when he takes drugs or alcohol or both he may under their influence commit a crime. But these by no means comprise all cases to which *Majewski* is applicable. Whether or not they represent more or less than a majority in any particular community is probably unknown, in the absence of statistical research.

Many and varied instances may be supposed (and one is necessarily very much in areas of supposition in this whole topic) in which ordinary notions of what is fair and just would be offered by such a conviction. Two instances will suffice: the young man or woman who under peer-group pressures, perhaps in the armed forces, perhaps after a sporting success, or at some reunion or initiation ceremony, for the first time drinks grossly to excess: again, the person who, under like pressures, is pursuaded for the first time to sample an hallucinogenic drug or, perhaps, although no newcomer to so-called "soft" drugs, knowingly takes what he believes to be such a drug but which in fact proves to be one of great potency. In such instances, not, I think farfetched, I would regard it as unfair and unjust that an accused, robbed of his faculties by resultant intoxication, should be deprived of the opportunity of having the evidence of the absence of the mental elements of the crime with which he is charged left to the jury.

So much for general notions of fairness and justice. That principle of the criminal law, that *mens rea* should accompany the *actus reus*, appears to me to be no less affronted by any rule which subtracts from the general requirement of a mental element in crime those cases which owe their origin to intoxication. No doubt even principles of the common law as fundamental as the insistence upon proof of mental element are subject to exceptions and criticism founded upon a lack of logic may readily enough be met by a principled exception. But a suggestion exception which operates by means of uncertain criteria, in a manner not always rational and which serves an end which I regard as doubtful of attainment is one which I view with suspicion.

I regard the *Majewski* principle as suffering from just such defects. Of the uncertainty of the criterion by which it operates, the distinction between crimes of specific intent and all other crimes, I will say more later. Its lack of wholly rational operation seems to me to arise from the fact that it fails to ensure, as it might be hoped that it would, that the drunken criminal, although spared conviction of a major offence because of lack of specific intent, will nevertheless not go free but will instead suffer conviction of some lesser offence which does not call for proof of a specific intent. For it to operate in that way, providing a suitable gradation of offence and punishment, would at least be rational; it could then always be said of it that while the drunken criminal may escape conviction on the more serious charge "there will be a lesser crime" to which the intoxication – however mind stealing – will be no defence" (*per* Lord Russell in *Majewski* [1977] AC at 498–9). His Lordship of course appreciated that it did not always so operate, hence the qualifying word "commonly" which precedes the passage which I have quoted. In some instances it will do so, especially so long as murder continues to be classified for this purpose as a crime of specific intent, despite the difficulties of definition which that appears to involve. But in a number of cases it will operate quite eccentrically, because of the particular category to which crimes are consigned by applying to them the test of specific intent. All attempts are apparently crimes of specific intent, yet if the actual crime be committed and not merely attempted it may very well not be; again, wounding or causing grievous bodily harm with intent requires specific intent, not so manslaughter or rape; theft involves a specific intent but not assault or malicious wounding. These are instances where the facts of a particular criminal incident might seem to call for some gradation, but the gradation which in fact results may run the wrong way. In many other cases *Majewski* will result in no gradation at all; for example, rape, and indecent assault are crimes of the same "grade", neither requiring a specific intent.

This is all, no doubt, attributable to the particular criterion, "specific intent", which has been adopted as determinative of the operation of the principle. Since the seriousness of the crime or its social consequences does not play any part in determining whether or not a crime is one of specific intent, it is hardly surprising that the operation of the principle may seem haphazard.

So far as the end sought to be attained is concerned this appears, in substance, to be that of the protection of the public from violence and the preservation of order. For that purpose the deterrent effect of the criminal law is invoked. Yet by the very nature of the case, concerned as it is with the grossly intoxicated, deterrence, if it operates at all, will only do so not at the time of the offence but at the earlier time when the drugs or alcohol are taken in excess. It would, in my view, require convincing evidence before one might conclude that, as a matter of human behaviour, the person who both becomes grossly intoxicated and also commits a crime while in that condition will be in any way discouraged from his initial act of becoming intoxicated by the knowledge that the fact of his intoxication will not be available for use in evidence at his trial to deny the presence of any mental element involved in his crime. Cases of "Dutch courage" and of a known tendency to be violent when intoxicated aside, the possibility of the commission of any crime will not normally be contemplated when the drink or drugs are taken. For this reason, if for no other, the particular state of the criminal law seems to me to be unlikely to be capable of either encouraging or deterring the eventual offence.

There may be a strong case for the creation of a new offence such as that suggested in recommendation 56 of the Butler Committee Report, a new offence which might indeed operate as some deterrent, but that is quite a different question.

It is for these reasons that I see no sufficient reason for distinguishing, as the *Majewski* principle does, between the self-induced and other states of intoxication. I have already twice referred to those cases which involve "Dutch courage", of which the facts of *Attorney-General for Northern Ireland v Gallagher* [1963] AC 349, [1961] 3 All ER 299, provide an instance, or in which there is knowledge on the accused's part, when he takes excessive quantities of alcohol or drugs, that he is prone to violence when intoxicated. They are, no doubt, prime instances in which an accused should not be able to gain any advantage from his intoxication; nor does he seem likely to in a jurisdiction where the *Majewski* principle has no operation. In the case of the former the necessary *mens rea* would seem to be supplied by the act of consciously becoming intoxicated so as to be better fitted for the contemplated crime. In the latter case there is surely recklessness. An accused's tendency to violent crime when intoxicated, known to him when he takes the fatal drink or drugs, would be evidence of recklessness sufficient on conventional principles to involve *mens rea*. If lack of contemporaneity is thought to be a difficulty, the analogy of the innocent agent, represented by the drunken state, as the mere instrument of the guilty mind, represented by the previously sober state may, as is suggested by Smith & Hogan: *Criminal Law* (4th ed) at 190, be thought to overcome it.

What I earlier described as the second notable feature of *Majewski*, the division of all crimes into two classes, those which do involve a specific intent and the rest, has probably occasioned as much controversy in journal articles and texts as any other feature of the case. That in itself supplies a reason for not adding to the volume of what has already been said about the various meanings which in the authorities, and notably in *Majewski* itself, have been preferred as definitive of "specific intent". I have already remarked upon the consequences of adopting as the *discrimen* for the operation of *Majewski* this notion of "specific intent", not elsewhere encountered as a term of art in the law. To this I would only add that if the development of the criminal law is seen as moving from early emphasis upon the *actus reus* to an increasing concern with the mental element in crime – *Majewski* at 480, 481 and 481–9 – the point in that gradual process which *Majewski* selects at which to call a halt, the frontier between crimes of specific intent and other crimes, seems, with all due respect, to be unfortunate. It is a point neither clearly defined nor easily recognisable, the selection of which does not reflect or give effect to any coherent attitude either as to the relative wrongfulness of particular conduct or the degree of social mischief which that conduct is thought to involve; it seems an inappropriate response to natural concern lest intoxication be used as a device to escape punishment for crime.

In the court below, Young CJ was assisted to his conclusion by *Thomas v R* (1937) 59 CLR 279. The passage from the judgment of Dixon J, at 309, which Young CJ cited in his judgment, merits repetition as particularly apposite. "The truth appears to be that a reluctance on the part of courts has repeatedly appeared to allow a prisoner to avail himself of a defence depending simply on his own state of knowledge and belief. The reluctance is due in great measure, if not entirely, to a mistrust of the tribunal of fact – the jury. Through a feeling that, if the law allows such a defence to be submitted to the jury, prisoners may too readily escape by deposing to conditions of mind and describing sources of information, matters upon which their evidence cannot be adequately tested and contradicted, judges have been misled into a failure steadily to adhere to principle. It is not difficult to understand such tendencies, but a lack of confidence in the ability of a tribunal correctly to estimate evidence of states of mind and the like can never be sufficient ground for excluding from inquiry the most fundamental element in a rational and humane criminal code". Unless reliance is placed upon juries, properly instructed, to "estimate evidence of states of mind" relevant to that "most fundamental element in a rational and humane criminal code", the state of mind of the accused, the consequence will be that described by Lord Hailsham in *Director of Public Prosecutions v Morgan* [1976] AC 182 at 213, juries will "in effect be told to find an intent where none existed or where none was proved to have existed". His Lordship, in the different circumstances of the case then before him said that he could not in conscience bring himself to sanction such a view of the law. The conclusion arrived at by the Full Court of the Victorian Supreme Court in the present case avoids such a view and should be upheld.

In the present case evidence of intoxication should, in my view, have been allowed to go to the jury. It, together, with any other evidence, such as acts and words spoken by the accused, will form the material upon which a jury will then perform "its proper function of deciding on all the evidence, including that of intoxication, whether the Crown has in fact discharged its onus" – *R v Kamipeli* [1975] 2 NZLR 610 at 614. It is upon the properly instructed jury that reliance should be placed to ensure that only when intoxication has truly deprived the accused of the mental element which the law has prescribed as requisite for commission of the particular crime will it avail the accused.

I would grant special leave and dismiss the appeal.

4.90 In *R v Martin*[31] the High Court held that *O'Connor* applied to homicide. *O'Connor's* case establishes that evidence of intoxication may be relevant whenever it is necessary to prove the mental element of a crime. The prosecution is required to prove in manslaughter, no less than, in other crimes, that the actions of the accused upon which it relies were at least voluntary, since manslaughter is not only the unlawful, but also the voluntary, killing of another without intent.

Intent

4.91 An intent which is aided by alcohol is nonetheless an intent; *R v Sheehan*[32]. Such an intent remains valid.

31 (1984) 58 ALJR.
32 [1975] 2 All ER 960.

4.92   *A-G for Northern Ireland v Gallagher*
[1963] AC 349; [1961] 3 All ER 299; [1961] 3 WLR 619;
(1961) 45 Cr App R 316
House of Lords, 1961

Facts: The defendant suffered from a mental illness which manifested itself in periodic explosive outbursts. These outbursts were likely when the defendant consumed alcohol. On the day of his release from a mental hospital he purchased a knife and a bottle of whiskey and was seen cycling towards his home. Some two hours later he arrived in a neighbour's house and said he had killed his wife, the greater part of the bottle of whiskey having been consumed either before or after the killing or both.

Lord Denning: My Lords, I think the law on this point should take a clear stand. If a man, whilst sane and sober, forms an intention to kill and makes preparation for it, knowing it is a wrong thing to do, and then gets himself drunk so as to give himself Dutch courage to do the killing, and whilst drunk carries out his intention, he cannot rely on this self-induced drunkenness as a defence to a charge of murder, nor even as reducing it to manslaughter. He cannot say that he got himself into such a stupid state that he was incapable of an intent to kill. So also when he is a psychopath, he cannot by drinking rely on his self-induced defect of reason as a defence of insanity. The wickedness of his mind before he got drunk is enough to condemn him, coupled with the act which he intended to do and did do.

Possible Solution

4.93 There may be many circumstances where the taking of drugs or alcohol may, in itself, be an act of criminal negligence. There may also be circumstances where such an act amounts to recklessness. Where the accused is aware, from his past behaviour or the observation of others, or simply by the application of intelligence, that alcohol produces in him behaviour where he may be violent or might otherwise behave in an apparently criminal manner, this foresight coupled with the unjustified taking of the risk amounts to recklessness. There may be situations where that is not so. Either the accused may have no prior experience of his actions while intoxicated or may be ignorant as to the effect that alcohol may have or may give no thought to the matter at all. Criminal negligence does not require foresight but recklessness does. As criminal negligence only suffices for the crime of manslaughter the accused must for all other crimes requiring recklessness (such as assault), have had foresight of his actions. The solution is to make it an offence carrying a potentially severe penalty for a person to act dangerously while intoxicated. In *R v O'Connor*, Barwick CJ suggested that there should be a statutory provision which gave a jury the right to bring in an alternative verdict on a new charge of self-induced intoxication.

4.94 *Report of the Butler Committee on Mentally Abnormal Offenders*
1979 Cmnd 6244

We propose that it should be an offence for a person while voluntarily intoxicated to do an act (or make an omission) that would amount to a dangerous offence if it were done or made with the requisite state of mind for such an offence. The prosecution would not charge this offence in the first instance, but would charge an offence under the ordinary law. If the evidence of intoxication were given at the trial for the purpose of negativing the intent or other mental element required for the offence, the jury would be directed that they may return a verdict of not guilty of that offence but guilty of the offence of dangerous intoxication if they find that the defendant did the act (or made the omission) charged that by reason of the evidence of intoxication they are not sure that at the time he had the state of mind required for the offence, and they are sure that his intoxication was voluntary.

Code Options

4.95 *Model Penal Code*

Section 2.08   Intoxication

(1) Except as provided in subsection (4) of this section, intoxication of the actor is not a defence unless it negatives an element of the offence.

(2) When recklessness establishes an element of the offence, if the actor, due to self-induced intoxication, is unaware of a risk of which he would have been aware that had he been sober, such unawareness is immaterial.

(3) Intoxication does not, in itself, constitute mental disease within the meaning of section 4.01.

(4) Intoxication that (a) is not self-induced or (b) is pathological is an affirmative defence if by reason of such intoxication the actor at the time of his conduct lacks substantial capacity either to appreciate its criminality [wrongfulness] or to conform his conduct to the requirements of law.

(5) Definitions. In this section unless a different meaning plainly is required:

(*a*) "intoxication" means a disturbance of mental or physical capacities resulting from the introduction of substances into the body;

(*b*) "self-induced intoxication" means intoxication caused by substances that the actor knowingly introduces into his body, the tendency of which to cause intoxication he knows or ought to know, unless he introduces them pursuant to medical advice or under such circumstances as would afford a defense to a charge of crime;

(*c*) "pathological intoxication" means intoxication grossly excessive in degree, given the amount of the intoxicant, to which the actor does not know he is susceptible.

Further Materials

4.96   Ashworth *The 14th Report of the Criminal Law Revision Committee: Intoxication and General Defences* [1980] Crim LR 556.
Law Reform Commission of Victoria *Criminal Responsibility: Intention and Gross Intoxication* (Report No 6, 1986).
Singh *History of the Defence of Drunkenness in English Criminal Law* (1933) 49 LQR 528.
Colvin *Codification and Reform of the Intoxication Defence* (1983) 26 CLQ 43.

Insanity

4.97   Irish law lacks a definition of insanity. Where the accused is suffering from an insane delusion but only to the extent that he remains sane apart from that delusion, he is to be judged in accordance with the *M'Naghten Rules* of 1843; *Doyle v Wicklow County Council*[33]. The Oireachtas have not

---

33 [1974] IR 55 at 70.

responded to this decision by reforming the law to provide for a specific definition of insanity. Experience indicates that the encapsulation of the M'Naghten Rules by Sir James Stephen is used as the basis of directions to juries when this matter becomes an issue in a criminal trial.

4.98   ***Stephen – Digest of the Criminal Law (1894 Edition)***
                                     Article 28

INSANITY

No act is a crime if the person who does it is at the time when it is done prevented [either by defective mental power or] by any disease affecting his mind

(*a*) from knowing the nature and quality of his act; or,

(*b*) from knowing that the act is[34] wrong; [or[35],

(*c*) from controlling his own conduct, unless the absence of the power of control has been produced by his own default.]

But an act may be a crime although the mind of a person who does it is affected by disease, if such disease does not in fact produce upon his mind one or other of the effects above mentioned in reference to that act.

Illustrations

(1) A kills B under an insane delusion that he is breaking a jar. A's act is not a crime.

(2) A Kills B knowing that he is killing B, and knowing that it is wrong to kill B; but his mind is so imbecile that he is unable to form such an estimate of the nature and consequences of his act as a person of ordinary intelligence would form. A's act is not a crime if the words within the first set of brackets are law. If they are not it is.

(3) A kills B knowing that he is killing B, and knowing that it illegal to kill B; but under an insane delusion that the salvation of the human race will be obtained by his execution for the murder of B, and that God has commanded him (A) to produce that result by those means. A's act is a crime if the word "wrong" has the second of the two meanings ascribed to it in the note[36]. It is not a crime if the word "wrong" has the first of those two meanings.

(4) A suddenly stabs B under the influence of an impulse caused by disease, and of such a nature that nothing short of the mechanical restraint of A's hand would have prevented the stab. A's act is a crime if (*c*) is not law. It is not a crime if (*c*) is law.

(5) A suddenly stabs B under the influence of an impulse caused by disease, and of such a nature that a strong motive, as, for instance, the fear of his own immediate death, would have prevented the act. A's act is a crime whether (*c*) is or is not law.

(6) A permits his mind to dwell upon and desire B's death; under the influence of mental disease this desire becomes uncontrollable, and A kills B. A's act is a crime whether (*c*) is or is not law.

(7) A, a patient in a lunatic asylum, who is under a delusion that his finger is

---

34 The word "wrong" is variously interpreted as meaning: 1. Morally wrong. 2. Illegal. The practical effect of these differences is shown in Illustrations (4), (5), and (6).

35 The parts of the article bracketed are doubtful.

36 In extreme strictness this ought to be, "If the word 'wrong' has the first of these two meanings the criminality of the act would depend upon the question whether the jury thought that God's command under the circumstances altered the moral character of the act."

made of glass, poisons one of his attendants out of revenge for his treatment, and it is proved that the delusion had no connection whatever with the act. A's act is a crime.

Procedure

4.99 Insanity is, in effect, a finding that a person lacked the capacity to commit a crime. A person who is insane retains the physical capacity to bring about the external elements of a crime. The formula of Stephen (see para **4.98**) indicating that the mental capacity is absent in three specific situations accords with rational thinking on the subject. A person who stabs a man believing, because of mental illness, that he is slaughtering a bullock, lacks blame. A person whose faculty of judgment is so underdeveloped that he cannot know that killing another person is wrong, is deprived of the capacity of choice based on the reality of human social structures that is inherent in every normal person. A person who genuinely cannot control an impulse to steal, notwithstanding that he is aware of what he is doing and that stealing is wrong, cannot make a choice between pursuing a line of conduct and suppressing it which is in the essence of decisions. Wrongdoing is judged by the standards adopted by reasonable men; *Doyle v Wicklow County Council*[37]. One cannot blame a person for doing or failing to do something which he cannot prevent. One will, however, continue to blame those who were at fault in removing from themselves the capacity to control their actions or to know the nature of their own conduct; *R v Radford*[38]. Natural mental states, such as anger or drunkenness, which are transient in nature and which, in normal circumstances, are subject to control by the will are excluded from the defence of insanity.

4.100 A person found to be insane is held in the Central Mental Hospital pending a decision by the executive that he has recovered; *DPP v Gallagher*[39].

4.101   *Criminal Lunatics Act 1800*

1 Whereas persons charged with high treason, murder or felony, may have been or may be of unsound mind at the time of committing the offence wherewith they may have been or shall be charged, and by reason of such insanity may have been or may be found not guilty of such offence, and it may be dangerous to permit persons so acquitted to go at large: be it therefore enacted that in all cases where it shall be given in evidence upon the trial of any person charged with treason, murder or felony, that such person was insane at the time of the commission of such offence, and such person shall be acquitted, the jury shall be required to find specially whether such person was insane at the time of the commission of such offence, and to declare whether such person was acquitted by them on account of such insanity; and if they shall find that such person was insane at the time of the committing of such offence, the court before whom such trial shall be had, shall order such person to be kept in strict custody, in such place and in such manner as to the court shall seem fit, until His Majesty's pleasure shall be known; and it shall thereupon be lawful for His Majesty to give such order for the safe custody of such

37 [1974] IR 55 at 70.
38 (1985) 20A Crim R 388.
39 [1991] ILRM 339.

person, during his pleasure, in such place and in such manner as to His Majesty shall seem fit; and in all cases where any person before the passing of this Act, has been acquitted of any such offences on the ground of insanity at the time of the commission thereof, and has been detained in custody as a dangerous person by order of the court before whom such person has been tried, and still remains in custody, it shall be lawful for His Majesty to give the like order for the safe custody of such person, during his pleasure, as His Majesty is hereby enabled to give in the cases of persons who shall hereafter be acquitted on the ground of insanity.

4.102   *Lunacy (Ireland) Act 1821*

16   Persons indicted and acquitted on the Ground of Insanity at the Time of Commission of the Crime, may be detained in Custody

"And Whereas Persons charged with Offences in *Ireland* may have been or may be of unsound Mind at the time of committing the Offence wherewith they may have been or shall be charged, and by reason of such Insanity may have been or may be found not guilty of such Offences; and it may be dangerous to permit Persons in such cases to go at large;" Be it therefore enacted, That in all cases where it shall be given in Evidence on the Trial of any Person in *Ireland*, charged with Treason, Murder or any other Offence, that such Person was insane at the Time of the Commission of such Offence, and such Person shall be acquitted, the Jury shall be required to find specially whether such Person was insane at the time of the Commission of such Offence, and to declare whether such Person was acquitted by them on account of such Insanity; and if they shall find that such Person was insane at the time of the committing such Offence, the Court before whom the Trial shall be had, shall, if it shall be thought necessary or proper, order such Person to be kept in strict Custody, in such Place and in such Manner as to the Court shall seem fit, until the Pleasure of the Lord Lieutenant, or other Chief Governor or Governors of *Ireland* for the time being, shall be known; and it shall thereupon be lawful for the Lord Lieutenant, or other Chief Governor or Governors of *Ireland* for the time being, to give such Order for the safe Custody and Care of such Person, during the Pleasure of the Lord Lieutenant, or other Chief Governor or Governors of *Ireland* for the time being, in such Place and in such Manner as shall seem fit; and in all cases where any Person before the passing of this Act has been acquitted of any such Offences, on the Ground of Insanity at the time of the Commission thereof, and has been detained in Custody as a dangerous Person by Order of the Court before whom such Person has been tried or otherwise, and shall remain in Custody at the time of the passing of this Act, it shall be lawful for the Lord Lieutenant, or other Chief Governor or Governors of *Ireland* for the time being, to give the like Order for the safe Custody and Care of such Person, as the Lord Lieutenant, or other Chief Governor or Governors of *Ireland*, is or are by this Act enabled to give in the cases of Persons who shall hereafter be acquitted on the Ground of Insanity.

17   Criminals found insane at the Time of their Indictment, or of being brought up to be discharged for want of Prosecution, &c may be detained under Order of Courts, and Direction of Lord Lieutenant

And be it further enacted, That if any Person indicted in *Ireland* for any Offence shall be found to be insane, by a Jury lawfully impanelled for that Purpose, so that such Person cannot be tried upon such Indictment; or if, upon the Trial of any Person so indicted, such Person shall appear to the Jury charged with such Indictment to be insane, it shall be lawful for the Court before whom such Person shall be brought to be tried as aforesaid, to direct such Finding to be recorded, and thereupon to order such Person to be kept in strict Custody, and to be taken Care of, until the Pleasure of the Lord Lieutenant, or other Chief Governor or Governors of *Ireland* for the time being, shall be known; and if any Person charged with any Offence shall be brought before any Court to be discharged for Want of Prosecution, and such Person shall appear to be insane, it shall be lawful for such Court to order a Jury to be impannelled to try the Sanity of such Person; and if the Jury so impanelled shall find such Person to be insane, it shall be lawful for such Court to order such Person to be kept in strict Custody, in such Place and in such Manner as to such Court shall seem fit, until the Pleasure of the Lord Lieutenant, or other Chief Governor or Governors of *Ireland* for the time being, shall be known; and in all cases of Insanity so found, it shall be lawful for the Lord Lieutenant, or other Chief Governor or Governors of *Ireland* for the time being, to give the like Order for the safe Custody and Care of such Person so found to be insane, as the Lord Lieutenant, or other Chief Governor or Governors of *Ireland*, is or are by this Act enabled to give in the cases of Persons acquitted on the Ground of Insanity.

18 Such insane Criminals to be removed and detained in Lunatic Asylums, when provided

Provided always, and be it enacted, That whenever and as soon as there shall be a Lunatic Asylum built or maintained, either wholly or in part, in any County, County of a City or County of a Town, wherein such Prisoner, in any of the cases aforesaid, shall be tried or found insane as aforesaid, then and from thenceforth such insane Person shall, without Delay, be removed to such Asylum, and shall be kept therein so long as such Prisoner shall be detained in Custody.

4.103 *Lunatic Asylums (Ireland) Act 1845*

8 When Central Asylum established, the Lord Lieutenant empowered to order the Removal of Criminal Lunatics to such Asylum 1 & 2 G 4 c 33

And whereas by an Act passed in the Session of Parliament holden in the First and Second Years of the Reign of His late Majesty King *George* the Fourth, intituled *An Act to make more effectual Provision for the Establishment of Asylums for the Lunatic Poor, and for the Custody of Insane Persons charged with Offences*, in Ireland, it is amongst other things enacted, that it should be lawful for the Lord Lieutenant or other Chief Governor or Governors of *Ireland* for the Time being to give such Order for the safe Custody and Care of Criminals found insane as in the said Act mentioned, during the Pleasure of the Lord Lieutenant or other Chief Governor or Governors of *Ireland* for the Time being, in such Place and in such Manner as should seem fit; and it is by said Act further provided and enacted, that whenever and as soon as there should be a Lunatic Asylum built or maintained, either wholly or in part, in any County, County of City or County of a Town, wherein such Prisoner as therein mentioned should be tried or found insane as therein mentioned, then and from thenceforth such Insane Person should without Delay be removed to such Asylum so therein mentioned, and should be kept therein so long as such Prisoner should be detained in Custody; be it enacted, That whenever and as soon as the said Central Asylum shall be erected, and fit for the Reception of Criminal Lunatics, it shall be lawful for the Lord Lieutenant or other Chief Governor or Governors of *Ireland* to order and direct that all Criminal Lunatics then in Custody in any Lunatic Asylum or Gaol, or who shall thereafter be in Custody, shall be removed without Delay to such Central Asylum, and shall be kept therein so long as such Criminal Lunatics respectively shall be detained in Custody.

39   The Central Criminal Lunatic Asylum established in pursuance of the Lunatic Asylums (Ireland) Act 1845, shall be styled and known as the Central Mental
Hospital.

4.105   Psychiatric evidence is admissible only where the mental processes
of the accused are claimed to be outside the normal scope and experience of
ordinary people; *R v Turner*[40]. Where psychiatric evidence is presented by
the defence, it is usual that a psychiatrist nominated by the State will also
examine the accused and present a report to the court. A trial judge is
entitled to comment adversely on the failure of the defence to allow an
examination by a State nominated psychiatrist; *R v Malcolm*[41].

4.106   The burden of proof is on the accused to prove, on the balance of
probability, that at the time when he brought about the external element of
the crime, he was insane; *The People (DPP) v O'Mahony*[42].
   Insanity may also be relevant at the time when the trial is due to take
place. Here a different test is adopted. If the accused is not able to understand the indictment, the effect and nature of a plea of guilty or not guilty, to
challenge a juror to which he might wish to object, to instruct counsel and to
follow and understand the details of the evidence, he will be unfit to plead; *R
v Robertson*[43]. Here the burden of proof is on the defence, on the balance of
probabilities, if they assert unfitness to plead. If the prosecution assert that
the accused is fit to plead they must establish this beyond reasonable doubt;
R v Robertson[44].

4.107   It remains a possibility that the plea of insanity by an accused person
may be supported by an insufficiently trained psychiatrist. If the accused is
subsequently incarcerated but found to be sane, he should then be released.
A decision to keep the same person incarcerated in the Central Mental
Hospital would be subject to judicial review. The success of that proceeding
could not be predicted where an accused had earlier been found by a jury to
be insane on the balance of probability.

4.108   *Paul Carney – Anachorisms of our Criminal Insanity Laws*
                    Irish Times 13 January 1990

   The defence of insanity has been seldom raised up to now in Irish criminal trials. It
is therefore quite startling to look at the indictments tried in the Central Criminal
Court last term and find that a verdict of "guilty but insane" was sought by the
defence in four trials out of seven and achieved in three.
   It must have come to a surprise to the jurors trying these cases that they were
required to conduct their deliberations not under a modern mental health statute,
but under section 2 of the Trial of Lunatics Act 1883. This allows juries to bring in a
special verdict of guilty but insane where they find that the accused carried out the
acts for which they were charged but were insane at the time.

40 [1975] QB 834.
41 (1989) 50 CCC (3d) 172.
42 [1985] IR 51 at 522.
43 [1968] 3 All ER 557.
44 *Ibid* and generally see Ryan & Magee *The Irish Criminal Process*.

Insanity verdicts have only been sought in murder cases because of the mandatory penalty, formerly death and now penal servitude for life. Logically, a person found insane at the time of the commission of a homicide should be acquitted, released and dealt with if necessary under the Mental Treatment Acts. For historical reasons associated with the protection of the person of the monarch, the Criminal Lunatics Act 1800 provided that any person charged with high treason, murder or felony who was found not guilty by reason of insanity should be kept in strict custody during the King's pleasure.

Professor (now Mr Justice) Roderick J O'Hanlon, writing in the Irish Jurist in 1968, pointed out that historically, apart from female prisoners suffering from temporary puerperal mania, only one prisoner in 150 obtained release from Broadmoor where English "criminal lunatics" were detained.

The sentence of detention during His Majesty's pleasure was adapted in Ireland to detention "until the pleasure of the government be known". In 1973 this formula was successfully challenged on constitutional grounds in *The State (O) v O'Brien*. The Supreme Court held that the selection of punishment and the determination of the length of a sentence were integral parts of the administration of justice in criminal trials and that such functions were exercisable only by courts established under the Constitution.

Since *The State (O) v O'Brien* persons found guilty but insane have been sentenced to be detained "until further order of the court" and are committed to the Central Mental Hospital in Dundrum in secure hospital rather than prison conditions.

Serious crime in our jurisdiction necessarily involves "guilty knowledge". Insanity is a defence to the mental element. Historical reasons dealt with by Professor O'Hanlon explain why the jury records a verdict of "guilty but insane" rather than "not guilty by reason of insanity". Briefly stated, these are to discourage assassination, of the King in particular.

The State (O) v O'Brien means that persons found guilty but insane can go back to court whenever their doctors deem it appropriate and seek release on the grounds that their mental state has recovered and there is no longer any reason for their detention. As the verdict was in essence one of acquittal due to lack of or impaired intent no consideration of punishment should arise.

As well as the Criminal Lunatic Statutes the State inherited the well-known M'Naghten Rules in which the test of insanity is whether the accused knew the nature and quality of his act and if so whether he knew it was wrong. We also inherited a case law in which the following dicta are to be found:

"If you cannot resist an impulse in any other way we will hang a rope in front of your eyes and perhaps that will help" – Riddle J.

"My own opinion is that if a special divine order were given to a man to commit murder I should certainly hang him for it, unless I got a special divine order not to hang him" – Stephen LJ.

"I think that although the present law lays down such a definition of madness that nobody is hardly ever really mad enough to be within it, yet it is a logical and a good definition" – Baron Bramwell.

These quotations appear in Professor O'Hanlon's article and he goes on to say that all attempts to extend the scope of the defence of insanity beyond the confines of the M'Naghten Rules were unsuccessful in England. This, however, was remedied by statutory intervention in Ireland.

In Ireland there has been no statutory intervention and as usual it has been left to the judiciary to do the best it can. Judges cannot legislate and can only interpret the law if appropriate cases, supported by appropriate evidence come before them. Directions to juries in murder trials given by Mr Justice Henchy and Mr Justice Finlay (when judges of the High Court) and Mr Justice Gannon have added a third rule to the M'Naghten Rules.

In *DPP v Penny Ann Dorricott* (Central Criminal Court, 3 February 1982) Mr Justice Finlay asked the jury to consider as the third proposition (the first two being the M'Naghten Rules) whether the accused at the time did the act suffering from a disease of the mind which prevented her from exercising a free volition.

At first sight this direction looks like a "policemen at the elbow" test, but it appears to have been interpreted liberally by juries and to have worked well.

We should not have to rely on the judges for reform. If we had an Oireachtas we could take pride in we should not have on our statute book criminal lunatic statutes of the 1800s from the Westminster Parliament. That Parliament has replaced them. Ours has not.

(Table courtesy of Mr Patrick Morrissey, Registrar, Central Criminal Court.)

Pleas and verdicts in Central Criminal Court trials in Michaelmas Term 1989

Month	Number of Accused	Plea	Verdict
October 1989	1	Not guilty of murder but guilty of manslaughter	Not guilty of murder but guilty of manslaughter
	1	Not guilty by reason of mental illness	Guilty but insane
	1	Not guilty	Guilty but insane
November 1989	1	Not guilty of murder but guilty of manslaughter	Not guilty of murder but guilty of manslaughter
	1	Guilty but insane	Guilty of murder
	1	Not guilty by reason of insanity	Guilty but insane
December 1989	1	(a) Not guilty (b) Guilty of murder	Guilty of murder

History

4.109 The law on insanity is best understood in the context of its development through history.

4.110   *Roderick O'Hanlon – Not Guilty Because of Insanity*
(1968) Irish Jurist (ns) III 61

The charge of the trial judge to the jury never appears to feature in the law reports of modern times. This is a circumstance which, no doubt, is forced upon court reporters by the difficulty in giving adequate coverage to the decisions of the courts of appeal. Nevertheless it must be a matter of some regret, for important chapters in the development of the law have been written at this stage of proceedings, both civil and criminal, in the past. One recollects the important statement of the law on constructive malice by Stephen LJ in *Reg v Serné*, in 1887, and the authoritative statements of the law as to arson by Hawkins J in the cases of *Harris* (1881) and *Nattrass* (1882).

What has prompted the foregoing comment is the report in the Irish daily newspapers of the 1st December 1967, of the directions to the jury by Mr Justice Henchy, in the course of the trial of Edward Hayes at the Central Criminal Court on a charge of murdering Brigid Hayes, his wife at their home in Clonconane, Co

Limerick on October 15, 1965. The jury returned a verdict of guilty but insane, after an absence of 15 minutes. The charge of the trial judge appears from the newspaper reports to have contained a radical re-statement of the law as to insanity which – if followed – will have brought the law in this country very much into line with modern developments in the US and will have carried it well beyond the stage which has hitherto been reached in England.

In *The Irish Times* for December 1, 1967, the following extracts from the charge to the jury are reported:

"He [Mr Justice Henchy] stated that if the jury was satisfied that at the time of the attack the accused man's mind was so affected by illness that he was unable to restrain himself, a verdict of guilty but insane should be returned.

"The case seemed to be one in which Hayes, over a long period, had been labouring under a sense of grievance which had built up in his mind and which he sought to ventilate . . . He might have been under the delusion that he was a public executioner and would not know the moral nature of what he was doing.

"The issue of insanity was a very real issue." He went on: "I think you can agree that he is medically insane as his reasons given for killing are so irrational, motiveless and perverse that it is very hard to see that they came from the working of a normal mind.

"The workings of such a mind were so distorted and so far removed from rationality that he could take away the children's mother, and, for all practical purposes their father as well, in order to clear the name of the children. Such reasoning was not the same thinking of a rational man.

"He added that the accused man seemed to be so oppressed that he was driven by an inner compulsion so that he was without any control to find redress for grievances, real or imaginary. In that case the jury would find that the verdict would be guilty but insane. His wife's attempts to divert him from the grievances might be the reason that involved her."

In order to assess the importance of the *Hayes* case, a brief survey of the development of the law as to insanity in this country and in England from early times must be attempted.

The first records in the criminal law field show an attitude of intolerance towards the plea of insanity by way of defence. This is particularly so in the case of crimes where the person of the King was placed in jeopardy, and indeed attempts on the life of the Head of State or his Ministers have continued to exercise a distorting influence over the development of the law as to insanity down to our own times.

In the reign of King Alfred, high treason which took the form of killing or attempting to kill the king was not excused by the insanity of the offender. A statute of Henry VIII (33 Hen 8, c 20) decreed that a person attainted of treason who thereafter became insane, should nevertheless be executed.

The same ruthless attitude towards the insane is reflected in the statements of the law found in Coke and Hale. Coke accepts that insanity affords a defence to a criminal charge if the insanity is of such a degree that the person resembled a beast rather than a man. Hale, towards the end of 17th century, suggested that if the accused had the understanding of a child of 14, he should be convicted.

Coke's "wild beast" measure of insanity as an excusing factor persisted into the 18th century. Arnold, who was put on trial in 1724, for attempted murder of Lord Onslow, believed that his intended victim caused devils and imps to be introduced into his bedroom each night, to persecute him. The jury were told:

"It is not every kind of frantic humour that exempts from punishment. It must be a man that is totally deprived of understanding and memory and doth not know what he is doing, no more than an infant, than a brute or wild beast."

Arnold was convicted and sentenced to death, but the sentence was not carried into effect. A number of other celebrated killers fared less well in the second half of the 18th century and were convicted and executed in the teeth of evidence which clearly indicated a condition of mental abnormality.

The turning point was reached with *Hadfield's* case in 1800. Hadfield believed that it was necessary for him to sacrifice his life to save the world. To commit suicide would be sinful; accordingly he elected instead to commit some crime which would result in the imposition of the death penalty. He opened fire on George III in Drury Lane and was, no doubt, comforted by the fact that he was wide of the mark but had engaged in activity of a sufficiently treasonable character to qualify for public execution.

Erskine, who defended him, laid down a barrage against Coke and Hale, and the other protagonists of the "wild beast" theory of insanity. He argued, with a good deal of force, that the form of madness which the older writers accepted as a defence to a criminal charge had never existed in the world, save in the case of helpless and hopeless idiocy. He won over to his side the trial judge, Lord Kenyon, CJ, who eventually stopped the trial, telling the jury –

"If a man is in a deranged state of mind at the time, he is not criminally answerable for his acts."

The jury, by direction of the judge, returned a verdict of not guilty, the accused being under the influence of insanity at the time the act was committed.

This decision appeared to herald the arrival of a more enlightened era in the history of the criminal law, but it produced an immediate repercussion which has profoundly affected the entire development of the law as to insanity ever since. With the acquittal of Hadfield it appeared that the criminal law no longer afforded sufficient protection for the person of the King against attack. Accordingly, the Criminal Lunatics Act of 1800 (39 & 40 Geo 3, c 94), was passed, requiring the court to order any person charged with high treason, murder or felony, who was found not guilty because of insanity, to be kept in strict custody during the King's pleasure.

Up to that time, persons who were acquitted on the grounds of insanity had been entrusted to the care of their family or relatives. Henceforth, a successful plea of insanity in defence to a charge of high treason, murder, or other felony, must result in detention in a criminal lunatic asylum, probably for the remainder of the life of the accused. Kenny's *Criminal Law*, in a note to the 1944 edition, mentions that only about one prisoner in 150 ever obtained release from Broadmoor, apart from female prisoners suffering from temporary puerperal mania. (The position in this respect has since been radically altered in England by the Mental Health Act, 1959).

The tendency must inevitably have grown up to reserve the plea of insanity to cases of last resort, where the choice appeared to lie between the certainty of conviction of an offence involving the death penalty and the scarcely less fearful prospect of detention for life in a criminal lunatic asylum. Such a situation arose much more frequently during the early decades of the 19th century when over 200 offences still carried the death penalty. By 1861 the position had changed dramatically – only about four capital offences still remained. Only in this very limited group of cases was there scope for the law as to insanity to grow and develop. The plea was almost unknown as a defence to other criminal charges.

For the past century and more, the evolution of the criminal law in relation to insanity has been governed almost entirely by decisions in murder trials. This factor in turn must have tended to encourage the Courts to apply a fairly exacting test of insanity before exonerating an accused person from punishment for so heinous a crime. This trend emerged clearly with the formulation of the M'Naghten Rules in 1843 and with their subsequent interpretation by the Courts in England.

The more enlightened approach adopted by Lord Kenyon CJ in *Hadfield's* case was not followed consistently by the courts during the interval between the trial of

Hadfield and the enunciation by the Judges of the M'Naghten Rules. A good deal of uncertainty appears to have prevailed as to the proper form of direction to be given to the jury on the issue of insanity, and eventually Daniel M'Naghten's designs on the life of a Minister of State again led to a hardening of the attitude of the public, and in turn of the Courts, to the plea of insanity.

M'Naghten on the 20th January 1843, shot Edward Drummond, private secretary of Sir Robert Peel, Prime Minister, in the back as he walked up Whitehall. When put on trial he claimed that he believed he was subject to persecution by the Tory Party and that his life was thereby endangered. He thereupon shot Drummond, mistaking him for Peel.

The verdict in *M'Naghten's* case, "Not guilty on the ground of insanity" provoked so much dissatisfaction that in the same year the House of Lords summoned the Judges to answer a series of questions as to the law relating to insanity. The Judges protested against being required to declare the law otherwise than by the traditional method of judicial decision with reference to the facts of a particular case, but attended nonetheless before the House of Lords on 19 June, 1843, to give their answers.

The questions were five in number. The first four were concerned with the general issue of insanity as a factor excusing an accused person from criminal responsibility, and the last question was concerned with the admissibility of certain types of medical evidence in relation to insanity. As the wording of the questions and answers has been closely analysed in subsequent times, and has given rise to a number of conflicting decisions, the first four questions and the replies thereto are reproduced in full.

Q. 1—"What is the law respecting alleged crimes committed by persons afflicted with *insane delusions* in respect of one or more particular subjects or persons; as for instance where at the time of the commission of the alleged crime, the accused knew he was acting contrary to law, but did the act complained of with a view under the influence of insane delusion, of redressing or revenging some supposed grievance or injury, or of producing some supposed public benefit?

A. 1—"Assuming your Lordships' inquiries are confined to those persons who labour under such *partial delusions* only and are not in other respects insane, we are of opinion that notwithstanding the accused did the act complained of with a view under the influence of insame delusion, of redressing or revenging some supposed grievance or injury or of producing some public benefit, he is nevertheless punishable according to the nature of the crime committed if he knew at the time of committing such crime that he was acting *contrary to law*, by which expression we understand your lordships to mean the law of the land.

Q. 2—"What are the proper questions to be submitted to the jury where a person alleged to be afflicted with insane delusion respecting one or more particular subjects or persons is charged with the commission of a crime (murder, for example) and insanity is set up as a defence?

Q. 3—"In what terms ought the question be left to the jury as to the prisoner's state of mind at the time when the act was committed?

A. 2 & 3—"The jury ought to be told in all cases that every man is to be presumed to be sane and to possess a sufficient degree of reason to be responsiblity for his crimes until the contrary be proved to their satisfaction; and that to establish a defence on the ground of insanity it must be clearly proved that at the time of committing the act, the accused was labouring under such a *defect of reason* from *disease of the mind* as not to know the nature and quality of the act he was doing, or if he did know it, that he did not know he was doing what was *wrong*.

The mode of putting the latter part of the question to the jury on these occasions has generally been whether the accused at the time of doing the act knew the difference between right and wrong; which mode, though rarely if ever leading to any mistake with the jury is not, we conceive, so accurate when put generally and in the abstract as when put with reference to the party's knowledge of right and wrong in respect to the very act with which he is charged. If the question were to be put as to the knowledge of the accused solely and exclusively with reference to the law of the land it might tend to confound the jury by inducing them to believe that an actual knowledge of the law of the land was essential in order to lead to a conviction; whereas the law is administered on the principle that every one must be taken conclusively to know it, without proof that he does know it. If the accused was conscious that the act was one that he ought not to do, and if that act was at the same time contrary to the law of the land, he is punishable; and the usual course therefore has been to leave the question to the jury whether the accused had a sufficient degree of reason to know that he was doing an act that was wrong; and this course we think is correct, accompanied with such observations and explanations as the circumstances of each particular case may require."

Q. 4—"If a person under an insane delusion as to existing facts commits an offence in consequence thereof, is he excused?

A. 4—"The answer must of course depend on the nature of the delusion; but making the same assumption as we did before, namely that he labours under such partial delusion only and is not in other respects insane, we think he must be considered in the same situation as to responsibility as if the facts with respect to which the delusion exists were real. For example, if under the influence of his delusion he supposes another man to be in the act of attempting to take away his life and he kills that man as he supposes in self-defence, he would be exempt from punishment. If his delusion was that the deceased had inflicted a serious injury to his character and fortune and he killed him in revenge for such supposed injury, he would be liable to punishment."

It will be seen at once that Hadfield, on a strict application of the M'Naghten Rules, would have been convicted, and M'Naghten himself would have had a slim enough prospect of acquittal. Certainly a new and tougher era for the mentally unbalanced set in with the formulation of these rules in 1843, and even the enlightened Stephen LJ in the latter half of the 19th century had little time for the Hadfields of this world. "My own opinion," he commented, "is that if a special divine order were given to a man to commit murder, I should certainly hang him for it unless I got a special divine order not to hang him".

Soon after the Rules were formulated the great debate began as to whether they provided a comprehensive code of the law as to insanity. Did there exist forms of insanity not dealt with by the Rules, but which, nevertheless, could afford a defence to a criminal charge? In more recent times the further and more fundamental question has been posed as to whether the Rules should be regarded as having any binding force in view of the great advance in medical science relating to insanity since the Rules were formulated.

Defence lawyers contended that the Rules were concerned only with persons suffering from insane delusions and that the law should recognise the existence of non-delusional mental incapacity which deprived the accused person of the ability to control his actions. Sir James Stephen suggested that the law recognised the existence of such a defence, and even promoted a Homicide Law Amendment Bill to ensure that the plea of uncontrollable impulse would be admissible, but his proposed amendment never reached the statute book.

In the meantime, his brothers on the Bench had tended to close the ranks against any extension of the defence of insanity beyond the narrow confines of the M'Naghten Rules. The plea or *irresistible impulse* put forward in *Haynes*, 1 F & F 666, 1859, received short shrift from the trial judge, Baron Bramwell, who told the jury:

"The circumstances of an act being apparently motiveless is not a ground from which you can safely infer the existence of a powerful and irresistible influence or homicidal tendency . . . If an influence be so powerful as to be termed irresistible, so much the more reason is there why we should not withdraw any of the safeguards tending to counteract it. If the influence itself be held a legal excuse rendering the crime dispunishable you at once withdraw a most powerful restraint – law, forbidding and punishing its perpetration."

The same view was expressed even more pungently by Riddle J in a Canadian case in 1909 –

"If you cannot resist an impulse in any other way, we will hang a rope in front of your eyes, and perhaps that will help".

Baron Bramwell again turned up to defend the Rules before the Select Committee on Stephen's Homicide Law Amendment Bill in 1874, when he commented as follows:

"I think that although the present law lays down such a definition of madness that nobody is hardly every really mad enough to be within it, yet it is a logical and good definition."

All efforts to extend the scope of the defence of insanity beyond the confines of the Rules by judicial interpretation were unsuccessful in England. The rules of uncontrollable or irresistible impulse was finally rejected in the cases of *Kopsch* in (1925), 19 CAR 50, and *Flavell* in (1926), 19 CAR 141. The Privy Council in *Sodeman* [1936] 2 AER 1138, applied the same rule of law to the Dominions. The English Courts went still further, however, and declared that not only would the plea of irresistible impulse not be allowed, but that no form of mental abnormality could be accepted as a defence to a criminal charge unless it fell within the scope of the M'Naghten Rules. Lord Sankey, LC, delivering the judgment of the House of Lords in *Woolmington v DPP*, [1935] AC 462, said –

"M'Naghten's case stands by itself. It is the famous pronouncement on the law bearing on the question of insanity in cases of murder."

He appeared to treat the Rules as a comprehensive, all-embracing code, and this view was again expressed by the English Court of Criminal Appeal in *Windle*, [1952] 2 QB 826, where Lord Goddard CJ put the issue beyond further debate in delivering the judgment of the Court. He said –

"Mr Shawcross argued that the M'Naghten Rules only applied to delusions. The Court cannot agree with that. It is true that when the Judges were summoned to the House of Lords, the occasion had special reference to the case of *Reg v M'Naghten*, but the rules ever since that date have been generally applied to all cases of insanity, whatever might be the nature of the insanity or disease of the mind from which the person accused was suffering."

While the Courts in England were committing themselves to this interpretation of the meaning and scope of the Rules, considerable pressure was building up in legal and medical circles to modify or abandon the Rules and to bring the law as to insanity into line with the advances in medical knowledge on the question of mental abnormality.

A Committee on Insanity and Crime appointed by Lord Birkenhead, LC, and presided over by Atkin LJ, recommended in 1923 that it should be made clear that the law does recognise irresponsibility on the grounds of insanity where the act was committed under an impulse which the prisoner was by mental disease, in substance deprived of any power to resist. Opposite on the part of many of the judges prevailed over this recommendation, however, and the legislature did not adopt it.

The matter again came up for consideration by the Royal Commission on Capital Punishment, which reported in 1953 (with only one dissentient) that "the test of responsibility laid down by the M'Naghten Rules is so defective that the law on the subject ought to be changed."

On this occasion the Legislature acted on the recommendation and the English Homicide Act 1957, was enacted, which gave statutory recognition to the defence of "diminished responsibility", Section 2 of the Act providing that a verdict of manslaughter and not of murder should be returned in cases where the accused was suffering from such abnormality of mind (whether arising from a condition of arrested or retarded development of mind or any other inherent causes or induced by disease or injury) as substantially impaired his mental responsibility for his acts and omissions in doing or being a party to the killing."

This, in effect, left the M'Naghen Rules intact as the touchstone for the ordinary case where a plea of insanity was raised on behalf of the accused, but allowed in for the first time a form of mental abnormality or incapacity which did not come within the scope of the *Rules*, for the purpose of reducing a charge of murder to one of manslaughter, but not for the purpose of enabling the accused to qualify for a verdict of "guilty but insane".

So long as the death penalty was retained in murder cases this provision was of major importance; it must have lost much of its significance with the passing of the Murder (Abolition of Death Penalty) Act, 1965, since when, the imposition of life imprisonment for murder may not, in fact, involve a longer period in confinement than would be served by an accused person convicted of manslaughter.

Even the reforming zeal of Lord Gardiner, LC has not succeeded in driving the *M'Naghten Rules* from their *entrenched position in England* and what Dr F A Whitlock in "Criminal Responsibility and Mental Illness" (Butterworth, 1963) called "the long, uneasy flirtation between law and medicine" has not as yet culminated even in the shotgun wedding which the author felt might be forced upon the parties concerned "by a public impatient both with legal argument and psychiatric differences in open Court."

The law in *Ireland* on this important topic has gradually diverged from the course laid for it by Courts and Legislature in England. The same problem as to whether the Rules were to be regarded as a comprehensive code arose for consideration before the Courts here in the 1930s and resulted in a clear break with English precedent.

The first of a series of reported cases around this period was *A-G v O'Connor*, (1933) LJ Ir 130, where defence counsel asked that a question should be left to the jury as to whether the accused had acted under an uncontrollable impulse in committing the homicide which led to the charge of murder being brought against him. The President of the High Court (Sullivan P) refused the application on the ground that a defence of uncontrollable impulse was not recognised by law. The jury returned a verdict of insanity, and accordingly the case proceeded no further.

In *A-G v O'Brien*, [1936] IR 263, an appeal against the conviction of the accused for murder came before the Court of Criminal Appeal, presided over by Kennedy CJ. One of the grounds of appeal was that the trial judge should have left the defence of irresistible impulse to the jury. This plea was rejected on the ground that whether or not the defence was known to the law (which point was reserved by the Court for further consideration) there was no evidence to substantiate it in O'Brien's case. Kennedy CJ, in delivering the judgment of the Court dealt specifically with the scope and application of the M'Naghten Rules:

"The Judges in *M'Naghten's* case protested as to the inconvenience of being called on to express their opinions in the abstract, not in relation to the facts of a particular case and without argument or debate on the matter. The answers of the Judges to the questions have been the subject of vigorous dissent on the part of medical men and certain lawyers of distinction.

The questions *related to* crimes committed by persons 'afflicted with insane delusions in respect of one or more particular subjects or questions.' *It follows, in our opinion,* that *the opinions given by the Judges must in every case be read with the like specific limitation.* [But opinions given on the second and third questions have been commonly read as applying to the whole field of insanity, which is, of course, of far wider area and comprises a more extensive and varied range of cases of mental disease than thsoe which can be conveniently summed as affliction with insane delusion]. Hence the dissatisfaction expressed by many legal and medical persons with the opinions as so read with the wide and general interpretation wrongly given to them.

No doubt substantial grounds of objection in practice may be raised against admitting the defence of "irresistible impulse" . . . but the English Court of Criminal Appeal to the contrary notwithstanding, that is not sufficient to rule it out of consideration if it be shown to rest on any established principle of criminal law. It is not ours to make laws. We have only to ascertain and declare the law as it is, whether when ascertained it is found to be in the circumstances of our day deserving of approval or otherwise. If otherwise, we have a Legislature competent to alter or adapt it in the light of the latest science and of the conditions of the time in which we live."

No clearer statement could be required that, as far as this country is concerned, the *M'Naghten Rules are to be regarded as a comprehensive code of insanity* as a defence to criminal charges and certainly the express terms of the Rules, which have already been cited, appear to justify the view of our Court of Criminal Appeal rather than that of the Courts in England. Nevertheless, no significant break-through was achieved until the case of Edward Hayes in November last, when a defendant who was not professionally represented was given the benefit of a statement of the law of insanity which went far beyond the narrow confines of M'Naghten.

In the interim *O'Brien's* case was followed by *Boylan*, [1937] IR, where the Court of Criminal Appeal again reserved for further consideration the question whether, if irresistible impulse were established, it would afford any defence to the charge of murder. Curiously enough, Mr Justice O'Byrne, who had been a member of the Court of Criminal Appeal in *O'Brien's* case, was the trial judge in *Boylan's* case, and interposed, when defence counsel referred to irresistible impulse in addressing the jury, to say that irresistible impulse was no defence. As in *O'Brien's* case, however, the Court of Criminal Appeal held in *Boylan* that there was no evidence on which the jury could have found that the accused was incapable of controlling his acts, and consequently they were not required to decide whether such a defence was known to the law.

The outcome was again the same in *Manning*, 89 ILTR 155, in 1954, when an appeal was taken from a conviction for murder on the ground *(inter alia) that the trial judge was wrong in law in not leaving the defence of irresistible impulse to the jury*. In the absence of any evidence to support the defence the Court rejected the appeal, leaving over the question as to the availability of the defence of *irresistible impulse in law for a suitable occasion "if and when it arises"*. The same course was taken by the Court of Criminal Appeal in the unreported case of *A-G v McGrath* in 1960.

The next attempt to bring about a *confrontation between the Irish Courts and M'Naghten* was made in the case of *A-G v Michael McGlynn*, one of the rare cases where the plea of insanity was raised by way of defence to an indictable offence other than murder. The accused was tried on charges under the Larceny Act, 1916, in the Circuit Court in Co Kerry. A plea of insanity was raised on his behalf, and counsel for the defence contended that the trial judge, in directing the jury on the law relating to the plea, should not put it to them on the basis of the M'Naghten Rules, but in accordance with a new formula devised and put into effect in some of the Courts in the United States.

The trial judge (the President of the Circuit Court) stated a case for the opinion of the Supreme Court as to whether it was appropriate for him to direct the jury in accordance with the M'Naghten Rules, or if not, what directions should be given to the jury on the present *law of insanity*. The trial of the accused was suspended in the meantime.

The Supreme Court, however, decided that there was no jurisdiction to state a case once the prisoner had been given in charge of the jury on a criminal trial on indictment. It then ceased to be "a matter pending before a Circuit Court Judge" as referred to in Sec 16 of the Courts of Justice Act, 1947, dealing with the power to state a case from the Circuit Court to the Supreme Court. Accordingly the issue as to insanity remained unresolved, as it had previously done in the cases of *O'Brien, Boylan, Manning and McGrath.*

In other common law jurisdictions, however, dissatisfaction with the M'Naghten Rules had come to a head in a more positive manner. Developments in the United States were foreshadowed by the evidence given by Mr Justice Frankfurter before the Royal Commission into Capital Punishment, 1949–53. He said:

> "The M'Naghten Rules were rules which the Judges, in response to questions by the House of Lords, formulated in the light of the then existing psychological knowledge . . . I do not see why rules of law should be arrested at the state of psychological knowledge of the time when they were formulated . . . if you find rules that are, broadly speaking, discredited by those who have to administer them, which is, I think, the real situation, certainly with us – they are honoured in the breach and not in the observance – then I think the law serves its best interests by trying to be more honest about it . . . I think that to have rules which cannot rationally be justified except by a process of interpretation which distorts and often practically nullifies them, and to say the corrective process comes by having the Governor of a State charged with the responsibility of deciding when the consequences of the rule should not be enforced, is not a desirable system . . . I am a great believer in being as candid as possible about institutions. They are in large measure abandoned in practice, and therefore I think the M'Naghten Rules are in large measure shams. That is a strong word, but I think the M'Naghten Rules are very difficult for conscientious people and not difficult enough for people who say 'We'll just juggle them' . . . I dare to believe that we ought not to rest content with the difficulty of finding an improvement in the M'Naghten Rules . . ."

The Commission agreed: "In our view the test of criminal responsibility contained in the M'Naghten Rules cannot be defended in the light of modern medical knowledge. It is well established that there are offenders who know what they are doing and know that it is wrong (whether "wrong" is taken to mean legally *or* morally wrong) but are nevertheless so gravely affected by mental disease that they ought not to be held responsible for their actions. Examination of a number of individual cases in which a verdict of guilty but insane was returned, and rightly returned, has convinced us that there are few indeed where the accused can truly be said not to have known that his act was wrong."

Next followed the rejection of the McNaghten Rules as no longer adequate, by Judge David Bazelon (Chief Judge, US Court of Appeals for the District of Columbia Circuit) in the case of *Durham v United States*, 214 F 2d 862 (1954), in which he laid down the so-called "Durham Rule" – a new test of criminal responsibility.' It posited simply that an accused is not criminally responsible if his act was the product of mental disease or defect. The Court stated that "science of psychiatry now recognises that a man is an integrated personality and that reason, which is only one element in that personality, is not the sole determinant of behaviour".

The Durham Rule was considered in other States, and by the Federal Courts, but did not command as much support as might have been anticipated. Judge Bazelon explained this by suggesting that *Durham* touched an exposed nerve in the administration of criminal justice (Justice Stumbles on Science, *The Irish Jurist*, Vol 1, 1966, p 273.

A more significant development came with the decision of the United States Court of Appeals in New York in *United States v Freeman*, 357 F 2d 606 (1966). This is a decision of the court of the highest federal jurisdiction except for the Supreme Court of the United States, and is binding throughout the second federal circuit, comprising the states of New York, Vermont and Connecticut. It decided that the M'Naghten Rules should be abandoned as a test of criminal responsibility in cases where the sanity of the accused at the time of the commission of the offence was in issue, and should be replaced by a rule based on the American Law Institute's Model Penal Code.

Freeman had been convicted of selling narcotics and sentenced to five years' imprisonment. He was a drug addict and a confirmed alcoholic, and there was considerable psychiatric evidence as to impairment of his mental faculties. The trial jduge felt bound to follow the M'Naghten Rules, and did not consider the alternative Durham Rule. The Court of Appeal, however, ruled that it was not obliged to apply the M'Naghten test, being satisfied that the US Supreme Court had not ruled conclusively that M'Naghten was the true test of legal insanity.

The judgment of the Court was delivered by Judge Irving R. Kaufman, who accepted as correct the test of insanity formulated in the Model Penal Code, which runs as follows:

"A person is not responsible for criminal conduct if at the time of such conduct as a result of mental disease or defect he lacks substantial capacity either to appreciate the wrongfulness of his conduct or to conform his conduct to the requirements of the law."

He declared that the M'Naghten Rules "are not in harmony with modern medical science which is opposed to any concept which divides the mind into separate compartments – the intellect, the emotions and the will. The model penal code formulation views the mind as a unified entity and recognises that mental disease or defect may impair its functioning in numerous ways. The rule, moreover, reflects awareness that in the perspectives of psychiatry absolutes are ephemeral and gradations inevitable. By employing the telling word 'substantial' to modify 'incapacity' the rule emphasizes that any incapacity is not sufficient to justify avoidance of criminal responsibility, but that total incapacity is also unnecessary. The choice of the word 'appreciate' rather than 'know', in the first branch of the test also is significant. Mere intellectual awareness that conduct is wrongful, when divorced from appreciation or understanding of the moral or legal import of behaviour, can have little significance."

By this decision an important branch of the US Courts has moved away from the unreal world of the M'Naghten Rules into which, in the words of Baron Bramwell, hardly anyone was ever mad enough to gain admission. The same distinguished judge had advocated that every insane accused who broke the law should be convicted if he would not have yielded to his criminal impulse had there been a policeman at his elbow. Only the commonsense of the juryman has intervened between the lunatic and the rigour of this rule of law. Lord Cooper told the Royal Commission of 1953: "However much you charge a jury as to the M'Naghten Rules or any other test, the question they would put to themselves when they retire is: 'Is this man mad or is he not?'"

The foregoing survey of some of the major developments in the law of insanity in this country and in England and the United States may serve to highlight the importance of the case of Edward Hayes, referred to at the outset. It may well represent the adoption by the Courts generally in this country of a more enlightened approach to the issue of insanity in the criminal law courts than would be possible if the Courts continued to operate strictly within the confines of the M'Naghten Rules. Hayes, as already stated, was not professionally represented, but it should be pointed out that counsel for the Attorney-General, Mr A J Hederman, SC, in opening the case to the jury, put the issue of mental capacity to them on the basis subsequently adopted by the trial judge in his charge to the jury.

He also made submissions to the trial Judge, on behalf of the Attorney-General, as to the form in which the issue of insanity should be left to the jury and adopted the formula suggested by Sir James Stephen in his Digest of the Criminal Law to the following effect: "No act is a crime if the person who does it, at the time when it is done, is prevented, either by defective mental power or by any disease affecting his mind (a) from knowing the nature and quality of his act or (b) from knowing that the act is wrong, or (c) from controlling his own conduct, unless the absence of the power of control has been produced by his own default."

Mr Justice Henchy gave a considered judgment in relation to these submissions in which he reviewed the historical development of the defence of insanity. In relation to the question whether the third test suggested by Sir James Stephen (which goes outside the ambit of the M'Naghten Rules) should be left to the jury, he said:

"Now it seems to me that I should take the jury's verdict on that matter, on that ground, and I so decide, for this broad reason, that the essence of guilt, in a case such as this, is not alone that the accused man should have committed the act complained of, but that he should have done it with a guilty mind or that he should have *mens rea*.

"In the normal case, tried in accordance with the M'Naghten Rules, the test is solely one of knowledge: Did he know the nature and quality of his act or did he know that the act was wrong? The rules do not take into account the capacity of a man on the basis of his knowledge to act or to refrain from acting, and I believe it to be correct psychiatric science to accept that certain serious mental diseases, such as paranoia or schizophrenia, in certain cases enable a man to understand the morality or immorality of his act or the legality or illegality of it, or the nature and quality of it, but nevertheless prevent him from exercising a free volition as to whether he should or should not do that act.

"In the present case the medical witnesses are unanimous in saying that the accused man was, in medical terms, insane at the time of the act. However, legal insanity does not necessarily coincide with what medical men would call insanity, but if it is open to the jury to say, as say they must, on the evidence, that this man understood the nature and quality of his act, and understood its wrongfulness, morally and legally, but that nevertheless he was debarred from refraining from assaulting his wife fatally because of a defect of reason, due to his mental illness, it seems to me that it would be unjust, in the circumstances of this case, not to allow the jury to consider the case on those grounds."

What is achieved by the *Durham* and *Freeman* cases in the US and by the *Hayes* case in Ireland is a more acceptable assessment of the forms of mental abnormality which should afford exemption from criminal responsibility. This, of course, stops far short of providing a solution for the problems created by insanity in the criminal law field. The Court of Appeals which decided *Freeman* added the following comment to its judgment:

"We recognise our liability to determine at this point whether society possesses sufficient hospital facilities and doctors to deal with criminals who are found to be incompetent. But our function as judges requires us to interpret the law in the best interest of society as a whole. We therefore suggest that if there are inadequate facilities and personnel in this area, Congress, the state legislatures and federal and state executive departments should promptly consider bridging the gap." 357 F 2d at p 618.

Dr A Whitlock, in his work on criminal responsibility already referred to, was franker still in recognising not only the inadequacy of the facilities provided for treatment of social delinquents, but also the inability of medical science itself to cope with many of its problems in this particular sphere. He states: "There is nothing in current therapeutics to suggest that psychiatrists have particularly effective techniques in dealing with the socially deviant even when these methods are applied to those who have some measure of explicit mental abnormality, as in the case of the psychopathic offender."

With the virtual abolition of the death penalty in this country by the Criminal Justice Act, 1964, and in England by the Murder (Abolition of Death Penalty) Act, 1965, the plea of insanity has ceased to feature as an attempt on the part of the accused to cheat the gallows, aided and abetted by psychiatric evidence which was often regarded with doubt and suspicion by judges and public alike. We are thus free to consider, in a more normal atmosphere, the bearing of mental abnormality on criminal responsibility generally and one is conscious of a growing awareness of the need for more intensive research into the causes for socially deviant behaviour, and of the need for the provision of suitable institutions and courses of treatment to deal with it.

We in Ireland have certainly been laggards in these fields. The Commission of Inquiry on Mental Illness has recommended the establishment of a Department of Forensic Psychiatry. With the recognition by the Courts that more and more of the persons who come before them accused of offences should not be regarded as criminally responsible because of the presence of the element of mental abnormality, the problem of dealing with such cases is bound to become more acute and may help to create the conditions of urgency which alone appear to be capable of propelling our legislators into action.

ADDENDUM

Since the above article was written the plea of insanity was again raised in the trial of James Coughlan on a charge of murder, before Mr Justice Kenny and a jury in the Central Criminal Court. The State case was that Coughlan had attacked a 12-year-old boy and his eight-year-old sister while they were walking beside a stream at Ballyclough, Co Limerick; had knocked them into the river and had held the boy under the water until he drowned.

The trial judge was asked by defence counsel, Mr Thomas Finlay, SC, to leave the issue of insanity to the jury in the same form in which it had been dealt with in the *Hayes* case.

Mr Justice Kenny is reported to have given as his view that the issue for the jury in any case where the plea of insanity was relied upon was the following – 'Was the act caused by disease of the mind?' The course he proposed to take was to leave that broad general issue to the jury, while stating by way of example of acts so caused by disease of the mind which exempted from criminal responsibility the three cases cited by Sir James Stephen – these being cases where the accused did not know the nature or the quality of the act, or did not know that what he was doing was wrong, or was prevented by defective mental power or by any disease affecting his mind from controlling his own conduct, unless the absence of the power of control was produced by his own default.

A verdict of guilty but insane was returned by the jury after an absence of ten minutes. (*The Irish Times*, 28th June 1968).

The approach of Kenny J to the problem appears, if anything, to go further than that of Henchy J in the *Hayes* case, since it does not necessarily confine the defence of insanity even within the bounds of the three tests laid down by Sir James

Stephen, but recognises the possibility of a valid defence of insanity being raised even in a case which does not appear to fall strictly within the Stephen formula.

Modern Approach

4.111   In *Doyle v Wicklow County Council*[45] the Supreme Court substantially adopted Professor O'Hanlon's analysis.

4.112   ***Doyle v Wicklow County Council***
                                          [1974] IR 55
                                       Supreme Court, 1973

Facts: This case concerned an application for compensation under the Criminal Injury Code. A seventeen year old youth set fire to and burned an abattoir but there was evidence that the youth was suffering from a mental disorder. Certain questions were submitted by way of case stated to the Supreme Court which resulted in that court considering the correct test for the defence of insanity in a criminal trial which was held to be the standard applicable in such an application.

Medical evidence was presented that the youth was suffering from a mental disorder which led him to believe that for setting fire to the abattoir he should not be charged or punished, although he knew his act was one forbidden by society or contrary to law. His reason for this belief was his love of animals, to the killing of which he was very much opposed. He had a conviction that humans did not need animals for food and that they should not be killed.

Griffin J: . . . Neither this Court nor its predecessor, the Supreme Court of Justice, has had to decide the extent to which the McNaghten rules apply or whether they are the sole and exclusive test for determining the insanity of an accused person.

Whilst insanity has always exempted from criminal responsibility a person doing an act which would otherwise be a crime, the approach of the courts and writers to the question of insanity has become less rigid with the passage of time, as might be expected.

In my opinion, the McNaghten rules do not provide the sole or exclusive test for determining the sanity or insanity of an accused. The questions put to the judges were limited to the effect of insane delusions and I would agree with the opinion expressed by the Court of Criminal Appeal in *Attorney General v O'Brien*[46] that the opinions given by the judges must be read with the like specific limitation.

The questions and answers were also directed to *knowledge*, and this matter was considered by Mr Justice Henchy in *The People (Attorney General) v Hayes* (Central Criminal Court – 30th November, 1967).

In that case the accused was charged with the murder of his wife. Submissions were made by counsel on behalf of the Attorney General as to the form in which the issue of insanity should be left to the jury, and in the course of his considered judgment in relation to these submissions Henchy J said:— "In the normal case, tried in accordance with the McNaghten rules, the test is solely one of knowledge: did he know the nature and quality of his act or did he know that the act was wrong? The rules do not take into account the capacity of a man on the basis of his knowledge to act or to refrain from acting and I believe it to be correct psychiatric science to accept that certain serious mental diseases, such as paranoia or schizophrenia, in certain cases enable a man to understand the morality or immorality of his act or the legality or illegality of it, or the nature and quality of it,

45 [1974] IR 55.
46 [1936] IR 263.

but nevertheless prevent him from exercising a free volition as to whether he should or should not do that act. In the present case the medical witnesses are unanimous in saying that the accused man was, in medical terms, insane at the time of the act. However, legal insanity does not necessarily coincide with what medical men would call insanity, but if it is open to the jury to say, as say they must, on the evidence, that this man understood the nature and quality of his act, and understood its wrongfulness, morally and legally, but that nevertheless he was debarred from refraining from assaulting his wife fatally because of a defect of reason, due to his mental illness, it seems to me that it would be unjust, in the circumstances of this case, not to allow the jury to consider the case on those grounds." I would adopt what was said by Mr Justice Henchy as being a correct statement of the law on this matter.

Code Options

4.113 *Model Penal Code*

Mental Disease or Defect Excluding Responsibility
4.01 (1) A person is not responsible for criminal conduct if at the time of such conduct as a result of mental disease or defect he lacks substantial capacity either to appreciate the criminality (wrongfulness) of his conduct or to conform his conduct to the requirements of the law.

(2) As used in this article, the terms "mental disease or defect" do not include an abnormality manifested only by repeated criminal or otherwise anti-social conduct.

4.114 *Law Reform Commission of Canada Draft Criminal Code, 1986*

No one is liable for his conduct if, through disease or defect of the mind, he was at the time incapable of appreciating the nature, consequences or legal wrongfulness of such conduct.

4.115 *Canadian Criminal Code*

16 (1) No person shall be convicted of an offence in respect of an act or omission on his part while that person was insane.

(2) For the purposes of this section, a person is insane when the person is in a state of natural imbecility or has disease of the mind to an extent that renders the person incapable of appreciating the nature and quality of an act or omission or of knowing that the act or omission is wrong.

(3) A person who has specific delusions, but is in other respects sane, shall not be acquitted on the ground of insanity unless the delusions caused that person to believe in the existence of a state of things that, if it existed, would have justified or excused the act or omission of that person.

(4) Everyone shall, until the contrary is proved, be presumed to be and to have been sane.

Further Materials

4.116 Stuart *Canadian Criminal Law: A Treatise* (2nd edition, 1987) p 316–373.
Fingarette *Diminished Mental Capacity as a Criminal Law Defence* (1974) 37 MLR 264.
Dell *Wanted: An Insanity Defence that can be used* [1983] Crim LR 431.
Wells *Whither Insanity?* [1983] Crim LR 787.
Wasik *Codification: Mental Disorder and Intoxication under the Draft Criminal Code* [1986] 50 JCL 393.

Automatism

4.117   The defence of insanity is concerned with the consciousness of the accused while committing the act. The defence of automatism is concerned with whether or not that act was voluntary. It is a basic principle of criminal law that a person cannot be made criminally responsible unless there was an alternative course of action open to him; *Kilbride v Lake*[47]. An alternative course of action is not open to a person who, although he may be dimly aware of what he is doing, has no control over his actions. Obvious examples include the driver who is attacked by a swarm of bees, the sleepwalker and the person precipitated into a state of unconsciousness through the forced administration of drugs.

In early law the principle that a crime had to be committed voluntarily was established, though left undeveloped. Hale indicates that if a man is forced to kill another by his arm being taken while it is holding a weapon and struck against the victim, he is not guilty[48]. The exploration of the functions of the mind which took place over the last century indicated that, apart from insanity, a person might cause the external element of a crime by an involuntary action precipitated inside his organism. The defence of automatism requires that the action of the accused was done by his body without any control by his mind; *Bratty v A-G for Northern Ireland*[49]; *R v Rabey*[50]; *R v Radford*[51].

4.118   Clearly, where the involuntary conduct was caused by the fault of the accused, for example, in taking alcohol or drugs, he must rely on the defence of intoxication; *R v Lipman*[52]; (see paras **4.81–4.82**).

4.119   Reasons of policy have dictated a substantial qualification to the defence of automatism which, as it is interpreted in England, amounts almost to a negation of the defence. If the involuntary action of the accused is caused by an internal factor, it should be characterised within the classification of insanity; *Bratty v A-G for Northern Ireland*[53]. Transient states caused by external factors are more properly described as automatism; *R v Quick*[54]. A mental disorder which manifests itself in violence and which is prone to recur is classified as a disease of the mind; *Bratty v A-G for Northern Ireland*[55]. Automatism is, therefore, strictly caused by external factors. These external factors will be discounted if they amount only to the ordinary stresses and disappointments of life, such as disappointment in love or marital stress; *R v Rabey*[56]; *R v T*[57].

47 [1962] NZLR 590.
48 1 Hale pc 434.
49 [1963] AC 386 at 401, 409.
50 (1980) 15 CR (3d) 225.
51 (1985) 20 A Crim R 388.
52 [1970] 1 QB 152.
53 [1963] AC 386.
54 [1973] QB 910.
55 [1963] AC 386.
56 [1980] 15 Cr (3d) 225.
57 [1990] Crim LR 256.

4.120 The distinction between the defences of insanity and automatism has become crucial in cases where diabetics claim the defence of automatism for crimes committed while suffering the effects of either hypoglycaemia (low blood-sugar level) or hyperglycaemia (high blood-sugar level) and has resulted in somewhat artificial distinctions being drawn by the English Courts.

4.121 In *R v Quick*[58], self-administered insulin injections were held to be an external factor which should have resulted in the issue of automatism being left to the jury. This, however, ignores the underlying condition which necessitated the injections.

4.122 In *R v Hennessy*[59] the Court of Appeal placed the emphasis on the underlying condition of hyperglycaemia and held it to be "M'Naughten insanity". The distinction relied upon was that the external factor in *R v Quick*[60], lowering the blood-sugar level, might have been the insulin injections administered earlier in the day, whereas the high blood-sugar level in cases of hyperglycaemia was caused by an inherent defect which, when not corrected by insulin, was a disease. If this disease then causes a malfunction of the mind, the case may fall within the M'Naughten rules. The court held that the stress, anxiety and depression resulting from employment and marital problems, to which the defendant attributed his condition, could no doubt be the result of external factors but that they were not in themselves, either separately or collectively, external factors of the kind capable in law of causing or contributing to a state of automatism. In this the court relied on the House of Lords idea of external factors in *R v Sullivan*[61] per Lord Diplock: ". . . some external physical factor such as a blow on the head causing concussion or the administration of an anaesthetic for therapeutic purposes". Stress, anxiety and depression constitute a state of mind which is prone to recur and they lack the feature of novelty or accident which is the basis of Lord Diplock's definition.

4.123 In *R v Bailey*[62] the court addressed the issue of self-induced automatism. If a diabetic fails to take food after an insulin injection and as a result of the hypoglycaemic condition which results he commits an assault, he will have a valid defence of automatism to a crime of basic intent, as defined in *DPP v Majewski*[63] (see para **4.84**) unless the prosecution can prove the necessary degree of recklessness. This would require proof that the diabetic appreciated, not only that he might lose consciousness but that such a failure might lead to aggressive, unpredictable and uncontrollable conduct and he nevertheless deliberately runs the risk or otherwise disregards it.

58 [1973] QB 910.
59 [1989] 2 All ER 9.
60 [1973] QB 910.
61 [1984] AC 156 at 172.
62 [1983] 2 All ER 503.
63 [1977] AC 443.

4.124 *R v Falconer*
(1989) 46 A Crim R 83
Court of Criminal Appeal Western Australia, 1989

Facts: The accused was the wife of the deceased. Her evidence was that he was a violent man. In January 1988 Mrs Falconer discovered that he was pursuing another woman. In July 1988 she discovered that one of her daughters had been abused by the deceased while she was between the ages of 7 and 15. She then learned that her youngest daughter had also been subjected to sexual interference. On the 18th August she obtained a non-molestation order from the local court. The deceased became violent as a consequence. Following an apparent legal settlement the accused occupied the family home. She was, however, terrified of her husband's return and took stringent precautions to ensure that he could not enter the house. On the 2nd October 1988 he came to take possession of certain personal items. When he was not handed the bolts to his rifles he hit the accused. He offered to return to the house on Sunday the 9th October 1988 to fix some tiles which had apparently become dislodged in a storm. By this stage the accused was half her normal weight, was physically and emotionally drained and had become obsessive in her fear of her husband. When he came to the house as he had indicated the accused shot him dead. She later told the police that she must have shot her husband. But she did not remember how it happened save that he was laughing at her and had reached out for her hair. Evidence was given indicating that she had, at the time of the killing, been in a disassociative state which amounted to non-insane automatism. The Court of Criminal Appeal indicated that the issue of voluntariness should have been left to the jury.

Malcolm CJ: . . . . The issue sought to be raised at the trial was whether, at the time the shooting occurred, the appellant was not acting voluntarily but was in a state of automatism, although she was completely sane. The foundation for this issue is s 23 of the *Criminal Code* (WA) which provides that:

"Subject to the express provisions of this Code relating to negligent acts and omissions, a person is not criminally responsible for an act or omission which occurs independently of the exercise of his will, or for an event which occurs by accident.

Unless the intention to cause a particular result is expressly declared to be an element of the offence constituted, in whole or part, by an act or omission, the result intended to be caused by an act or omission is immaterial.

Unless otherwise expressly declard, the motive by which a person is induced to do or omit to do an act, or to form an intention, is immaterial so far as regards criminal responsibility."

The state of automatism which is not the product of a disease of the mind is variously referred to as non-insane automatism, sane automatism, disassociative or dissociative automatism or disassociative or dissociative or disassociated state. Dr Schioldann-Nielsen, a psychiatrist with specialist experience in forensic psychiatry gave evidence that in such a state the person acts involuntarily. He also said that the state could occur suddenly in previously normal people who have been exposed to sharply occurring emotional strain, or stress, or any trauma. Dr Schioldann-Nielsen was of the opinion that the appellant was sane at all material times. He had first seen the appellant the day after the shooting. In his opinion the progressive worsening of the appellant's distress and general mental state in the period leading up to the day of the shooting, the physical attack on her by Mr Falconer and his sexual advance to her on that day, coupled with his taunt that "the court won't believe the girls; won't believe you and the girls", could have caused the appellant to panic. Dr Schioldann-Nielsen said "that could have been the mechanism which released the full-blown disassociative state, so to speak". In his opinion, the appellant's description of what then happened and her recitation of the events "could be fully consistent with a person in such a disorder" (that is, in a dissassociative state). Dr Schioldann-Nielsen did not proffer any opinion as to what may have in fact occurred because he was not there.

Dr Finlay-Jones had recently examined the appellant and found her to be sane. He substantially agreed with the evidence of Dr Schioldann-Nielsen. Dr Finlay-Jones was of opinion that automatism could be induced by an external force such as a blow on the head. He was also of opinion that psychological factors could act as an external force to cause automatic behaviour, and that such behaviour could also be caused without any evidence of internal or external stress. In the case of the appellant there was evidence of more than psychological stress; there was evidence of conflict. Based on the appellant's account of the events leading up to her husband's death on 9 October 1988. Dr Finlay-Jones noted that the appellant said her husband had laughed at her saying: "They won't believe you and the girls because they did not believe Erin." Dr Finlay-Jones regarded that as "crucial". It was "the third and perhaps the most immediate example of something she could no longer really dodge, that her husband was sexually corrupt". This was evidence of severe stress, combined with evidence of conflict because the appellant still loved her husband. As Dr Finlay-Jones described it:

"I think she was faced with an intolerable dilemma at that moment, that on the one hand it is undeniable that he is, to use her words: 'a filthy bastard and yet I love him. Possibly by extension that makes me filthy too.' She is faced with what I would call a psychological conflict, I think it is in that setting of psychological conflict that a person is capable of losing control of the mind, of acting – perhaps quite briefly – in an automatic way. I think that her inability to remember what happened next is consistent with that."

As to the psychological conflict, Dr Finlay-Jones said that Mr Falconer's behaviour, as the appellant recounted it, also acted, in his opinion, to put her into conflict. As she described it on that day he was at one moment polite, kind, and considerate to her. Then he would suddenly switch and try to hit her, or yell abuse at her. He would then act frightened and say he did not want to go to gaol and appear to be different yet again. According to Dr Finlay-Jones, the appellant's description of what happened when her recollection returned and how she felt was consistent with the reports of people who have been in disassociated states. Such persons are seemingly conscious but mentally unaware. In that particular way the mind of a person in a disassociated state does not go with his or her act.

Having heard the evidence the learned Commissioner made the following finding:

"I have reviewed this evidence given by the doctors because it is essential to a determination on whether the evidence of automatism should be left to the jury. It seems to me clear that the evidence of the doctors that there was no external factor or factors in evidence on 9 October 1988 which caused the psychological conflict within the accused, which was capable of causing her to act in an automatic way."

The learned Commissioner considered that, once he had made that finding, he was bound on the authorities to rule that, in the absence of evidence of any external factor, the evidence of stress, anxiety and depression were not separately or together capable in law of causing or contributing to a state of automatism. The relevant authorities referred to by the learned Commissioner were *Tsigos* [1965] NSWR 1607; *Joyce* [1970] SASR 184; *Isitt* (1977) 67 Cr App R 44; *Sullivan* [1984] AC 156; (1983) 77 Cr App R 176; and *Hennessy* [1989] 1 WLR 287; [1989] 2 All ER 9. In particular, the learned Commissioner referred to the following passage in the judgment of the Lord Chief Justice, Lord Lane in *Hennessy* (at 294; 14):

"In our judgment, stress, anxiety and depression can no doubt be the result of the operation of external factors, but they are not, it seems to us, in themselves separately or together external factors of the kind capable of law of causing or contributing to a state of automatism. They constitute a state of mind which is prone to recur. They lack the feature of novelty or accident, which is the basis of the distinction drawn by Lord Diplock in *Sullivan* (at 156, 172; 177, 182). It is contrary to the observations of Devlin J, to which we have just referred in *Hill v Baxter* [1958] 1 QB 277 at 285; (1957) 42 Cr App R 51 at 59. It does not, in our judgment, come within the scope of the exception of some external physical factor such as a blow on the head or the administration of an anaesthetic."

The learned Commissioner rejected a submission by counsel for the appellant that the external factors referred to in *Hennessy* and the other cases mentioned, were not limited to factors such as a blow on the head and that the factors in play in the present case were in truth external, rather than internal. Counsel had relied on the note of *Wiseman* (1972) 46 ALJ 412, in which automatism had been left to the jury in circumstances where the accused had suffered a series of shattering emotional experiences, which had brought her mind to a disassociative state.

The learned Commissioner concluded:

"I cannot regard the report of *Wiseman* as being sufficient authority for Mr Singleton's proposition. In my opinion, the statements in *Sullivan* and in *Hennessy* make it clear that in the present case the accused's disassociative state, if it existed, was a consequence of entirely internal factors and not external factors. The evidence of Dr Finlay-Jones was really to that effect. I consider myself, then, bound by authority to rule that automatism is not open as a defence in this case."

Counsel for the appellant made two submissions. First, he submitted that there were in fact external factors at play in the present case, which justified the issue of automatism being left to the jury. Secondly, he submitted that on the authorities the question whether an act was voluntary or not was a question of fact and that if a state of automatism could, as a matter of fact, be induced by factors other than external factors, the authorities which held that factors other than external which induced a state of automatism were not capable in law of causing or contributing to a state of automatism should not be followed.

The reason for the distinction between the external factors and internal factors in the context of automatism is to be found in the application of the definition of legal insanity in the M'Naghten Rules as stated in *M'Naghten*'s case (1843) 10 Cl & Fin 200; 8 ER 718. The M'Naghten Rules are:

1. "Every man is presumed to be sane, and to possess a sufficient degree of reason to be responsible for his crimes, until the contrary be proved to the satisfaction of the jury."
2. "To establish a defence on the ground of insanity, it must be clearly proved that, at the time of the committing of the act, the party accused was labouring under such a defect of reason, from disease of the mind, as not to know the nature and quality of the act he was doing, or, if he did know it, that he did not know what he was doing was wrong."

These rules are reflected in ss 26 and 27 of the *Criminal Code*. These sections are as follows:

"26. Every person is presumed to be of sound mind, and to have been of sound mind at any time which comes in question, until the contrary is proved.
27. A person is not criminally responsible for an act or omission if at the time of doing the act or making the omission he is in such a state of mental disease or natural mental infirmity as to deprive him of capacity to under-

stand what he is doing, or of capacity to control his actions, or of capacity to know that he ought not to do the act or make the omission.

A person whose mind, at the time of his doing or omitting to do an act, is affected by delusions on some specific matter or matters, but who is not otherwise entitled to the benefit of the foregoing provisions of this section, is criminally responsible for the act or omission to the same extent as if the real state of things had been such as he was induced by the delusions to believe to exist."

The principal difference between the M'Naghten Rules and the Code provisions is that unlike s 27 of the Code the M'Naghten Rules contain no reference to the capacity of an accused to control his or her actions: *Wray* (1930) 33 WALR 67.

In the context of automatism, if the accused did not know the nature and quality of his act because of something other than a defect of reason from disease of the mind, then his act may not be properly described as voluntary. In such a case he would be entitled to be acquitted on the ground that the Crown had failed to prove beyond a reasonable doubt that the relevant act was voluntary. This is the significance of non-insane automatism. If the failure to realise the nature and quality of the act was due to a defect of reason from disease of the mind, then according to the M'Naghten Rules, the accused would be not guilty, but insane: see s 2 of the *Trial of Lunatics Act* 1883 (UK) as amended by the *Criminal Procedure (Insanity) Act* 1964 (UK). This is the signficance of insane automatism: see *Bratty v A-G (Northern Ireland)* [1963] AC 386 at 409–410; (1961) 46 Cr App R 1 at 16–18 per Lord Denning is approved and explained by Barwick CJ in *Ryan* (1967) 121 CLR 205 at 215; cf *Hennessy* (at 291; 12) per Lane LCJ.

The rationale of the distinction lies in the need to protect the community from the recurrent conduct of persons suffering from a disease of the mind. As Lord Diplock said in *Sullivan* (at 172; 182):

"I agree with what was said by Devlin J in *Kemp* [1957] 1 QB 399 at 407; (1956) 40 Cr App R 121 at 127–128, that 'mind' in the M'Naghten Rules is used in the ordinary sense of the mental faculties of reason, memory and understanding. If the effect of a disease is to impair these faculties so severely as to have either of the consequences referred to in the latter part of the rules, it matters not whether the aetiology of the impairment . . . itself is permanent or is transient and intermittent, provided that it subsisted at the time of commission of the act."

This explains why in so many cases the question is whether the function of the mind was disturbed by disease, being an internal factor, or by some external factor. The distinction is highlighted by reference to the facts in *Hennessy* and those in the earlier decision in *Quick* [1973] QB 910; (1973) 57 Cr App R 722. In *Hennessy* the accused suffered from diabetes which, unless his level of blood sugar was kept down by insulin, meant he was likely to suffer from hyperglycaemia causing impairment of awareness leading to coma. That likelihood would be increased by anxiety or stress. In *Hennessy*, notwithstanding the accused's depression and marital troubles, which had caused stress and anxiety it was held that the hyperglycaemia was a disease which affected the mind of the accused. In *Quick* a similar mental condition was found to be not due to diabetes, but to the use by the accused of insulin, which was an external factor. As Lawton LJ explained (at 922–923; 734–736):

"A malfunctioning of the mind of transitory effect caused by the application to the body of some external factor such as violence, drugs, including anaesthetics, alcohol and hypnotic influences cannot fairly be said to be due to disease. Such malfunctioning, unlike that caused by a defect of reason from disease of the mind, will not always relieve an accused from criminal responsibility . . . In this case Quick's alleged mental condition, if it ever existed, was not caused by his diabetes but by his use of the insulin prescribed by his doctor. Such malfunctioning of his mind as there was, was caused by an external factor and not by a bodily disorder in the nature of a disease which disturbed the working of his mind. It follows in our judgment that Quick was entitled to have his defence of automatism left to the jury and that Bridge J's ruling as to the effect of the medical evidence called by him was wrong."

The English cases no doubt reflect the common law, but I have difficulty with the proposition that any particular factor which expert medical evidence suggests may cause or contribute to automatism should be left incapable in law of causing or contributing to automatism. There are, however, cases in which the issue of non-insane automatism induced by psychological disturbance or emotional stress has been left to the jury. These include *Kay* (1970) 3 CCC (2d) 84; *Wiseman* (1972) 46 ALJ 412; *Pantelic* (1974) 21 FLR 253; and *Sproule* (1975) 26 CCC (2d) 92.

The issue was considered by the Supreme Court of Canada in *Rabey* (1980) 54 CCC (2d) 1. In that case the appellant had been charged with causing bodily harm with intent to wound arising out of an incident in which one student hit another with a rock taken from a geology lab. The appellant raised automatism based on a pyschological blow which he was said to have suffered from reading a letter in which a girl to whom he was emotionally attached had referred to him as a "nothing". It was alleged that this, coupled with a meeting the next day in which the girl told him he was "only a friend", had produced a state of automatism. The expert evidence was not in agreement. The defence psychiatrist thought he had been in "a dissociative state" at the time of the attack, which was not a disease of the mind and was not likely to recur. The Crown's expert thought the appellant was simply in a state of rage. He was of the view, however, that if he had "dissociated" at the time he was suffering from a disease of the mind because the "dissociative state" was a subdivision of hysterical neurosis which was a mental illness. The trial judge, sitting without a jury, acquitted the appellant on the ground that there was a reasonable doubt concerning the state of automatism.

The Crown appealed to the Ontario Court of Appeal, which allowed the appeal and ordered a new trial: *Rabey* (1977) 37 CCC (2d) 461. The judgment of the court was delivered by Martin JA who (at 477–478) drew the distinction between insanity and sane automatism as follows:

"In general, the distinction to be drawn is between a malfunctioning of the mind arising from some cause that is primarily internal to the accused, having its source in his psychological or emotional make-up, or in some organic pathology, as opposed to a malfunctioning of the mind, which is the transient effect produced by some specified external factor such as, for example, concussion. Any malfunctioning of the mind, or mental disorder having its source primarily in some subjective condition or weakness internal to the accused (whether fully understood or not) may be a 'disease of the mind' if it prevents the accused from knowing what he is doing, but transient disturbances of consciousness due to certain specific external factors do not fall within the concept of disease of the mind."

Martin JA said (at 482):

"In my view, the ordinary stresses and disappointments of life which are the common lot of mankind do not constitute an external cause constituting an explanation for malfunctioning of the mind which takes it out of the category of a 'disease of the mind'."

Martin JA accepted that on the facts the "dissociative state" arose because of disease of the mind and that automatism should not have been considered. He then said (at 482):

"I leave aside, until it becomes necessary to decide them, cases where a dissociative state has resulted from emotional shock without physical injury, resulting from such causes, for example, as being involved in a serious accident although no physical injury has resulted; being the victim of a murderous attack with an uplifted knife . . . seeing a loved one murdered or seriously assaulted . . . Such extraordinary external events might reasonably be presumed to affect the average normal person without reference to the subjective make-up of the person exposed to such experience."

On appeal to the Supreme Court of Canada in *Rabey*, the majority judgment was delivered by Ritchie J who approved of the approach adopted by Martin JA. The minority judgment delivered by Dickson J also appears to have accepted the distinction drawn by Martin JA. Dickson J stressed that the accused had not raised the issue of insanity and was entitled to rely on the presumption of sanity. Because the accused had issued involuntariness the burden was on the Crown to show insanity. The finding of insanity was reached in the absence of pathological symptoms of any previously existing or ongoing psychiatric disorder. On the medical evidence accepted by the trial judge the prospect of recurrence of "dissociation" was extremely remote. There was no finding of any psychosis, neurosis or personality disorder. Dealing with the question of psychological blow (at 28) Dickson J said:

"I cannot accept the notion that an extraordinary external event, that is, an intense emotional shock, can cause a state of dissociation or automatism, if and only if all normal persons . . . would react in that way. If I understand the quoted passage correctly, an objective standard is contemplated for one of the possible causes of automatism, namely, psychological blow, leaving intact the subjective standard for other causes of automatism, such as physical blow, or reaction to drugs."

Dickson J (at 29) pointed out that if X has a brittle skull and sustains a concussion which causes him to run amok he has a valid defence of automatism. So too, where he has an irregular metabolism which has induced an unanticipated and violent reaction to a drug. If a subjective standard is applied in these cases, why not in psychological blow situations? Dickson J accepted, however, that there must have been some kind of psychological shock. Consequently "dissociation" caused by a low stress threshold and surrender to anxiety could not fairly be said to result from a psychological blow. Likelihood of recurrence was not the decisive factor because: "A condition organic in nature, which causes an isolated act of unconscious violence could well be regarded as a case of temporary insanity." (See footnote 34 at 17.)

It seems that both the majority and the minority in *Rabey* recognised the possibility that a psychological blow which created extraordinary degree of emotional stress or shock or psychological disturbance could create a state of non-insane automatism.

Many of the relevant authorities were recently reviewed by King CJ in *Radford* (1985) 42 SASR 266 at 272–276; 20 A Crim R 388 at 394–397. As to the necessity of external factors King CJ said (at 276; 397–398):

"There is no reason in principle for making a distinction between disturbance of the mental faculties by reason of stress caused by external factors and disturbance of the mental faculties caused by the effects of physical trauma or somnambulism. The significant distinction is between the reaction of an unsound mind to its own delusions or to external stimuli on the one hand and the reaction of a sound mind to external stimuli, including stress producing factors, on the other hand. I appreciate that if it is true that a state of depersonalisation or disassociation is not itself a disease of the mind, although it may result from mental illness, the result may be that certain cases of unwilled acts which would formerly have been treated as the result of temporary insanity and would have founded verdicts of not guilty on the ground of insanity, will now result in outright acquittals. I do not see any reason to shrink from that consequence. The consequence of a verdict of not guilty by reason of insanity is detention during the Governor's pleasure. If a person was not morally responsible for the action which is the subject of the charge because the action was an unwilled automatic act, he should not suffer conviction or punishment. If he is not mentally ill and there is therefore no reason to suppose that the act will be repeated, detention for the protection of others is pointless and an embarrassment to the mental health authorities."

That is a passage with which I respectfully agree and which I adopt: see also *Hall* (1988) 36 A Crim R 368 at 371–372 per Roden J.

The difficulty with which the courts have been faced is the precise point of distinction between insane automatism the produce of a "mental disease" and non-insane automatism which is not. The existence of the distinction has been recognised in very many cases. In Queensland, where the Code provisions are identical to those in Western Australia it has been strongly suggested that in the context of automatism, there were not distinct defences of involuntariness and insanity, but only one relevant defence, namely, insanity: *Foy* [1960] Qd R 225 at 237–238 per Philp J. This view was based upon a wider view of "mental disease" which was derived from M Hale, *Pleas of the Crown* which was said to be unaffected by the M'Naghten Rules. Wanstall J (at 247) agreed with this part of the judgment of Philp J. These views were, however, obiter and difficult to reconcile with the recognition in the common law of the distinction between insane and non-insane automatism. The views so expressed were questioned by the majority in *Cooper v McKenna* [1960] Qd R 406 at 418–419 per Stable J, with whom Matthews J agreed. The historical approach by Philp J to the interpretation of "mental disease" was also criticised by the Court of Appeal in *Quick* (at 922; 734). The defence of non-insane automatism was recognised in England (albeit without enthusiasm) by a Court of Criminal Appeal constituted by five judges in *Harrison-Owen* [1951] 2 All ER 726 at 727–728 per Lord Goddard CJ. Where the defence was raised it was held that the issue of voluntariness should be left to the jury on the basis that the onus was on the Crown to prove the relevant act was voluntary. The defence was recognised in Western Australia in *Holmes* [1960] WAR 122 in a trial in which Jackson SPJ (as he then was) directed the jury on the issue of voluntariness under s 23 where automatism was raised. The accused was suffering from hardening of the arteries and a consequent reduction in the blood supply to the brain, exacerbated by stress. The jury were also directed to consider insanity even though that defence had been deliberately excluded by defence counsel. Jackson SPJ (at 125) gave as an example of non-insane automatism a person under the influence of an epileptic fit. This was contrary to what was said in *Foy* and inconsistent with the judgment of Stable J in *Cooper v McKenna* and the characterisation of psychomotor epilepsy in *Bratty v A-G (Northern Ireland)* [1963] AC 386; (1961) 46 Cr App R 1. These differences illustrate the difficulties involved in making the necessary distinctions: see R S O'Regan, "Automatism and Insanity Under the Australia State Criminal Codes" (1978) 52 ALJ 208; P Fairall, "Automatism" (1984) 8 Crim LJ 335; Lederman, "Non-insane and Insane Automatism: Reducing the Significance of a Problematic Distinction" (1985) 34 ICLJ 819.

In the present case the medical evidence was that the appellant was sane, although the question whether she was suffering from "mental disease" within the meaning of s 27 of the Code was not explored. For present purposes, I am prepared to assume that the defence raised should be classified as non-insane automatism and that a direction under s 23 only was appropriate, although further inquiry may have led to a direction under s 27.

At all events the evidence in this case was that:

(*a*) the appellant had separate from her husband for the reason, among others, that he had a history of using violence towards her, including hitting her and grabbing her by the hair;

(b) the appellant had recently discovered that her husband had sexually assaulted two of their daughters and this had caused her great stress;

(c) criminal charges had been preferred against the appellant's husband and she had shown an increasing level of fear at what he might do to her or to her daughters;

(d) in the week preceding the shooting she had demonstrated fear, depression, emotional disturbance and an apparently changed personality;

(e) on the day of the shooting, according to the appellant, her husband had
   (i) entered the appellant's house unexpectedly;
   (ii) sexually assaulted the appellant;
   (iii) demonstrated dramatic changes of mood;
   (iv) taunted her with the suggestion that neither the daughters nor the appellant would be believed in court; and
(v) reached out at her apparently to grab her by the hair.

From that point the appellant said she remembered nothing until she found herself on the floor with her shotgun by her and her husband dead on the floor nearby. The medical evidence was that on her account of the circumstances her conduct and behaviour before and after the shooting were consistent with a disassociative state or non-insane automatism.

It was a question of law for the learned Commissioner whether the evidence disclosed a sufficient foundation for the defence of automatism to be left to the jury. The relevant question was whether there was evidence upon which the jury would be entitled to entertain a reasonable doubt as to the voluntary quality of the act attributed to the accused: *Ryan* (at 217) per Barwick CJ; cf *Bratty v A-G (Northern Ireland)* [1963] AC 386; (1961) 46 Cr App R 1; *Hill v Baxter* [1958] 1 QB 277 at 285; (1957) 42 Cr App R 51 at 59, per Devlin J. It was submitted by counsel for the respondent that the evidence only disclosed the possibility that the appellant was acting in a disassociative state and that there was no expert evidence that at the time of the shooting the appellant was in such a state. The mere possibility that she was is not enough: *Tsigos* [1965] NSWR 1607 at 1609 per Walsh J; and at 1631 per Moffit J; *Foy* [1960] Qd R 225 at 239 per Philp J; and *Joyce* [1970] SASR 184 at 190–191. In my opinion, however, the expert evidence did go further than raise a mere possibility. Dr Schioldann-Nielsen said that in his opinion the factors he described could have caused the appellant to panic and this "could have been the mechanism which released the full-blown disassociatve state". The appellant's description of what happened "could be fully consistent with a person in such a disorder". He did not offer an opinion concerning what in fact occurred because he was not there. Dr Finlay-Jones' evidence was likewise that the appellant's description was consistent with her being in a disassociated state. She was in a state of psychological conflict which created a setting consistent with her acting in an automatic way.

The evidence given by the experts was based upon the appellant's out of court statements to them rather than her evidence at the trial. For present purposes, however, it is sufficient to say that there was no apparent inconsistency between what she told them and her evidence at the trial. Given that the appellant's evidence concerning what happened was believed, I am of opinion that the evidence was such that, if accepted by the jury, would have entitled them to entertain a reasonable doubt as to the voluntary quality of the acts attributed to the appellant. As Barwick CJ said in *Ryan* (at 217):

"If voluntariness is not conceded and the material to be submitted to the jury wheresoever derived provides a substantial basis for doubting whether the deed in question was a voluntary or willed act of the accused, the jury's attention must be specifically drawn to the necessity of deciding beyond all reasonable doubt that the deed charged as a crime was the voluntary or willed act of the accused. If it was not then for that reason, there being no defence of insanity, the accused must be acquitted. No doubt care will be taken by the presiding judge that the available material warrants the raising of this specific issue. In doing so, he will of course have in mind that the question for him is whether upon that material a jury would be entitled to entertain a reasonable doubt as to the voluntary quality of the act attributed to the accused . . . Although a claim of involuntariness is no doubt easily raised, and may involve nice distinctions, the accused, if the material adduced warrants that course, is entitled to have the issue properly put to the jury."

In *Schultz* [1982] WAR 171; (1981) 5 A Crim R 234, the only live issue on a charge of wilful murder was that of intent. The appellant sought to adduce evidence from the psychologist and from a psychiatrist to establish that the appellant was of borderline mentally defective intelligence. It was contended that the evidence was relevant to intent, but the trial judge ruled the evidence inadmissible. This Court held that the evidence was relevant and admissible. Burt CJ (with whom Wickham and Jones JJ agreed) said (at 174; 237):

"Unless there are authorities to the contrary, in my opinion the evidence was relevant and, when led by the appellant, admissible. Once it be acknowledged that there is no legal presumption that a man intends the probable consequences of his acts and that in every case the finding to be made is specifically and exclusively as to the intention of a particular person at a particular moment of time, then, as it seems to me, all facts personal to the person concerned which have bearing or which in the judgment of reasonable men have a bearing upon the operation of his mind are relevant to that finding. Of course, facts which go no way to distinguish the person concerned from his fellows need not be made the subject of evidence because they require no proof. But such facts as do distinguish the person concerned from his fellows in a way which could, in the judgment of reasonable men, weaken an inference as to intent otherwise based upon the facts found would seem to me to be relevant to that question and if those facts cannot without the aid of expert opinion evidence be made known to the jury then such evidence directed to their proof is relevant and apart from special rules which may operate to exclude it, as, for example, when the evidence goes only to 'disposition' and is sought to be led by the Crown, it is admissible evidence. Whether the evidence proposed to be called satisfies that test, as it controls admissibility, is a question for the judge. It is a question of law although it will call for the exercise of a discretionary judgment to answer it."

The issue in the present case was whether the jury, if satisfied, that the appellant shot her husband, could infer that she did so with the intention to kill him. The question whether the shooting was a conscious or voluntary act of will on the part of the appellant was highly relevant to the issue of intent.

The evidence of the assault on the day of the shooting and Mr Falconer's taunting of the appellant, given her general emotional and mental state was, on the medical evidence before the court capable of giving rise to involuntary conduct. Consequently, the evidence derived in that way, coupled with the appellant's own evidence gave rise to an issue of voluntariness which should have been left to the jury.

In my opinion the appellant is entitled to succeed on ground 1.

Code Options

4.125   *Model Penal Code*

Section 2.01.   Requirement of Voluntary Act; Omission as Basis of Liability; Possession as an Act.

(1) A person is not guilty of an offence unless his liability is based on conduct that includes a voluntary act or the omission to perform an act of which he is physically capable.

(2) The following are not voluntary acts within the meaning of this section:

(*a*) a reflex or convulsion;
(*b*) a bodily movement during unconsciousness or sleep;
(*c*) conduct during hypnosis or resulting from hypnotic suggestion;
(*d*) a bodily movement that otherwise is not a product of the effort or determination of the actor, either conscious or habitual.

(3) Liability for the commission of an offence may not be based on an omission unaccompanied by action unless:

(*a*) the omission is expressly made sufficient by the law defining the offence; or
(*b*) a duty to perform the omitted act is otherwise imposed by law.

(4) Possession is an act, within the meaning of this section, if the possessor knowingly procured or received the thing possessed or was aware of his control thereof for a sufficient period to have been able to terminate his possession.

Further Materials

4.126 Fox *Physical Disorder Consciousness and Criminal Liability* (1963), 63 Colum Law Rev 645.
Holland *Automatism and Criminal Responsibility* (1982) 25 CLQ 95.

Infancy

4.127 Criminal law is essentially an adult business. Prisons are designed to punish and rehabilitate mature offenders. Children have no place within a system which may corrupt them further or which may break an undeveloped spirit. It should be the policy of the law to keep children as far away from the criminal process as possible. A juvenile first-time offender who admits the offence may be cautioned and placed under the care of a juvenile liaison officer, without the need for formal prosecution. Regrettably, circumstances arise where children commit crimes and deny their involvement, often with the full connivance of misguided parents. In those circumstances the law may have to arbitrate as to whether a child committed a crime. Where the child must be prosecuted on indictment the court rituals remain unchanged. For a summary prosecution the District Court inquires into the offence applying the same standards as in the case of an adult but with less formality. See generally the Children Act 1908 as amended by the Children Act 1941.

4.128 Criminal law is concerned with blame. The notion of blameworthiness presents itself in an especially difficult way in the case of children. They may be used by unscrupulous adults as willing or unwilling tools for the commission of crime. Children may themselves engage in crime but it may often be that their motivation does not stem from wickedness but from peer pressure, the social acceptance of delinquent behaviour in the communities where they live, or an insufficient understanding of what their conduct involves. This latter consideration has led to special rules in dealing with child offenders. Regrettably, Irish law has remained unreformed since 1922. This is the responsibility of our politicians.

4.129   *Archbold – Criminal Pleading Evidence and Practice*
26th Edition, 1922

Infants under seven. Infants under the age of discretion are not punishable by any criminal prosecution whatever; 1 Hale, 27: 1 Hawk, c 1, s 1: and see Mirror, c 4, s 16 (Selden Soc. Publ, vol 7): 1 Russ Cr (7th ed) 58 (f). A child under the age of seven years cannot be guilty of any criminal offence; for, under that age an infant is, by incontrovertible presumption of law, *doli incapax*, and cannot be endowed with any discretion. Reg. 309 b; 1 Hale, 27, 28; 4 Bl Com 23: Mirror, c 4, s 6; Fost. 349: Reniger v. Fogossa, 1 Plowd. 1: R v Carter [1774] 1 Cowp 220, 223: Marsh v Loader, 14 CB (NS) 535: 1 Russ Cr (7th ed) 58.

Infants between seven and fourteen. Between the ages of seven and fourteen years a child is presumed not to have reached the age of discretion and to be *doli incapax*; but this presumption may be rebutted by strong and pregnant evidence of a mischievous discretion, expressed in the maxim *malitia supplet cetatem*; for the capacity to commit crime, do evil and contract guilt, is not so much measured by years and days, as by the strength of the delinquent's understanding and judgment. 4 Bl. Com 23: 1 Hale, 25, 27. Thus, it has been said that an infant eight years of age might be indicted for murder, and hanged on conviction; Dalt. c 147; and an infant between the age of eight and nine years was executed for arson, it appearing that he was actuated by malice and revenge, and had perpetrated the offence with craft and cunning. 1 Hale, 25 n. So a girl of thirteen was burnt for killing her mistress; 1 Hale, 26; and where an infant nine years of age killed an infant of the like age, and confessed the felony, it appearing upon examination that he had hid both the blood and the body, the justices were of opinion that he might lawfully be hanged, but respited the judgment that he might be pardoned. Fitz. Cor 57. See *R v York*, Fost. 70; 4 Bl Com 24: *R v Wild*, 1 Mood 452. Under the present law sentence of death may not be pronounced or recorded against a person under sixteen (8 Edw 7, c 67, s 103). In criminal proceedings against a person under fourteen, the evidence of a mischievous discretion, to rebut the *primá facie* presumption of law arising from nonage, should be clear and strong beyond all doubt and contradiction. 4 Bl Com 23: 1 Hale, 25, 27: *R v Vamplew*, 3 F&F 520 *R v Gorrie*, 83 JP 136. Where a child between the age of seven and fourteen years is indicted for felony, two questions are to be left to the jury: first, whether he committed the offence; and secondly, whether at the time he had a guilty knowledge that he was doing wrong. *R v Owen*, 4 C&P 236: *R v Smith*, 1 Cox 260; and see *R v Gorrie*, supra. The fact that the child did the acts constituting the elements of the offence is not in itself any evidence whatever of the guilty state of mind which is essential for conviction. *R v Kershaw*, 18 TLR 357; 37 LJ Newsp 120, Bucknill, J. An infant under fourteen is presumed by law to be unable to commit a rape, and therefore cannot be found guilty of it as a principal in the first degree; for though in other felonies *malitia supplet cetatem*, yet, as to this particular act, the law presumes him impotent, as well as wanting in discretion. This presumption was not affected by 9 G 4, c 31, ss 16, 17 (rep.), which first made the offence complete upon proof of penetration, without evidence of emission; *R v Groombridge*, 7 C&P 582; nor by the present enactment, 24 & 25 Vict c 100, s 63, by which 9 G 4, c 31, is superseded: *R v Waite* [1892] 2 QB 600; 61 LJ (MC) 189; 17 Cox, 554. Nor is any evidence admissible to show that the defendant had in fact arrived at the full state of puberty, and could commit the offence. *R v Philips*, 8 C&P 736: *R v Jordan*, 9 C&P 118: *R v Brimilow*, Id 366; 2 Mood 122 In *R v Brimilow* it was held that the boy had been properly convicted of an assault under 1 Vict c 85, s 11 (rep.). Nor can a boy under fourteen be convicted of an assault with intent to commit a rape. *R v Eldershaw*, 3 C&P 396. This doctrine has been extended to other offences involving carnal knowledge. *R v Waite*, supra. But a boy under fourteen may be a principal in the second degree in a rape, or like offence, if he aids and assists in the commission of the offence, and it appears that he had a mischievous discretion; for the excuse of impotency will not apply in such a case. 1 Hale, 630: *R v Eldershaw*, 3 C&P 396. See *R v Allen*, 1 Den. 364; 2 C&K 869; 18 LJ (MC) 72; 3 Cox, 270: *R v Williams* [1893] 1 QB 320; 62 LJ (MC) 69. Whether where there is evidence of guilty knowledge he may be held to be an accomplice appears to be doubtful. See *R v Cratchley*, 9 Cr App R 232; and *R v Tatam*, 15 Cr App R 132.

In *R v Sutton*, 3 A&E 597; 5 N&M 353, there are dicta to the effect that under certain circumstances an infant under fourteen might be liable to indictment in respect of public duties arising out of his occupation of property.

Infants of Fourteen or over. The incapacity of infants to commit crime ceases upon their attaining the age of fourteen years, at which age they are presumed by the law to be *doli capaces*, and capable of distinguishing good from evil, and are, with respect to their criminal actions, subject to the same rule of construction as others of more mature age. 1 Hale, 25; Doct and Stu c 26; Co Litt 79, 171, 247; Dalt c 147; 1 Hawk c 1, n (1). But for the purposes of punishment a distinction is drawn between adults and young persons (of fourteen and under sixteen), and juvenile adults (of sixteen and under twenty-one). See 8 Edw 7, c 67, ss 102, 103, and 8 Edw 7, c 59, ss 1–4.

In some misdemeanours and offences which are not capital an infant is said to be privileged by reason of his nonage, if under twenty-one, because laches is not to be attributed to him. Co Litt 357; 4 Bl Com 22. But inasmuch as an infant is liable in tort, it is difficult to understand the grounds of this early distinction as to misdemeanours when an infant over seven could be liable for felony. An infant who is indicted for any notorious breach of the peace, as riot, forcible entry, battery, or for perjury or cheating, or the like, is equally liable as a person of full age; because, upon his trial, the court, *ex officio*, ought to consider whether he was *doli capax*, and had discretion to do the act with which he is charged. 1 Hale, 20, 21; 4 Bl Com 22; 3 Bac Abr, Infancy (H). An infant, though incapable of making a contract of bailment, has been held liable to indictment for larceny as a bailee. *R v M'Donald*, 15 QBD 323. But an infant cannot lawfully be adjudicated bankrupt, and consequently cannot be convicted as a bankrupt of an offence under s. 159 of the Bankruptcy Act, 1914 (4 & 5 Geo 5, c 59), which depends on the existence of bankruptcy and the existence of valid debs by the infant. *R v Wilson*, 5 QBD 28; 49 LJ (MC) 13; *Lovell v Beachamp* [1894] AC 607; 63 LJ (QB) 802.

4.130 Examples of the application of these principles include: *Green v Cavan County Council*[64] and *Monagle v Donegal County Council*[65]. Where a child is between seven and fourteen, evidence of a mischievous discretion may be gathered from the nature of the act itself, the intelligence and understanding of the child and the behaviour of the child immediately subsequent to the offence; *JM v Runeckles*[66]. It is not necessary to prove that the child knew that what he had done was morally wrong, he must know that it was seriously wrong in the sense of it being not merely naughty or mischievous; *JM v Runeckles*, above. Incapacity due to infancy ceases upon

---

64 [1959] Ir Jur Rep 75.
65 [1961] Ir Jur Rep 37.
66 (1984) 79 Cr App R 255.

a person attaining the age of fourteen. The younger the child the stronger is the presumption; *B v R*[67]. After the age of fourteen the defence of infancy is unavailable.

4.131 The institution to which a person under the age of twenty one may be sent to by the courts depends on a number of factors such as age (always taken at the time of the court appearance), character, nature of the offence and the availability of a suitable place. This last factor has become increasingly important in recent years due to the lack of suitable places of detention for young people caused by insufficient funds being made available for this type of expenditure due to the prevailing economic climate.

In brief there are five alternatives:

(1)   Industrial schools
These may be used for non-offenders up to the age of fifteen when in need of care and attention and for offenders between the ages of seven and fifteen. The upper age limit may be extended by two years in certain circumstances. Offenders under twelve must be sent here and normally first offenders of good character would also be sent to these schools.

(2)   Reformatory schools
These overlap to some extent with industrial schools. They are for offenders between the ages of twelve and seventeen. All offenders above the age of fifteen are sent here. An offender can be detained in these schools for a period of two to four years but, in any case, not beyond nineteen years of age unless, for the offender's welfare, the age limit is extended in which case the age limit is twenty one.

(3)   St Patrick's Institution
This was formerly known as Borstal. In 1970 two further centres opened, Shanganagh Castle at Shankill in County Dublin and Loughan House at Blacklion in County Cavan. Both are 'open' institutions. A person between seventeen and twenty one may be sent to these institutions instead of prison. In certain circumstances sixteen year olds may be sent to these places.

(4)   Prison
Persons over seventeen years of age may be sent to prison. There is also a provision whereby a child who is certified as being so unruly and depraved that he cannot be detained elsewhere may be sent to prison. The maximum period a person under seventeen may be detained in prison is three months.

(5)   Detention Centre or Remand Home
Persons under seventeen years may be sent to St Lawrence's School in Finglas, Dublin, which was formerly Marlborough House, having been refused bail or as a short term alternative to other forms of detention. The maximum period of detention in this institution is one month.

67 (1958) 44 Cr App R 1.

Code Options

4.132 *Model Penal Code*

Section 4.10 Immaturity Excluding Criminal Conviction: Transfer of Proceedings to Juvenile Court.

(1) A person shall not be tried for or convicted of an offence if:

(*a*) at the time of the conduct charged to constitute the offence he was less than sixteen years of age [, in which case the Juvenile Court shall have exclusive jurisdiction*]; or

(*b*) at the time of the conduct charged to constitute the offence he was sixteen or seventeen years of age, unless:

   (i) the Juvenile Court has no jurisdiction over him, or
   (ii) the Juvenile Court has entered an order waiving jurisdiction and consenting to the institution of criminal proceedings against him.

(2) No court shall have jurisdiction to try or convict a person of an offence if criminal proceedings against him are barred by subsection (1) of this section. When it appears that a person charged with the commission of an offence may be of such an age that criminal proceedings may be barred under subsection (1) of this section, the Court shall hold a hearing thereon, and the burden shall be on the prosecution to establish to the satisfaction of the Court that the criminal proceeding is not barred upon such grounds. If the Court determines that the proceeding is barred, custody of the person charged shall be surrendered to the Juvenile Court, and the case, including all papers and processes relating thereto, shall be transferred.

Further Materials

4.133 Mitchell *A Report on the Law and Procedures Regarding the Prosecution and Disposal of Young Offenders, October 1977 (commissioned by the Director of Public Prosecutions).*

Consent

4.134 Look at this in the light of what is said about consent and sexual offences (chapter 6).

Mistake of Fact

4.135 The defence of mistake cannot be considered in isolation from an analysis of the elements of an offence. Where an element of an offence is defined in terms of absolute liability a mistake cannot absolve the accused of responsibility. An example is the offence of underage sexual intercourse where, traditionally, it has been held that a mistaken belief that the girl is above the proscribed aged does not constitute a defence; *R v Prince*[68]. This is further discussed in the context of sexual offences in chapter 6. Where an offence may be committed by negligence, for example, careless driving, then a negligent mistake cannot absolve the accused of responsibility.

68 (1875) LR 2 CCR 154.

Where the offence is manslaughter, which may be committed by criminal negligence, a mistake arrived at in a criminally negligent fashion cannot absolve the accused of responsibility.

4.136 *R v Foxford*
[1974] NI 181
Court of Appeal Northern Ireland, 1974

Facts: The accused, a soldier, was charged with the manslaughter of a twelve year old boy while on night patrol duty in a hostile area. There had been some disturbances in the area before the shooting and the accused's defence was that he had fired in self-defence at a gunman who had just shot at his patrol.

In finding the accused guilty of manslaughter the trial judge held that there was no evidence to support the accused's allegation that the boy had fired at the patrol and considered it doubtful if the accused saw the deceased at all. Firing a rifle at night, without proper aim, into a street where members of the public had been, constituted gross negligence.

He subsequently appealed on a number of matters arising from the conduct of the trial and the conviction was quashed on other grounds.

Kelly J: . . . The defence is that the accused lawfully fired his rifle at Kevin Heatley in self-defence and in defence of the members of his patrol and therefore in the prevention of crime because Kevin Heatley was in fact a gunman who had immediately before discharged an armed low velocity shot from a hand-gun at the accused and his patrol . . .

. . . If I accept the facts alleged by the Crown then the categories of manslaughter which call for consideration are (1) the commission of an unlawful and dangerous act which clearly subjects another to the risk of some harm and which causes death, and (2) the commission of an act containing an element of criminal negligence resulting in death – although it does seem to me that these varieties of involuntary manslaughter overlap to some extent in the particular circumstances of this case.

. . . As to (2) it is well established that the degree of negligence essential to this variety of manslaughter must go well beyond that degree of negligence which founds civil liability. It must be gross or criminal negligence.

. . . In considering the defence raised I remind myself of section 3 of the Criminal Law Act (Northern Ireland) 1967 which states:—

"A person may use such force as is reasonable in the circumstances in the prevention of crime . . .".

Another conclusion of fact which could be arrived at in this case is that the accused made an honest, albeit unreasonable, mistake of fact in believing that the deceased was armed with a pistol and had fired at him when this was not the case and that the accused returned fire at the deceased honestly believing that these facts were true. In these circumstances, I believe that it is only if this mistake was so wholly unreasonable, as to amount to gross or criminal negligence, that the accused can be convicted of manslaughter. See the text in *Smith and Hogan* (3rd ed.) at p 263 which appears to go further than the dicta in *R v Rose* (1884) 15 Cox CC 540 and *R v Chisam* (1963) 47 Cr App R 130, but which I respectfully adopt as the proper test in such circumstances.

. . . I am satisfied beyond reasonable doubt that the accused did fire an unaimed shot from the west side of Main Avenue from his rifle in the manner described by those Crown witnesses who saw him and that he did this without cause or justification. I can find no evidence to support the allegation of the accused that Kevin Heatley had a gun and fired a shot at the accused and his patrol and I am quite satisfied that this was not the case. Nor do I accept that the accused at any time believed that the deceased had a gun or had fired a gun. I think it is extremely doubtful if he saw Kevin Heatley at all.

To fire an SL rifle in the circumstances I have found, is an unlawful act and a dangerous one and one which clearly must subject others to the risk of harm. And the accused in so doing must have realised that his action was likely to harm if not frighten someone. Furthermore, to fire a SL rifle at night without proper aim into a street where members of the public had been and might still be about was negligence of the grossest kind. I have no doubt but that the conduct of which I have found him guilty amounts in law to manslaughter.

Negating the Mental Element

4.137   At common law it appears to have been the position that a mistake could only constitute a defence if it was reasonable in the circumstances; *R v Tolson*[69].

4.138   *C S Kenny – Outlines of Criminal Law*
                          11th Edition, 1922

We may fairly regard this state of mind as always arising from mistake or some other form of ignorance; (eg, taking from the hat-stand in your club another man's umbrella in mistake for your own). Blackstone speaks of there being also a class of cases in which it arises from (what he calls) Misfortune; apparently with the idea of distinguishing, from acts done with the expectation that no unlawful result would follow on them, some acts done with the expectation of their being followed by no result at all. But it does not seem possible to draw accurately any such line of demarcation. And inasmuch as, even were it drawn, the legal treatment of the two classes would present no points of difference, all distinction between them may well be disregarded here.

Our criminal law often allows mistake or ignorance to afford a good defence by showing, even where there has been an *actus reus*, that no sufficient *mens rea* preceded it. But such a defence can only arise when three conditions are fulfilled.

(1) The first condition is that the mistake must be of such a character that, had the supposed circumstances been real, they would have prevented any guilt[70] from attaching to the person in doing what he did. Therefore it is no defence for a burglar, who breaks into No 5, to show that he mistook that house for No 6; or that he did not know that nine o'clock had already struck. Similarly, on an indictment for assaulting a constable "in the discharge of his duty", the fact that the assailants did not know of his official character will be no defence for them. On the other hand, it will be no offence[71] to lay violent hands upon a person, whom you reasonably, though mistakenly, suppose to be committing a burglary[72]. The cases of *Reg v Prince* and *Reg v Tolson*, which we have already discussed[73], afford important illustrations of this principle.

(2) A further condition is that the mistake must be a reasonable one. This will be mainly a question of fact. But in extreme cases the jury may be assisted by the judge's directions as to some mistakes being clearly reasonable and some others clearly unreasonable. Of the former class an illustration is related by Sir Michael

---

69 (1889) 23 QBD 168.
70 As to whether this means legal guilt or merely moral guilt, *Outlines of Criminal Law* at p 41.
71 As to stabbing a supposed corpse, see LQR for 1920, p 7.
72 *Rex v Levett*, Cro Car, 538 (KSC 26).
73 *Outlines of Criminal Law* at pp 41, 48.

Foster[74]. A man, before going to church, fired off his gun, and left it empty. But during his absence some person went out shooting with the gun; and, on returning, left it loaded. The owner, late in the same day, took up the gun again; and in doing this, touched the trigger. The gun went off, and killed his wife, who was in the room. Foster held that in these circumstances the man had reasonable grounds to believe that the weapon was not loaded. The case might well have been otherwise if weeks, instead of hours, had elapsed between his firing off the gun and his subsequently handing it without taking any pains to see whether it had meanwhile been loaded again[75]. Similarly in an American case[76], where a constable was charged with arresting a man unlawfully, it appeared that the man had fallen down in the street in a fit, and his friends had first tried to revive him by administering whiskey, and then had gone away to seek help. The constable was acquitted; for the fact that the man smelt of whiskey afforded reasonable ground for supposing his insensibility to be due to intoxication (which would quite have been a lawful ground for taking him into custody).

On the other hand, no belief which has now come to be currently regarded as an obsolete superstition can be treated as a mistake sufficiently reasonable to excuse a crime which it may give rise to. Thus in 1880, at Clonmel, a woman who had placed a child naked on a hot shovel, in the honest belief that it was a deformed fairy sent as a substitute for the real child, (who would be restored if the changeling were thus imperilled), was convicted and was sentenced to imprisonment. So, in 1895, again at Clonmel, were men who had caused the death of the wife of one of them by holding her over a fire and searing her with a red hot poker, in the honest expectation of thereby exorcising a demons that was supposed to possess her[77]. And even people who break the law in consequence of a belief that they are obeying a Divine command, are legally regarded as actuated by a mistake which is "unreasonable". Illustrations are afforded in America by the prosecutions of Mormons for polygamy[78]; and in England by the prosecutions of the "Peculiar People" for withholding medical aid[79] from their sick children. (At the same time it must be remembered that some religious delusions may be of so extreme a character as to be evidence of insanity, and to afford a good defence upon that ground[80].)

(3) The final condition is, that the mistake, however reasonable, must not relate to matters of law but to matters of "fact". For a mistake of law, even though inevitable, is not allowed in England to afford any excuse for crime, *Ignorantia juris neminem excusat*[81]. The upmost effect it can ever have is that it may occasionally, like drunkenness[82], rebut the existence of the peculiar form of *mens rea* which some particular kind of crime may require. Thus larceny can only be committed when a thing is stolen without even the appearance of right to take it;

74 Foster 265 (KSC 27).
75 Contrast *Reg v Jones*, 12 Cox 628 (KSC 28); *The State v Hardie*, 10 Runnells 647 (KSC123); cases where a mistaken belief that the firearms were unloaded was unreasonable.
76 *Commonwealth v Presby*, 14 Gray 65.
77 In 1894 an Indian was convicted in Canada who had killed a man under the belief of his being an evil spirit that would attack human beings; *Reg v Mackekequonabe*, 2 Canadian Crim CA 138.
78 *Reynolds v United States*, 98 US 145 (KSC 31).
79 Kenny *Outlines of Criminal Law* at p 122.
80 *Rev v Hadfield*, 27 St Tr Compare CC Sess Pap CLIV 357.
81 For a discussion of the justifications that may be offered for this severe rule, see *Austin's Jurisprudence*, Lect XXV, and Markby's *Elements of Law*, secs 269, 270. Perhaps after considering them all, the student may still feel compelled, with the late Prof Henry Sidgwick, to regard the rule as "not a realisation of ideal justice, but an exercise of Society's right of self-preservation". For the milder principles adopted in Roman Law see *Justinian's Digest*, XXII 6, and *Lindley's Jurisprudence*, p 24 and App xix.
82 Kenny *Outlines of Criminal Law* at p 61.

and accordingly, a *bona fide* mistake of law, if based upon reasonable grounds, – like that of a woman who gleans corn in a village where it is the practice to do so – will afford a sufficient defence[83]. Similarly a mortgagor who, under an invalid but *bona fide* claim of right, damages the fixtures in the house which he has mortgaged, will not be guilty of "malicious" damage[84]. Apart, however, from these exceptional offences, the rule which ignores mistakes of law is applied with rigour. A sailor has been convicted of an offence that had been forbidden only by an Act of Parliament of which he could not possibly know, since it was enacted when he was far away at sea, and the offence was committed before the news of its enactment could reach him[85]. Frenchmen, who had acted as seconds in a fatal duel here, have similarly been committed for trial on a charge of murder, although their own land practised duelling and they did not know that English law forbade it[86]. Various Italians have recently been punished in London for keeping lotteries, in spite of their urging that in Italy every little village possesses a lottery sanctioned by the State, and that they had no idea that the English law could be different. It is therefore easy to see that a veterinary surgeon's mistaken belief that an operation, which he knows to be painful and purposeless[87], is nevertheless unpunishable legally, will afford him no defence for performing it. Again, where a Parliamentary elector, who had a qualification in each of three polling-districts of the same county constituency and accordingly was on the register of each, voted at all the three respective polling-stations, but in the honest and not unnatural belief that he could legally do so, he was held by Stephen J, to have no legal defence for this criminal conduct[88].

These mistakes are reasonable enough; yet they afford no excuse. Nor would they do so, even if the prisoner could shew that he had taken pains to obtain a lawyer's advice and had been misled by it. Still less, therefore, can any excuse be conferred by legal errors that are unreasonable. Some such occasionally occur in connexion with the law of Marriage. In a trial for bigamy, which I witnessed at the Central Criminal Court in 1883, it appeared that not only the prisoner himself, but also his first wife and all her family, had believed his marriage with her to be void, because the wedding-ring was only of brass and not of gold. In a much more recent case, where the first marriage was between a Catholic and a Protestant, the parties had believed it to be invalid because they had gone through a Roman Catholic marriage alone, and had not superadded a Protestant ceremony[89].

But although mistakes of law, unreasonable or even reasonable, thus leave the offender punishable for the crime which he has blundered into, they may of course afford good grounds for inflicting on him a milder punishment[90].

Reasonableness

4.139 The requirement that a mistake should be reasonable was formulated at a time when the accused was not entitled to give evidence. It is possible to see the requirement as a historical anarchism which constituted merely an aid to the jury in determining, in the absence of evidence from the

---

83 *Ibid* at p 203.
84 *Reg v Croft*, [1889] CCC Sess Pap CXI 202.
85 *Rex v Bailey*, R and R 1 (KSC 29). Cf p 519 infra.
86 Barronet's Case, 1 E and B 1. French law forbids it.
87 In England dishorning adult cattle without anaesthetic was illegal, *Ford v Wiley*, LR 23 QBD 203, when still legal in Scotland and Ireland; see now 9 & 10 Geo 5, c 54. It is an embarrassing but unsettled question whether the Jewish mode of slaughtering cattle is illegal in England.
88 *Reg v Hearn*, CCC Sess Pap CIII 561.
89 Cf LR [1893] p 85.
90 *Rex v Esop*, 7 C and P 456.

accused, whether his excuse is credible. Alternatively, it may be the policy of the law to ensure that only mistakes which could reasonably be made will excuse. If it were otherwise, people might be allowed too wide a latitude in the commission of crime. That attitude, however, punishes people merely on the basis of their negligence. A mistake which is totally unreasonable will rarely be accepted as being genuine by a jury. The jury is entitled to have regard to the presence or absence of reasonable grounds for a mistake in determining whether or not an accused genuinely fell into an error which renders his conduct blameless. That generalised approach is encapsulated in s 2 of the Criminal Law (Rape) Act 1981 which is referred to in the chapter on sexual offences. In Australia where a mistake deprived the accused of mental culpability his mistake need merely have been honest. Where a mistake consisted of a positive assertion of justification or excuse it had to be both honest and reasonable[91]. Australian law may now be developing towards the acceptance of mistake, whether as an element of the offence or as asserting a positive justification or excuse, on the basis only that it is genuine; *R v He Kaw Te*[92]. In England a mistaken belief which, if true, would have made the accused's actions innocent relieves him of liability notwithstanding that the mistake may have been unreasonable; *Beckford v R*[93]. The classic example is of the person who sees another being assaulted, goes to the aid of that person in an appropriately forceful fashion and later discovers that he is obstructing a plain-clothes police officer in the course of trying to effect a difficult arrest; *R v Williams*[94].

4.140   It is submitted that the supposed requirement that a mistake be reasonable contravenes the standard of fairness implied by the Constitution. Society may fairly blame a person for making a mistake. It is possible for the Oireachtas to extend the grounds of criminal liability by the creation of an offence of causing harm to persons or property in a criminally negligent fashion. This would impose an objective standard, albeit a high one, of fault on the community. In the absence of such an offence it contravenes the analysis of criminal liability based on subjective blame to convert the definition of intent or recklessness, which is the foundation of the vast bulk of indictable crime, into mere negligence. A person who genuinely takes action in a situation where, if he was correct, he could suffer no criminal penalty is not blameworthy. The imposition of a requirement of reasonableness on that mistake imposes blame through the artificial means of substituting carelessness for intention or recklessness.

Unconstitutionality

4.141   A person may have committed a crime by bringing about the external element, (having, at the time, the necessary mental element) have no defence at common law, and yet be entitled to be acquitted. The manner of his arrest and conviction or the law under which it is sought to convict him

91 *O'Connor and Fairall* p 45–62.
92 (1985) 59 ALJR 620.
93 [1988] AC 130.
94 [1987] 3 All ER 411.

may infringe the provisions of the Constitution. The guarantee of procedural fairness contained in Article 38 of the Constitution has proved more fruitful in allowing accused persons avenues of escape from conviction than arguments that the law, under which they are sought to be convicted is, itself, unconstitutional. Matters of procedure and evidence are outside the scope of this work.

It is worth noting that in a trial of offences an accused is entitled to constitutional justice. The rights which that concept comprises are applied more rigorously the graver the offence which is to be tried; *The State (Healy) v Donoghue*[95]. The concept of procedural fairness can work in favour of the prosecution. The Court of Criminal Appeal has held unconstitutional the common law rule making a wife incompetent to give evidence against her husband on a charge of incest. The basis of the decision was that the rule infringed the right of the family to seek vindication from the courts following an attack being made on one of its members; *The People (DPP) v JT*[96].

4.142 The Oireachtas is committed under Article 40, and in the Preamble to the Constitution, to providing order in society through the instrument of justice. By analogy with the natural law provisions implied into the personal rights section of the Constitution, it is possible to argue that certain acts which have not been declared by common law or statute to be criminal are nonetheless so wrong in their nature as to constitute a crime against the fundamental human law adopted by the Constitution; *Attorney-General (SPUC) v Open Door Counselling Limited*[97]. Judicial activism has not yet extended to the creation of criminal offences. The law remains in the ruined state that neglect by the Oireachtas has generated.

4.143 An appeal that a criminal provision is unconstitutional must cross a number of fundamental hurdles to be successful. The accused must firstly have exhausted all aspects of the case with a non constitutional element and in raising the constitutional point must be so directly affected by it as to entitle the accused to seek relief; *Cahill v Sutton*[98]. Acts of the Oireachtas passed subsequent to 1937 are presumed not to conflict with the Constitution; *The State (Sheerin) v Kennedy*[99]. An Act will not be declared unconstitutional if it is possible to construe it in a constitutional manner; *East Donegal Co-Operative v A-G*[1]. Finally, provisions of the Constitution cannot be picked at random from the text for the purpose of declaring an Act to be inconsistent with the fundamental law. Where there is a conflict between constitutional rights this must be resolved in favour of those rights which are more fundamental. Rights may only be declared on a reading of the purpose and objective of the Constitution from its entire text; *Murray v Ireland*[2].

95 [1976] IR 325.
96 (1988) 3 Frewen 141.
97 [1985] ILRM 449.
98 [1980] IR 269.
99 [1966] IR 379.
 1 [1970] IR 317.
 2 [1985] IR 532.

4.144   *McGee v Attorney General*
                                      [1974] IR 284
                                  Supreme Court, 1973

Facts: Section 17 of the Criminal Law (Amendment) Act 1935 made it a criminal
offence, carrying a penalty of six months imprisonment, to sell contraceptives or
import them into the State. Mrs McGee was aged 27 years and had four children.
She had been told that another pregnancy could put her health at grave risk. She
attempted to import some contraceptive jelly from England but this was seized by
Custom Officials.

Walsh J: . . . It is a matter exclusively for the husband and wife to decide how
many children they wish to have; it would be quite outside the competence of the
State to dictate or prescribe the number of children which they might have or
should have. In my view, the husband and wife have a correlative right to agree to
have no children. This is not to say that the State, when the common good requires
it, may not actively encourage married couples either to have larger or smaller
familes.
    . . . the rights of a married couple to decide how many children, if any, they will
have are matters outside the reach of positive law where the means employed to
implement such decisions do not impinge upon the common good or destroy or
endanger human life. It is undoubtedly true that among those persons who are
subject to a particular moral code no one has a right to be in breach of that moral
code. But when this is a code governing private morality and where the breach of it
is not one which injures the common good then it is not the State's business to
intervene. It is outside the authority of the State to endeavour to intrude into the
privacy of the husband and wife relationship for the sake of imposing a code of
private morality upon that husband and wife which they do not desire.
    In my view, Article 41 of the Constitution guarantees the husband and wife
against any such invasion of their privacy by the State. It follows that the use of
contraceptives by them within that marital privacy is equally guaranteed against
such invasion and, as such, assumes the status of a right so guaranteed by the
Constitution. If this right cannot be directly invaded by the State it follows that it
cannot be frustrated by the State taking measures to ensure that the exercise of
that right is rendered impossible. I do not exclude the possibility of the State being
justified where the public good requires it (as, for example, in the case of a
dangerous fall in population threatening the life or the essential welfare of the
State) in taking such steps to ensure that in general, even if married couples could
not be compelled to have children, they could at least be hindered in their
endeavours to avoid having them where the common good required the maintenance or increase of the population.
    . . . Similarly it is not impossible to envisage a situation where the availability of
contraceptives to married people for use within marriage could be demonstrated
to have led to or would probably lead to such an adverse effect on public morality
so subversive of the common good as to justify State intervention by restricting or
prohibiting the availability of contraceptives for use within marriage or at all. In
such a case it would have to be demonstrated that all the other resources of the
State had proved or were likely to prove incapable to avoid this subversion of the
common good while contraceptives remained available for use within marriage.
    In my opinion, s 17 of the Act of 1935, in so far as it unreasonably restricts the
availability of contraceptives for use within marriage, is inconsistent with the
provisions of Article 41 of the Constitution for being an unjustified invasion of the
privacy of husband and wife in their sexual relations with one another. The
fundamental restriction is contained in the provisions of sub-s 3 of s 17 of the Act
of 1935 which lists contraceptives among the prohibited articles which may not be
imported for any purposes whatsoever. On the present state of facts, I am of

opinion that this provision is inconsistent with the Constitution and is no longer in force.

. . . So far I have considered the plaintiff's case only in relation to Article 41 of the Constitution; and I have done so on the basis that she is a married woman but without referring to her state of health. I now turn to the claim made under Article 40 of the Constitution. So far as this particular Article is concerned, and the submissions made thereunder, the state of health of the plaintiff is relevant. If, for the reasons I have already given, a prohibition on the availability of contraceptives for use in marriage generally could be justified on the grounds of the exigencies of the common good, the provisions of s 1 of Article 40 (in particular, the proviso thereto) would justify and would permit the State to discriminate between some married persons and others in the sense that, where conception could more than ordinarily endanger the life of a particular person or persons or particular classes of persons within the married state, the law could have regard to this difference of physical capacity and make special exemptions in favour of such persons. [I think that such an exemption could also be justified under the provisions of s 3 of Article 40 on the grounds that one of the personal rights of a woman in the plaintiff's state of health would be a right to be assisted in her efforts to avoid putting her life in jeopardy.] I am of opinion also that not only has the State the right to do so but, by virtue of the terms of the proviso to s 1 and the terms of s 3 of Article 40, the State has the positive obligation to ensure by its laws as far as is possible (and in the use of the word "possible" I am relying on the Irish text of the Constitution) that there would be made available to a married woman in the condition of health of the plaintiff the means whereby a conception which was likely to put her life in jeopardy might be avoided when it is a risk over and above the ordinary risks inherent in pregnancy. It would, in the nature of things, be much more difficult to justify a refusal to do this on the grounds of the common good than in the case of married couples generally.

. . . Both in its preamble and in Article 6, the Constitution acknowledges God as the ultimate source of all authority. The natural or human rights to which I have referred earlier in this judgment are part of what is generally called the natural law. There are many to argue that natural law may be regarded only as an ethical concept and as such is a re-affirmation of the ethical content of law in its ideal of justice. The natural law as a theological concept is the law of God promulgated by reason and is the ultimate governor of all the laws of men. In view of the acknowledgment of Christianity in the preamble and in view of the reference to God in Article 6 of the Constitution, it must be accepted that the Constitution intended the natural human rights I have mentioned as being in the latter category rather than simply an acknowledgment of the ethical content of law in its ideal of justice. What exactly natural law is and what precisely it imports is a question which has exercised the minds of theologians for many centuries and on which they are not yet fully agreed. While the Constitution speaks of certain rights being imprescriptible or inalienable, or being antecedent and superior to all positive law, it does not specify them. Echoing the words of O'Byrne J in *Buckley and Others (Sinn Féin) v The Attorney General*[3], I do not feel it necessary to enter upon an inquiry as to their extent or, indeed, as to their nature. It is sufficient for the court to examine and to search for the rights which may be discoverable in the particular case before the court in which these rights are invoked.

In a pluralist society such as ours, the courts cannot as a matter of constitutional law be asked to choose between the differing views, where they exist, of experts on the interpretation by the different religious denominations of either the nature or extent of these natural rights as they are to be found in the natural law. The same considerations apply also to the question of ascertaining the nature and extent of

3 [1950] IR 67, 82.

the duties which flow from natural law; the Constitution speaks of one of them when it refers to the inalienable duty of parents to provide according to their means for the religious, moral, intellectual, physical and social education of their children: see s 1 of Article 42. In this country it falls finally upon the judges to interpret the Constitution and in doing so to determine, where necessary, the rights which are superior or antecedent to positive law or which are imprescriptible or inalienable. In the performance of this difficult duty there are certain guidelines laid down in the Constitution for the judge. The very structure and content of the Articles dealing with fundamental rights clearly indicate that justice is not subordinate to the law. In particular, the terms of s 3 of Article 40 expressly subordinate the law to justice. Both Aristotle and the Christian philosophers have regarded justice as the highest human virtue. The virtue of prudence was also esteemed by Aristotle as by the philosophers of the Christian world. But the great additional virtue introduced by Christianity was that of charity – not the charity which consists of giving to the deserving, for that is justice, but the charity which is also called mercy. [According to the preamble, the people gave themselves the Constitution to promote the common good with due observance of prudence, justice and charity so that the dignity and freedom of the individual might be assured. The judges must, therefore, as best they can from their training and their experience interpret these rights in accordance with their ideas of prudence, justice and charity.] It is but natural that from time to time the prevailing ideas of these virtues may be conditioned by the passage of time; no interpretation of the Constitution is intended to be final for all time. It is given in the light of prevailing ideas and concepts. . . .

Henchy J: . . . The dominant feature of the plaintiff's dilemma is that she is a young married woman who is living, with a slender income, in the cramped quarters of a mobile home with her husband and four infant children, and that she is faced with a considerable risk of death or crippling paralysis if she becomes pregnant. The net question is whether it is constitutionally permissible in the circumstances for the law to deny her access to the contraceptive method chosen for her by her doctor and which she and her husband wish to adopt. In other words, is the prohibition effected by s 17 of the Act of 1935 an interference with the rights which the State guarantees in its laws to respect, as stated in sub-s 1 of s 3 of Article 40?

The answer lies primarily in the fact that the plaintiff is a wife and a mother. It is the informed and conscientious wish of the plaintiff and her husband to maintain full marital relations without incurring the risk of a pregnancy that may very well result in her death or in a crippling paralysis. Section 17 of the Act of 1935 frustrates that wish. It goes further; it brings the implementation of the wish within the range of the criminal law. Its effect, therefore, is to condemn the plaintiff and her husband to a way of life which, at best, will be fraught with worry, tension and uncertainty that cannot but adversely effect their lives and, at worst, will result in an unwanted pregnancy causing death or serious illness with the obvious tragic consequences to the lives of her husband and young children. And this in the context of a Constitution which in its preamble proclaims as one of its aims the dignity and freedom of the individual; which in sub-s 2 of s 3 of Article 40 casts on the State a duty to protect as best it may from unjust attack and, in the case of injustice done, to vindicate the life and person of every citizen; which in Article 41, after recognising the family as the natural primary and fundamental unit group of society, and as a moral institution possessing inalienable and imprescriptible rights antecedent and superior to all positive law, guarantees to protect it in its constitution and authority as the necessary basis of social order and as indispensable to the welfare of the nation and the State; and which, also in Article 41, pledges the State to guard with special care the institution of marriage, on which the family is founded, and to protect it against attack.

Section 17, in my judgment, so far from respecting the plaintiff's personal rights, violates them. If she observes this prohibition (which in practice she can scarcely avoid doing and which in law she is bound under penalty of fine and imprisonment to do), she will endanger the security and happiness of her marriage, she will imperil her health to the point of hazarding her life, and she will subject her family to the risk of distress and disruption. These are intrusions which she is entitled to say are incompatible with the safety of her life, the preservation of her health, her responsibility to her conscience, and the security and well-being of her marriage and family. If she fails to obey the prohibition in s 17, the law, by prosecuting her, will reach into the privacy of her marital life in seeking to prove her guilt.

In my opinion, s 17 of the Act of 1935 violates the guarantee in sub-s 1 of s 3 of Article 40 by the State to protect the plaintiff's personal rights by its laws; it does so not only by violating her personal right to privacy in regard to her marital relations but, in a wider way, by frustrating and making criminal any efforts by her to effectuate the decision of her husband and herself, made responsibly, conscientiously and on medical advice, to avail themselves of a particular contraceptive method so as to ensure her life and health as well as the integrity, security and well-being of her marriage and her family. Because of the clear unconstitutionality of the section in this respect, I do not find it necessary to deal with the submissions made in support of the claim that the section violates other provisions of the Constitution.

4.145   *Norris v Attorney-General*
                                    [1984] IR 36
                                 Supreme Court, 1983

Facts: The plaintiff was a homosexual who sought a declaration that s 61 and s 62 of the Offences Against the Person Act 1861, and s 11 of the Criminal Law Amendment Act 1885 were inconsistent with the Constitution. Essentially his argument was that he had a private right to sexual expression and that this was infringed by these enactments in a manner which was inconsistent with the Christian and democratic nature of the State.

O'Higgins CJ: . . . The plaintiff is now and has been, since 1967, a lecturer in English at Trinity College, Dublin. He is aged 38 and is unmarried. Although born in Leopoldville, in the former Belgian Congo, he is an Irish citizen. He has asserted in his statement of claim and in evidence that he is congenitally and irreversibly homosexual in outlook and disposition, that he is neither sexually attracted to nor has he any interest in women, that he desires a sexual relationship based on his congenital orientation and that for him any heterosexual relationship, such as that of marriage, is not open or possible.

He claims that at any early age his realisation of his own feelings and disposition, and a growing awareness of public attitudes and of the state and sanctions of the criminal law, not only caused him considerable anxiety and distress but also led to a profound nervous illness which required protracted medical care and counselling. When he recovered from his illness, he decided to declare hismelf publicly as a homosexual and, with other homosexual men and women, formed an association known as the Irish Gay Rights Movement, of which he became chairman.

. . . He indicated in evidence the reforms and changes which he wished to achieve, which would provide protection for the young and incapacitated, but would free from all criminal sanctions homosexual conduct carried out in private between consenting male adults. Lest it be thought that this Court could or should consider the merits of such proposed reforms or express any view thereon, I desire to make it clear that such is not and can never be a function of this Court. The sole function of this Court, in a case of this nature, is to interpret the Constitution and the law and to declare with objectivity and impartiality the result of that interpretation on the claim being considered.

At the core of the plaintiff's challenge to the impugned legislation is the assertion that the State has no business in the field of private morality and has no right to legislate in relation to the private sexual conduct of consenting adults. It is the plaintiff's case that to attempt to do so is to exceed the limits of permissible interference and to shatter that area of privacy which the dignity and liberty of human persons require to be kept apart as a haven for each citizen. Accordingly, the plaintiff says that any legislation which purports to do so is *de facto* inconsistent with the Constitution. Apart from this, however, the plaintiff has advanced other grounds of alleged inconsistency which must be considered. I propose in the first place to deal with these other grounds and then to return to what appears to be the plaintiff's main submission.

As already mentioned, the plaintiff argues that the impugned legislation is inconsistent with Article 40, s 1, of the Constitution in that it discriminates against male citizens who are homosexual. I understand his complaint in this respect to be confined to the Act of 1885. In case I am incorrect in this respect, however, I would like to express the view that such an argument is scarcely entertainable in relation to the impugned sections of the Act of 1861. The act which constitutes buggery can only be committed by males. It is designated as a crime whether it is committed with a male or a female. It follows that the prohibition applies to the act irrespective of whether it is committed by a homosexual or by a heterosexual male. No discrimination could be involved.

As to gross indecency, however, the prohibition only applies to such conduct between males. Does the fact that it does not apply to gross indecency between females involve a discrimination which would be prohibited by Article 40, section 1, I do not think so. The legislature would be perfectly entitled to have regard to the difference between the sexes and to treat sexual conduct or gross indecency between males as requiring prohibition because of the social problem which it creates, while at the same time looking at sexual conduct between females as being not only different but as posing no such social problem. Furthermore, in alleging discrimination because the prohibition on the conduct which he claims he is entitled to engage in is not extended to similar conduct by females, the plaintiff is complaining of a situation which, if it did not exist or were remedied, would confer on him no benefit or vindicate no right of his which he claims to be breached. I do not think that such an argument should be entertained by this Court. For the same reasons, I would reject the plaintiff's complaint that there is discrimination in the fact that the laws of the State do not apply criminal sanctions to heterosexual conduct outside marriage between consenting adults.

The plaintiff has also submitted that the blanket prohibition of homosexual conduct effected by the legislation threatens his physical and mental health through frustration and disorientation arising from his congenital disposition. For this reason the plaintiff asserts that his right to bodily integrity is endangered. In my opinion this submission is not a sound one. If the legislation is otherwise valid and within the competence of the legislature to enact, it cannot be rendered inoperative merely because compliance with it by the plaintiff is difficult for, or harmful to, him due to his innate or congenital disposition. In this respect the exigencies of the common good must prevail. The plaintiff also alleges that this legislation and, in particular, s 11 of the Act of 1885, impairs his rights of freedom of expression and freedom of association which are guaranteed by Article 40, s 6, of the Constitution. I do not accept this submission. Freedom of expression and freedom of association are not guaranteed as absolute rights. They are protected by the Constitution subject to public order and morality. Accordingly, if the impugned legislation is otherwise valid and consistent with the Constitution, the mere fact that it prohibits the plaintiff from advocating conduct which it prohibits or from encouraging others to engage in such conduct or associating with others for the purpose of so doing, cannot constitute a breach of the Constitution.

I now turn to what I have described as the core of the plaintiff's case. This is the claim that the impugned legislation constitutes an unwarranted interference with his private life and thereby infringes his right to privacy. This claim is based on the philosophical view, attributed to John Stuart Mill, that the law should not concern itself in the realm of private morality except to the extent necessary for the protection of public order and the guarding of citizens against injury or exploitation. It is a view which received significant endorsement in the report of the Wolfenden Committee on Homosexual Offences and Prostitution. That committee's report, furnished to the British Parliament in 1957, contained the following statement in support of its recommendation for limited decriminalisation:—

"There remains one additional counter argument which we believe to be decisive, namely, the importance which society and the law ought to give to individual freedom of choice in action in matters of private morality. Unless a deliberate attempt is to be made by society, acting through the agency of the law, to equate the sphere of crime with that of sin, there must remain a realm of private morality and immorality, which is, in brief and crude terms not the law's business. To say this is not to condone or encourage private immorality."

The Wolfenden Committee had been established by the Scottish Home Office and, although it recommended (in effect) the removal of criminal sanctions from homosexual conduct when carried out in private between adult responsible males, the British Parliament was very slow to accept that recommendation and to act upon it. It was not until the Sexual Offences Act 1967 (which was introduced as a private member's bill) that the law was changed in England and Wales; in Scotland the change was not made until the passing of the Criminal Justice (Scotland) Act 1980. In relation to Northern Ireland, the British Parliament declined to act until compelled to do so as a result of the recent decision of the European Court of Human Rights in *Dudgeon v United Kingdom*. The caution shown by successive British Governments and Parliaments is understandable because what was proposed was a significant reversal of legislative policy in an area in which deep religious and moral beliefs were involved.

From the earliest days, organised religion regarded homosexual conduct, such as sodomy and associated acts, with a deep revulsion as being contrary to the order of nature, a perversion of the biological functions of the sexual organs and an affront both to society and to God. With the advent of Christianity this view found clear expression in the teachings of St. Paul, and has been repeated over the centuries by the doctors and leaders of the Church in every land in which the Gospel of Christ has been preached. To-day, as appears from the evidence given in this case, this strict view is beginning to be questioned by individual Christian theologians but, nevertheless, as the learned trial judge said in his judgment it remains the teaching of all Christian Churches that homosexual acts are wrong.

In England, buggery was first treated as a crime by the statute 25 Hen. VIII c 6, having been previously dealt with only in the ecclesiastical courts. In Ireland, it first received statutory condemnation in the statute of the Irish Parliament 10 Chas I, sess 2, c 20. Subject to statutory changes as to punishment, it continued to be prohibited and punished as a crime in accordance with the provisions of the Act of 1861 which were complemented by the later provisions of the Act of 1885. While those statutory provisions have now been repealed in the entire of the United Kingdom, the question in this case is whether they ceased to operate in Ireland at the time of the enactment of the Constitution in 1937.

In the course of the trial of this action in the High Court, reference was made to the Wolfenden Report, to the Kinsey Survey on homosexual behaviour conducted in the United States and to a similar survey conducted in Sweden. No such survey has been conducted in Ireland, but the trial judge, on the evidence he heard was prepared to conclude that there is probably a large number of people in this country with homosexual tendencies. Of these, however, only a small number are exclusively homosexual in the sense that their orientation is congenital and irreversible. It is this small group (of those with homosexual tendencies) who must look to the others for the kind of relationship, stable or promiscuous, which they seek and desire. It follows that the efforts and activities of the congenital must tend towards involving the homosexually orientated in more and more deviant sexual acts to such an extent that such involvement may become habitual. The evidence in this case and the text-books produced as part thereof indicate how sad, lonely and harrowing the life of a person, who is or has become exclusively homosexual, is likely to be. Professor West in his work, Homosexuality Re-Examined, states at p 318:— "Exclusive homosexuality forces a person into a minority group; cuts off all prospect of fulfilment through a family life with children and hampers participation in mainstream social activities which are mostly geared to the needs of heterosexual couples." He goes on to talk of those, whose life centres on short-term liaisons, as facing loneliness and frustration as they lose their sexual attractiveness with advancing age. Other authors, also referred to, indicate the instability of male homosexual relations, the high incidence of suicide attempts and the depressive reactions which frequently occur when a relationship ends (Harrison; Reid, Barrett & Hewer). These are some of the consequences which, experience has indicated, tend to follow on a lifestyle which is exclusively homosexual.

Apart from these sad consequences of exclusive homosexuality, unfortunately there are other problems thereby created which constitute a threat to public health. Professor West in his work already mentioned, which was published in a revised form in England over ten years after the decriminalisation of homosexual conduct, says at p 228:— "Far from being immune from venereal infection, as many used to like to believe, male homosexuals run a particularly high risk of acquiring sexually transmitted diseases." The author goes on to show that in the post-decriminalisation decade in Britain many forms of venereal disease (syphilis, gonorrhoea, urethritis and intestinal infection) have shown an alarming increase in males, and that this is attributable directly to the increase in homosexual activity and conduct. In relation to syphilis, the author gives this serious warning:— "A promiscuous homosexual with such a reservoir of infection can transmit the disease, in all innocence, to a whole sequence of victims before the carrier is discovered. The diagnosis at this stage is not always obvious, even when suspected, since blood tests for this infection do not usually become positive until some weeks after the primary chancre has appeared." He might well have added that, in the case of the novice or the new entrant into homosexual activity, reticence or shame might well delay further the tracing and discovery of the carrier.

Apart from these known consequences of fairly widespread homosexual behaviour and conduct, one other matter of particular importance should be noted. This is the effect of homosexual activity on marriage. It has to be accepted that, for the small percentage of males who are congenitally and irreversibly homosexual, marriage is not open or possible. They must seek such partnerships as they can amongst those whose orientation disposes them to homosexual overtures. But for those so disposed or orientated, but not yet committed, what effect will the acceptance of such overtures be likely to have on marriage? Again, precise information in relation to Ireland is not available. One can only look to what the Wolfenden Committee said in its report (para 55) before the changes in the law occurred in the United Kingdom:— "The second contention, that homosexual behaviour between males has a damaging effect on family life, may well be true. Indeed we have had evidence that it often is: cases in which homosexual behaviour on the part of the husband has broken up a marriage are by no means rare, and there are also cases in which a man in whom the homosexual component is relatively weak, nevertheless, derives such satisfaction from homosexual outlets that he does not enter upon a marriage which might have been successfully and happily consummated. We deplore this damage to what we regard as the basic unit of society."

That view was based on the limited experience available to the Committee prior to any changes in the law. It indicates, however, that homosexual activity and its encouragement may not be consistent with respect and regard for marriage as an institution. I would not think it unreasonable to conclude that an open and general increase in homosexual activity in any society must have serious consequences of a harmful nature so far as marriage is concerned.

I have been speaking of homosexuality and of its possible consequences in accordance with what, in my view, can be gathered from the evidence in this case. What I have said can be summarised as follows.

(1) Homosexuality has always been condemned in Christian teaching as being morally wrong. It has equally been regarded by society for many centuries as an offence against nature and a very serious crime.

(2) Exclusive homosexuality, whether the condition be congenital or acquired, can result in great distress and unhappiness for the individual and can lead to depression, despair and suicide.

(3) The homosexuality orientated can be importuned into a homosexual lifestyle which can become habitual.

(4) Male homosexual conduct has resulted, in other countries, in the spread of all forms of venereal disease and this has now become a significant public-health problem in England.

(5) Homosexual conduct can be inimical to marriage and is *per se* harmful to it as an institution.

In the United Kingdom the decisive factor in bringing about decriminalisation of homosexuality was the acceptance of the view advocated by the Wolfenden Committee, and repeated in this case by the plaintiff, that homosexuality was concerned only with private morality and that the law had no business in entering into that field. Whether such a view can be accepted in Ireland depends not on what was done by a sovereign parliament in the United Kingdom but on what our Constitution ordains and requires.

The preamble to the Constitution proudly asserts the existence of God in the Most Holy Trinity and recites that the people of Ireland humbly acknowledge their obligation to "our Divine Lord, Jesus Christ." It cannot be doubted that the people, so asserting and acknowledging their obligations to our Divine Lord Jesus Christ, were proclaiming a deep religious conviction and faith and an intention to adopt a Constitution consistent with that conviction and faith and with Christian beliefs. Yet it is suggested that, in the very act of so doing, the people rendered inoperative laws which had existed for hundreds of years prohibiting unnatural sexual conduct which Christian teaching held to be gravely sinful. It would require very clear and express provisions in the Constitution itself to convince me that such took place. When one considers that the conduct in question had been condemned consistently in the name of Christ for almost two thousand years and, at the time of the enactment of the Constitution, was prohibited as criminal by the laws in force in England, Wales, Scotland and Northern Ireland, the suggestion becomes more incomprehensible and difficult of acceptance.

But the plaintiff says that the continued operation of such laws was inconsistent with a right of privacy which he enjoys. Here, in so far as the law and the State are concerned, he asserts a "no go area" in the field of private morality. I do not accept this view either as a general philosophical proposition concerning the purpose of law or as having particular reference to a right of privacy under our Constitution. I regard the State as having an interest in the general moral wellbeing of the community and as being entitled, where it is practicable to do so, to discourage conduct which is morally wrong and harmful to a way of life and to values which the State wishes to protect.

A right of privacy or, as it has been put, a right "to be let alone"' can never be absolute. There are many acts done in private which the State is entitled to condemn, whether such be done by an individual on his own or with another. The law has always condemned abortion, incest, suicide attempts, suicide pacts, euthanasia or mercy killing. These are prohibited simply because they are morally wrong and regardless of the fact, which may exist in some instances, that no harm or injury to others is involved. With homosexual conduct, the matter is not so simple or clear. Such conduct is, of course, morally wrong, and has been so regarded by mankind through the centuries. It cannot be said of it, however, as the plaintiff seeks to say, that no harm is done if it is conducted in private by consenting males. Very serious harm may in fact be involved. Such conduct, although carried on with full consent, may lead a mildly homosexually orientated person into a way of life from which he may never recover. As already indicated, known consequences are frustration, loneliness and even suicide. In addition, it is clearly established that an increase in the practice of homosexuality amongst males increases the incidence of all forms of venereal disease, including the incapacitating and often fatal disease of syphilis. Surely, in the light of such possible consequences, no one could regard with equanimity the freeing of such conduct from all legal restraints with the certain result that it would increase and its known devotees multiply. These, however, are not the only considerations.

There is the effect of homosexuality on marriage. As long ago as 1957 the Wolfenden Committee acknowledged, in relation to Great Britain, the serious harm such conduct caused to marriage not only in turning men away from it as a partnership in life but also in breaking up existing marriages. That was the conclusion reached as to the state of acts before the criminal sanctions were removed. One can only suspect that, with the removal of such sanctions and with the encouragement thereby given to homosexual conduct, considerably more harm must have been caused in Great Britain to marriage as an institution. In Ireland, in this respect, the State has a particular duty. Article 41, s 3, sub-s 1, of the Constitution provides:— "The State pledges itself to guard with special care the institution of Marriage, on which the Family is founded, and to protect it against attack." Surely, a law which prohibits acts and conduct by male citizens of a kind known to be particularly harmful to the institution of marriage cannot be regarded as inconsistent with a Constitution containing such a provision.

On the ground of the Christian nature of our State and on the grounds that the deliberate practice of homosexuality is morally wrong, that it is damaging to the health both of individuals and the public and, finally, that it is potentially harmful to the institution of marriage, I can find no inconsistency with the Consititution in the laws which make such conduct criminal . . .

Finlay P and Griffin J concurred.

The laws in question were later found to be inconsistent with the European Convention on Human Rights; see *Norris v Ireland*[4]. The Law Reform Commission have recommended the complete reform of the law on homosexuality in their report on Child Sexual Abuse[5].

4.146   *King v The Attorney-General*
                    [1981] IR 233
                  Supreme Court, 1980

Facts: The plaintiff was found guilty of two offences of "loitering with intent" under the Vagrancy Act 1824 (as amended by the Prevention of Crimes Act 1871 and the Penal Servitude Act 1891). He was also convicted of possession of

4 Eur Court HR 26 October 1988, series A No 142
5 (LRC 32–1990).

house-breaking implements with intent to steal. The proof of intent is often difficult. It may be inferred from the acts and declarations of the accused assisted by the presumption that the person intends the natural and probable consequences of his acts. It may also be expressly proved by the accused's own admission. The intent portion of the offence of "loitering with intent" was proved by the prosecution establishing that intent from the circumstances of the known character of the accused. This meant, unlike in the vast majority of other criminal offences, the prosecution were entitled to make reference to the accused's previous convictions for the purpose of proving his guilt. Thus where two persons, A and B, were seen by a Garda wandering around a deserted street in the middle of the night, A, if he had just been released from serving a prison sentence, was more likely to be convicted than B, despite the fact that they were each engaged in precisely the same activity. The offence was struck down by the High Court, and on appeal by the Supreme Court, as unconstitutional. A strange effect of this decision was that the State stopped prosecuting prostitutes for various offences of solicitation. This was because the provisions in question contained a reference to the accused being "a common prostitute". Apparently the office of the Chief State Solicitor received advice to the effect that this status provision infringed the principle in King's case. That advice was, it is submitted, wrong. The element of being a common prostitute was proved from the prosecution leading evidence proving solicitation on other occasions. It was not necessary to refer to a woman's previous convictions. The effect of this advice has been to considerably weaken the law of protecting women from sexual exploitations. This strange example of law making without judicial decision requires reform. Details proposals in that regard are contained in the Law Reform Commission Report on Vagrancy and Selected Offences of 1985 which like the majority of the reports, awaits implementation.

McWilliam J [High Court]: . . . The requirements of the offences with which the plaintiff was charged were that he should be a suspected person or a reputed thief, that he should have been loitering in a public place, and that he should have had an intent to commit a felony, *ie*, to steal. But no proof of any act showing an intent to commit a felony was necessary as the statute provides that such intent may be established from the bad character of the plaintiff and the circumstances of the case. I may observe that the expression "loitering" is somewhat indefinite and that, without the other ingredients, it could not possibly constitute an offence in any way; so that doing something which is a perfectly lawful act on the part of any other citizen may be the foundation of an offence on the part of a suspected person or a reputed thief. As no proof of any act showing intent to commit a felony is necessary, a person could be convicted for doing an otherwise lawful act mainly because he was a suspected person or a reputed thief.

The concept of justice appears in Article 34, s 1, of the Constitution which commences:— "Justice shall be administered in courts established by law by judges appointed in the manner provided by this Constitution . . .." In *The State (Healy) v Donoghue* the Chief Justice said at p 348 of the report:— "In the first place the concept of justice, which is specifically referred to in the preamble in relation to the freedom and dignity of the individual, appears again in the provisions of Article 34 which deal with the courts. It is justice which is to be administered in the courts and this concept of justice must import not only fairness, and fair procedures, but also regard to the dignity of the individual." He went on to adopt the view expressed by Mr Justice Gannon in the High Court at p 333:— "Before dealing with the submissions on the grounds on which the conditional orders were made, I think I should say at the outset that it appears to me that the determination of the question of whether or not a court of local and limited jurisdiction is acting within its jurisdiction is not confined to an examination of the statutory limits of jurisdiction imposed on the court. It appears to me that this question involves also an examination of whether or not the court is performing the basic function for which it is established – the administration of justice. Even if all the formalities of the statutory limitation of the court be complied with and if court procedures are formally satisfied, it is my opinion that the court in such instance is not acting within its jurisdiction if, at the same time, the person accused is deprived of any of his basic rights of justice at a criminal trial." At p 349 of the report the Chief Justice said:— "Being so considered, it is clear that the words 'due course of law' in Article 38 make it mandatory that every criminal trial shall be conducted in accordance with the concept of justice, that the procedures applied shall be fair, and that the person accused will be afforded every opportunity to defend himself."

In delivering the judgment of the Supreme Court in *The Criminal Law (Jurisdiction) Bill, 1975* (the Chief Justice said at p 152 of the report:— "The provisions of Article 38, s 1, of the Constitution, stating that no person shall be tried on a criminal charge save in due course of law, require fair and just treatment for the person so charged, having due regard to the rights of the State to prosecute for the offence charged and to ensure that the person so charged will stand his trial. The phrase 'due course of law' requires a fair and just balance between the exercise of individual freedoms and the requirements of an ordered society."

Mr Justice Kenny included the right to free movement within the State amongst the personal rights which are defended and vindicated by Article 40, s 3, sub-s 1, of the Constitution: see *Ryan v The Attorney General* at p 313. This appears to me to include moving slowly, dawdling or stopping for a time. Article 40, s 1, specifically provides that all citizens shall, as human persons, be held equal before the law. It appears to me also that amongst these citizens are to be included those who have been previously convicted, at any rate when acting in any capacity which is not directly concerned with their previous conviction. One of the concepts of justice which the courts have always accepted is that evidence of character or of previous convictions shall not be given at a criminal trial except at the instigation of the accused, as that could prejudice the fair trial of the issue of the guilt or innocence of the accused. In *The People (Attorney General) v O'Callaghan* Ó Dálaigh CJ said at p 509 of the report:— "The courts owe more than verbal respect to the principle that punishment begins after conviction, and that every man is deemed to be innocent until tried and duly found guilty."

In *R v Harris* Humphreys J said at p 113 with regard to the amendment made by s 15 of the Act of 1871:— "That obviously allows, in such a case, something to be given in evidence which would otherwise according to the common law of England, not be admissible, this is, laying before the tribunal of fact evidence of the previous bad character of the accused person although he had not himself put his character is issue." In *R v Goodwin* the same judge, when giving the judgment of the Court of Criminal Appeal in England in a case concerning s 7 of the Act of 1871, said at pp 523–4:— "The provisions of s 7 are unusual in that they require that the jury shall know that the man whom they are trying has been previously convicted, and is likely, according to what is known of him, to commit the offence with which he is charged. On most charges, the greatest care is taken to keep precisely that fact from the knowledge of the jury. That being so, whenever a charge under s 7 is brought the judge and everyone else concerned in the case should be meticulously careful to see that the accused person is not convicted except upon clear and unmistakable evidence that he has committed the particular offence charged against him."

Those cases are very relevant when considering whether the constitutional concept of justice, which imports fairness and fair procedures, is or is not observed in the case of a prosecution under s 4 of the Act of 1824, as amended. Although I accept the proposition that a Justice is less likely to be prejudiced than a jury, evidence of previous character and convictions is bound to affect anyone's mind to a greater or lesser extent; it appears to me that the provision enabling such evidence to be given was included to enable a Justice to convict in the absence of other satisfactory evidence.

There are two ways in which that part of s 4 of the Act of 1824, as amended, offends against the provisions of the Constitution. First, the provisions that evidence may be given of the known character of the accused and that no evidence need be given of any act showing, or tending to show, intent are contrary to the concept of justice which is implicit in the Constitution. Secondly, that part of the section offends against the provision that all citizens shall be held equal before the law, since a suspected person or a previously convicted person can be prevented from doing what it is perfectly lawful for any other citizen to do, *ie* walk slowly, dawdle or stop altogether in a public street.

Henchy J [Supreme Court]: Section 4 of the Act of 1824, as originally enacted, created a wide variety of offences. In the present case, however, we are concerned only with so much of the amended s 4 as was in force in Saorstát Éireann immediately before the coming into operation of the Constitution, and which was applied against the plaintiff so as to produce the convictions in respect of loitering. The judge correctly held that all other offences or matters purported to be dealt with in the sections in question are outside the scope of the constitutional argument in this case.

The question, therefore, is whether there is an inconsistency with the Constitution in the relevant parts of s 4 of the Act of 1824, as amended. Those parts (in so far as they are the basis of the charges of "loitering with intent") have been strung together in the judgment and order under appeal. I adopt that version, with some minor changes, as follows:—

". . . every suspected person or reputed thief, frequenting [or loitering about or in] any river, canal or navigable stream, dock or basin, or any quay, wharf or warehouse near or adjoining thereto, on any street, highway or avenue leading thereto, or any place of public resort, or any avenue leading thereto, or any street, or any highway or any place adjacent to a street or highway, with intent to commit felony . . . shall be deemed a rogue and vagabond, within the true intent and meaning of this Act; and it shall be lawful for any Justice of the Peace to commit such offender (being thereof convicted before him by the confession of such offender, or by the evidence on oath of one or more credible witness or witnesses) to the House of Correction, there to be kept to hard labour for any time not exceeding three calendar months . . . and . . . in proving the intent to commit a felony it shall not be necessary to show that the person suspected was guilty of any particular act or acts tending to show his purpose or intent, and he may be convicted if from the circumstances of the case, and from his known character as proved to the Justice of the Peace or court before whom or which he is brought, it appears to such justice or court that his intent was to commit a felony . . ."

It will be seen that, in order to secure a conviction in a prosecution such as this, it is necessary to prove that the accused was a suspected person or a reputed thief and that he was frequenting, or loitering in, any of the named types of places or areas with intent to commit a felony. To prove the intent to commit a felony, no overt act is necessary: instead, that intent may be inferred from the circumstances and from his known character (*ie* previous convictions) as proved to the court.

In my opinion, the ingredients of the offence and the mode by which its commission may be proved are so arbitrary, so vague, so difficult to rebut, so related to rumour or ill-repute or past conduct, so ambiguous in failing to distinguish between apparent and real behaviour of a criminal nature, so prone to make a man's lawful occasions become unlawful and criminal by the breadth and arbitrariness of the discretion that is vested in both the prosecutor and the judge, so indiscriminately contrived to mark as criminal conduct committed by one

293

person in certain circumstances when the same conduct, when engaged in by another person in similar circumstances, would be free of the taint of criminality, so out of keeping with the basic concept inherent in our legal system that a man may walk abroad in the secure knowledge that he will not be singled out from his fellow-citizens and branded and punished as a criminal unless it has been established beyond reasonable doubt that he has deviated from a clearly prescribed standard of conduct, and generally so singularly at variance with both the explicit and implicit characteristics and limitations of the criminal law as to the onus of proof and mode of proof, that it is not so much a question of ruling unconstitutional the type of offence we are now considering as identifying the particular constitutional provisions with which such an offence is at variance.

I shall confine myself to saying, without going into unnecessary detail, that the offence, both in its essential ingredients and in the mode of proof of its commission, violates the requirement in Article 38, s 1, that no person shall be tried on any criminal charge save in due course of law; that it violates the guarantee in Article 40, s 4, sub-s 1, that no citizen shall be deprived of personal liberty save in accordance with law – which means without stooping to methods which ignore the fundamental norms of the legal order postulated by the Constitution; that, in its arbitrariness and its unjustifiable discrimination, it fails to hold (as is required by Article 40, s 1) all citizens to be equal before the law; and that it ignores the guarantees in Article 40, s 3, that the personal rights of citizens shall be respected and, as far as practicable, defended and vindicated, and that the State shall by its laws protect as best it may from unjust attack and, in the case of injustice done, vindicate the life, good name, and property rights of every citizen.

Kenny J: . . . I am convinced that the whole of the part of the Act of 1824 which I have quoted is inconsistent with the Constitution. It is a fundamental feature of our system of government by law (and not by decree or diktat) that citizens may be convicted only of offences which have been specified with precision by the judges who made the common law, or of offences which, created by statute, are expressed without ambiguity. But what does "suspected person" mean? Suspected of what? What does "reputed thief" mean? Reputed by whom? It does not mean a person who has been convicted of theft, for then "convicted thief" would have been the appropriate words. So one is driven back to the conclusion that it is impossible to ascertain the meaning of the expressions. In my opinion, both governing phrases "suspected person" and "reputed thief" are so uncertain that they cannot form the foundation for a criminal offence.

There is Irish authority for the proposition that a person may be convicted of a criminal offence only if the ingredients of, and the acts constituting, the offence are specified with precision and clarity. O'Byrne J in delivering the judgment of the Court of Criminal Appeal in *The Attorney General v Cunningham*, said at p 32 of the report:— ". . . the court must have regard to the fundamental doctrine recognised in these courts that the criminal law must be certain and specific, and that no person is to be punished unless and until he has been convicted of an offence recognised by law as a crime and punishable as such." O'Byrne J quoted those words and approved of them when he was a judge of this Court: see *The People (Attorney General) v Edge* at p 142.

Article 38, s 1, of the Constitution provides:— "No person shall be tried on any criminal charge save in due course of law." If the ingredients of the offence charged are vague and uncertain, the trial of an alleged offence based on those ingredients is not in due course of law. On this ground I am of opinion that the part of s 4 of the Act of 1824 which I have quoted is inconsistent with the Constitution.

O'Higgins CJ concurred.

Griffin J and Parke J agreed with Henchy J.

4.147 In Canada the relationship between the criminal law and constitutional justice has been much litigated. In particular the concept of constitutional fairness has been focused on the rules of substantive criminal law, as expressed in the Code. Any potential injustice to an accused person arising from the operation of the rules of criminal law has been resolved by a finding of unconstitutionality. It might be thought that a similar analysis of Irish criminal law should uncover rules of law and procedure which are unjust in their operation. The amorphous nature of Irish criminal law has rendered litigation, in many case, unnecessary. As we see throughout the course of this work the rules of substantive criminal law are often unclear and choices can usually be made between varying concepts. Criminal procedure is in a similar position. The judiciary involved in the decision making process on the rules of criminal law are Circuit Court judges. Decisions are not reserved and written opinions are rarely given. For the most part, practice reveals, the judges of the circuit court are guided by the spirit of *The People (DPP) v Murray*[6]. Generally, a subjective approach to the analysis of the elements of a crime and the possible existence of a defence is taken. Elements of strict liability are discounted and a subjective approach to the concepts of intent and recklessness is taken. The only exception, in general practice, has been that the element of age in offences relating to sexual exploitation is taken as being one of absolute liability. In the context of this approach accused persons have little scope for litigation having regard to the previously stated rule that points of a non constitutional nature must be exhausted before the Constitution is explored. In Canada the situation is in marked contrast as the rules of criminal law have been written down in the form of a code. The certainty of the rules precludes their being adopted or bent in an attempt to give substantial justice where the possibility of unfairness arises[7].

4.148   *Canadian Criminal Code*

11   No civil remedy for an act or omission is suspended or affected by reason that the act or omission is a criminal offence.

15   No person shall be convicted of an offence in respect of an act or omission in obedience to the laws for the time being made and enforced by persons in de facto possession of the sovereign power in and over the place where the act or omission occurs.

19   Ignorance of the law by a person who commits an offence is not an excuse for committing that offence.

Further Materials

4.149   Redmond *The Criminal Law Jurisdiction Act and the Constitution* Ir Jur XIII (ns) 67.
Morgan *The Emergency Powers Bill Reference* Ir Jur XIII (ns) 67, XIV (ns) 22.

---

6 [1977] IR 360.
7 See generally *Kirkness* (1990) 60 CCC (3d) 97 SC; *Logan* (1990) 58 CCC (3d) 391 SC; *Rodney* (1990) 58 CCC (3d) 408 SC; *JJC* (1990) 59 CCC (3d) 1 SC; Ellis – Don Ltd (1990) 61 CCC (3d) 423 CA Ontario; *Dubois* 1990 62 CCC (3d) 90 CA Quebec.

Law Reform Commission *Report on Vagrancy in Relation to Offences*, 1985
(LRC 11 – 1985).
Forde *Constitutional Law of Ireland* (1987) chapter 13.

Provocation

4.150 Provocation is a defence special to murder. In England the defence
has not been extended to such offences as assault with intent to murder or
attempted murder; *Holmes v DPP*[8]. This approach is supported in Canada;
R v Campbell[9]. The situation in Australia is more complex with a trend in the
direction of allowing provocation to be pleaded as a defence to attempted
murder and the various statutory variations of that crime, such as wounding
with intent to murder[10].

4.151 The essence of provocation is a sudden loss of self-control in an
accused person to the extent that he is unable to prevent himself from
intentionally killing another person; *R v Thornton*[11]. As such, the law is a
concession to human frailty.

4.152 The policy of the law may also take into account that the deceased
may be partially responsible for his own death in having provoked the
"murderous attack". The one principle which has remained unshaken in the
history of the defence is that the accused must have acted under a temporary
suspension of reason; his intent to kill or seriously injure the victim over-
whelmed his ability to think and to control himself.

Development

4.153 The emergence of objective rules in dealing with a situation of
violent passion was particularly inappropriate in relation to the defence of
provocation. The strength of people's emotions vary and the possibility of
triggering off a violent psychic upheaval depends on the character and
background of each individual person. Someone from a particular ethnic
background may be seriously upset if called by the disparaging word vulgarly
applied to that group. A similar remark would not at all upset someone from
a different background. Objectivity was cast in the form of a rule which
required (1) that the accused actually lose self-control and (2) that a reasonable or ordinary person would have reacted similarly.

The reasonable man test reached its high water mark in England in the case
of *Bedder v DPP*[12]. The House of Lords held that an eighteen year old
sexually impotent youth was not to be judged in the context of these
characteristics but as a sexually able ordinary adult. The deceased was a
prostitute. She had jeered at the accused on account of his impotence and
had kicked him in the testicles.

8 [1946] AC 588.
9 (1977) 58 CCC (2d) 6.
10 O'Connor and Fairall p 192–203.
11 *The Independent*, 30 July 1991.
12 [1954] 2 All ER 801.

4.154 In the face of a storm of academic criticism the Court of Criminal Appeal in Ireland sought an alternative. Neither the New Zealand Crimes Act 1961, nor the case of *R v McGregor*[13] were argued before the court. Instead a dissenting judgment of Murphy J in *Moffa v R*[14] was used.

4.155   *The People (DPP) v Sean MacEoin*
                                          [1978] IR 27
                              Court of Criminal Appeal, 1978

Kenny J: The accused, Seán MacEoin, was tried in the Central Criminal Court before Mr Justice Butler and a jury on the charge that on the 25th April, 1976, he murdered Patrick Hyland; he was found guilty. The accused applied unsuccessfully for a certificate of leave to appeal and he now appeals to this Court. At the end of the argument, the Court said that leave to appeal would be given, that the application for leave would be treated as the hearing of the appeal, which would be allowed, and that a new trial would be ordered. The Court indicated that it would give its reasons for its decision at a later date this we now do.

As the accused, when giving evidence, admitted that he had struck the deceased with a hammer, and as his counsel told the jury in his closing speech that the only issue they had to decide was whether the accused was guilty of murder or manslaughter, it is not necessary to deal with the history of the relationship between the two men in any detail. In 1973 the accused was serving a sentence of imprisonment in Mountjoy; he met the deceased there and became friendly with him. The deceased invited the accused to the deceased's flat at No 12B Upper Seán MacDermott Street, Dublin, and the accused visited him there periodically. At the beginning of April, 1976, the deceased requested the accused to come to live with him in the flat and the accused agreed to do this; the accused moved his belongings from where he was living and went to reside in the flat. Both of them were unmarried. The deceased drank heavily and, when drunk, spoke loudly to himself and became aggressive.

On Saturday the 25th April, 1976, the accused was not working and he went to a number of public houses; he went back to the flat at intervals and, when he did, he found the deceased there. The accused had about 14–20 pints of stout during the day before he finally returned to the flat at about 11.30 pm where he found the deceased sitting at a table with a bottle of wine on it and talking to himself. The accused made up a makeshift bed for himself (there was only one bed in the flat) and got into it. After some time the deceased came towards the bed shouting:— "You are going" and "You are going now." When the accused sat up in the bed, the deceased produced a hammer from behind his back and hit the accused on the head with it. The hammer fell on the floor and the two of them struggled for it. The accused got it and the deceased started to punch him. In evidence the accused said that he was terrified because the deceased looked dangerous; he then said:— "I simmered over and I completely lost control of myself." He hit the deceased on the head with the hammer and the deceased fell on the floor. The accused then stooped down and in a rage hit the deceased a number of blows (which he estimated from three to six) with the hammer on the head and killed him.

The accused now appeals to this Court on the grounds that the trial judge's charge to the jury on the issue of provocation was incorrect and that the judge's answer to the jury was erroneous when they returned and asked for "a clear definition of murder and manslaughter." His counsel also advanced the argument that the view expressed by the trial judge and in all the reported English cases (that the provocation relied on had to be such that it would provoke a reasonable man

13 [1962] NZLR 1069.
14 (1977) 13 ALR 225.

and that, in addition, it actually provoked the accused) was not the law in this country. Counsel asked us to abandon the "objective" test and to declare that the law was that if what was relied on as provocation actually provoked the accused (whether it would provoke a reasonable man or not) the prosecution had to prove beyond reasonable doubt that it did not.

Section 4 of the Criminal Justice Act 1964, is the background to much of the trial judge's charge. That section reads:—

"(1) Where a person kills another unlawfully the killing shall not be murder unless the accused person intended to kill, or cause serious injury to, some person, whether the person actually killed or not.

(2) The accused person shall be presumed to have intended the natural and probable consequences of his conduct; but this presumption may be rebutted."

The first passage in the trial judge's charge to which objection is taken arose out of his explanation to the jury of s 4, sub-s 2, of the Act of 1964. That passage reads:— ". . . and so in this case if it is established to your satisfaction that the accused man struck the deceased repeatedly over the head with a hammer to the extent of causing the type of fractures that have been described in the evidence, then the only logical – the only reasonable – result of that action must be either to kill or to cause serious bodily harm. But that is a presumption which can be rebutted and the suggested rebuttal in this case is that, although it is conceded that the accused did in fact rain these blows with a hammer on Paddy Hyland's head, at the time he was so terrified for his own safety that he was acting in self defence and that he was so provoked by the attack which Paddy Hyland had made on him that he suffered loss of control over his own mind so as to inhibit him, to prevent him, to render him unable to form any intention and, least of all, an intention either to kill or cause serious bodily harm."

The trial judge thus told the jury that the provocation had to be such that it made the accused unable to form an intention to kill or cause serious bodily harm. Indeed, the view which the judge expressed to the jury later was that if there was an intention to kill despite the provocation they should find the accused guilty of murder, and that it was only when the provocation removed the desire to kill or cause serious bodily injury that it could reduce the crime to manslaughter. This was the law which was expressed by Viscount Simon in *Holmes v Director of Public Prosecutions* at p 598 of the report and which was stated in the 34th edition (1959) of Archbold's Criminal Pleading, Evidence and Practice at para 2503 in a passage which is based upon Viscount Simon's speech. However, in our view it is incorrect; the provocation relied on usually is one, if not the sole, cause of the formation of the intention to kill or cause serious injury to another. To speak of provocation negativing or depriving a man of the intention to kill or cause serious injury is to confuse cause and result.

The passage in Viscount Simon's speech is inconsistent with the advice of the Privy Council in *Attorney-General for Ceylon v Perera* in which Lord Goddard, at p 206 of the report, said:— "The defence of provocation may arise where a person does not intend to kill or inflict grievous bodily harm but his intention to do so arises from sudden passion involving loss of self-control by reason of provocation. In *Lee Chun-Chuen v The Queen* Lord Devlin, when giving the advice of the Privy Council, said at p 228 of the report:— "Their Lordships think it right to reaffirm the law as stated by Lord Goddard and to do so with special reference to Lord Simon's dictum, to which Lord Goddard did not advert." The same view was expressed by Gibbs J in the High Court of Australia in *Straker v The Queen* at p 108 of the report:— If the directions of the learned trial judge on the subject of intention led the jury to think that they could not return a verdict of manslaughter by reason of provocation if they were satisfied that the appellant had an intention to kill or to cause grievous bodily harm, the directions would, of course, have been erroneous."

It follows that the dichotomy which the trial judge in this case put before the jury on three occasions between the existence of an intention to kill or cause serious injury and the effect of provocation does not exist, and that an intention to kill or cause serious injury is consistent with provocation and does not prevent this defence from reducing murder to manslaughter unless the prosecution prove that the accused was not provoked.

This would be sufficient to dispose of this appeal, but on the retrial, the question will arise as to whether the provocation must be acts or words which would cause a reasonable man to be provoked so that he temporarily loses control of himself and which actually cause the accused to cease to be master of himself (the objective test) or whether it is sufficient for him to raise a case that he was provoked by what was done or said whether it was such as would provoke a reasonable man or not (the subjective test). Therefore, we consider that we should deal with this ground.

The objective test was first explicitly stated (p 338) by Keating J in *R v Welsh*:— "The law is, that there must exist such an amount of provocation as would be excited by the circumstances in the mind of a reasonable man, and so as to lead the jury to ascribe the act to the influence of that passion." The best modern statement of this view is to be found in the judgment of Devlin J (as he then was) in *R v Duffy*:— "Provocation is some act, or series of acts, done by the dead man to the accused which would cause in any reasonable person, and actually causes in the accused, a sudden and temporary loss of self-control, rendering the accused so subject to passion as to make him or her for the moment not master of his mind." This formulation of the objective test has been approved by the House of Lords and the Privy Council on many occasions: *Mancini v Director of Public Prosecutions; Holmes v Director of Public Prosecutions; Bedder v Director of Public Prosecutions* and *Lee Chun-Chuen v The Queen*. It had become so much part of the accepted doctrine of the courts in England that it was accepted by the legislature there by s 3 of the Homicide Act 1957, which provides:— "Where on a charge of murder there is evidence on which the jury can find that the person charged was provoked (whether by things done or by things said or by both together) to lose his self-control, the question whether the provocation was enough to make a reasonable man do as he did shall be left to be determined by the jury; and in determining that question the jury shall take into account everything both done and said according to the effect which, in their opinion, it would have on a reasonable man." The effect of this section is thus stated at para 2499 of the 36th (1966) edition of Archbold's Pleading, Evidence and Practice in Criminal Cases:— "The test to be applied is whether the provocation was sufficient to deprive a reasonable man of his self-control; not whether it was sufficient to deprive of his self-control the particular person charged." The objective test was also approved by a majority of the High Court of Australia in *Moffa v The Queen* – with a strong dissenting judgment from Mr Justice Murphy. We were not referred to any Irish authority on the matter and so we have now to determine which test should be applied.

The objective test is profoundly illogical; we assume that the reasonable man whom it propounds as the criterion is not the accused. If he were, the question would not be whether the reasonable man would be provoked but whether the accused was provoked. But what are the characteristics of this reasonable man? Is he to be endowed with the knowledge and temperament of the accused? Words which would have no effect on the abstract reasonable man may be profoundly provocative to one having knowledge of what people say about him. A hot-tempered man may react violently to an insult which a phlegmatic one would ignore. These are difficulties which those who support the objective test have never attempted to answer.

The objections to the objective test have been so cogently stated by Murphy J in his dissenting judgment in *Moffa v The Queen* that I hope that a somewhat lengthy quotation from his judgment (at p 242 of the report) will be excused:—

"The 'reasonable' or 'ordinary' man test
This test requires the accused's behaviour to be of the standard which a reasonable or ordinary man would exhibit. This is used in addition to the subjective test . . .

Objections to the Test
The test cannot withstand critical examination. It is not clear whether the reasonable or ordinary man, if he was subjected to the same provocation, would (or might) have lost control, or would have lost control to the extent of killing the deceased, or would have lost control to the extent of killing in the manner he did. Is he a complete stranger subjected to the provocative conduct or a person in the same circumstances as the accused? To be in the same circumstances, he should be taken to be in the same relationship with the deceased (in this case, a marital relationship) and must have experienced the relationship. In a case such as this, he should have lived the life of the accused, or it would be impractical to speak of what a reasonable or ordinary man would do in the circumstances. For example, it might have been an unbearable insult to a person of the accused's origin to be called 'a black bastard.' Once the full circumstances are taken into account, the objective test disappears because it adds nothing to the subjective test. For this reason, those who adhere to the objective test have rigidly excluded individual peculiarities of the accused (for example, low intelligence, impotence, pugnacity)."

Our law as to one aspect of self-defence was stated by the Supreme Court in *The People (Attorney General) v Dwyer* and provides a useful analogy on the so-called objective or reasonable-man test. In that case the accused was charged with and convicted of murder. The killing occurred in the course of a brawl in which many (including the accused and the dead person) were involved. The trial judge told the jury that if the accused, though acting in self-defence, killed through using more force than was reasonably necessary in the circumstances, the verdict should be guilty of murder. This direction was approved by this Court. The accused's contention was that if he used the amount of force which he thought necessary, he should not be convicted of murder even if a reasonable man would think it was excessive. Here again we have the contrast between the subjective and the objective test. On appeal the Supreme Court decided that when self-defence is raised, the correct charge to a jury is that if they come to the conclusion that the accused used more force than was reasonably necessary but no more than he honestly believed to be necessary they should return a verdict of guilty of manslaughter. This seems to us to have been a decisive rejection of the objective test in a branch of law closely allied to provocation.

The application of the objective test to provocation has been severely criticised in many text-books of high repute and by eminent writers on criminal law. In the standard text-book on criminal law (Smith and Hogan) the authors submit the test to a devastating analysis and suggest that it should be abolished and a purely subjective criterion applied – see the second edition of that work at pp 213–215. The same approach is adopted in Russell on Crime (12th ed., ch. 29) and by Professor Glanville Williams in an article entitled "Provocation and the Reasonable Man" in the 1954 volume of the Criminal Law Review.

In the opinion of this Court the objective test in cases of provocation should be declared to be no longer part of our law. If the accused raises the defence that he was provoked and establishes that and nothing more, we do not mean that the prosecution must prove beyond reasonable doubt that he was not provoked. The nature of the provocation may not justify the force used judged by the accused's state of mind. But the inquiry to be made by the judge first and then by the jury must centre not on the reasonable man but on the accused and his reaction to the conduct or words which are said to be provocative.

When the defence of provocation is raised, we think that the trial judge at the close of the evidence should rule on whether there is any evidence of provocation which, having regard to the accused's temperament, character and circumstances, might have caused him to lose control of himself at the time of the wrongful act and whether the provocation bears a reasonable relation to the amount of force used by the accused.

If there is evidence on which the jury could reach a decision favourable to the accused on this issue, the trial judge should allow the defence to be considered by the jury and should tell them that, before they find the accused guilty of murder, the prosecution must establish beyond reasonable doubt that the accused was not provoked to such an extent that, having regard to his temperament, character and circumstances, he lost control of himself at the time of the wrongful act. Then the jury should be told that they must consider whether the acts or words, or both, of provocation found by them to have occurred, when related to the accused, bear a reasonable relation to the amount of force he used. If the prosecution prove beyond reasonable doubt that the force used was unreasonable and excessive having regard to the provocation, the defence of provocation fails.

Provocation can never reduce a wrongful killing to anything except manslaughter: it can never justify an acquittal. For these reasons we allowed this appeal and directed a new trial.

Proportionality

4.156 In *Mancini v DPP*[15], Viscount Simon stated "In short, the mode of resentment must bear a reasonable relationship to the provocation if the offence is to be reduced to manslaughter". It follows that if the victim attacked the accused with his fists a reply could not be made with a gun or a dagger. The Privy Council in *Phillips v R*[16] and the Court of Appeal in *R v Brown*[17] rejected the test of proportionality as a separate element. The manner in which a reply to provocation had been made was a consideration to be taken into account in deciding how the average or reasonable man would have reacted to the provocation offered him. Neither case was cited to the Court of Criminal Appeal in *The People (DPP) v MacEoin*[18]. The Court instead referred to out-of-date text books. The modern test, used in common law countries, is as to whether an ordinary man, sharing the accused's permanent characteristics, would have been provoked by what was done to the extent of losing his self-control and doing what the accused did. It is impossible to construe the test of proportionality as set out by the Court of Criminal Appeal in *MacEoin*.

4.157   *Johnson v R*
                       (1976) 11 ALR
                 High Court of Australia, 1976

Facts: The two accused were convicted of the murder of their father. There was a background of violence and bitterness prior to the incident in which the father was killed. That morning the deceased had attempted to evict the accused from the house. There was further unpleasantness later in the day. The accused spent most of the evening in a hotel, and returned home shortly after midnight. An argument started with the deceased who again tried to evict them from the house. The

15 [1942] AC 1 at 9.
16 [1969] 2 AC 130.
17 [1972] 2 QB 229.
18 [1978] IR 27.

accused stated that the deceased made a sudden and unreasonable attack upon one brother (Peter), breaking his nose and commencing to choke him. The other brother (Phillip) came to his aid, and kicked the father in the face. The deceased then attacked Phillip. Phillip armed himself with knives from the kitchen and fought with the deceased until "something seemed to snap". He kicked and jumped on the deceased while he was on the floor. The deceased died of abdominal and cerebral haemorrhage. His injuries were extensive. Peter initially made a statement in which he said he had been involved in the fighting. At the trial he gave evidence that he had been unconscious or dazed at all relevant times. In finding him guilty of murder the jury clearly rejected the evidence given by him at the trial.

The trial judge directed the jury that for the accused to have a defence of provocation the actions of the deceased must have been reasonably calculated to deprive an ordinary person of the power of self-control, that they must in fact have deprived the accused of self-control, that the act causing death must have been done suddenly in the heat of passion, and that the retaliation must have been commensurate with the provocation offered. The accused appealed to the High Court.

Barwick CJ: The importance of the fatal act having been taken in the heat of passion may also be related to the proportion of that act to the provocation and to whether the provocative act or situation is such as would lead an ordinary man to lose his self-control so as to do an act of the kind of the fatal act done by the accused. If an ordinary man would not be so far affected, there is no case for operative provocation. The accused's act, though done during his loss of self-control, will be accounted as due to malice.

I do not pause to discuss the consequences in connection with the objective test of loss of self-control of exchanging the ordinary man for the reasonable man in the expression of that element of operative provocation. In relation to the element of loss of self-control, not a condition of applied reason, my own preference is for the objective element to be related to the ordinary man. The objective test is, in my view, better related to human nature than to reason and thus to the ordinary man. So to relate it will be to increase the area in which, by use of the objective test, acts in fact done by an accused, hypersensitive or of unusual temperament, though in fact done whilst out of self-control, cannot qualify as acts done under provocation. But, none the less, the adoption and proper application of the objective test of loss of self-control better fits the administration of justice than the adoption of a subjective test. What seeming injustice may result from the use of the objective test must be left to the wisdom and discretion of the Executive.

My reading of the early cases relating to provocation leads me to the opinion that it was then conceived that there were degrees of loss of self-control; that the description "loss of self-control" was not of an absolute state; this acceptance that there are degrees of loss of self-control was consistent with the later adoption of the view that whether the accused had relevantly lost self-control depended on whether the ordinary man would, in like circumstances, have lost self control to the point of doing an act of the kind and degree by which the accused killed the deceased. Disproportion between the provocative act and the fatal act might result in the conclusion that an ordinary man would not have so far lost self-control in like circumstances. The provocation in that case is relevantly inoperative. The notion that a state of loss of self-control is relative is basic to the concept of the objective test. That test properly applied keeps provocation within bounds. I can see little warrant for applying a test of reasonableness to the acts of a man who has justifiably ie, satisfying the objective test, lost his self-control. First to find such justifiable loss of self-control and then to measure according to reason what the person so out of self-control did, seems to me to be an erroneous step. But I can understand, once the objective test of the lack of self-control has been adopted, that it is necessary to consider in applying it whether an ordinary man would have lost self-control to the requisite extent by reason of the provocation before it is possible to reduce the crime to manslaughter. East's reference to an act of provocation which might heat the blood to a proportionate degree of resentment and keep it boiling to the moment of the commission of the fatal act is understandable, in my opinion, on the footing that the act of resentment must in fact have been the act of a man out of self-control in circumstances where an ordinary man would have lost self-control to the point of doing an act of that kind and degree (see *Pleas of the Crown* (1803), vol 1; p 238). It thus relates both to the extent as well as to causality of the loss of self-control. Keating J's remarks in *R v Welsh* (1869) 11 Cox CC 336 at 339, are in my opinion, to a like effect: "Something which might naturally cause an ordinary and reasonably minded man to lose his self-control and commit such an act".

Having considered the reported cases and the writings on this matter I have come to the conclusion that the proportion of the fatal act to the provocation is part of the material on which the jury should consider whether the provocation offered the accused was such as would have caused an ordinary man, placed in all the circumstances in which the accused stood, to have lost his self-control to the point of doing an act of the kind and degree of that by which the accused killed the deceased. That proportion is not, in my opinion, a separate matter to be considered after it has been decided that an ordinary man would have lost self-control in the circumstances by reason of the provocation. The relationship of the fatal act to the provocation is perhaps best expressed by saying that the provocation must be such as would lead an ordinary man in the accused's circumstances to so lose his self-control as to do an act of the kind and degree as the act by which the accused killed the deceased.

Background to the Loss of Self-control

4.158   Motives of revenge are inconsistent with the defence of provocation; *R v Duffy*[19]. However, the provocative act or acts must be seen against the background of the relationship between the deceased and the accused. In some circumstances there may be a lapse of time between a provocative incident and the loss of self-control.

4.159   *The Queen v R*
                            (1981) 28 SASR 321
                  Supreme Court of South Australia, 1981

Facts: The deceased was asleep when killed by the accused. They were husband and wife. The accused had been subjected by her husband to violent and domineering behaviour during the course of her marriage. Shortly before the killing the victim had taken one of his daughters away in a car and raped her. This incident caused the daughter to relate to the accused a history of sexual abuse by her husband of all their daughters. At midnight the deceased had attempted to violently force his sexual attentions on his wife. He then attempted a reconciliation after which he went to sleep. The accused sat on the edge of the bed smoking for some time. She then went out and got an axe. She struck the victim killing him.

King CJ: The loss of self-control which is essential, is not to be confused with the emotions of hatred, resentment, fear or revenge. If the appellant, when in control of her mind and will, decided to kill the appellant because those emotions or any of

19 [1949] 1 All ER 932.

them had been produced in her by the enormity of the deceased's past behaviour and threatened future behaviour or because she considered that that was the only way in which she or her children could be protected from the deceased's molestations in the future, the crime would nevertheless be murder. The law of a well ordered and civilised society cannot countenance deliberate killing, even to the extent of treating it as extenuated, as a response to the conduct of another however abhorrent that conduct might be. Nor can society countenance killing a person as a means of averting some apprehended harm in the future. The law of course permits the use by a person of force, even to the extent of inflicting death, if that is necessary to defend that person against immediately threatened harm. But the law has always and must always set its face against killing by way of prevention of harm which is merely feared for the future. Other measures which are peaceful and lawful must be resorted to in order to deal with threats of future harm. Self-defence is therefore not in question in this case. Moreover, the history of incest occurring in the absence of the appellant cannot of itself amount to provocation, even though recounted to her later. Words or conduct cannot amount to provocation unless they are spoken or done to or in the presence of the killer (*R v Fisher* (1837) 8 C&P 182 (173 ER 452); *R v Mouers* (1921) 57 DLR 569; *R v Terry* [1964] VR 248; *R v Arden* [1975] VR 449), although, of course, such words or conduct may be important as part of the background against which what is said or done by the deceased to the killer is to be assessed.

In determining whether the deceased's actions and words on the fatal night could amount to provocation in law, it is necessary to consider them against the background of family violence and sexual abuse. I have reached the conclusion that, at least on the version of the facts most favourable to the appellant, it was open to a reasonable jury to take the view that an ordinary person possessing those characteristics of the appellant which rendered her susceptible, might suffer, in consequence of the deceased's words and actions on the fatal night, a loss of self-control to the extent of doing what the appellant did. The deceased's words and actions in the presence of the appellant on the fatal night might appear innocuous enough on the face of them. They must, however, be viewed against the background of brutality, sexual assault, intimidation and manipulation. When stroking the appellant's arm and cuddling up to her in bed, and when telling her that they could be one happy family and that the girls would not be leaving, the deceased was not only aware of his own infamous conduct but must also have at least suspected that the appellant knew or strongly suspected that, in addition to the long history of cruelty, he had habitually engaged in sexual abuse of her daughters. The implication of the words was therefore that this horror would continue and that the girls would be prevented from leaving by forms of intimidation and manipulation which were only too familiar to the appellant. In this context it was, in my opinion, open to the jury to treat the words themselves and the caressing actions which accompanied them as highly provocative and quite capable of producing in an ordinary mother endowed with the natural instincts of love and protection of her daughters, such a loss of self-control as might lead to killing. A jury might find, to adopt the words of Dixon J in *Parker v R* (1963) 111 CLR 610 at 630, "all the elements of suddenness in the unalleviated pressure and the breaking down of control" as the night's events reached their climax in the bed.

Self-Induced Provocation

4.160 The accused may pursue a course of unlawful conduct which has as its natural result extreme annoyance to another person. Where that occurs the legal policy behind provocation may be inappropriate. It may not be necessary to make a concession to human frailty where the provocation was induced by the accused man.

4.161 *Edwards v R*
[1973] AC 648; [1973] 1 All ER 152; [1972] 3 WLR 893;
(1973) 57 Cr App R 157; [1972] Crim LR 782
Privy Council, 1972

Facts: The accused had followed the victim to Hong Kong with the intention of blackmailing him. The response of the victim was, according to the accused, to attack him with a knife and stab him. The accused then took possession of the knife and, in a fit of passion, killed the victim.

Lord Pearson: . . . No authority has been cited with regard to what may be called "self-induced provocation." On principle it seems reasonable to say that—

(1) a blackmailer cannot rely on the predictable results of his own blackmailing conduct as constituting provocation sufficient to reduce his killing of the victim from murder to manslaughter, and the predictable results may include a considerable degree of hostile reaction by the person sought to be blackmailed, for instance vituperative words and even some hostile action such as blows with a fist;

(2) but if the hostile reaction by the person sought to be blackmailed goes to extreme lengths it might constitute sufficient provocation even for the blackmailer;

(3) there would in many cases be a question of degree to be decided by the jury.

In the present case, if the appellant's version of the facts be assumed to be correct. Dr. Coombe, the person sought to be blackmailed, did go to extreme lengths, in that he made a violent attack on the appellant with a knife, inflicting painful wounds and putting the appellant's life in danger. There was evidence of provocation and it was fit for consideration by the jury: *Parker v The Queen* [1964] AC 1369, 1392. The burden of proof would be on the prosecution to satisfy the jury that the killing was unprovoked. If the evidence raised in their minds a reasonable doubt whether it was provoked or not, the proper verdict would be a conviction for manslaughter: *Bullard v The Queen* [1957] AC 635.

Common Law Test

4.162 In contrast with the entirely subjective test, wrapped up with the supposed test of proportionality, laid down by the Court of Criminal Appeal in *The People (DPP) v MacEoin*[20] (see para **4.148**) the test at common law is a more appropriate guide.

4.163 *R v Camplin*
[1978] AC 705; [1978] 2 All ER 168; [1978] 2 WLR 679;
(1978) 67 Cr App R 14; [1978] Crim LR 432
House of Lords, 1978

Facts: The defendant, a fifteen year old youth killed a middle-aged Pakistani by splitting his skull with a large rimless frying pan. At the time the two of them were alone in the latter's flat. The defendant claimed that having been buggered by his victim despite his resistance he (the victim) then began laughing at him, whereupon the defendant lost his self-control and fatally attacked him.

Lord Diplock: My Lords, the doctrine of provocation in crimes of homicide has always represented an anomaly in English law. In crimes of violence which result in injury short of death, the fact that the act of violence was committed under provocation which had caused the accused to lose his self-control does not affect

20 [1975] IR 27.

the nature of the offence of which he is guilty. It is merely a matter to be taken into consideration in determining the penalty which it is appropriate to impose. Whereas in homicide provocation effects a change in the offence itself from murder for which the penalty is fixed by law (formerly death and now imprisonment for life) to the lesser offence of manslaughter for which the penalty is in the discretion of the judge.

The doctrine of provocation has a long history of evolution at common law. Such changes as there had been were entirely the consequence of judicial decision until Parliament first intervened by passing the Act of 1957. Section 3 deals specifically with provocation and alters the law as it had been expounded in the cases, including three that had been decided comparatively recently in this House, viz., *Mancini v Director of Public Prosecutions* [1942] AC 1; *Holmes v Director of Public Prosecutions* [1946] AC 588 and *Bedder v Director of Public Prosecutions* [1954] 1 WLR 1119. One of the questions in this appeal is to what extent propositions as to the law of provocation that are laid down in those cases and in particular in *Bedder* ought to be treated as being of undiminished authority despite the passing of the Act.

For my part I find it instructive to approach this question by a brief survey of the historical development of the doctrine of provocation at common law. Its origin at a period when the penalty for murder was death is to be found, as Tindal CJ, echoing Sir Michael Foster [*Crown Cases and Crown Law* (1746) pp 315–316], put it in *Rex v Hayward* (1833) 6 C&P 157, 159, in "the law's compassion to human infirmity." The human infirmity upon which the law first took compassion in a violent age when men bore weapons for their own protection when going about their business appears to have been chance medley or a sudden falling out at which both parties have recourse to their weapons and fight on equal terms. Chance medley as a ground of provocation was extended to assault and battery committed by the deceased upon the accused in other circumstances than a sudden falling out; but with two exceptions actual violence offered by the deceased to the accused remained the badge of provocation right up to the passing of the Act of 1957. The two exceptions were the discovery by a husband of his wife in the act of committing adultery and the discovery by a father of someone committing sodomy on his son; but these apart, insulting words or gestures unaccompanied by physical attack did not in law amount to provocation.

The "reasonable man" was a comparatively late arrival in the law of provocation. As the law of negligence emerged in the first half of the 19th century he became the anthropomorphic embodiment of the standard of care required by the law. It would appear that Keating J in *Reg v Welsh* (1869) 11 Cox CC 336 was the first to make use of the reasonable man as the embodiment of the standard of self-control required by the criminal law of persons exposed to provocation; and not merely as a criterion by which to check the credibility of a claim to have been provoked to lose his self-control made by an accused who at that time was not permitted to give evidence himself. This had not been so previously and did not at once become the orthodox view. In his *Digest of the Criminal Law* published in 1877 and his *History of the Criminal Law of England* published in 1883 Sir James Fitzjames Stephen makes no reference to the reasonable man as providing a standard of self-control by which to decide the question whether the facts relied upon as provocation are sufficient to reduce the subsequent killing to manslaughter. He classifies and defines the kinds of conduct of the deceased that alone are capable in law of amounting to provocation; and appears to treat the questions for the jury as being limited to (1) whether the evidence establishes conduct by the deceased that falls within one of the defined classes; and, if so, (2) whether the accused was thereby actually deprived of his self-control.

The reasonable man referred to by Keating J was not then a term of legal art nor has he since become one in criminal law. He (or she) has established his (or her) role in the law of provocation under a variety of different sobriquets in which the noun "man" is frequently replaced by "person" and the adjective "reasonable" by "ordinary," "average" or "normal." At least from as early as 1914 (see *Rex v Lesbini* [1914] 3 KB 1116) the test of whether the defence of provoation is entitled to succeed has been a dual one; the conduct of the deceased to the accused must be such as (1) might cause in any reasonable or ordinary person and (2) actually causes in the accused a sudden and temporary loss of self-control as the result of which he commits the unlawful act that kills the deceased. But until the Act of 1957 was passed there was a condition precedent which had to be satisfied before any question of applying this dual test could arise. The conduct of the deceased had to be of such a kind as was capable in law of constituting provocation; and whether it was or not was a question for the judge, not for the jury. This House so held in *Mancini v Director of Public Prosecutions* [1942] AC 1 where it also laid down a rule of law that the mode of resentment, as for instance the weapon used in the act that caused the death, must bear a reasonable relation to the kind of violence that constituted the provocation.

That he was only 15 years of age at the time of the killing is the relevant characteristic of the accused in the instant case. It is a characteristic which may have its effects on temperament as well as physique. If the jury think that the same power of self-control is not to be expected in an ordinary, average or normal boy of 15 as in an older person, are they to treat the lesser powers of self-control possessed by an ordinary, average or normal boy of 15 as the standard of self-control with which the conduct of the accused is to be compared?

It may be conceded that in strict logic there is a transition between treating age as a characteristic that may be taken into account in assessing the gravity of the provocation addressed to the accused and treating it as a characteristic to be taken into account in determining what is the degree of self-control to be expected of the ordinary person with whom the accused's conduct is to be compared. But to require old heads upon young shoulders is inconsistent with the law's compassion to human infirmity to which Sir Michael Foster ascribed the doctrine of provocation more than two centuries ago. The distinction as to the purposes for which it is legitimate to take the age of the accused into account involves considerations of too great nicely to warrant a place in deciding a matter of opinion, which is no longer one to be decided by a judge trained in logical reasoning but is to be decided by a jury drawing on their experience of how ordinary human beings behave in real life.

It seems to me that as a result of the changes effected by section 3 a jury is fully entitled to consider whether an accused person, placed as he was, only acted as even a reasonable man might have acted if he had been in the accused's situation. There may be no practical difference between, on the one hand, taking a notional independent reasonable man but a man having the attributes of the accused and subject to all the events which surrounded the accused and then considering whether what the accused did was only what such a person would or might have done, and, on the other hand, taking the accused himself with all his attributes and subject to all the events and then asking whether there was provocation to such a degree as would or might make a reasonable man do when he (the accused) in fact did.

In my view it would now be unreal to tell a jury that the notional "reasonable man" is someone without the characteristics of the accused: it would be to intrude into their province. A few examples may be given. If the accused is of particular colour or particular ethnic origin and things are said which to him are grossly insulting it would be utterly unreal if the jury had to consider whether the words would have provoked a man of different colour or ethnic origin – or to consider how such a man would have acted or reacted. The question would be whether the accused if he was provoked only reacted as even any reasonable man in his situation would or might have reacted. if the accused was ordinarily and usually a very unreasonable person, the view that on a particular occasion he acted just as a reasonable person would or might have acted would not be impossible of acceptance.

It is not disputed that the "reasonable man" in section 3 could denote a reasonable person and so a reasonable woman. If words of grievous insult were addressed to a woman, words perhaps reflecting on her chastity or way of life, a consideration of the way in which she reacted would have to take account of how other women being reasonable women would or might in like circumstances have reacted. Would or might she, if she had been a reasonable woman, have done what she did?

In the instant case the considerations to which I have been referring have application to a question of age. The accused was a young man. Sometimes in the summing up he was called a boy or a lad. He was, at the time of the events described at the trial, under 16 years of age; he was accountable in law for the charge preferred against him. More generally in the summing up he was referred to as a young man; that would appear to me to have been appropriate.

The jury had to consider whether a young man of about the same age as the accused but placed in the same situation as that which befell the accused could, had he been a reasonable young man, have reacted as did the accused and could have done what the accused did. For the reasons which I have outlined the question so to be considered by the jury would be whether they considered that the accused, placed as he was, and having regard to all the things that they found were said, and all the things that they found were done, only acted as a reasonable young man might have acted, so that, in compassion, and having regard to human frailty, he could to some extent be excused even though he had caused a death.

Raising Provocation

4.164 The accused does not have to expressly state that he lost self-control. This may be inferred from all the circumstances; *Van den Hoek v R*[21]. In *The People (DPP) v MacEoin*[22], (see para **4.155**) the judge is required to rule, as a matter of law, at the close of the defence case whether there is sufficient evidence of provocation to go to a jury. It is the duty of the trial judge to direct the jury on provocation even though the defence has not been expressly relied on by the accused; *R v Lee Chun-Chuen*[23].

4.165   *Van Den Hoek v R*
                          (1986) 69 ALR 1
                   High Court of Australia, 1986

Facts: The deceased was the husband of the accused. They had separated and were living apart but Mr Van Den Hoek had returned to the house. He entered the house in an aggressive mood and told the accused that he wanted a divorce. He said: "I want it now" and "I am going to kill you". He then produced a knife and came towards the applicant who ran through the house in an attempt to avoid him. She went into the bathroom and he followed. She backed away and started lashing out with her legs, he slipped and fell. In her own words: "He dropped the knife and I was so scared I bend down picked the knife and stabbed and ran. I didn't know what happened". The question arose as to whether the defence of provocation should have been left to the jury.

21 (1986) 69 ALR 1.
22 [1978] IR 27.
23 [1963] AC 220 at 233.

Mason J: . . . The evidence was sufficient to raise the defence for the determination of the jury. The applicant testified that she was terrified by the deceased's attack on her. The uncontradicted medical evidence established, not only that she was in a state of extreme anxiety, but also that her condition was such that her ability to think and relate to what was happening had been impaired. True it is she did not testify to her sudden loss of self-control. But the absence of self-control may be inferred from her state of fear and anxiety. That the loss of self-control was sudden and temporary and that it was caused by the acts of the deceased, deposed to by the applicant, might also be reasonably inferred. In passing I should mention that Kennedy J's comment "She was not angry" does not precisely reflect the applicant's evidence. She certainly stated that she was not angry when the deceased demanded a divorce, but she was at no time asked whether she was angry when the struggle occurred in the bathroom and continued outside.

The failure of an accused person to testify to loss of self-control is not fatal to a defence of provocation or a case in which self-defence is raised. Because the admission of loss of self-control is bound to weaken, if not destroy, self-defence, the law does not place the accused in a dilemma (*Lee Chun-Chuen* at 232–3). The jury's capacity to infer loss of self-control from appropriate facts is underscored by the comment of Lord Devlin, speaking for the Judicial Committee, in *Lee Chun-Chuen* (at 233) that a jury would be entitled to infer loss of self-control from facts suggesting a possible loss of self-control, even if the accused expressly denied loss of temper, especially when the nature of the main defence would account for the falsehood. Of course, an admission of fear is not as antagonistic to self-defence as an admission of anger. Nonetheless the point remains that the absence of direct evidence of loss of self-control is explicable when self-defence is an issue with the result that the jury is entitled to infer it in the absence of direct evidence.

It has been repeatedly held that if there is material on which a jury, acting reasonably, could find manslaughter as a result of provocation, it is the duty of the trial judge to put the issue to the jury, even if there is no suggestion at the trial that the issue should be put to the jury (*Parker* at 681; *Pemble v R* (1971) 124 CLR 107 at 117–18).

In the result I agree with the judgment of Burt CJ in the Court of Criminal Appeal on the issue of provocation.

Code Options

4.166 *Model Penal Code*

210.3(1)(b)   A criminal homocide constitutes manslaughter when a homocide which would otherwise be murder is committed under the influence of extreme mental or emotional disturbance for which there is reasonable explanation or excuse. The reasonableness of such explanation or excuse shall be determined from the viewpoint of a person in the actor's situation under the circumstances as he believes them to be.

4.167   *Canadian Criminal Code*

232(1)   Culpable homicide that otherwise would be murder may be reduced to manslaughter if the person who committed it did so in the heat of passion caused by sudden provocation.

(2)   A wrongful act or insult that is of such a nature as to be sufficient to deprive an ordinary person of the power of self-control is provocation for the purposes of this section if the accused acted on it on the sudden and before there was time for his passion to cool.

(3)   For the purposes of this section, the questions

(*a*)   whether a particular wrongful act or insult amounted to provocation, and (*b*) whether the accused was deprived of the power of self-control by the provocation that he alleges he received,

are questions of fact, but no one shall be deemed to have given provocation to another by doing anything that he had a legal right to do, or by doing anything that the accused incited him to do in order to provide the accused with an excuse for causing death or bodily harm to any human being.

(4) Culpable homicide that otherwise would be murder is not necessarily manslaughter by reason only that it was committed by a person who was being arrested illegally, but the fact that the illegality of the arrest was known to the accused may be evidence of provocation for the purpose of this section.

Further Materials

4.168 Ashworth *Self-Induced Provocation and the Homocide Act* [1973] Crim LR 483.
Ashworth *The Doctrine of Provocation* (1976) 35 Camb LJ 292.
Brett *The Physiology of Provocation* [1970] Crim LR 634.
Charleton *Offences Against the Person* (1992), chapter 4.
Audridge *Self-Induced Provocation in the Court of Appeal* (1991) 50 JCL 94.

Chapter 5

HOMICIDE

Introduction

5.01 The law relating to murder and manslaughter originally developed from the one common law concept of homocide[1]. Homicides were then classified as those which were justifiable and those which were excusable. The former did not carry the penalty of forfeiture of property. Murder came to develop an additional distinct element from manslaughter; malice aforethought. This concept had a highly technical meaning, as can be seen from the quotation from Coke which follows at para **5.13**. It has since been resolved into a statutory definition contained in s 4 of the Criminal Justice Act 1964. The relationship between the elements of murder and manslaughter and their historical development is explained by Kaye in – *The Early History of Murder and Manslaughter*[2].

Inter-Relationship of Murder to Manslaughter

5.02 At common law a verdict of guilty of a felony could not be returned as an alternative verdict. Because murder and manslaughter were originally the one offence of homicide it is possible, as an exception to this rule, for a jury to return a verdict of guilty of manslaughter where the accused is charged with murder.

In the majority of murder trials the issue is not whether the accused killed the victim, but whether in killing he intended to kill or cause serious injury. As intention is, as we have seen in chapter 1, a subjective concept it is always open to a jury to find that the prosecution have failed to prove intention beyond reasonable doubt. Consequently, a manslaughter verdict is always open.

5.03 Situations can arise where the issue of a verdict of manslaughter has not been raised. For example, the accused may be charged with having killed

1 Stephen *History of the Criminal Law of England* chapter 26.
2 (1967) 83 LQR 365–395, 569–601.

the victim by exploding a bomb in a crowded public place. The accused may defend the case solely on the basis that he had nothing to do with the outrage. In the circumstances there would be nothing to rebut the presumption that the accused intended the natural and probable consequences of his actions; s 4 of the Criminal Justice Act 1964. If, on the other hand, the accused admits exploding the bomb but claims that he had given a warning to the Gardaí, which was later ignored, and which was designed to ensure that no one was hurt, the issue of intent to kill or cause serious injury will be central to the trial. In two early cases the Court of Criminal Appeal took the view that if there was no evidence on which a manslaughter verdict might be returned on a charge of murder, the trial judge should direct the jury that they cannot find a verdict of manslaughter; *The State v Felix McMullen*[3] and *The People (A-G) v Mary Ann Cadden*[4]. Both of these cases were decided under the felony-murder rule, which was abolished by s 4 of the Criminal Justice Act 1964.

5.04 If there is evidence which can support a finding of manslaughter the trial judge must instruct the jury that this verdict is available on a charge of murder; *R v Porritt*[5]. It is not necessary for the trial judge to inform the jury that a verdict of manslaughter is open where no evidence supports such a possible verdict and where the issue has not been raised by counsel; *R v Fazal*[6]; *R v Kearney*[7]; *R v Maxwell*[8]. A trial judge may always express an accurate view that, on the evidence, a verdict of manslaughter cannot reasonably be found by a jury hearing a murder case, though he must not withdraw the decision from the jury; *R v Gammage*[9]. It has also been held by the Federal Court of Australia that a trial judge may decline to accept a jury's verdict of manslaughter and ask them to reconsider it in the light of the evidence and any further direction he things it desirable to give. On a reconsideration a verdict of manslaughter must be accepted; *R v Tajber*[10]. The jury should consider the issue as to whether the accused is guilty of murder first. If he is acquitted on this charge they should then proceed to consider manslaughter; *R v Saunders*[11].

Legislation

5.05 The legislation on homocide does not comprise a code. It disjointedly deals with various aspects of the law which have been amended piecemeal.

3 [1925] 2 IR 9.
4 (1956) 1 Frewen 157 (1957) 91 ILTR 97 CCA.
5 [1961] 1 WLR 1169.
6 (1990) 91 Cr App R 256.
7 (1989) 88 Cr App R 380.
8 [1990] 1 All ER 801.
9 (1969) 44 ALJR 36.
10 (1986) 23 A Crim R 189.
11 [1988] AC 148.

Criminal Justice Act 1964

5.06

Malice

4—(1) Where a person kills another unlawfully the killing shall not be murder unless the accused person intended to kill, or cause serious injury to, some person, whether the person actually killed or not.

(2) The accused person shall be presumed to have intended the natural and probable consequences of his conduct; but this presumption may be rebutted.

Short title

11 —This Act may be cited as the Criminal Justice Act 1964.

Criminal Justice Act 1990

5.07
Abolition of death penalty

1 No person shall suffer death for any offence.

Sentence for treason and murder

2 A person convicted of treason or murder shall be sentenced to imprisonment for life.

Special provision in relation to certain murders and attempts

3 (1) This section applies to—

(*a*) murder of a member of the Garda Síochána acting in the course of his duty,
(*b*) murder of a prison officer acting in the course of his duty,
(*c*) murder done in the course or furtherance of an offence under section 6, 7, 8 or 9 of the Offences against the State Act 1939, or in the course or furtherance of the activities of an unlawful organisation within the meaning of section 18 (other than paragraph (*f*)) of that Act, and
(*d*) murder, committed within the State for a political motive, of the head of a foreign State or of a member of the government of, or a diplomatic officer of, a foreign State,

and to an attempt to commit any such murder.

(2) (*a*) Subject to *paragraph (b)*, murder to which this section applies, and an attempt to commit such a murder, shall be a distinct offence from murder and from an attempt to commit murder and a person shall not be convicted of murder to which this section applies or of an attempt to commit such a murder unless it is proved that he knew of the existence of each ingredient of the offence specified in the relevant paragraph of *subsection (1)* or was reckless as to whether or not that ingredient existed.
(*b*) Save as otherwise provided by this Act, the law and proceedure relating to murder and an attempt to commit murder shall apply to the offence.

(3) In this section—

"diplomatic officer" means a member of the staff of a diplomatic mission of a foreign State having diplomatic rank;

"prison" means any place for which rules or regulations may be made under the Prisons Acts 1826 to 1980, section 7 of the Offences against the State (Amendment) Act 1940, section 233 of the Defence Act 1954, section 2 of the Prisoners of War and Enemy Aliens Act 1956, or section 13 of the Criminal Justice Act 1960;

"prison officer" includes any member of the staff of a prison and any person having the custody of, or having duties in relation to the custody of, a person detained in a prison.

Minimum period of imprisonment for treason and murder, and attempts, to which *section 3* applies

4 Where a person (other than a child or young person) is convicted of treason or of a murder or attempt to commit a murder to which *section 3* applies, the court—

- (*a*) in the case of treason or murder, shall in passing sentence specify as the minimum period of imprisonment to be served by that person a period of not less than forty years,
- (*b*) in the case of an attempt to commit murder, shall pass a sentence of imprisonment of not less than twenty years and specify a period of not less than twenty years as the minimum period of imprisonment to be served by that person.

Restrictions on power to commute or remit punishment or grant temporary release

5 (1) The power conferred by section 23 of the Criminal Justice Act 1951, to commute or remit a punishment shall not, in the case of a person serving a sentence passed on him on conviction of treason or of murder to which *section 3* applies or an attempt to commit such a murder, be exercisable before the expiration of the minimum period specified by the court under *section 4* less any reduction of that period under *subsection (2)* of this section.

(2) The rules or practice whereby prisoners generally may earn remission of sentence by industry and good conduct shall apply in the case of a person serving a sentence passed on him on conviction of treason or of murder to which *section 3* applies or an attempt to commit such a murder as if he had been sentenced to a term of imprisonment equal to the minimum period specified by the court under *section 4*, and that period shall be reduced by the amount of any remission which he has so earned.

(3) Any power conferred by rules made under section 2 of the Criminal Justice Act 1960 (including that section as applied by section 4 of the Prisons Act 1970), to release temporarily a person serving a sentence of imprisonment shall not, in the case of a person serving a sentence passed on him on conviction of treason or of murder to which *section 3* applies or an attempt to commit such a murder, be exercisable during the period for which the commutation or remission of his punishment is prohibited by *subsection (1)* of this section unless for grave reasons of a humanitarian nature, and any release so granted shall be only of such limited duration as is justified by those reasons.

Procedure in cases of murder, and attempts, to which *section 3* applies

6 (1) Where a person is accused of murder to which *section 3* applies or of any attempt to commit such a murder, he shall be charged in the indictment with murder to which that section applies or, as the case may be, with an attempt to commit such a murder.

(2) A person indicted for murder to which *section 3* applies may—

(*a*) if the evidence does not warrant a conviction for such murder but warrants a conviction for murder, be found guilty of murder,

(*b*) if the evidence does not warrant a conviction for murder but warrants a conviction for manslaughter, be found guilty of manslaughter.

(3) A person indicted for an attempt to commit a murder to which *section 3* applies may, if the evidence does not warrant a conviction for such an attempt but warrants a conviction for an attempt to commit murder, be found guilty of an attempt to commit murder.

5.08 *Offences Against the Person Act 1861*

Conspiring or soliciting to commit murder

4 All persons who shall conspire, confederate, and agree to murder any person, whether he be a subject of Her Majesty or not, and whether he be within the Queen's dominions or not, and whosoever shall solicit, encourage, persuade, or endeavour to persuade, or shall propose to any person, to murder any other person, whether he be a subject of Her Majesty or not, and whether he be within the Queen's dominions or not, shall be guilty of a misdemeanour, and being convicted thereof shall be liable, at the discretion of the court, to be kept in penal servitude for any term not more than 10 and not less than 3 years, – or to be imprisoned for any term not exceeding two years with or without hard labour.

Manslaughter

5 Whosoever shall be convicted of manslaughter shall be liable, at the discretion of the court, to be kept in penal servitude for life or for any term not less than three years or to be imprisoned for any term not exceeding two years, with or without hard labour, or to pay such fine as the court shall award, in addition to or without any such discretionary punishment as aforesaid.

Indictment for murder or manslaughter

6 In any indictment for murder or manslaughter, or for being an accessory to any murder or manslaughter, it shall not be necessary to set forth the manner in which or the means by which the death of the deceased was caused, but it shall be sufficient in any indictment for murder to charge that the defendant did feloniously, wilfully, and of his malice aforethought kill and murder the deceased; and it shall be sufficient in any indictment for manslaughter to charge that the defendant did feloniously kill and slay the deceased; and it shall be sufficient in any indictment against any accessory to any murder or manslaughter to charge the principal with the murder or manslaughter (as the case may be) in the manner herein-before specified, and then to charge the detendant as an accessory in the manner heretofore used and accustomed.

Excusable homicide

7 No punishment or forfeiture shall be incurred by any person who shall kill another by misfortune or in his own defence, or in any other manner without felony.

Petit treason

8 Every offence which before the commencement of the act of the ninth year of King *George* the Fourth, Chapter Thirty-one, would have amounted to petit treason, shall be deemed to be murder only, and no greater offence; and all persons guilty in respect thereof, whether as principals or as accessories, shall be dealt with, indicted, tried, and punished as principals and accessories in murder.

Murder or manslaughter abroad

9 Where any murder or manslaughter shall be committed on land out of the United Kingdom, whether within the Queen's Dominions or without, and whether the person killed were a subject of Her Majesty or not, every offence committed by any subject of Her Majesty, in respect of such case, whether the same shall amount to the offence of murder or of manslaughter, or of being accessory to murder or manslaughter, may be dealt with, inquired of, tried, determined, and punished in any county or place in *England* or *Ireland* in which such person shall be apprehended or be in custody, in the same manner in all respects as if such offence had been actually committed in that county or place; provided that nothing herein contained shall prevent any person from being tried in any place out of *England* or *Ireland* for any murder or manslaughter committed out of *England* or *Ireland*, in the same manner as such person might have been tried before the passing of this act.

Provision for the trial of murder and manslaughter where the death or cause of death only happens in England or Ireland

10 Where any person, being feloniously stricken, poisoned, or otherwise hurt upon the sea, or at any place out of *England* or *Ireland*, shall die of such, stroke, poisoning, or hurt in *England* or *Ireland*, or, being feloniously stricken, poisoned, or otherwise hurt at any place in *England* or *Ireland*, shall die of such stroke, poisoning, or hurt upon the sea, or at any place out of *England* or *Ireland*, every offence committed in respect of any such case, whether the same shall amount to the offence of murder or manslaughter, or of being accessory to murder or manslaughter, may be dealt with, inquired of, tried, determined, and punished in the county or place in *England* or *Ireland* in which such death, stroke, poisoning, or hurt shall happen, in the same manner in all respects as if such offence had been wholly committed in that county or place.

Attempts to murder

Administering poison, or wounding with intent to murder

11 Whosoever shall administer to or cause to be administered to or to be taken by any person any poison or other destructive thing, or shall by any means whatsoever wound or cause grievous bodily harm to any person, with intent in any of the cases aforesaid to commit murder, shall be guilty of felony, and being convicted thereof shall be liable, at the discretion of the court, to be kept in penal servitude for life or for any term not less than three years, or to be imprisoned for any term not exceeding two years, with or without hard labour, and with or without solitary confinement.

Destroying or damaging a building with gunpowder, with intent to murder

12 Whosoever, by the explosion of gunpowder or other explosive substance, shall destroy or damage any building with intent to commit murder, shall be guilty of felony, and being convicted thereof shall be liable, at the discretion of the court, to be kept in penal servitude for life or for any term not less than three years, or to be imprisoned for any term not exceeding two years, with or without hard labour, and with or without solitary confinement.

Setting fire to or casting away a ship with intent to murder

13 Whosoever shall set fire to any ship or vessel or any part thereof, or any part of the tackle, apparel, or furniture thereof or any goods or chattels being therein, or shall cast away or destroy any ship or vessel, with intent in any of such cases to commit murder, shall be guilty of felony, and being convicted thereof shall be liable, at the discretion of the court, to be kept in penal servitude for life or for any term not less than three years, – or to be imprisoned for any term not exceeding two years, with or without hard labour, and with or without solitary confinement.

Attempting to administer poison, or shooting or attempting to shoot, or attempting to drown, &c., with intent to murder

14 Whosoever shall attempt to administer to or shall attempt to cause to be administered to or to be taken by any person any poison or other destructive thing, or shall shoot at any person, or shall, by drawing a trigger or in any other manner, attempt to discharge any kind of loaded arms at any person, or shall attempt to drown, suffocate, or strangle any person with intent, in any of the cases aforesaid, to commit murder, shall, whether any bodily injury be effected or not, be guilty of felony, and being convicted thereof shall be liable, at the discretion of the court, to be kept in penal servitude for life or for any term not less than three years, – or to be imprisoned for any term not exceeding two years, with or without hard labour, and with or without solitary confinement.

By any other means attempting to commit murder

15 Whosoever shall, by any means other than those specified in any of the preceding sections of this Act, attempt to commit murder, shall be guilty of felony, and being convicted thereof shall be liable, at the discretion of the court, to be kept in penal servitude for life or for any term not less than three years, – or to be imprisoned for any term not exceeding two years, with or without hard labour, and with or without solitary confinement.

Letters threatening to murder

Sending letters treatening to murder

16 Whosoever shall maliciously send, deliver, or utter, or directly or indirectly cause to be received, knowing the contents thereof, any letter or writing threatening to kill or murder any person, shall be guilty of felony, and being convicted thereof shall be liable, at the discretion of the court, to be kept in penal servitude for any term not exceeding ten years and not less than three years, – or to be imprisoned for any term not exceeding two years, with or without hard labour, and with or without solitary confinement, and, if a male under the age of sixteen years, with or without whipping.

5.09 The penalty for manslaughter is discretionary. The penalty for murder, and for murder to which s 3 of the Criminal Justice Act 1990 applies, is mandatory. This imposes an obligation on the trial judge to sentence in accordance with the statute; *The People (AG) v Murtagh*[12].

5.10 Homicide is lawful if it occurs in self-defence (see paras **4.06–4.08**). Homicide is manslaughter, and not murder, if excessive force is used in self-defence but the accused believed that the force he used was no more

12 [1966] IR 361.

than was reasonably necessary for that purpose (see paras **4.23–4.28**). Force can also be used lawfully in effecting an arrest. A killing in such circumstances would probably be only justified where there was proportionality between the violence actually used and the crime under investigation, or the mischief which the officer sought to avoid; *R v Turner*[13]. Where the victim provokes the accused so that he is no longer the master of his own mind, such a killing, though intentional, will be manslaughter (see paras **4.150–4.159**).

5.11 The requirement that the victim should die within a year and a day of being stricken by the accused has effectively been replaced by the modern rules relating to causation. These will be dealt with subsequently. At common law the victim must be "any reasonable creature in being". This only means that he should be a human being. This is not without its problems and is dealt with below. The common law requirement that the killing should occur "under the King's Peace" indicates that the court should have jurisdiction to try the accused. The phrase also indicates that the killing of an alien enemy is lawful if it occurs in the course of a battle.

The Elements of Murder

5.12 Murder is distinguished from manslaughter by the mental element. Otherwise the elements are the same. In the absence of a complete definition the analysis by Chief Justice Coke best expresses the elements of homicide.

5.13   *Lord Coke – Institutes of the Law of England*
                               Volume 3

Murder is when a man of sound memory, and of the age of discretion, unlawfully killeth within any county of the realm, any reasonable creature in *rerum natura* under the King's Peace, with malice aforethought either expressed by the party or implied by law, so as the party wounded or hurt, etc. die of the wound or hurt, etc. within a year and a day after the same . . . Malice prepense is where one compasseth to kill, wound, or beat another, and doth it *cedato animo*. This is said in law to be malice aforethought prepensed – malitia praecogitata . . . [malice aforethought is implied in three cases] (1) If one kills another without any provocation on the part of him that is slain . . . (2) If a magistrate, or known officer, or any other that hath lawful warrant and in doing or offering to do his office or to execute his warrant is slain, this is murder by malice implied by law . . . (3) In respect of the person killing, if A assault B to rob him and in resisting A killeth B this is murder by malice implied albeit he never saw or knew him before. If a prisoner by the duress of the gaoler cometh to an untimely death, this is murder in the gaoler, and the law implieth malice in respect of the cruelty . . . If the sheriff or other officer where he ought to hang the party attaineth according to his judgment and his charge rule against the law, and of his own wrong burn or behead him, or *eo converso* the law in this case implies malice in him. Some manslaughters be voluntary, and not of malice aforethought upon some sudden falling out. *Delinquens per iram provacatus punira debet mitius*. Another, for distinction's sake is called manslaughter. There is no difference between murder and manslaughter,

13 VR 30.

but that the one is upon maliceaforethought and the other upon a sudden occasion and therefore is called chance Medely.

5.14 The requirement for the accused to be "a man of sound memory and of the age of discretion" is that he should be sane and of the age of responsibility in criminal law. The punishment of children and young persons convicted of homocide is within ss 102 and 104 of the Children Act 1908 as amended by the first schedule to the Criminal Justice Act 1990.

Causation

5.15 The principles gleaned from homocide cases are of general application in deciding issues of causation in criminal law. Causation has nothing whatever to do with the mental element of crime. It is essential for the prosecution to establish that the accused caused the death of the victim. The task of the defence in arguing that the accused did not intend to kill or cause serious injury to the victim will be made easier if his contribution to the death was remote from that occurrence or was less than total. The two elements are, however, in law, mutually exclusive.

Two common law rules may not have survived the enactment of the Constitution. A death caused by the accused giving perjured evidence against the victim, whereby the victim is convicted of a crime and executed is not murder at common law. The rule is so lacking in rational justification as to be unsustainable. The rule that the accused is not responsible for the death of the victim when he dies a year and a day after been stricken reflects the undeveloped state of medical science at the time when it was formulated. In Pennsylvania the Supreme Court has held that the rule does not apply where there is otherwise adequate proof of causation; *Commonwealth v Ladd*[14]. Death by execution caused by perjured evidence was thought not to be murder or manslaughter at common law. This rule is no longer relevant as the death penalty has been abolished.

General Statement

5.16 The accused will legally have caused the death of the victim if his act, or acts, substantially contributed to the subsequent death, taking into account the time at which, and the manner in which the death occurred. It is a function of the judge to decide whether there is any evidence reasonably capable of supporting the conclusion that the accused's act was still a substantially contributing factor at the time when the victim died, having regard to the manner of his death; Howard *Criminal Law*[15]. In Canada the Supreme Court has held that the accused will be liable for the victim's death where the act or acts of the accused were "a contributing cause . . . outside the small *de minimis* range"; *R v Smithers*[16].

14 (1960) 402 Pa 164, 166A (2d) 501.
15 (4th edition 1982) 29.
16 (1977) 34 CCC (2d) 427.

R v Hallett
                                   [1969] SASR 141
                         Supreme Court of South Australia, 1969

Facts: Hallett and the deceased Whiting were spending a weekend at the beach.
The accused alleged that during the course of the weekend the victim had made
homosexual advances to him culminating in the accused being forced to lie down
under knife-point to accept the deceased's advances. A fight ensued and the knife
was knocked out of the deceased's hand. The deceased ran into the sea in an
alleged attempt to commit suicide. The accused claimed to have rushed in to save
him but the fight recommenced in the water. The accused responded by choking
the deceased and leaving him unconscious at the water's edge. The accused then
fell asleep. On awakening he found the victim had drowned. The trial judge
instructed the jury that where the victim died as a result of an act or event which
could not have occurred but for the infliction of the injury by the accused then if
the subsequent act was a natural consequence of that act, the accused would be
liable. If, on the other hand, the act was not a natural consequence, causation
would not be proved. Before the Supreme Court it was argued that the jury should
have been told that unless they were satisfied that the victim's death ensued as a
result of the injury which the accused inflicted on him and the leaving of the victim
at the edge of the sea, they could not be satisfied that the accused had caused the
death of the victim. It was further argued that the jury had to be satisfied that it was
not the involuntary intervention of sleep on the part of the accused which altered
the situation from a safe one, so far as the victim was concerned, to a hazardous
one.

Bray CJ: . . . We disagree with this argument. Some confusion has sometimes
arisen particularly in the older cases, between the factors relevant when considering causation and those relevant when considering the necessary mental state
required to constitute the crime of murder. Compare 1 *Russell on Crime* (12th ed,
1964), p 413. The learned judge in a passage not quoted was at pains to point out
to the jury the necessity to separate the two questions. Foresight by the accused of
the possibility or probability of death or grievous bodily harm from his act, though
very relevant to the question of malice aforethought, has nothing to do with the
question of causation. The death of the deceased is the material event. The
question to be asked is whether an act or series of acts (in exceptional cases an
omission or series of omissions) consciously performed by the accused is or are so
connected with the event that it or they must be regarded as having a sufficiently
substantial causal effect which subsisted up to the happening of the event, without
being spent or without being in the eyes of the law sufficiently interrupted by some
other act or event. It does not matter on the question of causation whether or not
the accused after the commission of his act fails to appreciate or takes unavailing
steps to avoid its probable consequences or mistakenly thinks he has taken such
steps or fails to take such steps through some supervening factor unless that supervening factor so interrupts the effect of the original act as to prevent that original
act from being in the eyes of the law the cause of death. In this case if the deceased
was drowned and violent acts consciously performed by the accused had a causal
effect which continued up to the moment of drowning, it does not matter, so far as
causation is concerned, whether he lay unconscious on the beach until the tide
covered him or whether while unconscious he rolled down the slope into the water
or even whether in a state of insufficient consciousness he staggered further into
the water. Only if he consciously entered the water would it in our view be even
arguable that the chain of causation had been broken. (Compare the American
cases cited in Howard *Australian Criminal Law* (1965), p 32). And his Honour
expressly left this possibility to the jury. In our view, it is irrelevant on the question
of causation, assuming the appellant's story to be true, whether or not he thought

he had placed Whiting in a position of safety, whether or not it was reasonable for him to think so, whether or not he foresaw or ought to have foreseen that the deceased might be reached by the tide and drowned, whether or not the appellant was to blame for going to sleep, or whether or not he could or would have saved the life of the deceased if he had not gone to sleep. We say this because it was the act of the appellant in reducing the deceased to unconsciousness which, on his own story, originated the chain of events which led to drowning.

The only question, it seems to us, which can be raised in this connection is whether the action of the sea on the deceased can be regarded as breaking the chain of causation. We do not think it can. In the exposure cases the ordinary operation of natural causes has never been regarded as preventing the death from being caused by the accused. Such are the cases mentioned by Hale, Hawkins and East (1 *Hale PC* 431; 1 *Hawkins PC*, c 13, s 6; 1 *East PC* 226), of the infant being placed in the orchard and being killed by a kite, or the infant being placed in a pig sty and eaten by the pigs . . . In these cases, of course, the *actus reus* was the exposure of the helpless victim by itself; in the instant case the *actus reus* on the appellant's story is one stage further removed and consists of the violence exercised by him on the deceased in the water. Hence the questions raised by Mr Elliott's argument as to whether the situation in which the appellant left the unconscious Whiting on the water's edge was a safe one or a hazardous one, or was only turned from a safe one to a hazardous one by the involuntary intervention of sleep are irrelevant when considering causation. . . .

We are not concerned to deny that there may be cases where the extraordinary as opposed to the ordinary operation of natural forces might be regarded as breaking the chain of causation, as in the case of the earthquake referred to in the passage from Smith and Hogan cited by the learned judge. So here if the deceased had been placed in a situation safe from the ordinary operations of the sea and had been engulfed by a extraordinary tidal wave as the result of an earthquake in the sea it may be that the earthquake and not the act of the appellant would be regarded as the cause of death. But we cannot regard the ordinary operations of the tides at Tumby Bay, whether known to the appellant or not, as being such a supervening cause.

For these reasons the direction of the learned judge on this topic was not such as to call for the intervention of this Court. His Honour might have directed the jury in terms of the passage from *R v Bristow* [1960] SASR 210, citing *R v Smith* [1959] 2 QB 36; [1959] 2 All ER 193 (C-MAC), that if at the time of death the original wound (here the original violence in the water referred to in the accused's story) was still an operating cause and a substantial cause the death could be said to be the result of this, even if some other cause, such as the action of the water, was still operating and that only if it could be said that the original violence was merely the setting in which the action of the sea operated could it be said that the death did not result from that violence. *Bristow's* case is after all binding upon the judges of this Court unless the Full Court for some reason sees fit to depart from it. His Honour did in substance, though not in precise words, so direct. He told the jury specifically that the act of the accused must be a substantial cause. He did not use the word operational; but his remarks about the death by drowning postulate that the accused was still unconscious from the violence used by the appellant when he was involved with the sea, either by the action of the tide or by rolling down the slope or by both. If this was so, clearly the violence which preceded the unconsciousness was still operational. His Honour, by clear inference if not expressly, told the jury that if the deceased had remained conscious and gone out and drowned himself the violence of the accused would not have been the cause of death. If his Honour erred in referring to the question of foreseeability in this context that could only operate in favour of the appellant. . . .

If the deceased was unconscious as a result of the assault and drowned by the sea in any of the circumstances mentioned by his Honour then we do not think it matters whether the appellant left him in a position of mortal peril or not, or whether subsequent drowning was a consequence which might or might not have been expected to occur in the normal course, apart of course from extraordinary events like the tidal wave we mentioned previously. But all this could only operate in the accused's favour. . . .

Accordingly the appeal on the question of causation fails. The argument for the appellant is fallacious in two ways: firstly, in that it assumes that the relevant act of the appellant was the leaving of the deceased on the beach and not the violence in the water reducing him to unconsciousness, and secondly, because the chain of causation could not be broken by the appellant's omissions to take further measures for the safety of the deceased, even if such omissions were contrary to his original intention and were excused by his inadvertently falling asleep. . . .

5.18 In *Evans and Gardiner*[17] the victim died eleven months after a stabbing from which he had apparently fully recovered. It was held that once the death took place within a year and a day of the original injury the principles of causation remained the same no matter what the gap in time was between the act or omission of the accused and the death of the deceased. In *R v Smith*[18] the victim, following a stabbing, had a 75% chance of recovery which was considerably diminished because of poor medical treatment. It was held that the accused had substantially contributed to the victim's death. In *R v Jordan*[19] the accused escaped liability where, following a stabbing, the victim almost recovered from his wound. He was negligently administered an antibiotic to which he was intolerant. This administration was resumed notwithstanding that it had been discontinued for that very reason. In *R v Cheshire*[20] the Court of Appeal rejected as incorrect a direction by a trial judge that subsequent medical treatment could interrupt a chain of causation where it was reckless, in the sense that the doctors "could not care less". Negligence in the treatment of a victim need not be the immediate cause of death. Such treatment only excluded the responsibility of the accused where it was so independent of his acts, and in itself so potent in causing death, that the contribution made by the accused to that death became insignificant.

Mitigation by the Victim

5.19 It would appear that the tortfeasor is entitled to expect the victim to mitigate his loss. An accused under criminal law is not so entitled. If the victim dies from a refusal to accept obvious treatment or from compounding his own injuries by neglect the accused will still be liable once his original act was a substantial contributing cause to the victim's death.

5.20   *R v Flynn*
                                      (1867) 16 WR 319 (Ir)
                                   Central Criminal Court, 1867

Facts: This case was tried before Mr Justice O'Brien at the County Mayo Assizes (Summer, 1867). The indictment was for manslaughter, and charged the prisoner with having killed John Tracey. It appeared from the evidence that on Sunday, 24th March, a fight took place between the prisoner and his friends on

17 (No 2) (1976) VR 523.
18 [1959] 2 QB 35.
19 (1956) 40 Cr App R 152.
20 [1991] 3 All ER 670.

one side and the deceased and his friends on the other; that stones were thrown and sticks used at both sides; that after the fight was over the prisoner threw a stone at the deceased which struck him on the forehead over the right eye, and knocked him down; that the deceased then got up and went into a public-house; that in about two hours afterwards the deceased, his father, and his brothers, and also the prisoner, waked together to the police-barracks, which was about two miles distant; that the prisoner went there for the purpose of making a complaint against the Traceys; that the deceased went to bed about the middle of the night at the barracks; and that he and the prisoner remained at the barracks that night. It also appeared that on the following morning (Monday), the deceased rode from the police-barracks to his own house, a distance of about four miles; that he was then very weak and went to bed. That late on the following (Tuesday) night Dr Burke having been sent for attended the deceased; that the doctor did not see the deceased again till after his death, which occurred on Thursday; that the deceased was buried on the following Saturday; and that on the following Thursday the body was taken out of the grave, when Dr Burke made a *post mortem* examination of it in the coffin at the inquest. Dr Burke on his examination at the trial stated that when he attended the deceased on Tuesday night he examined him; that the deceased was lying in bed throwing his arms about quite unconsciously; that he had a large contused wound over the right eyebrow about an inch long; that there was considerable blackness of the skin all about the right eye; that the pupils of both eyes were enlarged and dilated; that the doctor examined him minutely and opened the wound to see if there was a fracture; that he found none on the outer table of the skull, and could not examine the inner table; that in the doctor's opinion the deceased was then labouring under compression of the brain, and that he discovered no other appearance of injury or blow on the body of the deceased. On Thursday 4th April, the doctor made a *post mortem* examination of the body of the deceased at the inquest, and the doctor stated that he then found a fracture of the inner table of the skull of the deceased which exactly corresponded with the external injury over the eye; that the vessels of the brain were considerably congested, and there was a clot of blood underneath the fracture; that the outer table of the skull was not fractured; that a violent fall might have caused the injury to the inner table; that the outer table would have been more likely to have been injured than the inner table by a blow, and that the injury to the inner table would have been more likely to have been caused by a fall than a blow of a stone, but that a blow of a stone or blunt instrument would have produced the fracture. The doctor further stated that in his opinion the deceased might have been able to walk to the police-barracks after he received the fracture, but that the reaction caused by walking would have accelerated his death, and that but for such exertion the deceased would have had better chances of recovery. The doctor further stated that in his opinion the death of the deceased was caused by compression of the brain; that the fracture of the skull was, in his opinion, sufficient to have caused that compression of the brain and consequent death of the deceased; but that the fact of the deceased having walked to the police-barracks on the Sunday night in question and having gone home next morning on horseback (as stated in the evidence) accelerated the reaction which brought on the compression of the brain; and that the deceased would have been more likely to recover if he had not walked to the police-barracks and ridden home next morning. The doctor further stated that he could not form an opinion whether the blow and injury which caused the fracture of the skull would have caused death of the deceased had he not so walked and ridden, or whether such walking and riding was or was not contributory to his death, or whether he would have recovered, but for such walking and riding; but that in his opinion the injury which the deceased received from the blow was sufficient to have caused his death even if he had not so walked and ridden.

It was contended for the prisoner that even if he had struck the deceased with the stone still there was not sufficient evidence to go to the jury to establish that the death of the deceased was occasioned by and owing to the blow of the stone so as to warrant the conviction of the prisoner, and that there was not sufficient evidence to show that the deceased would have died from the effects of the blow if he had not walked to the police-barracks and ridden home the following morning, as already mentioned, or to show that his death was not occasioned by or owing to the exertion and reaction caused by such walking and riding. And it was contended that the learned judge should direct the jury to acquit the prisoner, or that, at all events, he should tell them they should acquit him unless they were of opinion that the deceased would have died from the effects of the blow even if he had not walked to the barracks or afterwards ridden home as already stated.

Counsel for the Crown contended, on the other hand, that it appeared from the evidence that the blow of the stone and not such walking and riding was the cause of the death of the deceased.

The learned judge told the jury that if they were of opinion that the prisoner struck the deceased with the stone, as stated in the evidence, and if they also believed Dr Burke's evidence as to the cause of the death of the deceased, then they should find the prisoner guilty, even though they were unable to form an opinion whether or not the deceased would have died from the effects of the blow in case he had not walked to the barrack and afterwards ridden home, as mentioned in the evidence, but were of opinion that in such cases he *might* not have died from the effects of the blow.

The jury, acting on this direction, found the prisoner guilty, but recommended him to mercy on the grounds of the great provocation he had received.

The learned judge thereupon sentenced him to twelve months' imprisonment, and now submitted to the Court whether he should have directed an acquittal or whether the above decision was erroneous.

O'Malley, for the prisoner, cited *Johnson's* case and *Brown's* case, 1 Lewin CC 164, 165. Where it cannot be said clearly what was cause of death, the prisoner is entitled to an acquittal. At all events, it was for the jury to say what was the cause of death.

Harrison Q.C., Solicitor-General, Blake, Q.C., for the Crown, cited 1 Hale PC 428; *Rex v Ren*, Kel 26; *Rex v Holland*, 2 Moo & R 351. *Johnson's* case has been disapproved of: See the editor's note 1 Lewin CC 164, and Roscoe on Crim Ev 661, 6th edn.; *Rex v Martin*, 5 C&P 130. This is an attempt to import the doctrine of contributory negligence into a criminal case, which will not be permitted: *Reg v Swindall*, 2 C&K 230.

Pigot CB: In this case the question is a very narrow one, but on such a subject as the law of homicide it is very important that no doubt should exist, especially on so important a question as what is to be regarded as the cause of death. The passage from 1 Hale PC 428, cited during the argument by the Solicitor-General, bears very closely on the question:— "But if a man receives a wound which is not in itself mortal, but, either for want of helpful appliances or neglect thereof, it turns to a gangrene or a fever, and that gangrene or fever be the immediate cause of death, yet this is murder or manslaughter in him that gave the stroke or wound, for that, though it were not the immediate cause of his death, yet if it were the mediate cause thereof, and the fever or gangrene was the immediate cause of his death, yet the wound was the cause of the gangrene or fever, and so, consequently, is *causa causati*." *Edward Rew's* case, Kelyng's Rep. 26, is also very much in point, where "it was resolved that if one gives wounds to another, who neglects the cure of them, or is disorderly, and doth not keep that rule which a person wounded should do, yet, if he die, it is manslaughter or murder, according as the case is in the person who gave the wounds, because if the wounds had not been the man had not died; and, therefore, neglect or disorder in the person who gave the wounds shall not excuse the person who gave them." These authorities seem to lay down the rule to this effect, that if a man who has received a serious blow or hurt does not alter his ways on that account, but continues to go through the ordinary course of life which he has been accustomed to pursue, that shall not exonerate the giver of the blow from his liability if such conduct has had the effect of causing death. But if, on the other hand, his acts subsequent to the blow have been so far out of his ordinary course as to give rise to a distinct set of circumstances causing a new mischief, there the new mischief will be regarded as he *causa causati*, and not the original blow. The question is, what did the wounded man do which made that mortal which was not mortal before? Here the man walked to the police-barracks two miles off, and rode home four miles off the next day. It is difficult to say that this was "disorderly" conduct although in reference to the wound it was disorderly. We think, therefore, that the cause of death was clearly referable to the blow of the stone, and that the subsequent conduct of the deceased was not such as to excuse the prisoner from the result of his act. There still remains the question of the form of the judge's charge, and although I think it would have been better to have left to the jury distinctly the question whether the blow was the cause of death notwithstanding the other circumstances in the case, yet, in substance, this charge is in entire accordance with the law. The learned judge, in fact, told the jury that, if the doctor was to be believed, the blow was the cause of death. The doctor does not say in terms that the blow was the cause of death, but there is nothing in the evidence to cause the injury except the blow, and there was no injury except the blow. The doctor says the injury might have been caused by a fall; but there is no evidence of a fall except what was caused by the blow. The doctor says, by a short chain of causation, the blow caused the fracture, and the fracture caused death. We are, therefore, of opinion that the conviction should be affirmed.

5.21   *R v Blaue*
[1975] 3 All ER 446; [1975] 1 WLR 1411; (1975) 61 Cr App R 271;
[1976] Crim LR 648 CA
Court of Appeal England, 1975

Facts: The victim was stabbed by the accused with a knife. She lost a large quantity of blood. She was advised that a blood transfusion was necessary. For religious reasons she refused to accept it. She died the following day.

Lawton LJ: . . . When the judge came to direct the jury on this issue he did so by telling them that they should apply their common sense. He then went on to tell them they would get some help from the cases to which counsel had referred in their speeches. He reminded them of what Lord Parker CJ had said in *R v Smith*[21] and what Maule J had said 133 years before in *R v Holland*[22]. He placed particular reliance on what the latter judge had said. The jury, he said, might find it "most material and most helpful". He went on:

> "This is one of those relatively rare cases, you may think, with very little option open to you but to reach the conclusion that was reached by your predecessors as members of the jury in *R v Holland*, namely "Yes" to the question of causation that the stab was still, at the time of this girl's death, the operating cause of death – or a substantial cause – of death. However, that is a matter for you to determine after you have withdrawn to consider your verdicts."

Counsel for the appellant has criticised that direction on three grounds: first, because *R v Holland* should no longer be considered good law; secondly, because *R v Smith*, when rightly understood, does envisage the possibility of unreasonable

---

[21] [1959] 2 All ER 103; [1959] 2 QB 35.
[22] (1841) 2 Mood & R 351.

conduct on the part of the victim breaking the chain of causation; and thirdly because the judge in reality directed the jury to find causation proved although he used words which seemed to leave the issue open for them to decide.

In *R v Holland* the defendant, in the course of a violent assault, had injured one of his victim's fingers. A surgeon had advised amputation because of danger to life through complications developing. The advice was rejected. A fortnight later the victim died of lockjaw: ". . . the real question is", said Maule J, "whether in the end the wound inflicted by the prisoner was the cause of death?" That distinguished judge left the jury to decide that question as did the judge in this case. They had to decide it as juries always do, by pooling their experience of life and using their common sense. They would not have been handicapped by a lack of training in dialectics or moral theology.

Maule J's direction to the jury reflected the common law's answer to the problem. He who inflicted an injury which resulted in death could not excuse himself by pleading that his victim could have avoided death by taking greater care of himself: see Hale[23]. The common law in Sir Matthew Hale's time probably was in line with contemporary concepts of ethics. A man who did a wrongful act was deemed *morally* responsible for the natural and probable consequences of that act. Counsel for the appellant asked us to remember that since Sir Matthew Hale's day the rigour of the law relating to homicide has been eased in favour of the accused. It has been – but this has come about through the development of the concept of intent, not by reason of a different view of causation. Well-known practitioner's textbooks, such as Halsbury's Law[24] and Russell on Crime[25], continue to reflect the common law approach. Textbooks intended for students or as studies in jurisprudence have queried the common law rule. See Hart and Honoré, Causation in the Law,[26] and Smith and Hogan[27].

There have been two cases in recent years which have some bearing on this topic; *R v Jordan* and *R v Smith*. In *R v Jordan* the Court of Criminal Appeal, after conviction, admitted some medical evidence which went to prove that the cause of death was not the blow relied on by the prosecution but abnormal medical treatment after admission to hospital. This case has been criticised but it was probably rightly decided on its facts. Before the abnormal treatment started the injury had almost healed. We share Lord Parker CJ's opinion that *R v Jordan* should be regarded as a case decided on its own special facts and not as an authority relaxing the common law approach to caustion. In *R v Smith* the man who had been stabbed would probably not have died but for a series of mishaps. These mishaps were said to have broken the chain of causation. Lord Parker CJ in the course of his judgment, commented as follows:

"It seems to the court that if, at the time of death the original wound is still an operating cause and a substantial cause, then the death can properly be said to be the result of the wound, albeit that some other cause of death is also operating. Only if it can be said that the original wounding is merely the setting in which another cause operates can it be said that the death does not result from the wound. Putting it another way, only if the second cause is so overwhelming as to make the original wound merely part of the history can it be said that the death does not flow from the wound.'

The physical cause of death in this case was the bleeding into the pleural cavity arising from the penetration of the lung. This had not been brought about by any decision made by the deceased girl but by the stab wound.

---

23 Pleas of the Crown (1800), pp 427, 428.
24 3rd Edn, vol 10, p 706.
25 12th Edn (1964), vol 1, p 30.
26 1959, pp 320, 321.
27 Criminal Law (3rd Edn, 1973), p 214.

Counsel for the appellant tried to overcome this line of reasoning by submitting that the jury should have been directed that if they thought the girl's decision not to have a blood transfusion was an unreasonable one, then the chain of causation would have been broken. At once the question arises – reasonable by whose standards? Those of Jehovah's Witnesses? Humanists? Roman Catholics? Protestants of Anglo-Saxon descent? The man on the Clapham omnibus? But he might well be an admirer of Eleazar who suffered death rather than eat the flesh of swine or of Sir Thomas Moore who, unlike nearly all his contemporaries, was unwilling to accept Henry VIII as Head of the Church in England. Those brought up in the Hebraic and Christian traditions would probably be reluctant to accept that these martyrs caused their own deaths.

As was pointed out to counsel for the appellant in the course of argument, two cases, each raising the same issue of reasonableness because of religious beliefs, could produce different verdicts depending on where the cases were tried. A jury drawn from Preston, sometimes said to be the most Catholic town in England, might have different views about martyrdom to one drawn from the inner suburbs of London. Counsel for the appellant accepted that this might be so; it was, he said, inherent in trial by jury. It is not inherent in the common law as expounded by Sir Matthew Hale and Maule J. It has long been the policy of the law that those who use violence on other people must take their victims as they find them. This in our judgment means the whole man, not just the physical man. It does not lie in the mouth of the assailant to say that his victim's religious beliefs which inhibited him from accepting certain kinds of treatment were unreasonable. The question for decision is what caused her death. The answer is the stab wound. The fact that the victim refused to stop this end coming about did not break the causal connection between the act and death.

If a victim's personal representatives claim compensation for his death the concept of foreseeability can operate in favour of the wrongdoer in the assessment of such compensation; the wrongdoer is entitled to expect his victim to mitigate his damage by accepting treatment of a normal kind: see *Steele v R George & Co Ltd*[28]. As counsel for the Crown pointed out, the criminal law is concerned with the maintenance of law and order and the protection of the public generally. A policy of the common law applicable to the settlement of tortious liability between subjects may not be, and in our judgment is not, appropriate for the criminal law.

The issue of the cause of death in a trial for either murder or manslaughter is one of fact for the jury to decide. But if, as in this case, there is no conflict of evidence and all the jury has to do is to apply the law to the admitted facts, the judge is entitled to tell the jury what the result of that application will be. In this case the judge would have been entitled to have told the jury that the appellant's stab wound was an operative cause of death. The appeal fails.

Suicide

5.22 Causation has been held to occur where the victim died by committing suicide subsequent on a bestial attack by the accused; *Stephenson v State*[29]. Causation also occurs where the accused kills the victim by a fright; *R v Towers*[30]. Similarly, causation occurs where the victim dies trying to escape

28 [1942] 1 All ER 447, [1942] AC 497.
29 (1933) 205 Ind 141, 179 NE 633.
30 (1874) 12 Cox 530.

from the accused, owing to a well-grounded apprehension that the accused is going to inflict serious physical injury on him or her; *R v Donovan*[31].

Fear

5.23   Cases such as *R v Lewis*[32] and *R v Mackie*[33] follow closely the principles stated by Lord Coleridge in *R v Halliday*[34]. This, like *R v Lewis*, was a case of causing grievous bodily harm: "When a man creates in another man's mind an immediate sense of danger, which causes such person to try to escape, and in so doing he injures himself, the person who creates such a state of mind is responsible for the injuries". It is clear, however, that if a man has done acts which would make him criminally liable for causing grievous bodily harm, and death results from these acts, he is guilty of manslaughter. *R v Mackie* differs from other authorities because in those cases the evading action taken by the victim, jumping out of a window, was much more likely to result in bodily harm than that taken by the victim in *R v Mackie*, simply going downstairs. In *R v Mackie* the victim was only three years old and the jury in that case by their verdict of guilty must have found that any reasonable person would have expected the victim to have been caused some harm. In *R v Boswell*[35] the victim was electrocuted while fleeing across a railway line. The accused had knocked the victim to the ground and kicked him repeatedly. When the victim managed to get up he was chased by the accused. The evidence was that he had shouted "I will kill you", or words to that effect. The judge directed the jury that before they could return a verdict of manslaughter they must be satisfied in relation to the following elements:

(1)   that in the moments immediately before his death the victim was in fear of being physically hurt;
(2)   that because of that fear he tried to escape from an attack being made upon him or from an anticipated further attack by the accused;
(3)   that it was a reasonable fear on his part, not just some purely fanciful or wholly unjustified fear;
(4)   that the fear in his mind was caused by the actions of the accused;
(5)   that the accused's actions, which caused that fear, including any threats uttered by him, were unlawful;
(6)   that the accused when kicking or uttering threats, foresaw that the victim might try to escape and in so doing might suffer some physical harm, not necessarily serious harm, but some harm.

5.24   The close relationship between this type of case and those involving a course of conduct is illustrated by the similar approach taken by the Court of Appeal in *R v Church* (see para **5.51**). While issues of causation can be crucial in determining whether an unlawful killing has occurred, it must be borne in mind that even if the jury are satisfied that the accused caused the victim's death, all the essential elements of the offence must still be proved; *R v Jennings* [1990] Crim LR 588.

31 (1850) 4 Cox 399.
32 [1970] Crim LR 647.
33 (1973) 57 Cr App R.
34 (1889) 61 L7 701.
35 [1973] Crim LR 307.

5.25 In *R v Arobieke*[36] the victim was also electrocuted fleeing across a railway line. In that case the Court of Appeal squashed the accused's conviction for manslaughter. There had been a history of animosity between the accused and the victim. While with a group of his friends the deceased has spotted the accused, and had become apprehensive and so walked away alone. A prosecution witness had testified that the victim had walked onto the platform and looked about nervously before getting on a train. The accused had walked along the opposite platform looking into the train before going back to the ticket barrier. The victim then ran down the platform and crouched down close to where he had subsequently descended to the tracks. The trial judge had instructed the jury that they must be satisfied that the accused was on the platform when the victim was on the train and had looked for him, intending to physically hurt or threaten him with violence, that the victim had seen the accused behaving in that manner and reasonably apprehended that he was in imminent danger of physical attack and that the defendant's conduct in relation to the victim was such that any reasonable person would recognise it as being likely to subject the victim to the risk of some harm, albeit not serious. The Court of Appeal held there was no evidence of any assault. Nor was there an unlawful act. Thus the jury could not have concluded an intention to physically hurt or assault the accused. An essential ingredient for this species of manslaughter is that an unlawful act should take place. To look onto a train is not an unlawful act. In normal parlance it may be said that the defendant's actions "caused" the victim to flee and thereby to lose his life but an essential element of the crime was absent. Assault is discussed at paras **7.35–7.44**, and assault manslaughter at paras **5.53–5.54**.

Birth and Death

5.26 Some protection is given to a human being prior to being born. This protection is not absolute and remains in a state of unreform since 1922.

5.27   *Stephen – History of the Criminal Law of England*
Chapter 26

Homicide obviously means the killing of a human being by a human being; but each member of this definition suggests a further question. When does a human being begin to be regarded as such for the purposes of this definition? What kind of an act amounts to a killing?

With regard to the first question the line must obviously be drawn either at the point at which the foetus begins to live or at the point at which it begins to have a life independent of its mother's life, or at the point when it has completely proceeded into the world from its mother's body. It is almost equally obvious that for the purposes of defining homicide the last of these three periods is the one which it is more convenient to chose. The practical importance of the distinction is that it draws the line between the offence of procuring abortion and the offences of murder and manslaughter as the case may be. The conduct, the intentions and the motives which usually lead to the one offence are so different from those which lead to the others, the effects of the two crimes are also so dissimilar, that it is well

36 [1988] Crim LR 314.

to draw a line which makes it practically impossible to confuse them. The line has in fact been drawn at this point by the law of England; but one defect has resulted which certainly ought to be remedied. The specific offence of killing a child in the act of birth is not provided, as it ought to be. It was proposed by the Criminal Code Commissioners of Canada to remove this defect (see section 2.1.2 of the Draft Code) by making such an act a specific offence punishable with extreme severity, as it borders on murder, though the two should not be confounded.

5.28   ***R v Hutty***
[1953] VLR 338
High Court of Victoria, 1953

Barry J: Legally a person is not in being until he or she is born in a living state. A baby is fully and completely born when it is completely delivered from the body of its mother and it has a separate and independent existence in the sense that it does not derive its power of living from its mother. It is not material that the child still be attached to the mother by the umbilical cord; that does not prevent it from having a separate existence. But it is required . . . that the child should have an existence separate from and independent of its mother and that occurs when the child is fully extruded from its mother's body and is living by virtue of the functioning of its own organs.

5.29 If an accused does an act to the mother of the victim, while the victim is in the womb, and the victim is subsequently born alive, but dies as a result of these injuries the accused will be guilty of either murder or manslaughter depending on his intention; *R v Kwok Chak Ming*[37]. The Court of Criminal Appeal has held this principle not to apply in a case of threatening to kill a foetus in the womb by bringing about a miscarriage in the mother, under s 16 of the Offences Against the Person Act 1861; *R v Tait*[38].

Abortion

5.30   *Offences Against the Person Act 1861*

58 Every woman, being with child, who, with intent to procure her own miscarriage shall unlawfully administer to herself any poison or other noxious thing, or shall unlawfully use any instrument or other means whatsoever with the like intent, and whosoever, with intent to procure the miscarriage of any woman, whether she be or be not with child, shall unlawfully administer to her or cause to be taken by her any poison or other noxious thing, or shall unlawfully use any instrument or other means whatsoever with the like intent shall be guilty of felony, and on being convicted thereof, shall be liable, to be kept in penal servitude for life.

59 Whosoever shall unlawfully supply or procure any poison or other noxious thing, or any instrument or thing whatsoever, knowing that the same is intended to be unlawfully used or employed with intent to procure the miscarriage of any woman, whether she be or be not with child, shall be guilty of a misdemeanour, and being convicted thereof shall be liable to be kept in penal servitude for any period not less than three years and not exceeding five years.

37 [1963] HKLR 349, and generally *see Williams Textbook of Criminal Law* (2nd edition), chapter 11.
38 [1989] 3 All ER 682.

60 If any woman shall be delivered of a child, every person who shall, by any secret disposition of the body of the said child, whether such child died before, at, or after its birth, endeavour to conceal the birth thereof, shall be guilty of a misdemeanour, and being convicted thereof shall be liable at the discretion of the court, to be imprisoned for any term not exceeding two years, with or without hard labour: provided, that if any person tried for the murder of any child shall be acquitted thereof, it shall be lawful for the jury by whose verdict such person shall be acquitted, to find, in case it shall so appear in evidence, that the child had recently been born, and that such person did, by some secret disposition of the dead body of such child, endeavour to conceal the birth thereof: and thereupon the court may pass such sentence as if such person had been convicted upon an indictment for the concealment of the birth.

5.31 *Constitution*

Article 40.3.3 The State acknowledges the right to life of the unborn and, with due regard to the equal right to life of the mother, guarantees in its laws to respect, and, as far as practicable, by its laws to defend and vindicate that right.

5.32 In *R v Bourne*[39] MacNaughten J held that an abortion was not unlawful if it was done for the purpose of preserving the life of the mother. That view was possible if the doctor was of opinion, on reasonable grounds and with adequate knowledge, that the probable consequences of the continuation of the pregnancy would be to make the mother a physical or mental wreck. That judgement was made on a defence which was contained in the Infant Life (Preservation) Act 1929 which is not part of our legislation. Similarly, in *R v Davidson*[40] Menhennitt J held that an abortion was not unlawful where the doctor believed on reasonable grounds that the operation was necessary to preserve the woman from a serious danger to her life or physical or mental health (not being merely the normal dangers of pregnancy and of child birth) which the continuance of the pregnancy would entail and in the circumstances not out of proportion to the danger to be averted[41].

5.33 *Attorney General v X*
[1992] ILRM 401

Facts: X was a school girl of fourteen and a half years of age. Since she was thirteen she had been sexually molested by the father of one of her friends. In December 1991 an act of sexual intercourse took place and she discovered she was pregnant two months later. As will be seen from the judgments of the Supreme Court she was extremely distraught and became suicidal. The question for the Supreme Court was as to whether she was entitled to terminate her pregnancy. An additional issue arose as to whether a pregnant woman had the right to travel from the jurisdiction for the purpose of seeking an abortion elsewhere. This latter issue was not decided by the court because they decided in favour of X on the first issue.

39 [1939] 1 KB 687.
40 [1969] VR 667.
41 Further see Charleton *Offences Against the Person* (1992) chapter 5.

Finlay CJ:

Submissions of the Attorney General on these two issues

With regard to the submission that by reason of the absence of legislation vindicating and defending the right identified and guaranteed in Article 40.3.3° the court had no power or function to protect that right by any particular order, counsel on behalf of the Attorney General relied upon the judgment on Kenny J in *The People v Shaw* [1982] IR 1. He also relied on the judgment delivered by me, with which the other members of the Court agreed, in *The Attorney General (SPUC) v Open Door Counselling Ltd* [1988] IR 593. He submitted that it would be quite inconsistent with the obligation and right of the Courts to uphold the Constitution and the rights therein identified and guaranteed, if it were not empowered to act without the intervention in any particular instance of the Oireachtas.

With regard to the question of the true interpretation of the provisions of Article 40.3.3°, it was submitted on behalf of the Attorney General, firstly, that the terms of that sub-section must not be interpreted in isolation from the other provisions of the Constitution. That the use of the phrase 'due regard' and of the phrase 'as far as practicable' necessarily involved, for the interpretation of the provisions of the sub-section of the Article, a consideration of the entire provisions of the Constitution, of the principles in accordance with which the courts should approach its interpretation, and with the need for harmonisation between this particular provision of the Commission and other rights and obligations identified, granted or guaranteed by it. In this context reliance was placed by counsel on the judgments of this Court in *McGee v The Attorney General* [1974] IR 284; on the judgment of O'Higgins CJ in *The State (Healy) v Donohoe* [1976] IR 326 and the judgment of O'Higgins CJ in *The State (Director of Public Prosecutions) v Walsh* [1981] IR. Having regard to the principles thus laid down by this Court, it was submitted on behalf of the Attorney General that the phrases 'due regard' and 'as far as practicable' contained in the sub-article of the Constitution made it necessary that in interpreting this sub-article one looked elsewhere at the position of a woman who is a mother and a member of a family group and a member of society in the terms of the rights and obligations which, as such, she may have, together with, in relevant cases, the rights and obligations of her parents as well.

Having regard to these principles, it was submitted that the true test to be applied was that under the terms of the sub-article if it was established in any case that the continuation of the life of the unborn constituted a risk of immediate or inevitable death to the mother the termination of the pregnancy would be justified and lawful.

Such a test, it was urged, had due regard to the principles which had been submitted and to the rights and obligations and constitutional situation of the mother as a life in being.

It was consequently contended that the test proposed on behalf of the defendants of a real and substantial danger to the life of the mother, as justifying the termination of the pregnancy, was disproportionate and even having regard to the considerations which it was conceded were relevant, was a failure to approach sufficiently equality between the two rights concerned.

On behalf of the Attorney General it was further submitted that even if the test for reconciliation of the right to life of the unborn and of the mother proposed by the defendants were correct the evidence adduced on behalf of the defendants did not establish a risk complying with that test.

Article 40.3.3° of the Constitution as inserted by the Eighth Amendment

"The State acknowledges the right to life of the unborn and, with due regard to the equal right to life of the mother, guarantees in its laws to respect, and, as far as practicable, by its laws to defend and vindicate that right."

In *The State (Quinn) v Ryan* [1965] IR 70 Ó Dálaigh CJ, with whose judgment the other members of the court agreed, stated as follows:—

"It was not the intention of the Constitution in guaranteeing the fundamental rights of the citizen that these rights should be set at naught or circumvented. The intention was that rights of substance were being assured to the individual and that the courts were the custodians of these rights. As a necessary corollary it follows that no one can with impunity set these rights at naught or circumvent them, and that the courts' powers in this regard are as ample as the defence of the Constitution requires."

In his judgment in *The People v Shaw* [1982] IR 1 Kenny J, stated as follows at p 62 of the report:—

"When the People enacted the Constitution of 1937, they provided (Article 40.3) that the State guaranteed in its laws to respect, and, as far as practicable, by its laws to defend and vindicate the personal rights of the citizen and that the State should, in particular, by its laws protect as best it might from unjust attack and in the case of injustice done, vindicate the life, person, good name and property rights of every citizen. I draw attention to the use of the words 'the State'. The obligation to implement this guarantee is imposed not on the Oireachtas only, but on each branch of the State which exercises the powers of legislating, executing and giving judgment on those laws: Article 6. The word 'laws' in Article 40.3, is not confined to laws which have been enacted by the Oireachtas, but comprehends the laws made by judges and by ministers of State when they make statutory instruments or regulations."

In my judgment in *The Attorney General (SPUC) v Open Door Counselling Ltd* [1988] IR 593 at p 622, dealing with the guarantee contained in Article 40.3.3° of the Constitution, having quoted from the decision of Ó Dálaigh CJ in *The State (Quinn) v Ryan* [1965] IR 70 as applicable to an issue which arose in that case concerning the *locus standi* of the plaintiff to maintain the proceedings, I stated as follows:—

"If it is established to the satisfaction of the court that the admitted activities of the defendants constitute an assistance to pregnant women within the jurisdiction to go out of the jurisdiction for the purpose of having an abortion, then, that is an activity which directly threatens the right to life of the unborn, not only in a single case but in all cases of women who are assisted by those activities to have an abortion.

If, therefore, the jurisdiction of the courts is invoked by a party who has a *bona fide* concern and interest for the protection of the constitutionally guaranteed right to life of the unborn, the courts as the judicial organ of government of the State would be failing in their duty as far as practicable to vindicate and defend that right if they were to refuse relief upon the grounds that no particular pregnant woman who might be affected by the making of an order was represented before the courts."

Having regard to these statements of the law expressed by this Court and to the principles underlining them, I have no doubt that the submission that the courts are in any way inhibited from exercising a function to vindicate and defend the right to life of the unborn which is identified and guaranteed by Article 40.3.3° of the Constitution by reason of a want of legislation is incorrect and that the appeal of the defendants upon this ground must fail.

Interpretation of Article 40.3.3°

In the course of his judgment in *McGee v The Attorney General* [1974] IR 284 Walsh J stated as follows at p 318 of the report:—

"In this country, it falls finally upon the judges to interpret the Constitution and in doing so to determine, where necessary, the rights which are superior or antecedent to positive law or which are imprescriptible or inalienable. In the performance of this difficult duty there are certain guidelines laid down in the Constitution for the judge. The very structure and content of the Articles dealing with fundamental rights clearly indicate that justice is not subordinate to the law. In particular, the terms of s 3 of Article 40 expressly subordinate the law to justice. Both Aristotle and the Christian philosophers have regarded justice as the highest human virtue. The virtue of prudence was also esteemed by Aristotle, as by the philosophers of the Christian world. But the great additional virtue introduced by Christianity was that of charity – not the charity which consists of giving to the deserving, for that is justice, but the charity which is also called mercy. According to the preamble, the people gave themselves the Constitution to promote the common good, with due observance of prudence, justice and charity so that the dignity and freedom of the individual might be assured. The judges must, therefore, as best they can from their training and their experience interpret these rights in accordance with their ideas of prudence, justice and charity. It is but natural that from time to time the prevailing ideas of these virtues may be conditioned by the passage of time; no interpretation of the Constitution is intended to be final for all time. It is given in the light of prevailing ideas and concepts."

In the course of his judgment in *The State (Healy) v Donoghue* [1976] IR 326, O'Higgins CJ stated as follows at p 347 of the report:—

"The preamble to the Constitution records that the people seeking to promote the common good, with due observance of prudence, justice and charity, so that the dignity and freedom of the individual may be assured, true social order attained, the unity of our country restored and concord established with other nations, do hereby adopt, enact, and give to ourselves this Constitution.

In my view, this preamble makes it clear that rights given by the Constitution must be considered in accordance with concepts of prudence, justice and charity, which may gradually change or develop as society changes and develops and which fall to be interpreted from time to time in accordance with prevailing ideas. The preamble envisages a Constitution which can absorb or be adapted to such changes. In other words, the Constitution did not seek to impose for all time the ideas prevalent or accepted with regard to these virtues at the time of its enactment. Walsh J expressed this view very clearly in *McGee v The Attorney General* when he said at p 319 of the report. . . ."

The learned Chief Justice then quoted from that portion of the judgment of Walsh J which I have set out above in this judgment. I not only accept the principles set out in these two judgments as correct and appropriate principles which I must follow in interpreting the provisions of this subsection of the Constitution, but I find them particularly and peculiarly appropriate and illuminating in the interpretation of a sub-article of the Constitution which deals with the intimate human problem of the right of the unborn to life and its relationship to the right of the mother of an unborn child to her life.

I accept the submission made on behalf of the Attorney General, that the doctrine of the harmonious interpretation of the Constitution involves in this case a consideration of the constitutional rights and obligations of the mother of the unborn child and the interrelation of those rights and obligations with the rights and obligations of other people and, of course, with the right to life of the unborn child as well.

Such a harmonious interpretation of the Constitution carried out in accordance with concepts of prudence, justice and charity, as they have been explained in the judgment of Walsh J in *McGee v The Attorney General* [1974] IR 284 leads me to the conclusion that in vindicating and defending as far as practicable the right of the unborn to life but at the same time giving due regard to the right of the mother to life, the court must, amongst the matters to be so regarded, concern itself with the position of the mother within a family group, with persons on whom she is dependent, with, in other instances, persons who are dependent upon her and her interaction with other citizens and members of society in the areas in which her activities occur. Having regard to that conclusion, I am satisfied that the test proposed on behalf of the Attorney General that the life of the unborn could only be terminated if it were established that an inevitable or immediate risk to the life of the mother existed, for the avoidance of which a termination of the pregnancy was necessary, insufficiently vindicates the mother's right to life.

I, therefore, conclude that the proper test to be applied is that if it is established as a matter of probability that there is a real and substantial risk to the life, as distinct from the health, of the mother, which can only be avoided by the termination of her pregnancy, such termination is permissible, having regard to the true interpretation of Article 40.3.3° of the Constitution.

Has the appellant by evidence satisfied this test?

With regard to this issue, the findings of fact made by the learned trial judge in the High Court are as follows:—

"When the defendant learned that she was pregnant she naturally was greatly distraught and upset. Later she confided in her mother that when she learned she was pregnant she had wanted to kill herself by throwing herself downstairs. On the journey back from London she told her mother that she had wanted to throw herself under a train when she was in London, that as she had put her parents through so much trouble she would rather be dead than continue as she was. On the 31st January, in the course of a long discussion with a member of the Garda Síochána, she said: 'I wish it were all over; sometimes I feel like throwing myself downstairs.' And in the presence of another member of the Garda Síochána, when her father commented that the 'situation was worse than a death in the family' she commented: 'Not if it was me'."

On the day of her return from London the defendant's parents brought her to a very experienced clinical psychologist. He explained in his report that he had been asked to assess her emotional state; that whilst she was co-operative she was emotionally withdawn; that he had concluded that she was in a state of shock and that she had lost touch with her feelings. She told him that she had been crying on her own, but had hidden her feelings from her parents to protect them. His opinion was that her vacant, expressionless manner indicated that she was coping with the appalling crisis she faced by a denial of her emotions. She did not seem depressed, but he said that she 'coldly expressed a desire to solve matters by ending her life.' In his opinion, in her withdrawn state 'she was capable of such an act, not so much because she is depressed but because she could calculatingly reach the conclusion that death is the best solution.' He considered that the psychological damage to her of carrying a child would be considerable, and that the damage to her mental health would be devastating. His report was supplemented by oral testimony. He explained in the course of his consultation with the defendant she had said to him: 'It is hard at fourteen to go through the nine months' and that she said: 'It is better to end it now than in nine months' time.' The psychologist understood this to mean that by ending her life she would end the problems through which she was putting her parents with whom she has a very strong and loving relationship.

The psychologist who gave oral evidence as well as submitting a report, (which was admitted by agreement in evidence before the learned trial judge) stated that when he had interviewed this young girl and was anxious to have a continuing discussion with her parents who accompanied her and not having anybody available to remain with the young girl in the waiting room, his view of the risk of her committing suicide was so real, on his past experience in this field of medicine, that notwithstanding its obvious inappropriateness he requested her to remain in the room while he discussed the problem with her parents.

I am satisfied that the only risk put forward in this case to the life of the mother is the risk of self-destruction. I agree with the conclusion reached by the learned trial judge in the High Court that that was a risk which, as would be appropriate in any other form of risk to the life of the mother, must be taken into account in reconciling the right of the unborn to life and the rights of the mother to life. Such a risk to the life of a young mother, in particular, has it seems to me, a particular characteristic which is relevant to the question of whether the evidence in this case justifies a conclusion that it constitutes a real and substantial risk to life.

If a physical condition emanating from a pregnancy occurs in a mother, it may be that a decision to terminate the pregnancy in order to save her life can be postponed for a significant period in order to monitor the progress of the physical condition, and that there are diagnostic warning signs which can readily be relied upon during such postponement.

In my view, it is common sense that a threat of self-destruction such as is outlined in the evidence in this case, which the psychologist clearly believes to be a very real threat, cannot be monitored in that sense and that it is almost impossible to prevent self-destruction in a young girl in the situation in which this defendant is if she were to decide to carry out her threat of suicide.

I am, therefore, satisfied that on the evidence before the learned trial judge, which was in no way contested, and on the findings which he has made, that the defendants have satisfied the test which I have laid down as being appropriate and have established, as a matter of probability, that there is a real and substantial risk to the life of the mother by self-destruction which can only be avoided by termination of her pregnancy.

It is for this reason that, in my view, the defendants were entitled to succeed in this appeal, and the orders made in the High Court have been set aside.

Right to travel

I accept that where there exists an interaction of constitutional rights the first objective of the courts in interpreting the Constitution and resolving any problem thus arising should be to seek to harmonise such interacting rights. There are instances, however, I am satisfied, where such harmonisation may not be possible and in those instances I am satisfied, as the authorities appear to establish, that there is a necessity to apply a priority of rights.

Notwithstanding the very fundamental nature of the right to travel and its particular importance in relation to the characteristics of a free society, I would be forced to conclude that if there were a stark conflict between the right of a mother of an unborn child to travel and the right to life of the unborn child, the right to life would necessarily have to take precedence over the right to travel. I therefore conclude that the submission made that the mother of the unborn child had an absolute right to travel which could not be qualified or restricted, even by the vindication or defence of the right to life of the unborn, is not a valid or sustainable submission in law.

Furthermore, for the reasons set out by me earlier in this judgment concerning the ample powers of the court, even in the absence of legislation, to vindicate and defend the right to life of the unborn, I reject also the submission that the power of the court to interfere with the right to travel of the mother of an unborn child is in any way limited or restricted by the absence of legislation, except in so far as such absence of legislation may be a relevant factor on the questions of ineffectiveness or futility of the granting of orders restricting travel.

The order made in the High Court in this case was an order prohibiting the travelling by the mother of the unborn child outside the State for a period of nine months. At the commencement of the submissions made on behalf of the Attorney General it was indicated that the Attorney General no longer sought to stand over that precise order but was content instead, if the court concluded that a restriction on the right to travel could and should be applied, that it would be confined to an injunction restraining the mother from travelling outside the State for the purpose of having an operation of abortion carried out.

It was stated by counsel on behalf of the Attorney General that whilst the Attorney General was in his case seeking the more limited order of restraining travel, not in general but for the purpose of having an abortion performed, he did not concede that the more extensive order might not be appropriate in another case.

It is a principle to the making of orders by the courts by way of injunction that the court should avoid making a futile or unenforceable order. That principle would *prima facie* apply to injunctions made in order to protect constitutional rights in the same way as it applies to injunctions made in the protection of rights arising under private law. Furthermore, the duty which is imposed upon the State under the terms of Article 40.3.3° of the Constitution which is being discharged by the courts in granting injunctions in the context with which I am now concerned, is a duty to vindicate and defend the right of the unborn to life 'as far as practicable.' This duty, with that qualification, must it seems to me necessarily apply in any event to the discretions vested in the court the principle that it cannot and should not make orders which are futile, impractical or ineffective.

It is therefore necessary to examine the submissions made that orders, either in the form made in the High Court in this case or even in the more limited form now contended for by counsel on behalf of the Attorney General, are orders which are so incapable of supervision or enforcement that they must be deemed to be futile and, therefore, never orders which can properly be made by the courts.

I would accept that in a great number of instances, living in a country which has a land frontier and in an age which has such wide and varied facilities of travel, the making of orders restraining an individual from travelling out of the jurisdiction either for a specified time or for a specified purpose would be impossible to supervise and impossible to enforce except in the negative sense of possible imposition of punishment or sanctions after the order had been disobeyed. The imposition of such penalties, except to the extent that they might provide a deterrent, would not be an effective defence of the right of the unborn to life.

Whilst this is so, it is clear that in the instant case the orders made in the High Court, firstly, by way of an interim injunction and subsequently by way of a permanent injunction, were orders which until they were discharged by the ruling of this Court on appeal were wholly effective to achieve the purpose for which they were made. The fact that they were so effective was entirely due to the strikingly commendable attitude of all of the three defendants in this case, notwithstanding the anguish which they were suffering, of being willing and anxious to abide by the lawful orders of the court. It may, unfortunately, be true that a great number of people exist who would not have such a proper approach to the orders made by a court in pursuance of the defence of the right to life of the unborn.

Having regard, however, to the obligation of the courts to vindicate and defend that right and to use every power which they may have in an attempt to achieve that objective I do not consider that it can be said that a mere expectation that a significant number of people may be unwilling to obey the orders of a court could deprive that court from attempting, at least, in appropriate cases to discharge its constitutional duty by the making of an injunction restricting, to some extent, the right to travel of an individual.

Hederman J: . . . . The death of a foetus may be the indirect but foreseeable result of an operation undertaken for other reasons. Indeed it is difficult to see how any operation, the sole purpose of which is to save the life of the mother, could be regarded as a direct killing of the foetus, if the unavoidable and inevitable consequences of the efforts to save the mother's life leads to the death of the foetus. But like all examples of self-defence, of which this would be one, the means employed to achieve the self-protection must not go beyond what is strictly necessary. The most significant aspect of the provisions of Artile 40.3 and of the Eighth Amendment is the objective of protecting of human life which is the essential value of every legal order and central to the enjoyment of all other rights guaranteed by the Constitution. The constitutional provisions amount to a dedication to the fundamental value human life. The Eighth Amendment establishes beyond any dispute that the constitutional guarantee of the vindication and protection of life is not qualified by the condition that the life must be one which has achieved an independent existence after birth. The right of life is guaranteed to every life born or unborn. One cannot make distinctions between individual phases of the unborn life before birth, or between unborn and born life. Clearly the State's duty of protection is far reaching. Direct State interference in the developing unborn life is outlawed and furthermore the State must protect and promote that life and above all defend it from unlawful interference by other persons. The State's duty to protect life also extends to the mother. The natural connection between the unborn child and the mother's life constitutes a special relationship. But one cannot consider the unborn life only as part of the maternal organism. The extinction of unborn life is not confined to the sphere of private life of the mother or family because the unborn life is an autonomous human being protected by the Constitution. Therefore the termination of pregnancy other than a natural one has a legal and social dimension and requires a special responsibility on the part of the State. There cannot be a freedom to extinguish life side by side with a guarantee of protection of that life because the termination of pregnancy always means the destruction of an unborn life. Therefore no recognition of a mother' right of self-determination can be given priority over the protection of the unborn life. . .

. . . Abortion as a medical procedure is unique in that it involves three parties. It involves the person carrying out the procedure, the mother and the child. It is inevitable that if the procedure is adopted the child's life is extinguished. Therefore before that decision is taken it is obvious that the evidence required to justify the choice being made must be of such a weight and cogency as to leave open no other conclusion but that the consequences of the continuance of the pregnancy will, to an extremely high degree of probability, cost the mother her life and that any such opinion must be based on the most competent medical opinion available. In the present case neither this Court nor the High Court has heard or seen the mother of the unborn child. There has been no evidence whatever of an obstetrical or indeed of any other medical nature. There has been no evidence upon which the Court could conclude that there are any obstetrical problems, much less serious threats to the life of the mother of a medical nature. What has been offered is the evidence of a psychologist based on his own encounter with the first defendant and on what he heard about her attitude and behaviour from other persons, namely, the Garda Síochána and her parents. This led him to the opinion that there is a serious threat to the life of the first defendant by an act of self-destruction by reason of the fact of being pregnant. This is a very extreme reaction to pregnancy, even to an unwanted pregnancy. But as was pointed out in this Court in *SPUC v Grogan* [1989] IR 734 the fact that a pregnancy is unwanted was no justification for terminating it or attempting to terminate it. If there is a suicidal tendency then this is something which has to be guarded against. If this young person without being pregnant had suicidal tendencies due to some other cause then nobody would doubt that the proper course would be to put her in such care and under such supervision as would counteract such tendency and do everything possible to prevent suicide. I do not think the terms of the Eighth Amendment or indeed the terms of the Constitution before the Amendent would absolve the State from its obligation to vindicate and protect the life of a person who had expressed the intention of self-destruction. This young girl clearly requires loving and sympathetic care and professional counselling and all the protection which the State agencies can provide or furnish.

There could be no question whatsoever of permitting another life to be taken to deal with the situation even if the intent to self-destruct could be traced directly to the activities or the existence of another person.

It has not been argued that the words "having regard to the equal right to life of the mother" should be construed more widely than preserving the life of the mother and should be construed to be wide enough to include a situation where the best expert opinion is to the effect that the continuance of the pregnancy would be to make the mother a physical wreck. I do not think the word "life" in this context is to be construed any differently from the word "life" in the earlier part of the same Article though the State would be obliged to do all it reasonably possibly can to take steps to prevent anybody becoming a physical or a mental wreck, short of taking innocent life to achieve it. Fortunately the court does not have to decide this matter now but has to decide the matter in the context of a threat of suicide. Suicide threats can be contained. The duration of the pregnancy is a matter of months and it should not be impossible to guard the girl against self-destruction and preserve the life of the unborn child at the same time. The choice is between the certain death of the unborn life and a feared substantial danger of death but no degree of certainty of the mother by way of self-destruction.

On the vital matter of the threat to the mother's life there has been a remarkable paucity of evidence. In my opinion the evidence offered would not justify this Court withdrawing from the unborn life the protection which it has enjoyed since the injunction was granted.

Since this hearing commenced the solicitors for the defendants sought particulars as to how the plantiff would or could enforce the injunction preventing the first defendant from leaving the jurisdiction. In reply to these requisitions the Attorney General directed that counsel on his behalf should submit to the Supreme Court that, in the event of its dismissing the appeal by the defendants, that Court should alter the order of the High Court insofar as it is unconditionally restraining the first defendant from leaving the jurisdiction (*ie* from leaving it under any circumstances or for any purpose). Instead it is considered that it would be sufficient to make an order restraining her from leaving the jurisdiction for the purpose of having an abortion outside the State.

In these new circumstances, unless the court could make an injunction of the nature already granted by Costello J, prohibiting the defendant from leaving the jurisdiction, it could not effectively discharge its constitutional obligation of protecting the unborn life. If the defendants were to travel out of the jurisdiction and the first defendant had an abortion, the court could only deal with the question of contempt of court if the defendants returned to the jurisdiction, but could not restore the unborn life. Therefore this Court should not grant the injunction at (b) in the terms now sought by the Attorney General.

I would uphold the order of the High Court at paragraphs (a) and (c) of his order and would make no order in respect of paragraph (b).

McCarthy J: . . . It is not a question of balancing the life of the unborn against the life of the mother, if it were, the life of the unborn would virually always have to be preserved, since the termination of pregnancy means the death of the unborn; there is no certainty, however high the probability, that the mother will die if there is not a termination of pregnancy. In my view, the true construction of the Amendment, bearing in mind the other provisions of Article 40 and the fundamental rights of the family guaranteed by Article 41, is that, paying due regard to the equal right to life of the mother, when there is a real and substantial risk attached to her survival not merely at the time of application but in contemplation at least throughout the pregnancy, then it may not be practicable to vindicate the right of life of the unborn. It is not a question of a risk of a different order of magnitude; it can never be otherwise than a risk of a different order of magnitude.

On the facts of the case, which are not in context, I am wholly satisfied that a real and substantial risk that the girl might take her own life was established; it follows that she should not be prevented from having a medical termination of pregnancy.

This conclusion leads inevitably to the recognition that the wording of the Amendment contemplates abortion lawfully taking place within this State. In *SPUC v Grogan* [1989] IR 734, I said at p 770 of the report:—

"In the course of argument, counsel for the defendants submitted that the wording of the Eighth Amendment itself recognised that there could, in certain circumstances, be a lawful abortion in this State. The constitutional guarantee by the State is 'in its laws to respect, and, as far as practicable, by its laws to defend and vindicate' the right to life of the unborn. No relevant law has been enacted by the Oireachtas since the Eighth Amendment came into force, the direct criminal law ban on abortion still deriving from the Offences Against the Person Act 1861. As was pointed out by the Chief Justice in the *Open Door Counselling* case at p 625: 'If the Oireachtas enacts legislation to defend and vindicate a constitutionally guaranteed right it may well do so in wider terms than are necessary for the resolution of any individual case'.

It is unfortunate that the Oireachtas has not enacted any legislation at all in respect of this constitutionally guaranteed right."

In the course of argument, counsel for the Attorney General acknowledged that the Amendment does envisage the carrying out of a lawful abortion within the State. In my view, he was correct in so doing. From the wording of that portion of his judgment which I have cited, I conclude that Costello J also considered that there could be circumstances in which an abortion within the State might lawfully be carried out.

Before the enactment of the Amendment, the provisions of s 58 of the Offences Against the Person Act 1861, made it a criminal offence to procure a miscarriage. The terms were wide enough to make the act of the prospective mother or any one taking part in the procedure guilty of an offence. Abortion, for any purpose, was unlawful. The Eighth, like any Amendment to the Constitution, originated in the legislature and, in this instance, was initiated by the executive. The relevant Bill was passed by both houses of the Oireachtas and in accordance with the Constitution, it was then voted on by the People in a referendum. Its purpose can be readily identified – it was to enshrine in the Constitution the protection of the right to life of the unborn thus precluding the legislature from an unqualified repeal of s 58 of the Act of 1861 or otherwise, in general, legalising abortion. The guarantee to the unborn was qualified by the requirement of due regard to the right to life of the mother and made less than absolute by recognising that the right could only be vindicated as far as practicable. The guarantee was secured by the commitment of the State in its laws to respect and by its laws to defend and vindicate that right. I agree with the Chief Justice that the want of legislation pursuant to the amendment does not in any way inhibit the courts from exercising a function to vindicate and defend the right to life of the unborn. I think it reasonable, however, to hold that the People when enacting the Amendment were entitled to believe that legislation would be introduced so as to regulate the manner in which the right to life of the unborn and the right to life of the mother could be reconciled.

In the context of the eight years that have passed since the Amendment was adopted and the two years since *Grogan's* case the failure by the legislature to enact the appropriate legislation is no longer just unfortunate; it is inexcusable. What are pregnant women to do? What are the parents of a pregnant girl under age to do? What are the medical profession to do? They have no guidelines save what may be gleaned from the judgments in this case. What additional considerations are there? Is the victim of rape, statutory or otherwise, or the victim of incest, finding herself pregnant, to be assessed in a manner different from others? The Amendment, born of public disquiet, historically divisive of our people, guaranteeing in its laws to respect and by its laws to defend the right to life of the unborn, remains bare of legislative direction. Does the right to bodily integrity, identified in *Ryan v Attorney General* [1965] IR 294 and adverted to by Walsh J in *SPUC v Grogan* [1989] IR 734 at p 767, involve the right to control one's own body? Walsh J graphically describes part of the problem:—

"When a woman becomes pregnant she acquires rights which cannot be taken from her, namely, the right to protect the life of her unborn child and the right to protect her own bodily integrity against any effort to compel her by law or by persuasion to submit herself to an abortion. Such rights also carry obligations the foremost of which is not to endanger or to submit to or bring about the destruction of that unborn life. There is no doubt that, particularly in the case of an unmarried pregnant woman, intense pressures of a social kind may be brought to bear upon her to submit to an abortion, even from her peers or her parents. There may even be specious arguments of an economic nature ranging from those of the neo-Malthusian type to those which would seek to determine for economic reasons that the population should be structured in a particular way even to the point of deciding that the birth of too many persons of one sex should be prevented. The destruction of life is not an acceptable method of birth control. The qualification of certain pregnancies as being 'unwanted' is likewise a totally unacceptable criterion. The total abandonment of young children or old persons or of those who by reason of infirmity, mental or physical, or those who are unable to look after themselves too often occurs throughout the world. There is clear evidence that they are unwanted by those who abandon them. That would however provide no justification whatever for their elimination. On the economic plane there are, no doubt, some distorted minds which could make a case for the elimination of what they would regard as old useless and unproductive human units. To be unwanted is not justification for the destruction of one's life."

Since the Amendment contemplates lawful abortion, how may the State still, as far as practicable, vindicate the right to life of the unborn? Legislation may be both negative and positive: negative, in prohibiting absolutely or at a given time, or without meeting stringent tests: positive by requiring positive action. The State may fulfil its role by providing necessary agencies to help, to counsel, to encourage, to comfort, to plan for the pregnant woman, the pregnant girl or her family. It is not for the courts to programme society; that is partly, at least, the role of the legislature. The courts are not equipped to regulate these procedures.

The right to travel

Such a right has been identified in *The State (M) v The Attorney General* [1979] IR 73 as one of the unenumerated rights, all of which enjoy the same guarantee as contained for those expressed in Article 40. If the purpose of exercising the right to travel is to avail of a service, lawful in its own location, but unlawful in Ireland, is the right curtailed or abolished because of that local illegality and/or because of the guarantee in the Amendment? If it were a matter of a balancing exercise, the scales could only tilt in one direction, the right to life of the unborn, assuming no threat to the life of the mother. In my view, it is not a question of balancing the right to travel against the right to life; it is a question as to whether or not an individual has a right to travel – which she has. It cannot, in my view, be curtailed because of a particular intent. If one travels from the jurisdiction of this State to another, one, temporarily, becomes subject to the laws of the other State. An agreement, commonly called a conspiracy, to go to another State to do something lawfully done there cannot, in my opinion, permit of a restraining order. Treason is thought to be the gravest of crimes. If I proclaim my intent to go to another country there to plot against the Government here, I may, by some extension of the law against sedition, be prosecuted and, consequently, subject to detention here, but I cannot be lawfully prevented from travelling to that other country there to plot the overthrow, since that would not be a crime in the other country. I go further. Even if it were a crime in the other country, if I proclaim my intent to explode a bomb or shoot an individual in another country, I cannot lawfully be prevented from leaving my own country for that purpose.

The reality is that each nation governs itself and enforces its own criminal law. A court in one State cannot enjoin an individual leaving it from wrongdoing outside it in another State or States. It follows that, insofar as it interferes with the right to travel, there is no jurisdiction to make such an order. In this context, I cannot disregard the fact that, whatever the exact numbers are, there is no doubt that in the eight years since the enactment of the Amendment, many thousands of Irish women have chosen to travel to England to have abortions; it is ironic that out of those many thousands, in one case of a girl of fourteen, a victim of sexual abuse and statutory rape, in the care of loving parents who chose with her to embark on further trauma, having sought help from priest, doctor and gardai, and with an outstanding sense of responsibility to the law of the land, should have the full panoply of the law brought to bear on them in their anguish.

In short

(1) The Attorney General acted properly in bringing the matter before the court.
(2) The terms of the Eighth Amendment, now contained in Article 40.3.3° contemplate lawful abortion within the State.
(3) Despite the absence of regulating legislation, the judicial arm of Government must seek to enforce the guarantee.
(4) On the facts of this case, the mother is not to be prevented from having an abortion.
(5) In any event, she cannot be lawfully prevented from leaving the State, whatever her purpose in doing so.
(6) The failure of the legislature to provide for the regulation of Article 40.3.3° has significantly added to the problem.

It was for these reasons that I agreed that the order of the High Court should be set aside.

Egan J: . . . In the present case Costello J accepted that there was a risk that X might take her own life. He held, however, that it was much less and of a different order of magnitude than the certainty that the life of the unborn would be terminated if an injunction were not granted. Even although that be so, however, can it be said that he applied the proper test? I would regard it as a denial of the mother's right to life if there was a requirement of certainty of death in her case before a termination of the pregnancy would be permissible.

In my opinion the true test should be that a pregnancy may be terminated if its continuance as a matter of probability involves a real and substantial risk to the life of the mother. The risk must be to her life but it is irrelevant, in my view, that it should be a risk of self-destruction rather than a risk to life for any other reason. The evidence establishes that such a risk exists in the present case.

. . . The right to travel can only effectively arise in reference to an intention to procure an unlawful abortion and must surely rank lower than the right to life of the unborn. It may well be that proof of an intention to commit an unlawful act cannot amount to an offence but I am dealing with the question of an unborn within the jurisdiction being removed from the jurisdiction with the stated intention of depriving it of its right to life. In the face of a positive obligation to defend and vindicate such a right it cannot reasonably be argued that a right to travel *simpliciter* can take precedence over such a right, (I again emphasize that the question of European Community law is not being considered).

It may well be that instances of a declared intention and proof of such would be very rare indeed and there is also the position that the supervision of a court order would be difficult but these considerations must, in my opinion, yield precedence to the defence and vindication of the right to life.

Having regard to the construction and meaning, however, of the Eighth Amendment and my opinion that an abortion in this case would not be unlawful, I was satisfied that the orders made in the High Court should be set aside.

O'Flaherty J: . . . I believe the sub-section is clear in the following respects:—

(i) Abortion, as such, certainly abortion on demand, is not something that can be legalised in this jurisdiction.

(ii) Promotional propaganda in respect of abortions abroad is prohibited. *The Attorney General (SPUC) v Open Door Counselling Ltd* [1988] IR 593.

(iii) The legislators when they come to enact legislation must have due regard to the mother's right to life – a right protected throughout the Constitution in any event. Until legislation is enacted to provide otherwise, I believe that the law in this State is that surgical intervention which has the effect of terminating pregnancy *bona fide* undertaken to save the life of the mother where she is in danger of death is permissible under the Constitution and the law. The danger has to represent a substantial risk to her life though this does not necessarily have to be an imminent danger of instant death. The law does not require the doctors to wait until the mother is in peril of immediate death.

I believe the instant case to come within this principle.

Having regard to the principles of interpretation that in my judgment should apply, the further question to be asked is whether officers of the State are obliged to invoke what may be called the police power of the State to interfere with the freedom of the individual, especially the individual's freedom of movement in and out of the jurisdiction?

I leave aside the entitlement of the Oireachtas to enact legislation in regard to the provision and take it as self-executing in the absence of such legislation. I believe that its positive thrust is that the State should provide every practical assistance to pregnant women who find themselves unwillingly in that situation to help them make a decision which is in accordance with the Constitution and the law. The responsibility for this devolves primarily on the executive branch of government pending the enactment of legislation; but, in addition, no effort of heart or mind or resource should be spared by all citizens to provide encouragement for such mothers.

The State's role in such a case should be a positive rather than a negative one. In particular, I do not believe that the court should grant an injunction to interfere to this extraordinary degree with the individual's freedom of movement. In this case the injunction granted also involves, in my judgment, an unwarranted interference with the authority of the family.

It should be known that once an injunction is granted by a court it is an order that must be obeyed. If there is a failure to obey the order, then that disobedience may be punished by the imposition of various penalties, including the possibility of imprisonment or fines. To say that it is unlikely that such penalties would ever be invoked in this case is no answer; the fact is that such severe remedies are available.

Such a regime is impossible to reconcile with a Constitution one of the primary objects of which, as stated in its Preamble, is to assure the dignity and freedom of the individual.

I join with the other members of the court in agreeing that the Attorney General acted correctly in seeking the opinion of the High Court in the circumstances of this case.

For futher discussion see Charleton *Judicial Discretion in Abortion: The Irish Perspective* 6 ILJF (1992) 4.

5.34 *Infanticide Act 1949*

Infanticide

1 (1) On the preliminary investigation by the District Court of a charge against a woman for the murder of her child, being a child under the age of twelve months, the Justice may, if he thinks proper, alter the charge to one of infanticide and send her forward for trial on that charge.

(2) Where, upon the trial of a woman for the murder of her child, being a child under the age of twelve months, the jury are satified that she is guilty of infanticide, they shall return a verdict of infanticide.

(3) A woman shall be guilty of felony, namely, infanticide if—

(*a*) by any wilful act or omission she causes the death of her child, being a child under the age of twelve months, and

(*b*) the circumstances are such that, but for this section, the act or omission would have amounted to murder, and

(*c*) at the time of the act or omission the balance of her mind was disturbed by reason of her not having fully recovered from the effect of giving birth to the child or by reason of the effect of lactation consequent upon the birth of the child

and may for that offence be tried and punished as for manslaughter.

(4) Section 60 of the Offences Against the Person Act 1861, shall have effect as if the reference therein to the murder of any child included a reference to infanticide.

Short title

2 This Act may be cited as the Infanticide Act 1949.

Death

5.35 In 1976 the Conference of Medical Royal Colleges and their Faculties of the United Kingdom resolved that where it is established that there is irreversible brain damage, in the sense that none of the vital centres of the brain stem are still functioning, the patient is to be accounted dead. A decision to cease artificial support should, in practice, be taken by two doctors[42]. It does not interrupt the chain of causation if a medical practitioner disconnects a life support machine because, by generally accepted medical criteria, the victim was dead; *R v Malcherek*[43].

42 [1976] 2 BMJ 1187, [1977] Crim LR 443.
43 [1981] 2 All ER 422.

5.36   ***R v Green and Harrison***
(1988) 43 CCC (3d) 413
Supreme Court of British Columbia, 1988

Facts: The deceased was shot in the head by two different persons. One accused
put forward the defence that the deceased was already dead when he shot him.

Wood J: In this case the issue of when death, as an event, occurs is raised in the
evidence by the statements of the accused Green who told police that Roche
Charles Frie, the person named in the indictment, was already dead when he
"pumped two bullets into him".

The evidence establishes that three bullets were fired into the head of Mr Frie.
All three individually were fatal wounds in the sense that no amount of treatment
could have saved Mr Frie's life if any one – and only one – had been inflicted alone.
As I understand the evidence all three bullets severely damaged the base of the
brain and/or the brain stem from which the respiratory function is controlled. As a
consequence with the first shot fired, whichever one it was, Mr Frie likely ceased
breathing. The evidence however is also capable of supporting the conclusion that
his heart would have continued to beat for anywhere from three to five minutes
after the first shot. The opinion of Dr Currie to this effect is supported by his
finding that all three bullet tracks showed evidence of arterial bleeding, a phe-
nomena which can only occur as long as the heart beats.

On the evidence as a whole it is open to the jury to conclude that Harrison fired
the first shot to the top of Mr Frie's head and that Green then, some time
thereafter, fired two more shots to the left side of Mr Frie's head – one through and
the other behind his ear. If Mr Frie was already dead when the first of these two
shots were fired then Green cannot be convicted of murder except by virtue of the
application of s 21(1), which the Crown relies upon in its theory that Green aided
and abetted Harrison in the killing. Thus it becomes crucial for the jury to know,
as a matter of law, when death can be said to occur.

Mr Brunear urges me to accept the wisdom of both the medical profession and
the Law Reform Commission on this subject and to instruct the jury that death
takes place when a person becomes brain dead in the medical sense of that term.
Mr Van Alstine argues that the traditional approach to the question should
prevail, namely, that life continues until all vital functions of the human body
ceased to operate.

In recent years the medical profession has been concerned with this question
for obvious reasons. As the miracle of human transplants has become almost
routine the need for live donors of organs has grown. The moral or ethical
implications not to mention the legal consequences of removing vital organs from
one not yet dead in order to save the life of another, who but for such help must
die, have troubled doctors, lawyers, philosophers and theologians alike.

The Law Reform Commission, in its report on the criteria for the determination
of death, has sought to address this specific problem and has proposed a legislative
definition of when death occurs, based on the best advice and assistance it has been
able to receive from all interested groups. That proposal – and it is nothing more
than that – emphasizes brain function as the criterion by which death is
determined. Thus the common expression "brain dead" which was bandied about
during the cross-examination of Dr Currie. From the evidence it would appear
that the medical profession considers a person to be brain dead when 24 hours of
continuous EEG monitoring produces no sign of any brain activity whereas the
Law Reform Commission proposed that the "irreversible cessation of brain
function be determined by the prolonged evidence of spontaneous circulatory and
respiratory function".

As I have said both the medical profession and the Law Reform Commission are
principally concerned with the moral and legal issues arising out of artificially

345

sustained life and human transplant procedures. The legal issues raised are approached from what is primarily a civil law point of view – in other words the administration of the criminal law does not appear to have been of paramount concern in the approach taken by either group.

The suggestion that brain death or the irreversible cessation of brain function be the legal standard for determining when death occurs may be suitable in the medical context and even in the civil law context, but in my view it is a completely impractical standard to apply in the criminal law. The present case is a good example of why it is not feasible to apply such a concept to the criminal law. If the onus is on the Crown to satisfy this jury beyond a reasonable doubt that Mr Frie was still alive – that is to say that his brain function had not yet irreversibly ceased – when the accused Green "pumped" two bullets into him, it can be seen that such an onus would be impossible to discharge – unless someone had happened to come along with an EEG monitor and applied same to Mr Frie either before or immediately after the two shots allegedly fired by Green.

On the face of it I see no reason why the same legal definition of death must be applied to both a civil and a criminal context. Indeed there are good reasons why the same criteria should not apply. The criminal law seeks to deter the incidence of, *inter alia*, violent crime by holding accountable those whose conduct endangers the lives and safety of others. The civil law, in the context under discussion, seeks to ensure that societies' moral and personal values are not compromised in the pursuit of *bona fide* efforts to prolong or save meaningful life.

In *R v Kitching and Adams* (1976), 32 CCC (2d) 159, [1976] 6 WWR 697 (Man CA), the Manitoba Court of Appeal considered the issue from the opposite perspective. There the accused, who were convicted of manslaughter, caused serious injury to the deceased who thereafter was kept alive artificially until his kidneys were removed for transplant purposes at which point the life-support system was disconnected and he died. The issue in that case was the cause of death – not when death occurred. The Court of Appeal, therefore, did not have to deal with the issue before me. However, I did find the discussion of the general issue by Mr Justice O'Sullivan at pp 172–5 of the report helpful in deciding on the approach to take in the matter at bar.

In my view the criminal law should, whenever possible, strive for certainty and simplicity in its approach to such definitional problems. The traditional criterion described by Mr Justice O'Sullivan at p 172 of the report has both virtues: "Traditionally, both law and medicine have been unanimous in saying that it is not safe to pronounce a man dead until after his vital functions have ceased to operate. The heart has always been regarded as a vital organ."

I adopt that traditional approach in this case. I propose to tell this jury that as a matter of law Mr Frie was alive so long as any of his vital organs – which would include his heart – continued to operate. It will, of course, be for them to decide, on the evidence, whether any of Rocky Frie's vital organs continued to function after the first shot was fired into his head. If they conclude that no vital organs continued to function after the first shot, or if they are left with a reasonable doubt on that issue then they must give the accused Green the benefit of that doubt and conclude that Mr Frie was dead before the second and third shots were fired.

Suicide

5.37 Suicide is at common law the murder of self. A person aiding and abetting a suicide is guilty of murder. The same principle applies to the mutual aid involved in a suicide pact. Attempted suicide is a misdemeanour.

5.38   *R v Joseph Abbott*
                        (1903) 67 JP 151
                  Central Criminal Court, 1903

Facts: The accused bought aqua-fortis and he and his wife took the poison because of depression over unemployment. A police officer administered emetic to both. It was successful in the case of the accused, but not in the case of his wife.

Kennedy J: The law is quite clear. If two parties mutually agree to commit suicide, and only one accomplishes that object, the survivor is guilty of murder. Was there such an agreement here? If so, there can only be one verdict. "A person who administers poison to another with the intention of killing him is guilty of murder if that person dies, and if two persons agree that they will each take poison, each person is a principal and each is guilty. A case has been cited by the learned counsel for the prisoner which is said to warrant the statement that a consideration for such an agreement must be proved, but I have no hesitation in saying that this is not the law of the land. The entering into the agreement to kill themselves was illegal. It is contrary to the law of the land to commit suicide, and if two persons meet together and agree so to do, and one of them dies, it is murder in the other" (Field J, in *R v Jessop* (1887), 16 Cox CC, at p 206). If you think there was such an agreement it is your duty to find a verdict of guilty of wilful murder.

The accused was found guilty but the jury recommended mercy. The accused was sentenced to death.

5.39   *Suicide Bill 1991*

Suicide to cease to be a crime

1 The rule of law whereby it is a crime for a person to commit suicide is hereby abrogated.

Criminal liability for complicity in another's suicide

2 (1) A person who aids, abets, counsels or procures the suicide of another, or an attempt to commit suicide, shall be liable on conviction on indictment to imprisonment for a term not exceeding ten years.
    (2) If on the trial of an indictment for murder or manslaughter it is proved that the accused aided, abetted, counselled or procured the suicide of the person in question, the jury may find him guilty of that offence.

Short title

3 This Act may be cited as the Suicide Act 1991.

5.40 The provisions of the Suicide Bill 1991 are self-explanatory. Under the Bill it is no longer an offence for a person to commit suicide, or, it follows, to attempt suicide. A person who assists another in committing suicide, for example, by supplying him with strychnine knowing that it is to be used for the purpose of suicide, is guilty of a special offence contrary to s 2 of the Bill. This would apply, as in the case of *Abbott*, to the survivor of a suicide pact. A verdict of guilty on an offence of aiding suicide may be returned on an indictment for murder or manslaughter. If a person begs the accused to aid him in committing suicide the assistance of the accused must not go beyond encouragement or providing him with the means to end his own life. If the accused goes so far as to kill the person who wishes to die he is guilty of murder. An example of aiding suicide, contrary to s 2 of the Suicide Bill 1991, would be where poison is supplied, as in the previous example, or where the accused informs the person as to how he may best effect his purpose, knowing that this information will be acted upon. An example of murder would be where the accused, himself, injects the poison into the person's arm. In the case of a suicide pact an agreement to die together is caught by s 2. The survivor will be guilty of an offence contrary to that section. If the suicide pact involves each of the participants killing the other, for example by simultaneously firing shot guns, and one survives the survivor is guilty of murder because he has killed the other.

This Bill was first laid before the Oireachtas in November 1991 by a number of opposition senators. Despite the clear need for reform of the criminal law in this country the Bill was defeated at the second stage presumably as the grounds that Bills which are not Government approved are not to be passed into law. Why it was deemed necessary to block a perfectly straightforward piece of necessary legislation remains unclear. One is forced to the conclusion that our political representatives lack genuine committment to reforming our legal system. The irony of the matter is that at the time of writing the Minister for Justice has indicated that he will be dealing with the issue by way of legislation. If this actually occurs one wonders how much the minister's version will differ from the legislation originally proposed in 1991?

The Mental Element in Murder

5.41 The mental element in murder is no longer malice aforethought. It is, instead, an intent to kill or cause serious injury to some person.

In ordinary language one intends to do something when one means to do it. When one has made a decision to do something it is one's purpose to do that thing. This suffices as a working definition of intention in most cases. The decision may have been made, or the purpose may have been formed, either long before the act in question or virtually simultaneously with it.

Problems arise in what is called oblique intention. This occurs where what the accused means to do may appear to be separate from and independent of his true purpose. The purpose of the accused, for example, may well be to explode a bomb on a plane in order to destroy its cargo. It is only a philosopher who would consider that there would be any divergence between the accused's knowledge of the ultimate death of the passengers and crew of that plane, and what he meant to do. At the other extreme, the accused may intend to do something although it is so difficult that it becomes highly improbable. For example, the accused may wish to kill a family member by administering an extremely weak dose of a deadly poison. The point is that the accused intends death whether he can achieve it or not. If he does succeed his intention is no more as real than if he had failed.

Reality and Intent

5.42 Reality does play some part in these considerations. A person is presumed to have intended the natural and probable consequences of his conduct. The person in question is the accused. This test is a subjective one which takes into account the accused's mentality, his state of intoxication, his age and all the other personal circumstances and idiosyncrasies which shape his approach to a decision.

Experience indicates that accused persons will often try to escape the consequences of their action by alleging they did not intend them. It has occurred in many murder trials that the accused has admitted stabbing the victim in the heart but has then claimed that he never intended to kill or cause him serious injury. The law as to criminal negligence will ensure, almost invariably, that in those circumstances the accused would be guilty of manslaughter at least.

It is impossible to look into the accused's mind. His intent is to be inferred, beyond reasonable doubt, from all of the surrounding circumstances. If a particular intent can be inferred from the natural and probable consequences of the accused's action then he may have to defend himself by giving evidence as to what he personally intended. It is often in these circumstances that the jury will be able to see how the accused's mind does, and did, work. The more inescapable death or serious injury was as a consequence of the accused's actions the more difficult it will be for him to say that he did not intend that consequence. The more remote or unlikely such an eventuality is from the consequences of the accused's actions the less likely it will be that he will be either charged with murder or forced into a position of having to give evidence to explain his conduct. The amateur soccer goalkeeper who intends to make a marvellous, but highly improbable, penalty save, would always have intended it. Nothing is more natural or probable than playing a sport with the purpose of achieving the best results. The industrial spy who places an incendiary device in a rival's briefcase intends to destroy the materials in that briefcase. If the briefcase is put in a cargo hold of a plane and causes a fire which ultimately leads to a crash and the death of passengers, that improbable result will leave the accused with little to explain. The terrorist who places a bomb in a plane carrying military equipment may actively hope that the pilot and crew will escape. If they do not the natural and probable consequence of the explosion is the death of the crew and passengers. The more likely an event is, the stronger becomes the conclusion that the accused intended it. Yet, even in the most glaringly obvious circumstances the accused may escape liability for murder, if not manslaughter. This is because the test is purely subjective. However hard it is for the ordinary person to do something and intend something else, or to divide their mind between intending one action and knowing that another consequence will, in all probability, occur, an accused is, in our law, entitled to be judged by the state of his or her own mind. For an analysis see the judgments of the Court of Criminal Appeal in *The People (DPP) v Douglas and Hayes* reproduced at para **2.05**, and *The People (DPP) v Murray* reproduced at para **1.31**.

English Approach

5.43 In England the question of intent generally, and in murder cases in particular, has been the subject of much debate. As the law in this country most closely follows that jurisdiction a short discussion followed by the leading case on the subject at the present time, is appropriate. In 1961 the House of Lords decided that there was an irrevocable presumption of law that a person foresees and intends the natural consequences of his act. The person in question is the reasonable or ordinary man. Thus, where a youthful or slightly deranged offender had killed, then if the circumstances were such that a reasonable or ordinary person would have foreseen and intended the consequence of death or serious injury, the accused would be guilty of murder; *DPP v Smith*[44]. This approach appears never to have been taken in this jurisdiction and was widely criticised. The decision in *DPP v Smith* was expressly not followed in Australia; *Parker v R*[45]. An objective approach is inconsistent with s 4 of the Criminal Justice Act 1964 and the decision of the Court of Criminal Appeal in *The People (DPP) v Douglas and Hayes*[46]. Operating the presumption that an accused intends the natural and probable consequences of his action amounts to no more than a statement that the jury are entitled to view the accused as having ordinary perceptions of the consequences of his actions until such time as there is anything to indicate to the contrary. If there is, the prosecution must prove, beyond reasonable doubt, that the accused intended the result which he brought about.

In 1975 the House of Lords decided that intention was equivalent to a foresight by the accused that death or grievous bodily harm was a highly probable result of his actions; *R v Hyam*[47]. This decision equated intention with recklessness. In general, in the criminal law, intention and recklessness are alternative states of mind for the commission of offences. Where a particular crime specifies as its mental element an intention to do the act, it cannot be committed by unjustifiably taking a foreseen risk; acting recklessly. Crimes which specifically require an intent to do a particular act include all attempts, murder, and such offences as wounding or causing grievous bodily harm with intent contrary to s 18 of the Offences Against the Person Act 1861. In contrast, the offence of maliciously wounding or inflicting grievous bodily harm, contrary to s 20 of the Offences Against the Person Act 1861 may be committed by either intent or recklessness; *R v Charles*[48]. In 1985 the House of Lords reversed to the decision in *Hyam*. They held that in most cases the question of intention should be left to the good sense of the jury; *R v Maloney*[49]. In 1986 the House of Lords held that the greater the probability of a consequence occurring the more likely it was that it was so foreseen and thus the more likely it was that it was intended; *R v Hancock and Shankland*[50].

Summary

5.44 Thus the vital question is what was on the accused's mind? The more likely it was that a particular result would occur the more likely it is that the accused foresaw it and intended it. That is only commonsense. The higher the degree of such foresight in the accused's mind the more likely it was that

44 [1961] AC 290.
45 (1963) 111 CLR 610.
46 [1985] 1 LRM 25.
47 [1975] AC 55.
48 (1892) 17 Cox 499.
49 [1985] AC 905.
50 [1986] AC 455.

he had made a decision to bring about that consequence. The presumption that the accused intends the natural and probable consequences of his action is of assistance only in interpreting evidence. In the final analysis the question remains whether the accused intended to bring about the consequences with which he is charged. In an ordinary case, where the accused is alleged to have stabbed or shot the deceased, a direction as to the likely consequences of the accused's actions would be unnecessary, according to the reasoning of the House of Lords. The jury in such a case is considering whether the accused meant to do what he did. It is submitted that as a minimum necessary direction the jury should be told this. In cases of oblique intent where the accused kills the victim as a result of purposefully doing an action in which the victim is caught up, more precise directions may be necessary. The crystallisation of the law in *R v Nedrick*, which follows, is therefore of particular relevance.

5.45   ***R v Nedrick***
[1986] 3 All ER 1; [1986] 1 WLR 1025; (1986) 83 Cr App R 267;
[1986] Crim LR 792
Court of Appeal England, 1986

Facts: The accused killed a child who was asleep in a house. He intended to burn the child's mother out of her house. To do so he poured paraffin through the letter box and set it alight when it was obvious that the house was inhabited.

Lord Lane CJ: On 25 January 1985 in the Crown Court at Stafford the appellant, was convicted by a majority verdict of murder and was sentenced to life imprisonment. The jury were discharged from returning verdicts on two further counts, one of arson with intent to endanger life and the other of arson being reckless as to life being endangered.

On 20 May 1986, having declined to apply the proviso, we substituted for the verdict of murder a verdict of guilty of manslaughter and passed therefore a sentence of 15 years' imprisonment under the provisions of s 3 of the Criminal Appeal Act 1968. We now give our reasons.

The case for the Crown was that the appellant had a grudge against a woman called Viola Foreshaw, as a result of which, after threats that he would 'burn her out', he went to her house in the early hours of 15 July 1984, poured paraffin through the letter box and onto the front door and set it alight. He gave no warning. The house was burnt down and one of Viola Foreshaw's children, a boy aged 12 called Lloyd, died of asphyxiation and burns.

After a number of interviews during which he denied any responsibility, the appellant eventually confessed to the police that he had started the fire in the manner described adding. 'I didn't want anyone to die, I am not a murderer; please tell the judge; God knows I am not a murderer.' When asked why he did it, he replied, 'Just to wake her up and frighten her.'

The appellant's defence, rejected by the jury, was that he had neither started the fire not made any admissions to that effect.

The sole effective ground of appeal is that the judge misdirected the jury on the intent necessary to establish a charge of murder. This is the direction which he gave:

'It is not necessary to prove an intention to kill; the Crown's case is made out if they prove an intention to cause serious injury, that is sufficient . . . There is, however, an alternative state of mind which you will have to consider. If, when the accused performed the act of setting fire to the house, he knew that it was highly probable that the act would result in serious bodily injury to somebody inside the house, even though he did not desire it, desire to bring that result about, he is guilty of murder. If you are sure that he did the unlawful and deliberate act, and if you are sure that that was his state of mind, then, again, the prosecuton's case in the alternative of murder would be established.'

The direction was given before the publication of the speeches in the House of Lords in *R v Moloney* [1985] 1 All ER 1025, [1985] AC 905 and *R v Hancock* [1980] 1 All ER 641, [1980] AC 455. In the light of those speeches it was plainly wrong. The direction was based on a passage in *Archbold's Pleading Evidence and Practice in Criminal Cases* (41st edn, 1982) p 994, para 17–18 which has been repeated in the 42nd edn (1985) para 17–18. That passage was expressly disapproved in *R v Moloney* [1985] 1 All ER 1025 at 1030, [1985] AC 905 at 925–926, in that it equates foresight with intention, whereas foresight of consequences, as an element bearing on the issue of intention in murder . . . belongs not to the substantive law but to the law of evidence' (see [1985] 1 All ER 1025 at 1038, [1985] AC 905 at 928 per Lord Bridge). The judge was in no way to blame of course for having directed the jury in this way.

What then do a jury have to decide so far as the mental element in murder is concerned? They simply have to decide whether the defendant intended to kill or do serious bodily harm. In order to reach that decision the jury must pay regard to all the relevant circumstances, including what the defendant himself said and did.

In the great majority of cases a direction to that effect will be enough, particularly where the defendant's actions amounted to a direct attack on his victim, because in such cases the evidence relating to the defendant's desire or motive will be clear and his intent will have been the same as his desire or motive. But in some cases, of which this is one, the defendant does an act which is manifestly dangerous and as a result someone dies. The primary desire or motive of the defendant may not have been to harm that person, or indeed anyone. In that situation what further directions should a jury be given as to the mental state which they must find to exist in the defendant if murder is to be proved?

We have endeavoured to crystallise the effect of their Lordships' speeches in *R v Moloney* and *R v Hancock* in a way which we hope may be helpful to judges who have to handle this type of case.

It may be advisable first of all to explain to the jury that a man may intend to achieve a certain result whilst at the same time not desiring it to come about. In *R v Moloney* [1985] 1 All ER 1025 at 1037, [1985] AC 905 at 926 Lord Bridge gave an illustration of the distinction:

'A man who, at London Airport, boards a plane which he knows to be bound for Manchester, clearly intends to travel to Manchester, even though Manchester is the last place he wants to be and his motive for boarding the plane is simply to escape pursuit.'

The man who knowingly boards the Manchester aircraft wants to go there in the sense that boarding it is a voluntary act. His desire to leave London predominates over his desire not to go to Manchester. When he decides to board the aircraft, if not before, he forms the intention to travel to Manchester.

In *R v Hancock* the House decided that the *R v Moloney* guidelines require a reference to probability. Lord Scarman said ([1986] 1 All ER 641 at 651, [1986] AC 455 at 473):

'They also require an explanation that the greater the probability of a consequence the more likely it is that the consequence was foreseen and that if that consequence was foreseen the greater the probability is that that consequence was also intended.'

When determining whether the defendant had the necessary intent, it may therefore be helpful for a jury to ask themselves two questions. (1) How probable was the consequence which resulted from the defendant's voluntary act? (2) Did he foresee that consequence?

If he did not appreciate that death or serious harm was likely to result from his act, he cannot have intended to bring it about. If he did, but thought that the risk to which he was exposing the person killed was only slight, then it may be easy for the jury to conclude that he did not intend to bring about that result. On the other hand, if the jury are satisfied that at the material time the defendant recognised that death or serious harm would be virtually certain (barring some unforeseen intervention) to result from his voluntary act, then that is a fact from which they may find it easy to infer that he intended to kill or do serious bodily harm, even though he may not have had any desire to achieve that result.

As Lord Bridge said in *R v Moloney* [1985] 1 All ER 1025 at 1036, [1985] AC 905 at 925:

'. . . the probability of the consequence taken to have been foreseen must be little short of overwhelming before it will suffice to establish the necessary intent.'

Later he uses the expression 'and moral certainty' (see [1985] 1 All ER 1025 at 1037 [1985] AC 905 at 926) and says, 'will lead to a certain consequence unless something unexpected supervenes to prevent it' (see [1985] 1 All ER 1025 at 1039, [1985] AC 905 at 929).

Where the charge is murder and in the rare cases where the simple direction is not enough, the jury should be directed that they are not entitled to infer the necessary intention unless they feel sure that death or serious bodily harm was a virtual certainty (barring some unforeseen intervention) as a result of the defendant's actions and that the defendant appreciated that such was the case.

Where a man realises that it is for all practical purposes inevitable that his actions will result in death or serious harm, the inference may be irresistible that he intended that result, however little he may have desired or wished it to happen. The decisions is one for the jury to be reached on a consideration of all the evidence.

Attempted Murder

5.46 The intent in attempted murder is confined to an attempt to kill. An intent to cause serious injury is insufficient. This topic is dealt with at paras **2.04–2.05**.

Coincidence of Mental Element with External Element

5.47 Generally, the mental element and the external elements of a crime must coincide in point of time (see para **1.17**). Controversy has been created by the situation of an accused person who fails in his intention to kill but later, not being aware of the fact that the victim is still alive, succeeds in his earlier purpose of killing the victim. An alternative situation is where an accused person stuns the victim with a blow and then trusses them in such a way that they later die from suffocation. Had the victim died from the blow the accused would be guilty of either murder or manslaughter, depending on the intent which accompanied that act. However, the insertion of the gag, the real cause of death, was not done with an intention of causing any harm whatsoever.

5.48 This problem has parallels in other areas of the criminal law. In *Fagan v Metropolitan Police Commissioner*[51] the accused was told by a police officer to park his car at a particular spot. He drove his car onto the policeman's foot. He refused for some time to reverse from that position. He was convicted of assaulting a police officer in the due execution of his duty. On appeal he maintained that the initial act of driving onto the policeman's foot was not an assault, because it was not intentional and that the refusal to remove his car was merely an omission. His appeal failed, James J giving the view of the majority:

> "There was an act constituting battery which at its inception was not criminal because there was no element of intention but which became criminal from the moment the intention was formed to produce the apprehension which was flowing from the continuing act. The fallacy of the appellant's argument is that it seeks to equate the facts of this case with such a case as where a motorist has accidentally run over a person and, that action having been completed, fails to assist the victim with the intent that the victim should suffer".

Essentially, the law differentiates between crimes which may be committed by one act or omission (for example, larceny, murder or forgery) and those which are continuing in their nature (for example, crimes of possession). The offence of possessing a firearm with intent does not require an immediate coincidence of that intention with the first moment of possession. The intent to possess may be conditional, for example, that the firearm should be used for the purpose of endangering life if the occasion arises; *R v Bentham and Others*[52].

5.49 In *Thabo Meli v The Queen*[53] the Privy Council construed separate acts as constituting one transaction. There was thus complete coincidence between the mental and the external elements of the crime. The victim had been taken to a hut where he was struck over the head with the intention that he should be killed. His unconscious body was then rolled over a small cliff to give the death an appearance of accident. Medical evidence indicated that the accused had not succeeded in killing the deceased in the hut, or on rolling him over the cliff, but that he had later died from exposure. Lord Reid said:

> ". . . it is said that, while the first act was accompanied by *mens rea*, it was not the cause of death; but the second act, while it was the cause of death, was not accompanied by *mens rea*; . . . it appears to their Lordships impossible to divide up what was really one transaction in this way. There is no doubt that the accused set out to do all these acts in order to achieve their plan and as parts of their plan; and it is too refined a ground of judgment to say that, because they were under a misapprehension at one stage and thought that their guilty purpose had been achieved before in fact it was achieved, therefore they are to escape the penalties of the law . . .".

51 [1969] 1 QB 439.
52 [1973] 1 QB 357.
53 [1954] 1 WLR 228.

5.50   *R v Ramsay*
                         [1967] NZLR 1005
                   Court of Appeal New Zealand, 1967

Facts: The defendant admitted knocking the victim unconscious, gagging her
and placing her in the boot of his car, never realising "there was any risk to her at
all". When he went to release her he discovered she was dead and he then hid the
body in an offal pit. The remains were discovered some three weeks later and the
accused was subsequently charged with and convicted of murder. Medical evidence was unable to establish whether death had resulted from the blow on the
head or the subsequent gagging. In his summing-up the trial judge had relied
heavily on the decision in *Thabo Meli*.

McCarthy J: . . . and so it seems to me that while it may sometimes be useful to
view conduct as a whole to ascertain whether there was a dominating intention
running throughout a series of acts which can fairly be taken as the intention
actuating the fatal act, nevertheless when it comes to ascertaining knowledge of
the likely consequences of a particular act, one does not get the same help from
looking at a course of conduct in that way. A course of conduct doubtless
sometimes reveals a persisting intention sufficiently plainly to enable one to say
without doubt that every part of that conduct was directed by that intention; but
we doubt whether one can ever determine from the overall character of a sequence
of actions what knowledge there was in the mind of the actor of the likely
consequences of a particular act. To ascertain that knowledge one should look at
the act as an individual act, though not in isolation from the surrounding facts,
including, naturally, prior conduct of the accused . . . Telling the jury . . . that so
long as they were satisfied that the inserting of the gas was part of the course of
conduct and followed on as a natural result of and was part of what he was doing,
then it was sufficient even if the appellant did not know it would kill her or was
likely to kill her . . .
   The jury were entitled to have regard to all the appellant's actions of that night,
not because they made up one indivisible course of action, but because and to the
extent that they assist to reveal the state of mind including knowledge of likely
consequences, at the moment of the commission of the act which caused
death . . .

5.51   In *R v Church*[54] the series of acts doctrine propounded in *Thabo Meli*
was used by the Court of Appeal. In that case the accused struck and
attempted to strangle a woman. She fell unconsciousness and the accused,
on a cursory examination believing her dead, threw her into a river where
she drowned. In *Attorney-General's Reference (No 4 of 1980)*[55] a question
was posed for the Court of Appeal as to whether it was necessary, in order to
found a conviction of an accused who had killed another by one or other of
two or more different acts (each of which was a sufficient act to establish
manslaughter), to prove which act caused the death. The court answered
the question in the negative without citing any authority for a proposition
which they said was clear beyond argument[56].

54 [1966] 1 QB 59.
55 [1981] 1 WLR 705.
56 See also *R v Le Brun* [1991] 3 WLR 653.

Manslaughter

5.52 Manslaughter occurs where the accused kills the victim in one of the following circumstances:

(1) intending to kill or cause serious injury while lacking self-control through an act of provocation;
(2) being in a situation where he is entitled to use force against the victim but uses more force than was objectively necessary but no more than he honestly believed to be necessary;
(3) where the death of the victim is caused by a criminally negligent act or omission;
(4) by an assault;
(5) by a criminal and dangerous act.

Categories 1 and 2 are dealt with in the chapter on defences.

Assault Manslaughter

5.53 It is manslaughter for the accused to kill the victim by an assault intended to hurt or cause an injury of a more than trivial character but which is not intended to be a serious injury.

5.54   *R v Holzer*
[1968] VR 481
Supreme Court of Victoria, 1968

Facts: The accused was tried for manslaughter. The evidence showed that a companion of the accused picked a fight with a companion of the victim. The accused punched the deceased in the mouth causing him to fall backwards and hit his head on the roadway. He later died of these injuries. The punch itself caused a half inch long tear in the membrane of the deceased's lip. The accused said in the course of his evidence "I didn't hope to cause any real serious harm but when I threw the punch at him I hit him in the mouth and it would have cut his lip or bruised his lip or something . . . in my opinion it would just cut his lip and tell him to wake himself up". The ruling that follows is as to the appropriate direction in relation to manslaughter in these circumstances.

Smith J: The authorities relating to involuntary manslaughter are in an unsettled state, but I do not think that, sitting here in a trial court, it would be appropriate for me to assume the role of innovator or law reformer in this field. My task, as I see it, is to assess where the weight of authority lies and, so far as practicable, to reconcile conflicts in relevant authorities. We are not here concerned with any possible doctrine of felony manslaughter; furthermore, we are not here concerned with the doctrine of manslaughter by criminal negligence, under which, as I understand the law founded upon the House of Lords' decision in *Andrews v Director of Public Prosecutions* [1937] AC 576, [1937] 2 All ER 552, the accused must be shown to have acted not only in gross breach of duty of care but recklessly, in the sense that he realised that he was creating an appreciable risk of really serious bodily injury to another or others and that nevertheless he chose to run the risk. What we are here concerned with is, first, the doctrine of manslaughter by the intentional infliction of bodily harm, and secondly, the doctrine of manslaughter by an unlawful dangerous act.

Under the first of those doctrines the law, as I see it, is that a person is guilty of manslaughter if he commits the offence of battery on the deceased and death results directly from the commission of that offence, and the beating or other application of force was done with the intention of inflicting on the deceased some physical injury not merely of a trivial or negligible character, or, it would seem, with the intention of inflicting pain, without more injury or harm to the body than is involved in the infliction of pain which is not merely trivial or negligible.

In relation to the unlawful dangerous act doctrine, the unlawful act, it seems clear, must consist of a breach of the criminal law. The weight of authority, as it appears to me, is against the view that the accused must be shown to have acted with realisation of the extent of the risk which his unlawful act was creating. Authorities differ as to the degree of danger which must be apparent in the act. The better view, however, is I think that the circumstances must be sure that a reasonable man in the accused's position, performing the very act which the accused performed, would have realised that he was exposing another or others to an appreciable risk of really serious injury. The view which I have expressed, that realisation of the risk created does not have to be proved against the accused, is a factor in persuading me that the degree of apparent danger must be that which I have attempted to define, and that it is not sufficient, as it was held to be in *R v Church* [1966] QB 59, [1965] 2 All ER 72 (CCA), to show there was a risk of some harm resulting, albeit not serious harm. I may add that although, under the doctrine to manslaughter by unlawful dangerous act, *mens rea* is necessary, this requirement, in my view is satisfied by proof of an intention to commit the assault or other criminally unlawful act of which the accused has been guilty. On that aspect I would refer to *R v Lamb* [1967] 2 QB 981, [1967] 2 All ER 1282 (CA).

Gentlemen, in view of what I have just been saying in giving this ruling, in view of what was said yesterday, and, I might add, in view of the state of the evidence, my impression in relation to the present case is that upon an application here of the *Mamote* doctrine (*Mamote-Kulang v R* 111 CLR 62, [1964] ALR 1046) the real issue would be whether the blow was struck with an intention to do Harvey (the deceased) some physical injury not merely of a trivial or negligible character, and that on an application here of the unlawful dangerous act doctrine the real issue would be whether the blow was a dangerous one in the sense that a reasonable man in the accused's situation, striking that blow in the circumstances, would have realised he was exposing Harvey to an appreciable danger of really serious injury. That is, as I see it, the application of the ruling on the present facts.

[His Honour directed the jury in accordance with this ruling as follows:]

As the Crown has to satisfy you beyond reasonable doubt of all the elements that are necessary to make up the crime of manslaughter the next thing that needs to be done is to tell you what are the elements of that crime of manslaughter so far as those elements are relevant to the present case. The law says, in the first place, that the crime of manslaughter is committed if three elements are present. The first is an unlawful assault and battery committed by the accused on the deceased; and that the expression "assault and battery" means, in law, an intentional application of physical force to the deceased's body in a hostile manner without his consent and without lawful justification or excuse. Counsel for the accused here has told you, and rightly in my view, that upon the accused's own account, given in evidence before you, if every word of it is correct, there was here no lawful justification or excuse for his striking the blow that he admits he struck on Harvey's face, and that, accordingly, there was here present the first of the three necessary elements, namely, an unlawful assault and battery by the accused on Harvey. The second of the three elements is that Harvey's death in fact resulted from the blow, from the assault and battery. Once again, as his counsel has told you, and rightly as I consider, on the accused's own account given in his evidence before you that element is undisputed and the evidence, you may think, is perfectly clear that the death did in fact result from the assault. The first two of the three elements, therefore, you may consider, are not really in dispute and do not

357

require any examination or investigation by you. The third of the three elements is that the blow, the assault and battery, was given or committed by the accused with the intention of doing Harvey some physical injury, not merely of a trivial or negligible character. The intended injury need not be a serious injury. Indeed, if it were a serious injury that was intended we would be in the field of murder, not manslaughter. The injury intended may be of a minor character but it must not be merely trivial or negligible. There is an alternative way in which it would be open to you here to find that the charge of manslaughter had been made out. That would be if, in addition to the first two elements which I have mentioned to you and which you may think are clearly established, but without the third element I have already mentioned of intent to do physical injury . . . there was, instead, this further element that the blow, the assault, was a dangerous act, in the sense that a reasonable man in the accused's situation, striking this blow in those circumstances, would have realised that he was exposing Harvey to an appreciable danger of some really serious injury. You will see that this alternative method of proving manslaughter does not call for proof of any particular intention on the part of the accused. It looks instead at what a reasonable man in this situation would have realised and to establish manslaughter in this alternative way it must appear that this reasonable man in the accused's situation would have realised that he was exposing Harvey to an appreciable danger of some really serious injury. You will see, therefore, that in this alternative way of establishing manslaughter, as proof of any intent to injure is not called for, the law formulates the test by reference to really serious injury, whereas in the first way of constituting manslaughter, which I put to you where intent to injure is proved, it is sufficient for the Crown to prove an intention to do some physical injury which may be minor, although it must not be merely trivial or negligible . . . in law the crime of manslaughter is committed if three elements are established. The first is an unlawful assault and battery, that is to say a blow or other intentional application of physical force to the victim's body in a hostile manner without his consent, and without lawful justification or excuse. The second is that the victim's death in fact results from that unlawful act. The third is that that unlawful act was done with the intention of doing the victim some physical injury, which need not be serious, but may be of a minor character provided that it is not merely of a trivial or negligible kind.

I told you that the defence here had informed you that they did not dispute that the first two elements out of those three were established. As to the third element, that the unlawful act was done with the intention of doing some physical injury, not merely of a trivial or negligible kind, the reason for saying that the intention must not be to inflict merely trivial or negligible injury is that there is a principle of law that the law does not concern itself with trifles. Something which strictly amounts to a physical injury, some harm to the body, may nevertheless be so slight that no sensible person would pay any attention to it. It may be so slight that the law would regard it as trifling. Just to take an illustration, it might be a scuff mark on the back of man's hand caused by a fingernail or drawing some object across it. It might be said that if you slap a man's hand hard enough to cause it to tingle, ache slightly, perhaps go red, you are interfering with the blood supply, and you are doing some bodily harm to him. It might be said that, strictly speaking, there is a physical injury, but you might think it fairly to be regarded as trifling. It is because of those considerations that the law says that the third requirement in law for establishing the crime of manslaughter is an intention to do some physical injury which, though it may be merely minor, must not be of a trivial or negligible character. If the third of those elements of manslaughter is not established, the law says that the crime may nevertheless be established if, instead of that third element, the Crown establishes that the unlawful act was one which a reasonable man in the accused's situation, doing that unlawful act, would have realised was exposing the victim to an appreciable danger of some really serious injury. The Crown does not have to show that the reasonable man would have realised that there was a certainty of serious injury, or even a probability of serious injury, but the Crown does have to show that the reasonable man would have realised that he was exposing the victim to an appreciable danger of some really serious injury.

Criminal Negligence

5.55 Manslaughter by criminal negligence and manslaughter by an unlawful and dangerous act stand as the only examples in our criminal law where the accused may be found guilty of a serious criminal offence without the necessity of the prosecution proving that the accused was aware that his conduct might bring about the external element of a crime. In the context of criminal negligence the inadvertence of the accused must be so bad that any reasonable person, in the situation of the accused, would have realised, if he thought about it at all, that what he was doing incurred a high degree of risk of causing substantial personal injury to others. However, in contrast to the definition applied to intention and recklessness, the accused need never have thought about the matter at all.

5.56   *The People (A-G) v John Dunleavy*
                            [1948] IR 95
                  Court of Criminal Appeal, 1947

Davitt J: This is an application by John Dunleavy for leave to appeal against his conviction on an indictment for manslaughter at the Dublin Circuit Criminal Court on 5th February 1947, and against a sentence of eighteen calendar months' imprisonment imposed upon him therefor by the learned Circuit Court Judge, Judge McCarthy. The accused was indicted that, on the 1st May 1946, he unlawfully killed John Ryan. The case for the prosecution was that, about midnight on that date, the deceased man, while cycling along the main thoroughfare leading from Whitehall to Santry, on his own left-hand side of the road, within seven feet of the kerb, was run down by a motor taxi-cab driven by the accused. It was not alleged that the accused was driving at a fast rate of speed; in fact the evidence was that he was proceeding slowly; but the gravamen of the case against him was that, on an unlighted stretch, close to the city, of a main traffic artery over forty feet wide, he was driving without lights and without six or seven feet of the kerb on his own right-hand side.

The case for the applicant is that the learned Circuit Court Judge, in charging the jury, did not adequately or properly instruct them as to what constituted the crime of manslaughter by negligent driving, and as to what it was necessary for the prosecution to establish before the accused could be properly convicted.

The learned Circuit Court Judge based his instruction to the jury, as to the degree of negligence which the prosecution had to establish, mainly upon the observations of Hewart LCJ in *Bateman*'s case[57]. It is unnecessary fully to quote his instruction which is careful and conscientious and not very brief. The pith of his remarks is contained in the following passage: "In order to establish criminal liability the facts must be such that, in the opinion of the jury, the negligence of the accused went beyond a mere matter of compensation between subjects and

57 19 CR App R 8.

showed such a disregard for the lives and safety of others as to amount to a crime against the State and conduct deserving punishment; and, gentlemen, in the net result, what you have to decide is: did the accused, on the night of the 1st May, drive his car in such a way that his conduct was a danger to the public, in accordance with the statement of this Court?" The learned judge did not explicitly tell the jury that a high degree of negligence on the part of the accused was essential.

Considering the charge as a whole, we are of the opinion that the jury were not instructed with sufficient clearness as to the different degrees of negligence, fraught with different legal consequences, of which a person may be guilty in driving upon the highway nor of the very high degree of negligence on the part of an accused person, which the prosecution must establish in order to justify a conviction.

The crime of manslaughter, and in particular manslaughter by negligence, does not very readily lend itself to the task of precise and concise definition. It is, therefore, a matter of considerable difficulty to devise any brief formula of words, in which to instruct a jury, as to what constitutes this crime, which will be accurate and sufficient, and at the same time satisfactory for use upon all occasions. What is the most suitable direction must, to some extent, depend upon the circumstances of the particular case and the general course of the trial. It is well to bear in mind, as pointed out by Caldecote LCJ in *R v Bonnyman*[58], that what a jury requires is not a legal disquisition but a straightforward direction which will aid their common sense in arriving at a verdict upon the particular charge.

Notwithstanding the many fatal accidents which have accompanied the development of fast mechanised transport, there are few recently reported cases dealing with manslaughter upon the highway. During the earlier part of the last century, trial judges usually approached the question of manslaughter from one or other of four points of view. Some considered that the crime was committed if death was occasioned by a trespass, or an act which was unlawful, or by negligence which amounted to an illegality. Others considered whether the fatal negligence was in breach of a duty tending to the preservation of life. Simple negligence or ordinary carelessness occasioning death was, in some cases, considered to amount to manslaughter. Some judges on the other hand took the view that ordinary carelessness was not enough, and that the negligence causing death had to be "culpable" or "gross" or "criminal" before the felony could be committed.

The view that a simple act of ordinary carelessness which occasions death, in driving upon the highway, can justify a conviction for manslaughter, has not been acted upon for many years; and has been expressly negatived in many authoritative opinions, some of them very recent. The creation by statute of such minor offences as careless or inconsiderate driving has rendered the doctrine of the unlawful act as a basis for the felony of manslaughter no longer serviceable in this connection. The modern approach to the matter is exemplified in the case of *Tinline v White Cross Insurance*[59]. There Bailhache J said (at p 330): "The crime of manslaughter in a case like this consists in driving a motor-car with gross or reckless negligence. Ordinary negligence does not make a man liable for manslaughter. No one as been able to define where the dividing line is to be drawn, but everyone agrees that it requires a high degree of negligence to make the offence manslaughter." What appears to be an attempt at definition is the well-known passage from *Bateman*'s case[60]. Having referred to the practice of certain trial judges of explaining to juries in manslaughter cases that, to justify a conviction,

58 28 Cr App R 131, at p 134.
59 [1921] 3 KB 327.
60 19 Cr App R 8.

the negligence estabished must be "culpable," "criminal," "gross," or "wicked," or deserving of some such epithet, the Lord Chief Justice continued (at p 11): "But, whatever epithet be used and whether an epithet be used or not, in order to establish criminal liability the facts must be such that, in the opinion of the jury the negligence of the accused went beyond a mere matter of compensation between subjects and showed such disregard for the life and safety of others as to amount to a crime against the State and conduct deserving punishment." That the Lord Chief Justice attached particular importance to this passage is to be inferred from the circumstance that later in his opinion (at p 13) he repeats it almost word for word. In *Andrew*'s case[61] he again refers to it and suggests that the last clause might, with advantage, be amended so as to read: And showed such a disregard for the life and safety of others as to amount to a crime against the State and to call for a conviction." Though it is implicit in his opinion, it is in fact nowhere therein expressly stated that, to justify a conviction for manslaughter by negligence, it is necessary for the prosecution to establish on the part of the accused a high degree of negligence.

This Court is of the opinion that, with or without the amendment the passage quoted, taken by itself, cannot be regarded as a satisfactory instruction to a jury as to the standard to apply in determining whether the negligence established in a particular case of death occasioned by negligent driving, is sufficient to justify a conviction for manslaughter. One might reasonably suppose that any jury empanelled to try a case of manslaughter would be aware that the defendant was charged with a crime; that they should not convict him unless they believed him guilty; and that conviction for crime usually entails punishment of some kind. It can add very little to their knowledge to tell them that the negligence established must amount to a crime, must call for a conviction, and must deserve punishment.

It does assist a jury to tell them that the negligence must go beyond a mere matter of compensation and be such as to show a disregard for the life and safety of others. This direction does not, however, explain with sufficient clearness the high degree of negligence which is necessary. Negligence which exceeds the minimum requisite to establish civil liability may fall far short of what is necessary to establish manslaughter, and nevertheless be such as to show a certain disregard for the life and safety of others.

The matter is clearly and correctly dealt with in *Andrews*'s case. Having subjected the well-known passage from *Bateman*'s case to some not very stringent criticism, Lord Atkin proceeds to state that, in this class of case, simple negligence is not enough; that, for the purposes of the criminal law, there are different degrees of negligence and that a very high degree of negligence must be proved before the felony of manslaughter is established; that the degree of negligence which would be sufficient to establish the offence of dangerous driving under s 11 of the Road Traffic Act 1930, is not necessarily sufficient to establish manslaughter; and that it would be a misdirection to tell the jury that they might convict the accused if they were satisfied that the death in question was occasioned while the accused was committing, and because he was committing, an unlawful act such as the offence of dangerous driving. In that case, as is permissible in England, a count for dangerous driving was included in the indictment. This circumstance in no way prevents Lord Atkin's remarks from applying with undiminished force to cases where a charge of manslaughter is alone preferred. Section 11 of the Road Traffic Act 1930, is, in terms, very similar to our own Road Traffic Act 1933, s 51. Lord Atkin's remarks as to the danger of equating the negligence sufficient for dangerous driving with that required for manslaughter are therefore of equal application here. He suggested that if any epithet were, in

---

61 [1937] AC 576.

this class of case, to be used to qualify the negligence required, the word "reckless" while not entirely satisfactory appeared to be the most appropriate. This view was later, in *Bonnyman*'s case shared by Caldecote LCJ.

The effect shortly stated of these four cases: *Tinline, Bateman, Andrews* and *Bonnyman* appears to be that a jury is properly directed, in this class of case, if they are told that simple negligence, in the sense of ordinary carelessness, is not enough that a higher degree of negligence, such as would justify a conviction for the statutory offence of dangerous driving, is not necessarily sufficient; and that to justify a conviction for manslaughter, the jury must be satisfied that the fatal negligence was of a very high degree and of such as to be reckless or to amount to a reckless disregard for the life and safety of others. Such a direction has, we believe, been used upon many occasions by trial judges in this country; and is, upon the whole, reasonably sound and workmanlike. It is not, however, in our opinion wholly free from criticism.

To say that a person is driving with a reckless disregard for life means that he does not care whether he kills anybody or not. Such a state of mind will ordinarily, but perhaps not universally, amount to general malice sufficient to justify a conviction for murder. To say that a person is driving with a reckless disregard for the safety of others, may mean no more than that he does not care whether or not he puts them in danger. This may amount to no more than dangerous driving. To associate these two ideas is not to achieve the desired mean, but possibly to import an ambiguity. On the other hand, if the reference to recklessness is merely omitted, the jury are hardly given all the assistance which they are entitled to expect.

This Court is of the opinion that a more satisfactory way of indicating to a jury the high degree of negligence necessary to justify a conviction for manslaughter, is to relate it to the risk or likelihood of substantial personal injury resulting from it, rather than to attach any qualification to the word "negligence" or to the driver's disregard for the life or safety of others. In this connection the American case of *Commonwealth v Welansky*[62], a decision of the Supreme Court of Massachusetts, is of very considerable interest.

If the negligence proved is of a very high degree and of such a character that any reasonable driver, endowed with ordinary road sense and in full possession of his faculties. would realise, if he thought at all, that by driving in the manner which occasioned the fatality he was, without lawful excuse, incurring, in a high degree, the risk of causing substantial personal injury to others, the crime of manslaughter appears clearly to be established.

It may reasonably be assumed that any juror, sworn to try a case of manslaughter by negligent driving, will be aware that prosecutions of drivers for minor traffic offences, and civil actions for damages for personal injuries sustained in collisions upon the highway, are matters of common occurrence. Bearing this in mind, we are of opinion that whatever words are used by the trial judge in his charge, the jury should be given clearly to understand as follows:

(a) That negligence in this connection means failure to observe such a course of conduct as experience shows to be necessary if, in the circumstances, the risk of injury to others is to be avoided, failure to behave as a reasonable driver would.

(b) That they must be satisfied that negligence upon the part of the accused was responsible for the death in question.

(c) That there are different degrees of negligence, fraught with different legal consequences; that ordinary carelessness, while sufficient to justify a verdict for a plaintiff in an action for damages for personal injuries, or a conviction on prosecution in the District Court for careless or inconsiderate

---

62 55 North Eastern Reporter, 2nd Series, 902.

driving, falls far short of what is required in a case of manslaughter; and that the higher degree of negligence which would justify a conviction on prosecution in the District Court for dangerous driving is not necessarily sufficient.

(*d*) That before they can convict of manslaughter, which is a felony and a very serious crime, they must be satisfied that the fatal negligence was of a very high degree; and was such as to involve, in a high degree, the risk or likelihood of substantial personal injury to others.

The learned Circuit Court Judge, in his careful and conscientious charge to the jury, placed far too much reliance upon the passage quoted from *Bateman*'s case and did not clearly impress upon them the necessity of being satisfied that the negligence proved against the applicant was of a very high degree. His instructions, taken as a whole, may reasonably have left the jury under the impression that, if the conduct of the applicant amounted to no more than the unlawful act of dangerous driving within the meaning of s 51 of the Road Traffic Act 1933, this was necessarily sufficient to justify a conviction for manslaughter.

For these reasons we consider that there has been a misdirection, and have seen fit to reverse the conviction and order a new trial.

5.57 The judgment in *Dunleavy* was approved by the Supreme Court of Victoria in *Nydam v R*[63]. The interpretation placed on the judgment was a requirement that the act which in fact caused the death of the victim occurred in circumstances where there was a great falling short of the standard of care required of a reasonable man in the circumstances and a high degree of risk or likelihood of the occurrence of death or serious bodily injury if that standard of care was not observed. The House of Lords have also approved the objective test in manslaughter in holding that it is not necessary for the accused to foresee any harm to the victim; *DPP v Newbury & Jones*[64].

Criminal and Dangerous Act

5.58 The doctrine of criminal and dangerous act manslaughter occurred as a development of constructive malice. In the early period of the common law any unlawful act or omission which caused the death of the victim amounted to manslaughter. The rule was subsequently modified to require the accused to be committing a criminal offence; *The People (A-G) v Maher*[65]. Howard in his book, *Criminal Law*[66], makes the point that the unlawful and dangerous act rule is only applied in circumstances where the act of the accused was so dangerous that it became unlawful. There are, however, authorities against this proposition; *R v Buck*[67] and *R v Newton*[68]. Not every unlawful act, which is at the same time dangerous, gives rise to liability for manslaughter. Otherwise a dangerous driver would automatically be guilty of manslaughter. It is possible that on a full review the Court of Criminal Appeal in *Dunleavy* might have abolished this category completely. It is clear that it remains.

---

63 [1977] VR 430.
64 [1976] 2 All ER 365.
65 (1936) 71 ILTR 60.
66 (Sydney 4th edition 1982) at p 112.
67 (1960) 44 Cr App R 213.
68 [1958] Crim LR 600 at 612.

5.59   ***The People (A-G) v Crosbie and Meehan***
                              [1966] IR 490
                       Court of Criminal Appeal, 1966

Kenny J: John Crosbie, Patrick Meehan, James Meehan and William Bolger were
tried in the Central Criminal Court before Mr Justice Henchy and a jury in March,
1966, on a charge that they murdered Noel Murphy on the 21st of May 1965. After
a trial which lasted nine days the jury convicted John Crosbie and James Meehan
of manslaughter and acquitted Patrick Meehan and William Bolger. The four
accused had been tried with two others, Patrick Bradley and Michael Fagan, in the
Central Criminal Court in November, 1965, when Mr Justice Budd directed the
jury to find Patrick Bradley and Michael Fagan not guilty and the jury disagreed
on the charge against the four accused. An application for a certificate for leave to
appeal against conviction and sentence by counsel for John Crosbie and James
Meehan was refused by the trial judge and they applied to this Court for leave to
appeal. The arguments on the hearing of the appeal ended on the 27th July and the
court then stated that the applications for leave to appeal were refused and that the
court would give its reasons at a later date.

Christopher Noel Murphy was killed on the 21st of May, 1965, during a fight in
what is called "the read room" in the docks in Dublin. The dockers seeking work
meet in this room and those who are to be employed for the shifts during the day
hear their names being read out by the representatives of the stevedores. Murphy
was killed at 8.30 am when there were about 500 persons in this room. His death
was caused by a stab-wound inflicted on him by Crosbie who made a statement to
the Guards in which he admitted that he had a knife with him at the time of the
fight. There was abundant evidence on which the jury would have been entitled to
find that the stab wound which caused Murphy's death was inflicted by Crosbie. A
large number of witnesses were called by the prosecution: some of them had been
in the read room when the fight occurred and the accounts which they gave of the
sequence of the events differed in some details.

The accused, James Meehan and Patrick Meehan, are brothers. James lived at
15 Edenmore Grove, Raheny, Dublin, with two of his sisters, Ellen and Jean.
Crosbie lived beside the Meehans, at 17 Edenmore Grove, Raheny; Patrick
Meehan did not live in Raheny. James Meehan's two sisters worked in a café at
Burgh Quay and in May, 1965, a man called Christopher Meier, who went to this
café, had been offensive to them. They complained about this to James and
Patrick Meehan and to Crosbie and on Wednesday, the 19th May, Crosbie
assaulted Meier at the Labour Exchange in Gardiner Street. Crosbie intended to
go to England on the evening of Friday, the 21st May, and the two Meehans,
William Bolger and he decided that they would attack Meier in the read room on
the Friday morning, the 21st May, when they knew he would be there. The four of
them met on Friday morning and went into the read room. Crosbie was carrying a
knife but there was no evidence that any of the other three accused knew this.
James Meehan had a spanner which he described in his statement as being about a
foot long and which he said he had "to defend myself."

It is now necessary to give a description of the read room. There are three
entrances into it, two on the east side and one on the west side. The two on the east
are at the northern and southern ends of the east side while the entrance on the
west side (called the stevedores' door) is approached through a porch which is a
small room at the south-west corner with doors on the north and south side of it.
The two doors on the eastern side were sliding doors, while the stevedores' door
was on hinges. The porch was five feet by four feet and the northern and southern
doors in it were closed throughout the fight. The read room was 75 feet, 6 inches,
long and 68 feet wide. There are four stands in the room and from these the
representatives of the stevedores, having climbed some steps, read the names of
the dockers. Crosbie entered the read room by the lower door on the east side

when Meier was standing near the stevedores' door. The two Meehans, Bolger and Crosbie passed where Noel Murphy was standing and went towards Meier who was struck with a bar by James Meehan. Meier then ran towards the lower door on the eastern side of the room and escaped. Crosbie and the two Meehans were then attacked by three brothers, Liam Callaghan, Tony Callaghan and Joseph Callaghan, and Crosbie and James Meehan were driven into the porch. When Meier fled, Noel Murphy went down towards the porch and there was evidence that Noel Murphy was trying to separate Crosbie and one of the Callaghans in the porch while another of the witnesses said that Noel Murphy had got to the entrance of the porch when he was stabbed. Noel Murphy then staggered from the door of the porch into the read room. Crosbie came to the door of the porch leading into this room and Noel Murphy then said when Crosbie was standing near him: "He has a knife, he stabbed me." There was no evidence that either of the Meehans or Bolger was near Crosbie or Noel Murphy when this remark was made. Crosbie, who had a knife in his hand, was then attacked by Michael Murphy who succeeded in getting it from him. Noel Murphy died on the 21st May as the result of a stab-wound on the right-hand side of his chest.

In a statement which Crosbie made to the Guards he said: "I ran towards Myers (meaning Meier) and I got a wallop at his back with the bar. Then a melee started, someone jumped on my back. I tried to hit the man who jumped on me. I don't think I struck him. I know the man who jumped on my back but I don't like to give his name. Somebody also jumped in on me and a crowd dragged me into an alley way leading out of the read room. I didn't get a chance to see who they were and I cannot name any of them. There was a general struggle in the alley way. Two or three were holding on to me. We struggled out of the doorway. The crowd were kicking and shouting and punching. They had a hold of me by the arm and the back of the neck. I could not do anything so I pulled out the knife. I had the knife in my hand. I pulled it out on a swing with my left hand and as I did a man jumped back away from me and cried out: 'He has a knife, he has a knife.'" In a statement which James Meehan made to the Guards he said: "I approached Mears, my friends were standing behind me. I made a blow with the wrench at Mears and I missed. I made a second blow at him and I hit him on the shoulder. A general fight then developed. I was pushed into a doorway in the reading room by three brothers of the Callaghans and a few others. One of them was a fellow named Noel Murphy, a docker who lives on the south side of the city."

The trial judge gave the jury careful directions about the intent necessary to constitute the crime of murder, the inferences which they could draw about the common design of Crosbie, the Meehans and Bolger to attack Meier and to defend themselves against a counter-attack by Meier's supporters, self-defence and provocation and as to the circumstances in which the killing of Noel Murphy could be manslaughter.

Counsel for Crosbie said that the trial judge had misdirected the jury about the ingredients of manslaughter when he told them that they should apply the standard of the reasonable man when deciding whether Crosbie had done a dangerous act in producing the knife. Counsel asked the court to hold that the much discussed decision in *Director of Public Prosecutions v Smith*[69] was wrong and he cited the scathing criticism of it in the 1964 edition of Russell on Crime. The passages in the judge's charge to which counsel objected were: "The prosecution have to show that he (meaning Crosbie) did the fatal stabbing and that at the time he did it he intended not to cause death or serious injury but to cause an injury less than that or to use the knife for the purpose of frightening" (p 17). "If you have not got this consideration of self-defence or inevitable accident, then you simply ask yourself the question: Did he kill him with the knife and at the time did he intend

69 [1961] AC 290.

to cause him any injury or to use the knife for any purpose against the deceased man?" (p 18). "If you use a knife as a weapon for the purposes of causing serious injury intentionally and death results it is murder. If you carry a knife for the purpose of frightening somebody and you kill that person in the process . . . that would be manslaughter unless one is covered by self-defence" (p 34). "If you do not find him (meaning Crosbie) guilty of murder, you then consider the case of manslaughter. For that the prosecution must prove that he did the fatal assault, that he stabbed this man fatally and at the time he did so he intended not to cause serious injury but some injury less than that. You could also find him guilty of manslaughter if he killed under provocation; if his intention was not to cause serious injury, that he unlawfully caused an injury less than serious; or was using a knife to frighten or terrorise or put off others including, Noel Murphy . . . then you could find him guilty of manslaughter" (p 56). The trial judge was asked to recall the jury when he completed his charge and when they returned, the Judge, in the course of his remarks to them, said: "I told you that if you found Crosbie not guilty of murder you pass on to the question of whether he is guilty of manslaughter and for that the State must prove he killed the deceased man with a knife and that, at the time he did so, he did the act with the intention of either causing him injury less than serious injury or that he had the intention of frightening or terrifying him at the time. That is correct, gentlemen, subject to this being made clear to you . . . that if you use something for the purpose of frightening or annoying somebody, it must be an act which, in the opinion of a reasonable person, is something likely to injure: the sort of use of a knife which, in the estimation of a reasonable person, is calculated to run a person, against whom he is using it, into the risk of some injury of some kind or whether if you are satisfied he took out the knife, not for the actual purpose of killing or committing serious injury – or if necessary any physical injury – but for the purpose of annoying or frightening the deceased man or any person around, but, if you think, in doing that, he should have realised that, in taking out the knife and using it in that way, a reasonable person would expect or feel that he could cause injury to some of them, then he is guilty of manslaughter."

A person who produces a knife with the intention of intimidating or frightening another and not for self-defence commits an assault and the act done is therefore unlawful. When a killing resulted from an unlawful act, the old law was that the unlawful quality of the act was sufficient to constitute the offence of manslaughter. The correct view, however, is that the act causing death must be unlawful and dangerous to constitute the offence of manslaughter. The dangerous quality of the act must however be judged by objective standards and it is irrelevant that the accused person did not think that the act was dangerous. In the opinion of this Court the statement of the law in *R v Larkin*[70], a decision of the Court of Criminal Appeal in England, at p 219, is correct in so far as it deals with the offence of manslaughter: "If a person is engaged in doing a lawful act, and in the course of doing that lawful act behaves so negligently as to cause the death of some other person, then it is for the jury to say, upon a consideration of the whole of the facts of the case, whether the negligence proved against the accused person amounts to manslaughter, and it is the duty of the presiding judge to tell them that it will not amount to manslaughter unless the negligence is of a very high degree; the expression most commonly used is unless it shows the accused to have been reckless as to the consequences of the act. That is where the act is lawful. Where the act which a person is engaged in performing is unlawful, then, if at the same time it is a dangerous act, that is, an act which is likely to injure another person, and quite inadvertently he causes the death of that other person by that act, then he is guilty of manslaughter."

---

70 [1943] 1 All ER 217.

Counsel for Crosbie said that this view meant that a person could be guilty of manslaughter when he had no intent to do serious injury, that an intent to do serious injury was thereby attributed to a person accused of manslaughter and could not be rebutted while the effect of s 4 of the Criminal Justice Act 1964, is that the intent to do serious injury could be rebutted when the offence charged is murder. But the question in manslaughter is not whether the accused intended to do serious injury, for if he did, he is guilty of murder. The relevant intention in manslaughter is the deliberate doing of an act which is unlawful and which, judged by objective standards, is dangerous. Thus in a charge of manslaughter caused by the dangerous driving of a motor car, it is not a defence that the accused driver did not think that the driving was dangerous.

In the opinion of this Court, the judge's charge in relation to manslaughter by Crosbie was correct.

5.60 The unlawful and dangerous act need not necessarily be directed or aimed at the victim; *R v Goodfellow*[71]. Two recent cases in the English Court of Appeal have dealt with both aspects of the unlawful and dangerous act rule in manslaughter. In *R v Ball*[72] the accused admitted unlawfully assaulting the victim by firing a gun at a range of 12 yards. He claimed that the assessment of danger must be based on his mistaken belief that he was firing a blank and not on the fact of his having fired a live cartridge. Dismissing the appeal the court held that where the act was unlawful the question for the jury was whether it was also dangerous in the sense that all sober and reasonable people would inevitably realise that it would subject the victim to the risk of some harm, albeit not serious harm. Questions of gross or criminal negligence were not material. In manslaughter arising from an unlawful and dangerous act, the accused's state of mind was relevant only to establish: (1) that the act was committed intentionally; and (2) that it was an unlawful act. Once 1 and 2 were established, the question of whether the act was dangerous was to be judged by the standard of a sober and reasonable man.

Omission

5.61 A killing can occur by virtue of an omission as well as an act. If an omission is made deliberately with the intention of causing death or serious injury then, if the accused is under a duty to do the act, the killing will be murder. If, on the other hand, the killing is due to criminal neglect it will be manslaughter; *R v Stone and Dobinson*[73]. It is not an offence to stand by and watch people kill themselves. An omission is only equivalent to an act in criminal law if the accused was under a duty to act. That duty can arise by virtue of contract, blood relationship, or the voluntary assumption of responsibility. The modern trend is for the courts to move away from these separate categorisations and to look instead at the complete facts of the case to determine whether or not an accused should be liable for an omission to act.

71 (1986) 83 Cr App R 23.
72 [1989] Crim LR 730.
73 [1977] QB 358.

5.62   *R v Taktak*
                                (1988) 34 A Crim R 334
                    Court of Criminal Appeal New South Wales, 1988

Facts: The accused hired a prostitute for a party. When he left her at the party he
went away and was later telephoned by one of the party goers to say that they had
finished with her. When he arrived she was unconscious due to heroin consumption. He took her by taxi to a place where he made ineffectual attempts to treat
her. Some time later he made two attempts to call a doctor but the girl was dead
when medical help eventually arrived. It was argued on appeal that no duty of care
arose in these circumstances. The appeal was dismissed and the following judgment proposes a broader principle for finding a duty of care which accords with the
approach already adopted in *R v Stone and Dobbinson.*

Carruthers J: . . . the evidence led by the Crown was capable of satisfying the jury
beyond reasonable doubt that the appellant owed a duty of care in law to Miss
Kirby. That duty flowed from his taking her unconscious body into his exclusive
custody and control and thereby removing her from the potentiality of appropriate
aid from others. The legal principles are, I think, conveniently stated in 40 Am Jur
2d, par 90 at 383: "Generally speaking, the affirmative legal duty which is the vital
element of a homicide charge based upon failure to supply medical or surgical
attention may exist, first, where a statute imposes a duty to care for another; the
second, where one stands in a certain status or relationship to another; the third,
where one has assumed a contractual duty to care for another; and fourth, where
one has voluntarily assumed the care of another and has so secluded the helpless
person as to prevent others from rendering aid".

5.63   It may be that the courts will see fit to impose a test of reasonableness
as to whether a person should act in a given set of circumstances. The virtues
of a hero are not required of the ordinary person and it would seem that a
proper test would be that liability for an omission would occur where it is
reasonable to infer the relationship between the accused and the victim gave
rise to a duty in the accused to act to safeguard health. A duty to rescue
might be imposed where the accused could make reasonable efforts to
rescue the victim without endangering his own safety.

Code Options

5.64   *Draft Criminal Code*
                    Adopted by the Criminal Law Revision Committee

Murder

56   A person who kills another—

   (*a*) intending to kill; or

   (*b*) intending to cause serious injury and being aware that he may kill; [or

   (*c*) intending to cause fear of death or serious injury and being aware that he
      may kill,]

   is guilty of murder, unless section 58, 60, 61, 65 or 67 applies.

Manslaughter

57   (1) A person is guilty of manslaughter where—

   (*a*) he kills or is a party to the killing of another with the fault specified in
      section 56 but section 58 (diminished responsibility), 60 (provocation) or 61
      (use of excessive force) applies; or

(*b*) he is not guilty of murder by reason only of the fact that, because of voluntary intoxication, he is not aware that death may be caused or believes that an exempting circumstance exists; or

(*c*) he kills another—
  (i) intending to cause serious injury; or
  (ii) being reckless whether death or serious injury will be caused.

(2) Where section 58 applies the jury shall return a verdict of "guilty of manslaughter by reason of diminished responsibility" and in any other case they shall return a verdict of "guilty of manslaughter."

Jurisdiction over murder and manslaughter

62 A person is guilty of murder or manslaughter (if section 56 or 57 applies) where—

(*a*) he causes a fatal injury to another person to occur within the ordinary limits of criminal jurisdiction, whether his act is done within or outside and whether the death occurs within or outside those limits;

(*b*) he kills another person anywhere in the world by an act done within the ordinary limits of criminal jurisdiction; or

(*c*) being a British citizen, he kills another person anywhere in the world by an act done anywhere in the world.

Attempted manslaughter

63 A person who attempts or is a party to an attempt to kill another, where section 58, 60 or 61 would apply if death were caused, is not guilty of attempted murder but is guilty of attempted manslaughter.

Liability of party not having defence

64 The fact that one person is, by virtue of section 58, 60, 61, 63 or 67, not guilty of murder or attempted murder shall not affect the question whether any other person is so guilty.

Killing in pursuance of suicide pact

65 (1) A person who, with the fault specified in section 56, kills another or is a party to the other being killed by a third person is not guilty of murder but is guilty of an offence under this section if he is acting in pursuance of a suicide pact between him and the other.

(2) "Suicide pact" means a common agreement between two or more persons having for its object the death of all of them, whether or not each is to take his own life, but nothing done by a person who enters into a suicide pact shall be treated as done by him in pursuance of the pact unless it is done while he has the settled intention of dying in pursuance of the pact.

(3) A person who in pursuance of a suicide pact attempts or is a party to an attempt to kill another is not guilty of attempted murder but is guilty of an attempt to commit an offence under this section.

Complicity in suicide

66 A person who procures, assists or encourages suicide committed or attempted by another is guilty of an offence.

Infanticide

67 (1) A woman who, with the fault specified in section 56 or section 57(1)(*c*), kills or is a party to the killing of her child by an act done when the child is under the age of twelve months and when the balance of her mind is disturbed by reason of the effect of giving birth or of circumstances consequent upon that birth, is not guilty of murder or manslaughter but is guilty of infanticide.

(2) A woman who, in the circumstances specified in subsection (1), attempts or is a party to an attempt to kill her child is not guilty of attempted murder but is guilty of attempted infanticide.

(3) A woman may be convicted of infanticide (or attempted infanticide) although the jury is uncertain whether the child had been born and had an existence independent of her when his death occurred (or, in the case of an attempt, when the act was done).

Threat to kill or cause serious injury

68 A person who makes to another a threat, intending that other to fear that it will be carried out, to kill or cause serious injury to that other or a third person is guilty of an offence.

Causing death

69 For the purposes of sections 56 to 62, 65 and 67, a person does not cause the death of another unless—

(*a*) that other has been born and has an existence independent of his mother when his death occurs (whether or not he was born or had an independent existence at the time of the infliction of any injury causing death); and

(*b*) the death occurs within a year and a day after the day on which any act causing death was done by that person or on which any fatal injury resulting from such an act was sustained by that other (and, where the fatal injury was done to an unborn child, within a year and a day after the day on which he was born and had an independent existence).

Abortion

70 A person who terminates the pregnancy of a woman otherwise than in accordance with the provisions of section 1 of the Abortion Act 1967 is guilty of an offence.

Self-abortion

71 (1) A pregnant woman who terminates her pregnancy otherwise than in accordance with the provisions of section 1 of the Abortion Act 1967 is guilty of an offence.

(2) Notwithstanding section 54 (impossibility), a woman who is not pregnant cannot be guilty of an attempt to commit an offence under this section.

Supplying article for abortion

72 A person who supplies or procures any article knowing that it is to be used with intent to terminate the pregnancy of a woman, whether she is pregnant or not, commits an offence.

Child destruction

73 (1) A person who intentionally kills a child capable of being born alive before it has an existence independent of its mother is guilty of child destruction, unless the act which causes death is done in good faith for the purpose only of preserving the life of the mother.

(2) The fact that a woman had at any material time been pregnant for twenty-eight weeks or more shall be *prima facie* proof that she was at that time pregnant of a child capable of being born alive.

(3) A person who is found not guilty of murder or manslaughter (or attempted murder or manslaughter) of a child by reason only of the fact that the jury are uncertain whether the child had been born and had an existence independent of his mother when his death occurred (or, in the case of an attempt, when the act was done) shall be convicted of child destruction (or attempted child destruction).

Further Materials

5.65 O'Connor *Capital Murder and the Supreme Court* XIV Ir Jur (1979) 329.
Anon *Negligence as a Constituent of Manslaughter: The Decision of the Court of Criminal Appeal in Dunleavy's Case* XIV Ir Jur (1948) 9, 18.
Smith *A Note on Intention* [1990] Crim LR 85.
Ashworth *Reforming the Law of Murder* [1990] Crim LR 75.
Gough *The Mental Element in the Crime of Murder* (1988) 104 LQR 30.
Williams *The Mens Rea for Murder: Leave it Alone* (1989) 105 LQR 387.
Report of the House of Lords Select Committee on Murder and Life Imprisonment (ISBN 0 10 486889 9).

Dangerous Driving Causing Death

5.66 This offence of negligence is considered at paras **1.33–1.38**. Further see Charleton *Offences Against the Person* (1992), chapter 4.

Euthanasia

5.67 It is murder for a medical person to administer treatment to a patient for the purpose of ending their life. It is not a defence that the patient asked, for whatever reason, for their life to be ended. A medical person may administer pain killing drugs to keep a very sick person comfortable. At some stage the dose may have to be dangerously high to effect this purpose. Tolerance of a drug (particularly morphine) may necessitate large doses. If such a dose kills there will be no offence unless the doctor intended thereby to cause death. Almost always his or her intention will be to attempt to relieve intolerable pain. Morphine can have the effect, particularly at the large dosages needed to relieve exquisite pain, of putting a patient in a coma. Recovery may never occur. In this state the terminally ill are usually not fed, except to relieve discomfort. Death is allowed to take its natural course while pain is kept at bay by pain relieving drugs. It may be, there is a double effect in a high dose of morphine; relieving pain and causing a usually terminal coma. A doctor is entitled to choose this course in an appropriate case. Extreme pain in a terminal illness makes this choice appropriate. There is no justification, however, in using a drug with intent to kill. Some drugs will cause death almost immediately and any pain relieving effect is achieved through death alone. Such an action is equivalent to shooting a patient and is murder. The medical properties of drugs are well known and there can be little room for dispute as to what is genuinely pain relieving or what merely shortens life. In *R v Cox* (The Independent, 10 September 1992) a doctor was requested by a dreadfully ill patient to take her life. He administered a drug which had no effect but to kill. He was convicted of attempted murder as the body was burned before a post-mortem examination could have been completed. While his action was understandable, his intent was clear. Probably his compassionate judgment was clouded by a desire to relieve terrible suffering. This was a different case where another consultant would have chosen a high dose of morphine.

Chapter 6

SEXUAL OFFENCES

Outline

6.01 At common law intercourse was only lawful where it occurred between husband and wife. The expression 'unlawful sexual intercourse', when it occurs in the statutes, therefore refers to that which occurs in an extra-marital context; *R v Chapman*[1]. It is only within certain specified circumstances that extra-marital sexual intercourse is criminal. Even before the reforms introduced by the Criminal Law (Rape) (Amendment) Act 1990 a man was not entitled to use more than "gentle violence" on his wife for the purpose of obtaining her consent to intercourse; *McN v McN*[2]; *G v G*[3]. Nor could a husband force his wife to consent to unusual sexual acts as part of the marriage contract; *R v Kowalski*[4].

6.02 To a large extent the criminal law on sexual practices mirrored the Judeo-Christian ethic. Until recently, some States in the United States retained fornication as a criminal offence. Until 1967 in the United Kingdom homosexual acts between consenting adults carried a penalty of life imprisonment. This continues to be the situation here. As we shall subsequently see, the status of that law has been put in doubt by the obligations of the State to conform to the European Convention on Human Rights.

Essentially, men and women of heterosexual orientation are entitled to consent to sexual conduct short of intercourse after the age of fifteen; s 12 of the Criminal Law (Amendment) Act 1935. A girl can validly, in law, consent to sexual intercourse after she has attained her 17th birthday (see para **6.31**). Homosexual acts and sexual acts with animals are banned in their entirety. Bestiality remains proscribed as the law is unaffected by any intentional obligation of the State. Apart from these limitations men and women are entitled to engage in any sexual conduct which does not actually

---

1 [1959] 1 QB 100.
2 [1936] IR 177.
3 [1924] AC 349.
4 [1988] Crim LR 124.

cause physical or, it is submitted, mental harm; *R v Donovan*[5]; and see *R v Browne*[6], and see also para **4.05**.

Legitimacy of Legal Intervention

6.03 The law has a legitimate interest in interfering in the conduct of human sexual practices. People develop psychically and physically from a state of sexual immaturity. Freud argued that infants, and very young children, had their sexual energy channelled into pleasure apart from the sexual organs. Neither Freud nor any serious thinker subsequently has argued that children were capable of, or benefited from, adult sexual experience. Some people argue that although homosexual interest is a natural part of human sexual development that an orientation of interest in one's own sex can be fixed by practice. This is thought to be especially so where an adult interferes with a child and turns what may be a tentative experiment into an act of uninhibited indulgence.

Apart from the lack of development associated with youth some people may, through accident or illness, be unable to understand the nature of sexual intercourse or to protect themselves against the predatory intentions of others. Experience of various kinds of sexual crime has demonstrated to the writer that, of all the forms of sexual conduct proscribed by the law, incest appears to cause the most lasting and deep-seated harm to the personality of the victim. Incest cases are usually categorised by years of abuse often commencing in early childhood. It may be that the scale of the damage is attributable, in part, to the repetition of abuse. Nature has set between parents and children a barrier by which the children demand privacy, especially in sexual matters, and has orientated the species away from the possibility of reproduction with close blood relations. In the context of incestuous abuse experience indicates that the closer the exploitative sexual practices come to intercourse, or its equivalent, the more harm is done.

It is apparent, on any rational analysis, that the law has good reason for interfering in the area of sexual conduct. The course of everyday life indicates the strength of the instincts which drive people into intimate physical contact with one another and the necessity of using the criminal law to divert this energy away from being the cause of grave harm to others.

6.04 *Wolfenden Committee on Homosexual Offences and Prostitution* Cmnd 247, 1957

[The function of the criminal law in the field of sexual relations is] to preserve public order and decency, to protect the citizen from what is offensive and injurious and to provide sufficient safeguards against exploitation and corruption of others, particularly those who are especially vulnerable because they are young, weak in body or mind, inexperienced or in a state of special physical, official or economic dependence.

It is not, in our view, the function of the law to intervene in the private lives of citizens or to seek to enforce any particular pattern of behaviour further than is necessary to carry out the purposes we have outlined.

5 [1934] 2 QB 498.
6 'The Independent', 20 February 1992.

6.05 Sexual relations are made criminal by reason of (a) blood relationship, (b) mental illness, (c) sexual orientation, (d) age, and (e) real or legally implied lack of consent.

Blood Relationship

6.06 Incest has been a criminal offence since 1908. The Act outlawing this conduct remains adequate in itself. It is, however, obvious that it needs to be extended to adoptive relationships and that its scope should include sexual acts which fall short of intercourse.

6.07   *Punishment of Incest Act 1908*
as amended by s 12 of the Criminal Law Amendment Act 1935

1 (1) Any male person who has carnal knowledge of a female person, who is to his knowledge his grand-daughter, daughter, sister, or mother, shall be guilty of a misdemeanour, and upon conviction thereof shall be liable, at the discretion of the court, to be kept in penal servitude for any term not less than three years and not exceeding seven years, or to be imprisoned for any time not exceeding two years with or without hard labour: Provided that if, on an indictment for any such offence, it is alleged in the indictment and proved that the female person is under the age of fifteen years, the same punishment may be imposed as may be imposed under section 1 of the Criminal Law Amendment Act 1935 (which deals with the defilement of girls under fifteen years of age).

(2) It is immaterial that the carnal knowledge was had with the consent of the female person.

(3) If any male person attempts to commit any such offence as aforesaid, he shall be guilty of a misdemeanour, and upon conviction thereof shall be liable at the discretion of the court to be imprisoned for any time not exceeding two years with or without hard labour.

(4) On the conviction before any court of any male person of an offence under this section, or of an attempt to commit the same, against any female under twenty-one years of age, it shall be in the power of the court to divest the offender of all authority over such female, and, if the offender is the guardian of such female, to remove the offender from such guardianship, and in any such case to appoint any person or persons to be the guardian or guardians of such female during her minority or any less period:

Provided that the High Court may at any time vary or rescind the order by the appointment of any other person as such guardian, or in any other respect.

2 Any female person of or above the age of seventeen years who with consent permits her grandfather, father, brother, or son to have carnal knowledge of her (knowing him to be her grandfather, father, brother, or son, as the case may be) shall be guilty of a misdemeanour, and upon conviction thereof shall be liable, at the discretion of the court, to be kept in penal servitude for any term not less than three years, and not exceeding seven years, or to be imprisoned with or without hard labour for any term not exceeding two years.

3 In this Act the expressions "brother" and "sister", respectively, include half-brother and half-sister, and the provisions of this Act shall apply whether the relationship between the person charged with an offence under this Act and the person with whom the offence is alleged to have been committed, is or is not traced through lawful wedlock.

4 (1) An offence under this Act shall be deemed to be an offence within, and subject to, the provisions of the Vexatious Indictments Act 1859, and any Act amending the same.

(2) A court of quarter sessions shall not have jurisdiction to enquire of, hear, or determine any indictment for an offence against this Act, or for an attempt to commit any such offence.

(3) If, on the trial of any indictment for rape, the jury are satisfied that the defendant is guilty of an offence under this Act, but are not satisfied that the defendant is guilty of rape, the jury may acquit the defendant of rape and find him guilty of an offence under this Act, and he shall be liable to be punished accordingly.

If, on the trial of any indictment for an offence under this Act, the jury are satisfied that the defendant is guilty of any offence under section 1 of the Criminal Law Amendment Act 1935, but are not satisfied that the defendant is guilty of an offence under this Act, the jury may acquit the defendant of an offence under this Act and find him guilty of an offence under section 1 of the Criminal Law Amendment Act 1935, and he shall be liable to be punished accordingly.

(4) Section 4 of the Criminal Evidence Act 1898, shall have effect as if this Act were included in the schedule to that Act.

5 All proceedings under this Act are to be held in camera.

6 No prosecution for any offence under this Act shall be commenced without the sanction of His Majesty's Attorney-General, but this section shall not apply to any prosecution commenced by or on behalf of the Director of Public Prosecutions.

7 This Act shall not extend to Scotland.

8 This Act may be cited as the Punishment of Incest Act 1908, and shall come into operation on the first day of January, one thousand nine hundred and nine.

6.08   *Status of Children Act 1987*

44 Any presumption of law as to the legitimacy or illegitimacy of any person is hereby abrogated.

45 [applies only to civil proceedings]

46 (1) Where a woman gives birth to a child – (a) during a subsisting marriage to which she is a party, or (b) within the period of ten months after the termination, by death or otherwise, of a marriage to which she is a party, then the husband of the marriage shall be presumed to be the father of the child unless the contrary is proved on the balance of probabilities.

(2) Notwithstanding subsection (1) of this section, where a married woman, being a woman who is living apart from her husband under – (a) a decree of divorce a *mensa et thoro*, or (b) a deed of separation, gives birth to a child more than ten months after the decree was granted or the deed was executed, as the case may be, then her husband shall be presumed not to be the father of the child unless the contrary is proved on the balance of probabilities.

(3) Notwithstanding subsection (1) of this section, where – (a) the birth of a child is registered in a register maintained under the Births and Deaths Registration Acts 1863–1987, and (b) the name of the person is entered as the father of the child on the register so maintained, then the person whose name is so entered shall be presumed to be the father of the child unless the contrary is proved on the balance of probabilities.

(4) For the purposes of subsection (1) of this section "subsisting marriage" shall

be construed as including a voidable marriage and the expression "the termination, by death or otherwise, of a marriage" shall be construed as including the annulment of a voidable marriage.

47 (1) The evidence of a husband or wife shall be admissible in any proceedings to prove that marital intercourse did or did not take place between them during any period.

(2) the proviso to section (3) of the Evidence Further Amendment Act 1869, is hereby repealed.

Reform

6.09 The crime of incest traces the forbidden relationship through blood. This is unfortunate as step-fathers are, according to the studies cited in Appendix I to the Law Reform Commission Consultation Paper on Child Sexual Abuse 1989, far more likely to abuse their step-children than are natural fathers. The English Criminal Law Revision Committee in their fifteenth report[7], recommended that the crime of incest be extended to adopted children and step-children but not to foster children or de facto adopted children or other children in respect of whom a person is in a position of trust or authority[8]. It is submitted that as the damage in incest cases comes in large measure from the abuse of the position of authority and trust that a parent has over a child, that the crime should extend to all situations where a person can reasonably be found to be exercising the role of a parent.

The English approach to sentencing in incest cases is set out in *Attorney-General's Reference (No 1 of 1989)*[9].

6.10 The prohibition on incest should clearly extend to sexual acts apart from intercourse. Practice in the criminal court has, in recent years, thrown up many cases where daughters have been sexually abused by their fathers. In many cases this abuse has fallen short of full sexual intercourse. In other cases the acts of abuse have been at least equivalent in gravity to sexual intercourse, the abuse taking the form, for example, of oral sex.

Theoretically, it is possible for a child of over fifteen years to consent to indecent acts, short of intercourse, with a parent. In practice, the writer has never seen defence of consent argued in this context. The standard response to these allegations is that no abuse ever took place. It is also usually the case that sexual abuse begins in a mild form when the child is relatively young and progresses beyond the fifteenth birthday. Consent would rarely, therefore, be a valid defence; as an admission of sexual conduct with a child under the age of fourteen supplies the evidence for a charge of sexual assault.

Children rarely complain of sexual abuse by a parent until they mature into young adults. They respond to abuse by withdrawing. This process is often driven by a feeling that a mother may be unsympathetic or by threats uttered by the abusing father. A complaint sometimes comes with the insight developed in the later teen years. It can also be precipitated by the discovery, or suspicion, that the father has begun abusing a younger

---

7 1984 (Cmnd 9213).
8 *Ibid* at para 8.25–8.35 of the Report.
9 [1989] 3 All ER 571.

sibling. In one case, in which the writer prosecuted, a complaint was even-tually made years after the abuse of a daughter had stopped. She discovered that her father had begun to abuse her own daughter while taking her out on walks.

6.11   The Court of Criminal Appeal has held that the rule of common law which prohibits a spouse from testifying against another on a charge of incest is inconsistent with the Constitution, as it infringes the protection which must be afforded to the family under our law; *The People (DPP) v JT*[10].

Further Materials

6.12   Bailey and Blackburn *The Punishment of Incest Act 1908: A Case Study of Law Creation* [1979] Crim LR 708.
Bailey and McCabe *Reforming the Law of Incest* [1979] Crim LR 749.

Mental Illness

6.13   A person may be so mentally ill that they can never consent to sexual intercourse. The test generally accepted in the common law world is that propounded by the Supreme Court of Victoria in *R v Morgan*[11]. There the Court indicated that in order to prove absence of consent it must be proved that the victim had not sufficient knowledge or understanding to comprehend (a) that what is proposed be done is the physical act of penetra-tion of her body by the male organ, or, if that is not proved (b) that the act of penetration proposed is one of sexual connection as distinct from an act of a totally different character (such as a surgical operation to improve the singing voice). Where consent is absent due to an absence of understanding as to its nature, an act of sexual intercourse will be rape and an indecent act will be a sexual assault.

The test is difficult to fulfil in practice. Consequently, the law has created a new form of sexual offence the elements of which proscribe sexual inter-course with a mentally defective woman. Regrettably, the defects of this law are many and obvious. It is limited to sexual intercourse; no assistance is given in allowing mentally ill victims who do not understand the nature of the oath to give unsworn evidence; rape is a defence to the charge and the description and categorisation of the victim is outdated and offensive. Notwithstanding calls for reform and a detailed treatment by the Law Reform Commission, the Oireachtas has remained unmoved. The legislation is therefore reproduced as an example of a useless law.

6.14   *Criminal Law Amendment Act 1935*

4 (1) Any person who, in circumstances which do not amount to rape, unlaw-fully and carnally knows or attempts to have unlawful carnal knowledge of any woman or girl who is an idiot, or an imbecile, or is feeble-minded shall, if the circumstances prove that such person knew at the time of such knowledge or attempt that such woman or girl was then an idiot or an imbecile or feeble-minded

10 (1988) 3 Frewen 141.
11 [1970] VR 337.

(as the case may be), be guilty of a misdemeanour and shall be liable on conviction thereof to imprisonment for any term not exceeding two years.

(2) No prosecution for an offence which is declared by this section to be a misdemeanour shall be commenced more than twelve months after the date on which such offence is alleged to have been committed.

6.15 The definitions are not explicitly taken from English law existing at the time of this Act, but the definitions appear to be parallel.

6.16 *Mental Deficiency Act 1913*

Definition of defectives.

1   The following classes of persons who are mentally defective shall be deemed to be defectives withing the meaning of this Act—

(*a*) Idiots; that is to say, persons so deeply defective in mind from birth or from an early age as to be unable to guard themselves against common physical dangers;

(*b*) Imbeciles; that is to say, persons in whose case there exists from birth or from an early age mental defectiveness not amounting to idiocy, yet so pronounced that they are incapable of managing themselves or their affairs, or, in the case of children, of being taught to do so;

(*c*) Feeble-minded persons; that is to say, persons in whose case there exists from birth or from an early age mental defectiveness not amounting to imbecility, yet so pronounced that they require care, supervision, and control for their own protection or for the protection of others, or, in the case of children, that they by reason of such defectiveness appear to be permanently incapable of receiving proper benefit from the instruction in ordinary schools;

(*d*) Moral imbeciles; that is to say, persons who from an early age display some permanent mental defect coupled with strong vicious or criminal propensities on which punishment has had little or no deterrent effect.

6.17 *Mental Treatment Act 1945*

253   Where the person in charge of a mental institution or a person employed therein ill-treats or wilfully neglects a patient in the institution, or a person having charge, whether by reason of any contract or of any tie of relationship, marriage, or otherwise, of a person of unsound mind ill-treats or wilfully neglects such person of unsound mind, he shall be guilty of an offence under this section and shall be liable, on summary conviction thereof, to a fine not exceeding one hundred pounds or to imprisonment for a term not exceeding 6 months or, at the discretion of the court, to both such fine and such imprisonment, or on conviction thereof on indictment, to a fine not exceeding two hundred pounds or, at the discretion of the court, to imprisonment for a term not exceeding two years or to both such fine and such imprisonment.

254   Where – (a) A person has been convicted on indictment of a misdemeanour under section 4 of the Criminal Law Amendment Act, 1935 (No 6 of 1935), and (b) the judge is satisfied that at the time when the misdemeanour was committed – (i) such person had the care or charge of the woman or girl in relation to whom the misdemeanour was committed, or (ii) such person was carrying on a mental institution and such woman or girl was a patient therein, or (iii) such person was employed as an officer or servant in a mental institution or an institution for the detention of persons of unsound mind and such woman or girl was a patient or prisoner therein, the said section 4 shall have effect as if it provided that such person should be liable on such conviction to penal servitude for any term not exceeding five years nor less than three years or to imprisonment for any term not exceeding two years.

6.18 *Mental Treatment Act 1961*

35 The following sentence is hereby added to section 253 of the Principal Act: "In this section the word 'ill-treats' shall be construed as including a reference to striking or otherwise assaulting."

6.19 *Criminal Evidence Act 1992*

See below in relation to the oath, s 26 at para **6.43**.

Further Materials

6.20 Law Reform Commission *Discussion Paper on Sexual Offences Against the Mentally Handicapped* (LRC 33 – 1990).
Charleton *Criminal Law – Protecting the Mentally Sub-Normal against Sexual Exploitation* (1984) 6 DULJ NS 165 [Note that the year in which the case is referred to in that article was heard by the Circuit Court was 1983 and not 1973 as stated mistakenly in the text].
Charleton *Offences Against the Person* (1992) chapter 8.

Sexual Orientation

6.21 Homosexual practices are still subject to the criminal law. The law remains unreformed despite detailed recommendations by the Law Reform Commission. The wording of the legislation, in itself, indicates an attitude which has lost currency.

6.22 *Offences Against the Person Act 1861*
as amended by the Statute Law Revision Act 1892

61 Whosoever shall be convicted of the abominable crime of buggery, committed either with mankind or with any animal shall be liable to be kept in penal servitude for life.

62 Whosoever shall attempt to commit the said abominable crime, or shall be guilty of any assault with intent to commit the same, or of any indecent assault upon any male person shall be guilty of a misdemeanour, and on being convicted thereof shall be liable to be kept in penal servitude for any term not exceeding ten years.

6.23 Buggery, at common law, consists of intercourse by a man or woman with an animal, per anum or per vaginam, or of intercourse between men and women, or men, per anum; *R v Bourne*[12].

---

12 (1952) 36 Crim LR 125.

6.24   *Criminal Law Amendment Act 1885*

11 Any male person who, in public or private, commits, or is a party to the commission of, or procures or attempts to procure the commission by any male person of, any act of gross indecency with another male person, shall be guilty of a misdemeanour, and being convicted thereof shall be liable at the discretion of the Court to be imprisoned for any term not exceeding two years, with or without hard labour.

6.25 Gross indecency clearly implies some act going beyond mere indecency. It has been held that physical contact is not necessary for the offence to be committed; *R v Hunt*[13].

6.26   *Norris v The Attorney-General*
[1984] IR 36
Supreme Court, 1983

This judgment is reproduced at para **4.145**.

The Law Reform Commission has recommended that:

(1) Sections 61 and 62 of the Offences Against the Person Act 1861 and Section 11 of the Criminal Law Amendment Act 1885 should be repealed at para 4.29;
(2) In general the same legal regime should obtain for consensual homosexual activity as for heterosexual and that, in particular, no case had been established for providing that the age of consent, ie seventeen, should be any different;
(3) It follows from the above recommendation that the defence of reasonable mistake as to the age of the victim would apply equally to homosexual activity;
(4) Anal penile penetration of boys and girls between the ages of fifteen and seventeen should continue to be an offence; at para 4.31, Report on Child Sexual Abuse (LRC 32 – 1990).

6.27 The legal situation becomes even more inconsistent on a contemplation of the Prohibition of Incitement to Hatred Act 1989. The long title of this Act describes it as "An Act to prohibit incitement to hatred on account of race, religion, nationality or sexual orientation". The following definition of hatred is contained in s 1(1): "'Hatred' means hatred against a group of persons in the State or elsewhere on account of their race, colour, nationality, religion, ethnic or national origins, membership of the travelling community or sexual orientation".

Further Materials

6.28 The Wolfenden Committee *Report on Homosexual Offences and Prostitution* 1957 (Cmnd 247).
Norris v Ireland, Eur Court HR 26 October 1988, Series A No 142.
Dudgeon v UK, Eur Court HR 22 October 1981, Series A No 45, (1981) 4 EHRR 149.

13 [1950] 2 All ER 291.

6.28   *Sexual offences*

J Clifford Hindley *The Age of Consent for Male Homosexuals* [1986] Crim
LR 595.
Law Reform Commission *Consultation Paper on Child Sexual Abuse* 1989.
Law Reform Commission *Report on Child Sexual Abuse* (LRC 32 – 1990).

Age

6.29   Prosecutions for the sexual abuse of children have increased in the
late 1980's. This may not indicate an increase in the incidence of this terrible
crime but rather a more frequent reporting of the offence. This may be due
to sympathetic reception and an increased awareness that help may be
available. Dealing with these cases poses the question of how a child can be
sexually abused, frequently over a period of several years, without other
members of the family being aware of the crime. Such suffering is caused in
the victim by this crime that it, when mixed with abused parental dominance, evokes a fear of reporting. The victim is often isolated by inappropriate feelings of guilt and, as a result, the offender is free to continue with
his crime. In some cases, one suspects, the mother is aware of the abuse but
is herself under the dominance of the offender.

These cases are notoriously difficult to prove. The prosecution are often
left in circumstances where they have no corroborating evidence of the
victim's testimony. Notwithstanding the fact that abuse of different siblings
can take place over a period of years the evidence of only one child, without
the supporting testimony of the others, has usually been allowed by the trial
judge. Sometimes the rule against similar fact evidence, as it is called, has
been carried to bizarre lengths. Commonsense would indicate that an unnatural tendency in a parent to abuse a child is not simply evidence that one
child was abused but is evidence that all the children of the family, at least of
that sex, are at risk. The conduct of these cases reflects the uncertainty of the
law of evidence. Most recently the House of Lords have reviewed the similar
fact rule and in an enlightened judgment indicated that striking similarity is
not necessarily the feature which allows the evidence of one victim to be
admissible in support of the evidence of another victim. In revising the test
the House of Lords have required that the supporting evidence must be so
probative as to outweigh the automatic prejudicial effect of the revelation on
one criminal charge that the accused had previously been involved in a
similar kind of offence; *R v P*[14].

Mistake

6.30   Where the offender and victim are unrelated the situation can often
emerge that a young person has an appearance older than their actual age.
Judgments are reproduced indicating the various approaches that may be
taken to the problem as to whether age, in this context, is an element of
absolute liability or whether an offender to be worthy of blame for this
offence must be knowing or reckless as to whether the victim was below the
age for sexual intercourse or intimate conduct.

14 [1991] 3 All ER 337.

6.31   *Criminal Law Amendment Act 1935*

1 (1) Any person who unlawfully and carnally knows any girl under the age of fifteen years shall be guilty of a felony, and shall be liable on conviction thereof to penal servitude for life or for any term not less than three years or to imprisonment for any term not exceeding two years.

(2) Any person who attempts to have unlawful carnal knowledge of any girl under the age of fifteen years shall be guilty of a misdemeanour, and shall be liable, in the case of a first conviction of such misdemeanour, to penal servitude for any term not exceeding five years nor less than three years or to imprisonment for any term not exceeding two years or, in the case of a second or any subsequent conviction of such misdemeanour, to penal servitude for any term not exceeding ten years nor less than three years or to imprisonment for any term not exceeding two years.

2 (1) Any person who unlawfully and carnally knows any girl who is of or over the age of fifteen years and under the age of seventeen years shall be guilty of a misdemeanour and shall be liable, in the case of a first conviction of such mis-demeanour, to penal servitude for any term not exceeding five years nor less than three years or to imprisonment for any term not exceeding two years or, in the case of a second or any subsequent conviction of such misdemeanour, to any term of penal servitude not exceeding ten years nor less than three years or to imprison-ment for any term not exceeding two years.

(2) Any person who attempts to have unlawful carnal knowledge of any girl who is of or over the age of fifteen years and under the age of seventeen years shall be guilty of a misdemeanour, and shall be liable, in the case of a first conviction of such misdemeanour, to imprisonment for any term not exceeding two years or, in the case of a second or any subsequent conviction of such misdemeanour, to penal servitude for any term not exceeding five years nor less than three years or to imprisonment for any term not exceeding two years.

(3) No prosecution for an offence which is declared by this section to be a misdemeanour shall be commenced more than twelve months after the date on which such offence is alleged to have been committed.

3 If upon the trial of any indictment for rape, or any offence made a felony by section 1 of this Act, the jury shall be satisfied that the defendant is guilty of an offence under section three of the Criminal Law Amendment Act 1885, or under either section 1 or section 2 of this Act, or of an indecent assault, but are not satisfied that the defendant is guilty of the felony charged in such indictment, or of an attempt to commit the same, then and in every such case the jury may acquit the defendant of such felony, and find him guilty of such offence as aforesaid, or of an indecent assault (as the case may be), and thereupon such defendant shall be liable to be punished in the same manner as if he had been convicted for such offence as aforesaid, or for the misdemeanour of indecent assault, as the case may be.

14 It shall not be a defence to a charge of indecent assault upon a person under the age of fifteen years to prove that such person consented to the act alleged to constitute such indecent assault.

6.32   *R v Prince*
(1875) 13 Cox CC 138
Court for Crown Cases Reserved England 1875

Facts: The accused was charged with the offence of abducting an unmarried girl under the age of sixteen out of the possession of her lawful guardian contrary to section 55 of the Offences Against the Person Act 1861. The girl was fourteen but looked older than sixteen. She had told Prince that she was eighteen, he believed her and that belief was reasonable. The Court held that a reasonable belief that the girl's age was such that it was not a criminal offence to abduct her, was not a defence to this charge.

Blackburn J: . . . The question, therefore, is reduced to this, whether the words in 24 & 25 Vict c 100, s 55, that whosoever shall unlawfully take "any unmarried girl being under the age of sixteen, out of the possession of her father" are to be read as if they were "being under the age of sixteen, and he knowing she was under that age." No such words are contained in the statute, nor is the word "maliciously," "knowingly," or any other word used that can be said to involve a similar meaning. The argument in favour of the prisoner must, therefore, entirely proceed on the ground that in general a guilty mind is an essential ingredient in a crime, and that where a statute creates a crime the intention of the legislature should be presumed to be to include "knowingly" in the definition of the crime; and the statute should be read as if that word were inserted, unless the contrary intention appears. We need not inquire at present whether the canon of construction goes quite so far as above stated, for we are of opinion that the intention of the legislature sufficiently appears to have been to punish the abductor, unless the girl, in fact, was of such an age as to make her consent an excuse irrespective of whether he knew her to be too young to give an effectual consent, and to fix that age at sixteen. The section in question is one of a series of enactments beginning with s 50 forming a code for the protection of women and the guardians of young women. These enactments are taken with scarcely any alteration from the repealed statute 9 Geo 4, c 31, which had collected them into a code from a variety of old statutes all repealed by it. Section 50 enacts that "whosoever shall unlawfully and carnally know and abuse any girl under the age of ten years, shall be guilty of felony." Section 51 "Whosoever shall unlawfully and carnally know and abuse any girl being above the age of ten years and under the age of twelves years, shall be guilty of a misdemeanor." It seems impossible to suppose that the intention of the legislature in those two sections could have been to make the crime depend upon the knowledge by the prisoner of the girl's actual age. It would produce the monstrous result that a man who had carnal connection with a girl in reality not quite ten years old, but whom he, on reasonable grounds, believed to be a little more than ten, was to escape altogether. He could not, in that view of the statute, be convicted of the felony, for he did not know her to be under ten. He could not be convicted of the misdemeanour because she was, in fact, not above the age of ten. It seems to us that the intention of the legislature was to punish those who had connection with young girls though with their consent, unless the girl was, in fact, old enough to give a valid consent. The man who has connection with a child relying on her consent does it at his peril if she is below the statutable age.

6.33   ***R v Peters***
[1956] VLR 743
Supreme Court of Victoria 1956

Herring CJ: In this case, the application is for leave to appeal against conviction on the ground that the accused person who was convicted under s 44(1) of the Crimes Act 1928 of carnally knowing a girl over and above the age of ten years and under the age of sixteen years, believed on reasonable grounds that she was over sixteen. She told him that she was over sixteen. The learned judge in directing the jury said: "Any man who has intercourse with a girl under sixteen unless he is married to her is guilty of a crime, and it does not matter if he thought she was twenty or twenty-five – that girl undoubtedly looks more than thirteen. She has matured quickly. He may have been misled. She agrees she told him she was seventeen and he believed her but that is not a defence. I tell you that, gentlemen, as a matter of law and you should keep it in mind. It is no defence to him to this charge that he believes she was seventeen or any other age. It may make a great difference to me in a certain event but it does not concern you. It is no defence at all that he believed she was seventeen, eighteen or nineteen. I tell you that as a matter of law, and if I am wrong I will be put right."

In directing the jury in that way the learned judge was doing what has been done in these courts ever since *Gibson*'s case in 1885. In *R v Gibson* (1885) 11 VLR 94, the Full Court of Victoria followed the decision of the court in England in *R v Prince* (1875) LR 2 CCR 154. In *Prince*'s case the charge was one of unlawfully taking an unmarried girl under the age of sixteen out of the possession and against the will of her father. Sixteen judges sat on the matter and the view that prevailed, expressed, I think, by Blackburn J, was that the sole question was the intention of the legislature: whether it was or was not intended by the legislature that the crime should depend upon the knowledge or belief of the man charged as to the girl's age. The court came to the conclusion that the legislature could not have intended to make the crime depend upon the knowledge of the prisoner of the girl's actual age. It was this view that was adopted by the Full Court in *Gibson*'s case, where the offence was indecent assault on a girl under the age of twelve, the court taking the view that the legislature did not intend that *bona fide* ignorance of the age of a girl in this or in any of the other cases coming under the same head should be an excuse. The majority in *Prince*'s case said that a man, who has connexion with a child, relying on her consent, does it at his peril, if she is below the statutory age. The Full Court in *Gibson*'s case adopted this statement and since then in Victoria this principle has been applied in cases falling under s 44(1) and kindred sections. It is too late now to apply to this court to adopt a different view. The application is dismissed.

6.34   *The People v Francisco Hernandez*
                    (1964) 393 P (2d) 673; 39 Cal Rep 361
                    Supreme Court of California 1964

Peek J: The rationale of the *Ratz* decision, [115 Cal 132, relying on *Prince* supra] rather than purporting to eliminate intent as an element of the crime, holds that the wrongdoer must assume the risk; that, subjectively, when the act is committed, he consciously intends to proceed regardless of the age of the female and the consequences of his act, and that the circumstances involving the female, whether she be a day or a decade less than the statutory age, are irrelevant. There can be no dispute that a criminal intent exists when the perpetrator proceeds with utter disregard of, or lack of grounds for, a belief that the female has reached the age of consent. But if he participates in a mutual act of sexual intercourse, believing his partner to be beyond the age of consent, with reasonable grounds for such belief, where is the criminal intent? In such circumstances he has not consciously taken any risk. Instead he has subjectively eliminated the risk by satisfying himself on reasonable evidence that the crime cannot be committed. If it occurs that he has been misled, we cannot realistically conclude that for such reason alone the intent with which he undertook the act suddenly becomes more heinous.

While the specific contentions herein made have been dealt with and rejected both within and without this state, the courts have uniformly failed to satisfactorily explain the nature of the criminal intent present in the mind of one who in good faith believes he has obtained a lawful consent before engaging in the prohibited act. As in the *Ratz* case the courts often justify convictions on policy reasons, which, in effect, eliminate the element of intent. The legislature, of course, by making intent an element of the crime, has established the prevailing policy from which it alone can properly advise us to depart. [The judge then referred to *The People v Vogel* 46 Cal 2d 798 which held that a reasonable belief that someone was married was a defence to a charge of bigamy] . . .

We are persuaded that the reluctance to accord to a charge of statutory rape the defence of a lack of criminal intent has no greater justification than in the case of other statutory crimes, where the legislature has made identical provision with respect to intent. "At common law an honest and reasonable belief in the existence of circumstances, which, if true, would make the act for which the person is indicted an innocent act, has always been held to be a good defence . . . So far as I am aware it has never been suggested that these exceptions do not apply to the case of statutory offences unless they are excluded expressly or by necessary implication." (*Matter of Application of Ahart*, 172 Cal 762, 764–765, 159 P 160, 161–162, quoting from *R v Tolson* [1889] 23 QBD 168, sc, 40 Alb LJ 250). Our departure from the views expressed in *Ratz* is in no manner indicative of a withdrawal from the sound policy that it is in the public interest to protect the sexually naive female from exploitation. No responsible person would hesitate to condemn as untenable a claim to good faith belief in the age of consent of an "infant" female whose obviously tender years preclude the existence of reasonable grounds for that belief. However, the prosecutrix in the instant case was but three months short of eighteen years of age and there is nothing in the record to indicate that the purposes of the law as stated in *Ratz* can be better served by foreclosing the defence of a lack of intent. This is not to say that the granting of consent by even a sexually sophisticated girl known to be less than the statutory age is a defence. We hold only that in the absence of a legislative direction otherwise, a charge of statutory rape is defensible wherein a criminal intent is lacking.

Legislative Intent

6.35 Section 4 of the Criminal Law Amendment Act 1885, made it a felony, punishable by penal servitude for life or two years imprisonment, to have sexual intercourse with a girl under thirteen years, and by s 5 a misdemeanour punishable by two years imprisonment, to have sexual intercourse with a girl under sixteen years. It was a statutory defence to the misdemeanour charge that the accused had reasonable cause to believe the girl to be sixteen years or more. The Criminal Law Amendment Act 1935 raised these ages to fifteen and seventeen years, respectively, but did not incorporate any statutory defence of reasonable mistake as to age. That Act also removed all such defences in the sections, remaining in force, of the Criminal Law Amendment Act 1885. A clear legislative intent to make sexual offences with the young crimes of strict liability can therefore be discussed. An argument can be made that such strict liability, where on the accused's view of events he was innocent, infringes the fundamental principles of justice. This argument has been accepted in Canada; *R v Roche*[15].

Reform

6.36 The Law Reform Commission have made recommendations following a review of the law in this area.

6.37 *Law Reform Commission Report on Child Sexual Abuse 1990*
LRC 32 – 1990

Mandatory Reporting

1 For the purpose of a mandatory reporting law we recommend . . . the definition of child sexual abuse proposed by the Western Australia Task Force in its 1987 Report, viz:

15 (1985) 46 CR 3rd 130 (Ontario Supreme Court).

"(i) intentional touching of the body of a child for the purpose of the sexual arousal or sexual gratification of the child or the person;

(ii) intentional masturbation in the presence of the child;

(iii) intentional exposure of the sexual organs of a person or any other sexual act intentionally performed in the presence of the child for the purpose of sexual arousal or gratification of the older person or as an expression of aggression, threat or intimidation towards the child; and

(iv) sexual exploitation, which includes permitting, encouraging or requiring a child to solicit for or to engage in prostitution or other sexual act as referred to above with the accused or any other person, persons, animal or thing or engaging in the recording (on video-tape, film, audio tape, or other temporary or permanent material), posing, modelling or performing of any act involving the exhibition of a child's body for the purpose of sexual gratification of an audience or for the purpose of any other sexual act (referred to in sub-paragraphs (i) and (ii) above)." Para 1.10 (Para 2.11).

The Criminal Law

34 The expression "carnal knowledge" used in the Criminal Law (Amendment) Act 1935 should be replaced by the expression "sexual intercourse", as defined in section 1(2) of the Criminal Law (Rape) Act 1981. Para 4.05 (para 4.06).

Unlawful Sexual Intercourse

35 It should continue to be an offence, save in certain circumstances, for any male to have sexual intercourse with a girl under the age of 17 years. Para 4.07 (paras 4.05, 4.06).

36 In the case of a girl between the ages of 15 and 17, sexual intercourse should be a criminal offence only where the male participant is "a person in authority" as defined in para 46 below or at least five years older than the girl in question. Para 4.12 (paras 4.19 to 4.22).

37 The maximum penalty for an offence of unlawful sexual intercourse with a girl between the ages of 13 and 17 should be seven years imprisonment. This represents an increase from five years penal servitude where the girl is aged between 15 and 17 and a reduction from penal servitude for life where the girl is aged between 13 and 15. Para 4.10 (para 4.13).

38 A person who has sexual intercourse with a girl under the age of 13 years should be liable to penal servitude for life. Accordingly, the relevant age of the girl in this context should be lowered from 15 to 13. Para 4.09 (para 4.12).

Offence of Child Sexual Abuse

39 A new offence of "child sexual abuse" or "sexual exploitation" should be created to replace the present offence of "indecent assault with consent". The definition should be based on the Western Australian definition of child sexual abuse which we have recommended for adoption in civil proceedings in para 1 above. Only sexual activity engaged in for the sexual gratification of the accused or another, or as an expression of aggression, threat or intimidation should constitute an offence. In any prosecution for the offence, the onus should be on the accused to establish that he had no improper motive. The offence should be prosecutable summarily or on indictment at the election of the DPP. Depending on the nature of the offence, the maximum penalty should be between 5 and 7 years imprisonment. Para 4.19 (para 4.07).

40 It should only be possible to commit the offence referred to in the previous paragraph with a child under 15 years of age. However the conduct in question should also be a criminal offence when committed with a boy or girl of 15 or 16 years of age where the perpetrator is a 'person in authority' as defined in para 46 below. Para 4.20 (para 4.22).

Mistake

41 In a prosecution for a consensual sexual offence, there should be a defence available to the accused that he genuinely believed at the time of the act, on reasonable grounds, that the girl had attained the age of consent or an age attracting a less serious penalty. In arriving at a conclusion as to whether he did so believe, the court should be entitled to take into account whether there were reasonable grounds on which he could hold such a belief. Paras 4.14 to 4.15 (paras 4.15 to 4.17).

Liability of Girl or Boy

42 There should be no change in the present law that where a person is charged with having sexual intercourse or sexual activity falling short of intercourse with a girl under a specified age, the girl is not subject to any criminal liability. The same should apply to any offence of anal penetration committed by a person in authority or by a person five years older than the boy in question or other sexual activity with boys under a specified age. Para 4.23 (para 4.21).

'Person in Authority'

46 A "person in authority" should be defined as a parent, stepparent, grandparent, uncle or aunt, any guardian or person *in loco parentis* or any person responsible, even temporarily, for the education, supervision or welfare of a person below the age of 17. Para 4.11 (paras 4.10, 4.20).

Ritual Abuse

6.38 It is, in practice, extremely difficult to secure a conviction solely on the evidence of a child. The view is still prevalent in the community that children through the exercise of their imagination invent claims of sexual abuse against adults. In the community there is also a tendency to treat the testimony of children with less credibility than that of an adult. Section 30 of the Children Act 1908, as amended by s 28(2) of the Criminal Justice (Administration) Act 1914 enables a child of tender years who does not, in the opinion of the court, understand the nature of the oath, to give evidence not upon oath if, in the opinion of the court, a child has sufficient intelligence to justify the reception of the evidence and understands the duty of speaking the truth; *The People (A-G) v O'Sullivan*[16].

6.39 With the increase in reporting of cases of child sex abuse members of juries are more ready to believe that a child has been subjected to abuse for the purpose of the perverse sexual gratification of an adult. Where children are very young the evidence may need to be drawn from them in a specialised manner. Because of the vulnerability of children, their incompletely developed personality and the threat of violence or abandonment which may accompany abuse, expression to complaint is not readily given. Specialised interviewing techniques, often involving the use of anatomically correct dolls, are used to investigate the cases where physical signs show a suspicion of abuse.

The most intractable problem in the area of investigation concerns claims

16 [1930] IR 552.

that children have been subjected to ritual sexual abuse. In its most extreme form ritual sexual abuse involves children in satanic ceremonies[17]. Many regard the claims made by the alleged victims of ritual abuse as being so fantastic as to be beyond credibility. Others blame suggestive interviewing techniques as implanting into the minds of children details which may supplement genuine claims of abuse with ritualistic overtones that may have special appeal to the imagination of abused and vulnerable children. No such cases have yet come for prosecution before the Irish courts. In England the Official Solicitor reported that allegations of ritual abuse were upheld in four wardship cases involving 24 children over the two years to September 1991. These cases represented a tiny minority of some 2,000 child abuse cases handled in the period. Allegations of ritual abuse had featured in 48 cases involving 130 children in that period. Some had yet to come to court. In the majority of those cases ritual abuse was not found. In many cases that finding was unnecessary as it was sufficient for the court to make a finding of abuse without further investigating the claim in order to classify it as ritual abuse. Some of these 48 cases were rejected entirely.

6.40 Where children who have had no contact with one another make a claim of ritual abuse describing details common to their cases the tendency may be to accept that such abuse has taken place. Other factors can, however, produce this consistency. The children may have been interviewed by one interviewer, or team of interviewers, who have use similar suggestive questioning. Alternatively, evangelical groups have been blamed on spreading the scare of ritual abuse through a community; the sensitive intelligence of children may incorporate the details given onto their own real experiences of being abused.

Where children are very young the use of the blunt instrument of criminal law can be positively harmful. Cases of sexual abuse, whether ritual or otherwise, against young children are usually contested by the civil standard of proof on the balance of probability in applications by health boards to remove children from the custody of their parents. The experience of the writer in prosecuting cases of abuse against children in the criminal court would not indicate that the conviction of the offender is likely in the absence of strong independent corroborative evidence supporting the testimony of the child.

Helping the Child Victim to Give Evidence

6.41 The recommendations of the Law Reform Commission in their Report on Child Sexual Abuse[18] have found expression in the Criminal Justice (Evidence) Act 1992. The Commission proposed that the ordinary depositions, taken in the District Court, should be video-recorded and that the prosecution should be permitted to show the tape to the jury as the evidence of the child. They further proposed the early interview of the child by a suitably trained examiner and that a recording of this interview could be played as evidence in chief with the child being made available only for cross-examination. It was also proposed that the court of trial should have the power to appoint, for special reasons, a child-examiner, through whom

17 Smith and Pazder *Michelle Remembers* (London 1981).
18 (LRC 32–90).

all questions would be asked. The Commission also recommended that s 30 of the Children Act 1908 should be repealed; it would be replaced by a provision enabling the court to hear the evidence of children without requiring them to take an oath, or to affirm. The court must, however, be satisfied that the child is competent to give evidence in the sense of being capable of giving an intelligible account of events.

6.42 It is extremely difficult for a witness to describe the core elements of a distressing experience. One of the best ways to allow a child's testimony to develop naturally, and thus to be successful, is through an examination-in-chief which leads from background material, such as schooling and family, to the incidents of abuse. To allow a child to be cross-examined without having given evidence-in-chief might leave them unprepared, both mentally and in terms of their approach, to the subsequent questioning. It is also difficult to see that the use of a video tape, on its own, can be of assistance in cases where convictions are so rare. Experience indicates that juries are very reluctant to act on the evidence of a child in the absence of strong corroborative evidence linking the accused to the commission of the offence. If a case is prosecuted for the purpose of convicting a guilty offender then a case must be capable of being proved beyond reasonable doubt. That very high standard of proof is very difficult to achieve merely by playing the jury a video of a child's testimony.

Legal rules cannot operate independently of the community. It is only when ordinary people are more willing to accept as true an account of sexual abuse from a child, that more convictions will result. Leaving the jury with evidence consisting of a video tape will not assist in breaking through the collective doubt as to the veracity of children who complain that they have been sexually abused.

Obviously, the Commission, in proposing a child examiner, are hoping for a diminution in the trauma of giving evidence. Some people are very good at communicating with children and some are very bad. There is a case to be made for the Bar Council and the Law Society to allow only those persons who have shown themselves to be sensitive and able in child abuse cases to conduct them. With the implementation of the "child examiner" procedure one can foresee a plethora of appeals resulting which consist of complaints of a mistranslation of the questions of the cross-examiner by the child examiner. One can also see defence counsel arguing with the jury, in a closing address, for a reasonable doubt on the basis that if he or she had been allowed to conduct an examination in the way that he or she thought best that more of "the truth" might have been uncovered. These doubts as to the wisdom of these proposals, as translated into law by the Criminal Law (Evidence) Act 1992 may be fanciful. It should, however, be remembered that it will be for the ordinary people who make up juries to indicate whether or not these procedures can work.

6.43   *Criminal Evidence Act 1992*

Offences to which Part III applies

11   This Part applies to—

(*a*) a sexual offence,
(*b*) an offence involving violence or the threat of violence to a person, or

(*c*) an offence consisting of attempting or conspiring to commit, or of aiding, abetting, counselling, procuring or inciting the commission of, an offence mentioned in *paragraph (a)* or *(b)*.

Evidence through television link by persons under 17 years

12 (1) In any criminal proceedings, unless the court sees good reason to the contrary, a person other than the accused may give evidence, whether from within or outside the State, through a live television link if the person is under 17 years of age and the offence or one of the offences charged is an offence to which this Part applies.

(2) Evidence given under *subsection (1)* shall be videorecorded.

(3) While evidence is being given through a live television link pursuant to *subsection (1)*, neither the judge, nor the barrister or solicitor concerned in the examination of the witness, shall wear a wig or gown.

Evidence through intermediary

13 (1) Where—

(*a*) a person is accused of an offence to which this Part applies, and

(*b*) a person under 17 years of age is giving, or is to give, evidence through a live television link,

the court may, on the application of the prosecution or the accused, if satisfied that, having regard to the age or mental condition of the witness, the interests of justice require that his examination-in-chief, cross-examination or re-examination, or any part thereof, be conducted through an intermediary, direct that any such examination be so conducted.

(2) An intermediary referred to in *subsection (1)* shall be appointed by the court and shall be a person who, in its opinion, is competent to act as such.

Procedure in District Court in relation to certain offences

14 (1) Where—

(*a*) a person is before the District Court charged with an offence to which this Part applies,

(*b*) the person in respect of whom the offence is alleged to have been committed is a person under 17 years of age,

(*c*) the offence is not being tried summarily or is not being dealt with on a plea of guilty, and

(*d*) it is proposed to give evidence at the trial by means of a videorecording as mentioned in *section 15(1)(b)*,

the prosecution shall, in addition to causing the documents mentioned in *section 6(1)* of the Criminal Procedure Act 1967, to be served on the accused—

(i) notify him that it is proposed so to give evidence, and

(ii) give him an opportunity of seeing the videorecording in advance of the preliminary examination.

(2) If at a preliminary examination of an offence to which this Part applies the person in respect of whom the offence is alleged to have been committed is available for cross-examination, any statement made by him on a videorecording mentioned in *section 15(1)(b)* may be considered by the judge of the District Court conducting the preliminary examination.

Videorecording as evidence at trial

15 (1) Subject to *subsection (2)*—

(*a*) a videorecording of any evidence given by a person under 17 years of age through a live television link at the preliminary examination of an offence to which this Part applies, and

(*b*) a videorecording or any statement made by a person under 14 years of age (being a person in respect of whom such an offence is alleged to have been committed) during an interview with persons who are in the opinion of the court appropriately qualified for the purpose,

shall be admissible at the trial of the offence as evidence of any fact stated therein of which direct oral evidence by him would be admissible:

Provided that, in the case of a videorecording mentioned in *paragraph (b)*, either—

(i) it has been considered in accordance with *section 14(2)* by the judge of the District Court conducting the preliminary examination of the offence, or

(ii) the person whose statement was videorecorded is available at the trial for cross-examination.

(2) Any such videorecording or any part thereof shall not be admitted in evidence as aforesaid if the court is of opinion, having regard to all the circumstances, that in the interests of justice the videorecording concerned or that part ought not to be so admitted.

(3) In estimating the weight, if any, to be attached to any statement contained in such a videorecording regard shall be had to all the circumstances from which any inference can reasonably be drawn as to its accuracy or otherwise.

(4) In this section "statement" includes any representation of fact, whether in words or otherwise.

Transfer of proceedings

16 In any proceedings for an offence to which this Part applies in any circuit or district court district in relation to which *sections 12 to 15* or *section 28* are not in operation the court concerned may, if in its opinion it is desirable that evidence be given in the proceedings through a live television link or by means of a video-recording, by order transfer the proceedings to a circuit or district court district in relation to which those provisions are in operation and, where such an order is made, the jurisdiction of the court to which the proceedings have been transferred may be exercised—

(*a*) in the case of the Circuit Court, by the judge of the circuit concerned, and

(*b*) in the case of the District Court, by the judge of that court for the time being assigned to the district court district concerned.

Identification evidence

17 (1) Where—

(*a*) a person is accused of an offence to which this Part applies,

(*b*) the person in respect of whom the offence is alleged to have been committed is a person under 17 years of age, and

(*c*) it is proposed to give evidence at the trial that the accused has been identified as being the offender by that person or another person under that age during an identification parade or other identification procedure,

it shall be presumed, until the contrary is proved, that the person so identified is the accused.

(2) In proceedings referred to in *subsection (1)* the accused shall not, without

the leave of the court, give or adduce evidence in rebuttal of the presumption referred to therein unless he has informed the prosecution of his intention to do so at least 7 days before the trial.

(3) This section shall not apply unless its terms have been communicated in writing to the accused at least 21 days before the trial.

Application of Part III to persons with mental handicap

18 The references in *sections 12(1), 13(1)(b), 14(1)(b), 15(1)(a)* and *17(1)(b)* to a person under 17 years of age and the reference in *section 15(1)(b)* to a person under 14 years of age shall include references to a person with mental handicap who has reached the age concerned.

Competence and Compellability of Spouses and Former Spouses to give Evidence

Definitions (Part IV)

19 In this Part—

"decree of judicial separation" includes a decree of divorce *a mensa et thoro* or any decree made by a court outside the State and recognised in the State as having the like effect;
"former spouse" includes a person who has been granted a decree of judicial separation in respect of his marriage to the accused.

Competence of spouses and former spouses to give evidence

20 The spouse or a former spouse of an accused shall be competent to give evidence at the instance—

(*a*) subject to *section 24*, of the prosecution, and
(*b*) of the accused or any person charged with him in the same proceedings.

Compellability to give evidence at instance of prosecution

21 (1) The spouse of an accused shall, subject to *section 24*, be compellable to give evidence at the instance of the prosecution only in the case of an offence which—

(*a*) involves violence, or the threat of violence, to—
　(i) the spouse,
　(ii) a child of the spouse or of the accused, or
　(iii) any person who was at the material time under the age of 17 years,
(*b*) is a sexual offence alleged to have been committed in relation to a person referred to in *subparagraph (ii)* or *(iii)* of *paragraph (a)*, or
(*c*) consists of attempting or conspiring to commit, or of aiding, abetting, counselling, procuring or inciting the commission of, an offence falling within *paragraph (a)* or *(b)*.

(2) A former spouse of an accused shall, subject to *section 25*, be compellable to give evidence at the instance of the prosecution unless—

(*a*) the offence charged is alleged to have been committed at a time when the marriage was subsisting and no decree of judicial separation was in force, and
(*b*) it is not an offence mentioned in *subsection (1)*.

(3) The reference in *subsection (1)* to a child of the spouse or the accused shall include a reference to—

    (*a*) a child who has been adopted by the spouse or the accused under the Adoption Acts 1952 to 1991, or, in the case of a child whose adoption by the spouse or the accused has been effected outside the State, whose adoption is recognised in the State by virtue of those Acts, and

    (*b*) a person in relation to whom the spouse or the accused is in *loco parentis*.

Compellability to give evidence at instance of accused

22   Subject to *section 24*, the spouse or a former spouse of an accused shall be compellable to give evidence at the instance of the accused.

Compellability to give evidence at instance of co-accused

23   (1) Subject to *section 24*—

    (*a*) the spouse of an accused shall be compellable to give evidence at the instance of any person charged with the accused in the same proceedings only in the case of an offence mentioned in *section 21(1)*,

    (*b*) a former spouse of an accused shall be compellable to give evidence at the instance of any person charged with the accused in the same proceedings unless—

        (i) the offence charged is alleged to have been committed at a time when the marriage was subsisting and no decree of judicial separation was in force, and

        (ii) it is not an offence mentioned in *section 21(1)*.

    (2) *Subsection (1)* is without prejudice to the power of a court to order separate trials of persons charged in the same proceedings if it appears to it to be desirable in the interests of justice to do so.

Saving

24   Where spouses (being either a husband and wife or persons who were formerly husband and wife) are charged in the same proceedings, neither shall at the trial be competent by virtue of *section 20(a)* to give evidence at the instance of the prosecution, or be compellable by virtue of *section 21, 22* or *23* to give evidence, unless the spouse or former spouse is not, or is no longer, liable to be convicted at the trial as a result of pleading guilty or for any other reason.

Right to marital privacy

25   Nothing in this Part shall affect any right of a spouse or former spouse in respect of marital privacy.

PART V

Miscellaneous

Oath or affirmation not necessary for child etc., witness

26   (1) Notwithstanding any enactment, in any criminal proceedings the evidence of a person under 14 years of age may be received otherwise than on oath or affirmation if the court is satisfied that he is capable of giving an intelligible account of events which he has observed.

    (2) If any person whose evidence is received as aforesaid makes a statement material in the proceedings concerned which he knows to be false or does not believe to be true, he shall be guilty of an offence and on conviction shall be liable to be dealt with as if he had been guilty of perjury.

(3) *Subsection (1)* shall apply to a person with mental handicap who has reached the age of 14 years as it applies to a person under that age.

Abolition of requirement of corroboration for unsworn evidence of child, etc

27 (1) The requirement in section 30 of the Children Act 1908, of corroboration of unsworn evidence of a child given under that section is hereby abolished.

    (2)(*a*) Any requirement that at a trial on indictment the jury be given a warning by the judge about convicting the accused on the uncorroborated evidence of a child is also hereby abolished in relation to cases where such a warning is required by reason only that the evidence is the evidence of a child and it shall be for the judge to decide, in his discretion, having regard to all the evidence given, whether the jury should be given the warning.

    (*b*) If a judge decides, in his discretion, to give such a warning as aforesaid, it shall not be necessary to use any particular form of words to do so.

(3) Unsworn evidence received by virtue of *section 26* may corroborate evidence (sworn or unsworn) given by any other person.

Evidence through television link by persons outside State

28 (1) Without prejudice to *section 12(1)*, in any criminal proceedings a person other than the accused who is outside the State may, with the leave of the court, give evidence through a live television link.

(2) Evidence given under *subsection (1)* shall be videorecorded.

(3) Any person who while giving evidence pursuant to *subsection (1)* makes a statement material in the proceedings which he knows to be false or does not believe to be true shall, whatever his nationality, be guilty of perjury.

(4) Proceedings for an offence under *subsection (3)* may be taken, and the offence may for all incidental purposes be treated as having been committed, in any place in the State.

Copies of documents in evidence

29 (1) Where information contained in a document is admissible in evidence in criminal proceedings, the information may be given in evidence, whether or not the document is still in existence, by producing a copy of the document, or of the material part of it, authenticated in such manner as the court may approve.

(2) It is immaterial for the purposes of *subsection (1)* how many removes there are between the copy and the original, or by what means (which may include facsimile transmission) the copy produced or any intermediate copy was made.

(3) In *subsection (1)* "document" includes a film, sound recording or videorecording.

Further Materials

6.44 *R v Metro News Limited* (1986) 53 CR (3d) 289.
Card *Sexual Relations with Minors* [1975] Crim LR 370.

Rape

6.45 It is only with the enactment of the Criminal Law (Rape) (Amendment) Act 1990 that the attitude to rape which partially blames the crime on the victim has been swept away.

An Old-Fashioned View

6.46 It is instructive to compare modern legislation and attitudes with those prevailing two centuries ago. It is important for us to sound the elements of this attitude in order to determine whether any trace of it still influences our approach to this crime.

6.47 *Lord Hale – Pleas of the Crown, Volume 1*

Rape is the carnal knowledge of any woman above the age of ten years against her will, and of a woman-child under the age of ten years with or against or will. The essential words in an indictment of rape are *rapuit et carnaliter cognovit*, but *carnaliter cognovit*, nor any other circumlocution without the word *rapuit* are not sufficient in a legal sense to express rape . . .

To make a rape there must be an actual penetration or *res in re*, (as also in buggery) and therefore *emissio seminis* is indeed an evidence of penetration, but singly of itself it makes neither rape nor buggery, but it is only an attempt of rape or buggery, and it is severely punished by fine and imprisonment . . .

But the least penetration makes it rape or buggery, yet although there be not *emissio seminis* . . .

If A actually ravisheth a woman, and B and C were present, aiding and abetting, they were all equally principals, and all subject to the same punishment both at common law and since the statute of *Westminster 2 de quo infra*.

It appears by Bracton, *ubi supra*, that in an appeal of rape it was a good exception *guod ante diem et annum contentas in appello habuit eam ut concubinam et amicam, et inde ponit se super patriam*, and the reason was, because that unlawful cohabitation carried a presumption in law, that it was not against her will.

But this is no exception at this day, it may be an evidence of an assent, but it is not necessary that it should be so, for the woman may forsake that unlawful course of life.

But the husband cannot be guilty of a rape committed by himself upon his lawful wife, for by their mutual matrimonial consent and contract the wife hath given up herself in this kind unto her husband, which she cannot retract.

A the husband of B intends to prostitute her to a rape by C against her will and C accordingly doth ravish her, A being present, and assisting to this rape: in this case these points were resolved, 1. That this was a rape in C notwithstanding the husband assisted in it, for tho in marriage she hath given up her body to her husband, she is not to be by him prostituted to another. 2. That the husband being present, aiding and assisting, is also guilty as principal in rape, and therefore, although the wife cannot have an appeal of rape against the husband, yet he is indictable for it at the King's suit as a principal. 3. That in this case the wife may be a witness against her husband, and accordingly she was admitted, and A and C were both executed . . .

An infant under the age of fourteen years is presumed by law unable to commit a rape, and therefore it seems cannot be guilty of it, and tho in other felonies *malitia supplet aetatem* in some cases as hath been shown, yet it seems as to this fact the law presumes him impotent, as well as wanting discretion.

But he may be a principal in the second degree as aiding and assisting, though under fourteen years, if it appears by sufficient circumstances, that he had a mischievous discretion, as well as in other felonies. [Hale next deals with the age of consent which, at the time, was twelve years stating that intercourse with a girl under that age was rape whether she consented or not]

But if she were above the age of twelve years, and consented upon menace of death, if she consented not, this is not a consent to execute a rape . . .

The party ravished may give evidence upon oath, and is in law a competent witness; but the credibility of her testimony, and how far forth she is to be believed, must be left to the jury, and is more or less credible according to the circumstances of fact that concur in that testimony.

For instance if the witness be of good fame, if she presently discovered the offence and made pursuit after the offender, showed circumstances and signs of the injury whereof many are of the nature, that only women are the most proper examiners and inspectors, if the place, wherein the fact was done, was remote from people, inhabitants or passengers, if the offender fled for it; these and the like are concurring evidences to give greater probability to her testimony, when proved by others as well as herself.

But on the other side, if she concealed the injury for any considerable time after she had opportunity to complain, if the place where the fact was supposed to be committed, were near to inhabitants, or common resource or passage of passengers, and she made no outcry when the fact was supposed to be done, when and where it is probably she might be heard by others; these and the like circumstances carry a strong presumption, that her testimony is false or feigned . . .

It is true rape is a most detestable crime, and therefore ought severely and impartially to be punished with death; but it must be remembered, that it is an accusation easily to be made and hard to be proved, and harder to be defended by the party accused, tho never so innocent.

I shall never forget a trial before myself of a rape in the county of Sussex.

There had been one of that county convicted and executed for a rape in that county before some other judges and three assizes before, and I suppose very justly: some malicious people seeing how easy it was to make out such an accusation, and how difficult it was for the party accused to clear himself, furnished the two assizes following with many indictments of rapes, wherein the parties accused with some difficulty escaped.

At the second assizes following there was an antient wealthy man of about fifty-three years old indicted for a rape which was fully sworn against him by a young girl of fourteen years, and a concurrent testimony of her mother and father, and some other relations. The antient man, when he came to his defence, alleged that it was true the fact was sworn, and it was not possible for him to produce witnesses to the negative; but yet, he said, his very age carried a great presumption that he could not be guilty of that crime; but yet he had one circumstance more, that he believed would satisfy the court and the jury, that he neither was nor could be guilty; and being demanded what that was, he said, he had above seven years last past been afflicted with a rupture so hideous and great, that it was impossible he could carnally know any woman nether had he upon that account, during all that time carnally known his own wife, and offered to show the same openly in court; which for the indecency of it I declined, but appointed to the jury to withdraw into some room to inspect this unusual evidence; and they accordingly did so, and came back and gave an account if it to the court, that it was impossible he should have to do with any woman in that kind, much less to commit a rape, for all his bowels seemed to be fallen down into those parts, that they could scarce discern his privities, the rupture being full as big as the crown of a hat, whereupon he was acquitted.

Again, at Northampton assizes, before one of my brother justices upon the *nisi prius*, a man was indicted for the rape of two young girls not above fourteen years old, the younger somewhat less, and the rapes fully proved, tho' peremptorily denied by the prisoner, he was therefore to the satisfaction of the judge and jury convicted; but before judgment it was most apparently discovered, that it was but a malicious contrivance, and the party innocent; he was therefore reprieved before judgment.

I only mention these instances, that we may be the more cautious upon trials of offences of this nature, wherein court and jury may with so much ease be imposed upon without great care and vigilance; the heinousness of the offence many times transporting the judge and the jury with so much indignation, that they are over hastily carried to the conviction of the person accused thereof, by the confident testimony sometimes of malicious and false witnesses.

Attitudes

6.48 Enormous changes have occurred since the time of Hale in both the attitude to rape and in its definition. It is outside the scope of this work to discuss procedure and evidence but brief mention will be made of some of these points, which, as appears from their context, apply to sexual offences other than rape.

Mental Element

6.49 In 1976 the House of Lords decided in *DPP v Morgan*[19] that the mental element in rape was an intention to have sexual intercourse without the consent of the victim; or, the equivalent intention, of having intercourse not caring whether the victim consented or not. A similar result was reached in Canada in *R v Pappajohn*[20]. This had already been accepted in Victoria; *R v Burles*[21]. In the result; where the accused believed, no matter how unreasonably, that the victim was consenting, he must, notwithstanding that she did not consent, be acquitted. A jury is, however, under no obligation to believe an obviously false story. They may judge what they are told by the accused against their view of what an ordinary or reasonable person would have believed in the circumstances and as against how he would have behaved.

6.50   *R v Saragozza*
                                   [1984] VR 187
                          Supreme Court of Victoria 1984

Starke J: Once it is accepted that it is an element of the crime of rape that the accused either was aware that the woman was not consenting, or else realised that she might not be and determined to have intercourse whether she was consenting or not, the conclusion is inescapable that a man who believes that the woman is consenting cannot be guilty of the offence; for the existence of this belief is inconsistent with the presence of the mental element of the crime. Logic then insists that the reasonableness of the belief bears only on whether the accused in fact held it. As the Full Court observed in *R v Flannery and Prendergast* [1969] VR 31, at p 33, the existence of a belief that the woman was consenting necessarily negatives an awareness that the woman was not consenting or a realisation that she might not be and a determination to have intercourse whether she was consenting or not. [is a sufficient mental element for the crime of rape].

6.51 Following on the decision in *Morgan*, the Heilbron Committee sought to emphasise that not every unreasonable excuse a rapist could come up with would entitle him to an acquittal. In so doing they were simply restating a fundamental principle of the criminal law; that in deciding whether or not an accused held a particular belief they were entitled to test that belief against the possibility of an ordinary person, in similar circumstances to the accused, making the same mistake.

19 [1976] AC 182.
20 [1980] 2 SCR 120.
21 [1947] VLR 392.

6.52   *Report of the Advisory Group on the Law of Rape*
Cmnd 6352, 1975

81 Notwithstanding our conclusions that *Morgan*'s case is right in principle, we nevertheless feel that legislation is required to clarify the law governing intention in rape cases, as it is now settled. We think this for two principle reasons. The first is that it would be possible in future cases to argue that the question of recklessness did not directly arise for decision in *Morgan*'s case, in view of the form of the question certified: to avoid possible doubts the ruling on recklessness needs to be put in statutory form.

82 Secondly, it would be unfortunate if a tendency were to arise to say to a jury "that a belief, however unreasonable, that the woman consented, entitled the accused to acquittal." Such phrase might tend to give an undue or misleading emphasis to one aspect only and the law, therefore, should be statutorily restated in a fuller form which would obviate the use of these words.

83 We think that there would be advantage if this matter could also be dealt with by a statutory provision which would – (i) declare that (in cases where the question of belief is raised) the issue which the jury have to consider is whether the accused at the time when sexual intercourse took place believed that she was consenting, and (ii) make it clear that, while there is no requirement of law that such a belief must be based on reasonable grounds, the presence or absence of such grounds is a relevant consideration to which the jury should have regard, in conjunction with all the other evidence, in considering whether the accused genuinely had such a belief.

6.53   *Criminal Law (Rape) Act 1981*

2 (1) A man commits rape if – (*a*) he has unlawful sexual intercourse with a woman who at the time of the intercourse does not consent to it, and (*b*) at that time he knows that she does not consent to the intercourse or he is reckless as to whether she does or does not consent to it, and references to rape in this Act and any other enactment shall be construed accordingly.

(2) It is hereby declared that if at a trial for a rape offence the jury has to consider whether a man believed that a woman was consenting to sexual inter-course, the presence or absence of reasonable grounds for such a belief is a matter to which the jury is to have regard, in conjunction with any other relevant matters, in considering whether he so believed.

Recklessness in Rape

6.54 Recklessness was discussed by the Supreme Court in the case of *The People (DPP) v Murray*[22] and the relevant extracts are reproduced at para **1.31**. The Supreme Court make it clear that recklessness involves the accused taking a serious and unjustifiable risk; such a risk must be apparent to the accused. Awareness of the risk, coupled with the determination not to consider it further, is an equivalent mental condition. There is no argument to be made in favour of the proposition that the risk must be so high as to require the accused to consider that the victim is probably not consenting. Any question of doubt may be resolved, in those intimate circumstances, by a simple question. Therefore, it is submitted that a risk is serious, and that the accused is thus reckless, if he is aware of a possibility that the victim may

22 [1977] IR 360.

not be consenting. The availability of an easy answer to this question means that a disregard of this risk is unjustifiable, involving as it does the possible violation of another person's mental and physical integrity.

6.55 As people share broadly similar perceptions and experiences it is legitimate to judge whether or not a belief was genuinely held by comparing it with the circumstances alleged to give rise to it. In that context s 2(2) does not introduce a special category of mental element. It affirms that common-sense should be used in considering whether there is a reasonable possibility of truth in an accused's account of how he came to have sexual intercourse with an alleged rape victim. The correct method of dealing with this subsection in the English context was elucidated by the Court of Appeal in *R v Satnam*[23].

The External Circumstances

6.56 The external circumstance of rape consists of an act of sexual intercourse by a man with a woman who does not consent to that act. In that context the definition of sexual intercourse, the meaning of consent and when consent may be withdrawn are fundamental.

6.57 *Offences Against the Person Act 1861*

48 Whosoever shall be convicted of the crime of rape shall be guilty of felony, and being convicted thereof shall be liable to be kept in penal servitude for life.

63 Whenever, on the trial for any offence punishable under this Act, [which includes rape under s 48] it may be necessary to prove carnal knowledge, it shall not be necessary to prove the actual emission of seed in order to constitute a carnal knowledge shall be deemed complete upon proof of penetration only.

6.58 *Criminal Law (Rape) Act 1981*

1 (2) In this Act references to sexual intercourse shall be construed as references to carnal knowledge as defined in s 63 of the Offences Against the Person Act, 1861, so far as it relates to natural intercourse (under which such intercourse is deemed complete on proof of penetration only).

6.59 *The People (A-G) v Dermody*
[1956] IR 307
Court of Criminal Appeal 1956

Maguire CJ: . . . The next point taken is that the evidence did not justify a finding of rape. The evidence of the prosecutrix was that the male organ of her assailant went into her vagina a "wee bit" and while the jury might have rejected this and concluded that in the circumstances this did not happen, this Court cannot hold that they were not entitled to accept this evidence and that what happened amounted to penetration. It is submitted that the learned judge did not correctly direct the jury as to what amounted to penetration. In the view of this Court, his direction on this matter was correct and proper. It should hardly be necessary to say that in law if the male organ is proved to have entered the opening of the vagina this amounts to penetration even if there is no emission. The law as stated in the

23 (1983) 78 Cr App R 149.

earliest case cited, *Rex v Russen*[24], is still the law. If penetration is proved, though not of sufficient depth to penetrate the hymen, still this was sufficient to constitute the crime of rape. In other words, proof of the rupture of the hymen is unnecessary. There has been, however, a change brought about by the Statute, 9 Geo 4, c 31, and re-enacted in the Offences Against the Person Act 1861, that it is no longer necessary to prove emission in order to establish rape or carnal knowledge, that the offence may be established on proof of penetration only.

6.60   ***Kaitamaki v R***
[1985] AC 147; [1984] 2 All ER 435; [1984] 3 WLR 137;
(1984) 79 Cr App R 251; [1984] Crim LR 564;
[1984] 81 LSG 97 1915 PC;
Privy Council, on Appeal from New Zealand 1984

Facts: The accused gave evidence that during the course of a second bout of intercourse he became aware that the woman was not consenting. He did not desist. The direction to the jury was that if the accused continued with the act having realised that the woman was not willing, it was rape. The case is an authority for the proposition that consent to sexual intercourse, or to any other intimate act, may be withdrawn at any time.

Lord Scarman: The appellant's counsel submits that by the criminal law of New Zealand if a man penetrates a woman with her consent he cannot become guilty of rape by continuing the intercourse after a stage when he realises that she is no longer consenting.

The submission raises a question as to the true construction of ss 127 and 128 of the Crimes Act 1961. Section 127 defines sexual intercourse and is in these terms:

"For the purposes of this Part of this Act, sexual intercourse is complete upon penetration; and there shall be no presumption of law that any person is by reason of his age incapable of such intercourse."

Section 128 defines rape and, so far as is material, is in these terms:

"*Rape*—(1) Rape is the act of a male person having sexual intercourse with a woman or girl—(*a*) Without her consent . . ."

Counsel for the appellant took one point only; but he submitted that it was all he needed. He relied on the defiition is s 127 to establish the proposition that rape is penetration without consent; once penetration is complete the act of rape is concluded. Intercourse, if it continues, is not rape, because for the purposes of the Act it is complete on penetration.

The Court of Appeal by a majority rejected the submission, expressing the opinion that the purpose of s 127 was to remove any doubts as to the minimum conduct needed to prove the fact of sexual intercourse. "Complete' is used in the statutory definition in the sense of having come into existence, but not in the sense of being at an end. Sexual intercourse is a continuing act which only ends with withdrawal. And the offence of rape is defined in s 128 as that of "having" intercourse without consent.

Their Lordships agree with the majority decision of the Court of Appeal, and with the reasons which they gave for rejecting the appellant's submission and for construing the two sections in the way in which they did. As Lord Brightman observed in the course of argument before the Board, s 127 says "complete", not "completed". The Board was referred not only to the two Australian cases discussed by the Court of Appeal (*R v Salmon* [1969] SASR 76 and *R v Mayberry*

---

24 1 East PC 439.

[1973] Qd R 211) but to a third one, *Richardson v R* [1978] Tas SR 178. None of these cases is directly in point because each is concerned with statutory provisions which differ from the two sections of the New Zealand statute with which this appeal is concerned. Their Lordships rest their view on the true construction, as they see it, of the two sections already quoted of the Crimes Act 1961.

This case is an authority for the obvious proposition, which is self-evident, that a woman may withdraw her consent to any form of sexual relations at any time.

Consent

6.61 The other external element requires that the consent of the woman be absent. It is important to focus on the simplicity of this element. Once there is no consent to sexual intercourse the act is rape if the accused knew or was reckless as to this fact.

6.62 *Criminal Law (Rape) (Amendment) Act 1990*

9 It is hereby declared that in relation to an offence that consists of or includes the doing of an act to a person without the consent of that person any failure or omission by that person to offer resistance to the act does not of itself constitute consent to the act.

6.63 *Criminal Law Amendment Act 1885*

4 Whereas doubts have been entertained whether a man who induces a married woman to permit him to have connexion with her by personating her husband is or is not guilty of rape, it is hereby enacted and declared that every such offender shall be deemed to be guilty of rape.

6.64 The absence of consent to sexual intercourse is an objective fact. The accused's view as to the existence, or non-existence, of this fact is subjective. As has been stated an honest, though unreasonable, mistake that the woman was consenting is a defence to rape. The old common law definition is therefore obsolete; the sole question on the external element is whether or not the woman consented to the act of sexual intercourse; *R v Olugboja*[25].

Consent cannot be implied by a prior sexual relationship but must be actively given in respect of each act. It is rape to have sexual intercourse with a woman who is asleep; *R v Mayers*[26]. The individualised nature of consent is emphasised by the statutory rules restricting questions as to sexual experience with other partners, and, by a more recent amendment, with the accused. Consent is also absent, as we noted in the introduction to this chapter, where understanding of the nature of sexual intercourse or of the physical act is absent. This may be due to either youth or mental handicap.

6.65 Submission to an act of sexual intercourse does not necessarily imply consent. Submission at the point of a knife, or as a result of the threat of any other form of serious harm, has been rejected in law, and is in practice

25 (1981) 73 Cr App R 344.
26 (1872) 12 Cox 311.

rejected by juries, as consent. This attitude has been given statutory expression in s 9 of the 1990 Rape Act.

6.66 At common law fraud as to the nature and quality of the act, and as to the identity of the partner vitiates consent. This means that although consent was apparently present, because it was induced by a fundamental deceit it is legally absent. Fraud as to the attributes of a partner (that, for example, he is a solicitor) does not vitiate consent; *R v Papadimitropoulos*[27]. Consent induced by a pretence that the partner is the woman's husband is no true consent because it is a fraud as to the identity of her partner; *R v Dee*[28]. Similarly a pretence that sexual intercourse is an act of a different character, such as a voice operation, renders consent invalid; *R v Williams*[29].

In summary:

(1) There is no consent where the victim does not understand the character of sexual intercourse as penetration or that penetration is a sexual act.

(2) There is no consent where the victim is tricked into a misunderstanding as to the nature of sexual intercourse and believes it, as a result, to be an act of a different character (such as a necessary act of hygiene).

(3) There is no consent where the accused impersonates the husband or lover of the victim. Here the victim is consenting to have sexual intercourse with a different person and cannot, therefore, be consenting to have sexual intercourse with the accused.

(4) There is no consent where the victim is forced to submit to sexual intercourse by the threat of violence or by any other serious threat. Submission is not consent.

(5) Consent induced by deceit as to a person's attributes is a valid consent because in that instance the victim consents to have sexual intercourse with the accused, notwithstanding the fact that she is mistaken in her belief that he is very rich or, according to the Australian case of *Papadimitropoulos*, that he is her husband. This kind of deceit may be the lesser crime of unlawfully procuring sexual intercourse. This is discussed subsequently at para **6.81**.

6.67   ***Law Reform Commission Report on Rape 1988***
                    LRC 24 – 1988

16   (b) The Absence of Consent
In the Consultation Paper, we said that we were not aware of any problems having arisen as a result of the "non-definition" of consent and that the law should be left as it is.

While no cases have been drawn to our attention in which the present law created serious difficulty, it was represented to us that it was certainly capable of doing so. The Irish Association for Victim Support was strongly of the opinion that the absence of a definition had influenced verdicts. It would be accordingly advantageous if the legislature were to clarify the law so as to put it beyond doubt that consent obtained by force or fraud was not consent. It was urged that there was a real danger of juries equating a failure to offer physical resistance with consent.

27 (1957) 98 CLR 249.
28 (1884) 15 Cox 5791 LR IR 468.
29 [1923] 1 KB 340.

17 We think that there is considerable merit in these arguments. As we pointed out in the Consultation Paper, the law has been put beyond doubt by legislation in Western Australia, New Zealand and Canada. We think that the case has been established for making similar provision in this jurisdiction. Accordingly, we recommend that legislation should provide that:

1 "Consent" means a consent freely and voluntarily given and, without in any way affecting or limiting the meaning otherwise attributable to those words, a consent is not freely and voluntarily given if it is obtained by force, threat, intimidation, deception or fraudulent means.

2 A failure to offer a physical resistance to a sexual assault does not of itself constitute consent to a sexual assault.

Special Defences

6.68 The special defences to rape, which had long outlived their usefulness, were finally abolished in the Rape Act 1990.

6.69 *Criminal Law (Rape) (Amendment) Act 1990*

5 (1) Any rule of law by virtue of which a husband cannot be guilty of the rape of his wife is hereby abolished.
(2) Criminal proceedings against a man in respect of the rape by him of his wife shall not be instituted except by or with the consent of the Director of Public Prosecutions.

6 Any rule of law by virtue of which a male person is treated by reason of his age as being physically incapable of committing an offence of a sexual nature is hereby abolished.

Note on Procedure

6.70 Rape trials were subjected to criticism on the basis that the focus of discovering guilt shifted from the accused onto the victim. Rape is an especially difficult crime as the pivot of the offence is whether or not the victim consented. The presence or absence of consent means that either the woman who complains of the offence is either the victim of a dreadful crime or is acting from deranged or spiteful motives. An acquittal does not mean that the jury have resolved matters in favour of the latter proposition. It simply means that they have failed to find in the prosecution case sufficient evidence to convince them of guilt beyond reasonable doubt.

Attitudes from the time of Lord Hale indicated that rape was an offence which could easily be fabricated but which was difficult to disprove. Later developments in the law of evidence removed any burden of disproof from the accused. The practical approach of juries to crime indicates that as a matter of fact, though not as a matter of law, there are circumstances where they require to hear an explanation from the accused. It can happen that a person is less than convincing in his evidence. This may occur for reasons unconnected with the offence and may be due to confusion, lack of intelligence or poor expression. If the prosecution can catch the accused lying he is likely to be convicted. A lie on a peripheral issue may not necessarily indicate guilt. Every person indicted before a jury on a criminal offence is in peril of being convicted. The Criminal Procedure Act 1967 provides that a

District Justice must examine the documents relating to a criminal case against an accused, including the witness statements, and decide whether or not there is a sufficiently weighty case to put him on trial. Where a person is returned for trial there may be circumstances where he feels it is in his own interest to give evidence. If his testimony is equivocating or if he is caught in apparent circumstances of untruth by the prosecution he is in grave danger of a conviction.

False Reporting

6.71 There are, of necessity, special rules in relation to sexual offences. It seems to have been genuinely believed that women would invent rape allegations against men for reasons of spite. This attitude was expressed even in a student text book on forensic medicine. There may be strong reasons why a person wishes to unjustly accuse another of a criminal offence. Such a wicked action, and such a burdensome undertaking, is usually motivated by extreme emotion. Intimate human relationships flow from the deepest passions. It is therefore possible that disappointment, or betrayal, in a relationship can sometimes be the source of a false rape allegation. While the writer's experience is that such false allegations are extremely rare, juries have acquitted accused men, for this apparent reason, not infrequently.

The Warning

6.72 The old law was that a jury should be warned that it was dangerous to convict on the uncorroborated testimony of a complainant in a sexual offence unless there was corroboration, independent of that testimony, which indicated that the accused was guilty of the offence. If consent is the issue in the trial (and it almost always is) then marks consistent with forcible sexual intercourse can corroborate rape. For this reason the apparent victims of recently discovered rapes are always medically examined and a careful note is made of any injury. It is helpful to present those injuries on a body map.

Even severe injuries can be sought to be explained away by an accused person on the basis of rough sex. Medical testimony is therefore vital to a properly presented prosecution case. The distress of the alleged victim can be corroboration, though it constitutes very weak evidence, in this regard, and a jury should be wary of relying on it; *The People (DPP) v Mulvey*[30]. A confession of rape, or sexual assault, can corroborate such a complaint. Silence cannot be corroboration. A lie told by an accused may be corroboration where it is deliberate, related to a material issue, shown to be a lie by evidence other than that which requires to be corroborated and provided the motive for the lie is a realisation of guilt and a fear of the truth; *R v Lucas*[31].

Evidence that the victim, at the first reasonable opportunity, made a complaint consistent with her testimony is not, in any circumstances, corroboration of that testimony. It is merely evidence of the consistency of her allegations; *R v Osborne*[32].

30 [1987] IR 502.
31 [1981] QB 720.
32 [1905] 1 KB 551.

405

7   (1) Subject to any enactment relating to the corroboration of evidence in criminal proceedings, where at the trial on indictment of a person charged with an offence of a sexual nature evidence is given by the person in relation to whom the offence is alleged to have been committed and, by reason only of the nature of the charge, there would, but for this section, be a requirement that the jury be given a warning about the danger of convicting the person on the uncorroborated evidence of that other person, it shall be for the judge to decide in his discretion, having regard to all the evidence given, whether the jury should be given the warning; and accordingly, any rule of law or practice by virtue of which there is such a requirement as aforesaid is hereby abolished.

(2) If a judge decides, in his discretion, to give such a warning as aforesaid, it shall not be necessary to use any particular form of words to do so.

6.74   Even with the abolition of the mandatory warning, corroboration is of importance in sexual offences. The more evidence the better. Any independent testimony which tends to prove that the accused committed the crime is welcome in an attempt to vindicate the right to justice of the victim of any crime. Prior to the 1990 Act the jury had to be warned "in unmistakable terms" (per Maguire CJ in *The People (A-G) v Cradden*[33]), that it was dangerous to convict on the uncorroborated testimony of the prosecutrix, and that they should weigh her evidence with great care; *The People (A-G) v Williams*[34]. It is submitted that this form of warning would now be unjust to the victim. The legislature have placed the complainants in sexual cases on the same footing as those who complain of other crimes.

It is a useful exercise, however, to indicate whether or not there is any independent evidence supporting the prosecution case and, if it is absent, to point out that the jury should not lose sight of the fact that the prosecution's case consists of the testimony of one individual. This account may have been denied on oath by the accused. Even such a mild warning may be inappropriate, it is submitted, where the medical evidence indicates a forced act of sexual intercourse. Where there are any factors identified either on the prosecution or defence cases, that would indicate an extremity of passion that might lead to a false allegation these may usefully be identified by the trial judge and a jury directed to consider these factors by bringing to bear on them their collective wisdom and experience of intimate human relations[35].

Accomplices

6.75   Where the victim is a willing participant in incest, homosexual acts or underage sexual intercourse, or where the victim is under fifteen and cannot legally, but does, in fact, consent to sexual intimacy the accomplice warning must be given. This indicates that it is dangerous to convict on the evidence of an accomplice, where it is not corroborated, because an accomplice can have special reasons to unjustly draw others into the consequences of complicity in an admitted criminal offence.

33 [1955] IR 130 at 141 CCA.
34 [1940] IR 195.
35 On the former law see O'Connor *The Mandatory Warning Requirement in Respect of Complaints in Sexual Cases in Irish Law*, The Irish Jurist, Vol 20 1985.

The Complaint

6.76 A complaint of a sexual offence made at the first opportunity which *reasonably afforded* itself and which was not elicited by leading, inducing or intimidating questions, can be led as evidence of the consistency of the victim's testimony; *R v Osborne*[36]. This does not constitute corroboration that the accused committed the offence. It merely assists the jury in deciding the weight to be attached to the victim's testimony. If an early complaint is made it is clearly inconsistent with a later allegation of fabrication and shows a constant insistence that consent was absent.

Protecting the Victim

6.77 It was formerly possible to criticise rape trials as being an enquiry into the guilt of the victim rather than the guilt of the accused. Clearly, since the issue at rape trials is whether the victim consented or not, some enquiry must be made. Since s 3 of the Criminal Law (Rape) Act 1981, as amended by the 1990 Act, the issue of the alleged victim's experience with any person including the accused except, of course, on the occasion to which the charge relates, can only be raised with the leave of the trial judge. This exclusion applies in any trial for sexual assault offences.

6.78   *Criminal Law (Rape) Act 1981*
as amended by s 13 of the Criminal Law (Rape) (Amendment) Act 1990

3   (1) If at a trial any person is for the time being charged with a sexual assault offence to which he pleads not guilty, then, except with the leave of the judge, no evidence shall be adduced and no question shall be asked in cross-examination at the trial, by or on behalf of any accused person at the trial, about any sexual experience (other than that to which the charge relates) of a complainant with any person; and in relation to a sexual assault tried summarily pursuant to *section 12(a)* *subsection (2)(a)* shall have effect as if the words "in the absence of the jury" were omitted, *(b) subsection (2)(b)* shall have effect as if for the references to the jury there were substituted references to the court and *(c)* this section (other than this paragraph) and *subsections (3)* and *(4)* of *section 7* shall have effect as if for the references to the judge there were substituted references to the court.

(2) *(a)* The judge shall not give leave in pursuance of *subsection (1)* for any evidence or question except on an application made to him, in the absence of the jury, by or on behalf of an accused person. *(b)* The judge shall give leave if, and only if, he is satisfied that it would be unfair to the accused person to refuse to allow the evidence to be adduced or the question to be asked, that is to say, if he is satisfied that, on the assumption that if the evidence or question was not allowed the jury might reasonably be satisfied beyond reasonable doubt that the accused person is guilty, the effect of allowing the evidence or question might reasonably be that they would not be so satisfied.

(3) If, notwithstanding that the judge has given leave in accordance with this section for any evidence to be adduced or question to be asked in cross-examination, it appears to the judge that any question asked or proposed to be asked (whether in the course of so adducing evidence or of cross-examination) in reliance on the leave which he has given is not or may not be such as may properly be asked in accordance with that leave, he may direct that the question shall not be asked or, if asked, that it shall not be answered except in accordance with his leave given on a fresh application under this section.

36 [1905] 1 KB 551.

(4) Nothing in this section authorises evidence to be adduced or a question to be asked which cannot be adduced or asked apart from this section.

6.79 The purpose of the enactment seems to be that where prior sexual experience, either with the accused or with another, is introduced simply to besmirch the character of the alleged victim it should be excluded. Where it is introduced to show that the victim was more likely to have consented to sexual intercourse, or that the accused mistook her as so consenting, it should be admitted. The approach of the Court of Appeal in England is towards excluding matters relevant to credit only when deciding, as a matter of logic, as to whether a particular enquiry will assist the court on the question as to whether the alleged victim consented or not; *R v Viola*[37].

The complainant is entitled to anonymity in sexual offence cases, as is the accused, subject to the interests of justice requiring that the accused or complainant be named; ss 7 and 8 of the Rape Act 1981 as amended by ss 14 and 16 of the Rape Act 1990. Those proceedings must be held in private subject to press representation and the right of the victim, and of the accused if under 18 years, to bring a friend or relative; s 11 of the Rape Act 1990.

Alternative to Rape

6.80 An interesting alternative to the charge of rape was enacted in Victorian times. The only relevant comment made on the section which follows was by Lord Hewart CJ in delivering the judgment of the Court of Criminal Appeal in *R v Williams*[38], where he said "It is obvious that these words go beyond a case of rape. It is easy to imagine a case which would come within the comprehensive scope of these words and yet fail to come within a charge of rape".

6.81 *Criminal Law Amendment Act 1885*
as amended by s 8 of the Criminal Law (Amendment) Act 1935

3 Any person who—
(1) By threats or intimidation procures or attempts to procure any woman or girl to have any unlawful carnal connexion, either within or without the Queen's dominions; or
(2) By false pretences or false representations procures any woman or girl, not being a common prostitute or of known immoral character, to have any unlawful carnal connexion, either within or without the Queen's dominions; or
(3) Applies, administers to, or causes to be taken by any woman or girl any alcoholic or other intoxicant or any drug, matter, or thing, with the intent to stupefy or overpower so as thereby to enable any person to have unlawful carnal connexion with such woman or girl,

shall be guilty of a misdemeanour, and being convicted thereof shall be liable at the discretion of the court to be imprisoned for any term not exceeding two years, with or without hard labour.

Provided that no person shall be convicted of an offence under this section upon

37 (1982) Cr App R 125 and see further Charleton *Offences Against the Person* (1992) chap 8.
38 [1923] 1 KB 340.

the evidence of one witness only, unless such witness be corroborated in some material particular by evidence implicating the accused.

Sexual Assault

6.82 Sexual assault is the old crime of indecent assault relabelled in words more appropriate to the current use of language. Sexual assault is defined as an assault accompanied by circumstances which are objectively indecent. This objective mental element requires an intentional act on the part of the accused. The elements of the offence thus are:

(1) That the accused intentionally assaulted the victim.

(2) That the assault, or the assault and the circumstances accompanying it, are capable of being considered by right-minded persons as indecent.

(3) That the accused intended to commit such an assault as is referred to in (2) above.

6.83 *Criminal Law (Rape) (Amendment) Act 1990*

2 (1) The offence of indecent assault upon any male person and the offence of indecent assault upon any female person shall be known as sexual assault.

(2) A person guilty of sexual assault shall be liable on conviction on indictment to imprisonment for a term not exceeding 5 years.

(3) Sexual assault shall be a felony.

3 (1) In this Act "aggravated sexual assault" means a sexual assault that involves serious violence or the threat of serious violence or is such as to cause injury, humiliation or degradation of a grave nature to the person assaulted.

(2) A person guilty of aggravated sexual assault shall be liable on conviction on indictment to imprisonment for life.

(3) Aggravated sexual assault shall be a felony.

6.84 It is an objective fact whether the aggravating circumstances mentioned in s 3 are present. There is no apparent intention to make the elements of the offence which distinguish a sexual assault from an aggravated sexual assault ones of strict liability. It follows that for an aggravated sexual assault to be proved an accused must have intended an assault of that nature. Although recklessness is excluded as a possible mental element for a sexual assault, or an assault in aggravating circumstances, this will not cause difficulty as the nature of these acts is obviously entirely purposive. It requires an active decision for a person to physically accost another in the sexually explicit manner required by the definition of the offence.

6.85 *R v Court*
[1987] QB 156; [1986] 1 All ER 120; [1987] 3 WLR 1029;
(1986) 84 Cr App R 210 CA; [1987] 1 WLR 1136; [1989] AC 28;
[1988] 2 WLR 1071; [1988] 2 All ER 221; (1988) 87 Cr App R 144 HL
House of Lords 1988

Facts: The appellant, an assistant in a shop, struck a 12 year old girl visitor some 12 times, for no apparent reason as she thought, outside her shorts on her buttocks. In response to a question by the police as to why the appellant had done so, he said "I don't know – buttock fetish." He was tried on a count charging indecent assault contrary to s 14(1) of the Sexual Offences Act 1956. He pleaded guilty to assault, denied that it was indecent and submitted that his statement about "buttock fetish" should be excluded as being a secret uncommunicated motive and could not make indecent an assault not overtly indecent. The trial judge refused to exclude the statement, the appellant did not give evidence and he was convicted. The Court of Appeal (Criminal Division) dismissed the appellant's appeal against conviction, and he then appealed to the House of Lords.

Lord Ackner: It cannot, in my judgment, have been the intention of Parliament, that an assault can, by a mere mistake or mischance, be converted into an indecent assault, with all the opprobium which a conviction for such an offence carries.

It was common ground before your Lordships, and indeed it is self evident, that the first stage in the proof of the offence is for the prosecution to establish an assault. The "assault" usually relied upon is a battery, the species of assault conveniently described by Lord Lane CJ in *Faulkner v Talbot* [1981] 1 WLR 1528, 1534 as "any intentional touching of another person without the consent of that person and without lawful excuse. It need not necessarily be hostile or rude or aggressive, as some of the cases seem to indicate." But the "assault" relied upon need not involve any physical contact but may consist merely of conduct which causes the victim to apprehend immediate and unlawful personal violence. In the case law on the offence of indecent assault, both categories of assault feature.

It also was common ground before your Lordships, as it was in the Court of Appeal, that if the circumstances of the assault are *incapable* of being regarded as indecent, then the undisclosed intention of the accused could not make the assault an indecent one. The validity of this proposition is well illustrated by *Reg v George* [1956] Crim LR 52.

Again it was common ground that if, as in this case, the assault involved touching the victim, it was not necessary to prove that she was aware of the circumstances of indecency or apprehended indecency. An indecent assault can clearly be committed by the touching of someone who is asleep or unconscious.

The conduct of the appellant in assaulting the girl by spanking her was only *capable* of being an indecent assault. To decide whether or not right-minded persons might think that assault was indecent, the following factors were clearly relevant – the relationship of the defendant to his victim – were they relatives, friends or virtually complete strangers? How had the defendant come to embark on this conduct and *why* was he behaving in this way? Aided by such material, a jury would be helped to determine the quality of the act, the true nature of the assault and to answer the vital question – were they sure that the defendant not only intended to commit an assault upon the girl, but an assault which was indecent – was such an inference irresistible?

I would accordingly dismiss the appeal and answer the certified question as follows:

"On a charge of indecent assault the prosecution must prove: (1) that the accused intentionally assaulted the victim; (2) that the assault, or the assault and the circumstances accompanying it, are capable of being considered by right-minded persons as indecent; (3) that the accused intended to commit such an assault as is referred to in (2) above."

I would add that evidence, if any, of the accused's explanation for assaulting the victim, whether or not it reveals an indecent motive, is admissible both to support or negative that the assault was an indecent one and was so intended by the accused.

Section 4 Rape

6.86 The debate prior to the Rape Act 1990 was essentially as to whether the victim of an offence of a sexual character, which did not amount to sexual intercourse, would be discouraged by the inappropriate labelling of such an offence as a mere indecent assault. The response of the Oireachtas was to create the new offences of sexual assault and aggravated sexual assault and, in accordance with the modern use of language, to indicate that certain forms of grievous sexual assault amounted to a form of rape.

6.87   *Criminal Law (Rape) (Amendment) Act 1990*

4   (1) In this Act "Rape under section 4" means a sexual assault that includes –
(*a*) penetration (however slight) of the anus or mouth of the penis, or (*b*) penetration (however slight) of the vagina by any object held or manipulated by another person.
(2) A person guilty of rape under section 4 shall be liable on conviction on indictment to imprisonment for life.
(3) Rape under section 4 shall be a felony.

6.88   *Law Reform Commission Report on Rape 1988*
LRC 24 – 1988

We accordingly recommend that the crime of rape should be defined by statute so as to include non-consensual sexual penetration of the vagina, anus and mouth of a person by the penis of another person or of the vagina or anus of a person by an inanimate object held or manipulated by another person and that in this form the crime should be capable of being committed against men and women.

6.89   The Criminal Law (Rape) (Amendment) Bill 1988 contained no provisions changing the statutory definition of rape. This approach followed the views of two members of the Commission who dissented from the recommendation contained in para 14[39]. The acts described in s 4(1)(*a*) and 4(1)(*b*) of the Act were contained in the Bill as acts included under the new offence of "aggravated sexual assault". However, during its passage through the Oireachtas the Bill was amended to create the new offence of "Rape under section 4".

The offence of s 4 rape, as it now exists, is merely a sexual assault incorporating one or other of the aggravating elements in s 4. As such, the prior discussion of sexual assault is completely appropriate.

Protecting Children

6.90   Lawyers are worried as to whether a child who willingly consents to sexually touching another person, without being touched in return, is protected as a victim by the application of the offence of sexual assault to these circumstances. It is submitted that this worry is misplaced. There can be almost no circumstances, which can be imagined as occurring in practice, where a child will accept an invitation to engage in sexual conduct with another person without that other person touching the child in the course of those acts.

6.91   *Law Reform Commission Consultation Paper on*
Child Sexual Abuse 1989

4.04   In the area of non-consensual offences, there is clearly a need for an offence of procuring an act of indecency with a young person. A child may be compelled as

---

39 See the report at paras 50–52.

a result of a threat, or of having been otherwise put in fear, to perform an indecent act with an adult, eg fellatio, which would not strictly speaking constitute an indecent assault by that adult. At present, such acts have to be charged as assaults or not at all. This class of activity has a "consensual dimension" and also and at the moment the similar offence of gross indecency under s 11 of the Criminal Law Amendment Act 1885 may be charged against males only.

Sentencing

6.92 The commission of a crime of rape will usually lead to the imposition of a severe sentence. Rape is always a serious offence. Sexual assaults can vary in their gravity. Suspended sentences have been given for sexual assault particularly where the first report is made after an interval of several years. This latter approach may not be correct as, it is submitted, the trauma to the victim may resurface even years after the offence. A complaint made long after the abuse usually coincides with the re-eruption of such suffering.

6.93   *The People (DPP) v Tiernan*
                                      [1988] IR 250
                                  Supreme Court, 1988

Finlay CJ: This is an appeal brought to the Supreme Court by the appellant against the decision of the Court of Criminal Appeal, delivered on the 13th January, 1986, dismissing his application for leave to appeal against a sentence of twenty-one years' penal servitude imposed on him for rape. It is brought pursuant to a certificate issued by the Attorney General on the 9th March, 1987, pursurant to s 29 of the Courts of Justice Act 1924. The grounds upon which the Attorney General certified that the decision of the Court of Criminal Appeal involved a point of law of exceptional public importance, and that it was desirable in the public interest that an appeal should be taken to the Supreme Court, were that it involved the guidelines which the courts should apply in relation to sentences for the crime of rape. The grounds of appeal are as follows:—

"(a) that the learned trial judge erred in principle in imposing a sentence which was far in excess of any sentence which had heretofore been imposed for the crime of rape or, indeed, any crime except perhaps one incident of kidnapping and false imprisonment,

(b) that the learned trial judge erred in principle in imposing a sentence which was far in excess of the conventional period a person might expect to serve who was sentenced to life imprisonment,

(c) that while the crime of rape was heinous, the court should have regard to degrees of seriousness, and that this crime lacked any element of premeditation,

(d) that the learned trial judge did not have sufficient regard to the fact that the accused made a statement admitting his guilt in pleading guilty, and

(e) that the learned trial judge did not have sufficient regard to the need that the accused should some day be rehabilitated in society."

Although the certificate of the Attorney General states that the point of law he certified was the guidelines which the courts should apply in relation to sentences for the crime of rape, having regard to its appellate jurisdiction this Court dealt only with the issues arising under the grounds of appeal submitted in this individual case and did not receive submissions nor reach any decision with regard to questions which might be applicable to cases of rape which had different facts and circumstances surrounding them. As counsel for the Director of Public

Prosecutions submitted, the certificate must be read as stating the point of law to be whether on the application of the correct principles this sentence was appropriate.

Many of the considerations, however, which arise for determination on this appeal will hopefully be of assistance to judges having responsibility to decide on sentences appropriate on convictions for rape.

The crime of rape must always be viewed as one of the most serious offences contained in our criminal law even when committed without violence beyond that constituting the act of rape itself. In *Attorney General v Conroy* [1965] IR 411 this Court stated that the nature of the offence was such as to render unconstitutional any statutory provision which could permit it ever to be regarded as a minor offence.

The act of forcible rape not only causes bodily harm but is also inevitably followed by emotional, psychological and psychiatric damage to the victim which can often be of long term, and sometimes of lifelong duration.

In addition to those damaging consequences, rape can distort the victim's approach to her own sexuality. In many instances, rape can also impose upon the victim a deeply distressing fear of sexually transmitted disease and the possibility of a pregnancy and of a birth, whose innocent issue could inspire a distress and even a loathing utterly alien to motherhood.

Rape is a gross attack upon the human dignity and the bodily integrity of a woman and a violation of her human and constitutional rights. As such it must attract very severe legal sanctions.

All these features, which I mention in summary and not as an attempted comprehensive account of the character of rape, apply even when it is committed without any aggravating circumstance. They are of such a nature as to make the appropriate sentence for any such rape a substantial immediate period of detention or imprisonment.

Whilst in every criminal case a judge must impose a sentence which in his opinion meets the particular circumstances of the case and of the accused person before him, it is not easy to imagine the circumstance which would justify departure from a substantial immediate custodial sentence for rape and I can only express the view that they would probably be wholly exceptional.

The facts of this case

Unfortunately, the facts of the rape to which this appellant pleaded guilty contain very many aggravating circumstances. They are:—

(1) It was a gang rape, having been carried out by three men.
(2) The victim was raped on more than one occasion.
(3) The rape was accompanied by acts of sexual perversion.
(4) Violence was used on the victim in addition to the sexual acts committed against her.
(5) The rape was performed by an act of abduction in that the victim was forcingly removed from a car where she was in company with her boyfriend, and her boyfriend was imprisoned by being forcingly detained in the boot of the car so as to prevent him assisting her in defending herself.
(6) It was established that as a consequence of the psychiatric trauma involved in the rape the victim suffered from a serious nervous disorder which lasted for at least six months and rendered her for that period unfit for work.
(7) The appellant had four previous convictions, being:—

    (*a*) for assault occasioning actual bodily harm,
    (*b*) for aggravated burglary associated with a wounding,
    (*c*) for gross indecency, and
    (*d*) for burglary.

Of this criminal record, particularly relevant as an aggravating circumstance to a conviction for rape are the crimes involving violence and the crime involving indecency.

The above summary of the facts surrounding the crime in this case reveals that very many though not all of the most serious aggravating circumstances which can be attached to the crime of rape were present.

The submissions

In the course of the submissions the Court was referred to a number of decisions in the common law jurisdictions namely: *R v Pui* [1978] 2 NZLR 193; *The People (DPP) v Carmody* [1988] ILRM 370; *R v Billam* [1986] 1 WLR 349; *R v McCue* [1987] Crim LR 345; *R v Gibson* [1987] Crim LR 346; *R v Birch* [1988] Crim LR 182; *R v Sullivan* [1988] Crim LR 188; *R v Pawa* [1978] 2 NZLR 190; *R v Puru* [1984] 2 NZLR 248; *The People (Attorney General) v O'Driscoll* (1972) 1 Frewen 351 and *R v Robert Shaw* (1986) 3 Cr App R 77.

In particular, stress was laid upon the decision in England of Lord Lane CJ in *R v Billam* [1986] 1 WLR 349, and in New Zealand by Woodhouse P of the Court of Appeal in Wellington, in *R v Puru* [1984] 2 NZLR 248.

It is necessary to emphasise that these decisions, while very helpful, were delivered in cases in which the structure and matters before the courts were wholly different from the instant appeal. Both the Criminal Division of the Court of Appeal in London, in *R v Billam*, and the Court of Appeal in New Zealand, in *R v Puru*, were dealing with cases where a number of different decisions were brought before them for review or consideration, and where evidence was submitted of overall patterns or tendencies in the imposition of sentences within their jurisdiction for rape. The specific purpose of this form of multiple appeal in the case of *R v Billam* was to seek from the Criminal Division of the Court of Appeal a broad statement on policy, almost amounting to a range or tariff of appropriate sentences for rape of different kinds.

Having regard to the absence of any statistics or information before this Court in this appeal concerning any general pattern of sentences imposed for the crime of rape within this jurisdiction, general observations on such patterns would not be appropriate. Furthermore, having regard to the fundamental necessity for judges in sentencing in any form of criminal case to impose a sentence which in their discretion appropriately meets all the particular circumstances of the case (and very few criminal cases are particularly similar), and the particular circumstances of the accused, I would doubt that it is appropriate for an appellate court to appear to be laying down any standardisation or tariff of penalty for cases. I would, however, adopt with approval the general propositions that neither a victim's previous sexual experience nor the fact that she could be considered to have exposed herself by imprudence to the danger of being raped could conceivably be considered as a mitigating circumstance in any rape.

The mitigating circumstances in rape are indeed limited.

It would appear to be suggested under ground (c) of the appeal in this case that the lack of an element of premeditation could be considered in some way to be a mitigating circumstance. It is a relevant circumstance, though one, in my view, of very limited importance, but is better described, in my opinion, as the absence of aggravating circumstance, rather than the existence of a mitigating circumstance.

The only single mitigating circumstance which arises in this case, I am satisfied, is the fact that when interviewed by the Garda Síochána the appellant immediately admitted his complicity in the crime and made a full statement. His attitude at that time was followed by a plea of guilty.

A plea of guilty is a relevant factor to be considered in the imposition of sentence and may constitute, to a lesser or greater extent, in any form of offence, a mitigating circumstance.

I have no doubt, however, that in the case of rape an admission of guilt made at an early stage in the investigation of the crime which is followed by a subsequent plea of guilty can be a significant mitigating factor. I emphasise the admission of guilt at an early stage because if that is followed with a plea of guilty it necessarily makes it possible for the unfortunate victim to have early assurance that she will not be put through the additional suffering of having to describe in detail her rape and face the ordeal of cross-examination.

Such an admission of guilt may, depending upon the circumstances under which it is made and the extent of the evidence apparent to an accused person as being available against him, also be taken in some circumstances as an indication of remorse and therefore as a ground for a judge imposing sentence to have some expectation that if eventually restored to society, even after a lengthy sentence, the accused may possibly be rehabilitated into it.

The necessity for consideration of this possibility has been underlined by the Court of Criminal Appeal in *The People (Attorney General) v O'Driscoll* (1972) 1 Frewen 351.

Conclusion

With regard to the individual grounds of the appeal submitted, I have come to the following conclusions.

(a) The fact that this sentence was in excess of sentences which have been recorded in respect of the crime of rape, even if satisfactorily established to the Court, it not, in my view, a ground by itself for varying the sentence. For over one hundred years the maximum sentence provided by statute for the crime of rape is penal servitude for life. It must, therefore, follow that the imposition of a sentence of twenty-one years could not of itself be considered wrong in principle.

(b) What is described in this ground as the conventional period a person who has been sentenced to life imprisonment might expect to serve is a matter of a policy pursued by the Executive at given times and subject to variation at the discretion of the Executive. It cannot, therefore, in my view, properly be taken into consideration by a court in imposing sentence.

(c) I have already indicated that insofar as this ground might be considered as an assertion that the lack of any element of premeditation was a mitigating circumstance, it would be incorrect, but if it is directed towards a suggestion that an element of premeditation is an aggravating circumstance which did not apply to this crime, I would accept that it is true.

(d) I have already dealt with the importance which, in my view, exists with regard to a statement admitting guilt and a plea of guilty made by a person charged with rape. I am satisfied that a consideration of the principles enunciated on this ground, coupled with the desirability of contemplating that the accused should some day be rehabilitated into society, mentioned at ground (e), lead to a conclusion that notwithstanding the extraordinarily serious nature of the crime of rape and notwithstanding the multiple aggravating circumstances which surrounded this particular rape, it is possible to conclude that the sentence of twenty-one years imposed in the Circuit Court and affirmed in the Court of Criminal Appeal did not have sufficient regard to the admission of guilt and the plea of guilty. I would have little hesitation in upholding a sentence of twenty-one years on the facts of this case had this appellant put the victim to a trial and to the ordeal of giving evidence. When he did not, under circumstances from which it is possible to infer that he might have had some chance of escaping conviction for want of identification on a trial, it seems to me that the sentence is excessive. I have already emphasised the importance to be attached in a rape case to any early admission of guilt followed by a plea of guilty.

In these circumstances I would allow this appeal on the basis that the appropriate sentence for the offence in this case is seventeen years' penal servitude. I would therefore reduce the period of penal servitude from twenty-one years to seventeen years, the period having commenced on the 8th October, 1985.

Further Materials

6.94 Law Reform Commission Consultation Paper on Rape, 1987.
Law Reform Commission Report on Rape, 1988 (LRC 24 – 1988).
Law Reform Commission Consultation Paper on Child Sexual Abuse, 1989.
Criminal Law Revision Committee (England) Report on Sexual Offences, 1984 (Cmnd 9213).
Honoré *Sex Law*, London 1978.
Temkin *Rape and the Legal Process*, London 1987.
Boyle, M Bertrand, C Lacerd-Lamontagne and R Chamai *A Feminist Review of Criminal Law*, Canada 1985.
Brooks *Marital Consent in Rape* [1989] Crim LR 877.
Sullivan *The Need for a Crime of Sexual Assault* [1989] Crim LR 331.
Charleton *Offences Against the Person* (1992), chapter 8.

Chapter 7

OTHER CONCEPTS

7.01 This chapter explores some further concepts which are fundamental to criminal liability. These have not been mentioned in earlier chapters and those concepts do not inter-relate.

Possession

7.02 Possession is a particular element of certain offences which by-pass the need for an accused to have a criminal intent. Instead, liability is based on the physical proximity existing between the accused and an outlawed object, where he intends to exercise control over it. Possession is basic to the code of offences concerned with the control of drugs, firearms, explosives, offensive weapons and other forms of contraband.

7.03   ***Williams v Douglas***
                 (1949) 78 CLR 521
            High Court of Australia, 1949

Facts: The accused was arrested in a location which was not physically proximate to the contraband he was alleged to be possessing. The substance in question, gold, was hidden by the accused in a communal bathroom at the hotel where he was staying. It was not beyond interference by another person.

Latham CJ, Dixon and McTiernan JJ: . . . The magistrate dismissed the complaint on the ground that at the material time the defendant did not have actual possession of the gold or exclusive possession of the place where it was found, namely, the bathroom. He considered there was no evidence that the defendant placed the gold where it was found or that he alone knew it was there. He said that, on the contrary, it seemed that somebody else must have known the whereabouts of the gold, otherwise the detective sergeant would not have found it.

In reversing this decision the Full Court took the view that the magistrate drew the wrong deductions from the facts before him. Their Honours were of opinion that the only possible inference on the facts was that the applicant was in possession of the parcel of gold hidden under the bath. There was no suggestion that anyone else could have put it there. He claimed it when it was found, and it was suffiently obvious that he could get it when he wished.

The application for special leave was supported upon the ground that this decision was inconsistent with what was laid down in this Court in *Moors v Burke*[1] and that the principles explained in that decision were applicable to s 36 of the *Gold Buyers Act* 1921–1948. It was further submitted that the question which is raised was one of considerable importance in the administration of s 36 of the Act. *Moors v Burke* was decided upon what is now s 40 of the *Police Offences Act 1928* (Vict). That section deals with the unexplained possession of personal property suspected to be stolen. As the section was originally framed it spoke of "possession," but in *Tatchell v Lovett*[2], Hood J had construed the word "possession" as meaning possession in fact, an as not extending to any form of constructive possession. The Victorian Legislature gave effect to this decision by placing the word "actual" before "possession" and it was upon the section in that form that *Moors v Burke* was decided. Section 36 of the *Gold Buyers Act* is directed to the analogous but by no means identical purpose of throwing upon persons who are proved to be engaged or to have entered into transactions with gold the onus of justifying their legality. Section 36 applies to a peson engaged in a number of transactions. It applies if he offers gold for sale or for smelting; if he has gold in his possession or control; if he has sold any gold; if gold has been smelted for him. It further applies if in a prosecution under the section against some other person he states that he gave or entrusted or is alleged to have given or entrusted the gold to the defendant. In any of these circumstances the section provides that he may be required by a licensed gold buyer or a licensed gold assayer to whom the gold is or was offered or by whom it was bought or smelted or by any member of the police force or by a justice to satisfy him that he came lawfully by the gold or that it was obtained from a claim, place or works mentioned in an entry signed by him. If he does not satisfy the person who so calls upon him, then proceedings for an offence against the Act may be taken against him. Upon the hearing of the proceedings, unless the defendant proves to the satisfaction of the magistrate that he honestly came by the gold he is to be convicted of an offence.

It is plain that these provisions are founded upon the principle that a person who is closely connected by some transaction of an objective description with gold and deals with it either by sale or analogous dealing or by having it in his control and possession should have the onus thrown upon him of accounting for his connection with the gold. If the word "possession" were given the extended meaning of which it is capable in the law it would include many cases of constructive possession where the real connection of the accused with the gold was ambiguous and uncertain, and where it would not be fair to throw so great an onus upon him. In the context it therefore appears right to construe the words "possession or control" as referring to *de facto* possession and actual control and not to extend the word "possession" to constructive possession.

The result is much the same as if the word "actual" had been written before the word "possession," but *de facto* possession is a conception which is itself much more extensive than that of physical custody. It is wide enough to include any case where the person alleged to be in possession has hidden the thing effectively so that he can take it into his physical custody when he wishes and where others are unlikely to discover it except by accident. The present case therefore depends on a question of fact, namely, whether the applicant had hidden the gold under the bath. It seems clear enough that whoever hid it there chose an effective hiding place and that when concealed there the gold was at his command. The fact that at some periods of the day the bathroom might be in use by other persons, so that for the time being the applicant could not obtain access to it, is unimportant. It is not as if he was entirely excluded from access to it for any lengthy period. Even if the

1 (1919) 26 CLR 265.
2 (1908) VLR 645.

applicant had not himself hidden it, it would be enough if an accomplice had done so with his knowledge, or after hiding it has communicated the hiding place to him for the purpose of enabling him to find the gold. The difference between the view of the magistrate and that of the Full Court is simply upon the proper inference to be drawn, and the magistrate appeared to be of opinion that there were reasonable hypotheses consistent with someone else than the applicant or his accomplice having hidden the gold. Possibly the magistrate may have taken the view that an accomplice may have hidden the gold but failed to acquaint the applicant with the hiding place.

These are not questions on which it would be proper to give special leave to appeal, and that would be a sufficient ground for refusing the application. But in any case the view of the Full Court upon the question of fact seems preferable to that of the magistrate. The magistrate's opinion involved not a reasonable hypothesis, but merely a speculative hypothesis. For these reasons the application should be refused. The Supreme Court awarded to the complainant the costs of the appeal from the magistrate to that court. The correctness of this exercise of the discretion of the Supreme Court was contested but that is not a matter upon which special leave would be granted.

Rich J: The phrase in the section we are called upon to interpret is "possession or control." Possession does not mean actual physical possession or manual detention. "Suppose I request a bystander to hold anything for me, it still remains in my possession. So also possession may be required or retained over goods which are in the manual detention of a third person": *R v Sleep*[3], per Willes J. And the phrase possession and control denotes the right and power to deal with the article in question. In the instant case the question resolves itself into one of fact. In any given case it is necessary to take into consideration all the circumstances and the nature of the thing the subject of the inquiry. In the circumstances of this case as the accused claimed the gold when it was "discovered" I consider that the inferences which can be drawn are that the accused knew that the gold was concealed under the bath, that it was placed there by himself or an accomplice and to use the words of Dwyer CJ that "he could have got it when he wished." He had it as effectually under his control or his *de facto* possession as if he had locked it in a box in the bathroom, a box of which he and he alone had the key, or if you like he and an accomplice alone had keys.

The application should be dismissed.

7.04   *Minister for Posts and Telegraphs v Campbell*
[1966] IR 69
Case Stated to the High Court from the District Court, 1966

Facts: The prosecution proved that a TV licence inspector called to a cottage and found a television set on a table. No licence had been issued to the person occupying the cottage.

Davitt P: This is a consultative case stated by District Justice M. J. C. Keane under the provisions of the Courts (Supplemental Provisions) Act, 1961, s 52. The facts as stated are briefly as follows: – the defendant, Christopher Campbell, was charged on summons before the District Justice, the complaint being that he, on the 9 March, 1964, at Clane in the County Kildare did unlawfully keep or have in his possession certain apparatus for wireless telegraphy, to wit, a television set, contrary to statute. The Wireless Telegraphy Act 1926, by s 3, sub-s 1, provides that subject to certain exceptions, which are not in this case material, no person shall keep or have in his possession any apparatus for wireless telegraphy save in so

3 (1861) Le & Ca 44 [169 ER 1296].

far as such keeping or possession is authorised by a licence granted under the Act. By sub-s 3 it provides that every person who keeps or has in his possession any such apparatus in contravention of the section shall be guilty of an offence. On the 9 March, 1964, Thomas Brown, an inspector for the Department of Posts and Telegraphs, called to a cottage near Clane and, after speaking to a woman there, inspected the cottage and found on a table therein a television set. According to a certificate of valuation, signed by the secretary of Kildare County Council, issued under the provisions of the Local Government (Ireland) Act 1898, s 54, sub-s 10, and dated the 12 August 1964, the defendant, Christopher Campbell, was the rated occupier of the cottage. No licence under the Act had been issued to anyone named Christopher Campbell in the Clane area or was in force on the 9 March 1964.

The District Justice was, of course, satisfied that the television set was an apparatus requiring a licence under the Act, but was not satisfied that the facts established in evidence were sufficient to prove that the defendant on the 9 March 1964, kept it or had it in his possession. He accordingly stated this Case and asks whether he would be correct in law in convicting the defendant. It would be more consistent if he asked whether he would be correct in acquitting him.

In my opinion a person cannot, in the context of a criminal case, be properly said to keep or have possession of an article unless he has control of it either personally or by someone else. He cannot be said to have actual possession of it unless he personally can exercise physical controll over it; and he cannot be said to have constructive possession of it unless it is in the actual possession of some other person over whom he has control so that it would be available to him if and when he wanted it. Normally speaking, a person can properly be said to be in possession of the contents of his own dwelling-house, but only if he is aware of what it contains. He cannot properly be said to be in control or possession of something of whose existence and presence he has no knowledge. Assuming, for the sake only of the argument, that the evidence established that the cottage was the defendant's dwelling-house, there is in this case no evidence as to how the television set came to be there, how long it was there, or whether the defendant was ever at any time aware of its presence or existence. There is therefore no evidence that it was ever actually in his control or possession. There is no evidenc as to who was the woman who was present in the house on the occasion of Mr Brown's visit, or as to what was her relation, if any, to the defendant. There is nothing to indicate that he had any control over her actions. There are therefore no grounds for concluding that he had constructive possession of the television set. As far as the evidence goes, the set may have been placed in the cottage without his knowledge or consent.

I have assumed for the sake of argument that the cottage was the defendant's dwelling-house. The statutory declaration as to service endorsed upon the summons indicates that the Garda who made it was in a position to prove that it was his last and most usual place of abode when it would appear that on the 3 September 1964, service was effected at the cottage upon the defendant's wife. The Garda did not, however, give this evidence before the District Justice; and the only evidence relied on to prove that the cottage was his dwelling-house was the evidence that he was the rated occupier. A person may be the rated occupier of a cottage without dwelling in it. If the defendant did live in the cottage, or even stayed there occasionally, and the television set was there at any material time, he could hardly remain unaware of its presence. The evidence does not establish that the set was in the cottage at any time other than on the occasion of Mr Brown's visit on the 9 March 1964. It does not establish that the defendant was there on that occasion or at any time that day or at any time on any other day.

In my opinion the view of the District Justice, as indicated in the case stated, is quite correct. The onus resting upon the prosecution of establishing that the defendant kept or had possession of the set was not discharged; and he would not be correct in law in convicting the defendant upon the evidence adduced. These views are in accordance with the decision of the Court of Criminal Appeal in the case of *The People v John Nugent and Joseph Byrne* (1964; unreported).

Safe Keeping

7.05 Possession may occur where the accused has an article in the hands of an agent or where it is left by another at a particular location and where, at some future stage, he will be able to exercise control over it; *R v Peaston*[4]. Where a person gives an article into the custody of another person for safe-keeping he continues to have possession of it; *Sullivan v Earl of Caithness*[5].

Joint Possession

7.06 The mental element of possession is an intention to exercise control, either exclusively or in common design with others, over the article in question; *R v Cavendish*[6]. Where several persons are found in proximity to an object it may be impossible to say which of them was in possession. This problem is peculiar to the law relating to the physical possession of objects. It does not tend to occur in other factual situations. It is rare, for example, for a dead person to be found, obviously killed through stab wounds, and for three or four persons to be standing nearby holding bloody knives.

7.07
R v Whelan
[1972] NI 153
Court of Criminal Appeal Northern Ireland, 1971

Facts: The RUC raided a house in Belfast occupied by fourteen people. In a small room upstairs the three accused were found in three different beds. On searching the room the police found a revolver and some rounds of ammunition on the top of a chest of drawers. These were covered by men's clothing. The three accused were the only adult males in the house. On questioning they denied possession of the firearm and asserted that the police had planted the gun in an effort to "frame" them.

Lowry LCJ: While it is always necessary, as the learned trial judge advised the jury, when two or more are jointly tried, to consider each charge separately against each accused, it is accepted by all that in this particular case the two alternatives on the facts were either that all three men were guilty or that they must be acquitted, and the reason for that was that it was quite impossible to say that one man in particular was at any material time the person in possession of the gun.

The Crown had to prove, considering that the possession was not direct physical possession, a number of things including the intent of each of the accused to be in possession of the gun, what the learned trial judge referred to as his assent to being in control of it, and it was conceded, as I say, that in order to do that the Crown could not rely on anyone's physical possession and had to rely, therefore, on the surrounding circumstances. It is quite proper to regard those circumstances as consisting of what happens before, during or after the point of time to which the charge relates since what one is trying to ascertain is the mental attitude of the accused person.

4 (1978) 69 Cr App R 203.
5 [1976] QB 966.
6 [1961] 2 All ER 856.

The Crown relied, in the first place, on the smallness of the room, on the fact that these accused men, who are brothers, were the only adult males and the fact that this room was, as it seems, their bedroom as well as that of three small boys, whose ages are not quite clearly ascertained. The other occupants of the house seem to have been women or children who slept in other rooms. On the hearing of the appeal and at the trial something was made of the fact that there were other occupants of the house and other juvenile occupants of the room. Were that the only difficulty in the way of the Crown, it seems to me that the jury would have ample justification for disregarding to all intents and purposes the persons in the other parts of the house and indeed the persons in the room other than the three brothers who had been charged, but even narrowing the case to this extent, it seems to the court that the difficulty facing the Crown in sustaining the proposition that there is a prima facie case is that one cannot attribute the possession to any one of these three men and, therefore, one has on that basis to consider whether there is evidence on which they could properly be held to have been jointly in possession.

The first group of facts which, as it was submitted, led to that conclusion, was the presence of the three men in this their own bedroom and the presence of the gun on a chest of drawers covered by male clothing which appeared to be not cast-off clothing, but clothing in current use. The second set of facts which, it is submitted, supported the conclusion that the gun was in joint possession, was what passed after the gun was discovered by the police. Without detailing what every accused person said, two of them, almost immediately after the discovery, alleged, in different words, that the gun had been planted by the police and the third man took up this allegation at the police station some seven hours later. It seems to us that the conduct of the accused persons in making this allegation, (for which, by the way, no grounds have emerged from the evidence), has received too much emphasis as an argument in favour of their being in joint possession of the gun. No doubt it does point to an attempt (which is not alleged to have been founded on fact) to exculpate whoever might be the guilty party or parties by putting the blame on those conducting the search, but it seems to us firstly that it is not clear that this indicates a concerted attempt to do that and secondly (if it does indicate such an attempt) that it would be equally consistent with the fact of one man possessing the gun and the other two, his brothers, attempting to help him out of his difficulties.

Now those are the two groups of facts on which the Crown has relied and which seem to have influenced the learned trial judge in refusing to accede to the submission that there was no evidence to go before the jury. Every argument of logic and commonsense would indicate that there was a very strong case that at least one of these men was in possession of this gun, and it is quite clear that none of them has a licence or permit to have the gun and no explanation is forthcoming as to what the gun was doing in this house. It appears to the court, however, that this is a case which could well be approached on the basis that guilt existed in the alternative, that is to say, that one, or possibly two, of these men might have been guilty while the remaining two or one, as the case may be, were or was innocent of the offences which have been included in the indictment and that the difficulty, in fact the impossibility, of laying the blame conclusively at the door of one accused is not a warrant for permitting or inviting a finding of guilty against each of them.

So far I have said that we are dealing with the case where a direction was sought at the end of the Crown case and in our opinion a direction ought to have been granted at that stage on the ground that while there was very strong evidence that somebody was guilty of an offence in connection with this gun, there was absolutely no indiction which individual was guilty and insufficient evidence on which to found the inference that all three were in possession of the gun.

That is not quite the end of the matter. It has been established, certainly since *R v Power* [1919] 2 KB 572, that evidence given during the case for the defence may supplement gaps in the Crown case so that one must view the evidence as a whole if the trial proceeds to a verdict. Here each accused elected not to give sworn evidence but to make a short statement from the dock, as was his right. It is possible in some cases that an inference may be drawn either favourably or unfavourably according to what is said and to the manner in whih the accused elects to make his statement. This could increase the weight of the case against an accused person, but when, as we have found here, there was *no* cogent evidence which would have justified the conclusion that these men were guilty of possessing a weapon, nothing (apart from an admission) which they said or failed to say consequently could make a difference to that.

Therefore, our conclusion is that there was at the end of the case no evidence on which the jury, properly directed, could find the verdicts of guilty, which they did. That disposes of the case, but I must briefly refer to the learned trial judge's charge. In our opinion it was a conspicuously fair charge intended to place clearly before the jury the dilemma, namely, that the jury really in practice had to find all three men guilty or all three men not guilty. The trial judge also took care to say that if the jury could not decide who was in possession of the gun, they they were bound to acquit all three of the accused. In short, any deficiences which have been found in the charge seem to us to be directly due to the initial logical difficulty that the case was allowed to proceed when there was (as we consider) no evidence on which the jury could reach a conclusion adverse to the accused. The charge was bound to be made against that difficult background, but it was quite clear that the learned trial judge was endeavouring to point out to the jury all the circumstances in which the men could be acquitted. The difficulty was, we are quite sure, for the jury that there appeared to be a very strong case that someone in the room was guilty of a serious offence. Therefore, if all three men were undistinguishably guilty or innocent, all three were likely to be found guilty, as indeed they were. We have already pointed out the reasons for saying that, even if one of these men may have been clearly guilty, that did not warrant subjecting all three to the risk of conviction which turned into a fact.

Accordingly, all the convictions must be quashed.

7.08   As with most problems in criminal law, the difficulty arising from the *Whelan* judgment was easily capable of solution. The response was the statutory provision which follows. The problem of joint possession can surface in a particularly acute way in drugs cases. Where two or three persons are stopped while driving in a car drugs may be found secreted in the dash board, under the carpet, or in some other location. Unless one or other of the suspects makes an admission of ownership or control over the drugs the principle in *Whelan*'s case will apply. As we have seen from *Campbell*'s case the mere fact of ownership of property is not, of itself, an indication of control of anything in or on it. While it may be common sense to suppose that the owner of the car, or the owner of the house, as the case may be, has possession of something hidden within it, this does not amount to proof beyond reasonable doubt. Unfortunately, the legislature has not followed the lead of Northern Ireland in solving this problem. It may be only a matter of time before legislature is forced to intervene.

7.09   *Northern Ireland (Emergency Provisions) Act 1973*

Onus of proof in relation to offences of possession

7   (1) Where a person is charged with possessing a proscribed article in such circumstances as to constitute an offence to which this section applies and it is proved that at the time of the alleged offence—

(*a*) he and that article were both present in any premises; or (*b*) the article was in premises of which he was the occupier or which he habitually used otherwise than as a member of the public;

the court may accept the fact proved as sufficient evidence of his possessing (and, if relevant, knowingly possessing) that article at that time unless it is further proved that he did not at that time know of its presence in the premises in question, or if he did know, that he had no control over it.

(2) This section applies to vessels, aircraft and vehicles as it applies to premises.

(3) I this section "proscribed article" means an explosive, firearm, ammunition, substance or other thing (being a thing possession of which is an offence under one of the enactments mentioned in *subsection (4)* below).

(4) This section applies to scheduled offences under the following enactments, that is to say—

The Explosive Substances Act 1883

Section 3, so far as relating to para (*b*) thereof (possessing explosive with intent to endanger life or cause serious damage to property).

Section 4 (possessing explosive in suspicious circumstances).

The Firearms Act (Northern Ireland) 1969

Section 1 (possessing firearm or ammunition without, or otherwise than as authorised by, a firearm certificate).

Section 4 (possessing machine gun or machine pistol or weapon discharging, or ammunition containing, noxious substance).

Section 14 (possessing firearm or ammunition with intent to endanger life or cause serious damage to property).

Section 15(2) (possessing firearm or imitation firearm at time of committing,or being arrested for, a specified offence).

Section 19(1) to (3) (possession of a firearm or ammunition by a person who has been sentenced to imprisonment, etc).

Section 19A (possessing firearm or ammunition in suspicious circumstances).

The Protection of the Person and Property Act
(Northern Ireland) 1969

Section 2 (possessing petrol bomb, etc, in suspicious circumstances).

7.10   *The People (DPP) v O'Shea (No 2)*
                        [1983] ILRM 592
                      Supreme Court, 1983

Facts: This was an appeal from an acquittal in the Central Criminal Court of an accused on a charge of possession of drugs contrary to the Misuse of Drugs Act 1977. The facts giving rise to the prosecution are summarised in the unanimous judgment of the Supreme Court.

Finlay P: The facts appearing from the transcript of evidence in this case purporting to support the charges made against this respondent may thus be summarised. On 25 August 1979 two members of the Garda Siochana approached a lay-by on the side of the Naas dual carriageway at Palmerstown, Kill, in the County of Kildare on which there were a two-ton motor-van and a large articulated lorry backed into each other. The Gardai approached two men who were standing close to the vehicle and observed in the case of one of the Gardai, one other man and in the case of the other, what he believed to be either two or three further men. After a short conversation one of the men at the scene threw a gun to one of the others who was being interviewed by Garda Stokes. Garda Stokes disarmed him and grappled with him and the man escaped into a Hillman car and drove with one other companion away from the scene of the incident. A third man who was being interviewed by Garda Dowd was arrested by him at the scene of the incident and brought into custody in the Garda car. A chase then ensued of the Hillman car in which the two men had escaped and eventually two men were captured after the car had crashed. None of these three persons was the respondent in this case. Neither of the guards sought to offer any identification of the respondent as being one of the persons at the scene of the incident. On examination of the van and articulated lorry, there were found in it a large number of containers of a substantial size marked electrical goods which on being opened and examined contained cannabis. In both vehicles there were also a number of cardboard boxes containing bananas. The finding of the vehicles and the apprehension of the three men who were at the scene took place in the very early hours of the morning of 25 August. On 27 August 1979 the respondent went to the house of a solicitor in Dun Laoghaire who contacted Detective Sergeant Walsh who is a member of the Drugs Unit of the Central Detective Unit Dublin Castle. As a result Detective Sergeant Walsh with Inspector Mullins came to the house of the solicitor and was introduced to the respondent who informed him that he had got innocently involved in the incident at Naas with the drugs which happened a few days previously and that he wanted to tell the truth about his involvement. After a short time, the respondent agreed to accompany the two Gardai to Dun Laoghaire Garda Station and repeated on arrival there that he wanted to tell the whole truth about his involvement and then dictated to the Gardai concerned a lengthy voluntary statement. This statement was the only evidence of any description associating the respondent with the incident which had occurred at the lay-by off the Naas dual carriageway.

Detective Sergeant Walsh in evidence stated that insofar as the facts set out in that statement could be checked, he checked them or had them checked and was satisfied that they were accurate. Insofar as they were not capable of being checked he was satisfied to accept their accuracy and he expressly stated that he was satisfied that the respondent in making this statement was telling him the truth. Reference was made in the statement to one person whom the respondent met after the incident at the lay-by and that person gave evidence and confirmed exactly the account given in the statement by the respondent.

It is necessary to quote the material part of that statement involving the incident the subject matter of the charges and it is as follows:

> We then drove back in the direction of Naas again and followed McCann into a lay-by off the Naas Road. At this point, we were facing in the direction of Dublin again. I saw a big lorry parked there with a car behind it with lights on. I was still in the cab of the van. I said to Hugh I was not getting out of the van. McCann then got in beside me in the van and ordered me out. I saw him put a gun in his pocket. It seemed to be a short black gun. I was really very nervous at this stage. McCann ordered me to get the car with its lights on to move off. That car did move away. I then jumped back into the cab of the van again. Hugh turned the van around and backed it up to the back of the big lorry. McCann told me to jump up onto the lorry. Boxes were then thrown to me from the back of the van. My worry now was to get the job finished as soon as possible and get out of there as I now knew there was something seriously wrong. Initially, I felt there were explosives involved but the boxes were fairly light and I just did not know what was happening. I finished the loading and I went towards McCann's car. I was just about alongside the car when I heard someone shout "Get them boys" or words to that effect. I immediately jumped into the ditch and rolled over. I expected there was going to be shooting. As I lay on the ditch I saw McCann's car being driven away and being chased by a police car.

One of the functions of a trial judge in a criminal trial is to reach a decision at the conclusion of the evidence tendered on behalf of the prosecution as to whether there is evidence which if accepted by a jury could as a matter of law lead to a conviction. This may frequently occur in practise in cases where there is a gap in the evidence tendered on behalf of the prosecution and where some vital link in the chain of proof is missing. It also arises in my view, however, and not infrequently, in cases where an apparent link in the chain of proof is so tenuous that it would clearly be perverse for a jury properly directed as to the onus of proof upon the prosecution to act upon it.

Detailed submissions were made to the court on behalf of the appellant in this case with regard to the precise extent and nature of the knowledge which must be associated with possession of drugs contrary to the Misuse of Drugs Act and to a lesser extent of firearms and ammunition contrary to the Firearms Act. In my view of the facts appearing from the transcript in this case, these questions do not fall to be decided and should not be decided in this case.

What is abundantly clear is that the account contained in the statement of the respondent, portion of which I have quoted, was entirely exculpatory and consistent only with his innocence. In the absence of any evidence otherwise implicating him in the commission of any of the crimes alleged against him to have permitted the case to go to the jury would have been to invite them to consider the possibility of convicting him by what could only be described as a perverse speculation. It was for these reasons that I was satisfied that the appeal of the appellants must be dismissed.

Knowledge

7.11 With most articles and substances their nature is apparent from their appearance. A gun looks like a gun. On occasion, however, substances such as controlled drugs, may resemble innocent household items. It seems consistent with the approach in *The People (DPP) v Murray*[7] (see para **1.31**) that before guilt can be established in respect of an illicit substance or an outlawed thing, the prosecution should be able to infer recklessness or knowledge as to the nature of that substance from the facts.

7.12   *Beaver v R*
                                        (1957) 118 CCC 129
                                Supreme Court of Canada, 1957

Facts: The accused sold a package containing Morphine to a police officer. He claimed that he had no knowledge that the substance contained in the package was a drug but that he believed it to be sugar or milk.

When the decisions as to the construction of the *Opium and Narcotic Drug Act* on which the respondent relies are examined it appears that two main reasons are assigned for holding that *mens rea* is not an essential ingredient of the offence created by s 4(1)(d), these being (i) the assumption that the subject-matter with which the Act deals is of the kind dealt with in the cases of which *Hobbs v Winchester Corp*, [1910] 2 KB 471, is typical and which are sometimes referred to as "public welfare offence cases", and (ii) by implication from the wording of s 17 of the Act.

As to the first of these reasons, I can discern little similarity between a statute designed, by forbidding the sale of unsound meat, to ensure that the supply available to the public shall be wholesome, and a statute making it a serious crime to possess or deal in narcotics; the one is to ensure that a lawful and necessary trade shall be carried on in a manner not to endanger the public health, the other to forbid altogether conduct regarded as harmful in itself. As a necessary feature of

7 [1977] IR 360.

his trade, the butcher holds himself out as selling meat fit for consumption; he warrants that quality; and it is part of his duty as trader to see that the merchandise is wholesome. The statute simply converts that civil personal duty into a public duty.

Has X possession of heroin when he has in his hand or in his pocket or in his cupboard a package which in fact contains heroin but which he honestly believes contains only baking soda? In my opinion that question must be answered in the negative. The essence of the crime is the possession of the forbidden substance and in a criminal case there is in law no possession without knowledge of the character of the forbidden substance. Just as in *R v Ashwell* (1885), 16 QBD 190, the accused did not in law have possession of the complainant's sovereign so long as he honestly believed it to be a shilling so in my illustration X did not have possession of heroin so long as he honestly believed the package to contain baking soda. The words of Lord Coleridge CJ in *R v Ashwell* at p 225, quoted by Charles J delivering the unanimous judgment of the Court of Criminal Appeal in *R v Hudson* (1943) 29 Cr App R 65 at p 71:

"In good sense it seems to me he did not take it till he knew what he had got; and when he knew what he had got, that same instant he stole it."

might well be adapted to my illustration to read: "In good sense it seems to me he did not have possession of heroin till he knew what he had got."

If the matter were otherwise doubtful I would be drawn to the conclusion that Parliament did not intend to enact that *mens rea* should not be an essential ingredient of the offence created by s 4(1)(*d*) by the circumstance that on conviction a minimum sentence of 6 months' imprisonment plus a fine of $200 must be imposed. Counsel informed us that they have found no other statutory provision which has been held to create a crime of strict responsibility, that is to say, one in which the necessity for *mens rea* is excluded, on conviction for which a sentence of imprisonment is mandatory. The legislation dealt with in *Hobbs v Winchester*, *supra*, provided that a sentence of imprisonment might, not must, be imposed on a convicted person.

It would, of course, be within the power of Parliament to enact that a person who, without any guilty knowledge, had in his physical possession a package which he honestly believed to contain a harmless substance such as baking soda but which in fact contained heroin, must on proof of such facts be convicted of a crime and sentenced to at least 6 months' imprisonment; but I would refuse to impute such an intention to Parliament unless the words of the statute were clear and admitted of no other interpretation. To borrow the words of Lord Keyon in *Fowler v Padget* (1798) 7 Term R 509 at p 514, 101 ER 1103; "I would adopt any construction of the statute that the words will bear, in order to avoid such monstrous consequences as would manifestly ensue from the construction contended for by the defendant."

The conclusion which I have reached on the main question as to the proper construction of the word possession makes it unnecessary for me to consider the other points raised by Mr Dubin in his argument as to the construction of s 4(1)(*d*). For the above reasons I would quash the conviction on the charge of having possession of a drug.

As to the charge of selling, as is pointed out by my brother Fauteux, the appellant's version of the facts brings his actions within the provisions of s 4(1)(*f*) since he and his brother jointly sold a substance represented or held out by them to be heroin; and I agree with the conclusion of my brother Fauteux that the conviction on the charge of selling must be affirmed.

7.13 An entirely different approach to this problem is taken in England; *Warner v Metropolitan Police Commissioner*[8].

8 [1969] 2 AC 256.

7.14   *Other concepts*

Possession Offences

7.14   Reference should be made to the various possession offences and the manner in which the wrong is described in the wording of the statute.

7.15   *Misuse of Drugs Act 1977*

1   (1) 'supply' includes giving without payment . . .

(2) For the purpose of this Act any controlled drug, pipe, utensil or document of which a person has control and which is in the custody of another who is either under the person's control or, though not under the person's control, acts on his behalf, whether as agent or otherwise, shall be regarded as being in the possession of the person and the provisions of *section 16* and *section 18* together with the provisions of this Act relating to the possession of controlled drugs shall be construed and have effect in accordance with the foregoing.

3   (1) Subject to *subsection (3)* of this section and *section 4(3)* of this Act, a person shall not have a controlled drug in his possession.

(2) A person who contravenes *subsection (1)* of this section shall be guilty of an offence.

(3) The Minister may by order declare that *subsection (1)* of this section shall not apply to a controlled drug specified in the order, and for so long as an order under this subsection is in force the prohibition contained in the said *subsection (1)* shall not apply to a drug which is a controlled drug specified in the order.

4   (3) It shall be lawful for any person, or a person of a class or description specified in regulations under this section, to have in his possession in prescribed circumstances or for prescribed purposes, as may be appropriate, a controlled drug specified therein, provided that any conditions specified in the regulations or attached to a licence under this Act and applicable in the particular case are complied with.

5   (1) For the purpose of preventing the misuse of controlled drugs, the Minister may make regulations:

(*a*) Prohibiting absolutely, or prohibiting subject to such conditions or exceptions as may be specified . . . (ii) The importation or exportation of controlled drugs.

15   (1) Any person who has in his possession, whether lawfully or not, a controlled drug for the purpose of selling or otherwise supplying it to another in contravention of regulations under *section 5* of this Act, shall be guilty of an offence.

(2) Subject to *section 29(3)* of this Act, in any proceedings for an offence under *subsection (1)* of this section, where it is proved that a person was in possession of a controlled drug and the court, having regard to the quantity of the controlled drug which the person possessed or to such matter as the court considers relevant, is satisfied that it is reasonable to assume that the controlled drug was not intended for the immediate personal use of the person, he shall be presumed, until the court is satisfied to the contrary, to have been in possession of the controlled drug for the purpose of selling or otherwise supplying it to another in contravention of regulations under *section 5* of this Act.

21   (1) A person who attempts to commit an offence under this Act, or who aids, abets, counsels or procures the commission of an offence under this Act, or who solicits or incites any other person to commit an offence under this Act shall be guilty of an offence.

(2) Any person who, whether by act or omission, contravenes or fails to comply with regulations under this Act shall be guilty of an offence.

(3) A person who, in purported compliance with any obligation to give information to which he is subject by virtue of regulations made under this Act, gives any information which he knows to be false in a material particular or recklessly gives information which is so false shall be guilty of an offence.

(4) Any person who by act or omission impedes or obstructs a member of the Garda Síochána or a person duly authorised under this Act in the lawful exercise of a power conferred by this Act shall be guilty of an offence and if, in the case of a continuing offence, the impediment or obstruction is continued after conviction, he shall be guilty of a further offence.

(5) Any person who conceals from a person lawfully exercising a power under section 24 of this Act any controlled drug, or who without reasonable excuse fails to produce any book, record or other document which he has been duly required to produce under that section, shall be guilty of an offence.

(6) Any person who contravenes a condition attached to a licence, permit of authorisation granted or issued by the Minister under this Act (other than section 24) or under regulations made under this Act shall be guilty of an offence.

(7) Any person who, for the purpose of obtaining, whether for himself or another, the grant, issue or renewal of a licence, permit of authorisation under this Act or under regulations made under this Act -

(*a*) makes any statement or gives information which he knows to be false in a material particular or recklessly gives information which is so false, or

(*b*) produces or otherwise makes use of any book, record or other document which to his knowledge contains any statement or information which he knows to be false in a material particular,

shall be guilty of an offence.

22 (1) In any proceedings for an offence under this Act, it shall not be necessary to negative by evidence the existence of any—

(*a*) order made under *section 2 (or 3)* of this Act,

(*b*) licence, permit or authorisation under this Act,

and accordingly the onus of proving the existence of any such licence, permit or authorisation shall be on the person seeking to avail himself thereof.

(2) In any proceedings for an offence under this Act it shall not be necessary for the prosecutor to prove that at the time of the offence—

(*a*) a defendant was not a person to whom regulations made under *section 4* of this Act applied,

(*b*) a defendant was a person to whom an exception under regulations made under *section 5* of this Act applied, and
in case a defendant claims that—

(i) by virtue of the said *section 4* he had lawfully in his possession a controlled drug,

(ii) he is a person to whom such an exception is applied,

the onus of proving such lawful possession, or that he is such a person, as may be appropriate, shall be on the defendant.

29 (1) In any proceedings for an offence under this Act in which it is proved that the defendant had in his possession or supplied a controlled drug, the defendant shall not be acquitted of the offence charged by reason only of proving only that he neither knew nor suspected nor had reason to suspect that the substance, product or preparation in question was the particular controlled drug alleged.

(2) In any such proceedings in which it is proved that the defendant had in his possession or supplied a controlled drug, or a forged prescription, or a duly issued prescription altered with "intent to deceive", it shall be a defence to prove that:

(*a*) he did not know and had no reasonable grounds for suspecting–
  (i) that what he had in his possession was a controlled drug or such a prescription, as may be appropriate, or
  (ii) that he was in possession of a controlled drug or such a prescription, as may be appropriate, or
(*b*) he believed the substance, product or preparation to be a controlled drug, or a controlled drug of a particular class or description, and that, if the substance, product or preparation had in fact been that controlled drug or a controlled drug of that class or description, he would not at the material time have been committing an offence under this Act.

7.16   *Misuse of Drugs Regulations 1988*

General prohibition

4   (1) Subject to the provisions of these Regulations a person shall not—

(*a*) produce a controlled drug,
(*b*) supply or offer to supply a controlled drug, or
(*c*) import or export a controlled drug.

(2)(*a*) Sub-article (1)(*c*) shall not apply to any drug specified in Schedule 4 or 5.
(*b*) Sub-article (1)(*b*) shall not apply to poppy straw.

Licences

5   A person so authorised by a licence granted by the Minister under section 14 of the Act and for the time being in force may, under and in accordance with the terms of the licence and in compliance with any conditions attached thereto—

(*a*) produce, supply, offer to supply, import, export or have in his possession any controlled drug to which the licence relates, or
(*b*) cultivate opium poppy or any plant of the genus Cannabis, or any plant of the genus Erythroxylon as may be specified in the lience.

Administration

6   It shall not be a contravention of the provisions of article 4(1)(*b*) for—

(*a*) any person to administer to another any drug specified in Schedule 5,
(*b*) a registered medical practitioner or registered dentist to administer to a patient any drug specified in Schedules 2, 3 or 4.
(*c*) any person, other than a registered medical practitioner or registered dentist, to administer to a patient, in accordance with the directions of a registered medical practitioner or registered dentist, any drug specified in Schedules 2, 3 or 4.

Exemption for practitioners, pharmacists, etc

7   (1) A practitioner or pharmacist may, when acting in his capacity as such, for the purpose of his profession or business—

(*a*) supply or offer to supply any drug specified in Schedules 2, 3, 4 or 5 to any person who may lawfully have that drug in his possession, or
(*b*) manufacture or compound any such drug.

(2) A person keeping open shop for the dispensing or compounding of medical prescriptions or for the sale of poisons may, when acting in his capacity as such, for

the purpose of his profession or business, at the premises at which he keeps open shop—

   (*a*) supply or offer to supply any drug specified in Schedules 2, 3, 4 or 5 to any person who may lawfully have that drug in his possession, or

   (*b*) manufacture or compound any such drug

provided that nothing in this article shall be construed as authorising a registered druggist to supply or offer to supply a controlled drug on foot of a medical prescription.

Supply in hospitals, etc

8 (1) A person may supply or offer to supply any drug specified in Schedules 2, 3, 4 or 5 to any person who may lawfully have that drug in his possession where the person so supplying or offering to supply the drug is a person acting in his capacity as—

   (*a*) the matron or acting matron of a hosiptal or nursing home which is wholly or mainly maintained by a public authority out of public funds or by a charity or by voluntary subscriptions, and the drug is a medical preparation,

   (*b*) the sister or acting sister for the time being in charge of a ward, theatre or other department in such a hospital or nursing home where the drug is a medical preparation supplied to her by a person responsible for the dispensing and supply of medicines at such hospital or nursing home,

   (*c*) a person in charge of a laboratory the recognised activities of which consist in, or include, the conduct of scientific education or research and which is attached to a university or a hospital referred to in para (*a*) of this sub-article, or a person in charge of any other laboratory engaged in the conduct of scientific education or research and which is attached to any other institution approved for the purpose by the Minister,

   (*d*) the State Chemist,

   (*e*) the Director of the Forensic Science Laboratory of the Department of Justice,

   (*f*) a public analyst appointed under section 10 of the Sale of Food and Drugs Act, 1875,

   (*g*) the Medical Director of the National Drugs Advisory Board,

   (*h*) a person employed or engaged in connection with any arrangements made for testing the quality or amount of the drugs, medicines and appliances supplied for the purpose of section 59 of the Health Act, 1970,

   (*i*) a person employed or engaged as an inspector in connection with a scheme for the licensing of manufacturers or wholesalers of medical preparations under the Health Acts 1947 to 1985,

   (*j*) a person authorised under and in accordance with Regulations made under section 65 of the Health Act, 1947 (as amended by section 39 of the Health Act, 1953 and by section 36 of the Act) for the purpose of enforcement and execution of the said Regulations,

   (*k*) a person appointed as an inspector by the Pharmaceutical Society of Ireland, acting under the directions in writing of the Registrar of the said Society;

provided that nothing in this sub-article shall be construed as authorising—

   (i) the matron or acting matron of a hospital or nursing home, having a pharmacist responsible for the dispensing and supply of medicines, to supply or offer to supply any drug, or

   (ii) a sister or acting sister for the time being in charge of a ward, theatre or other department to supply any drug otherwise than for administration to a patient in that ward, theatre or department in accordance with the directions of a registered medical practitioner or a registered dentist.

(2) A person who is authorised as a member of a group may, under and in accordance with the terms of his group authority and in compliance with any conditions attached thereto, supply or offer to supply any drug specified in Schedules 2, 3, 4 or 5 which is a medical preparation to any person who may lawfully have that drug in his possession.

(3) The owner of a ship, or the master of a ship which does not carry on board as part of her complement a registered medical practitioner, may supply or offer to supply any drug specified in Schedules 2, 3, 4 or 5 which is a medical preparation—

(*a*) to any member of the crew,
(*b*) to any person who may lawfully supply that drug; or
(*c*) to a member of the Garda Síochána or an officer of customs and excise for the purpose of destruction.

(4) The installation manager of an offshore installation may supply or offer to supply any drug specified in Schedules 2, 3, 4 or 5 which is a medical preparation—

(*a*) to any person on that installation, whether present in the course of his employment or not,
(*b*) to any person who may lawfully suply that drug; or
(*c*) to a member of the Garda Síochána or an officer of customs and excise for the purpose of destruction.

(5) A person whose name is for the time being entered in a register kept for the purposes of this sub-article by the Minister may, at the premises in respect of which his name is entered in the register and in compliance with any conditions subject to which his name is so entered, supply or offer to supply any drug specified in Schedules 3, 4 or 5 to any person who may lawfully have that drug in his possession.

7.17   *Firearms Acts 1925–1990*

Firearms Act 1925

1 The word "ammunition" (except where used in relation to a prohibited weapon) means ammunition for a firearm but also includes grenades, bombs, and other similar missiles whether the same are or are not capable of being used with a firearm, and also includes any ingredient or component part of any such ammunition or missile;

2 The provisions of this Act relating to ammunition shall be in addition to and not in derogation of any enactment relating to the keeping and sale of explosives.

Firearms Act 1990

4 (1) In the Firearms Acts 1925 to 1990, "firearm" means: (*a*) a lethal firearm or other lethal weapon of any description from which any shot, bullet or other missile can be discharged; (*b*) an air gun (which expression includes an air rifle and an air pistol) or any other weapon incorporating a barrel from which metal or other slugs can be discharged; (*c*) a crossbow; (*d*) any type of stun gun or other weapon for causing any shock or other disablement to a person by means of electricity or any other kind of energy emission; (*e*) a prohibited weapon as defined in section 1(1) of the Firearms Act, 1925; (*f*) any article which would be a firearm under any of the foregoing paragraphs but for the fact that, owing to the lack of a necessary component part or parts, or to any other defect or condition, it is incapable of discharging a shot, bullet or other missile or of causing a shock or other disablement (as the case may be); (*g*) save where the context otherwise requires, any component part of any article referred to in any of the foregoing paragraphs and, for the purposes of this definition, the following articles shall be deemed to be such component parts as aforesaid: (i) telescope sights with a light beam, or telescope sights, with an electronic light amplification device or an infra-red device, designed to be fitted to a firearm specified in paragraph (*a*), (*b*), (*c*) or (*e*), and (ii) a silencer designed to be fitted to a firearm specified in paragraph (*a*), (*b*) or (*e*).

Firearms Act 1964

24 (2) Where, in a prosecution for an offence under the Principal Act, possession, use or carriage of a firearm or ammunition by a person is proved, it shall not be necessary to prove that the person was not entitled to have in his possession, use or carry a firearm or ammunition.

25 In this section and the next two sections "imitation firearm" means anything which is not a firearm but has the appearance of being a firearm.

The portions of these Acts creating the most serious criminal offences are reproduced at paras **9.114–9.125**.

7.18 *Offences Against the Person Act 1861*

14 Whosoever shall . . . shoot at any person, or shall, by drawing a trigger or in any other manner, attempt to discharge any kind of loaded arms at any person . . . , with intent, in any of the cases aforesaid, to commit murder, shall, whether any bodily injury be effected or not, be guilty of felony; and being convicted thereof shall be liable to be kept in penal servitude for life.

18 Whosoever shall . . . shoot at any person, or, by drawing a trigger or in any other manner, attempt to discharge any kind of loaded arms at any person, with intent, in any of the cases aforesaid, to maim, disfigure, or disable any person, or to do some other grievous bodily harm to any person, or with intent to resist or prevent the lawful apprehension or detainer of any person, shall be guilty of felony to be kept in penal servitude for life.

19 Any gun, pistol, or other arms which shall be loaded in the barrel with gunpowder or any other explosive substance, and ball, shot, slug, or other destructive material, shall be deemed to be loaded arms within the meaning of this Act, although the attempt to discharge the same may fail from want of proper priming or from any other cause.

7.19 *Explosives Acts 1875, 1883 and*
The Dangerous Substances Act 1972
as amended

The Explosives Act 1875, the Explosives Substances Act 1883 and the Dangerous Substances Act 1972 (not yet in force) each contain separate definitions of what constitutes an explosive:

Explosives Act 1875

3 This Act shall apply to gunpowder and other explosives as defined by this section. The term "explosive" in this Act – (1) Means gunpowder, nitro-glycerine, dynamite, gun-cotton, blasting powders, fulminate of mercury of other metals, coloured fires, and every other substance, whether similar to those above mentioned or not, used or manufactured with a view to produce a practical effect by explosion or a pyrotechnic effect, and (2) includes fog-signals, fireworks, fuses, rockets, percussion caps, detonators, cartridges, ammunition of all descriptions, and every other adaptation or preparation of an explosive as above defined.

104 Her Majesty may, by Order in Council, declare that any substance which appears to Her Majesty to be specially dangerous to life or property by reason either of its explosive properties, or any process in the manufacture thereof being liable to explosion, shall be deemed to be an explosive within the meaning of this Act, and the provisions of this Act (subject to such exceptions, limitations and restrictions as may be specified in the Order) shall accordingly extend to such substance in like manner as if it were included in the term explosive in this Act.

Explosives Act 1883

9 (1) In this Act, unless the context otherwise requires, – the expression "explosive substance" shall be deemed to include any materials for making any explosive substance; also any apparatus, machine, implement, or materials used, or intended to be used, or adapted for causing, or aiding in causing, any explosion in or with any explosive substance; also any part of any such apparatus, machine or implement.

Dangerous Substances Act 1972

9 (1) In this Act, "explosive" means a substance of a kind used to produce a practical effect by explosion or a pyrotechnic effect or anything of which that substance is an integral part. (2) For the purpose of this Act, the Minister may by order define the composition, quality and character of any explosive, and may classify explosives.

The sections of these Acts creating the most serious criminal offences are reproduced at paras **9.109–9.113**.

The sections of these Acts creating the most serious criminal offences are reproduced at paras **9.109–9.113**.

7.20 Offences Against the Person Act 1861

12 Whosoever, by the explosion of gunpowder or other explosive substance, shall destroy or damage any building with intent to commit murder, shall be guilty of felony, and being convicted thereof shall be liable to be kept in penal servitude for life.

28 Whosoever shall unlawfully and maliciously, by the explosion of gunpowder or other explosive substance, burn, maim, disfigure, disable, or do any grievous bodily harm to any person, shall be guilty of felony, and being convicted thereof shall be liable, at the discretion of the court, to be kept in penal servitude for life or to be imprisoned and, if a male under the age of sixteen years, with or without whipping.

29 Whosoever shall unlawfully and maliciously cause any gunpowder or other explosive substance to explode, or send or deliver to or cause to be taken or received by any person any explosive substance or any other dangerous or noxious thing, or put or lay at any place, or cast or throw at or upon or otherwise apply to any person, any corrosive fluid or any destructive or explosive substance, with intent in any of the cases aforesaid to burn, maim, disfigure, or disable any person, or to do some grievous bodily harm to any person, shall, whether any bodily injury be effected or not, be guilty of felony, and being convicted thereof shall be liable, at the discretion of the court, to be kept in penal servitude for life or to be imprisoned and, if a male under the age of sixteen years, with or without whipping.

30   Whosoever shall unlawfully and maliciously place or throw in, into, upon, against, or near any building, ship or vessel any gunpowder or other explosive substance, with intent to do any bodily injury to any person, shall, whether or not any explosion take place, and whether or not any bodily injury be effected, be guilty of felony, and being convicted thereof shall be liable, at the discretion of the court, to be kept in penal servitude for any term not exceeding fourteen years and, if a male under the age of sixteen years, with or without whipping.

64   Whosoever shall knowingly have in his possession, or make or manufacture, any gunpowder, explosive substance, or any dangerous or noxious thing, or any machine, engine, instrument, or thing, with intent by means thereof to commit, or for the purpose of enabling any other person to commit, any of the felonies in this act mentioned, shall be guilty of misdemeanour, and being convicted thereof shall be liable, at the discretion of the court, to be imprisoned for any term not exceeding two years, with or without hard labour and, if a male under the age of sixteen years, with or without whipping.

Varying Words to Describe Possession

7.21   It can be seen from a reading of the Explosives Acts and the Firearms Acts that various different forms of wording are used to describe possession. It is difficult to understand why this is so. Each word of an Act must have a meaning. As differing words are used to describe what would seem, at first sight, to be a similar kind of relationship between a person and an article, each such word must have a different meaning. This construction must be put on the use of the three phrases in the Irish legislation of "possession", "having with" and "control". "Having with" is different in degree from "in possession". In *R v Kelt*[9] the Court of Appeal held that the distinction was one of fact and degree. They indicated that it was necessary when summing up a case in which the words "having with" were used to denote possession, that the judge should make it clear to the jury that possession was not enough; the law required the evidence to go a stage further and to establish that the accused had the article with him. The classic case of having a gun "with you" is when you are carrying it. However, the court concluded, even if the accused is not proved to have been carrying the gun he may have it "with him" if it is immediately available to him. In the result, if all that can be shown is possession in the sense that it is outside of a person's grab area, because it is merely in his house or in some other hiding place, mere possession is proved which is insufficient. A similar phrase "has with him" is also used in s 18(1) of the Firearms Act (Northern Ireland) 1969. In *R v Murphy*[10] Lord McDermott indicated that the firearm had to be with the offender. If the weapon is put down for a moment so that it can be retaken at once he continues to have it "with him". What the section does not cover is a more remote form of control which is enough to satisfy the test for possession. Lord McDermott gave the example of a burglar who drives to the scene of a crime and leaves his car with his pistol inside it on the road opposite the house he breaks into. When arrested the burglar will have an answer to a charge of "having a firearm with him" but none to a charge of having

9   (1977) 65 Cr App R 74.
10 [1971] N1 183.

possession. In *R v Pawlicki*[11] the Divisional Court, following this line of authority, indicated that a separation in terms of space did not mean that guns were not "with" the accused. It was sufficient that the guns were readily accessible to him at the time when he wanted them, in this case for the purpose of robbery.

It is difficult to say what the phrase "under his control" means. It clearly denotes a more personal form of possession than that which occurs when the accused possesses a weapon through the activity of an accomplice. It may be that by using the phrase the Oireachtas were excluding the normal application of the doctrine of common design.

Offensive Weapons

7.22   Another example of a scheme to control the use of dangerous articles is seen in the Firearms and Offensive Weapons Act 1990. The origin of this reform was the report of the Law Reform Commission on Vagrancy and Related Offences[12]. The purpose of the legislation is to ensure that dangerous articles, such as knives, flick-knives, hatchets, spears and crossbows are not possessed unless the person has a lawful excuse. A lawful excuse, in these circumstances, would be present where, for example, a butcher has possession of a large knife but is on his way to use it in his butcher's shop. In the absence of such an excuse a person in possession of such a weapon is guilty of an offence. The relevant sections are now quoted:

7.23   *Firearms and Offensive Weapons Act 1990*

Part III

Offensive Weapons

Possession of knives and other articles

9   (1) Subject to *subsections (2)* and *(3)*, where a person has with him in any public place any knife or any other article which has a blade or which is sharply pointed, he shall be guilty of an offence.

(2) It shall be a defence for a person charged with an offence under *subsection (1)* to prove that he had good reason or lawful authority for having the article with him in a public place.

(3) Without prejudice to the generality of *subsection (2)*, it shall be a defence for a person charged with an offence under *subsection (1)* to prove that he had the article with him for use at work or for a recreational purpose.

(4) Where a person, without lawful authority or reasonable excuse (the onus of proving which shall lie on him), has with him in any public place—

(a)   any flick-knife, or
(b)   any other article whatsoever made or adapted for use for causing injury to or incapacitating a person,

he shall be guilty of an offence.

(5) Where a person has with him in any public place any article intended by him unlawfully to cause injury to, incapacitate or intimidate any person either in a

---

11 The Independent, 6 April 1992.
12 (LRC 11–1985).

particular eventuality or otherwise, he shall be guilty of an offence.

(6) In a prosecution for an offence under *subsection (5)*, it shall not be necessary for the prosecution to allege or prove that the intent to cause injury, incapacitate or intimidate was intent to cause injury to, incapacitate or intimidate a particular person; and if, having regard to all the circumstances (including the type of the article alleged to have been intended to cause injury, incapacitate or intimidate, the time of the day or night, and the place), the court (or the jury as the case may be) thinks it reasonable to do so, it may regard possession of the article as sufficient evidence of intent in the absence of any adequate explanation by the accused.

(7)(*a*) A person guilty of an offence under *subsection (1)* shall be liable on summary conviction to a fine not exceeding £1,000 or to imprisonment for a term not exceeding twelve months or to both.

(*b*) A person guilty of an offence under *subsection (4)* or *(5)* shall be liable—

(i) on summary conviction, to a fine not exceeding £1,000 or to imprisonment for a term not exceeding twelve months or to both, or

(ii) on conviction on indictment, to a fine or to imprisonment for a term not exceeding five years or to both.

(8) In this section "public place" includes any highway and any other premises or place to which at the material time the public have or are permitted to have access, whether on payment or otherwise, and includes any club premises and any train, vessel or vehicle used for the carriage of persons for reward.

(9) In this section "flick-knife" means a knife—

(*a*) which has a blade which opens when hand pressure is applied to a button, spring, lever or other device in or attached to the handle, or

(*b*) which has a blade which is released from the handle or sheath by the force of gravity or the application of centrifugal force and when released is locked in an open position by means of a button, spring, lever or other device.

Trespassing with a knife, weapon of offence or other article

10 (1) Where a person is on any premises as defined in *subsection (2)* as a trespasser, he shall be guilty of an offence if he has with him—

(*a*) any knife or other article to which *section 9(1)* applies, or

(*b*) any weapon of offence (as defined in *subsection (2)*),

(2) In this section—

"premises" means any building, any part of a building and any land ancillary to a building;

"weapon of offence" means any article made or adapted for use for causing injury to or incapacitating a person, or intended by the person having it with him for such use.

(3) A person guilty of an offence under this section shall be liable—

(*a*) on summary conviction, to a fine not exceeding £1,000 or to imprisonment for a term not exceeding twelve months or to both, or

(*b*) on conviction on indictment, to a fine or to imprisonment for a term not exceeding five years or to both.

Production of article capable of inflicting serious injury

11 Where a person, while committing or appearing to be about to commit an offence, or in the course of a dispute or fight, produces in a manner likely unlawfully to intimidate another person any article capable of inflicting serious injury, he shall be guilty of an offence and shall be liable—

    (*a*) on summary conviction, to a fine not exceeding £1,000 or to imprisonment for a term not exceeding twelve months or to both, or

    (*b*) on conviction on indictment, to a fine or to imprisonment for a term not exceeding five years or to both.

Power to prohibit manufacture, importation, sale, hire or loan of offensive weapons

12   (1) Any person who—

    (*a*) manufactures, sells or hires, or offers or exposes for sale or hire, or by way of business repairs or modifies, or

    (*b*) has in his possession for the purpose of sale or hire or for the purpose of repair or modification by way of business, or

    (*c*) puts on display, or lends or gives to any other person,

a weapon to which this section applies shall be guilty of an offence.

(2) Where an offence under *subsection (1)* is committed by a body corporate and is proved to have been so committed with the consent or connivance of or to be attributable to any neglect on the part of a director, manager, secretary or other officer of the body corporate, the director, manager, secretary or other officer or any person purporting to act in such capacity shall also be guilty of an offence.

(3) A person guilty of an offence under this section shall be liable—

    (*a*) on summary conviction, to a fine not exceeding £1,000 or to imprisonment for a term not exceeding twelve months or to both, or

    (*b*) on conviction on indictment, to a fine or to imprisonment for a term not exceeding five years or to both.

(4) The Minister may by order direct that this section shall apply to any description of weapon specified in the order except any firearm subject to the *Firearms Acts*, 1925 to 1990.

(5) The Minister may by order amend or revoke an order made under this section.

(6) The importation of a weapon to which this section applies is hereby prohibited.

(7) Every order made under this section shall be laid before each House of the Oireachtas as soon as may be after it is made and, if a resolution annulling the order is passed by either such House within the next 21 days on which that House has sat after the order is laid before it, the order shall be annulled accordingly, but without prejudice to the validity of anything previously done thereunder.

Forfeiture of weapons and other articles

13   (1) Where a person is convicted of an offence under this Part, the court by or before which he is convicted may order any article in respect of which the offence was committed to be forfeited and either destroyed or otherwise disposed of in such manner as the court may determine.

(2) An order under this section shall not take effect until the ordinary time for instituting an appeal against the conviction or order concerned has expired or, where such an appeal is instituted, until it or any further appeal is finally decided or abandoned or the ordinary time for instituting any further appeal has expired.

Power of arrest without warrant

14   A member of the Garda Síochána may arrest without warrant any person who is, or whom the member, with reasonable cause, suspects to be, in the act of committing an offence under *section 9, 10 or 11*.

Search warrants

15 If a justice of the District Court or a Peace Commissioner is satisfied on the sworn information of a member of the Garda Síochána that there are reasonable grounds for suspecting that an offence under *section 12* has been or is being committed on any premises, he may issue a warrant under his hand authorising a specified member of the Garda Síochána, accompanied by such other members of the Garda Síochána as the member thinks necessary, at any time or times within one month from the date of the issue of the warrant, on production if so requested of the warrant, to enter, if need be by force, and search the premises specified in the warrant and to seize anything found there that he believes on reasonable grounds may be required to be used in evidence in any proceedings for an offence under *section 12* or an offence under the Customs Acts in relation to the importation into the State of a weapon to which *section 12* applies.

Power of search without warrant

16 (1) This section applies to a situation where a number of people are congregated in any public place (within the meaning of *section 9(8)*) and a breach of the peace is occurring, or a member of the Garda Síochána has reasonable grounds for believing that a breach of the peace has occurred, or may occur, in that place when the people were or are congregated there.

(2) If in a situation to which this section applies a member of the Garda Síochána suspects with reasonable cause that a person has with him any article in contravention of *section 9*, he may search him in order to ascertain whether this is the case.

(3) If in a situation to which this section applies a member of the Garda Síochána suspects with reasonable cause that some one or more of the people present has or have with him or them an article or articles in contravention of *section 9*, then, even if the member has no reason to suspect that any particular one of the people present has with him any such article, the member may search any of those people if he considers that a search is necessary in order to ascertain whether any of them has with him any such article or articles.

Extension of section 8 of Criminal Law Act 1976

17 Section 8 of the Criminal Law Act 1976, is herby amended by the insertion in *subsection (1)* after *paragraph (i)* of the following paragraph:

> "(*j*) an offence under *section 12(1)* of the *Firearms and Offensive Weapons Act 1990*.".

Repeal of portion of section 4 of Vagrancy Act 1824

18 Section 4 of the Vagrancy Act 1824 (as extended to Ireland by *section 15* of the Prevention of Crimes Act 1871), is hereby amended by the deletion of "or being armed with any gun, pistol, hanger, cutlass, bludgeon, or other offensive weapon," and "and every such gun, pistol, hanger, cutlass, bludgeon, or other offensive weapon,".

Code Options

7.24 *Canadian Criminal Code*

4 (3) For the purposes of this Act,

(*a*) a person has anything in possession when he has it in his personal possession or knowingly (i) has it in the actual possession or custody of another person, or (ii) has it in any place, whether or not that place belongs to or is

439

occupied by him, for the use or benefit of himself or of another person; and

(*b*) where one or two or more persons, with the knowledge and consent of the rest, has anything in his custody or possession, it shall be deemed to be in the custody and possession of each and all of them.

Permissive Offences

7.25   As we have seen in the context of manslaughter, the law does not require a person to intervene to prevent a crime. Modern statutes may reverse this trend in circumstances which indicate that a person bears a sufficient relationship of authority to a place in order to prevent an activity. The principle was laid down in *R v Coney*[13]. There a number of persons were charged with aiding and abetting an assault, in the shape of an illegal prize-fight at Ascot. The accused were present at the spectacle as members of an audience. They played no part in the organisation or production of the attraction and offered no help, inducement or encouragement for the fight to take place. They were convicted on the basis of mere presence. The Court for Crown cases reversed the conviction on appeal. Hawkins J was careful to indicate that participation in a criminal offence had to be active and intentional:

"Encouragement does not of necessity amount to aiding and abetting, it may be intentional or unintentional, a man may unwittingly encourage another in fact by his presence, by misinterpreted words, or gestures, or of his silence, non-interference, or he may encourage intentionally by expression, gestures, or actions intended to signify approval. In the latter case he aids and abets, in the former he does not. It is no criminal offence to stand by, a mere passive spectator of a crime, even of a murder. Non-interference to prevent a crime is not itself a crime".

7.26   *Gaming and Lotteries Act 1956*

Use of places for unlawful gaming

5   No person shall open, keep or use any building, room or place, enclosed or unenclosed, or permit it to be opened, kept or used for unlawful gaming or take part in the care and management of or in any way assist in conducting the business of any building, room or place so opened, kept or used.

7.27   *Pawnbrokers Act 1964*

Notification by Garda Síochána of lost and stolen property

35   (1) It shall be the duty of every Superintendent of the Garda Síochána to notify forthwith and to give a full description to all pawnbrokers within the district to which he is attached of any property lost, stolen or otherwise fraudulently obtained or disposed of.

(2) Where a pawnbroker is offered or shown or has in his possession property of a description notified to him under *subsection (1)* of this section, he shall without delay inform a member of the Garda Síochána at the nearest Garda Síochána station of the fact and shall take all reasonable steps to detain any person offering or showing such property and seize the property and to deliver the person and the

13 (1882) 8 QBD 534.

property as soon as practicable into the custody of a member of the Garda Síochána.

(3) A pawnbroker who fails to comply with a requirement of *subsection (2)* of this section shall be guilty of an offence.

7.28   *Intoxicating Liquor (Licensing) Act 1872*

13   If any licensed person permits drunkenness or any violent, quarrelsome, or riotous conduct to take place on his premises, or sells any . . . he shall be guilty of an offence.

14   If any licensed person knowingly permits his premises to be the habitual resort of or place of meeting of reputed prostitutes, whether the object of their so resorting or meeting is or is not prostitution, he shall if he allows them to remain thereon longer than is necessary for the purpose of obtaining reasonable refreshment, be guilty of an offence.

7.29   *Tansley v Painter*
[1969] Crim LR 139
Queen's Bench Divisional Court, 1969

Facts: D1 and D2 were charged with being in unauthorised possession of amphetamine sulphate, contrary to section 1 of the Drugs (Prevention of Misuse) Act 1964. The evidence was that both defendants had been sitting in D2's car, and that D2 was selling drugs from the car; amphetamine sulphate tablets were found in the car and the boot and a sample of D1's urine given shortly after his arrest showed the presence of amphetamine. D2 pleaded guilty to the offence, but D1 claimed that he knew nothing of the sale of the drugs nor that they were in the car. The justices disbelieved that evidence and admitted the evidence of the urine analysis notwithstanding D1's evidence that he had not given the sample willingly. They convicted him and he appealed.

Lord Parker CJ: . . . the question is not whether D1 knew what was going on but whether he was a party to a joint venture. Mere knowledge of what D2 was doing was not sufficient. There was no evidence entitling the justices to convict, although they had acted properly in admitting the evidence about the urine sample. That evidence could not support the conviction because D1 was not charged with possessing the amphetamine in the sample and the analysis was not evidence of possessing the amphetamine in the car; nor was it corroboration that D1 was in possession of the amphetamine.

Drugs

7.30   Very often, in drug prosecutions, a particular location would be used, on a temporary basis, to sell drugs. If the enterprise is managed effectively the Gardaí may not be able to obtain evidence as to who is actually involved in the dealing. A typical situation involves a house being taken over in a populated area where there would be large demand, such as a flat complex. The doors and windows are heavily locked and dealing takes place through a letter box or window after couriers have alerted those demanding drugs to the location. In order to counter the situation whereby even the tenant of a flat or house would escape notwithstanding his presence while this activity took place, the Misuse of Drugs Act 1977 reversed the principle in *R v Coney*[14].

14 *Ibid.*

7.31   *Misuse of Drugs Act 1977*
                      as amended by the Misuse of Drugs Act 1984

19   (1) A person who is the occupier or is in control or is concerned in the
management of any land, vehicle or vessel and who knowingly permits or suffers
any of the following to take place on the land, vehicle or vessel, namely—

  (*a*) the cultivation contrary to *section 17* of this Act of opium poppy or any
         plant of the genus Cannabis, (or any plant of the genus Erythroxylon),
  (*b*) the preparation of opium for smoking,
  (*c*) the preparation of cannabis for smoking,
  (*d*) the smoking of cannabis, cannabis resin or prepared opium,
  (*e*) the manufacture, production or preparation of a controlled drug in con-
         travention of regulations made under *section 5* of this Act,
  (*f*) the importation or exportation of a controlled drug in contravention of such
         regulations,
  (*g*) the sale, supply or distribution of a controlled drug in contravention of such
         regulations,
  (*h*) any attempt so to contravene such regulations, or
  (*i*) the possession of a controlled drug in contravention of *section 3* of this Act,
         shall be guilty of an offence.

Malice

7.32   Malice is an ancient concept in criminal law denoting a guilty state of
mind. It has fallen out of use in modern language. The concept of malice
aforethought was, for example, replaced by a statutory definition of intent in
the case of murder. Many older statutes employ the concept and it is thus of
importance to use the appropriate standard definition.

7.33   *R v Cunningham*
               [1957] 2 QB 396; [1957] 2 All ER 412; [1957] 3 WLR 76;
                          (1957) 41 Cr App R 155
                    Court of Criminal Appeal England, 1957

Facts: The appellant stole a gas meter and its contents from the cellar of a house
and in so doing fractured a gas pipe. Coal gas escaped, percolated through the
cellar wall to the adjoining house, and entered a bedroom with the result that W.,
who was asleep, inhaled a considerable quantity of the gas. The appellant was
charged on an indictment preferred under the Offences Against the Person Act
1861, s 23, with unlawfully and maliciously causing W to take a noxious thing,
namely, coal gas, so as thereby to endanger her life. The judge directed the jury
that "maliciously" meant "wickedly" – doing "something which he has no business
to do "and perfectly well knows it".

Byrne J: At the close of the case for the prosecution, Mr Brodie, who appeared for
the appellant at the trial and who has appeared for him again in this court,
submitted that there was no case to go to the jury, but the judge, quite rightly in
our opinion, rejected this submission. The appellant did not give evidence.
   The act of the appellant was clearly unlawful and therefore the real question for
the jury was whether it was also malicious within the meaning of section 23 of the
Offences against the Person Act 1861.
   Before this court Mr Brodie has taken three points, all dependent upon the
construction of that section. Section 23 provides:

"Whosoever shall unlawfully and maliciously administer to or cause to be administered to or taken by any other person any poison or other destructive or noxious thing, so as thereby to endanger the life of such person, or so as thereby to inflict upon such person any grievous bodily harm, shall be guilty of felony . . ."

Mr Brodie argued, first, that *mens rea* of some kind is necessary. Secondly, that the nature of the *mens rea* required is that the appellant must intend to do the particular kind of harm that was done, or, alternatively, that he must foresee that that harm may occur yet nevertheless continue recklessly to do the act. Thirdly, that the judge misdirected the jury as to the meaning of the word "maliciously." He cited the following cases: *Reg v Pembliton*,[15] *Reg v Latimer*[16] and *Reg v Faulkner*.[17] In reply, Mr Snowden, on behalf of the Crown, cited *Reg v Martin*.[18]

We have considered those cases, and we have also considered, in the light of those cases, the following principle which was propounded by the late Professor C. S. Kenny in the first edition of his Outlines of Criminal Law published in 1902 and repeated at p 186 of the 16th edition edited by Mr J. W. Cecil Turner and published in 1952:

["In any statutory definition of a crime, malice must be taken not in the old vague sense of wickedness in general but as requiring either (1) An actual intention to do the particular kind of harm that in fact was done; or (2) recklessness as to whether such harm should occur or not (ie, the accused has foreseen that the particular kind of harm might be done and yet has gone on to take the risk of it). It is neither limited to nor does it indeed require any ill will towards the person injured."]

The same principle is repeated by Mr Turner in his 10th edition of Russell on Crime at p 1592.

We think that this is an accurate statement of the law. It derives some support from the judgments of Lord Coleridge CJ and Blackburn J in *Pembliton's* case. In our opinion the word "maliciously" in a statutory crime postulates foresight of consequence.

In his summing-up Oliver J directed the jury as follows:

"You will observe that there is nothing there about 'with intention that that person should take it.' He has not got to intend that it should be taken; it is sufficient that by his unlawful and malicious act he causes it to be taken. What you have to decide here, then, is whether, when he loosed that frightful cloud of coal gas into the house which he shared with this old lady, he caused her to take it by his unlawful and malicious action. 'Unlawful' does not need any definition. It is something forbidden by law. What about 'malicious'? 'Malicious' for this purpose means wicked – something which he has no business to do and perfectly well knows it. 'Wicked' is as good a definition as any other which you would get."

"The facts which face you (and they are uncontradicted and undisputed; the prisoner has not gone into the box to seek to give any particular explanation) are these. Living in the house, which was now two houses but which had once been one and had been rather roughly divided, the prisoner quite deliberately, intending to steal the money that was in the meter . . . broke the gas meter away from the supply pipes and thus released the mains supply of gas at large into that house. When he did that he knew that this old lady and her husband were living

15 (1874) LR 2 CCR 119.
16 (1886) 17 QBD 359; 2 TLR 626; 55 LJMC 135.
17 (1877) 13 Cox 550.
18 (1881) 8 QBD 54; 14 Cox CC 633.

next door to him. The gas meter was in a cellar. The wall which divided his cellar from the cellar next door was a kind of honeycomb wall through which gas could very well go, so that when he loosed that cloud of gas into that place he must have known perfectly well that gas would percolate all over the house. If it were part of this offence – which it is not – that he intended to poison the old lady, I should have left it to you to decide, and I should have told you that there was evidence on which you could find that he intended that, since he did an action which he must have known would result in that. As I have already told you, it is not necessary to prove that he intended to do it; it is quite enough that what he did was done unlawfully and maliciously."

With the utmost respect to the learned judge, we think it is incorrect to say that the word "malicious" in a statutory offence merely means wicked. We think the judge was, in effect, telling the jury that if they were satisfied that the appellant acted wickedly – and he had clearly acted wickedly in stealing the gas meter and its contents – they ought to find that he had acted maliciously in causing the gas to be taken by Mrs Wade so as thereby to endanger her life.

In our view it should have been left to the jury to decide whether, even if the appellant did not intend the injury to Mrs Wade, he foresaw that the removal of the gas meter might cause injury to someone but nevertheless removed it. We are unable to say that a reasonable jury, properly directed as to the meaning of the word "maliciously" in the context of section 23, would without doubt have convicted.

In these circumstances this court has no alternative but to allow the appeal and quash the conviction.

7.34 From January 1992 the basic offences of malicious damage, contrary to s 51 of the Malicious Damage Act 1861 as amended by s 12 of the Criminal Justice Act 1951, have been abolished. In its place the Criminal Damage Act 1991 has introduced various offences of criminal damage. The legislation is reproduced later in this chapter. It can be seen from the wording of charges reproduced in chapter 9, and from the wording of the sections of the Offences Against the Person Act 1861 reproduced in this chapter in the context of assault, that malice is still an important concept. Certain sections of the Malicious Damage Act 1861 have been retained and these are reproduced at para **7.56**.

Assault

7.35 Assault is the basis of a series of offences the penalty for which is provided by the Offences Against the Person Act 1861.

7.36 *Offences Against the Person Act 1861*

18 Whosoever shall unlawfully and maliciously by any means whatsoever wound or cause any grievous bodily harm to any person, or shoot any person, or, by drawing a trigger or in any other manner attempt to discharge any kind of loaded arms at any person, with intent in any of the cases aforesaid, to maim, disfigure, or disable any person, or to do some other grievous bodily harm to any person, or with intent to resist or prevent the lawful apprehension or detainer of any person, shall be guilty of felony, and being convicted thereof shall be liable to be kept in penal servitude for life.

20 Whosoever shall unlawfully and maliciously wound or inflict any grievous bodily harm upon any other person, either with or without any weapon or instrument, shall be guilty of a misdemeanour, and being convicted thereof shall be liable to be kept in penal servitude for the term of five years.

27 Whosoever shall unlawfully abandon or expose any child, being under the age of two years, whereby the life of such child shall be endangered, or the health of such child shall have been or shall be likely to be permanently injured, shall be guilty of a misdemeanour, and being convicted thereof shall be liable to be kept in penal servitude for the term of five years.

31 Whosoever shall set or place, or cause to be set or placed, any spring gun, man trap, or other engine calculated to destroy human life or inflict grievous bodily harm, with the intent that the same or whereby the same may destroy or inflict grievous bodily harm upon a trespasser or other person coming into contact therewith, shall be guilty of a misdemeanour, and being convicted thereof shall be liable to be kept in penal servitude for the term of five years; and whosoever shall knowingly and wilfully permit any such spring gun, man trap, or other engine which may have been set or placed in any place then being in or afterwards coming into his possession or occupation by some other person to continue so set or placed, shall be deemed to have set and placed such gun, trap, or engine with such intent as aforesaid: provided that nothing in this section contained shall extend to make it illegal to set or place any gun or trap such as may have been or may be usually set or placed with the intent of destroying vermin: provided also, that nothing in this section shall be deemed to make it unlawful to set or place or cause to be set or placed, or to be continued set or placed, from sunset to sunrise, any spring gun, man trap, or other engine which shall be set or placed, or caused or continued to be set or placed, in a dwelling house, for the protection thereof.

38 Whosoever shall assault any person with intent to commit felony or shall assault, resist, or wilfully obstruct any Peace Officer, in the due execution of his duty, or any person act in aid of such officer, or shall assault any person with intent to resist or prevent the lawful apprehension or detainer of himself or of any other person for any offence, shall be guilty of a misdemeanour, and being convicted thereof shall be liable, at the discretion of the court, to be imprisoned for any term not exceeding two years, with or without hard labour.

47 Whosoever shall be convicted upon an indictment of any assault occasioning actual bodily harm shall be liable to be kept in penal servitude for the term of five years and whosoever shall be convicted upon an indictment for a common assault, shall be liable to be imprisoned for any term not exceeding one year, with or without hard labour.

Nature of Assault

7.37 In modern terminology the word "battery" has fallen out of use. An assault that occurs by creating the apprehension of immediate physical violence in the victim is now usually referred to as "psychic assault". The distinction between this kind of assault and battery is no longer valid but a discussion of the way in which an assault takes place is of use.

7.38   *C S Kenny – Outlines of the Criminal Law*
                                        11th edition, 1922

An "assault" is an unlawful attempt, or offer, with violence, to do a corporal hurt
to another[19]. A "battery" is an injury done to the person of a man in an angry,
revengeful, rude or insolent manner[20]. In other words, an assault is a movement
which attempts, or threatens, the unlawful application of force to another person;
whilst such an application itself, when actually effected, constitutes a battery.
Thus riding at a person is an assault, riding against him is a battery. A mere assault,
even without any battery, is not only a tort but also a misdemeanour. Hence if a
battery ensues, it does not enhance the degree of the crime; though it is important
as affording clear proof of the hostile intention of the movements which constitute
the assault. Usually, of course, both the two offences are committed together; and
the whole transaction is legally described as "an assault and battery". This became
shortened in popular language to "an assault"; and now the current speech even of
lawyers habitually uses that word as if synonymous with "battery".

Even in a battery, no actual harm need be done or threatened. The slightest
force will suffice, if it were exercised in a hostile spirit; thus merely spitting on a
person may amount to an indictable battery. The force applied (or threatened)
need not involve immediate contact between the assailant and the sufferer. Thus it
is sufficient if harm is done (or threatened) to a person's clothes without touching
his skin[21]. And, similarly, the hostile force may be exercised either directly or even
indirectly, as by striking a horse and thereby making it throw its rider[22].

To deprive another person of his liberty will usually involve either touching or
threatening to touch him; and thus the tort of false imprisonment usually involves
the crime of an assault[23]. But some bodily movement is essential to an assault or
battery; so that where there is only mere motionless obstruction[24] – as where a
cyclist is brought down by collision with a person who only stands still, however
wilfully, in front of him – no proceedings can be taken for assault. (The much
graver offence of "maliciously causing grievous bodily harm," may, however,
have been committed). Similarly, mere words, however threatening, can never
make an assault[25]. Yet they may unmake an assault; as in a case where a man laid
his hand menacingly on his sword, but at the same time said, "If it were not assize
time, I'd run you through the body[26]."

Alarm is essential to an assault. Hence if a person who strikes at another is so far
off that he cannot by possibility touch him, it is certainly no assault[27]. And it has
even been said that to constitute an assault there must, in all cases, be the means of
carrying the threat into effect[28]. Accordingly, whilst pointing a loaded pistol at a
person is undoubtedly an assault, it was held, in *Reg v James*[29], that it was no
assault to present an unloaded one. But in an earlier case, *Reg v St George*[30], it
was held, on the contrary, that if a person presents a firearm which he knows to be
unloaded at a man who does not know that it is unloaded, and who is so near that
(were it loaded) its discharge might injure him, an assault is committed.

---

19 Hawkins, PC c 62, s 1. An assault committed in a public place becomes an "Affray".
20 Ibid s 2. Cf Pollock on Torts, Bk II, chap 6.
21 Per Parke, B., in *Reg v Day*, 1 Cox 207.
22 Cf *Dodwell v Burford*, 1 mod 24.
23 I Hawk PC c 60, s 7; 4 Bl Comm 218.
24 *Innes v Wylie* 1 C and K 257.
25 I Hawk PC c 62, s 1.
26 *Tuberville v Savage* 1 Mod 3.
27 Com Dig Battery (C).
28 Per Tindal CJ, in *Stephens v Myers* (1830), 4 C and P 349.
29 (1844) 1 C and K 530.
30 (1840) 9 C & P 483; contrast 626.

This latter view, which makes the offence depend upon the alarm naturally (however mistakenly) aroused in the person threatened, is in accord with the Scotch law[31]; and it agrees with the predominance of authority in America, where this question has much more frequently come before the courts than in this country[32].

It may be regarded as now settled that poisoning, where the poison (as is usually the case) is taken by the sufferer's own hand, does not constitute an assault[33]. A contrary view was at one time taken in this country, and is still favoured in America[34]. But, on principle, it is essential to an assault that there should be a personal exertion of force by the assailant. If therefore the actual taking up of the cup or glass was the act of the person poisoned, there is no assault; even though he took it in consequence of the poisoner's false representation that it was harmless. This consideration seems to settle the controversy; irrespectively of the further arguments that poison, unlike an ordinary "battery", takes effect internally instead of externally, and acts chemically instead of mechanically. Hence, as we have seen[35], the statute 24 and 25 Vict c 100 distinguishes between the offence of causing bodily harm by an assault[36], and that of administering poison with intent to injure or annoy[37].

The exercise of force against the body of another man is not always unlawful[38]. The principal occasions on which (provided that the amount used is not more than is proportionate to the immediate need) it is legally justifiable are the following:

(1) In the furtherance of public authority; as in preventing a breach of the peace, or arresting a felon, or executing any process issued by a court of law. This has been already sufficiently considered in Homicide[39].

(2) In correcting either your own children, or the scholars or apprentices who have been placed under your authority. This right has also already been considered[40].

(3) In defending either (a) your person, or (b) your existing lawful possession of any property (whether it consist of lands or merely of goods).

"Nature prompts a man who is struck to resist; and he is justified in using such a degree of force as will prevent a repetition[41]." Nor is it necessary that he should wait to be actually struck, before striking in self-defence. If one party raise up a threatening hand, then the other may strike[42]. Nor is the right of defence limited to the particular person assailed; it includes all who are under any obligation, even though merely social and not legal, to protect him. The old authorities exemplify this by the cases of a husband defending his wife, a child his parent, a master his servant, or a servant his master[43]; (and perhaps the courts would now take a still

---

31 I Broun 394; and with Queensland law (QLR 1911, p 206).
32 See, for the liability, *Commonwealth v White* 100 Mass 407; and against it, *State v McKay* 44 Texas 43. In 1891 the Supreme Court of New South Wales pronounced for the liability (12 NSW 113); though in 1870 it had decided against it.
33 *Reg v Dilworth* 2 Moo and R 531; *Reg v Walkden* 1 Cox 282; *Reg v Hanson*, 2 C and K 912; and see per Hawkins, J., in *Reg v Clarence* LR 22 QBD at p 42.
34 *Commonwealth v Stratton* 114 Mass 303.
35 CS Kenny *Outlines of Criminal Law* pp 149–150.
36 Section 47.
37 Section 24.
38 Cf CS Kenny *Outlines of Criminal Law*, pp 102–111.
39 *Ibid* p 103.
40 *Ibid* p 109. It was upheld in 1910 for an apprentice as old as seventeen; Times, 30 November 1910.
41 Per Parke B, 2 Lewin 48.
42 *Ibid.*
43 Cf p 104, n 1 *supra*; *Reg v Rose* 15 Cox 540 (KSC 140).

more general view of this duty of the strong to protect the weak[44]). A familiar modern instance is the force exercised by the stewards of a public meeting, to remove those who persistently disturb it.

But the justification extends only to blows struck in sheer self-defence and not in revenge. Accordingly if, when all the danger is over and no more blows are really needed for defence, the defender nevertheless strikes one, he commits an assault and battery[45]. The numerous decisions that have been given as to the kind of weapons that may lawfully be used, to repel an assailant, are merely applications of this simple principle. Thus, as we have already seen[46], where a person is attacked with such extreme violence that his very life is in danger he is justified in even killing his assailant. But a mere ordinary assault must not be thus met by the use of firearms or other deadly weapons[47]. And, similarly, a knife is not usually a proper instrument of self-defence, but must only be employed where serious bodily danger is apprehended, or where a robbery (i.e., a theft by violence) is to be prevented[48]. Hence it is unjustifiable for a man to use it where the attack upon him is made with a mere strap. It should, however, be noted that where more force than was necessary has been used for self-defence, the case is not to be treated as if all the force employed had been illegal. The fact that part of it was justifiably exerted may, for instance, have the effect of reducing a charge of "wounding with intent to do grievous bodily harm" to one of mere unlawful wounding[49].

The right of self-defence extends, as we have said, to the defence not only of your person but also of your property, thus force may lawfully be used in expelling anyone who is trespassing in your house, or on your land, if no milder mode of getting rid of him would avail. Hence if his entry had itself been effected forcibly, as by a burglary or even by breaking open a gate, you may at once use force to expel him[50]. But in the case of an ordinary peaceful trespasser, it will not be until you have first requested him to depart, and he has failed to comply with the request, that you will be justified in ejecting him by the strong hand. Disturbance of an easement is a wrong in the nature of a trespass, and therefore force may be used to prevent it[51].

A similar right exists in the case of movable property. Force may accordingly be used to resist anyone who attempts to take away your goods from you[52]. And there is modern authority for saying that force may even be used to recapture your goods, after they have been actually taken out of your possession. But this alleged right to use force, not merely to protect an existing possession but to create one, is not beyond doubt[53]. In the case of real property it certainly does not exist. A landlord may commit an indictable offence by "forcibly entering" a house, although it is his own, if any full (though unlawful) possessor is excluding him[54]. For real property, unlike personal, is in no danger of being meanwhile destroyed, or lost, if the owner waits for the intervention of the law to recover it.

There is, again, a legal justification for the trifling degree of force involved in those petty instances of contact which inevitably arise in the ordinary social intercourse of everyday life[55]; such as tapping a friend's shoulder to attract his attention, or jostling past one's neighbour in a crowd. But, to be thus justifiable, these acts must be done *bona fide*, and with no unusual vehemence.

---

44 Bishop *Criminal Law of USA* 8th ed. 1 § 877.3. Cf 11, Mod 242.
45 *Reg v Driscoll* C and M 214 (KSC 151).
46 CS Kenny *Outlines of Criminal Law* p 103.
47 *Osborn v Veitch* 1 F and F 317 (KSC 150).
48 *Reg v Hewlett* 1 F and F 91 (KSC 150).
49 *Reg v Hunkey* 3 C and K 142.
50 *Green v Goddard* 2 Salk 641 (KSC 147).
51 *Bird v Jones* LR 7 QBD 742.
52 2 Rol Abr 548; *Green v Goddard* 2 Salk 641 (KSC 147).
53 See *Pollock on Torts* 6th ed at p 372.
54 *Newton v Harland* 1 M and G 744; cf LR 17 ChD at p 188.
55 *Hopper v Reeve* 7 Taunt 698.

(5) There is, further, a justification for acts that are done by consent of the person assaulted; unless the force be a breach of the peace, or be causelessly dangerous. *Volenti non fit injuria*. Hence seduction is no assault, either in the law of crime or even in that of tort[56].

But the consent must be given freely (i.e., without force, fear or fraud), and by a sane and sober person, so situated as to be able to form a reasonable opinion upon the matter to which consent is given[57]. For "fraud vitiates consent"; and accordingly an imposter who, by pretending to be a surgeon, induces an invalid to submit to be operated upon by him, will be guilty of assault, notwithstanding the consent which was nominally given. As regards the mental capacity to consent, it may be mentioned that, in the case of indecent assaults, the legislature has established a definite rule as to age, by enacting that consent given by a child of either sex under sixteen years of age shall not constitute a defence[58]. And, again, even the most complete consent, by the most competent person, will not suffice to legalise an assault which there are public grounds for prohibiting. Thus consent is no defence, criminally[59], for any assault that amounts to a breach of the peace. The public interests similarly preclude the consent of the person injured from affording any defence where the violence exercised (and consented to) involved some extreme and causeless injury to life, limb or health. If, therefore, one of the parties to a duel is injured, his consent is no excuse. Yet it is uncertain at what degree of danger the law thus takes away a man's right to consent to be placed in situations of peril, (as for instance, by allowing himself to be wheeled in a barrow along a tight-rope[60]). But in the case of a surgical operation carried out by a competent surgeon, however great be the risk, there will usually be adequate cause for running it; and so the patient's consent will be full justification for what would otherwise be an aggravated assault. And even injuries which are occasioned in the course of a mere game, if it be a lawful one and be played with due care, are not regarded as causeless[61].

These rules as to the amount of violence which constitutes an assault, and as to the circumstances which will excuse that violence, hold equally good in the law of tort and in the law of crime. But those two branches of law differ in their rules as to the state of mind which will render a man liable for the exercise of such violence as has been shown to be a forbidden act. In actions of tort, either intention or even mere negligence[62] – if the degree of negligence be gross – will suffice to render the wrong-doer liable to pay damages. But an assault will not render a man liable to criminal punishment unless it were committed with actual intention[63].

Forms of Assault

7.39   There are a vast number of forms of assault. These appear to be unnecessary. Some of them are stated in outdated language and further

---

56 *Pollock on Torts* 6th ed at p 226.
57 For a Submission is not always a Permission.
58 Criminal Law Amendment Act 1922.
59 *Reg v Coney* LR 8 QBD 534. 1 Vide supra, p 110. For the (disputed) effect of such consent upon the civil liability, see *Pollock on Torts* chap IV, s 11; *Kenny's Cases on Tort* at p 157.
60 But against juvenile acrobats, see the Children's Dangerous Performances Acts 1879 and 1897.
61 CS Kenny *Outlins of Criminal Law* at p 110.
62 *Weaver v Ward* Hobart 134; yet seen *Bigelow on Torts* 7th ed at p 374.
63 *Ackroyd v Barett* 11 TLR 115. But negligence in driving may, without any actual intention, suffice for the statutory misdemeanour of "causing bodily harm by wilful misconduct or wilful neglect when in charge of a carriage or vehicle" (eg even of a bicycle); 24 and 25 Vict c 100, s 35. In India, in the United States (*Wharton's Criminal Law* Bk IV, ch 8), and in Scotland (*Macdonald's Criminal Law* at p 154), negligence is held to be not sufficient to make assaults criminal.

7.39 *Other concepts*

offences are applicable to such specialised categories of victim as to appear ludicrous when read in modern language[64]. The Criminal Law Revision Committee indicated in its draft criminal code[65] that the law should be overhauled by the creation of three main offences:

(1) Intentionally causing serious injury, carrying a maximum of life imprisonment.
(2) Recklessly causing serious injury carrying a maximum penalty of five years imprisonment.
(3) Intentionally or recklessly causing injury carrying a maximum of three years imprisonment.

7.40 It is also necessary to seriously consider the application of the principle of criminal negligence in manslaughter to the causing of serious harm to others. There seems no reason in principle why a person can be convicted of manslaughter if, through his criminal negligence, death results to the victim. He can only be convicted of assault on the graver mental elements, which are more difficult to prove, of recklessness and intention, if his victim lives on, perhaps maimed for life.

Mental Element

7.41 Returning to first principles it seems obvious that where one offence is differentiated from another by the addition of an external element and a significantly increased penalty, the legislature is presumed to have intended that a mental element, in the form of either intention of recklessness, is required for the proof of that aggravating factor; *The People (DPP) v Murray*[66].

A series of cases had led to conflicting decisions in the Court of Appeal over the necessary mental element in offences under s 20 and s 47 of the Offences Against the Person Act 1861 (see para **7.36**). Clarifying the position, the House of Lords held that a verdict of assault occasioning actual bodily harm (s 47) might be returned merely upon proof of an assault together with proof of the fact that actual bodily harm was occasioned thereby. In order to establish the more serious offence under s 20, the prosecution must prove either that the defendant intended or that he actually foresaw that his act would cause physical harm to some person albeit it was only harm of a minor character. It is doubtful whether this approach could conform with the *Murray* decision.

7.42   *R v Savage and Parmenter*
[1991] 2 All ER 225; [1991] 2 WLR 408; (1991) 92 Cr App R 68 CA;
[1991] 4 All ER 698; [1991] 3 WLR 914 HL(E)
House of Lords, 1991

Lord Ackner: My Lords, these two appeals have been heard together, because they each raise the issue of the mental element which the prosecution have to

---

64 See further Charleton *Offences Against the Person* (1992) chapter 6.
65 (Cmnd) 1985.
66 [1977] IR 360.

450

establish in relation to offences under two sections of the Offences against the Person Act 1861, viz s 20, unlawfully and maliciously wounding or inflicting grievous bodily harm and s 47, assault occasioning actual bodily harm.

R v Savage

The facts and the decision of the Court of Appeal

On 3 October 1989 in the Crown Court at Durham the appellant, Mrs Savage was indicted and convicted on a single count of unlawful wounding contrary to s 20 of the Act, the particulars of the offence being that on 31 March 1989 she unlawfully and maliciously wounded Miss Beal. She was ordered to undertake 120 hours of community service. The victim, Miss Beal, was a former girlfriend of Mrs Savage's husband. There had been some bad feeling between these two young women, although they had never previously met. On the evening of 31 March 1989 they were both in the same public house, but not together. Mrs Savage pushed her way through to the table where Miss Beal was sitting with some friends. She had in her hand a pint glass which was nearly full of beer. Having said "Nice to meet you darling," she then threw the contents of the glass over Miss Beal. Unfortunately, not only was Miss Beal soaked by the beer, but, contrary to Mrs Savage's evidence, she must have let go of the glass, since it broke and a piece of it cut Miss Beal's wrist. The jury, by their verdict, concluded either that the appellant had deliberately thrown not only the beer but also the glass at Miss Beal or, alternatively, that while deliberately throwing the beer over Miss Beal, the glass has accidentally slipped from her grasp and it, or a piece of it, had struck Miss Beal's wrist, but with no intention that the glass should hit or cut Miss Beal. The material words of s 20 read: "20. Whosoever shall unlawfully and maliciously wound or inflict any grievous bodily harm upon any other person . . ." In the course of his summing up the recorder said:

> "It is alleged that on 31 March Mrs Savage unlawfully and maliciously wounded Tracey Beal. What does this mean? First of all it means that you must find Susan Savage did some unlawful action, unlawful in the sense that it was, not in self-defence and it was not a mere accident; malicious in the sense that it was deliberate and aimed against Tracey Beal, and that as a result of that unlawful, deliberate act aimed against Tracey Beal, Tracey Beal suffered a wound. . . . She went up to her . . . and threw deliberately the contents of a pint glass at her. That is an assault, that is an unlawful action aimed deliberately against Tracey Beal. Mrs Savage admits it. . . . If you were sure that in throwing the liquid from the glass she let go of the glass unintentionally, but in doing this unlawful act she let go of the glass and it struck Miss Beal, then that is a consequence of her unlawful act. If a wound resulted from it then that is unlawful wounding."

In the Court of Appeal reference was made to *Reg v Mowatt* [1968] 1 QB 421 and to the following statement in the judgment of Diplock LJ, giving the judgment of the court at p 426:

> "In the offence under s 20, and in the alternative verdict which may be given on a charge under s 18, for neither of which is any specific intent required, the word 'maliciously' does import upon the part of the person who unlawfully inflicts the wound or other grievous bodily harm an awareness that his act may have the consequence of causing some physical harm to some other person. That is what is meant by the 'particular kind of harm' in the citation from Professor Kenny. It is quite unnecessary that the accused should have foreseen that his unlawful act might cause physical harm of the gravity described in the section, ie, a wound or serious physical injury. It is enough that he should have foreseen that some physical harm to some person, albeit of a minor character, might result. In

451

many cases in instructing a jury upon a charge under s 20, or upon the alternative verdict which may be given under that section when the accused is charged under s 18, it may be unnecessary to refer specifically to the word 'maliciously.' "

The Court of Appeal observed that despite doubts which had been expressed about the above statement of the law, it was binding on the court and that the test imported by the words "maliciously" is a subjective and not an objective one. In the opinion of the Court of Appeal, it accordingly followed that the recorder was wrong to direct the jury that "malicious' meant deliberate and aimed at Tracey Beal with the result that a wound occurred. The recorder omitted to direct the jury that they had to find that Mrs Savage foresaw that some physical harm would follow as a result of what she did. The question as to whether she foresaw that her act was likely to cause some harm, other than wetting Miss Beal with the beer, was a question they should have been asked to consider. In view of this misdirection, the Court of Appeal quashed the verdict.

On 28 November 1990 the Court of Appeal gave leave to appeal, certifying the following points of law to be of general public importance:

"(1) Whether a verdict of guilty of assault occasioning actual bodily harm is a permissible alternative verdict on a count alleging unlawful wounding contrary to s 20 of the Offences Against the Persons Act 1861. (2) Whether a verdict of guilty of assault occasioning actual bodily harm can be returned upon proof of an assault and of the fact that actual bodily harm was occasioned by the assault. (3) If it is proved that an assault has been committed and that actual bodily harm has resulted from that assault, whether a verdict of assault occasioning actual bodily harm may be returned in the absence of proof that the defendant intended to cause some actual bodily harm or was reckless as to whether such harm would be caused."

Reg v Parmenter

The facts and the decision of the Court of Appeal

Paul Parmenter was born on 8 February 1988. Between that date and 11 May 1988 his father, the appellant, Philip Mark Parmenter caused his baby son to suffer injuries to the bony structures of the legs and right forearm. He was indicted on eight counts, six represented three paired alternatives, laid under s 18 and 20 of the Act, the seventh count alleged a separate offence under s 20, and the eighth count to which he pleaded guilty from the outset, alleged cruelty to a person under the age of 16. The only issue before the jury was whether Mr Parmenter had acted with the relevant intent, his case being that he did not realise that the way he handled the child would cause injury. At the conclusion of the trial in February 1989 at the Chelmsford Crown Court, Mr Parmenter was acquitted of the three s 18 offences and convicted of all four s 20 offences.

On the crucial issue of intent, the trial judge directed the jury as follows:

"Let me tell you what 'maliciously' means. First of all, let me tell you what it does not mean. If you and I meet in the corridor outside and we were discussing the word maliciously, one I rather expect would say, and I expect you would too, it means something like spiteful, something like that. That does not apply in the framework of this section of the Act of Parliament. Let me tell you what maliciously means, because in the circumstances of this case it is very important indeed. It is quite unnecessary that the accused should have foreseen that his unlawful act might cause physical harm of the type described in the section – and here comes the important part – it is enough that he should have foreseen that some physical harm to some person, albeit of a minor character, might result. Two of you are writing it down, I see. I say it again, like a shipping forecast; it is enough that he should have foreseen that some physical harm to some person, albeit of a minor character might result. That is what you have to consider. So, members of the jury, the questions that you have to ask yourselves on counts four, five and six only arise if he is not guilty on counts one, two and three, and they are these. Are we sure that he inflicted grievous bodily harm of the nature described in the indictment? If the answer to the question is yet then: are we sure that he should have foreseen that some physical harm, albeit of a minor character, might result? If the answer to that question is yes, he is guilty. If the answer to that question is no, he is not guilty.''

This direction was founded on *Reg v Mowatt* [1968] 1 QB 421 and in particular the following passage in the judgment, at pp 425–426:

"No doubt upon these facts the jury should be instructed that they must be satisfied before convicting the accused that he was aware that physical harm to some human being was a possible consequence of his unlawful act in wrenching off the gas meter. In the words of the court, 'maliciously in a statutory crime postulates foresight of consequence,' and upon this proposition we do not wish to cast any doubt. But the court in that case also expressed approval obiter of a more general statement by Professor Kenny, *Kenny's Outlines of Criminal Law*, 18th edn (1962), p 202 which runs as follows: 'in any statutory definition of a crime, "malice" must be taken not in the old vague sense of wickedness in general, but as requiring either (1) an actual intention to do the particular kind of harm that in fact was done, or (2) recklessness as to whether such harm should occur or not (ie the accused has foreseen that the particular kind of harm might be done, and yet has gone on to take the risk of it). It is neither limited to, nor does it indeed require, any ill will towards the person injured.'

"This generalisation is not, in our view, appropriate to the specific alternative statutory offences described in ss 18 and 20 of the Offences Against the Person Act 1861, and s 5 of the Prevention of Offences Act 1851, and if used in that form in the summing-up is liable to bemuse the jury. In s 18 the word 'maliciously' adds nothing. The intent expressly required by that section is more specific than such element of foresight of consequences as is implicit in the word 'maliciously' and in directing a jury about an offence under this section the word 'maliciously' is best ignored.

"In the offence under s 20, and in the alternative verdict which may be given on a charge under s 18, for neither of which is any specific intent required, the word 'maliciously' does import upon the part of the person who unlawfully inflicts the wound or other grievous bodily harm an awareness that his act may have the consequence of causing some physical harm to some other person. That is what is meant by 'the particular kind of harm' in the citation from Professor Kenny. It is quite unnecessary that the accused should have foreseen that his unlawful act might cause physical harm of the gravity described in the section, ie, a wound or serious physical injury. It is enough that he should have foreseen that some physical harm to some person, albeit of a minor character, might result."

It will be recalled that the final paragraph of the above quotation is that to which the Court of Appeal made specific reference in the *Savage* case.

The Court of Appeal then observed that at first sight it appeared that the direction given by the trial judge was quite unexceptionable, containing as it did a verbatim quotation from the *Mowatt* case [1968] 1 QB 421. However, on closer inspection it was apparent that he had inadvertently imparted a fundamental change to the principle laid down in *Mowatt*'s case. The Court of Appeal said [1991] 2 WLR 408, 411–412:

"It seems to us clear, when the judgment in *Mowatt* is read as a whole, that the court was stating two propositions, one positive and one negative. The positive proposition was that to found a conviction under s 20 it must be proved that the defendant *actually* foresaw that physical harm to some other person would be the consequnce of his act. This is subject to a negative qualification, that the defendant need not *actually* have foreseen that the harm would be as grave as that which in the event occurred.

"If one now returns to the summing up in the present case we find the judge posing the crucial question as follows: 'Are we sure that he inflicted grievous bodily harm of the nature described in the indictment? If the answer to the question is yes, then: are we sure that he should have foreseen that some physical harm, albeit of a minor character, might result? If the answer to that question is yes, he is guilty. If the answer to that question is no, he is not guilty.'

"In the judgment in *Mowatt* the words 'should have foreseen' were, we believe, intended to bear the same meaning as 'did foresee' or simply 'foresaw.' Read out of context, however, the ordinary meaning of the words 'should have' is 'ought to have.' By reading the passage to the jurors in isolation from its context the judge thus inadvertently created a real risk that the jurors would believe that they were being directed to ask themselves, not whether the appellant *actually* foresaw that his acts would cause injury, but whether he *ought to have* foreseen it. Indeed we would be prepared to go further and say that this is the natural understanding of the passage which we have just quoted. At any rate, whether we are right in this or not there was an ambiguity which went to the heart of the case, for while there was a possibility that the jury might feel doubt about whether the appellant actually intended to injure the child, there seems on the evidence to have been little room for question that, judged objectively, he 'should have' realised that what he did would lead to injury."

The Court of Appeal accordingly quashed the convictions on the four counts under s 20 (the trial judge had in fact fallen into the same error as that made by the judge in *Reg v Grimshaw* [1984] Crim LR 108). The court then had to consider whether they could and should substitute for the convictions which they had quashed, alternative verdicts of guilty under s 47 of the Act.

They then discovered that a curious situation had emerged, namely, that two different divisions of the Court of Appeal (Criminal Division) had, contemporaneously but unwittingly, delivered judgments on the necessary intent in section 47, but had unfortunately reached opposite conclusions, *Savage* was one of those cases and the other is *Reg v Spratt* [1990] 1 WLR 1073.

Reg v Spratt
The facts and the decision of the Court of Appeal

A young girl was struck twice whilst playing in the forecourt of a block of flats by two airgun pellets, which had been fired from a window by the appellant. He admitted to the police that he had fired a few shots out of the window, not in order to hit anyone, but to see how far the pellets would go. He was duly charged with an offence under s 47 of the Act to which he pleaded guilty. The basis of that plea, as was explained to the trial judge, was that the appellant accepted that he had been reckless, and that his recklessness took the shape of a failure to give any thought to the possibility of a risk. However, it was contended on his behalf that if he had known there were children in the area, he would not have fired the shots. The judge imposed a sentence of 30 months' imprisonment, against which the appellant appealed. When the matter came before the full court, the court itself raised the question whether, if the facts asserted on the appellant's behalf were true, he had in law committed the offence to which he had pleaded guilty. Subsequently leave was given to pursue an appeal against conviction. On the appeal it was argued for the Crown that the appellant ought objectively to have appreciated that there was a risk, and that this was enough to establish an offence under s 47, albeit that in the light of the decision of the Court of Appeal in *Reg v Cunningham* [1957] 2 QB 396, to which further reference will be made hereafter, this would not be sufficient for the purpose of s 20. The court, having considered a number of subsequent cases, including in particular three decisions of your Lordships' House, namely, *Reg v Caldwell* [1982] AC 341, *Reg v Lawrence (Stephen)* [1982] AC 510 and *Reg v Seymour (Edward)* [1983] 2 AC 493 concluded that the "subjective type of recklessness" furnished the test for ss 20 and 47 alike and that this had been decided by the Court of Appeal in *Reg v Venna* [1976] QB 421, also a case to which further reference will be made hereafter.

In *Reg v Spratt* [1990] 1 WLR 1073 McCowan LJ giving the judgment of the court said, at pp 1082–1083:

"Finally, Mr Arlidge argues that while *Reg v Venna* [1976] QB 421 says that *Cunningham* recklessness will amount to guilt under s 47, it does not say that nothing else will do. In other words, it is now possible to add on failure to give thought to the possibility of risk as also qualifying for guilt. We do not accept that interpretation of the decision in *Reg v Venna*. Moreover, we are not attracted by what would be the consequence of accepting Mr Arlidge's argument, namely that responsibility for the offence of assault occasioning actual bodily harm (in respect of which Parliament used neither the word 'maliciously' nor 'recklessly') would be wider than for the offence of unlawful wounding (in respect of which Parliament used the word 'maliciously')."

In relation to these two decisions, *Savage* and *Spratt*, the Court of Appeal in the *Parmenter* case [1991] 2 WLR 408 concluded that in one respect they were in harmony. Where the defendant neither intends nor adverts to the possibility that there will be any physical contact at all, then the offence under s 47 would not be made out. That is because there would have been no assault, let alone an assault occasioning actual bodily harm. Further there was no conflict where the defendant does advert to the possibility of harm, albeit not necessarily of the kind which actually happened. In such a case there clearly would be an assault. However, the two decisions were in conflict as to whether an intent is required in relation to the consequences of the assault. The Court of Appeal having decided to prefer the decision in the *Spratt* case, asked themselves whether there was implicit in the s 20 verdicts (given in the light of a direction in terms of "objective intent") a finding that the appellant subjectively intended or recognised the risk of physical harm. Understandably they concluded that the answer must be in the negative. Accordingly the court allowed the appeal, declining to substitute any other verdict on those counts where the convictions were quashed. The court concluded by observing, at p 417, that the authorities on the intent required in ss 20 and 47:

"can no longer live together, and that the reason lies in a collision between two ideas, logically and morally sustainable in themselves, but mutually inconsistent, about whether the unforeseen consequences of a wrongful act should be punished according to the intent (*Reg v Cunningham* [1957] 2 QB 396) or the consequences (*Reg v Mowatt* [1968] 1 QB 421)."

On 6 November 1990 the Court of Appeal granted leave to appeal to your Lordships' House and certified the following points of law to be of general public importance:

"(1)(a) Whether in order to establish an offence under s 20 of the Offences Against the Person Act 1861 the prosecution must prove that the defendant actually foresaw that his act would cause the particular kind of harm which was in fact caused, or whether it is sufficient to prove that (objectively) he ought so to have foreseen. (b) The like question in relation to s 47 of the Act. (2)(a) For the purposes of the answer to question (1)(a), whether the particular kind of harm to be foreseen may be any physical harm, or harm of (i) the nature, or (ii) the degree, or (iii) the nature and the degree of the harm which actually occurred? (b) The like question in relation to s 47 of the Act."

It will be observed that some of the certified questions in *Parmenter* overlap with those in *Savage*.

My Lords, I will now seek to deal with the issues raised by these appeals seriatim.

. . . 2. *Can a verdict of assault occasioning actual bodily harm be returned upon proof of an assault together with proof of the fact that actual bodily harm was occasioned by the assault, or must the prosecution also prove that the defendant intended to cause some actual bodily harm or was reckless as to whether such harm would be caused?*

Your Lordships are concerned with the mental element of a particular kind of assault, an assault "occasioning actual bodily harm." It is common ground that the mental element of assault is an intention to cause the victim to apprehend immediate and unlawful violence or recklessness whether such apprehension be caused: see *Reg v Venna* [1976] QB 421. It is of course common ground that Mrs Savage committed an assault upon Miss Beal when she threw the contents of her glass of beer over her. It is also common ground that however the glass came to be broken and Miss Beal's wrist thereby cut, it was, on the finding of the jury, Mrs Savage's handling of the glass which caused Miss Beal "actual bodily harm." Was the offence thus established or is there a further mental state that has to be established in relation to the bodily harm element of the offence? Clearly the section, by its terms, expressly imposes no such a requirement. Does it do so by necessary implication? It neither uses the word "intentionally" or "maliciously." The words "occasioning actual bodily harm" are descriptive of the word "assault," by reference to a particular kind of consequence.

In neither *Savage*, nor *Spratt* nor in *Parmenter*, was the court's attention invited to the decision of the Court of Appeal in *Reg v Roberts* (1971) 56 Cr App R 95. This is perhaps explicable on the basis that this case is not referred to in the index to the current, edition of *Archbold, Criminal Pleading, Evidence and Practice*, 43rd edn (1988). The relevent text, at para 20-117 states: "The *mens rea* required [for actual bodily harm] is that required for common assault" without any authority being provided for this proposition.

It is in fact *Roberts'* case which provides authority for this proposition, Roberts was tried on an indictment which alleged that he indecently assaulted a young woman. He was acquitted on that charge, but convicted of assault occasioning actual bodily harm to her. The girl's complaint was that while travelling in the defendant's car he sought to make advances towards her and then tried to take her coat off. This was the last straw, and although the car was travelling at some speed, she jumped out and sustained injuries. The defendant denied he had touched the girl. He had had an argument with her and in the course of that argument she suddenly opened the door and jumped out. In his direction to the jury the chairman of Quarter Sessions stated "If you are satisfied that he tried to pull off her coat and as a result she jumped out of the moving car then your verdict is guilty."

It was contended on behalf of the appellant that this direction was wrong since the chairman had failed to tell the jury that they must be satisfied that the appellant foresaw that she might jump out of the car as a result of his touching her, before they could convict. The court rejected that submission. The test, said the court, at p 102:

"Was it [the action of the victim which resulted in actual bodily harm] the natural result of what the alleged assailant said and did, in the sense that it was something that could reasonably have been foreseen as the consequence of what he was saying or doing? As it was put in one of the old cases, it had got to be shown to be his act, and if of course the victim does something so 'daft,' in the words of the appellant in this case, or so unexpected, not that this particular assailant did not actually foresee it but that no reasonable man could be expected to foresee it, then it is only in a very remote and unreal sense a consequence of his assault, it is really occasioned by a voluntary act on the part of the victim which could not reasonably be foreseen and which breaks the chain of causation between the assault and the harm or injury."

Accordingly no fault was found in the following direction of the chairman to the jury, at p 103:

"if you accept the evidence of the girl in preference to that of the man, that means that there was an assault occasioning actual bodily harm, that means that she did jump out as a direct result of what he was threatening her with, and what he was doing to her, holding her coat, telling her he had beaten up girls who had refused his advances, and that means that through his acts he was in law and in fact responsible for the injuries which were caused to her by her decision, if it can be called that, to get away from his violence, his threats, by jumping out of the car."

Thus once the assault was established, the only remaining question was whether the victim's conduct was the natural consequence of that assault. The words "occasioning" raised solely a question of causation, an objective question which does not involve inquiring into the accused's state of mind. In *Reg v Spratt* [1990] 1 WLR 1073 McCowan LJ said, at p 1082:

"However, the history of the interpretation of the Act of 1861 shows that, whether or not the word 'maliciously' appears in the section in question, the courts have consistently held that the *mens rea* of every type of offence against the person covers both actual intent and recklessness, in the sense of taking the risk of harm ensuing with foresight that it might happen."

McCowan LJ then quotes a number of authorities for that proposition. The first is *Reg v Ward* (1872) LR 1 CCR 356, but that was a case where the prisoner was charged with wounding with intent (s 18) and convicted of malicious wounding (s 20); next, *Reg v Bradshaw* (1878) 14 Cox CC 83, but that was a case where the accused was charged with manslaughter, which has nothing to do with a s 47 case. Then *Reg v Cunningham* [1957] 2 QB 396, is quoted, a case under s 23 of the Act concerned with unlawfully and maliciously administering, etc, a noxious thing which endangers life. And finally *Reg v Venna* [1976] QB 421 in which there was no issue as to whether in a s 47 case, recklessness had to extend to actual bodily harm. Thus, none of the cases cited were concerned with the mental element required in s 47 cases. Nevertheless, the Court of Appeal in *Reg v Parmenter* [1991] 2 WLR 408, 415, preferred the decision in *Reg v Spratt* [1990] 1 WLR 1073 to that of *Reg v Savage* (Note) [1991] 2 WLR 418 because the former was "founded on a line of authority leading directly to the conclusion there expressed."

My Lords, in my respectful view, the Court of Appeal in *Parmenter* were wrong in preferring the decision in *Spratt*'s case. The decision in *Roberts*' case, 56 Cr App R 95 was correct. The verdict of assault occasioning actual bodily harm may be returned upon proof of an assault together with proof of the fact that actual bodily harm was occasioned by the assault. The prosecution are not obliged to prove that the defendant intended to cause some actual bodily harm or was reckless as to whether such harm would be caused.

3. In order to establish an offence under s 20 of the Act, must the prosecution prove that the defendant actually foresaw that his act would cause harm, or is it sufficient to prove that he ought so to have foreseen?

Although your Lordships' attention has been invited to a plethora of decided cases, the issue is a narrow one. Is the decision of the Court of Criminal Appeal in *Reg v Cunningham* [1957] 2 QB 396 still good law, subject only to a gloss placed upon it by the Court of Appeal Criminal Division in *Reg v Mowatt* [1968] 1 QB 421, or does the later decision of your Lordships' House in *Reg v Caldwell* [1982] AC 341 provide the answer to this question?

. . . I think it is now convenient to go back in time to the decisions of the Court of Appeal in *Reg v Mowatt* [1968] 1 QB 421, to which reference has already been made. The facts of that case were simple. On 30 September 1966 in the early hours of the morning the defendant and a companion stopped a third man in the street and asked him whether there was a pub anywhere nearby. The defendant's companion then snatched a £5 note from the third man's breast-pocket and ran off. The third man chased him without success and returned to the defendant, grasping him by the lapels and demanding to know where his companion had gone. The defendant then struck the third man, knocking him down. Two police officers saw the defendant sit astride the third man and strike him repeated blows in the face, pull him to his feet and strike him again, knocking him down and rendering him almost unconscious. The defendant admitted inflicting the first blow but claimed it was self-defence. He was tried on an indictment which included a count for wounding with intent to do grievous bodily harm contrary to s 18 of the Offences Against the Person Act 1861. In summing up on this count the trial judge told the jury they were entitled to return a verdict of unlawful wounding under s 20 of the Act. However in his summing up, while explaining the meaning of the word "unlawfully" so far as it was relevant to the defence of self-defence, he gave no direction as to the meaning of "maliciously."

The importance of this case is that the Court of Appeal considered *Reg v Cunningham* and although modifying or explaining an important feature of that decision, in no way queried its validity. The judgment of the Court of Appeal to which I have already made references was, as previously stated, given by Diplock LJ. It is of course one of Mr Sedley's points, that although *Mowatt* was not referred to in *Caldwell*, it was most unlikely that its existence was overlooked, particularly by Lord Diplock. Diplock LJ observed [1968] 1 QB 421, 425, that "unlawfully and maliciously" was a fashionable phrase of parliamentary draftsmen in 1861. It ran as a theme, with minor variations, through the Malicious Damage Act 1861 (24 & 25 Vict c 97), and the Offences Against the Person Act passed in that year. He then referred to the "very special" facts in *Cunningham* and observed:

"No doubt upon these facts the jury should be instructed that they must be satisfied before convicting the accused *that he was aware* that physical harm to some human being was a possible consequence of his unlawful act in wrenching off the gas meter. In the words of the court, 'maliciously in a statutory crime postulates foresight of consequence,' and upon this proposition we do not wish to cast any doubt." (Emphasis added.)

Subsequently he added, at p 426:

"In the offence under s 20, an in the alternative verdict which may be given on a charge under s 18, for neither of which is any specific intention required, the word 'maliciously' does import upon the part of the person who unlawfully inflicts the wound or other grievous bodily harm an *awareness* that his act may have the consequence of causing some physical harm to some other person. That is what is meant by 'the particular kind of harm' in the citation from Professor Kenny. It is quite unnecessary that the *accused* should have foreseen that his unlawful act might cause physical harm of the gravity described in the section, ie, a wound or serious physical injury. It is enough that *he* should have foreseen that some physical harm to some person, albeit of a minor character, might result." (Emphasis added.)

Mr Sedley submitted that in *Caldwell's* case your Lordships' House could have followed either of two possible paths to its conclusion as to the meaning of "recklessly" in the Act of 1971. These were: (a) to hold that *Cunningham* (and *Mowatt*) were wrongly decided and to introduce a single test, wherever reckless-ness was an issue; or (b) to accept that *Cunningham*, (subject to the *Mowatt* "gloss" to which no reference was made), correctly states the law in relation to the

Offences Against the Person Act 1861, because the word "maliciously" in that statute was a term of legal art which imported into the concept of recklessness a special restricted meaning, thus distinguishing it from "reckless" or "recklessly" in modern "revising" statutes then before the House, where those words bore their then popular or dictionary meaning.

I agree with Mr Sedley that manifestly it was the latter course which the House followed. Therefore in order to establish an offence under s 20 the prosecution must prove either the defendant intended or that he actually foresaw that his act would cause harm.

4. *In order to establish an offence under s 20 is it sufficient to prove that the defendant intended or foresaw the risk of some physical harm or must he intend or foresee either wonding or grievous bodily harm?*

It is convenient to set out once again the relevant part of the judgment of Diplock LJ, in *Reg v Mowatt* [1968] 1 QB 421, 426. Having considered Professor Kenny's statement, which I have quoted above, he then said:

> "In the offence under s 20 . . . for . . . which [no] specific intent is required, the word 'maliciously' does import . . . an awareness that his act may have the consequence of causing some physical harm to some other person. That is what is meant by 'the particular kind of harm' in the citation from Professor Kenny. It is quite unnecessary that the accused should have foreseen that his unlawful act might cause physical harm of the gravity described in the section, ie, a wound or serious physical injury. *It is enough that he should have foreseen that some physical harm to some person, albeit of a minor character, might result.*" (Emphasis added.)

Mr Sedley submits that this statement of the law is wrong. He contends that properly construed, the section requires foresight of a wounding or grievous bodily harm. He drew your Lordships' attention to criticisms of the *Mowatt* decision made by Professor Glanville-Williams and by Professor J. C. Smith in their text books and in articles or commentaries. They argue that a person should not be criminally liable for consequences of his conduct unless he foresaw a consequence falling into the same legal category as that set out in the indictment.

Such a general principle runs contrary to the decision in *Roberts'* case, 56 Cr App R 95 which I have already stated to be, in my opinion, correct. The contention is apparently based on the proposition that as the *actus reus* of a s 20 offence is the wounding or the infliction of grievous bodily harm, the *mens rea* must consist of foreseeing such wounding or grievous bodily harm. But there is no such hard and fast principle. To take but two examples, the *actus reus* of murder is the killing of the victim, but foresight of grievous bodily harm is sufficient and indeed, such bodily harm, need not be such as to be dangerous to life. Again, in the case of manslaughter, death is frequently the unforeseen consequence of the violence used.

The argument that as s 20 and s 47 have both the same penalty, this somehow supports the proposition that the foreseen consequences must coincide with the harm actually done, overlooks the oft repeated statement that this is the irrational result of this piece-meal legislation. The Act "is a rag-bag of offences brought together from a wide variety of sources with no attempt, as the draftsman frankly acknowledged, to introduce consistency as to substance or as to form." (Professor Smith in his commentary on *Reg v Parmenter* [1991] CLR 43.)

If s 20 was to be limited to cases where the accused does not desire but does foresee wounding or grievous bodily harm, it would have a very limited scope. The *mens rea* in a s 20 crime is comprised in the word "maliciously." As was pointed out by Lord Lane CJ, giving the judgment of the Court of Appeal in *Reg v Sullivan* on 27 October 1980 (unreported save in [1981] Crim LR 46) the "particular kind of harm" in the citation from Professor Kenny was directed to "harm to the person" as opposed to "harm to property." Thus it was not concerned with the degree of the harm foreseen. It is accordingly in my judgment wrong to look upon the deicison in *Mowatt* [1968] 1 QB 421 as being in any way inconsistent with the decision in *Cunningham* [1957] 2 QB 396.

My Lords, I am satisfied that the decision in *Mowatt* was correct and that it is quite unnecessary that the accused should either have intended or have foreseen that his unlawful act might cause physical harm of the gravity described in s 20, ie a wound or serious physical injury. It is enough that he should have foreseen that some physical harm to some person, albeit of a minor character, might result.

7.43   *The People (DPP) v Messitt*
                              [1974] IR 406
                          Supreme Court, 1972

Facts: In this case two questions were certified by the Attorney General as being of general public importance to be answered. The questions were:

(1) Whether or not the injury alleged to have been intended by a person charged under s 18 of the Offences Against the Person Act 1861, i.e. to maim, disfigure or disable or to do some other grievous bodily harm, must be of a grave and permanent nature.
(2) Whether or not a wound, for the purposes of either s 18 or s 20 of the Offences Against the Person Act 1861, must be of such a nature as to involve a severence or penetration of the entire skin.

O Dalaigh CJ: . . . In this Court the appeal has been chiefly concerned with the second of the two questions certified by the Attorney General and, therefore, I propose to turn now to a consideration of that question.

It is hardly necessary to state the the Act of 1861 does not contain a definition of the term "wounding", nor is there any assistance to be got *ex visceribus* the statute. The text-book writers, however, have never been in doubt as to its meaning. The statement in Archbold's Pleading, Evidence and Practice in Criminal Cases (36th edn 1966, p 986), which is the most succinct and the clearest, is as follows: "The word 'wound' in s 18 includes incised wounds, punctured wounds, lacerated wounds, contused wounds, and gunshot wounds: see *Shea v R*[67]. But to constitute a wound within the statute, the continuity of the skin must be broken: *R v Wood*[68]; or, in other words, the outer covering of the body (that is, the *whole skin*, not the mere cuticle or upper skin) must be divided: *R v McLoughlin*[69]; *R v Beckett*[70]. But a division of the *internal* skin – eg within the cheek or lip – is sufficient to constitute a wound within the statute: *R v Smith*[71]; *R v Warman*[72]." See also Halsbury's Laws of England (1st edn, vol 9, p 600); Russell on Crime (9th edn, 1936, pp 532–535); and Hogan & Smith's Criminal Law (2nd edn, 1969, p 264).

The Offences Against the Person Act 1861 in its long title is expressed to be an Act to consolidate and amend the statute law of England and Ireland relating to offences against the person and, as already stated, ss 18 and 20 are a re-enactment of the provisions of 7 Wm 4 & 1 Vict, c 85 but with the words "stab or cut" deleted.

The normal rule of construction is that parliament in re-enacting the words of an earlier statute, in this case the word "wound", is deemed to be aware of the con-

67 (1848) 3 Cox CC 141.
68 (1830) 1 Mood CC 278.
69 (1838) 8 C&P 635.
70 (1836) 1 Mood & R 526.
71 (1837) 8 C&P 173.
72 (1846) 2 Car & Kir 195.

struction placed on those words by the courts and that, therefore, such contruction is a reliable dictionary as to the meaning of the words. If that rule is to be applied, the word "wound" in ss 18 and 20 of the Act of 1861 means that the whole skin, and not merely the upper skin, must be broken or divided. Counsel for the Attorney General has not called attention to any case where the interpretation of the word "wound" which was formulated in *McLoughlin's* case, has been departed from; and I can see no good reason why the law should now be disturbed after an interval of 134 years. Moreover, there need be no alarm or feeling that the law is left inadequate by this interpretation. The Act of 1861 saw to this; s 47 of that Act creates the offence of assault occasioning actual bodily harm and makes it punishable by imprisonment up to five years.

Therefore, it seems to me that the second question in the Attorney General's certificate should be answered in the affirmative.

I turn finally to a brief consideration of the first question in the Attorney General's certificate. I have already referred to the terms of s 18 of the Act of 1861. The use of the words "or to do some other grievous bodily harm" after the words "maim, disfigure or disable" indicate, if it were necessary to do so, that "maiming" and "disfiguring" and "disabling" are, severally, species of "grievous bodily harm." To maim is to do an injury to the body which causes loss of a limb or of the use of it; here it seems to me permanency is an element. But "disable" and "disfigure" do not necessarily imply permanency; indeed, modern surgical skills can go a great distance towards undoing what heretofore would formerly have been "disablement" or "disfigurement." Nor in the phrase "or to do some other grievous bodily harm" is there anything to indicate that bodily harm must be permanent. The only requirement is that it should be "grievous." I think the term "grave" has weightier connotations than "grievous" and that the two words are not wholly interchangeable. I see no reason to seek a definition of "grievous," but if one should be required I think Lord Kilmuir's "really serious" in *Director of Public Prosecutions v Smith*[73] is as simple and effective a definition as one could desire.

I find myself unable to offer an affirmative answer to the first question. Moreover, the question is not susceptible of a simple answer: such answer as I can give is set out discursively above.

Code Options

7.44   *Canadian Criminal Code*

265 (1) A person commits an assault when

(*a*) without the consent of another person, he applies force intentionally to that other person, directly or indirectly;

(*b*) he attempts or threatens, by an act or a gesture, to apply force to another person, if he has, or causes that other person to believe on reasonable grounds that he has, present ability to effect his purpose; or

(*c*) while openly wearing or carrying a weapon or an imitation thereof, he accosts or impedes another person or begs.

(2) This section applies to all forms of assault, including sexual assault, sexual assault with a weapon, threats to a third party or causing bodily harm and aggravated sexual assault.

(3) For the purposes of this section, no consent is obtained where the complainant submits or does not resist by reason of

(*a*) the application of force to the complainant or to a person other than the complainant;

73 [1961] AC 290, 334.

(*b*) threats or fear of the application of force to the complainant or to a person other than the complainant;

(*c*) fraud; or

(*d*) the exercise of authority.

(4) Where an accused alleges that he believed that the complainant consent to the conduct that is the subject-matter of the charge, a judge, if satisfied that there is sufficient evidence and that, if believed by the jury, the evidence would constitute a defence, shall instruct the jury, when reviewing all the evidence relating to the determination of the honesty of the accused's belief, to consider the presence or absence of reasonable grounds for that belief.

266 Every one who commits an assault is guilty of

(*a*) an indictable offence and is liable to imprisonment for a term not exceeding five years; or

(*b*) an offence punishable on summary conviction.

267 (1) Every one who, in committing an assault,

(*a*) carries, uses or threatens to use a weapon or an imitation thereof, or

(*b*) causes bodily harm to the complainant,

is guilty of an indictable offence and liable to imprisonment for a term not exceeding ten years.

(2) For the purposes of this section and sections 269 and 272, "bodily harm" means any hurt or injury to the complaint that interferes with the health or comfort of the complainant and that is more than merely transient or trifling in nature.

268 (1) Every one commits an aggravated assault who wounds, maims, disfigures or endangers the life of the complainant.

(2) Every one who commits an aggravated assault is guilty of an indictable offence and liable to imprisonment for a term not exceeding fourteen years.

269 Every one who unlawfully causes bodily harm to any person is guilty of an indictable offence and liable to imprisonment for a term not exceeding ten years.

It is obvious that reform is overdue. Simplification and a rational sentencing policy are essential. Causing serious harm by criminal negligence should also be an offence. It makes no sense that if the victim dies the accused will have committed manslaughter but if he lives, but without, for example, his legs, the accused must be proved to have committed some form of assault.

False Imprisonment

7.45 Since the decision of the Supreme Court in *The People (A-G) v Edge*[74] the law in respect of kidnapping has fallen into disuse in this jurisdiction. Instead the common law offence of false imprisonment, which carries the same penalty of life imprisonment, is used where a person is confined against their will.

74 [1943] IR 115.

7.46 *Archbold – Criminal Pleading Evidence in Practice*
26th edition, 1966

Evidence for the prosecution

All the prosecutor has to prove is the imprisonment: it is for the defendant to show that he was justified in what he did, and that the imprisonment was lawful.

Every confinement of the person is an imprisonment whether it be in a common prison or in a private house, or even by forcibly detaining one in the public streets: 2 Co Inst 482, 589. But merely preventing a man from proceeding along a particular way, when, without going along it, he may get to his desired destination, it is not an imprisonment: *Bird v Jones* 7 QB 742. Where the warrant is used merely as a summons, and no arrest is made thereon, and the party voluntarily goes before the magistrate, this, it seems, is not an imprisonment: *Arrowsmith v Le Mesurier* 2 B & P (NR) 211; *Barry v Adamson* 6 B & C 528. Where a man who had an idiot brother bedridden in his house kept him in a dark room without sufficient warmth or clothing, it was held not to be an imprisonment: *R v Smith* 2 C & P 449. Detention of a prisoner after expiry of his sentence is false imprisonment: *Migotti v Colvill* 4 CPD 233; and see *Moone v Rose* LR 4 QB 486. So is detention of a prisoner after acquittal: *Mee v Cruickshank* 20 Cox 210; and see *ante* § 2801. But detention in obedience to a specific order of court is not actionable if the exigency of the order or warrant is obeyed (*Greaves v Keene* 4 Ex D 73) and the order is valid on the face of it: *Henderson v Preston* 21 QBD 32. The offence would seem to be committed by mere detention without violence: see *R v Linsberg and Leies* 69 JP 107; *Hunter v Johnson*, 18 QBD 225.

If the prosecutor fail in proving the imprisonment, he may still prove the assault and battery, as directed *ante*, § 2637 *et seq*.

7.47 *Kane v The Governor of Mountjoy Prison*
[1988] ILRM 724
Supreme Court, 1988

Facts: This was an application pursuant to Article 40.4 of the Constitution. The applicant had been kept under close surveillance by the Gardaí who expected a warrant for his extradition to arrive. They wanted to be in a position to execute it. The accused claimed that this surveillance activity amounted to a deprivation of his personal liberty and, consequently, rendered his subsequent arrest unlawful.

Finlay CJ: . . . I have come to the following conclusions.

1. I am satisfied that the contention that the appellant continued in the detention of the Garda Síochána from the time he left Granard Garda Station until the time of his arrest for assault must fail. The essential feature of detention in this legal context is that the detainee is effectively prevented from going or being where he wants to go or be and instead is forced to remain or go where his jailer wishes him to remain or go. When the appellant left the Granard Garda station, the evidence clearly establishes that what he wanted to do was to go to Cavan. He was free to do so and he achieved his purpose. There is no evidence of any description which could lead to the conclusion that any member of the Garda Síochána for any reason wished that the appellant would go to Cavan.

The single incident accordingly, of his taking the lift from Granard to Cavan in the BCC car irrespective of how many members of the Garda Síochána were observing or following him on the making of that journey, makes it impossible to infer from the evidence that his detention had not by then ceased.

2. The position from the time of his arrival at the solicitor's office in Cavan remains, in my view, essentially the same, although the extent and nature of their surveillance altered. He, apparently, having consulted the solicitor, wished to see

his friend, Mr McKeown, and to go with him to his home at Swellen. This he achieved. It is difficult to conceive again on the evidence that members of the Garda Síochána had any particular reason to wish, or did wish that he should do that. He subsequently decided to walk in and out of Cavan, that he achieved, and eventually, with a number of associates, including members of Sinn Fein and persons believed by the Gardai to be members of, or supporters of the Provisional IRA, left Cavan in a car for a destination which is not known. Again it would be wholly unreal to infer from the evidence that this journey was at the wish of the Gardai. Having regard to the findings of fact, made by the learned trial judge, it appears to me to be an inescapable conclusion that had the car in which the appellant was travelling, been driven in a safe manner it would not have been prevented from going to whatever the chosen destination was. If a person desiring to make a secret journey is permitted to go where he wants to, but his route and destination are made known by observation, he is not in law being detained.

3. I accept the submission made on behalf of the appellant, that as far as privacy is concerned, overt surveillance may under certain circumstances be more onerous than covert surveillance. This is not always true, and indeed, one can conceive of circumstances in which the reverse would be true. I would be prepared to assume without deciding for the purpose of dealing with this submission that a right of privacy may exist in an individual, even while travelling in the public streets and roads.

I would agree with the view expressed by the learned trial judge, that if overt surveillance of the general type proved in this case were applied to an individual without a basis to justify it, it would be objectionable, and I would add, clearly unlawful. Overt surveillance including a number of Garda on foot, closely following a pedestrian, and a number of Garda cars, marked as well as unmarked, tailing a driver or passenger in a motor car would, it seems to me, require a specific justification arising from all of the circumstances of a particular case and the nature and importance of the particular police duty being discharged.

Such surveillance is capable of gravely affecting the peace of mind and public reputation of any individual and the courts could not, in my view, accept any general application of such a procedure by the police, but should require where it is put into operation and challenged, a specific adequate justification for it.

The issue raised by this submission therefore, in my view, involves a consideration of all the proven circumstances, background and facts of the case, as well as a consideration of the duty being discharged by the police and the nature of the surveillance which was proved to have occurred.

I am satisfied that there are no grounds for the distinction sought to be drawn between the duty of investigating or detecting crime and the duty of executing an extradition warrant. The State has a very clear interest in the expenditure and efficient discharge of the obligations reciprocally undertaken between it and other States for the apprehension of fugitive offenders. A member of the Garda Síochána aware of the intended issue and backing of an extradition warrant has a clear duty to take reasonable steps to ascertain, where it probably can be speedily executed, when it is obtained. The view expressed by the learned trial judge as to the more probable reason for the surveillance, which was applied to the appellant is supported by the evidence, but does not, in my view, affect the question of the justification for this surveillance.

In this case the appellant was originally arrested in circumstances which led to strong suspicion

    (*a*) he was a member of the IRA,
    (*b*) he had been in hiding, and
    (*c*) he was associated with arms found near-by.

He was furthermore arrested, in the course of a countrywide search for arms, believed by the authorities to represent a major danger to the security of the State.

For almost a day after his arrest he refused to give his name or address, despite an obligation imposed by the Offences Against the State Act to do so. When released, as he was in Granard, he was most unlikely for long to be on his own in seeking, as he was likely to do, to return to hiding. On the other hand, the likelihood then was that he would receive support and assistance by a tightly knit and efficient organisation of persons, who sympathised with him. That likelihood was, in my view, borne out by the facts as they eventually occurred.

Covert surveillance or even overt surveillance by a very limited number of persons following him at a discreet distance was most unlikely to be successful in keeping the Gardai aware of his whereabouts.

Consideration of the detailed evidence with regard to the events, which occurred between the appellant and his companions finally leaving the house at Swellen and his jump over the ditch at Lath indicates that notwithstanding the presence of possibly as many as ten or eleven guards of experience, who had available for their use up to three cars, that the car in which the appellant was travelling, was for most of its journey observed only by Garda Myles, who was very nearly on more than one occasion prevented from keeping it in sight.

Having regard to these considerations and to the nature of the duty which the Garda Síochána were carrying out on this afternoon, the extent and nature of the surveillance allocated by them to the appellant, was in my view, justified. I would accordingly dismiss this appeal.

McCarthy J (Hederman J concurring): In my view, the freedom of movement given to the appellant was limited so as to restrict his freedom of choice. The issue comes down to the question whether or not the gardai, who may lawfully "stake-out" a premises which they believe will be burgled, or who may lawfully and overtly or otherwise follow a suspect with a view to investigating or detecting crime may lawfully do the same in the reasonable expectation of the arrival of a valid extradition warrant. The issue narrows further if, as I do, one concludes that overt surveillance, which, by definition, does not impede the freedom of choice of movement, is a lawful invasion of privacy to whether or not the overt nature of the surveillance can be equally so justified. May the State authorities, in effect, say to the individual sought under an anticipated extradition warrant:

> You may go where you please but by our following you you will be unable to hide or to meet with people who might hide you because we understand an extradition warrant is on the way.

In my view, ordinarily, they may not. The duty of investigating or detecting crime is not the same as providing for the execution of an extradition warrant. The end result is as different in its nature as the surveillance may be. The critical matter is that the combination of interference with privacy and the impairment of freedom of choice of movement would be to provide for a circumstance that may never happen. Here the situation was quite different. A facsimile of the warrant had already been presented for "backing"; it was intended that the original would be "backed" and would be available for execution within a very short time. The procedure under the Act had not merely been set in motion; it was reaching finality. In the circumstances the Garda action, following on the events as set out in the judgment of the Chief Justice, was not excessive and, therefore, not unlawful.

I agree that the appeal be dismissed.

Extra-Territorial Offences

7.48 As we have seen in chapter 1 the criminal law extends to the territory of the State. There is no principle of international law which prevents a State from punishing one of its own citizens in respect of an act done in another jurisdiction. Some statutes have, exceptionally, so provided. At common law murder was an extra-territorial crime. It remains so pursuant to the Offences Against the Person Act 1861, as does bigamy. Other examples are included under the Explosives Act 1881 the main sections of which are reproduced at paras **9.109–9.112**. Two modern statutes extend the extra-territorial principle. Both of these arise from the activities of sectarian gangs in Northern Ireland.

The Criminal Law (Jurisdiction) Act 1976 was passed, in essence, as an alternative to extradition. It was considered, at the time, that the Constitution forbade the extraction of political offenders from this jurisdiction. The definition then put on political offences has not found favour with the courts in recent years[75]. The Criminal Law (Jurisdiction) Act 1976 essentially provides a mechanism whereby persons who commit certain terrorist-type crimes in Northern Ireland may be tried in this jurisdiction, as an alternative to extradition. It is outside the scope of this work to discuss the procedures of this Act; for a discussion see *The People (DPP) v Campbell Ryan Magee Sloan Fusco and McKee*[76].

The other main exception, again concerned with terrorist-type crime is the Extradition (European Convention on the Prevention of Terrorism) Act 1987. Section 5(1) of this Act makes it an offence to do, or attempt an act in a convention country which if done in Ireland would have constituted an offence involving either:

(1) An attack against the life, physical integrity or liberty of an internationally protected person;

(2) Involving kidnapping, the taking of a hostage or serious false imprisonment; or

(3) involving the use, to the endangerment of persons, of an explosive or automatic fire arm.

Under this section the nationality of the offender is irrelevant. Where, under s 5(2) the accused is a national of a convention country it is an offence to do, or attempt, an act anywhere in the world, which would have constituted an offence in his own jurisdiction and, if he had been an Irish citizen, would have amounted to the offence of murder or manslaughter or an offence under ss 2 or 3 of the Explosives Substances Act 1881 (as substituted by the Criminal Law (Jurisdiction) Act 1976) and which involved either categories 1, 2 or 3 above. The relevant text of these two Acts is now set out.

7.49   *Criminal Law (Jurisdiction) Act 1976*

Offences committed in Northern Ireland and related offences committed in State

2 (1) Where a person does in Northern Ireland an act that, if done in the State, would constitute an offence specified in the Schedule, he shall be guilty of an offence and he shall be liable on conviction on indictment to the penalty to which he would have been liable if he had done the act in the State.

(2) Where a person—

(a) in the State or in Northern Ireland, aids, abets, counsels or procures the commission of an offence under *subsection (1)* or *section 3*, or

75 See Charleton *Extradition from Ireland to the UK* (1989) 53 J Crim L 235.
76 (1983) 2 Frewen 131.

(*b*) in Northern Ireland, aids, abets, counsels or procures the commission of an offence specified in the Schedule,

he shall be guilty of, and may be indicted, tried and punished for, the relevant principal offence, and the following provisions of this Act relating to the commission of any such principal offence shall apply accordingly.

(3) Where a person—

(*a*) in the State or in Northern Ireland, attempts, conspires or incites another person to commit an offence under *subsection (1)* or *section 3*, or

(*b*) in Northern Ireland, attempts, conspires or incites another person to commit an offence specified in the Schedule,

he shall be guilty of an offence and he shall be liable on conviction on indictment to a penalty not greater than the penalty to which he would have been liable if he had been convicted of the relevant principal offence.

(4) Where a person has committed an offence under *subsection (1)* or *section 3* or attempted to commit any such offence, any other person who, in the State or in Northern Ireland, knowing or believing him to be guilty of the offence or attempt or of some other such offence or attempt, does without reasonable excuse any act with intent to impede his apprehension or prosecution in the State or in Northern Ireland shall be guilty of an offence.

(5) If, upon the trial on indictment of an offence under *subsection (1)* or *section 3* or an attempt to commit any such offence, it is proved that the offence charged (or some other offence of which the accused might on that charge be found guilty) was committed, but the accused is found not guilty of it, the accused may be found guilty of any offence under *subsection (4)* of which it is proved that he is guilty in relation to the offence charged (or that other offence).

(6) Where a person has committed an offence specified in the Schedule or attempted to commit any such offence, any other person who, in Northern Ireland, knowing or believing him to be guilty of the offence or attempt or of some other such offence or attempt, does without reasonable excuse any act with intent to impede his apprehension or prosecution in the State or in Northern Ireland shall be guilty of an offence.

(7) If, upon the trial on indictment of an offence specified in the Schedule or an attempt to commit any such offence, it is proved that the offence charged (or some other offence of which the accused might on that charge be found guilty) was committed, but the accused is found not guilty of it, the accused may be found guilty of any offence under *subsection (6)* of which it is proved that he is guilty in relation to the offence charged (or that other offence).

(8) A person committing an offence under *subsection (4)* or *(6)* with intent to impede another person's apprehension or prosecution shall be liable on conviction on indictment to imprisonment according to the gravity of the offence that the other person has committed or attempted to commit, as follows:

(*a*) in case that offence is murder, he shall be liable to imprisonment for a term not exceeding ten years;

(*b*) in case it is one for which a person (of full age and capacity and not previously convicted) may be sentenced to imprisonment for a term of fourteen years, he shall be liable to imprisonment for a term not exceeding seven years;

(*c*) in case it is not one included in *paragraph (a)* or *(b)* but is one for which a person (of full age and capacity and not previously convicted) may be sentenced to imprisonment for a term of ten years, he shall be liable to imprisonment for a term not exceeding five years;

(*d*) in any other case, he shall be liable to imprisonment for a term not exceeding three years.

(9) The enactments and rules of law as to when a person charged with an offence committed in the State may be convicted of another offence shall apply so as to enable a person charged with an offence under *subsection (1)* to be convicted of another offence, being an offence under that subsection, or of attempting to commit the offence charged or that other offence, and so as to enable a person charged with an offence under *section 3* to be convicted of attempting to commit that offence.

Escape from custody in Northern Ireland

3   (1)(*a*) A person who, in Northern Ireland, is charged with or convicted of—
   (i) an offence under the law of Northern Ireland consisting of acts (whether done in the State or in Northern Ireland) that also constitute an offence specified in the Schedule or an offence under *section 2*, or
   (ii) an offence under the law of Northern Ireland corresponding to this section,
   and who escapes from any lawful custody in which he is held in Northern Ireland shall be guilty of an offence.
   (*b*) The reference in *paragraph (a)* to an offence specified in the Schedule includes aiding, abetting, counselling or procuring the commission of an offence there specified, attempting, conspiring or inciting another person to commit an offence there specified or an offence of doing without reasonable excuse any act with intent to impede the apprehension or prosecution of a person who has, and whom the person in question knows or believes to have, committed an offence there specified.
   (*c*) The reference in *paragraph (a)* to lawful custody is a reference to any lawful custody in which the person concerned is held, for the purpose of the proceedings in relation to the offence under the law of Northern Ireland referred to in *paragraph (a)*, at any time between the bringing of a charge in relation to that offence and the conclusion of his trial (including any appeal or retrial) for that offence or in which he is held while serving a sentence imposed on his conviction for that offence.

(2) A person who escapes from lawful custody while in Northern Ireland pursuant to an order under *section 11(2)* shall be guilty of an offence.

(3) A person guilty of an offence under this section shall be liable on conviction on indictment to imprisonment for a term not exceeding seven years.

SCHEDULE

Common law offences

   1 Murder.

   2 Manslaughter.

   3 The common law offence of arson.

   4 Kidnapping.

   5 False imprisonment.

Malicious damage

   6 Any offence under the following provisions of the Malicious Damage Act 1861—

   (*a*) s 1 (setting fire to church etc);

(*b*) s 2 (setting fire to a dwelling house while a person is inside);

(*c*) s 3 (setting fire to house, outhouse or business or farming premises with intent to injure or defraud any person);

(*d*) s 4 (setting fire to railway station etc);

(*e*) s 5 (setting fire to any public building);

(*f*) s 6 (setting fire to other buildings);

(*g*) s 7 (setting fire to goods in certain buildings);

(*h*) s 35 (interference with railway).

Offences against the person

7 Any offence under the following provisions of the Offences Against the Person Act 1861—

(*a*) s 18 (wounding with intent to cause grievous bodily harm);

(*b*) s 20 (causing grievous bodily harm).

Explosives

8 Any offence under the following provisions of the Explosive Substances Act 1883—

(*a*) s 2 (causing explosion likely to endanger life or damage property);

(*b*) s 3 (possession etc of explosive substances);

(*c*) s 4 (making or possessing explosives in suspicious circumstances).

Robbery and burglary

9 Any offence under the following provisions of the Larceny Act 1916—

(*a*) s 23 (robbery);

(*b*) s 23B (aggravated burglary).

Firearms

10 Any offence under s 15 of the Firearms Act 1925 (possessing firearm or ammunition with intent to endanger life or cause serious injury to property).

11 Any offence under the following provisions of the Firearms Act 1964—

(*a*) s 26 (possession of firearm while taking vehicle without authority);

(*b*) s 27 (use of firearms to resist arrest or aid escape);

(*c*) s 27A (possession of firearm or ammunition in suspicious circumstances);

(*d*) s 27B (carrying firearm with criminal intent).

Unlawful seizure of aircraft and vehicles

12 Any offence under s 11 of the Air Navigation and Transport Act 1973 (unlawful seizure of aircraft).

13 Any offence under s 10 of this Act (unlawful seizure of vehicles).

7.50 *Extradition (European Convention on the Prevention of Terrorism) Act 1987*

Interpretation

1 (1) In this Act—

"the Act of 1965" means the Extradition Act 1965;

"convention country" means a country other than the State for the time being standing designated in an order under *section 2*;

469

"the Minister" means the Minister for Justice;

"serious offence" means an offence which, if the act constituting the offence took place in the State, would be an offence for which a person aged 21 years or over, of full capacity and not previously convicted may be punished by imprisonment for a term of 5 years or by a more severe penalty.

(2) References in this Act to an act include references to an omission and references to the doing of an act include references to the making of an omission.

(3) (*a*) A reference in this Act to a section is a reference to a section of this Act unless it is indicated that reference to some other enactment is intended.

(*b*) A reference in this Act to a subsection, paragraph or subparagraph is a reference to the subsection, paragraph of subparagraph of the provision in which the reference occurs unless it is indicated that reference to some other provision is intended.

(4) This Act applies, except where otherwise provided, in relation to an offence whether committed or alleged to have been committed before or after the passing of this Act.

Convention countries

2 (1) The Minister for Foreign Affairs may by order designate the countries which are parties to the European Convention on the Suppression of Terrorism, done at Strasbourg on the 27th day of January, 1977.

(2) The Minister for Foreign Affairs may by order amend or revoke an order under this section including an order under this subsection.

(3) An order under this section shall, as soon as may be after it is made, be laid before each House of the Oireachtas.

Certain offences not to be regarded as political offences

3 (1) For the purposes mentioned in *subsection (2)*—

(*a*) no offence to which this section applies and of which a person is accused or her been convicted outside the State shall be regarded as a political offence or as an offence connected with a political offence, and

(*b*) no proceedings outside the State in respect of an offence to which this section applies shall be regarded as a criminal matter of a political character.

(2) The purposes referred to in *subsection (1)* are—

(*a*) the purposes of Part II of the Act of 1965 in relation to any request for the surrender of a person made after the commencement of this Act by any convention country in relation to which that Part applies;

(*b*) the purposes of Part III of the Act of 1965 in relation to any warrant for the arrest of a person issued after the commencement of this Act in a place in relation to which that Part applies;

(*c*) the purposes of *section 24* of the Extradition Act 1870, and *section 5* of the Extradition Act 1873, in relation to the obtaining of evidence in the State for use in criminal proceedings instituted in a convention country after the commencement of this Act.

(3) (*a*) This section applies to—

(i) an offence within the scope of the Convention for the Suppression of Unlawful Seizure of Aircraft, done at The Hague on the 16th day of December, 1970,

(ii) an offence within the scope of the Convention for the Suppression of Unlawful Acts against the Safety of Civil Aviation, done at Montreal on the 23rd day of September, 1971,

(iii) a serious offence involving an attack against the life, physical integrity or liberty of an internationally protected person,

(iv) an offence involving kidnapping, the taking of a hostage or serious false imprisonment,

(v) an offence involving the use of an explosive or an automatic firearm, if such use endangers persons, and

(vi) any offence of attempting to commit any of the foregoing offences.

(*b*) References in this subsection to an offence include references to participation as an accomplice of a person who commits the offence.

(4) For the purposes of *subsection (3)(a)*:

(*a*) in *sub-paragraph (iii)* thereof, "an internationally protected person" has the meaning assigned to it by *subsection (5)*,

(*b*) in *sub-paragraph (iv)* thereof—

"an offence involving", in relation to kidnapping, the taking of a hostage or serious false imprisonment, includes any offence committed in the course thereof or in conjunction therewith;

"serious false imprisonment" means any false imprisonment involving danger, or prolonged or substantial hardship or inconvenience, for the person detained,

(*c*) in *sub-paragraph (v)* thereof—

"automatic firearm" means a firearm which is so designed or adapted that, if pressure is applied to the trigger, missiles continue to be discharged until pressure is removed from the trigger or the magazine containing the missiles is empty;

"explosive" means any article manufactured for the purpose of producing a practical effect by explosion or intended by the person using it for that purpose;

"an offence involving", in relation to the use of an explosive or an automatic firearm, includes any offence committed by means of the explosive or firearm.

(5) (*a*) In this section "an internationally protected person" means, in relation to any such offence as is mentioned in *subsection (3)(a)(iii)*, any of the following:

(i) a person who at the time of the commission of the offence is a Head of State, a member of a body which performs the functions of Head of State under the constitution of a State, a head of government or a minister for foreign affairs and is outside the territory of the State in which he holds office,

(ii) a person who at the time of the commission of the offence is a representative or an official of a State or an official or agent of an international organisation of an inter-governmental character, is entitled under international law to special protection from attack on his person, freedom or dignity and does not fall within *sub-paragraph (i)*,

(iii) a person who at the time of the commission of the offence is a member of the family of a person mentioned in *sub-paragraph (i)* or *(ii)* and—

(I) if the other person is mentioned in *sub-paragraph (i)*, is accompanying him, or

            (II) if the other person is mentioned in *sub-paragraph (ii)*, is a member of his household.

    (*b*) (i) If in any proceedings a question arises as to whether a person was at the relevant time an internationally protected person, a certificate signed by, or by a person authorised by, the Minister for Foreign Affairs and stating any fact relating to the question shall be evidence of that fact.

        (ii) A document purporting to be a certificate described in *sub-paragraph (i)* shall be deemed to be such a certificate, and to be signed by the person purporting to have signed it (and, in the case of such a document purporting to have been signed by a person authorised by the Minister for Foreign Affairs, to have been signed in accordance with the authorisation), unless the contrary is shown.

Certain other offences not to be regarded as political offences in certain circumstances

4 (1) (*a*) For the purposes mentioned in *paragraphs (a)* and *(b)* of *section 3(2)*, an offence to which this section applies and of which a person is accused or has been convicted outside the State shall not be regarded as a political offence or as an offence connected with a political offence if the court or the Minister, as the case may be, having taken into due consideration any particularly serious aspects of the offence, including—

        (i) that it created a collective danger to the life, physical integrity or liberty of persons,

        (ii) that it affected persons foreign to the motives behind it, or

        (iii) that cruel or vicious means were used in the commission of the offence,

is of opinion that the offence cannot properly be regarded as a political offence or as an offence connected with a political offence.

    (*b*) For the purposes mentioned in *section 3(2)(c)*, proceedings outside the State in respect of an offence to which this section applies shall not be regarded as a criminal matter of a political character.

  (2) (*a*) This section applies to—

        (i) any serious offence (other than an offence to which *section 3* applies) of which a person is accused or has been convicted outside the State—

           (I) involving an act of violence against the life, physical integrity or liberty of a person, or

          (II) involving an act against property if the act created a collective danger for persons,

        and

        (ii) any offence of attempting to commit any of the foregoing offences.

    (*b*) References in this subsection to an offence include references to participation as an accomplice of a person who commits the offence.

Jurisdiction in respect of certain offences committed outside the State

5 (1) If a person, whether an Irish citizen or not, does in a convention country an act which—

    (*a*) if he had done it in the State, would have constituted an offence, and

    (*b*) falls within the description of any of the offences referred to in *sub-paragraph (iii), (iv)* or *(v)* of *section 3(3)(a)*,

or attempts in a convention country to do any such act, he shall be guilty of the offence which the act or attempt would have constituted if he had done or made it in the State.

(2) If a person who is a national of a convention country but not an Irish citizen does outside the State and that convention country an act which—

(*a*) constitutes an offence under the law of that convention country,

(*b*) if he had been an Irish citizen, would have constituted the offence of murder or manslaughter or an offence under *section 2* or *3* or the Explosive Substances Act 1883 (as substituted by *section 4* of the Criminal Law (Jurisdiction) Act 1976), and

(*c*) falls within the description of any of the offences referred to in *sub-paragraph (iii)*, *(iv)* or *(v)* of *section 3(3)(a)*,

he shall be guilty of the offence which the act would have constituted if he had been an Irish citizen.

(3) (*a*) For the purposes of this section, any act done on board a ship, aircraft or hovercraft, when it is in or over the territory of a convention country, shall be treated as done in that country and any act done on board a ship, aircraft or hovercraft registered in a convention country shall be treated as done in that country and in the convention country (if any) in or over whose territory it is done.

(*b*) In *paragraph (a)* "territory" includes territorial seas.

(4) The provisions of the law of the State applied by virtue of this section to things done in any other country shall be read for the purposes of this Act with any necessary modifications.

(5) This section shall apply only to acts done after the commencement of this Act.

Proceedings by virtue of s 5

6 (1) Proceedings for an offence which is an offence by virtue of *section 5* may be taken in any place in the State and the offence may for all incidental purposes be treated as having been committed in that place.

(2) Where a person is charged with an offence referred to in *subsection (1)*, no further proceedings in the matter (other than any remand in custody or on bail) shall be taken except by or with the consent of the Director of Public Prosecutions.

(3) The Director of Public Prosecutions shall not take, or consent to the taking of, further proceedings such as are mentioned in *subsection (2)* in respect of an offence unless it appears to him that—

(*a*) a convention country in relation to which Part II of the Act of 1965 applies has made a request under that Part for the surrender of the person concerned for the purpose of trying him for an offence in respect of the act in question and the request has been finally refused (whether as the result of a decision of a court or otherwise), or

(*b*) a warrant has been issued by a judicial authority in a place in relation to which Part III of the Act of 1965 applies for the arrest of the person concerned for the purpose of trying him for an offence in respect of the act in question and it has been finally determined (whether as the result of a decision of a court or otherwise) that the warrant should not be endorsed for execution in the State under that Part or that the person concerned should not be delivered up in accordance with the warrant, or

(*c*) because of special circumstances (which may include the likelihood of a refusal such as is mentioned in *paragraph (a)* or of a determination such as is mentioned in *paragraph (b)*) it is expedient that proceedings should be taken against the person concerned for an offence under the law of the State in respect of the act in question.

(4) If a person would, but for this subsection, be required on conviction of an offence referred to in *subsection (1)* to be sentenced to death, he shall be sentenced to imprisonment for life.

(5) No proceedings shall be taken—

(*a*) under this section in respect of an act that constitutes an offence referred to in sub-s (1) and also an offence under *section 2* of the Criminal Law (Jurisdiction) Act 1976, or

(*b*) under *section 38* of the Act of 1965 in respect of an act that constitutes an offence by virtue of that section and also an offence referred to in *subsection (1)*.

Saving

11 Nothing in this Act shall prevent—

(*a*) an offence from being regarded as not being a political offence or as an offence connected with a political offence, or

(*b*) proceedings for an offence from being regarded as not being a criminal matter of a political character,

for the purposes mentioned in *subsection (2)* of *section 3* in circumstances or by reason of considerations other than those referred to in that section or *section 4*.

Criminal Damage

7.51 Offences of vandalism were previously dealt with under the Malicious Damage Act 1861. This was an extremely badly drafted piece of legislation. Its individual sections focused on particular types of arson or malicious damage. Each offence was defined within narrow terms and thus required a charge which precisely met the nature of the offence created. Even a slight mistake in identifying or drafting the charge would mean that the wrong section had been used thus entitling the accused to an automatic acquittal on the ground that he had not committed the particular offence charged.

On the 4 March 1986 three men were indicted before a jury in Portlaoise Circuit Court for the malicious damage of a statue contrary to s 39 of the Act. The motive for the crime was, apparently, a desire by the men to cause a section of the public to desist from praying before a statue which many people had claimed to experience as behaving as if it were alive. The press referred to this statue as "the moving statue". The charge chosen required that the roadside grotto be proved as "a place of divine worship". An acquittal was directed on the grounds that a grotto with a statue could not reasonably be so described in accordance with the section.

The Law Reform Commission, on examining the legislation, found that it was far too cumbersome and compartmentalised to be workable. They proposed, instead, that a generic offence of criminal damage would cover all forms of damage to property. Arson was to be retained as a separate offence.

The Criminal Damage Act 1991 essentially implements the recommendations of the Law Reform Commission. Offences are defined as occurring when the accused acts without lawful excuse. This, in itself, is defined in s 6. The accused must act with intent to cause damage to property or be reckless as to whether any property should be damaged. Recklessness is defined in s 2(6). Intent is not defined and the discussion on this topic in chapter 1 is therefore apposite. While all the offences contrary to s 2 carry the same penalty there are three basic offences. The simple offence of damaging property is clearly less serious than the other two offences of damaging property intending or being reckless as to whether the life of another would be thereby endangered, or the offence of damaging property with intent to defraud. This latter offence does not carry the defence of lawful excuse. In addition, these three separate offences may be committed by fire. It is thus appropriate to describe them on an indictment as offences of arson. It is an offence contrary to s 3 to threaten to damage property. It is an offence contrary to s 4 to possess an article with intent to damage property. It is an offence contrary to s 5 to operate a computer with intent to access data.

The Act is a fine example of law reform. Its provisions are clear and self-explanatory. It proceeds on a coherent basis which recognises and defines, in simple terms, both the mental and external elements of the offences created.

Certain sections of the Malicious Damage Act 1861 are retained. These use the term "maliciously" and the discussion in this chapter as to the mental element required by this topic is therefore appropriate. Essentially, it is no different from the mental element described in s 2 of the Criminal Damage Act 1991; it requires that the accused act with recklessness or intent. Both are subjective elements; *R v Cunningham*[77] (see para **7.33**).

7.52   *Law Reform Commission Report – Malicious Damage*
LRC 26–1988

1.   The present approach, of providing a long list of specific offences, should be replaced by a general offence in respect of criminal damage to another person's property, supplemented by a small number of other offences, dealing with liability in specific instances: para 15.

2.   The legislation should use the word "damage" in the substantive offence; a subsection should provide that this term includes cases where the interference consists wholly or partly of destroying, defacing or dismantling the property or rendering it inoperable or unfit for use: para 21.

3.   "Property" should be defined as embracing property of a tangible nature, whether real or personal, including money, and animals that are capable of being stolen; ss 40 and 41 of the *Malicious Damage Act 1861* should be retained: para 22.

4.   Property should be treated as belonging to any person (a) having the custody or control of it; (b) having in it any proprietary right or interest (not being an equitable interest arising only from an agreement to transfer or grant an interest); or (c) having a charge over it. Where property is subject to a trust, the persons to whom it belongs should be so treated as including any person having a right to enforce the trust. Property of a corporation sole should be so treated as belonging to the corporation notwithstanding a vacancy in the corporation: para 23.

5.   The same test of recklessness should apply to offences relating to criminal damage as we recommended should apply to the offence of handling unlawfully obtained property, in our Report on *Receiving Stolen Property*: para 30.

---

77 [1957] 2 QB 396.

6.   The legislation should make it an offence to destroy or damage property whether belonging to oneself or another with intent to defraud or with intent to endanger life or with recklessness in that regard: para 40.

7.   Arson should be retained as a separate offence. It should not carry a higher maximum penalty than other acts involving damage to property. The common law offence of arson should be abolished: para 42.

8.   The legislation should not include an offence of causing or risking a catastrophe, as provided for by s 220.2 of the Model Penal Code: para 46.

9.   The District Court should have juridiction to try summarily offences of criminal damage where the Director of Public Prosecutions so elects: para 47.

10.   Offences of malicious or criminal damage should not be scheduled for the purposes of the Offences Against the State Act 1939: para 54.

11.   In cases where the charge is of damaging property that is not one's own, it should be presumed until the contrary is shown that the property in question is not the property of the accused and that the owner, bailee or other person in possession of the property had not given the accused permission to damage it: para 55.

12.   For the purposes of the proposed legislation, a family home from which the accused is barred should be deemed to be the property of the spouse of the accused only: para 56.

13.   The doctrine of ouster of jurisdiction should have no application to the proposed offences: para 57.

14.   The maximum penalty for all criminal damage offences, whether by fire or otherwise, prosecuted on indictment, which do not involve intent to endanger life or recklessness as to whether life would be endangered should be ten years' imprisonment. Where such intent or recklessness exists, a life sentence would apply: para 58.

15.   The legislation should include a provision for the payment of compensation to victims of criminal damage and the related offences already proposed: para 59.

16.   In prosecutions for offences relating to damaging property or an ancillary threat or possession of anything with intent to damage property, other than an offence involving a threat to damage property in a way which the defendant knows is likely to endanger the life of another or involving an intent to use or cause or permit the use of something in his custody or under his control so as to damage property, the defendant is to be treated as having a lawful excuse—

   (*a*) if at the time of the act or acts alleged to constitute the offence he believed that the person or persons whom he believed to be entitled to consent to the damage to the property in question had so consented, or would have so consented to it if he or they had known of the damage and its circumstances; or

   (*b*) if he damaged or threatened to damage the property in question or, in the case of a charge for the offence recommended in para 18 below, intended to use or cause or permit the use of something to damage it, in order to protect himself or another person or property belonging to himself or another or a right or interest in property which was or which he believed to be vested in himself or another, and at the time of the act or acts alleged to constitute the offence he believed—

    (i) that he or such other person or the property, right or interest was in immediate need of protection; and

    (ii) that the means of protection adopted or proposed to be adopted were or would be reasonable having regard to all the circumstances.

The test should be that of the honesty, rather than the reasonableness, of the belief. This defence should be without prejudice to other existing defences: para 61.

17.   A person who without lawful excuse makes to another person a threat, intending that he or she would fear it would be carried out, (a) to damage any property belonging to that other person or a third person, or (b) to damage his own property in a way which he knows is likely to endanger the life of that other person or a third person, should be guilty of an offence: para 62.

18.   A person who has anything in his custody or under his control intending without lawful excuse to use it or cause or permit another to use it (a) to destroy or damage any property belonging to some other person, or (b) to destroy or damage his own or the user's property in a way which he knows is likely to endanger the life of some other person, should be guilty of an offence: para 63.

19.   There should be a power of arrest without warrant, by a member of the Gardai or any other person, in respect of the offences proposed, where, in either case, there is a reasonable belief that (a) such an offence has been committed and (b) the arrested person committed such offence: para 64.

20.   There should be a power to authorise a search warrant where there is reasonable cause to believe that a person has in his custody or under his control or in his premises anything which there is reasonable cause to believe has been used or is intended for use without lawful excuse (a) to damage property belonging to another, or (b) to damage any property in a way likely to endanger the life of another: para 65.

21.   Sections 35, 36, 47 and 48 of the Malicious Damage Act 1861, relating to offences in regard to railways and ships, should not be repealed, but the proposed legislation should provide for the same penalties for those offences as for offences under the proposed legislation: para 67.

7.53   *Criminal Damage Act 1991*

Interpretation

1   (1) In this Act—
"compensation order" has the meaning assigned to it by s 9(1);
"to damage" includes—

    (*a*) in relation to property other than data (but including a storage medium in which data are kept), to destroy, deface, dismantle or, whether temporarily or otherwise render inoperable or unfit for use or prevent or impair the operation of,

    (*b*) in relation to data—
        (i) to add to, alter, corrupt, erase or move to another storage medium or to a different location in the storage medium in which they are kept (whether or not property other than data is damaged thereby), or
        (ii) to do any act that contributes towards causing such addition, alteration, corruption, erasure or movement,

    (*c*) to do any act within the State that damages property ouside the State, (*d*) to do any act outside the State that damages property within the State, and

(*e*) to make an omission causing damage,

and cognate words shall be construed accordingly;

"data" means information in a form in which it can be accessed by means of a computer and includes a program;

"property" means—

(*a*) property of a tangible nature, whether real or personal, including money and animals that are capable of being stolen, and

(*b*) data.

(2) Property shall be treated for the purposes of this Act as belonging to any person—

(*a*) having lawful custody or control of it,

(*b*) having in it any proprietary right or interest (not being an equitable interest arising only from an agreement to transfer or grant an interest), or

(*c*) having a charge over it.

(3) Where, as respects an offence under s 2, 3(*a*) or 4(*a*)—

(*a*) the property concerned is a family home within the meaning of the Family Home Protection Act 1976, and

(*b*) the person charged—

(i) is the spouse of a person who resides, or is entitled to reside, in the home, and

(ii) is the subject of a protection order or barring order (within the meaning in each case of the Family Law (Protection of Spouses and Children) Act 1981) or is excluded from the home pursuant to an order under s 16(*a*) of the Judicial Separation and Family Law Reform Act 1989, or any other order of a court,

ss 2, 3(*a*) and 4(*a*) shall have effect as if the references therein to any property belonging to another, however expressed, were references to the home.

(4) Where property is subject to a trust, the persons to whom the property belongs shall be treated for the purposes of this Act as including any person having a right to enforce the trust.

(5) Property of a corporation sole shall be treated for the purposes of this Act as belonging to the corporation notwithstanding a vacancy in it.

(6) In this Act—

(*a*) a reference to any enactment shall, unless the context otherwise requires, be construed as a reference to that enactment as amended or extended by or under any subsequent enactment including this Act,

(*b*) a reference to a section is a reference to a section of this Act unless it is indicated that reference to some other enactment is intended,

(*c*) a reference to a subsection, paragraph or subparagraph is a reference to the subsection, paragraph or subparagraph of the provision in which the reference occurs unless it is indicated that reference to some other provision is intended.

Damaging property

2 (1) A person who without lawful excuse damages any property belonging to another intending to damage any such property or being reckless as to whether any such property would be damaged shall be guilty of an offence.

(2) A person who without lawful excuse damages any property, whether belonging to himself or another—

(*a*) intending to damage any property or being reckless as to whether any property would be damaged, and

(*b*) intending by the damage to endanger the life of another or being reckless as to whether the life of another would be thereby endangered,

shall be guilty of an offence.

(3) A person who damages any property, whether belonging to himself or another, with intent to defraud shall be guilty of an offence.

(4) An offence committed under this section by damaging property by fire shall be charged as arson.

(5) A person guilty of an offence under this section shall be liable—

(*a*) on summary conviction, to a fine not exceeding £1,000 or imprisonment for a term not exceeding 12 months or both, and

(*b*) on conviction on indictment—

(i) in case the person is guilty of arson under sub-s (1) or (3) or of an offence under sub-s (2) (whether arson or not), to a fine or imprisonment for life or both, and

(ii) in case the person is guilty of any other offence under this section, to a fine not exceeding £10,000 or imprisonment for a term not exceeding 10 years or both.

(6) For the purposes of this section a person is reckless if he has foreseen that the particular kind of damage that in fact was done might be done and yet has gone on to take the risk of it.

Threat to damage property

3 A person who without lawful excuse makes to another a threat, intending that that other would fear it would be carried out—

(*a*) to damage any property belonging to that other or a third person, or

(*b*) to damage his own property in a way which he knows is likely to endanger the life of that other or a third person,

shall be guilty of an offence and shall be liable—

(i) on summary conviction, to a fine not exceeding £1,000 or imprisonment for a term not exceeding 12 months or both, and

(ii) on conviction on indictment, to a fine not exceeding £10,000 or imprisonment for a term not exceeding 10 years or both.

Possessing any thing with intent to damage property

4 A person (in this section referred to as the possessor) who has any thing in his custody or under his control intending without lawful excuse to use it or cause or permit another to use it—

(*a*) to damage any property belonging to some other person, or

(*b*) to damage his own or the intended user's property—

(i) in a way which he knows is likely to endanger the life of a person other than the possessor, or

(ii) with intent to defraud,

shall be guilty of an offence and shall be liable—

(A) on summary conviction, to a fine not exceeding £1,000 or imprisonment for a term not exceeding 12 months or both, and

(B) on conviction on indictment, to a fine not exceeding £10,000 or imprisonment for a term not exceeding 10 years or both.

Unauthorised accessing of data

5 (1) A person who without lawful excuse operates a computer—

(*a*) within the State with intent to access any data kept either within or outside the State, or

(*b*) outside the State with intent to access any data kept within the State,

shall, whether or not he accesses any data, be guilty of an offence and shall be liable on summary conviction to a fine not exceeding £500 or imprisonment for a term not exceeding 3 months or both.

(2) Sub-s (1) applies whether or not the person intended to access any particular data or any particular category of data or data kept by any particular person.

"Without lawful excuse"

6 (1) This section applies to—

(*a*) any offence under s 2(1) or 5,

(*b*) any offence under s 3 other than one involving a threat by the person charged to damage property in a way which he knows is likely to endanger the life of another, and

(*c*) any offence under s 4 other than one involving an intent by the person charged to use, or cause or permit the use of, something in his custody or under his control to damage property in such a way as aforesaid.

(2) A person charged witn an offence to which this section applies shall, whether or not he would be treated for the purposes of this Act as having a lawful excuse apart from this subsection, be treated for those purposes as having a lawful excuse—

(*a*) if at the time of the act or acts alleged to constitute the offence he believed that the person or persons whom he believed to be entitled to consent to or authorise the damage to (or, in the case of an offence under s 5, the accessing of) the property in question had consented, or would have consented to or authorised it if he or they had known of the damage or the accessing and its circumstances,

(*b*) in the case of an offence under s 5, if he is himself the person entitled to consent to or authorise accessing of the data concerned, or

(*c*) if he damaged or threatened to damage the property in question or, in the case of an offence under s 4, intended to use or cause or permit the use of something to damage it, in order to protect himself or another or property belonging to himself or another or a right or interest in property which was or which he believed to be vested in himself or another and, at the time of the act or acts alleged to constitute the offence, he believed—

(i) that he or that other or the property, right or interest was in immediate need of protection, and

(ii) that the means of protection adopted or proposed to be adopted were or would be reasonable having regard to all the circumstances.

(3) For the purposes of this section it is immaterial whether a belief is justified or not if it is honestly held.

(4) For the purposes of sub-s (2) a right or interest in property includes any right or privilege in or over land, whether created by grant, licence or otherwise.

(5) This section shall not be construed as casting doubt on any defence recognised by law as a defence to criminal charges.

Proceedings

7 (1) Proceedings for an offence under s 2 or 5 alleged to have been committed by a person outside the State in relation to data kept within the State or other property so situate may be taken, and the offence may for all incidental purposes be treated as having been committed, in any place in the State.

(2) (*a*) Where a person is charged with an offence under s 2, 3 or 4 in relation to property belonging to another—

    (i) it shall not be necessary to name the person to whom the property belongs, and

    (ii) it shall be presumed, until the contrary is shown, that the property belongs to another.

(*b*) Where a person is charged with an offence under s 2 in relation to such property as aforesaid, it shall also be presumed, until the contrary is shown, that the person entitled to consent to or authorise the damage concerned had not consented to or authorised it, unless the property concerned is data and the person charged is an employee or agent of the person keeping the data.

(*c*) Para (*b*) shall apply in relation to a person charged with an offence under s 5 as if the reference to damage were a reference to access and with any necessary modifications.

(3) A person charged with an offence under s 2 in relation to data or an attempt to commit such an offence may, if the evidence does not warrant a conviction for the offence charged but warrants a conviction for an offence under s 5, be found guilty of that offence.

Jurisdiction of District Court

8 No rule of law ousting the jurisdiction of the District Court to try offences where a dispute of title to property is involved shall preclude that court from trying offences under this Act.

Compensation order

9 (1) On conviction of any person of an offence under s 2 of damaging property belonging to another, the court, instead of or in addition to dealing with him in any other way, may, on application or otherwise, make an order (in this Act referred to as a "compensation order") requiring him to pay compensation in respect of that damage to any person (in this section referred to as the "injured party") who, by reason thereof, has suffered loss (other than consequential loss).

(2) The compensation payable under a compensation order (including a compensation order made against a parent or guardian of the convicted person and notwithstanding, in such a case, any other statutory limitation as to amount) shall be of such amount (not exceeding £5,000 in the case of such an order made by the District Court or such other amount as may stand prescribed for the time being by law as the limit of that Court's jurisdiction in tort) as the court considers appropriate, having regard to any evidence and to any representations that are made by or on behalf of the convicted person or the prosecutor, and shall not exceed the amount of the damages that, in the opinion of the court, the injured party concerned would be entitled to recover in a civil action against the convicted person in respect of the damage concerned.

(3) A compensation order shall not be made unless both the injured party concerned and the approximate cost of making good the damage to it (or, where appropriate, of replacing it) are readily ascertainable at the time of the conviction concerned or within a reasonable period thereafter.

(4) In determining whether to make a compensation order against a person, and in determining the amount to be paid by a person under such an order, the court shall have regard—

(*a*) to his means, or
(*b*) in a case to which s 99 of the Children Act 1908 (which empowers a court to require a parent or guardian to pay any fine, damages or costs imposed on a child or young person), applies, the means of the parent or guardian,

so far as they appear or are known to the court.

(5) A compensation order may provide for payment of the compensation by such instalments and at such times as the court shall in all the circumstances consider reasonable.

(6) Where the court considers—

(*a*) that it would be appropriate both to impose a fine and to make a compensation order, but
(*b*) that the convicted person has insufficient means to pay both an appropriate fine and appropriate compensation,

the court may, if it is satisfied that the means are sufficient to justify its doing so, make a compensation order and, if it is satisfied that it is appropriate to do so having regard to the means that would remain after compliance with the order, impose a fine.

(7) At any time after a compensation order has ceased to be suspended by virtue of s 10(1) and before it has been complied with or fully complied with, the District Court may—

(*a*) on the application of the convicted person concerned—
  (i) reduce the amount to be paid, vary any instalment payable, or direct that no payments or further payments be made, under the order if it appears to the Court—
    (I) that the means of the convicted person are insufficient to satisfy the order in full, or
    (II) on being satisfied that the injured party concerned has been given an opportunity of making representations to the court on the issue and having regard to any such representations that are made by him or on his behalf, that the damage in respect of which the order was made is less than it was taken to be for the purposes of the order, and
  (ii) if any amount paid under the order exceeds the amount appearing to the Court to be reasonable compensation for the damage, order that the amount of the excess be repaid by the injured party to the convicted person, and, upon the making of such order, the compensation order shall cease to have effect,
  or
(*b*) on the application of the injured party concerned, increase the amount to be paid, the amount of any instalment or the number of instalments payable, under the order if it appears to the Court—
  (i) that the means of the convicted person are sufficient for the relevant purposes aforesaid, or
  (ii) on being satisfied that the convicted person concerned has been given an opportunity of making representations to the court on the issue and having regard to any such representations that are made by him or on his behalf, that the damage in respect of which the order was made is more than it was taken to be for the purposes of the order.

(8) A compensation order and an order under sub-s (7)(*b*) shall be treated for the purposes of enforcement as if they were orders made by the court concerned in

civil proceedings and, without prejudice to the provisions of sub-s (7), a compensation order shall be treated for those purposes as if it were an instalment order within the meaning of Part I of the Enforcement of Court Orders Act 1940.

(9) The references to damages in the aforesaid s 99 shall be construed as if they included references to compensation under a compensation order and sub-ss (5) and (6) of that section shall not apply in relation to a compensation order.

(10) This section is without prejudice to any other enactment which provides for the payment of compensation by a person convicted of an offence of damaging property or otherwise proved to have committed such an offence.

(11) The making of a compensation order against a parent or guardian of a convicted person shall not of itself give rise to any other liability on the part of the parent or guardian in respect of the damage concerned.

(12) In this section—

(a) references to conviction of a person include references to dealing with a person under s 1(1) of the Probation of Offenders Act 1907, and
(b) the third reference in sub-s (1), the first reference in sub-s (2) and the references in sub-ss (6)(b) and (7) to a convicted person, however expressed, include, in cases to which the aforesaid s 99 applies, references to his parent or guardian.

Suspension of compensation order pending appeal

10 (1) The operation of a compensation order shall be suspended—

(a) in any case, until the expiration of one month from the date of the conviction to which the order relates, and
(b) where notice of appeal, or of application for leave to appeal, against the conviction or sentence is given within one month from the date of the conviction, until the appeal or any further appeal therefrom is finally determined or abandoned or the ordinary time for instituting any further appeal has expired.

(2) Where the operation of a compensation order is suspended under sub-s (1)(b), the order shall not take effect if the conviction concerned is reversed on appeal.

(3) A court hearing an appeal against conviction or sentence may annul or vary the compensation order concerned.

(4) A person against whom a compensation order is made may appeal against the order to the court to which an appeal against the conviction concerned may be brought and sub-ss (1)(b) and (3) shall apply in relation to an appeal under this subsection as they apply, or would apply, to an appeal against the conviction.

(5) In this section references to conviction of a person include references to dealing with a person under s 1(1) of the Probation of Offenders Act 1907.

Effect of compensation order on civil proceedings

11 Where—

(a) a compensation order has been made in favour of a person in respect of damage to any property, and
(b) damages in respect of the damage fall to be assessed in civil proceedings, then—
    (i) if the damages, as so assessed, exceed any amount paid under the compensation order, the damages to be awarded shall not exceed the amount of that excess, and
    (ii) if any amount paid under the compensation order exceeds the

> damages, as so assessed, the court may order that the amount of the excess be repaid by that person to the person against whom the compensation order was made,

and, upon the award of damages or, as the case may be, the making of the order by the court, the compensation order shall cease to have effect.

Arrest without warrant

12 (1) This section applies to an offence under this Act other than s 5 or 13(4).

(2) Any person may arrest without warrant anyone who is or whom he, with reasonable cause, suspects to be in the act of committing an offence to which this section applies.

(3) Where an offence to which this section applies has been committed, any person may arrest without warrant anyone who is or whom he, with reasonable cause, suspects to be guilty of the offence.

(4) Where a member of the Garda Síochána, with reasonable cause, suspects that an offence to which this section applies or an offence under s 13(4) has been committed, he may arrest without warrant anyone whom he, with reasonable cause, suspects to be guilty of the offence.

(5) A member of the Garda Síochána may arrest without warrant anyone who is or whom he, with reasonable cause, suspects to be about to commit an offence to which this section applies.

(6) For the purpose of arresting a person under any power conferred by this section a member of the Garda Síochána may enter (if need be, by force) and search any place where that person is or where the member, with reasonable cause, suspects him to be.

(7) This section shall apply to an attempt to commit an offence as it applies to the commission of that offence.

(8) This section shall not prejudice any power of arrest conferred by law apart from this section.

Search warrant

13 (1) If a judge of the District Court is satisfied by information on oath of a member of the Garda Síochána that there is reasonable cause to believe that any person has in his custody or under his control or on his premises any thing and that it has been used, or is intended for use, without lawful excuse—

(*a*) to damage property belonging to another,
(*b*) to damage any property in a way likely to endanger the life of another or with intent to defraud, or
(*c*) to access, or with intent to access, data,

the judge may issue a search warrant mentioned in sub-s (2).

(2) A search warrant issued under this section shall be expressed and operate to authorise a named member of the Garda Síochána, accompanied by such other members of the Garda Síochána as may be necessary, at any time or times within one month of the date of issue of the warrant, to enter if need be by force the premises named in the warrant, to search the premises and any persons found therein, to seize and detain anything which he believes to have been used or to be intended for use as aforesaid and, if the property concerned is data or the search warrant has been issued on a ground referred to in sub-s (1)(*c*), to operate, or cause to be operated by a person accompanying him for that purpose, any equipment in the premises for processing data, inspect any data found there and extract information therefrom, whether by the operation of such equipment or otherwise.

(3) The Police (Property) Act 1897, shall apply to property which has come into the possession of the Garda Síochána under this section as it applies to property which has come into the possession of the Garda Síochána in the circumstances mentioned in that Act.

(4) A person who—

(*a*) obstructs or impedes a member of the Garda Síochána acting under the authority of a search warrant issued under this section, or

(*b*) is found on or at the premises specified in the warrant by a member of the Garda Síochána acting as aforesaid and who fails or refuses to give the member his name and address when required by the member to do so or gives him a name or address that is false or misleading,

shall be guilty of an offence and shall be liable on summary conviction—

(i) in the case of an offence under para (*a*), to a fine not exceeding £1,000 or imprisonment not exceeding 12 months or both, and

(ii) in the case of an offence under para (*b*), to a fine not exceeding £500.

Minor and consequential changes in existing law

14 (1) The common law offence of arson is hereby abolished.

(2) The Malicious Damage Act 1861, is hereby amended—

(*a*) by the substitution in s 37, for "Electric or Magnetic Telegraph", or "telegraph (within the meaning of the Telegraph Acts 1863 to 1916)", and

(*b*) by the substitution—

(i) in s 40, for the words from "shall be liable" to the end of the section, and

(ii) in s 41, for the words from "shall, on conviction thereof" to the end of the section,

of "shall be liable—

(*a*) on summary conviction, to a fine not exceeding £1,000 or imprisonment for a term not exceeding 12 months or both, and

(*b*) on conviction on indictment, to a fine not exceeding £10,000 or imprisonment for a term not exceeding 10 years or both.".

(3) The abolition by sub-s (1) of the common law offence of arson shall not affect the operation of s 2 of, and para 3 of the Schedule to, the Criminal Law (Jurisdiction) Act, 1976, and the repeal by s 15 of ss 1 to 7 of the Malicious Damage Act 1861, shall not affect the operation of those sections for the purposes of the said s 2 and para 6 of the said Schedule; and accordingly the said s 2 and the said Schedule shall have effect as if sub-s (1) and s 15 had not been enacted.

(4) On the commencement of this subsection—

(*a*) sub-s (3) shall cease to have effect,

(*b*) s 21(2) of, and para 3 of the Schedule to, the Criminal Law (Jurisdiction) Act 1976, shall be repealed, and

(*c*) the following paragraphs shall be substituted for para 6 of the said Schedule—

"*Criminal Damage*

6. Any offence under s 35 (interference with railway) of the Malicious Damage Act 1861.

6A. Any offence under sub-ss (1) and (4) or sub-ss (2) and (4) of s 2 of the Criminal Damage Act 1991 (arson).".

Repeal

15 The Malicious Damage Act 1861 (except ss 35 to 38, 40, 41, 47, 48, 58 and 72), is hereby repealed.

Short title and commencement

16 (1) This Act may be cited as the Criminal Damage Act 1991.

(2) This Act (except s 14(4)) shall come into operation one month after the date of its passing.

(3) Section 14(4) shall come into operation on such day as may be fixed therefor by order made by the Minister for Justice.

7.54 The element of "without lawful excuse" explained in s 6 is taken from the United Kingdom Criminal Damage Act 1971. The Law Commission, in their report on the matter, indicated that there was a clear distinction between the mental element and this element of unlawfulness[78]. In *R v Denton*[79] the matter was taken to extreme. The accused was held not guilty of arson where he set fire to his employer's property in the belief that he had been encouraged to do so to enable his employer to make a fraudulent claim against his insurance. It is difficult to see how subjective integration into a common design to destroy property for the purposes of fraud could possibly constitute a lawful excuse. In the context of ss 2, 3, 4 and 5 the phrase "a lawful excuse" indicates the existence of such property right, or permission, over the damaged article as would give the accused an entitlement to act either intending to damage it, or being reckless as to whether damage to it occurred. The civil law is relevant here only to the extent necessary for determining whether such an excuse existed for the purpose of the criminal law. In the law of tort a remedy of self-help can be exercised but only where the use of force is necessary because there is no reasonable alternative.

7.55 ***Lloyd v Director of Public Prosecutions***
[1991] 1 All ER 983
Divisional Court England, 1991

Facts: The accused parked his car in a private car park ignoring notices indicating that unauthorised parking would involve clamping. A levy of £25 was to be charged for unclamping an illegally parked vehicle. Mr Lloyd ignored these warnings. Late in the evening he discovered his car had been clamped. Coincidentally the security firm involved in unclamping cars had arrived to deal with another illegally parked vehicle. The accused refused to pay the £25 levy and left by taxi. He later returned and removed the clamp by using a disc cutter. He was charged with destroying or damaging the padlocks on the clamp without lawful excuse, intending to destroy or damage them or being reckless as to whether they would be destroyed or damaged, contrary to s 1(1) of the Criminal Damage Act 1971.

Nolan LJ: . . . [it has been submitted] that the immobilisation of the car was plainly unlawful thereafter and the appellant was at liberty to exercise his right of recaption using such reasonable force as was necessary to do so.

To my mind, it would be a truly absurd state of affairs if the appellant having consented to the risk of clamping, was at liberty to withdraw his consent with immediate effect once clamping had occurred and to proceed at once to recover his car by force. I am satisfied that this is not the law. Even assuming in the

78 Law Commission No 29 para 49.
79 [1982] 1 All ER 65.

appellant's favour that the refusal of South Coast Securities to let him remove his car, save on payment of £25, was an unlawful restraint, it would by no means follow that there was a lawful excuse for his subsequent action. He had a choice. He could have paid £25 under protest, removed his car and taken action against South Coast securities in the county court. Instead he chose to re-enter the car park, once again, quite plainly as a trespasser, and to retrieve his car by causing some £50–worth of damage to the property of South Coast Securities.

In my judgment, the suggestion that there was a lawful excuse for his action is wholly untenable. At worst what he had suffered was a civil wrong. The remedy for such wrongs is available in the civil courts. That is what they are there for. Self-help involving the use of force can only be contemplated where there is no reasonable alternative. Here . . . there was such an alternative . . .

It follows that I can express my conclusion more simply by saying, as I do, that in my judgment the present case is covered by the decision in *Stear v Scott* [Divisional Court, 28 March 1984]. I see no reason to suppose that the court in that case failed to have regard to the relevant authorities and principles . . . situations like these which have arisen in the present case are becoming increasingly common. They can cause intense irritation to both the motorist deprived of the use of his car, as he thinks, unreasonably, and to the landowner or other victim of the motorist's unauthorised parking. That makes it all the more necessary for it to be clearly stated that, at any rate as a general rule, if a motorist parks his car without permission on another person's property knowing that by doing so he runs the risk of being clamped, he has no right to damage or destroy the clamp. If he does so he will be guilty of a criminal offence.

7.56   *Malicious Damage Act 1861*

Injuries to Railway Carriages and Telegraphs

Placing Wood, &c on Railway with Intent to obstruct or overthrow any Engine, &c

35 Whosoever shall unlawfully and maliciously put, place, cast, or throw upon or across any Railway any Wood, Stone, or other Matter or Thing, or shall unlawfully and maliciously take up, remove, or displace any Rail, Sleeper, or other Matter or Thing belonging to any Railway, or shall unlawfully and maliciously turn, move, or divert any Points or other Machinery belonging to any Railway, or shall unlawfully and maliciously make or show, hide or remove, any Signal or Light upon or near to any Railway, or shall unlawfully and maliciously do or cause to be done any other Matter or Thing, with Intent, in any of the Cases aforesaid, to obstruct, upset, overthrow, injure, or destroy any Engine, Tender, Carriage, or Truck using such Railway, shall be guilty of Felony, and being convicted thereof shall be liable, at the Discretion of the Court, to be kept in Penal Servitude for Life or for any Term not less than Three Years, – or to be imprisoned for any Term not exceeding Two Years, with or without Hard Labour, and, if a Male under the Age of Sixteen, with or without Whipping.

Obstructing Engines or Carriages on Railways

36 Whosoever, by any unlawful Act, or by any wilful Omission or Neglect, shall obstruct or cause to be obstructed, any Engine or Carriage using any Railway, or shall aid or assist therein, shall be guilty of a Misdemeanor, and being convicted thereof shall be liable, at the Discretion of the Court, to be imprisoned for any Term not exceeding Two Years, with or without Hard Labour.

Injuries to Electric or Magnetic Telegraphs

37 Whosoever shall unlawfully and maliciously cut, break, throw down, destroy, injure, or remove any Battery, Machinery, Wire, Cable, Post, or other Matter or Thing whatsoever, being Part of or being used or employed in or about any Electric or Magnetic Telegraph, or in the working thereof, or shall unlawfully and maliciously prevent or obstruct in any Manner whatsoever the sending, Conveyance, or Delivery of any Communication by any such Telegraph, shall be guilty of a Misdemeanour, and being convicted thereof shall be liable, at the Discretion of the Court, to be imprisoned for any Term not exceeding Two Years, with or without Hard Labour: Provided that if it shall appear to any Justice, on the Examination of any Person charged with any Offence against this Section, that it is not expedient to the Ends of Justice that the same should be prosecuted by Indictment, the Justice may proceed summarily to hear and determine the same, and the Offender shall, on Conviction thereof, at the Discretion of the Justice, either be committed to the Common Gaol or House of Correction, there to be imprisoned only, or to be imprisoned and kept to Hard Labour, for any Term not exceeding Three Months, or else shall forfeit and pay such Sum of Money not exceeding Ten Pounds as to the Justice shall seem meet.

Attempt to injure such Telegraphs

38 Whosoever shall unlawfully and maliciously, by any overt Act, attempt to commit any of the Offences in the last preceding Section mentioned, shall, on Conviction thereof before a Justice of the Peace, at the Discretion of the Justice, either be committed to the Common Gaol or House of Correction, there to be imprisoned only, or to be imprisoned and kept to Hard Labour, for any Term not exceeding Three Months, or else shall forfeit and pay such Sum of Money not exceeding Ten Pounds as to the Justice shall seem meet.

Injuries to Cattle and other Animals

Killing or maiming Cattle

40 Whosoever shall unlawfully and maliciously kill, maim, or wound any Cattle shall be guilty of Felony, and being convicted thereof shall be liable, at the Discretion of the Court, to be kept in Penal Servitude for any Term not exceeding Fourteen and not less than Three Years, – or to be imprisoned for any Term not exceeding Two Years, with or without Hard Labour, and with or without Solitary Confinement.

Killing or maiming other Animals

41 Whosoever shall unlawfully and maliciously kill, maim, or wound any Dog, Bird, Beast, or other Animal, not being Cattle, but being either the Subject of Larceny at Common Law, or being ordinarily kept in a State of Confinement, or for any domestic Purpose, shall, on Conviction thereof before a Justice of the Peace, at the Discretion of the Justice, either be committed to the Common Gaol or House of Correction, there to be imprisoned only, or to be imprisoned and kept to Hard Labour, for any Term not exceeding Six Months, or else shall forfeit and pay, over and above the Amount of Injury done, such Sum of Money not exceeding Twenty Pounds as to the Justice shall seem meet; and whosoever, having been convicted of any such Offence, shall afterwards commit any of the said Offences in this Section before mentioned, and shall be convicted thereof in like Manner, shall be committed to the Common Gaol or House of Correction, there to be kept to Hard Labour for such Term not exceeding Twelve Months as the convicting Justice shall think fit.

Exhibiting false Signals, &c

47 Whosoever shall unlawfuly mask, alter, or remove any Light or Signal, or unlawfully exhibit any false Light or Signal, with Intent to bring any Ship, Vessel, or Boat into Danger, or shall unlawfully and maliciously do anything tending to the immediate Loss or Destruction of any Ship, Vessel, or Boat, and for which no Punishment is herein-before provided, shall be guilty of Felony, and being convicted thereof shall be liable, at the Discretion of the Court, to be kept in Penal Servitude for Life, or for any Term not less than Three Years, – or to be imprisoned for any Term not exceeding Two Years, with or without Hard Labour, and with or without Solitary Confinement, and, if a Male under the Age of Sixteen Years, with or without Whipping.

Removing or concealing Buoys and other Sea Marks

48 Whosoever shall unlawfully and maliciously cut away, cast adrift, remove, alter, deface, sink, or destroy, or shall unlawfully and maliciously do any Act with Intent to cut away, cast adrift, remove, alter, deface, sink, or destroy, or shall in any other Manner unlawfully and maliciously injure or conceal any Boat, Buoy, Buoy Rope, Peach, or Mark used or intended for the Guidance of Seamen or the Purpose of Navigation, shall be guilty of Felony, and being convicted thereof, shall be liable, at the Discretion of the Court to be kept in Penal Servitude for any Term not exceeding Seven Years and not less than Three Years, or to be imprisoned for any Term not exceeding Two Years, with or without Hard Labour, and with or without Solitary Confinement, and, if a Male under the Age of Sixteen Years, with or without Whipping.

Malice against Owner of Property unnecessary

58 Every Punishment and Forfeiture by this Act imposed on any Person maliciously committing any Offence, whether the same be punishable upon Indictment or upon summary Conviction, shall equally apply and be enforced, whether the Offence shall be committed from Malice conceived against the Owner of the Property in respect of which it shall be committed or otherwise.

Offences committed within the Jurisdiction of the Admiralty

72 All indictable Offences mentioned in this Act which shall be committed within the Jurisdiction of the Admiralty of *England* or *Ireland* shall be deemed to be Offences of the same Nature and liable to the same Punishments as if they had been committed upon the Land in *England* or *Ireland*, and may be dealt with, inquired of, tried, and determined in any County or Place in *England* or *Ireland* in which the Offender shall be apprehended or be in Custody, in the same Manner in all respects as if they had been actually committed in that County or Place; and in any Indictment for any such Offence, or for being an Accessory to such an Offence, the Venue in the Margin shall be the same as if the Offence had been committed in such County or Place, and the Offence shall be averred to have been committed "on the High Seas:" Provided that nothing herein contained shall alter or affect any of the Laws relating to the Government of Her Majesty's Land or Naval Forces.

Companies Offences

7.57 A company is a legal person. As such it possesses the power to buy and sell property, to enter into contracts and, essentially, to deal in the same way as an individual in commercial matters. The powers of the company are limited by its memorandum of incorporation. Since s 4 of the Companies Act, 1963, however, it is only where a person dealing with a company was aware that the dealing in question was outside the powers of the company as contained in its memorandum that such dealing will be void. In consequence, a person may generally presume, in any dealing with a company, that it is acting within the terms of its powers as defined by its memorandum.

Limited Liability

The type of company which concerns the criminal law is the limited liability company. The object of this entity is to allow persons who wish to engage in commerce to shelter behind an artificial legal entity. In normal circumstances, a person trading in the market place is liable to the full extent of his wealth for any obligation he enters into. If damages are awarded against a person for breach of contract it may result in the successful party mortgaging and selling that person's land, forcibly taking his goods or having an order made against him in the District Court that he should pay a periodic sum of money in satisfaction of the judgment. Remedies are also possible against a limited liability company. Where a person, however, trades through a limited liability company, it is only the assets of the company which can be made available in satisfaction of a judgment. The directors and shareholders are entirely free of personal responsibility. To the extent, therefore, that companies were set up in order to allow their directors and shareholders to retain their wealth securely, a company may be considered to have fraud as its object. Usually, in modern times, directors and shareholders of companies are required to give personal guarantees for any major debts which the company may enter into. If the company defaults in its obligations they will be liable by virtue of this separate contract.

Fraudulent Trading

7.58 Any reading of the newspapers will reveal that quite frequently companies collapse owing huge debts and without the assets to repay their creditors. If this occurs the company may be placed in liquidation and its assets distributed among the creditors. Some creditors will have security for their debts by way of a debenture but some will be unsecured. It is not uncommon for the costs of liquidation to eat up the entire assets of the company and for their to be nothing left over to satisfy creditors. Even if the assets of a company are large, by the time it is placed in liquidation the damage it would have done in drawing in goods or services on the promise of payment, while it is unable to meet these liabilities, will be such that only a tiny percentage of debts can be paid. The constant occurrence of this situation has led to the creation of offences whereby the controllers of a company will be liable where they trade knowing that a company will be unable to meet its liabilities. Unfortunately, this section has not resulted in any prosecution, successful or unsuccessful.

7.59   ***Companies Act 1963***
                            as inserted by s 137 of the
                            Companies Act 1990

Criminal liability of persons concerned for fraudulent trading of company

297   (1) If any person is knowingly a party to the carrying on of the business of a company with intent to defraud creditors of the company or creditors of any other person or for any fraudulent purpose, that person shall be guilty of an offence.

(2) Any person who is convicted of an offence under this section shall be liable – (a) on summary conviction to imprisonment for a term not exceeding twelve months or to a fine not exceeding £1,000 or to both, or (b) on conviction on indictment, to imprisonment for a term not exceeding seven years or to a fine not exceeding £50,000 or to both.

7.60   The essence of the section is the intent to defraud a person who is a creditor of the company or of any other person. While the phrase "of any other person" is unlimited in its scope, in practice it will relate to a scheme whereby the director of a company has attempted to hide his personal debts behind the limited liability of a company which he controls. In distinction to other sections of the Companies Acts, 1963–1990 liability is not limited to directors or shareholders. Any person may be a party to carrying on the business of a company for a fraudulent purpose.

Intent to defraud is discussed in greater detail in the context of forgery at paras **8.48–8.53**. In essence, it requires the accused to knowingly perpetrate some deceit or falsehood with a purpose of causing the person deceived to act to his loss. Usually, this deceit will take the form of a scheme which results in the victim losing his property to the deceiver. Equally, it may be a scheme where as a result of the deceit the victim parts with his property to someone else. Usually, the deceiver and the gainer from the transaction will be acting in conspiracy. Often, in the context of a company, the party that gains may be a separate legal entity apart from the deceiver and there may be no obvious reason as to why he will make a profit from the transaction. The essence of the section is, however, clear, and it is not necessary to prove that the deceiver gained a profit from his deceit, only that the victim lost as a result. In the context of section 297 it is not necessary that the fraudulent purpose be successful.

The offence is defined in terms of a mental element of an "intent to defraud" or "any fraudulent purpose". The evidence must be such as to establish that fraudulent purpose beyond reasonable doubt. This is usually only possible where the accused has acted in such a way as to make his fraudulent purpose clear. Uncovering such evidence may be as difficult as in any other criminal investigation. In the past this kind of prosecution was gravely hampered by the unreformed hearsay rule. This is now the subject of legislative reform in the shape of the Criminal Evidence Act 1992, which, unfortunately, may cause as many problems as it solves; it contains no residual exception allowing for the admission of hearsay evidence where it is sufficiently trustworthy.

Examples

7.61 Three civil cases decided under s 297, prior to its amendment by the Companies Act 1990, revealed the nature of the activity outlawed. In *Re Hunting Lodge Limited*[80] two directors were involved in selling the only remaining asset of a company which was then hopelessly insolvent. This asset consisted of a public house which was sold to a third party, O'C, who ostensibly paid £480,000. A secret arrangement for the payment of another £200,000 had been made. This, O'C was to pay directly into fictitious bank accounts held by the directors. Carroll J held the directors and O'C personally liable for this fraud holding that a single transaction was sufficient to constitute a "carrying on of the business of a company". In *Re Aluminium Fabricators Limited*[81], the directors of a company had deliberately maintained two sets of books in order to conceal from their accountants, the Revenue Commissioners, and their creditors, the fact that they were diluting the assets of the company by paying them to themselves. Obviously, this scheme would have the result that the Revenue Commissioners and their creditors would be deprived of taxation and payment for services. O'Hanlon J found that the business had been carried on with intent to defraud. A similar scheme was operated in *Re Kelly's Carpetdrome Limited*[82]. The controller of this company was involved in transferring the assets of the company into the control of the people behind the company. With that in mind an arrangement had been made for the destruction of records in order to deceive the Revenue Commissioners and render the company liable to pay less tax. In all of these three cases the persons involved were held personally liable for the company's debts. There is no doubt that on these facts, if the evidence had been available before a jury, an offence under s 297 was committed.

7.62 It may be helpful to contrast s 297 with s 297A. This now establishes civil liability where a person was, as an officer of the company, knowingly a party to carrying on the business of a company in a reckless manner. As our discussion of this topic in chapter 1 has indicated a reckless state of mind is insufficient to establish intent. Recklessness, in this context, will be the taking of a substantial risk, by the controllers of the company, that a creditor might be left unsatisfied due to the trading difficulties of the company. Intentionally carrying on the business for a fraudulent purpose in comparison, must involve a deliberate scheme to ensure that a creditor, such as the Revenue Commissioners, will remain unsatisfied. Usually, one of two schemes is involved. The assets of the company will be syphoned off so that little or nothing will be left to satisfy creditors, or, fraudulent books will be kept to deceive the Revenue Commissioners as to the profitability, and thus liability to tax, of the company.

Insider Dealing

7.63 A limited liability company has a share capital. This constitutes the means by which ownership of the company, and voting rights, are

---

80 [1985] ILRM 75.
81 High Court, unreported 13 May 1983.
82 High Court, unreported 1 July 1983.

determined. The document setting up the company will define the number of shares it is divided into. This number can be increased, or, exceptionally, decreased. In private companies the value placed on a share is usually nominal. The most common arrangement is to have a share capital divided into 100 ordinary £1 shares. The persons setting up the company purchase these shares for their stated value. In publically quoted companies, which are traded on a stock market, the share price is dependent on the trading performance and assets of a company. If the net assets of a company are, for example £1,000,000 and it achieves a profit of £100,000 each year then if it has 1,000,000 issued shares these may be traded at in or around £1.60. From time to time companies amalgamate with, or are taken over by other companies. These arrangements can make them part of a larger and more profitable group with vastly increased assets and can, in consequence, dramatically increase the price of a share. With inside knowledge it is possible to predict such a share movement and buy shares prior to the knowledge becoming public with a view to making a financial coup. Part V of the Companies Act 1990, for the first time, outlaws this conduct and, by s 111, makes it a criminal offence.

7.64 Identical provisions are used to make insider dealers civilly and criminally liable. This scheme is of dubious constitutional validity. Criminal liability is based on a civil standard of purely notional blame.

Essentially, an insider is prohibited from acquiring, disposing of, subscribing for or underwriting securities. This activity includes making or offering to make an agreement relating to any of those activities and inducing or attempting to induce any other person so to act. In this context securities include shares, debentures or other debt securities issued, or which are proposed to be issued, in Ireland or elsewhere and which are to be traded on a stock exchange. Consequently, an insider dealing in a private company is not a criminal offence as the shares will be traded outside the stock exchange. An insider, under s 108(11) is a person who is:

(a) An officer of the company or a related company;

(b) a shareholder of the company or a related company;

(c) the occupier of a position (including a public office) that may reasonably be expected to give him access to insider information, as defined by s 108(1) and (2) because of

    (i) a professional, business or other relationship with a company or

    (ii) his being an officer of a substantial shareholder in the company or a related company.

This prohibition extends beyond those who are connected with the company in this sense. Those who are in possession of relevant information from an insider are prohibited from dealing in securities if they are aware, or ought reasonably to have been aware, that the person from whom they received the information is prohibited from dealing. The insider is forbidden to pass on relevant information to any other person if he knows, or ought reasonably to know, that the other person will use that information in order to deal in securities, either himself or through an agent. The prohibition covers those who are in possession of information which is not generally available but, if it were, would be likely to materially affect the price of securities.

7.65 There are many ways in which insider trading may take place. Primarily, a director of the company will be aware that he is in possession of relevant information. For criminal liability, however, it is submitted, he must in addition know that the information, if generally available, would be likely materially to affect the price of the securities in which he proposes to deal. This interpretation is consistent with the decision in *The People (DPP) v Murray*[83]. In contrast, however, with the United Kingdom legislation the Company Securities (Insider Dealing) Act 1985, the requirement of knowledge is not explicit. Obviously, the Irish Act was modelled on its English predecessor and the legislature has deliberately chosen to leave out this mental element requirement. It may be, therefore, that the section can only be construed as one of strict liability. When one moves to the provisions dealing with the definition of an insider, one notes that the mental element is specifically excluded in the case of persons who occupy positions that may reasonably be expected to give him access to "insider information" by virtue of their professional or business relationship with a company, or with a substantial shareholder of the company. The situation becomes even more extreme in dealing with secondary insiders. These are forbidden to deal in securities in a company when they are in possession of relevant information if they have obtained it from someone who is also prohibited, if they are aware "or ought reasonably to be aware" that the person from whom they obtained the information is himself prohibited from dealing. The insider is forbidden to pass on information to a secondary insider if he knows or "ought reasonably to know" that the secondary insider will make use of the information for the purpose of insider dealing. The situation which emerges appears to be as follows:

(1) It is essential that any accused should actually engage in insider dealing.

(2) It is not necessary for the accused to know, or be reckless, that the information he is using for insider dealing is not generally available or, that if it were, it would be likely to materially affect the price of the securities he proposes to deal in.

(3) An insider extends to those occupying positions that might reasonably be expected to give them access to insider information.

(4) An insider commits an offence by passing on relevant information to a third party if he ought reasonably to have known that the third party will make use of the information for the purpose of insider dealing.

(5) A third party is prohibited form insider dealing if he ought reasonably to have been aware that the person from whom he obtained the information was himself prohibited from insider dealing.

7.66 The net effect of this is the establishment of a criminal liability which is based on the fact of insider dealing. While it is possible to construe the primary offence of insider dealing by an officer of the company as requiring recklessness or knowledge that general possession of the information would materially affect the price of the securities, this construction becomes impossible on a consideration of the definition of those who are insiders and those who receive information from insiders. Here, liability depends on

83 [1977] IR 360.

what a person ought reasonably to have known in the circumstances. Liability is therefore based upon the civil standard of negligence. The penalty for this offence, on indictment, is a maximum of ten years imprisonment and a fine of £200,000. If these provisions are given their ordinary meaning it is difficult to see how the imposition of criminal liability can be justified. In many instances covered by Part V of the Companies Act 1990, criminal liability is established merely on the basis of a transaction which, from a subjective viewpoint, could be entirely innocent but which, on an objective consideration, involved the accused failing to make an enquiry or failing to be aware of what a reasonable person would have been aware of in the circumstances. It is difficult to see the justice of these provisions. In so far as Part V of the Companies Act 1990 imposes criminal liability it may be unconstitutional. Under s 109 civil liability is imposed in these circumstances, in order to compensate those who have lost as a result of the insider dealing and to pay back the company for the loss it made as a result of the misuse of the information. These provisions can be justified as the civil standard of imposing liability for damages has always been based upon what a reasonable or ordinary person ought to have known or realised in a given set of circumstances. That has not been the standard in criminal offences, apart from those of a minor and regulatory nature.

7.67   *Companies Act 1990*

Insider Dealing

Interpretation

107 In this Part, except where the context otherwise requires—
"dealing", in relation to securities, means (whether as principal or agent) acquiring, disposing of, subscribing for or underwriting the securities, or making or offering to make, or inducing or attempting to induce a person to make or to offer to make, an agreement—

(*a*) for or relating to acquiring, disposing of, subscribing for or underwriting the securities; or
(*b*) the purpose or purported purpose of which is to secure a profit or gain to a person who acquires, disposes of, subscribes for or underwrites the securities or to any of the parties to the agreement in relation to the securities;

"director" includes a shadow director within the meaning of s 27;
"officer", in relation to a company, includes—

(*a*) a director, secretary or employee;
(*b*) a liquidator;
(*c*) any person administering a compromise or arrangement made between the company and its creditors;
(*d*) an examiner;
(*e*) an auditor; and
(*f*) a receiver;

"public office" means an office or employment which is remunerated out of the Central Fund or out of moneys provided by the Oireachtas or money raised by local taxation or charges, or an appointment to or employment under any commission, committee, tribunal, board or body established by the Government or any Minister of the Government or by or under any statutory authority;
"recognised stock exchange" includes, in particular, any exchange prescribed by the Minister which provides facilities for the buying and selling of rights or obligations to acquire stock;

"related company", in relation to a company, means any body corporate which is the company's subsidiary or holding company, or a subsidiary of the company's holding company;

"relevant authority", in relation to a recognised stock exchange, means—

(i) its board of directors, committee of management or other management body, or

(ii) its manager, however described;

"securities" means—

(a) shares, debentures or other debt securities issued or proposed to be issued, whether in the State or otherwise, and for which dealing facilities are, or are to be provided by a recognised stock exchange;

(b) any right, option or obligation in respect of any such shares, debentures or other debt securities referred to in para (a);

(c) any right, option or obligation in respect of any index relating to any such shares, debentures or other debt securities referred to in para (a); or

(d) such interests as may be prescribed;

"underwrite" includes sub-underwrite.

Unlawful dealings in securities by insiders

108 (1) It shall not be lawful for a person who is, or at any time in the preceding 6 months has been, connected with a company to deal in any securities of that company if by reason of his so being, or having been, connected with that company he is in possession of information that is not generally available, but, if it were, would be likely materially to affect the price of those securities.

(2) It shall not be lawful for a person who is, or at any time in the preceding 6 months has been, connected with a company to deal in any securities of any other company if by reason of his so being, or having been, connected with the first-mentioned company he is in possession of information that—

(a) is not generally available but, if it were, would be likely materially to affect the price of those securities, and

(b) relates to any transaction (actual or contemplated) involving both those companies or involving one of them and securities of the other, or to the fact that any such transaction is no longer contemplated.

(3) Where a person is in possession of any such information as is mentioned in sub-s (1) or (2) that if generally available would be likely materially to affect the price of securities but is not precluded by either of those subsections from dealing in those securities, it shall not be lawful for him to deal in those securities if he has received the information, directly or indirectly, from another person and is aware, or ought reasonably to be aware, of facts or circumstances by virtue of which that other person is then himself precluded by sub-s (1) or (2) from dealing in those securities.

(4) It shall not be lawful for a person at any time when he is precluded by sub-s (1), (2) or (3) from dealing in any securities, to cause or procure any other person to deal in those securities.

(5) It shall not be lawful for a person, at any time when he is precluded by sub-s (1), (2) or (3) from dealing in any securities by reason of his being in possession of any information, to communicate that information to any other person if he knows, or ought reasonably to know, that the other person will make use of the information for the purpose of dealing, or causing or procuring another person to deal, in those securities.

(6) Without prejudice to sub-s (3), but subject to sub-ss (7) and (8), it shall not be lawful for a company to deal in any securities at a time when any officer of that company is precluded by sub-s (1), (2) or (3) from dealing in those securities.

(7) Sub-s (6) does not preclude a company from entering into a transaction at any time by reason only of information in the possession of an officer of that company if—

    (*a*) the decision to enter into the transaction was taken on its behalf by a person other than the officer;

    (*b*) it had in operation at that time written arrangements to ensure that the information was not communicated to that person and that no advice relating to the transaction was given to him by a person in possession of the information; and

    (*c*) the information was not so communicated and such advice was not so given.

(8) Sub-s (6) does not preclude a company from dealing in securities of another company at any time by reason only of information in the possession of an officer of the first-mentioned company, being information that was received by the officer in the course of the performance of his duties as an officer of the first-mentioned company and that consists only of the fact that the first-mentioned company proposes to deal in securities of that other company.

(9) This section does not preclude a person from dealing in securities, or rights or interests in securities, of a company if—

    (*a*) he enters into the transaction concerned as agent for another person pursuant to a specified instruction of that other person to effect that transaction; and

    (*b*) he has not given any advice to the other person in relation to dealing in securities, or rights or interests in securities, of that company that are included in the same class as the first-mentioned securities.

(10) This section does not preclude a person from dealing in securities if, while not otherwise taking advantage of his possession of information referred to in sub-s (1)—

    (*a*) he gives at least 21 days' notice to a relevant authority of the relevant stock exchange of his intention to deal, within the period referred to in para (*b*), in the securities of the company concerned, and

    (*b*) the dealing takes place within a period beginning 7 days after the publication of the company's interim or final results, as the case may be and ending 14 days after such publication, and

    (*c*) the notice referred to in para (*a*) is published by the exchange concerned immediately on its receipt.

(11) For the purposes of this section, a person is connected with a company if, being a natural person—

    (*a*) he is an officer of that company or of a related company;

    (*b*) he is a shareholder in that company or in a related company; or

    (*c*) he occupies a position (including a public office) that may reasonably be expected to give him access to information of a kind to which sub-ss (1) and (2) apply by virtue of—

        (i) any professional, business or other relationship existing between himself (or his employer or a company of which he is an officer) and that company or a related company; or

        (ii) his being an officer of a substantial shareholder in that company or in a related company.

(12) For the purposes of sub-s (11) "substantial shareholder" means a person who holds shares in a company, the number of which is above the notifiable percentage for the time being in force under s 70.

(13) The prohibitions in sub-ss (1), (3), (4) and (5) shall extend to dealings in securities issued by the State as if the references in sub-ss (1), (9) and (11) (other

than paras (*a*) and (*b*) of the last mentioned subsection) to a company were references to the State.

Civil liability for unlawful dealing

109 (1) Where a person deals in or causes or procures another person to deal in securities in a manner declared unlawful by s 108 or communicates information in any such manner, that person shall, without prejudice to any other cause of action which may lie against him, be liable—

(*a*) to compensate any other party to the transaction who was not in possession of the relevant information for any loss sustained by that party by reason of any difference between the price at which the securities were dealt in in that transaction and the price at which they would have been likely to have been dealt in in such a transaction a the time when the first-mentioned transaction took place if that information had been generally available; and

(*b*) to account to the company that issued or made available those securities for any profit accuring to the first-mentioned person from dealing in those securities

(2) The amount of compensation for which a person is liable under sub-s (1) or the amount of the profit for which a person is liable to account under that subsection is—

(*a*) subject to para (*b*), the amount of the loss sustained by the person claiming the compensation or the amount of the profit referred to in sub-s (1)(*b*), as the case may be; or

(*b*) if the person so liable has been found by a court to be liable to pay an amount or amounts to any other person or persons by reason of the same act or transaction, the amount of that loss or profit less the amount or the sum of the amounts for which that person has been found to be liable.

(3) For the purposes of sub-s (2), the onus of proving that the liability of a person to pay an amount to another person arose from the same act or transaction from which another liability arose lies on the person liable to pay the amount.

(4) An action under this section for recovery of a loss or profit shall not be commenced after the expiration of 2 years after the date of completion of the transaction in which the loss or profit occurred.

Exempt transactions

110 (1) Nothing in s 108 shall prevent a person from—

(*a*) acquiring securities under a will or on the intestacy of another person; or

(*b*) acquiring securities in a company pursuant to an employee profit sharing scheme—

    (i) approved by the Revenue Commissioners for the purposes of the Finance Acts, and

    (ii) the terms of which were approved by the company in general meeting, and

    (iii) under which all permanent employees of the company are offered the opportunity to participate on equal terms relative to specified objective criteria;

(*c*) entering in good faith into a transaction to which sub-s (2) applies.

(2) This subsection applies to the following kinds of transactions—

(*a*) the obtaining by a director of a share qualification under s 180 of the Principal Act;

(*b*) a transaction entered into by a person in accordance with his obligations under an underwriting agreement;

(*c*) a transaction entered into by a personal representative of a deceased person, a trustee, or liquidator, receiver or examiner in the performance of the functions of his office; or

(*d*) a transaction by way of, or arising out of, a mortgage of or charge on securities or a mortgage, charge, pledge or lien on documents of title to securities.

(3) This Part shall not apply to transactions entered into in pursuit of monetary, exchange rate, national debt management or foreign exchange reserve policies by any Minister of the Government or the Central Bank, or by any person on their behalf.

Criminal liability for unlawful dealing

111 A person who deals in securities in a manner declared unlawful by s 108 shall be guilty of an offence.

Restriction on dealing

112 (1) Subject to sub-s (2), a person convicted of an offence under s 111 or this section shall not deal within the period of 12 months from the date of the conviction.

(2) Where a person convicted of an offence under sub-s (1) has, before the date of his conviction, initiated a transaction under which some element of performance remains to be rendered, sub-s (1) shall not prohibit him from completing the transaction where a relevant authority of a recognised stock exchange has indicated in writing, to the parties to the transaction, its satisfaction that—

(*a*) the transaction was initiated but not completed before the date of the conviction, and

(*b*) if the transaction were not concluded, the rights of an innocent third party would be prejudiced, and

(*c*) the transaction would not be unlawful under any other provision of this Part.

(3) A person who contravenes this section shall be guilty of an offence.

Duty of agents in relation to unlawful dealing

113 (1) A person shall not deal on behalf of another person if he has reasonable cause to believe or ought to conclude that the deal would be unlawful, within the meaning of s 108.

(2) A person who contravenes this section shall be guilty of an offence.

Penalties for offences under this Part

114 A person who commits an offence under this Part shall be liable—

(*a*) on summary conviction to imprisonment for a term not exceeding 12 months or to a fine not exceeding £1,000 or to both, or

(*b*) on conviction on indictment, to imprisonment for a term not exceeding 10 years or to a fine not exceeding £200,000 or to both.

Duty of recognised stock exchange in relation to unlawful dealing

115 (1) If it appears to a relevant authority of a recognised stock exchange that any person has committed an offence under this Part, such authority shall forthwith report the matter to the Director of Public Prosecutions and shall furnish to the Director of Public Prosecutions such information and give to him such access to and facilities for inspecting and taking copies of any documents, being information or documents in the possession or under the control of such authority and relating to the matter in question, as the Director of Public Prosecutions may require.

(2) Where it appears to a member of a recognised stock exchange that any person has committed an offence under this Part, he shall report the matter forthwith to a relevant authority of the recognised stock exchange concerned, who shall thereupon come under the duty referred to in sub-s (1).

(3) If it appears to a court in any proceedings that any person has committed an offence as aforesaid, and that no report relating to the matter has been made to the Director of Public Prosecutions under sub-s (1), that court may, on the application of any person interested in the proceedings concerned or of its own motion, direct a relevant authority of the recognised stock exchange concerned to make such a report, and on a report being made accordingly, this section shall have effect as though the report had been made in pursuance of sub-s (1).

(4) If, where any matter is reported or referred to the Director of Public Prosecutions under this section, he considers that the case is one in which a prosecution ought to be instituted and institutes proceedings accordingly, it shall be the duty of a relevant authority of the recognised stock exchange concerned, and of every officer of the company whose securities are concerned, and of any other person who appears to the Director of Public Prosecutions to have relevant information (other than any defendant in the proceedings) to give all assistance in connection with the prosecution which he or they are reasonably able to give.

(5) If it appears to the Minister, arising from a complaint to a relevant authority of a recognised stock exchange concerning an alleged offence under this Part, that there are circumstances suggesting that—

(*a*) the relevant authority ought to use its powers under this Part but has not done so, or

(*b*) that a report ought to be made to the Director of Public Prosecutions under sub-s (1), but that the relevant authority concerned has not so reported,

he may direct the relevant authority to use such powers or make such a report, and on a report being made accordingly, this section shall have effect as though the report had been made in pursuance of sub-s (1).

(6) Where the Minister gives a direction under sub-s (5), the relevant authority concerned shall communicate the results of its investigations, or a copy of its report under sub-s (1), as the case may be, to the Minister.

(7) A relevant authority of a recognised stock exchange shall not be liable in damages in respect of anything done or omitted to be done by the authority in connection with the exercise by it of its functions under this Part unless the act or omission complained of was done or omitted to be done in bad faith.

Co-operation with other authorities outside the State

116 (1) This section applies where a relevant authority of a recognised stock exchange receives a request for information from a similar authority in another Member State of the European Communities in relation to the exercise by the second-named authority of its functions under any enactment of the European Communities relating to unlawful dealing within the meaning of this Part, whether in the State or elsewhere.

(2) The relevant authority concerned shall, in so far as it is reasonably able to do so, and making use of its powers under this Part where appropriate, obtain the information requested and shall, subject to the following provisions of this section, provide such information accordingly.

(3) Where a relevant authority of a recognised stock exchange receives a

request under sub-s (1), it shall advise the Minister who, on being satisfied as to any of the matters referred to in sub-s (4), may direct the authority to refuse to provide all or part of the information requested.

(4) The matters referred to in sub-s (3) are that—

(*a*) communication of the information requested might adversely affect the sovereignty, security or public policy of the State;

(*b*) civil or criminal proceedings in the State have already been commenced against a person in respect of any acts in relation to which a request for information has been received under sub-s (1);

(*c*) any person has been convicted in the State of a criminal offence in respect of any such acts.

Authorised persons

117 (1) In this section and ss 118 and 121, "authorised person" means a person approved by the Minister to be an authorised person for the purposes of this Part being—

(*a*) the manager, however described, of a recognised stock exchange, or

(*b*) a person nominated by a relevant authority of a recognised stock exchange.

(2) Where an alleged offence under this Part is investigated by an authorised person, the relevant authorities of the recognised stock exchange concerned shall be under a general duty to ensure that potential conflicts of interest are avoided, as far as possible, on the part of any such authorised person.

(3) For the purpose of obtaining any information necessary for the exercise by a relevant authority of such exchange of the function referred to in s 115, an authorised person may, on production of his authorisation if so required, require any person whom he or such relevant authority has reasonable cause to believe to have dealt in securities, or to have any information about such dealings, to give the authorised person any information which he may reasonably require in regard to—

(*a*) the securities concerned,

(*b*) the company which issued the securities,

(*c*) his dealings in such securities, or

(*d*) any other information the authorised person reasonably requires in relation to such securities or such dealings,

and give him such access to and facilities for inspecting and taking copies of any documents relating to the matter as he reasonably requires.

(4) Every document purporting to be a warrant or authorisation and to be signed or authenticated by or on behalf of a relevant authority shall be received in evidence and shall be deemed to be such warrant or authorisation without further proof until the contrary is shown.

(5) An authorised person, or any person on whom he has made a requirement under this section, may apply to the court for a declaration under this section.

(6) The court, having heard such evidence as may be adduced and any representations that may be made by the authorised person and a person referred to in sub-s (5), may at its discretion declare—

(*a*) that the exigencies of the common good do not warrant the exercise by the authorised person of the powers conferred on him by this section, or

(*b*) that the exigencies of the common good do so warrant.

(7) Where the court makes a declaration under sub-s (6)(*a*), the authorised person shall, as soon as may be, withdraw the relevant requirement under this section.

(8) Where the court makes a declaration under sub-s (6)(*b*), the person on

whom the requirement was imposed shall, as soon as may be, furnish the required information to the authorised person.

(9) Where, in contravention of sub-s (8), a person refuses, or fails within a reasonable time, to comply with a requirement of an authorised person, the authorised person may certify the refusal under his hand to the court, and the court may, after hearing any statement which may be offered in defence, punish the offender in like manner as if he had been guilty of contempt of court.

Obligation of professional secrecy

118 (1) Information obtained by any of the following persons by virtue of the exercise by a recognised stock exchange of its functions under this Part shall not be disclosed except in accordance with law, namely—

(*a*) a relevant authority of the exchange,
(*b*) an authorised person, or
(*c*) any person employed or formerly employed by the exchange.

(2) Sub-s (1) shall not prevent a relevant authority of a recognised stock exchange from disclosing any information to the Minister, whether pursuant to a request under s 115(5) or otherwise, or to a similar authority in another Member State of the European Communities.

(3) Any person who contravenes sub-s (1) shall be guilty of an offence.

Extension of Council Directive 79/279/EEC

119 The provisions of Schedule C5(*a*) of Council Directive 79/279/EEC of 5 March 1979* coordinating the conditions for the admission of securities to official stock exchange listing, as given effect by the European Communities (Stock Exchange) Regulations 1984 (SI No 282 of 1984), shall also apply to securities within the meaning of s 107.

Annual report of recognised stock exchange

120 (1) An annual report shall be presented to the Minister on behalf of every recognised stock exchange on the exercise of the functions of the relevant authorities of the exchange concerned under this Part and, in particular, the report shall include—

(*a*) the number of written complaints received concerning possible contraventions of this Part,
(*b*) the number of reports made to the Director of Public Prosecutions under this Part,
(*c*) the number of instances in which, following the exercise of powers by authorised persons under this Part, reports were not made to the Director of Public Prosecutions, and
(*d*) such other information as may be prescribed.

(2) A copy of the report referred to in sub-s (1) shall, subject to sub-s (3), be laid before each House of the Oireachtas.

(3) If the Minister, after consultation with a relevant authority of the recognised stock exchange concerned, is of the opinion that the disclosure of any information contained in the report referred to in sub-s (1) would materially injure or unfairly prejudice the legitimate interests of any person, or that otherwise there is good reason for not divulging any part of such a report, he may lay the report under sub-s (2) with that information or that part omitted.

Power of Minister to make supplementary regulations

121 (1) If, in any respect, any difficulty arises in bringing any provision of this Part into operation or in relation to the operation of any such provision, the

Minister may by regulations do anything which appears to him to be necessary or expedient for removing that difficulty, for bringing the provision into operation, or for securing or facilitating its operation, and any such regulations may modify any provision of this Part so far as may be necessary or expedient for carrying such provision into effect for the purposes aforesaid.

(2) Without prejudice to the generality of sub-s (1), where the Minister considers it necessary or expedient to do so for the proper and effective administration of ss 115 and 117, he may make such regulations as he thinks appropriate in relation to—

(*a*) the powers of authorised persons, or

(*b*) the matters in respect of which, or the persons from whom, authorised persons may require information under this Part.

(3) Every regulation made by the Minister under this section shall be laid before each House of the Oireachtas as soon as may be after it is made and, if a resolution annulling the regulation is passed by either House within the next 21 days on which that House has sat after the regulation is laid before it, the regulation shall be annulled accordingly, but without prejudice to the validity of anything previously done thereunder.

Further Materials

7.68 McCormack *The New Companies Legislation* (1st ed, 1991) chapters 2, 5, 6, 7 and 12.
Keane *Company Law in the Republic of Ireland* (2nd ed, 1991) chapters 35, 36 and 37.
Ussher *Company Law in Ireland* (1st ed, 1986) chapters 7, 8, 9 and 13.

Official Secrets

7.69 The Official Secrets Act 1963 repealed the earlier Acts of 1911 and 1920. The most serious offence is contained in s 9. This applies to all persons, whether officials of the State or not, and makes it a criminal offence to deal in information relating to what can essentially be described as the defence of the State, in a manner prejudicial to the safety or preservation of the State. Under s 13 this offence is indictable and carries a possible penalty of seven years penal servitude. Section 2 defines the phrase "official information" which occurs in s 4. This section makes it an offence to communicate official information except without authorisation or in the course of the duties of a public office holder. The further defence of it being the duty of the accused "in the interest of the State to communicate it" might seem to provide a *carte blanche* to any person to disclose official secrets. It could be argued that this phrase requires the court to apply a subjective test as to whether the accused felt it was his duty in the interest of the State to communicate official information. Since, however, the absence of a duty in the interest of the State to communicate the information is part of the external element of the offence it should, it is submitted, be construed objectively. Thus, it is only where a reasonable or ordinary person would consider that a duty existed to communicate the information in the interest of the State that the accused is entitled so to act. Section 5 makes it an offence to disclose confidential information in official contract. Section 6 prohibits persons from retaining official documents, or any item containing official information, when he has no right to retain it or where he is not so required by his duty as the holder of a public office. Sections 7 and 8 contain various offences which protect public documents and public seals and stamps from forgery or improper use. Both of these offences operate through the creation of a residual offence of possession of these items which as we have seen, is a useful manner of constructing criminal liability. The relevant sections follow.

7.70   *Official Secrets Act 1963*

AN ACT TO PROVIDE FOR THE SAFEGUARDING OF OFFICIAL INFORMATION. [*5 February 1963*]

BE IT ENACTED BY THE OIREACHTAS AS FOLLOWS:

PART I

Preliminary

Short title

1   This Act may be cited as the Official Secrets Act 1963.

Interpretation

2   (1) In this Act—

"document" includes part of a document;

"Minister" means a member of the Government;

"model" includes design, pattern or specimen;

"official document" includes a passport, official pass, permit, document of identity, certificate, licence or other similar document, whether or not completed or issued for use, and also includes an endorsement thereon or addition thereto;

"official information" means any secret official code word or password, and any sketch, plan, model, article, note, document or information which is secret or confidential or is expressed to be either and which is or has been in the possession, custody or control of a holder of a public office, or to which he has or had access, by virtue of his office, and includes information recorded by film or magnetic tape or by any other recording medium;

"public office" means an office or employment which is wholly remunerated out of the Central Fund or out of moneys provided by the Oireachtas, or an appointment to, or employment under, any commission, committee or tribunal set up by the Government or a Minister for the purposes of any inquiry, but does not include membership of either House of the Oireachtas.

"sketch" includes a photograph or other mode of representing any place or thing;

"State authority" means the Attorney General, the Comptroller and Auditor General, the Revenue Commissioners, the Commissioners of Public Words in Ireland or the Irish Land Commission.

(2) In this Act—

expressions referring to communicating or receiving include any communicating or receiving, whether in whole or in part and whether the sketch, plan, model, article, note, document or information itself or the substance, effect or description thereof only be communicated or received;

expressions referring to obtaining or retaining any sketch, plan, model, article, note or document include the copying or causing to be copied of the whole or any part of any sketch, plan, model, article, note or document; and

expressions referring to the communication of any sketch, plan, model, article, note or document include the transfer or transmission thereof.

(3) A certificate given by a Minister under his seal that any official code word or password or any sketch, plan, model, article, note, document or information specified or indicated in the certificate is secret or confidential shall be conclusive evidence of the fact so certified.

Repeals

3 The Official Secrets Acts 1911 and 1920, are hereby repealed.

PART II

Official Information

Disclosure of official information

4 (1) A person shall not communicate any official information to any other person unless he is duly authorised to do so or does so in the course of and in accordance with his duties as the holder of a public office or when it is his duty in the interest of the State to communicate it.

(2) A person to whom sub-s (1) applies shall take reasonable care to avoid any unlawful communication of such information.

(3) A person shall not obtain official information where he is aware or has reasonable grounds for believing that the communication of such information to him would be a contravention of sub-s (1).

(4) In this section "duly authorised" means authorised by a Minister of State authority or by some person authorised in that behalf by a Minister or State authority.

Disclosure of confidental information in official contracts

5 (1) A person who is or has been—

(*a*) a party to a contract with a Minister or State authority or with any person on behalf of a Minister or State authority, or
(*b*) employed by such party,

shall not communicate to any third party any information relating to the contract and expressed therein to be confidential.

(2) A person to whom sub-s (1) applies shall take reasonable care to avoid any unlawful communication of such information.

(3) It shall be a good defence to a prosecution for a contravention of this section to prove that the communication was authorised in writing by the Minister or State authority or by the party contracting on behalf of the Minister or State authority.

Retention of documents and articles

6 (1) A person shall not retain any official document or anything which constitutes or contains official information when he has no right to retain it or when not required by his duty as the holder of a public office to retain it.

(2) A person shall comply with all directions issued by a Minister or the Secretary of a Department or any person authorised by a Minister under seal as to the return or disposal of any official document or anything which constitutes or

contains official information and which is in his possession or under his control and is specified or indicated in such directions.

(3) The Taoiseach may give directions as to the return or disposal of any original documents specified or indicated in such directions which constitute or contain official information and which are in the possession or under the control of any person who formerly held office as a Minister or Parliamentary Secretary and any such person shall comply with all such directions.

(4) Sub-ss (1) and (2) shall not apply to a person who formerly held an office to which sub-s (3) applies.

Offences relating to official dies, seals and stamps

7 (1) A person shall not—

(*a*) use or have in his possession or under his control, without lawful authority or excuse, any official die, seal or stamp or any die, seal or stamp so nearly resembling it as to be calculated to decieve, or

(*b*) counterfeit any official die, seal or stamp, or

(*c*) use or have in his possession or under his control, without lawful authority or excuse, any such counterfeit die, seal or stamp, or

(*d*) manufacture or sell or have in his possession for sale, without lawful authority or excuse, any official die, seal or stamp.

(2) In this section "official die, seal or stamp" means a die, seal or stamp of or belonging to, or used, made or provided by a Minister or State authority or any diplomatic or consular agent or other authority appointed by or acting under the authority of the Government.

Forgery, etc, of official documents

8 A person shall not—

(*a*) forge or, without lawful authority or excuse, alter or tamper with any official document, or

(*b*) use or have in his possession or under his control, without lawful authority or excuse, any forged, altered or irregular official document.

PART III

Communication of information to the prejudice of the safety or preservation of the State

Acts contrary to safety or preservation of State

9 (1) A person shall not, in any manner prejudicial to the safety or preservation of the State—

(*a*) obtain, record, communicate to any other person or publish, or

(*b*) have in his possession or under his control any document containing, or other record whatsoever of,

information relating to—

(i) the number, description, armament, equipment, disposition, movement or condition of any of the Defence Forces or of any of the vessels or aircraft belong to the State,

(ii) any operations or projected operations of any of the Defence Forces or of the Garda Síochána or of any of the vessels or aircraft belonging to the State,

    (iii) any measures for the defence or fortification of any place on behalf of the State,

    (iv) munitions of war, or

    (v) any other matter whatsoever information as to which would or might be prejudicial to the safety or preservation of the State.

(2) Where a person is charged with a contravention of this section it shall be a good defence to prove that the act in respect of which he is charged was authorised by a Minister or by some person authorised in that behalf by a Minister or was done in the course of and in accordance with his duties as the holder of a public office.

Communication with foreign agents or members of unlawful organisations

10 (1) Where a person is charged with a contravention of s 9, the fact that he has (whether within or outside the State) been in communication with or attempted to communicate with a foreign agent or with a member of an unlawful organisation shall be evidence that the act in respect of which he is charged has been done in a manner prejudicial to the safety or preservation of the State.

(2) A person shall, unless he proves the contrary, be deemed to have been in communication with a foreign agent or a member of an unlawful organisation if he has (whether within or outside the State) visited the address of a foreign agent or a member of an unlawful organisation or consorted or associated with such agent or member, or if (whether within or outside the State) the name or address of or any other information regarding a foreign agent or a member of an unlawful organisation has been found in his posession or has been supplied by him to any other person or has been obtained by him for any other person.

(3) Any address (whether within or outside the State) reasonably suspected of being an address used for the receipt of communications intended for a foreign agent or a member of an unlawful organisation, or any address at which such a person resides, or to which he resorts for the purpose of giving or receiving communications, or at which he carries on any business, shall be deemed to be the address of a foreign agent or a member of an unlawful organisation and communications addressed to that address to be communications with a foreign agent or a member of an unlawful organisation.

(4) In this section—

"foreign agent" includes any person who is or has been or is reasonably suspected of being or having been employed by a foreign power either directly or indirectly for the purpose of committing an act, (whether within or outside the State) prejudicial to the safety or preservation of the State, or who has or is reasonably suspected of having (whether within or outside the State) committed or attempted to commit any such act;

"member of an unlawful organisation" means any person who is or has been or is reasonably suspected of being or having been a member of an unlawful organisation within the meaning and for the purpose of the Offences Against the State Act 1939.

Harbouring offenders and failure to report offences

11 (1) A person shall not knowingly harbour any person whom he knows or has reasonable grounds for supposing to have contravened or to be about to contravene s 9.

(2) A person who becomes aware that there has been or is about to be contravention of s 9 shall forthwith disclose to a member of the Garda Síochána or of the Defence Forces any information in relation thereto which it is in his power to give.

Proceedings *in camera*

12   If in the course of proceedings, including proceedings on appeal, for an offence under s 9 or for an offence under Part II committed in a manner prejudicial to the safety or preservation of the State, application is made by the prosecution, on the ground that the publication of any evidence or statement to be given or made during any part of the hearing would be prejudicial to the safety or preservation of the State, that that part of the hearing should be *in camera*, the court shall make an order to that effect, but the verdict and sentence (if any) shall be announced in public.

PART IV

Legal proceedings and supplementary provisions

Offences

13   (1) A person who contravenes or attempts to contravene any provision of this Act shall, without prejudice to any other enactment, be guilty of an offence under this Act.

(2) A person shall be triable summarily for any offence under this Act and on conviction shall be liable to a fine not exceeding one hundred pounds or to imprisonment for a term not exceeding six months or to both.

(3) A person shall be triable on indictment for any offence under s 9 or for any offence under Part II committed in a manner prejudicial to the safety or preservation of the State, and on conviction shall be liable to imprisonment for a term not exceeding two years or to penal servitude for a term not exceeding seven years.

Restriction on prosecution

14   (1) Proceedings for any offence under this Act shall not be instituted except by or with the consent of the Attorney General.

(2) Before such consent is obtained a person charged with an offence under s 9 may be arrested, or a warrant for his arrest may be issued and executed, and he may be remanded in custody or on bail, but not in any case to a date later than eight days after he has been first remanded, and no further proceedings shall be taken until such consent is obtained.

Arrest without warrant

15   A person who is found contravening s 9 or who is reasonably suspected of having, or having attempted to, or being about to, contravene that section may be apprehended and detained in the same manner as a person who is found committing a felony.

Search warrants

16   (1) On his being satisfied that reasonable grounds exist for suspecting that there has been or is about to be a contravention of s 9 a justice of the District Court may issue a warrant to any member of the Garda Síochána to search any premises, place, vessel or aircraft.

(2) Where an officer of the Garda Síochána not below the rank of chief superintendent has reasonable grounds for believing that in the interest of the State immediate action is necessary, he may issue a search warrant having the same effect as a search warrant issued by a justice of the District Court.

(3) A search warrant issued under this section shall be expressed and shall operate to authorise a member of the Garda Síochána (not below the rank of inspector) named in the warrant together with any other persons named in the warrant and any other members of the Garda Síochána to enter, within one week

from the date of the warrant and if necessary by force, any premises, place, vessel or aircraft named in the warrant and search the same and every person found therein and seize any document or thing found therein or on such person which such member reasonably believes to be evidence of or to relate, directly or indirectly, to a contravention or intended contravention of s 9.

(4) A member of the Garda Síochána acting under the authority of a search warrant issued under this section may—

    (*a*) demand the name and address of any person found in the premises, place, vessel or aircraft named in the warrant, and

    (*b*) arrest without warrant any such person who refuses to give his name and address, or gives a false name or a false address.

(5) Any document seized under this section may be removed and retained for so long as the Minister for Justice thinks proper, and any other thing so seized may be removed and retained for a period of one month from the date of its seizure or, if proceedings are commenced within such period for an offence under this Act, until the conclusion of the proceedings, and thereafter the provisions of the Police (Property) Act 1897, shall apply to the thing so seized in the same manner as that act applies to property which has come into the possession of the Garda Síochána in the circumstances mentioned in that Act.

(6) Every person who obstructs a member of the Garda Síochána or other person acting under the authority of a search warrant issued under this section shall be guilty of an offence.

Obtaining information as to suspected offences

17 (1) Where an officer of the Garda Síochána not below the rank of chief superintendent has reasonable grounds for suspecting that an offence under s 9 has been committed and for believing that any person is able to furnish information as to the offence or suspected offence, he may apply to the Minister for Justice for permission to exercise the powers conferred by this subsection and, if such permission is granted, he may authorise a member of the Garda Síochána not below the rank of inspector to require the person believed to be able to furnish information to give any information in his power relating to the offence or suspected offence and if a person required in pursuance of such an authorisation to give information fails to comply with the requirement or knowingly gives false information he shall be guilty of an offence.

(2) Where any such officer has reasonable grounds for believing that in the interest of the State immediate action is necessary, he may exercise the powers conferred by sub-s (1) without applying for or being granted the permission of the Minister for Justice, but if he does so shall forthwith report the circumstances to the Minister.

Power to require the production of telegrams

18 (1) Where the Minister for Justice is of opinion that such a course is expedient in the interest of the State, he may, by warrant under his hand, require any person who owns or controls any telegraphic cable or wire, or any apparatus for wireless telegraphy, used for the sending or receipt of telegrams to or from any place out of the State, to produce to him, or to any person named in the warrant, the originals and transcripts, either of all telegrams, or of telegrams of any specified class or description, or of telegrams sent from or addressed to any specified person or place, sent or received to or from any place out of the State by means of any such cable, wire or apparatus, and all other papers relating to any such telegram as aforesaid, and that person shall comply with the requirement.

(2) In this section "telegram" has the same meaning as in the Telegraph Act 1869, and "wireless telegraphy" has the same meaning as in the Wireless Telegraphy Act 1926.

Chapter 8

PROPERTY OFFENCES

8.01 The law of dishonesty is essentially based on the Larceny Act 1916. While this is now the subject of a detailed review by the Law Reform Commission it has, in essence, worked well in this State since independence. In England it was necessary to replace the Act with the Theft Act 1968. Due to the problems which were discovered in that legislation, it was extensively amended in the Theft Act 1978. The difference in the way the Larceny Act 1916 worked in this jurisdiction, in contrast to England, appears to have been in the more pragmatic view that was taken of its provisions. In some ways the Larceny Act 1916 can be regarded at as a sentencing statute. In that Act, and in its predecessor, the Larceny Act 1861, precise attention was given to the manner in which society should respond to various forms of dishonesty. General stealing, contrary to s 2 of the Larceny Act 1916, carried a penalty of seven years imprisonment whereas the larceny of cattle, contrary to s 3 carried a penalty of fourteen years imprisonment. The reason for the disparity was related to the impossibility of guarding cattle against theft and the public disquiet that this form of dishonesty creates in rural areas where insurance against risk is rare. In the Larceny Act 1990 sentences for all these disparate offences were, in general, made subject to a maximum of ten years imprisonment. The law relating to receiving stolen property was also reformed, but in a manner which was inconsistent with the recommendations of the Law Reform Commission and which ignored the need to build criminal law on fundamental concepts.

Larceny

8.02 The Larceny Act 1916, and the associated legislation set out in the pages that follow, create seventeen different types of dishonesty offences.

Classification
(1) Simple Larceny
The accused takes the property of another person away with him intending to permanently deprive that person of that property, knowing

511

that the property belongs to that person and without believing that he has a legitimate entitlement to it (a claim of right made in good faith). This is the mental element of stealing which is an integral element of the offences which follow.

(2) Larceny from the Person
This is the same as in example 1 except that the stealing is from the person of the victim, for example, a pickpocketing or handbag snatch.

(3) Embezzlement
An item is given to the victim's secretary to pass onto him, but he keeps it for himself in the same manner as at example 1.

(4) Larceny by a Clerk or Servant
While in the employment of the victim the employee takes his property in the same manner as in example 1.

(5) Fraudulent Conversion
Money is given to the accused in order to expend it in a particular way but instead he pockets it in the same manner as in example 1.

(6) Obtaining by False Pretences
The accused wishes to obtain an article, but he does not have the money for it. So he pretends that, for example, a cheque is good, although he knows there is no money in his account to meet it. Again the mental element is otherwise the same as in example 1.

(7) Larceny by a Bailee
An article is hired out, or lent to the accused who then appropriates it to himself with the same mental element as in example 1.

(8) Larceny by a Trick
The accused has the intention of stealing, as in example 1, but in order to get his hands on the property makes a false representation, for example, that he wants to borrow it, or having borrowed the article replaces it by a copy which is less valuable. The mental element is the same as in example 1 with the addition of the intentional trick.

(9) Obtaining Credit by Fraud
The accused knows he cannot pay for an item but nonetheless orders it, for example, by mail order, or by selecting food from a menu in a restaurant. The mental element is the same as in example 1 with the accused intending to perpetrate the fraud for this purpose.

(10) Robbery
The accused uses force, or the threat of force, in order to steal from the victim. The mental element is the same as in example 1 and the accused also intends the use or threat of violence.

(11) Burglary in Order to Steal
The accused enters as a trespasser into a building. Burglary can be committed by either intending to steal, or by stealing having entered as a trespasser. The mental element in the case of stealing is the same as in example 1 but certain other offences are also included in the intent (rape, malicious damage, grievous harm to the person).

(12) Blackmail
In order to obtain property, with a view to stealing it, the accused menaces the victim by threatening him with unpleasant consequences.

(13) Forgery
In order to obtain property, with a view to stealing it, the accused alters a document. For example, an aunt of the accused dies and he produces to her solicitor a will which he has written himself, and which he represents as being his aunt's will, leaving her property to himself.

(14) False Accounting
The accused deliberately falsifies an accounting entry. Usually he would be employed on a task of keeping these accounts and usually his object would be to indicate that less money was received than was actually the case, and to keep the balance for himself. The offence consists of intentionally making the false entry with the mental element we shall subsequently consider.

(15) Counterfeit Offences
The accused has possession of, or passes over a bank note, or coinage knowing that it is false, his object being to receive value for that "money".

(16) Bribery
The accused wishes to obtain a favour from a public figure so he proffers money, or some other thing of value, to that person in order to get his way. It is also an offence to accept a bribe.

(17) Handling
The accused handles property knowing or believing it was previously stolen.

Reclassification

8.03   The English Theft Acts 1968 and 1978, made offences 1, 2, 3, 4, 5, 7, and 8 one offence. There is also a case to be made that obtaining by false pretences should simply be a species of theft. Where the accused succeeds in obtaining property by false pretences there is consent on the part of the owner to the transfer of possession in the property. This consent was obtained by fraud; it is arguable that this differentiates it from stealing. But this form of appropriation is as wrongful as any other and, in substance, it cannot be differentiated from any of the other forms of stealing. Obtaining credit by fraud may require the creation of a new offence. Robbery, burglary and blackmail are all distinct forms of stealing which have specific definitional elements appropriate to them. As we have seen in the case of sexual offences it is a legitimate task of the law to keep abreast with changes in language in order to ensure that specific offences are correctly labelled. The offence of robbery (involving as it does some form of violence), the offence of burglary (involving as it does the invasion of a person's home or property), and the offence of blackmail (involving menace to the victim), require to be maintained separately for the same reason that the new offence of "rape under s 4" was created by the Criminal Law (Rape) (Amendment) Act 1990. The victim is entitled to be treated as having been subjected to a crime of a particular gravity; the label attached to that crime should reflect the outrage of society and the wrong done to the victim. False accounting is a useful offence because it is capable of being proved without the need to go on to show his appropriation of the property, though this is usually the object of the transaction. Offences in relation to money are separate and distinct from all of these offences. The offence of bribery is also entirely separate from all of these.

The Law Reform Commission in their Discussion Paper on the *Law Relating to Dishonesty*[1] have provisionally recommended the creation of an offence of theft, defined as:

> "A person is guilty of theft who:
>
> (*a*) without the consent of the owner obtained other than by fraud or intimidation;
> (*b*) dishonestly; and
> (*c*) with intent permanently to deprive the owner thereof;
>
> appropriates property."

"Dishonesty" means an action without a claim of right made in good faith. There are also lengthy explanations of "appropriation" and "property". This offence coupled with new offences of "obtaining services by deception" and "making-off without payment" would replace offences 1 to 8 (inclusive) and 11. They also proposed a general offence of dishonesty; the so-called "sweeper offence" (see para **8.06**).

The other offences 9, 10 and 12–17 (inclusive) would remain, although in some cases considerably amended. The creation of some new offences are proposed.

Interchangeability

8.04   If the categories of the offences of dishonesty were mutually exclusive an unjust acquittal could occur were the wrong charge to be chosen for a particular set of facts. Categories 1, 2, 3, 4, 7 and 10 are all forms of simple larceny with additional elements. The other categories occur in defined circumstances which are easily identifiable. Burglary may also include larceny. The rule now is that if an offence incorporates simple larceny, category 1 may be chosen and it is not necessary to charge with the specific offence covering the additional aggravating elements. However, see *The State (A G) v Mills*[2] (see para **8.17**).

8.05   ***The State (Foley) v Carroll***
[1980] IR 150
High Court, 1979

Facts: The prosecutor had been charged in the District Court with the offence of stealing certain property "contrary to s 2 of the Larceny Act 1916". He was convicted of that offence and duly sentenced. He obtained in the High Court a conditional order of certiorari to quash his conviction on the ground that the facts proved at his trial established that at the time of the theft the property stolen belonged to his employer, and that the prosecutor should have been charged with stealing as a servant contrary to s 17 of the Act of 1916.

---

1 (April 1991).
2 [1955] 1 Frewen 153.

Finlay P: This is an application to make absolute, notwithstanding cause shown, a conditional order of certiorari made on the 24th October 1978, in respect of a conviction of the prosecutor in the District Court in Cork on the 11th November 1977. On that date the prosecutor was convicted on a charge of larceny contrary to s 2 of the Larceny Act 1916. The subject matter of the larceny was "a quantity of corrugated plastic sheeting to the value of £880 the property of Niall Sparks." On the hearing of this application it was established on the affidavits before me that Niall Sparks was at all material times a manager in the employment of Ward and Gladstone Ltd, and that that firm was the owner of the plastic sheeting. At all material times and in particular at the time of the commission of the offence, the prosecutor was in the employment of the same firm.

The submission made on behalf of the prosecutor is that these facts, which were established at the hearing of the charge, indicate that he had committed an offence under s 17 of the Act of 1916 and that, accordingly, the provisions of s 2 of the Act of 1916 (which relate to offences for which no special punishment is provided by statute) are inapplicable and that, therefore, the conviction is bad.

Section 2 of the Act of 1916 provides:— "Stealing for which no special punishment is provided under this or any other Act for the time being in force shall be simple larceny and a felony punishable with penal servitude for any term not exceeding five years."

In *The State (Simmonds) v The Governor of Portlaoise Prison* the Supreme Court decided that s 2 of the Act of 1916 does not create an offence. In the judgment of the Supreme Court, delivered by Ó Dálaigh CJ, it is stated as follows:— "Simple larceny is not an offence created by statute; it is an offence at common law. All that s 2 does is to designate the punishment for common-law larceny. The addition of the words 'contrary to s 2 of the Larceny Act 1916' does not render the indictment bad; as has been observed in the Court of Criminal Appeal in England, the reference to the section is unobjectionable and, indeed, convenient as it serves to direct attention to the fact that the charge is not one of compound or aggravated larceny and to the punishment which the offence charged carries; see Practice Point (Indictment for Larceny) 40 Cr App R 6. It has been the Irish practice to draw the indictment in the form used in this case. Archbold's Criminal Pleading, Practice and Evidence indicates that this is also the English usage. The position, therefore, is that there is no difference between larceny and larceny contrary to s 2 of the Larceny Act 1916; both expressions refer to the same offence – larceny at common law."

The relevant portions of s 17 of the Act of 1916 read as follows:— "Every person who (1) being a clerk or servant or person employed in the capacity of a clerk or servant (a) steals any chattel, money or valuable security belonging to or in the possession or power of his master or employer . . . shall be guilty of felony and on conviction thereof liable to penal servitude for any term not exceeding fourteen years."

Mr Ó Caoimh, on behalf of the respondent, in a careful and comprehensive analysis of the history of the crime known colloquially as larceny by a servant, urged upon me that it was at all times a common-law crime. He submitted that a servant who stole the property of his master committed the common-law crime of larceny and that, accordingly, s 17 of the Act of 1916 was a section which merely provided a special punishment for an offence specially described and consisting of a form of aggravated larceny. He submitted that, when the State chose to prosecute for simple larceny only a servant who stole his employer's goods, the servant was guilty of that larceny at common-law and could be convicted of it and receive the lesser sentence appropriate to simple larceny. In my view that argument is correct. The matter is dealt with in Hawkins's Pleas of the Crown (1824 ed., vol 1, p 143) as follows:— "Also it seems generally agreed, that one who has the bare charge or the special use of goods but not the possession of them; as a shepherd who looks after my sheep, or a butler who takes care of my plate, or a servant who keeps the key to my chamber, or a guest who has a piece of plate set before him in an inn, may be guilty of felony in fraudently taking away the same . . ." It is also dealt with in the 36th edition of Archbold's Pleading, Evidence and Practice at p 561 as follows:— "If a servant, who has merely the care and oversight of the goods of his master, as the butler of plate, the shepherd of sheep, and the like, takes them for himself, this is a larceny, even at common law: 1 Hale 506; because the goods, at the time they are taken, are deemed in law to be in the possession of the master, possession of the servant in such a case being the possession of the master."

By a series of statutes to which I have been referred (9 Geo 4, c 55; 12 & 13 Vict c 11; 24 & 25 Vict c 96) special punishments and provisions were made for various types of larceny by a clerk or servant. In my view, s 17 of the Larceny Act 1916, must be interpreted as the last of such special provisions. This is a section which does not create an offence but merely consolidates the existing law and provides a special punishment for the offence of larceny when it is committed by a servant.

If the State decides not to prosecute a person for some aggravated form of larceny but decides to prosecute him for simple larceny only, thus confining the sentence which can be imposed upon him, I can find no principle which would justify the assertion that the conviction for simple larceny is bad. If such were the case then a person charged with simple larceny could avoid conviction by establishing that the offence was aggravated by being accompanied by force, or carried out by use of a threat or whilst armed with an offensive weapon.

In these circumstances I am satisfied that the conviction in this case is good and that the sentence imposed, being within the limits contained in s 2 of the Act of 1916, is a valid sentence. Therefore, the cause shown must be allowed and the conditional order discharged.

8.06 The approach in the English Theft Acts 1968 and 1978, is to define in advance the circumstances in which a particular offence will apply. The choice of a wrong category therefore leads to acquittal. The modern approach is to retain the idea of a generic offence, such as that contained in s 2 of the Larceny Act 1916, and to allow further categories where these appear necessary for the proper labelling of offences in specific circumstances.

This approach was adopted in New Zealand, using Sir James Stephen's Draft Code, so that all larceny and embezzlement became fraudulent conversion, with the exception of larceny by a trick, which became obtaining by false pretences.

The Australian Capital Territory Crimes (Amendment) Ordinance (No. 4) of 1985, the purpose of which was to simplify the laws relating to larceny and associated offences enabling the courts to focus attention on the basic question of honesty or dishonesty instead of on technical questions and to reflect the commercial realities of the 20th century, adopted a "Theft Act" approach but incorporated some important departures from the English model.

The law must be clear enough to enable a lawyer to explain what conduct falls foul of the law. The Law Reform Commission have provisionally suggested that a person who dishonestly causes another to suffer financial prejudice, or a risk of prejudice, or who dishonestly makes a gain for himself or another, should be guilty of an offence, the so-called "sweeper offence". Where the law builds a detailed structure of offences on dishonest forms of behaviour, it should be readily possible to choose the appropriate charge and so warn the accused of the elements of the offence against which he must concentrate his defence. There is a balance to be struck between the automatic dismissal of a case where the prosecution erroneously chooses a form of charge and a requirement that justice be done by the courts hearing the factual basis of the case of dishonesty sought to be made out against a particular accused. That balance may be achieved by allowing amendment of the charge where the accused is not prejudiced or taken by surprise, coupled with a discretion to grant an adjournment, where this seems just, to allow either side time to prepare its case. In examining how the indictment rules in the Schedule to the Criminal Law (Administration) Act 1924 might operate if an all-embracing offence was created, the Law Reform Commission came to the conclusion that it would not affect a person's ability to defend himself. It would lessen the number of escape routes as it would no longer be possible to avail of some other "pigeon hole".

Fundamental principle

8.07 It is necessary to define a generic mental element for property offences. Offences which include stealing may all be based on that element. Where forgery is concerned the law has chosen between, in the various categories of offence, an intention to deceive or an intention to defraud. Offences of blackmail, false accounting and bribery are clearly such purposive acts that intention appears to be the only realistic element which could be applied to these offences. In the case of blackmail, it may be appropriate to retain a defence that what the accused sought to extract from the alleged victim was what he himself was entitled to and that the threat he made did not go beyond what he could lawfully have done.

8.08 The English Theft Acts 1968 and 1978 chose the principle of "dishonesty" as the general mental element in theft. The Criminal Law Revision Committee considered that a juror would recognise dishonesty in any individual set of facts. This was not a useful idea as, prior to a case being left to the consideration of a jury, the judge must rule whether or not there is sufficient evidence of the elements of the offence to allow a reasonable jury to convict. Dishonesty was thus defined and redefined by judges and appeal courts until the decision in *R v Ghosh*[3] which held that a finding of dishonesty should mean that what was done was dishonest according to the ordinary standards of reasonable and honest people and also that the accused realised that what he was doing was dishonest according to those standards.

The Law Reform Commission have provisionally recommended the use of the term "*dishonestly*" as its definition of theft but uses the tried and tested formula of "without a claim of right made in good faith" to define "dishonestly". They also suggest listing three situations which would not be considered dishonest and one which would, to assist in the application of this formula. This way the problems experienced with the Theft Act approach would be avoided.

Claim of right, made in good faith

8.09 The test in s 1(1) (the definition section) of the Larceny Act 1916 is that the accused should act "without a claim of right made in good faith".

---

3 [1982] QB 1053.

This is an entirely subjective test which allows the jury to make a subjective enquiry into the presence or absence of honest motives in the accused for the manner in which he dealt with the property.

8.10   *The People (DPP) v O'Loughlin*
                            [1979] IR 85; 113 ILTR 109
                         Court of Criminal Appeal, 1978

Facts: The accused was charged with stealing a muck-spreader. In a statement to Gardaí he admitted taking the machinery from a neighbour's farm yard but offered no excuse for what he had done. In giving evidence at his trial O'Loughlin attempted to state that he had taken the spreader because he believed that he was entitled to do so because this neighbour owed him money which he had refused to pay. After legal argument the trial judge refused to permit this evidence to be given and upon his conviction, he appealed to the Court of Criminal Appeal.

O'Higgins CJ: . . . Counsel sought to lead evidence that the applicant took the spreader in the belief that he was entitled to do so because its owner would not pay him money that was owing. In so ruling, the trial judge was of the opinion that to establish a claim of right (within the contemplation of s 1 of the Larceny Act 1916) the claim must be one known to the law. He was of the view that, as the law did not recogise a general right to take another's goods merely because a debt was owing, the suggested defence was inadmissible.

   In our opinion the trial judge was wrong in the view which he formed. The matter is dealt with fully in the decision of this Court in *The People (Attorney General) v Grey*. When dealing with the special facts in giving the judgment of the Court, O'Byrne J said at p 334 of the report:— "A claim by the applicant, that, in the circumstances that had arisen, he honestly believed that he was entitled to take the batteries and connectors for the purpose of supplying light to his residence was not expressly made. If it had been made in express terms, no doubt all proper and necessary directions with reference to it would have been given by the learned trial judge. It does, however, in our opinion, arise upon the evidence, and we are of opinion that it should, in the interests of justice, have been left to the jury with a direction that if the accused, when he took the batteries and connectors and applied same to his own use, honestly believed that he was entitled to do so, he ought to be acquitted even though his claim to be so entitled was not well founded in law or in fact. The absence of such a direction may, in our opinion, have led to a miscarriage of justice and, accordingly, we are of opinion that the applicant is entitled to have the convictions quashed."

   In so stating the law, the Court was following the earlier decision of the (English) Court of Criminal Appeal in *R v Bernhard* in which Charles J, in delivering the judgment of the Court, said at p 270 of the report:—

"We are, however, bound by a long series of decisions, many before and one at least subsequent, to the Larceny Act 1916, to hold that this view is incorrect, and that a person has a claim of right, within the meaning of the section, if he is honestly asserting what he believes to be a lawful claim, even though it may be unfounded in law or in fact. The material words in s 1 of the Larceny Act 1916, are declaratory of the common law, and a long and unbroken chain of authority supports this proposition."

   In this case, in our opinion, the question which should have been considered was not whether the claim being put forward was one known to the law but whether it was one in which the accused believed honestly and whether, with that honest belief, what he did could be excused. That was a matter to be decided by the jury. Accordingly, in our view, a miscarriage of justice took place once the judge declined to permit the applicant to put forward this defence. Accordingly, in our view, this ground of appeal is correct and the Court would be prepared, for this reason alone, to upset this conviction.

The definition of larceny

8.11 Larceny is defined in s 1 of the Larceny Act 1916. The worth of that definition is demonstrated by the ability of juries to understand and apply it when it is given, usually without further explanation, in the judge's direction. While a vast quantity of law has been grafted onto this definition, in its simple form, it remains the essential guide to those offences which it serves as a common definitional element.

8.12 *Larceny Act 1916*

1 For the purposes of this Act—

(1) A person steals who, without the consent of the owner, fraudulently and without a claim of right made in good faith, takes and carries away anything capable of being stolen with intent, at the time of such taking, permanently to deprive the owner thereof:

Provided that a person may be guilty of stealing any such thing notwithstanding that he has lawful possession thereof, if, being a bailee or part owner thereof, he fraudulently converts the same to his own use or the use of any person other than the owner:

(2) (i) the expression "takes" includes obtaining the possession—

(*a*) by any trick;

(*b*) by intimidation;

(*c*) under a mistake on the part of the owner with knowledge on the part of the taker that possession has been so obtained;

(*d*) by finding, where at the time of the finding the finder believes that the owner can be discovered by taking reasonable steps;

(ii) the expression "carries away" includes any removal of anything from the place which it occupies, but in the case of a thing attached, only if it has been completely detatched;

(iii) the expression "owner" includes any part owner, or person having possession or control of, or a special property in, anything capable of being stolen:

(3) Everything which has value and is the property of any person, and if adhering to the realty then after severance therefrom, shall be capable of being stolen:

Provided that—

(*a*) save as hereinafter expressly provided with respect to fixtures, growing things, and ore from mines, anything attached to or forming part of the realty shall not be capable of being stolen by the person who severs the same from the realty, unless after severance he has abandoned possession thereof; and

(*b*) the carcase of a creature wild by nature and not reduced into possession while living shall not be capable of being stolen by the person who has killed such creature, unless after killing it he has abandoned possession of the carcase.

8.13 *The People (DPP) v Morrissey*
[1982] ILRM 487
High Court, 1981

Facts: . . . The defendant ordered a piece of fresh meat at the meat counter of a supermarket where the meat was weighed and wrapped and the price put on the outside. The defendant put the meat in a bag and left the store where he was apprehended. The defendant admitted taking the meat but explained that he didn't know why he had done so because he had money to pay for it. The District Justice stated a case as to whether such facts sufficed to sustain a conviction on the charge of larceny contrary to s 2 of the 1916 Act.

Gannon J: The facts upon which this Court is now asked to advise show that after receiving the meat weighed and priced the defendant left the supermarket without disclosing that he had the meat in his possession and without paying for it at the cashier's desk. When approached outside he ran away and when detained he admitted taking the meat without paying for it and without explanation other than that 'he did not know why he had done so as he had plenty of money in his pocket.'

In the absence of any evidence to the contrary the only necessary inference from the giving of the meat with price marked to the defendant at the meat counter is that he was required to show the meat and to pay the designated price to the cashier before leaving and that he had accepted it with this knowledge. In the absence of evidence to the contrary the only necessary inference from his leaving the shop without disclosing his possession of the meat and without paying for it and running away is that at the time of leaving, if not at at the time of receiving the meat at the counter, he had the intention of depriving the owner of it and that he had obtained it fraudalently without the consent of the owner. Whether the intention was formed at the time of receiving the meat at the counter or when passing the cashier is immaterial as he did not have the true consent of the true owner at any stage of his taking and carrying away the meat.

In my opinion on the facts admitted or proved as set out in the case stated, the correct decision is that the offence as charged has been proved and conviction should follow and any contrary decision would be wrong in law.

8.14   The expression "anything capable of being stolen" which is expanded in s 1(3) (see para **8.12**) codifies the common law rules on what is the subject of larceny. The thing must be tangible, moveable, of value and the property of somebody. Real property and choses in action are not capable of being stolen. The question as to whether the thing taken is tangible or not is principally a question of fact and can be determined with the aid of expert testimony, where necessary. Things capable of being stolen include gas supplied by a gas company; *R v White*[4], water which is supplied by a water company; *Ferens v O'Brien*[5]: however, it would seem that electricity is not and the fraudulent abstraction of electricity is made an offence by s 10 (see para **8.18**). A person who wrongfully appropriates intangible property could indirectly be convicted by charging him with the larceny of the thing on which it is recorded, assuming that he also took this from the owner's possession; *R v Perry*[6]. For practical purposes the requirement that the thing be of value is unimportant as everything has some notional value; *R v Morris*[7].

8.15   To constitute larceny the taking must be without the owner's consent. The term owner is defined in s 1(2)(iii) (see para **8.12**). A part owner can be guilty of the larceny of his own goods, presuming he does not have the

4 [1853] Dears 203, 169 ER 696.
5 (1883) 11 QBD 21.
6 (1845) 1 C&K 725, 174 ER 1008.
7 (1840) 9 C&P 349; 173 ER 864.

consent of the other limited owners; *Rose v Matt*[8]. In cases where the owner facilitates the taking in order to trap the accused, a distinction is drawn between mere facilitation, where the taking is larceny *R v Egginton*[9], and a transfer of the goods, where the taking is not larceny; *R v Turvey*[10]. The capacity of an employee to consent to the taking of his employer's goods depends on his authority to deal with them. If a manager has complete authority then a shopper who he mistakenly undercharges cannot be guilty of larceny; *Lacis v Cashmarts*[11]. However, if the employee had only a limited authority, in similar circumstances, the owner's consent would be absent; *R v Middleton*[12]. If the accused believed the employee had the necessary authority, he would clearly have a claim of right made in good faith.

8.16 The phrase "with intent, at the time of such taking, permanently to deprive the owner thereof" makes it essential that the intent coincides with the taking; so that if the taking was innocent, the accused is not guilty of larceny regardless of his subsequent state of mind; *R v Leigh*[13]. See discussion of possession at paras **7.01–7.24**. In this regard a person cannot be guilty of larceny of goods until he has knowledge of them. However, a distinction between knowledge of the existence of the goods and knowledge of their qualities was made in *R v Hehir*[14]. Thus, where A pays to B a sum which B is aware is greater than A believes it to be, larceny is committed. However, if A pays to B a sum which is greater than that which both parties believe it to be, no offence is committed even though B subsequently converts the additional money on discovering the error. Where the accused's intention falls short of one to deprive permanently the taking is not larceny; *R v Crump*[15]. Personal enrichment is not necessary as long as the intent is to deprive the owner permanently. Destruction of the goods amounts to a permanent deprivation and an intent to destroy them suffices; *R v Wynn*[16]. Unless he "broke bulk" a bailee, at common law, could not commit larceny. Early statutory provisions are re-enacted in s 1(1) of the Larceny Act 1916 (see para **8.12**) which allow conviction of a bailee, or part-owner, where he forms the intent to deprive the owner after he has acquired possession. The accused must be under an obligation to return the goods to the owner or to deliver them to a third party. It is not necessary that the obligation be contractual; *R v McDonald*[17]. Larceny by a trick, or constructive taking, occurs where the victim is tricked into delivering goods to the accused. The trick need not be communicated to the victim but the accused must have the intent to deprive at the time of the delivery; *R v Rogers*[18].

8 [1951] 1 All ER 361.
9 (1801) 2 B&P 508. 126 ER 1410.
10 [1946] 2 All ER 60.
11 [1969] 2 QB 440.
12 (1873) LR 2 CCR 38.
13 (1800) 2 EAST PC 694.
14 [1895] 2 IR 709.
15 (1825) 1 C&P 658, 171 ER 1357.
16 (1849) 2 C&K 859, 175 ER 361.
17 (1885) 15 QBD 323.
18 (1841) 1 Cases on the Six Circuits 280.

8.17 Asportation was the common law term for "carries away", an expression which is expanded in s 1(2)(ii). Usually the carrying away will be self-evident in the taking but the fact that the two ingredients are separate is emphasised in the case law. The amount of asportation required is minimal and moving goods from one part of a vehicle to another is sufficient; *Willis v Lane*[19]. In *The People (A-G) v Mills*[20] the court held that larceny from the person under s 14 (see para **8.18**) requires "a complete separation or severance of the article from the owner's person"[21]. However, the court was unwilling to uphold a conviction of simple larceny under s 2 (see para **8.18**). Despite such a severance it would appear that the decision in *The State (Foley) v Carroll*[22] is to be preferred (see para **8.05**) with regard to interchangeability of offences. The former case contrasts with the decision in *R v Taylor*[23]. When the goods are attached, it is not sufficient to move them only as far as the rope or chain, by which they are attached allows; but there must be a complete severance; *R v Wilkinson*[24].

8.18   *Larceny Act 1916*

Simple larceny

2 Stealing for which no special punishment is provided under this or any other Act for the time being in force shall be simple larceny and a felony punishable with penal servitude for any term not exceeding five years, and the offender, if a male under the age of sixteen years, shall be liable to be once privately whipped in addition to any other punishment to which he may by law be liable.

Larceny of cattle

3 Every person who steals any horse, cattle, or sheep shall be guilty of felony, and on conviction thereof liable to penal servitude for any term not exceeding fourteen years.

Killing animals with intent to steal

4 Every person who wilfully kills any animal with intent to steal the carcase skin, or any part of the animal killed, shall be guilty of felony, and on conviction thereof liable to the same punishment as if he had stolen such animal, provided that the offence of stealing the animal so killed would have amounted to felony.

Larceny, &c., of Dogs

5 Every person who—

   (1) steals any dog after a previous summary conviction of any such offence; or
   (2) unlawfully has in his possession or on his premises any stolen dog, or the skin thereof, knowing such dog or skin to have been stolen, after a previous summary conviction of any such offence; or
   (3) corruptly takes any money or reward, directly or indirectly, under pretence or upon account of aiding any person to recover any stolen dog, or any dog which is in the possession of any person not being the owner thereof;

19 [1964] VR 293.
20 (1955) 1 Frewen 153.
21 (Davitt P at p 154).
22 [1980] IR 150.
23 [1911] 1 KB 874.
24 (1598) 2 East PC 556.

shall be guilty of a misdemeanour, and on conviction thereof liable to imprisonment for any term not exceeding eighteen months, with or without hard labour.

Larceny of wills

6 Every person who steals any will, codicil, or other testamentary instrument, either of a dead or of a living person, shall be guilty of felony, and on conviction thereof liable to penal servitude for life.

Larceny of documents of title to land and other legal documents

7 Every person who steals the whole or any part of—

(1) any document of title to lands; or

(2) any record, writ, return, panel, petition, process, interrogatory, deposition, affidavit, rule, order, warrant of attorney, or any original document of or belonging to any court of record, or relating to any cause or matter, civil or criminal, begun, depending, or terminated in any such court; or

(3) any original document relating to the business of any office or employment under His Majesty, and being or remaining in any office appertaining to any court of justice, or in any of His Majesty's castles, palaces, or houses, or in any government or public office;

shall be guilty of felony, and on conviction thereof liable to penal servitude for any term not exceeding five years.

Damaging fixtures, trees, &c., with intent to steal

8 Every person who—

(1) Steals, or, with intent to steal, rips cuts severs or breaks—

(a) any glass or woodwork belonging to any building; or

(b) any metal or utensil or fixture, fixed in or to any building; or

(c) anything made of metal fixed in any land being private property, or as a fence to any dwelling-house, garden or area, or in any square or street, or in any place dedicated to public use or ornament, or in any burial-ground:

(2) Steals, or, with intent to steal, cuts, breaks, roots up or otherwise destroys or damages the whole or any part of any tree, sapling, shrub, or underwood growing—

(a) in any place whatsoever, the value of the article stolen or the injury done being to the amount of one shilling at least, after two previous summary convictions of any such offence; or

(b) in any park, pleasure ground, garden, orchard, or avenue, or in any ground adjoining or belonging to any dwelling-house, the value of the article stolen or the injury done exceeding the amount of one pound; or

(c) in any place whatsoever, the value of the article stolen or the injury done exceeding the amount of five pounds:

(3) Steals, or with intent to steal, destroys or damages any plant, root, fruit, or vegetable production growing in any garden, orchard, pleasure ground, nursery-ground, hothouse, greenhouse or conservatory, after a previous summary conviction of any such offence;

shall be guilty of felony, and on conviction thereof liable to be punished as in the case of simply larceny.

Larceny of goods in process of manufacture

9 Every person who steals, to the value of ten shillings, any woollen, linen, hempen or cotton yarn, or any goods or article of silk, woollen, linen, cotton, alpaca or mohair, or of any one or more of those materials mixed with each other, or mixed with any other material, whilst laid, placed or exposed, during any stage, process or progress of manufacture in any building, field or other place, shall be guilty of felony and on conviction thereof liable to penal servitude for any term not exceeding fourteen years.

Abstracting of electricity

10 Every person who maliciously or fraudulently abstracts, causes to be wasted or diverted, consumes or uses any electricity shall be guilty of felony, and on conviction thereof liable to be punished as in the case of simple larceny.

Larceny, &c., of ore from mines

11 Every person who steals, or severs with intent to steal, the ore of any metal, or any lapis calaminaris, manganese, mundick, wad, black cawke, black lead, coal, or cannel coal from any mine bed or vein thereof, shall be guilty of felony and on conviction thereof liable to imprisonment for any term not exceeding two years with or without hard labour.

Larceny of postal packets, &c.

12 Every person who—

(1) steals a mail bag; or
(2) steals from a mail bag, post office, officer of An Post, or mail, any postal packet in course of transmission by post; or
(3) steals any chattel, money or valuable security out of a postal packet in course of transmission by post; or
(4) stops a mail with intent to rob the mail;

shall be guilty of felony and on conviction thereof liable to penal servitude for life.

Larceny in dwelling-houses

13 Every person who steals in any dwelling-house any chattel, money, or valuable security shall—

(*a*) if the value of the property stolen amounts to five pounds; or
(*b*) if he by any menace or threat puts any person being in such dwelling-house in bodily fear;

be guilty of felony and on conviction thereof liable to penal servitude for any term not exceeding fourteen years.

Larceny from the person

14 Every person who steals any chattel, money, or valuable security from the person of another shall be guilty of felony and on conviction thereof liable to penal servitude for any term not exceeding fourteen years.

Larceny from ships, docks, &c.

15 Every person who steals—

(1) any goods in any vessel, barge or boat of any description in any haven or any port of entry or discharge or upon any navigable river or canal or in any creek or basin belonging to or communicating with any such haven, port, river, or canal; or
(2) any goods from any dock, wharf or quay adjacent to any such haven, port, river, canal, creek, or basin; or

(3) any part of any vessel in distress, wrecked, stranded, or cast on shore, or any goods, merchandise, or articles of any kind belonging to such vessel;

shall be guilty of felony and on conviction thereof liable to penal servitude for any term not exceeding fourteen years.

Larceny by tenants or lodgers

16 Every person who, being a tenant or lodger, or the husband or wife of any tenant or lodger, steals any chattel or fixture let to be used by such person in or with any house or lodging shall be guilty of felony and on conviction thereof liable—

(*a*) if the value of such chattel or fixture exceeds the sum of five pounds, to penal servitude for any term not exceeding seven years;

(*b*) in all other cases, to imprisonment for any term not exceeding two years, with or without hard labour;

(*c*) in any case, if a male under the age of sixteen years, to be once privately whipped in addition to any other punishment to which he may by law be liable.

Clerks or Servants

8.19 The offence of embezzlement was created in response to the decision in *R v Bazeley*[25] which held that at common law a servant could not be guilty of larceny except where the property was in the actual or constructive possession of the master. Thus, where property was entrusted by a third party to a servant, on behalf of the master, misappropriation was not larceny. The distinction between larceny and embezzlement, which has been preserved by s 17 (see para **8.20**) is of little practical importance as s 44(2) of the Larceny Act 1916 allows for the substitution of verdicts.

Essentially, a clerk or servant is what would nowadays be termed an employee and is distinguished from an officer, agent or independent contractor who would be dealt with under s 20 and s 22 (see para **8.22**). The relationship need not be based on contract but may exist at will only, so that a volunteer could be held to be a clerk or servant; *R v Foulkes*[26]. Some of the old authorities on what constitutes this relationship may be found inadequate in the light of modern trends in civil law; *R v Negus*[27]. Factors such as the form of remuneration, the payment of tax and social insurance and the risk of profit and loss may influence the decision on whether or not the relationship exists which is normally a matter for the jury; *The People (A-G) v Warren*[28].

8.20 *Larceny Act 1916*

Larceny and embezzlement by clerks or servants

17 Every person who—

(1) being a clerk or servant or person employed in the capacity of a clerk or servant—

---

25 (1799) 2 Leach 835 168 ER 517.
26 (1875) 13 Cox CC 63.
27 (1873) LR 2 CCR 34.
28 [1945] IR 24 (1944) ILTR 173.

    (*a*) steals any chattel, money or valuable security belonging to or in the possession or power of his master or employer; or

    (*b*) fraudulently embezzles the whole or any part of any chattel, money or valuable security delivered to or received or taken into possession by him for or in the name or on the account of his master or employer:

(2) being employed in the public service of His Majesty or in the police of any place whatsoever—

    (*a*) steals any chattel, money, or valuable security belonging to or in the possession of His Majesty or entrusted to or received or taken into possession by such person by virtue of his employment; or

    (*b*) embezzles or in any manner fraudulently applies or disposes of for any purpose whatsoever except for the public service any chattel, money or valuable security entrusted to or received or taken into possession by him by virtue of his employment:

(3) being appointed to any office or service by or under a local marine board—

    (*a*) fraudulently applies or disposes of any chattel, money or valuable security received by him (whilst employed in such office or service) for or on account of any local marine board or for or on account of any other public board or department, for his own use or any use or purpose other than that for which the same was paid, entrusted to, or received by him; or

    (*b*) fraudulently withholds, retains, or keeps back the same, or any part thereof, contrary to any lawful directions or instructions which he is required to obey in relation to his office or service aforesaid;

shall be guilty of felony and on conviction thereof liable to penal servitude for any term not exceeding fourteen years, and in the case of a clerk or servant or person employed for the purpose or in the capacity of a clerk or servant, if a male under the age of sixteen years, to be once privately whipped in addition to any other punishment to which he may by law be liable.

Embezzlement by officer of an post

18 Every person who, being an officer of An Post, steals or embezzles a postal packet in course of transmission by post shall be guilty of felony and on conviction thereof liable—

    (*a*) if the postal packet contains any chattel, money or valuable security, to penal servitude for life:

    (*b*) in all other cases to penal servitude for any term not exceeding seven years.

Embezzlement, &c., by officers of the Bank of England or Ireland

19 Every person who, being an officer or servant of the Bank of England or of the Bank of Ireland, secretes, embezzles, or runs away with any bond, deed, note, bill, dividend warrant, warrant for the payment of any annuity, interest or money, security, money or other effects of or belonging to the Bank of England or Bank of Ireland and entrusted to him or lodged or deposited with the Bank of England or Bank of Ireland, or with him as such officer or servant, shall be guilty of felony and on conviction thereof liable to penal servitude for life.

Fraudulent Conversion

8.21   The essence of this offence is that the accused acquired the property in a fiduciary capacity and subsequently converted it wrongfully; *The People*

(A-G) v Singer[29]. If the fiduciary ownership was obtained by means of a false pretence there is no genuine entrustment; *The People (A-G) v Singer*[30]. It is in this respect that the offence differs from that of obtaining by false pretences (see para **8.24**) and the two offences are mutually exclusive; *The People (A-G) v Singer*[31].

8.22   *Larceny Act 1916*

Conversion

20 (1) Every person who—

(i) being entrusted either solely or jointly with any other person with any power of attorney for the sale or transfer of any property, fraudulently sells, transfers, or otherwise converts the property or any part thereof to his own use or benefit, or the use or benefit of any person other than the person by whom he was so entrusted; or

(ii) being a director, member or officer of any body corporate or public company, fraudulently takes or applies for his own use or benefit, or for any use or purposes other than the use or purposes of such body corporate or public company, any of the property of such body corporate or public company; or

(iii) being authorised to receive money to arise from the sale of any annuities or securities purchased, or transferred under the provision of Part V of the Municipal Corporations Act 1882, or under any Act repealed by that Act, or under the Municipal Corporation Mortgages &c. Act 1860, or any dividends thereon, or any other such money as is referred to in the said Acts, appropriates the same otherwise than as directed by the said Acts or by the Local Government Board or the Treasury (as the case may be) in pursuance thereof; or

(iv) (a) being entrusted solely or jointly with any other person with any property in order that he may retain in safe custody or apply, pay, or deliver, for any purpose or to any person, the property or any part thereof or any proceeds thereof; or

(b) having either solely or jointly with any other person received any property for or on account of any other person; fraudently converts to his own use or benefit, or the use or benefit of any other person, the property or any part thereof or any proceeds thereof; shall be guilty of a misdemeanour and on conviction thereof liable to penal servitude for any term not exceeding seven years.

(2) Nothing in paragraph (iv) of subsection (1) of this section shall apply to or affect any trustee under any express trust created by a deed or will, or any mortgagee of any property, real or personal, in respect of any act done by the trustee or mortgagee in relation to the property comprised in or affected by any such trust or mortgage.

Conversion by trustee

21 Every person who, being a trustee as hereinafter defined, of any property for the use or benefit either wholly or partially of some other person, or for any public or charitable purpose, with intent to defraud converts or appropriates the same or any part thereof to or for his own use or benefit, or the use or benefit of any person other than such person as aforesaid, or for any purpose other than such public or

---

29 (1960) 1 Frewen 214.
30 *Ibid.*
31 *Ibid.*

charitable purpose as aforesaid, or otherwise disposes of or destroys such property or any part thereof, shall be guilty of a misdemeanour and on conviction thereof liable to penal servitude for any term not exceeding seven years. Provided that no prosecution for any offence included in this section shall be commenced—

(a) by any person without the sanction of the Attorney General, or, in case that office be vacant, of the Solicitor-General;

(b) by any person who has taken any civil proceedings against such trustee, without the sanction also of the court or judge before whom such civil proceedings have been had or are pending.

Factors obtaining advances on the property of their principals

22 (1) Every person who, being a factor or agent entrusted either solely or jointly with any other person for the purpose of sale or otherwise, with the possession of any goods or of any document of title to goods contrary to or without the authority of his principal in that behalf for his own use or benefit, or the use or benefit of any person other than the person by whom he was so entrusted, and in violation of good faith—

(i) Consigns, deposits, transfers, or delivers any goods or document of title so entrusted to him as and by way of a pledge, lien, or security for any money or valuable security borrowed or received, or intended to be borrowed or received by him; or

(ii) Accepts any advance of any money or valuable security on the faith of any contract or agreement to consign, deposit, transfer, or deliver any such goods or document of title;

shall be guilty of a misdemeanour, and on conviction thereof, liable to penal servitude for any term not exceeding seven years: Provided that no such factor or agent shall be liable to any prosecution for consigning, depositing, transferring or delivering any such goods or documents of title, in case the same shall not be made a security for or subject to the payment of any greater sum of money than the amount which at the time of such consignment, deposit, transfer, or delivery, was justly due and owing to such agent from his principal, together with the amount of any bill of exchange drawn by or on account of such principal and accepted by such factor or agent.

(2) (a) Any factor or agent entrusted as aforesaid and in possession of any document of title to goods shall be deemed to have been entrusted with the possession of the goods represented by such document of title.

(b) Every contract pledging or giving a lien upon such document of title as aforesaid shall be deemed to be a pledge of and lien upon the goods to which the same relates.

(c) Any such factor or agent as aforesaid shall be deemed to be in possession of such goods or documents whether the same are in his actual custody or are held by any other person subject to his control, or for him or on his behalf.

(d) Where any loan or advance is made in good faith to any factor or agent entrusted with and in possession of any such goods or document of title on the faith of any contract or agreement in writing to consign, deposit, transfer, or deliver such goods or documents of title and such goods or documents of title are actually received by the person making such loan or advance, without notice that such factor or agent was not authorised to make such pledge or security, every such loan or advance shall be deemed to be a loan or advance on the security of such goods or documents of title and within the meaning of this section, though such goods or documents of title are not actually received by the person making such loan or advance till the period subsequent thereto.

(e) Any payment made whether by money or bill of exchange or other negotiable security shall be deemed to be an advance within the meaning of this section.

(*f*) Any contract or agreement whether made direct with such factor or agent as aforesaid or with any person on his behalf shall be deemed to be a contract or agreement with such factor or agent.

(*g*) Any factor or agent entrusted as aforesaid, and in possession of any goods or document of title to goods shall be deemed, for the purposes of this section, to have been entrusted therewith by the owner thereof, unless the contrary be shown in evidence.

8.23 *The People (A-G) v Singer*
(1960) 1 Frewen 214
Court of Criminal Appeal, 1960

Facts: The applicant was convicted of, inter alia, fraudulent conversion and obtaining money by false pretences. The charges arose from the operations of the notorious company Shanihan's Stamp Auctions Ltd. in the 1950's. Stamps were bought in and later sold by auction. Members of the public were invited by advertisement to invest in the purchase of stamps and were to receive the return of their money and, under certain conditions, profits. The company went into liquidation in 1959 with very substantial debts.

O Dalaigh CJ: In the opinion of this Court, false pretences contrary to section 32 and fraudulent conversion contrary to s 20, are mutually exclusive offences. In the case of fraudulent conversion the fiduciary element is the essential basis of the offence, and the entrustment is a genuine entrustment in which the fiduciary ownership has been lawfully obtained but which, so to speak, subsequently goes wrong. The term "conversion" of itself indicates this. Where the fiduciary ownership has been obtained by a false pretence made with intent to defraud there is no such genuine entrustment and the case falls with s 32 of the Larceny Act, 1916 and is excluded from s 20.

Obtaining by False Pretences

8.24 *Larceny Act 1916*

False pretences

32 Every person who by any false pretence—

(1) with intent to defraud, obtains from any other person any chattel, money, or valuable security, or causes or procures any money to be paid, or any chattel or valuable security to be delivered to himself or to any other person for the use or benefit or on account of himself or any other person; or

(2) with intent to defraud or injure any other person, fraudulently causes or induces any other person—

(*a*) to execute, make, accept, endorse, or destroy the whole or any part of any valuable security; or

(*b*) to write, impress, or affix his name or the name of any other person, or the seal of any body corporate or society, upon any paper or parchment in order that the same may be afterwards made or converted into, or used or dealt with as, a valuable security;

shall be guilty of a misdemeanour and on conviction thereof liable to penal servitude for any term not exceeding five years.

8.25 The essence of this offence is not larceny but the obtaining of property from another. Usually the accused will have the intent of permanently depriving the owner of that property but that is not necessarily the case. For example, a car may be obtained from a car hire company by the accused fraudulently pretending that he is the holder of a particular credit card which entitles the car hire company to charge against that account.

The false pretence must be one of existing fact and not one as to the future, so that statements of opinion and promises of future conduct cannot amount to false pretences; *R v Bryan*[32]. It must be established that the accused acted with intent to defraud and while proof of the accused's knowledge of the falsity of the representation supports a prima facie case of intent to defraud, the ultimate question is whether he intended to defraud and not merely that he knew that the representation was false; *The People (A-G) v Thompson*[33].

8.26 *Criminal Justice Act 1951*

10 A person who by any false pretence, with intent to defraud, obtains anything capable of being stolen or causes it to be delivered to himself or to any other person for the use or benefit or on account of himself or any other person, shall be guilty of a misdemeanour and on conviction shall be liable to penal servitude for a term not exceeding five years or to imprisonment for a term not exceeding two years.

8.27 This section which in substance re-enacts s 32 of the Larceny Act 1916 (see para **8.24**) uses the expression "anything capable of being stolen" rather than "chattel, money or valuable security" which is used in the 1916 Act.

8.28 *Debtors (Ireland) Act 1872*

13 Any person shall in each of the cases following be deemed guilty of a misdemeanour, and on conviction thereof shall be liable to be imprisoned for any time not exceeding one year, with or without hard labour; that is to say, (1) if in incurring any debt or liability he has obtained credit under false pretences, or by means of any fraud: . . .

8.29 This provision is important as it is not limited to false representations of past or present facts but can be used, for example, where a person orders and consumes a meal in a restaurant when he does not have the means to pay for it; *R v Jones*[34]. In such a case, he is not guilty under s 32 of the Larceny Act 1916 or s 10 of the Criminal Justice Act 1951 because his false representation relates to an intention as to the future.

While the conceptual differences between offences of larceny and false pretences are clear, in practice the evidence may not be very clear on the issue of passing ownership or possession. Prior to the Larceny Act 1916 this could have resulted in guilty defendants being acquitted since it was not possible to join felonies and misdemeanours in the same indictment. However, s 44 addresses this issue and allows substitution by a jury of a verdict of

32 (1857) Dears & B 265, 169 ER 1002.
33 (1960) 1 Frewen 201.
34 (1898) 1 QB 119.

guilty of larceny in a trial for obtaining by false pretences and vice versa. Similarly, an acquittal on either offence precludes a retrial on the alternative as the defendant would be in jeopardy in respect of both offences.

Reform

8.30 The Law Reform Commission has provisionally recommended the creation of a number of offences in this area of the law.

(1) Obtaining Services by Deception

This would consist of dishonestly obtaining services by deception, which is defined as: creating or reinforcing a false impression, including false impressions as to law, value, intention or other state of mind; but deception as to a person's intention to perform a promise shall not be inferred from the fact alone that he did not perform the promise. Preventing another from acquiring information which would affect his judgement of a transaction. Failing to correct a false impression which the deceiver previously created or reinforced or which the deceiver knows to be influencing another to whom he stands in a fiduciary or confidential relationship. Failing to disclose a known lien, adverse claim or other legal impediment to the enjoyment of property which he transfers or encumbers in consideration for the property obtained, whether such impediment is or is not valid, or is or is not a matter of official record. Deception would not, however, include falsity as to matters having no primary significance, or puffing by statements unlikely to deceive ordinary persons in the group addressed.

(2) Making-off without Payment

This would consist of making-off, knowing that payment on the spot is required or expected, dishonestly, with intent to avoid payment.

(3) Offences Against Banks

It should be an offence to use a cheque or credit card without the authority of the institution who issued it. (See also para **8.50**.)

Handling

8.31 It is a truism that there would be no thieves unless there were receivers. The commercial appropriation of property depends on the availability of rogues within criminal society to take stolen property and to sell it to either honest or dishonest people for a profit. Often, as in the case of car theft, the goods will be altered by having their identification marks removed. In the case of mass produced articles there is often no way of proving that something was stolen, other than these marks and cross-referencing them to records. Unfortunately, these records have been inadmissible to date, a fact which has now been changed by the Criminal Evidence Act 1992.

8.32   *Larceny Act 1916*
Section 33(1) as substituted by s 3 of
the Larceny Act 1990

Amendment of section 33 of Principal Act

3 The Principal Act is hereby amended by the substitution for s 33 of the following section:

"Handling stolen property

33   (1) A person who handles stolen property knowing or believing it to be stolen property shall be guilty of felony and shall be liable on conviction on indictment to imprisonment for a term not exceeding 14 years or to a fine or to both.
(2) For the purposes of this Act—

(*a*) a person handles stolen property if (otherwise than in the course of the stealing), knowing or believing it to be stolen property, he dishonestly—
  (i) receives the property, or
  (ii) undertakes or assists in its retention, removal, disposal or realisation by or for the benefit of another person, or
  (iii) arranges to do any of the things specified in subparagraph (i) or (ii) of this paragraph;
(*b*) where a person—
  (i) receives stolen property, or
  (ii) undertakes or assists in its retention, removal, disposal or realisation by or for the benefit of another person, or
    (iii) arranges to do any of the things specified in subparagraph (i) or (ii) of this paragraph,
  in such circumstances that it is reasonable to conclude that he knew or believed the property to be stolen property, he shall be taken to have so known or believed unless the court or the jury, as the case may be, is satisfied having regard to all the evidence that there is a reasonable doubt as to whether he so knew or believed; and
(*c*) believing property to be stolen property includes thinking that such property was probably stolen property.

(3) A person to whom this section applies may be indicted and convicted whether the principal offender has or has not been previously convicted or is or is not amenable to justice.".

8.33   *J Paul McCutcheon – Revision of the Larceny Act*
ICLJ 1991

Handling stolen propery

The old offence of receiving stolen goods was confined to cases where the accused knowingly acquired possession of stolen goods and the temporal coincidence of acquisition of possession and knowledge of the goods' provenance was crucial[35]. Moreover, a belief or suspicion as to their origin, or recklessness in that regard, did not satisfy the *mens rea* of the offence. For these reasons the law was considered to be seriously out of date, to present unreasonable obstacles to the prosecution of offenders and to be unduly favourable towards accused persons[36]. Hence its replacement by the new, more expansive offence of handling stolen property which departs from the traditional elements of possession and knowledge. Section 3 of the Act contains the ingredients of the offence[37], and its scope is elaborated in s 7. The offence as enacted differs from that recommended by the Law Reform Commission and it bears a close resemblence to its English counterpart[38]. In particular, the choice of knowledge or belief as the *mens rea* rather than knowledge or recklessness, as was recommended, follows the English legislative precedent. This was defended on the somewhat spurious ground that as

35 See LRC 23–1987 ch 2; McCutcheon, *The Larceny Act*, 1916 (Dublin, 1988) paras 152–161.
36 See LRC 23–1987 para 106.
37 Section 3 amends the 1916 Act by substituting a new s 33 (see para **8.32**).
38 Section 22, Theft Act 1968. See Smith, *The Law of Theft* (London, 1984) ch XIII; Griew, *The Theft Acts* 1968 and 1978 (London, 1986) ch 13.

a concept recklessness would prove too confusing for juries and that belief would be easier to apply[39]. Unlike the English equivalent, however, belief is defined to include thinking that the property was probably stolen property. The *actus reus* of the offence is expanded to include a wider range of activities within its scope. In this regard, it must be realised that handling does not necessarily require manual contact nor the acquisition of possession on the accused's part and it is better to think of the offence as being directed towards dishonest dealing in stolen property. It should be noted that the distinction between the principal offence and handling is preserved and, thus, it is not possible for an accused to be convicted of both offences arising out of the same set of facts[40]. Also preserved is the rule that the property must in fact have been stolen. Thus, if the alleged thief would be acquitted of the principal offence the accused must be acquitted of handling even where he is unaware of the facts which exculpate his confederate[41].

The *actus reus*

The intention of the Oireachtas to extend liability to most, if not all, forms of dishonest dealing in stolen property is evident from the all-embracing nature of the offence. Unlike the old law, handling includes both possessory and non-possessory conduct. The offence is further extended to those whose conduct is essentially accessory, facilitative or preparatory. The forms of conduct amounting to handling, which are set out in sub-s 2(*a*), are:

 (i) receiving
 (ii) undertaking the retention, removal, disposal or realisation of the property by or for the benefit of another
 (iii) assisting in the retention, removal, disposal or realisation of the property by or for the benefit of another
 (iv) arranging to do any of the foregoing

An initial point to observe is that the better view is that the section creates one offence only which can be committed in a number of different ways and, thus, it is sufficient to charge the accused with handling *simpliciter*[42]. But given the desirability of stating particulars of the offence in the indictment care will be required on the part of prosecutors who must navigate through this potential minefield. In *R v Nicklin*[43] it was held that a jury was precluded from returning a verdict of guilty by assisting in removal where the indictment alleged handling by receiving. The court went on to observe that ordinarily two alternative counts would suffice, namely handling by receiving and handling by undertaking or assisting in the retention, removal, disposal or realisation. A truncated version of the latter would normally suffice but again caution will be necessary. It remains to be seen whether this approach will commend itself to the Irish courts and whether they will exercise their power to amend indictments in a flexible manner. If not, it is conceivable that many prosecutions will fail as a result of improperly drafted indictments.

The old law is retained in as much as receiving is a form of handling. The extension of the law, therefore, is achieved by broadening the *actus reus* to include

---

39 See 392 *Dáil Debates*, cols 963–965.
40 See s 3(2)(a) which states that handling is committed 'otherwise than in the course of the stealing'.
41 This preserves the decision in *Walters v Lunt* [1951] 2 All ER 645 where a receiver of goods which had been taken by a child who was *doli incapax* was held to be not guilty.
42 *R v Nicklin* [1977] 2 All ER 444. Dicta in *R v Bloxham* [1983] 1 AC 109 to the effect that two offences are created have been heavily criticised; see Smith, *The Law of Theft* (London, 1984) para 399; Griew, *The Theft Acts 1968 and 1978* (London, 1986) para 13–43; Glanville Williams, *Textbook of Criminal Law* (London, 1983) pp 859–860.
43 [1977] 2 All ER 444.

the forms of conduct in (ii), (iii) and (iv) above within its scope. In *R v Bloxham*[44] it was stated that handling by retention, removal, disposal or realisation can be committed in one of two ways. The first is where the accused undertakes the activity *for the benefit* of another. The second is where the accused assists in conduct which is undertaken *by another*. Moreover, the mere fact that benefit to the other accrues is insufficient if the act was not undertaken for that person's benefit. In other words, benefit to the other must be the purpose or object of the act not merely a collateral incident. Assisting, which connotes helping or giving support, can be in respect of conduct by another or for another's benefit. For instance, A, knowing the full circumstances, helps B, a thief, carry stolen property to C, a fence. A assists in the removal *by B* and *for the benefit of C* and could be charged with either mode of handling.

'Retention', 'removal', 'disposal' and 'realisation' are not defined in the Act and their meanings will fall to be judicially determined. 'Retention' involves keeping the property and ensuring that it is not lost. Thus, a warehouse owner who stores stolen property on the thief's behalf is guilty of handling by retaining. In England the phrase has been the subject of some litigation. It has been held that what is required is conduct on the part of the accused which is intended or calculated to enable the property to be retained[45] and that a failure to disclose the existence of the property to the police is insufficient[46]. In *R v Pitchley*[47] the accused lodged money in a post office account on his son's behalf. He later became aware that the money was stolen and was held guilty as he assisted in its retention for the benefit of his son. 'Removal' clearly involves the transporting of the property and the significant point here is that it is not necessary to prove possession or control on the part of the accused. Thus, an employee who carries stolen property in his employer's truck is guilty of handling by assisting in the removal by another[48]. There is some dispute as to the meaning of 'disposal' but the better view is that it is confined to an alienation of the property, whether for value or not[49]. 'Realisation' suggests an exchange of the property for value, in which case it is already covered by the term 'disposal'[50]. 'Arranging' brings those whose participation is essentially preparatory within the scope of the law. An arrangement connotes a fixed or concluded agreement and it is doubtful whether preliminary enquiries or even an offer to deal in the property would be sufficient. The real utility of this provision is that it should facilitate the conviction of brokers who never come in contact with the property.

Stolen property

Section 7 of the Act elaborates on the scope of the offence. Section 7(1) provides that it is an offence to handle property whether it was stolen within the State or

---

44 [1983] 1 AC 109.
45 *R v Kanwar* [1982] 2 All ER 528.
46 *R v Brown* [1970] 1 QB 105. However, it was also held that failure to disclose is evidence that the accused permitted the property to remain on the premises and would support a conviction of handling by assisting in the retention.
47 (1972) 57 Cr App R 30.
48 The property is in the employer's possession (see *R v Reed* (1854) Dears 168, 257) and, thus, the accused has not received the property. It might be possible to charge him as an accessory to receiving by the employer, but the "removal" provision facilitates his being charged with handling as a principal.
49 See Glanville Williams, *Textbook of Criminal Law* (London, 1983) p 867. Griew, *The Theft Acts 1968 and 1978* (London, 1986) para 13–22 disagrees and suggests that "disposal" should include "destruction, dumping, transforming by heat or chemical means and distributing by way of gift' which overlaps considerably with malicious damage.
50 If this is the case, and it is difficult to imagine another reasonable meaning for "realisation", the term is redundant. Its inclusion in the section is probably the result of a legislative effort to be as comprehensive as possible by providing for potential unanticipated loopholes.

elsewhere[51]. Section 7(4) provides that stolen property includes property which was embezzled, fraudulently converted, obtained by false pretences or through extortion or blackmail. Section 7(3) provides that the property ceases to be stolen where it is restored to the person from whom it was stolen or to other lawful possession or custody or where a right to restitution of the property has been lost. Thus, where the police recover property it reverts to lawful custody and cannot be the subject of handling. A right to restitution will most likely be lost where the property was initially acquired under a voidable contract, as is the case with obtaining by false pretences[52]. If the property is passed to a *bona fide* purchaser for value without notice the owner loses the right to recover it[53] and, thus, it is no longer stolen property. The same proposition should apply in other cases where the owner would not be entitled in civil law to recovery of the property such as laches, ratification of the contract or statutory bar.

The most important provisions in s 7 is contained in sub-s 2, the effect of which is to provide for the conviction of those who deal with property into which the stolen property is converted. Under the old law the position in Ireland seemed to be that it was not an offence to receive the proceeds of a theft[54]. Section 7(2) makes it clear that it is an offence to handle both the original property and property into which it is converted. It must be proven (i) that the property which is the subject of the charge was in the hands of the thief or a handler and (i) that it represents the original property in the sense that it is the proceeds, direct or indirect, of a disposal or realisation of the original[55]. Thus, property can be traced through an indefinite number of conversions and the chain of transactions multiplies the number of things which represent the original. The chain is broken when an item is acquired innocently and, thus, it ceases to be in the hands of a thief or handler.

Mens rea

Two *mens rea* components are contained in s 3 and, of course, both must be established. The first is knowledge or belief that the property is stolen. Knowledge was the *mens rea* of the old offence and belief is the novel element. The selection of belief in preference to recklessness is controversial and will, no doubt, lead to difficulties in interpretation. Knowledge implies that the thing known is in fact true, whereas belief carries with it no such implication. Thus, I might believe in the American dream but I certainly do not know whether it exists. However, given the *actus reus* requirement that the property be stolen, the accused's belief must in fact be true. Thus, it would seem that the distinction between knowledge and belief is one of degree. In this respect, belief connotes something in the nature of a suspicion that the property is stolen. The degree of suspicion is indicated by the amplification of 'belief' in s 3(2)(c) to include 'thinking that such property was

---

51 This eliminates the problem which attended receiving property stolen in Northern Ireland; see *The People (Attorney General) v Ruttledge* [1978] IR 376; *The State (Gilsenan) v McMorrow* [1978] IR 360.
52 *Whitehorn Brothers v Davison* [1911] 1 KB 436; *Pearson v Rose and Young* [1951] 1 KB 275.
53 *Anderson v Ryan* [1967] IR 64.
54 This is the effect of the Circuit Court decision in *Attorney General v Farnan* (1933) 67 ILTR 208. However, it is arguable that the definition of "property" under the old s 46(1) was sufficiently broad to include property into which the original was converted. The English courts were of this view; see *D'Andrea v Woods* [1953] 1 WLR 1307. The point was never considered by an Irish court and, of course, is now a matter of historical interest only.
55 See LRC 23–1987 para 146.

probably stolen property'[56]. This implies that the suspicion be one of substantial proportions, and would clearly apply where the accused closed his eyes to the obvious[57].

The second component, contained in s 3(2)(a), is dishonesty. Quite what the purpose of its inclusion is uncertain, and it is conceivable that it adds nothing to the offence. After all if one deals in property knowing or believing it to be stolen it is not difficult to conclude that one acts dishonestly[58]. The choice of the term 'dishonestly' is unfortunate as it appears nowhere else in the Irish law of larceny. As a concept dishonesty was introduced by the Theft Act 1968 in substitution for that of fraud which operates under the larceny code. English decisions had interpreted fraud in the Larceny Act 1916 narrowly[59], whilst dishonesty has been interpreted more broadly[60]. But Irish authority on fraud suggests a broader interpretation than that adopted in England, one which is closer to 'dishonesty'[61]. The problem is that to employ both concepts is a source of potential confusion, especially as it would appear that their meanings are largely identical. Moreover, a possible unforeseen consequence of the dishonesty requirement is that claim of right should now be a defence to handling.

Conclusion

The Larceny Act 1990 exemplifies the difficulties faced where expansion of the law is an object of law reform. The addition of new categories of liability often occurs at the expense of clarity, precision and certainty. This is amply demonstrated by the new offence of handling. Whatever the criticisms that might have been directed at the old offence of receiving it did, at least, have the benefit of being precise. But now it has been replaced by an offence, the *actus reus* of which potentially accommodates 34 different modes of conduct. Moreover, the expansion of the *mens rea* and, in particular, the definition of belief to include thinking the property was probably stolen is hardly a model of conciseness. This is exacerbated by the habit of uncritical importation of Theft Act provisions into the Larceny Act despite the marked differences between the two codes. The confusing inclusion of the concepts both of fraud and dishonesty graphically illustrates this national legislative eccentricity and its consequent difficulties. There can be little doubt that the appellate courts will soon be called upon to throw light on the interpretation of various provisions of the Act. The points of especial difficulty which can be identified are the adequacy of indictments, the various modes of committing handling and *mens rea* of the offence.

The changes effected by the 1990 Act are the product of a manifest legislative desire to expand the scope of the law dealing with dishonesty. To an extent the Act is premature as it anticipates future reform of the larceny code generally. Such reform was contemplated by a number of contributors to the parliamentary debates on the Act and the matter is currently under review by the Law Reform

---

56 The Theft Act 1968 does not contain a similar provision and English courts have held that belief does not include a suspicion; see *R v Reader* (1977) 66 Cr App R 33; *R v Moys* (1984) 79 CR App R 72. No doubt the inclusion of the provision in the Irish Act is designed to circumvent those decisions.

57 See LRC 23–1987 paras 118–119.

58 Smith, *The Law of Theft* (London, 1984) para 415 suggests handling with knowledge would not be dishonest where the accused intends to return the property to the owner. But, even in the absence of a dishonesty requirement this would not amount to an offence. The accused would have lawful possession of the property on the basis of the owner's implied consent and, thus, the property would cease to be stolen under s 7(3).

59 *R v Williams* [1953] 1 QB 660; *R v Cockburn* [1958] 1 All ER 466.

60 *R v Feely* [1973] QB 530.

61 *The People (Attorney General) v Grey* [1944] IR 326; see McCutcheon, *The Larceny Act 1916* (Dublin, 1988) paras 23–29.

Commision. Although the final outcome is impossible to predict at this stage it is not difficult to imagine the Theft Act 1968 being adopted as the model for reform. This would be facilitated by the fact that the offences which have to date been removed, namely robbery, burglary, aggravated burglary and now handling, are based directly on their English equivalents. Whether that occurs or not remains to be seen but the case for comprehensive reform is unanswerable. The law has become an inelegant melange based on models which reflect radically different legal philosophies. It is time to decide which we wish to adopt and to enact the appropriate uniform statute.

Robbery

8.34 Robbery is larceny aggravated by the use, or threat of, force.

8.35 *Larceny Act 1916*
Section 23 as inserted by s 5 of
the Criminal Law (Jurisdiction) Act 1976

23(1) A person is guilty of robbery if he steals, and immediately before or at the time of doing so, and in order to do so, he uses force on any person or puts or seeks to put any person in fear of being then and there subjected to force.

(2) A person guilty of robbery, or of an assault with intent to rob, shall be liable on conviction on indictment to imprisonment for life.

8.36 *R v Dawson and James*
(1977) 64 Cr App R 170
Court of Appeal England, 1976

Facts: A sailor returning to his ship from shore leave was approached by three men. One stood behind him while the others stood alongside him. By nudging him continually the sailor was made to lose his balance, at which point the man standing behind reached into his pocket and removed his wallet. The three then ran off. The question posed on their appeal was whether there was enough evidence to go before the jury on the charge of robbery under s 8 of the Theft Act, 1968 which is identical to s 23 (as inserted by s 5 of the Criminal Law (Jurisdiction) Act 1976) of the Larceny Act 1916.

Lawton LJ: The choice of the word "force" is not without interest because under the Larceny Act 1916 the word "violence" had been used, but Parliament deliberately on the advice of the Criminal Law Revision Committee changed that word to "force." Whether there is any difference between "violence" or "force" is not relevant for the purposes of this case; but the word is "force." It is a word in ordinary use. It is a word which juries understand. The learned judge left it to the jury to say whether jostling a man in the way which the victim described to such an extent that he had difficulty in keeping his balance could be said to be the use of force. The learned judge, because of the argument put forward by Mr Locke went out of his way to explain to the jury that force in these sort of circumstances must be substantial to justify a verdict.

Whether it was right for him to put that adjective before the word "force" when Parliament had not done so we will not discuss for the purposes of this case. It was a matter for the jury. They were there to use their common sense and knowledge of the world. We cannot say that their decision as to whether force was used was wrong. They were entitled to the view that force was used.

We cannot say that this verdict was either unsafe or unsatisfactory. Accordingly the appeal is dismissed.

537

8.37 If the accused has a claim of right made in good faith he cannot be guilty of robbery but can be charged with an assault; *R v Skivington*[62]. Robbery is distinguished from blackmail by requiring the threat of force to be immediate. In blackmail the unpleasant consequence can be threatened as being far in the future.

Burglary

8.38 The most usual form of burglary is the case where the thief sneaks into a person's house in their absence, or while they are asleep or otherwise engaged, and steals their property. Burglary may also be committed by intention of the infliction, or attempted infliction of grievous bodily harm.

8.39   *Larceny Act 1916*
Section 23A and B as inserted by s 6 and 7 of the
Criminal Law (Jurisdiction) Act 1976

Burglary

23A   (1)   A person is guilty of burglary if—

 (*a*) he enters any building or part of a building as a trespasser and with intent to commit any such offence as is mentioned in subsection (2); or

 (*b*) having entered any building or part of a building as a trespasser, he steals or attempts to steal anything in the building or that part of it, or inflicts or attempts to inflict on any person therein any grievous bodily harm.

(2) The offences referred to in subsection (1)(a) are offences of stealing anything in the building or part of a building in question, of inflicting on any person therein any grievous bodily harm or raping any woman therein and of doing unlawful damage to the building or anything therein.

(3) References in subsections (1) and (2) to a building shall apply also to an inhabited vehicle or vessel, and shall apply to any such vehicle or vessel at times when the person having a habitation in it is not there as well as at times when he is there.

(4) A person guilty of burglary shall be liable on conviction on indictment to imprisonment for a term not exceeding fourteen years.

Aggravated burglary

23B   (1)   A person is guilty of aggravated burglary if he commits any burglary and at the time has with him any firearm or imitation firearm, any weapon of offence or any explosive; and, for this purpose—

 (*a*) "firearm" includes an airgun or air pistol, and "imitation firearm" means anything that has the appearance of being a firearm, whether capable of being discharged or not;

 (*b*) "weapon of offence" means any article made or adapted for use for causing injury to or incapacitating a person, or intended by the person having it with him for such use; and

 (*c*) "explosive" means any article manufactured for the purpose of producing a practical effect by explosion, or intended by the person having it with him for that purpose.

62 [1968] 1 QB 166.

(2) A person guilty of aggravated burglary shall be liable on conviction on indictment of imprisonment for life.

8.40   It must be established that the accused entered the building, or part thereof, which he was not entitled to enter, having at the time such knowledge or recklessness which, in law, made that entry unlawful; *R v Collins*[63]. The former law defined burglary as a breaking and entering. Under the new definition a person may enter as a trespasser notwithstanding the fact that he strolled through an open door. Under the old law even inserting one's finger through a window constituted an entry, but inserting an implement did not; *R v O'Brien*[64]. What is now required is an effective and substantial entry. This does not require that the entire body should enter the building or part thereof; *R v Brown*[65]. The Court of Appeal was inclined to emphasise that the entry should be effective for the purpose intended. Exceeding a right of entry makes a person a trespasser as is entry for a purpose other than that for which the invitation is given; *The People (DPP) v McMahon*[66]. The accused must know or be reckless as to the facts which make him a trespasser; *R v Jones and Smith*[67]. A building can be defined as a structure of considerable size which is intended to be permanent or at least to endure for a considerable time; *B&S v Leathley*[68].

Offences associated with burglary

8.41   *Larceny Act 1916*
Section 28 as inserted by s 2 of
the Larceny Act 1990

Amendment of section 28 of Principal Act

2   The Principal Act is hereby amended by the substitution for s 28 of the following section:

"Possession of articles

28   (1) A person who is, when not at his place of abode, in possession of any article with the intention that it be used in the course of or in connection with—

(*a*) larceny or burglary, or
(*b*) an offence under section 29, 30, 31 or 32 of this Act, or
(*c*) an offence under section 112 (which deals with taking a vehicle without lawful authority) of the Road Traffic Act 1961,

shall be guilty of felony and be liable on conviction on indictment to imprisonment for a term not exceeding 5 years or to a fine or to both.

(2) A person who is, without lawful authority or reasonable excuse, in possession of any article made or adapted for use in the course of or in connection with—

(*a*) larceny or burglary, or
(*b*) an offence under section 29, 30, 31 or 32 of this Act, or

63 [1973] QB 100.
64 (1860) 4 Cox 400.
65 [1985] Crim LR 212.
66 [1987] ILRM 87.
67 [1976] 3 All ER 54.
68 [1979] Crim LR 314.

(*c*) an offence under section 112 (which deals with taking a vehicle without lawful authority) of the Road Traffic Act, 1961,

shall be guilty of felony and be liable on conviction on indictment to imprisonment for a term not exceeding 5 years or to a fine or to both.

(3) Where a person is convicted of an offence under this section, the court may order that any article for the possession of which he was so convicted shall be forfeited and either destroyed or disposed of in such manner as the court may determine.

(4) An order under subsection (3) of this section shall not take effect until the ordinary time for instituting an appeal against the conviction or order concerned has expired or, where such an appeal is instituted, until it or any further appeal is finally decided or abandoned or the ordinary time for instituting any further appeal has expired.".

8.42   *Firearms and Offensive Weapons Act 1990*

Trespassing with a knife, weapon of offence or other article

10 (1) Where a person is on any premises as defined in *subsection (2)* as a trespasser, he shall be guilty of an offence if he has with him—

    (*a*) any knife or other article to which *section 9(1)* applies, or
    (*b*) any weapon of offence (as defined in *subsection (2)*).

    (2) In this section —

"premises" means any building, any part of a building and any land ancillary to a building;

"weapon of offence" means any article made or adapted for use for causing injury to or incapacitating a person, or intended by the person having it with him for such use.

    (3) A person guilty of an offence under this section shall be liable—

    (*a*) on summary conviction, to a fine not exceeding £1,000 or to imprisonment for a term not exceeding twelve months or to both, or
    (*b*) on conviction on indictment, to a fine or to imprisonment for a term not exceeding five years or to both.

8.43 The essence of these offences is the possession of articles which may be used in the commission of a crime[69].

The two offences created by the Larceny Act 1990, s 28(1) and (2), replace the previous section which had been amended to bring it into line with the changes effected in the offence of burglary by the Criminal Law (Jurisdiction) Act 1976. The two offences differ in the definition of the articles included. The first, and broader of the two, refers to "any article" but is linked to the intention of the accused with regard to the article. However, he must be in possession outside his place of abode. In the equivalent section of the English Theft Act 1968 "place of abode" was held to refer to the site where the accused intends to abide; *R v Bundy*[70]. The second offence uses a formula not unlike that employed in s 23B(1)(*b*) of the Larceny Act 1916. An article is made for a prohibited use if that is its primary purpose: the fact that it can be put to an innocent purpose does not take it

69 For a discussion on possession see chapter 7.
70 [1972] 2 All ER 382.

out of that category; *R v Simpson*[71]. While no proof of intent is required in this, the second offence, a defence of reasonable excuse or lawful authority is provided. While earlier offences of this nature were limited to burglary, they are now extended to larceny, demanding with menaces, obtaining by false pretences and taking a vehicle without consent, along with burglary.

Possession of implements

As we have seen in chapter 2 an attempt requires the accused to commit a proximate act to his intented crime. Criminals who are intent on committing burglary often have no particular target chosen before leaving on an expedition. They can wander around looking for a likely place that might be easily burgled. It is not an offence to "case the joint". In consequence the legislature implemented s 28 of the Larceny Act 1916 which made it an offence to go around at night prepared for burglary. Section 46(1) of the Act defined night as being between 9 pm and 6 am. The phrase "dangerous or offensive weapon or instrument" includes a loaded, unloaded, or imitation firearm; s 25(1) Firearms Act 1964. The limitations of this law led to its repeal and reform in s 2 of the Larceny Act 1990 (see para **8.41**). The repealed section is now quoted.

8.44   *Larceny Act 1916*

28 Every person who shall be found by night –

(1) armed with any dangerous or offensive weapon or instrument, with intent to commit any burglary; or

(2) having in his possession without lawful excuse (the proof whereof shall lie upon such person) any key, picklock, crow, jack, bit, or other implement of house-breaking; or

(3) having his face blackened or disguised with intent to commit any felony; or

(4) in any buildling with intent to commit any felony therein;
    shall be guilty of a misdemeanour and on conviction thereof liable –

  (a) if he has previously been convicted of any such misdemeanour or any felony, to penal servitude for any term not exceeding ten years;

  (b) in all other cases, to penal servitude for any term not exceeding five years.

Blackmail

8.45 Extortion is a better generic word for the offences which are technically described as demanding with menaces.

8.46   *Larceny Act 1916*

Demanding money &c., with menaces

29 (1) Every person who—

  (i) utters, knowing the contents thereof, any letter or writing demanding of any person with menaces, and without any reasonable or probable cause, any property or valuable thing;

  (ii) utters, knowing the contents thereof, any letter or writing accusing or threatening to accuse any other person (whether living or dead) of any

---

71 [1983] 1 WLR 1494.

crime to which this section applies, with intent to extort or gain thereby any property or valuable thing from any person;

(iii) with intent to extort or gain any property or valuable thing from any person accuses or threatens to accuse either that person or any other person (whether living or dead) of any such crime;

shall be guilty of felony, and on conviction thereof liable to penal servitude for life, and, if a male under the age of sixteen years, to be once privately whipped in addition to any other punishment to which he may by law be liable.

(2) Every person who with intent to defraud or injure any other person—

(a) by any unlawful violence to or restraint of the person of another, or
(b) by accusing or threatening to accuse any person (whether living or dead) of any such crime or of any felony,

compels or induces any person to execute, make, accept, endorse, alter, or destroy the whole or any part of any valuable security, or to write, impress, or affix the name of any person, company, firm or co-partnership, or the seal of any body corporate, company or society upon or to any paper or parchment in order that it may be afterwards made or converted into or used or dealt with as a valuable security, shall be guilty of felony and on conviction thereof liable to penal servitude for life.

(3) This section applies to any crime punishable with death, or penal servitude for not less than seven years, or any assault with intent to commit any rape, or any attempt to commit any rape, or any solicitation, persuasion, promise, or threat offered or made to any person, whereby to move or induce such person to commit or permit the abominable crime of buggery, either with mankind or with any animal.

(4) For the purposes of this Act it is immaterial whether any menaces or threats be of violence, injury, or accusation to be caused or made by the offender or by any other person.

Demanding with menaces, with intent to steal

30 Every person who with menaces or by force demands of any person anything capable of being stolen with intent to steal the same shall be guilty of felony and on conviction thereof liable to penal servitude for any term not exceeding five years.

Threatening to publish, with intent to extort

31 Every person who with intent—

(a) to extort any valuable thing from any person, or
(b) to induce any person to confer or procure for any person any appointment or office of profit or trust,
    (1) publishes or threatens to publish any libel upon any other person (whether living or dead); or
    (2) directly or indirectly threatens to print or publish, or directly or indirectly proposes to abstain from or offers to prevent the printing or publishing of any matter or thing touching any other person (whether living or dead);

shall be guilty of a misdemeanour and on conviction thereof liable to imprisonment, with or without hard labour, for any term not exceeding two years.

8.47 These sections contain a number of overlapping offences, extracted in piecemeal fashion from earlier legislation resulting in considerable confusion, which address the mischief of making improper threats in order to gain some benefit. The threat must be sufficient to influence a person of ordinary stability or courage; *R v Clear*[72]. A distinction has to be made between a threat and a demand in cases where reasonable and probable cause is a defence, as in s 29(1). What must be justified is the demand, not the threat; *Thorne v Motor Trade Association*[73]. It is not necessary that the victim receive the demand for an offence under s 30 to be complete; *R v Treacy*[74]. It is to be regretted that the opportunity to update and consolidate this area of the law, presented by the Larceny Act 1990 was not taken. Instead these offences were extended by criminalising acts preparatory to them (see para **8.41**).

Forgery

8.48 Forgery essentially consists of making or altering a document so that it can be used to deceive another and thus gain a benefit for the forger. The various offences of larceny require that another persons property should be expropriated. Forgery offences do not depend on the success of the criminal enterprise.

8.49 A forged document is of no value, other than as an object of curiosity, unless it is used as such. In order that the forger can achieve his purpose, which is usually to achieve the same benefit from the forged document that a genuine holder of it would have been entitled to, it must be shown to another person. This passing of a forged document as genuine is known as "uttering". It is also an offence to make a demand on a forged document; the various options for charging are set out in s 7 of the Forgery Act 1913.

The following example is taken from a series of cases tried before the Dublin Circuit Court in 1987. A woman goes into town to do some shopping and to meet friends. She leaves her handbag beside her while drinking a cup of coffee in a restaurant. It is stolen by a sneak thief. This criminal commits the crime of larceny. Criminal A roots through the handbag and finds a credit card. This is sold to criminal B. This criminal commits the crime of handling stolen property contrary to s 33(1) of the Larceny Act 1916 as inserted by s 3 of the Larceny Act 1990. Criminal B is an expert at imitating peoples signatures. She uses the credit card that day, and before the victim of the theft has a chance to ring the credit card company, to effect a number of expensive purchases. Every time she writes her name on the credit card docket she is making a forged document and, in the circumstances, clearly does so with intent to defraud the shop keeper and the credit card company. When, after having signed her assumed name, the criminal passes the document to the shop keeper she is uttering that document.

8.50 A major problem arises in the case of forgery which urgently requires reform. A series of cases have indicated that it is a profitable enterprise for cheques to be stolen in the course of transmission from insurance companies to those who have made claims on their policies. These cheques are bought for a particular sum by criminals operating forgery networks. A less signifi-

72 [1968] 1 QB 670.
73 [1937] AC 797.
74 [1971] AC 537.

cant criminal is used to go to a bank and open an account in the name of the payee of that cheque. Because the claimant on the insurance policy does not yet realise that his cheque was sent, but was stolen, the cheque clears and the money is lodged to the account of the criminal using the payee's assumed name. Three days later he withdraws most of the money. There is no law against using an assumed name and it is not a forgery where the thief subsequently uses that assumed name on a withdrawal form; the same physical person withdrew the money as made the original lodgment; *R v Moore*[75]. The Law Reform Commission have suggested that this gap should be plugged by reform, indicating that where the use of an assumed name is part of a fraudulent scheme, viewed as a whole, it is sufficient basis for the crime of forgery. More recently this form of deception has become less frequent due to the use of video cameras recording transactions by customers in banks. Although the transaction does not amount, technically, to forgery, it can amount to obtaining property by false pretences or to an attempt to commit that crime; (see para **8.24–8.30**). It is also the offence of handling stolen property (the cheque).

Mental element

8.51   The crime of forgery is based on the Forgery Act 1913. To constitute an offence of forgery the accused must intend to defraud or to deceive. Offences contrary to s 2 and s 4(1) of the Act require an intent to defraud; offences contrary to s 3, 4(2) and 5 require an intent to defraud or to deceive. The accused must know of the forged nature of the documents. In the absence of a confession this is usually not capable of direct proof (see para **8.61**). That knowledge is inferred from all the circumstances proved by the prosecution. It is most easily inferred if the accused, when he passes the forged document or instrument, gave a false name or address, as is usually the case. Equally, an inference of knowledge can be made from any other fact which is inconsistent with an innocent transaction, such as the accused assuming a different identity, either by way of disguise to his person, or disguise of his handwriting.

8.52   ***Welham v DPP***
[1961] AC 103, 44 Cr App R 124; [1960] 1 All ER 805;
[1960] 2 WLR 669; [1960] CLJ 199
House of Lords, 1960

Facts: The defendant, who was the manager of a motor dealers, submitted fictitious documents to finance companies and thereby obtained money. His defence was that he did not intend to defraud the finance companies but merely to circumvent restrictions on borrowing which prevented the finance companies making straight loans. He was convicted of uttering forged documents under s 6 of the Forgery Act 1913 and appealed.

Lord Radcliffe: Inevitably, the argument in this House concentrated much attention upon what was said by Buckley J in the course of his judgment in *In re London*

---

75 [1987] 3 All ER 825.

and Globe Finance Corporation Ltd[76], when he took occasion to point out the distinction as he saw it between an intention to deceive and an intention to defraud. The passage was criticised by the appellant's counsel as being either incomplete or inaccurate as an exhaustive statement of the law on this point: on the other hand, it was put forward on behalf of the Crown as being an authoritative exposition of the meaning of "intent to deceive" and "intent to defaud" in the crime of forgery, which must be taken as adopted and read into those phrases when they occur in the Act of 1913. I think that the criticism is misconceived and I think, on the other hand, that the argument for the Crown goes too far: but before I say more it is convenient to set out the familiar passage in full. "To deceive," he said, "is, I apprehend, to induce a man to believe that a thing is true which is false, and which the person practising the deceit knows or believes to be false. To defraud is to deprive by deceit: it is by deceit to induce a man to act to his injury. More tersely it may be put, that to deceive is by falsehood to induce a state of mind; to defraud is by deceit to induce a course of action."

Lord Denning: . . . Much valuable guidance is to be obtained from the dictum of Buckley J in the *Whittaker Wright* case, *In re London and Globe Finance Corporation*[77], but this has been criticised by modern scholars. It has even been hinted that it conceals within it the fallacy of the illegitimate antistrophe, which sounds, I must say, extremely serious. These scholars seem to think they have found the solution. "To defaud," they say, involves the idea of economic loss. I cannot agree with them on this. If a drug addict forges a doctor's prescription so as to enable him to get drugs from a chemist, he has, I should have thought, an intent to defraud, even though he intends to pay the chemist the full price and no one is a penny the worse off.

What is the common element in all these cases? It is, I think, best expressed in the definition given by East in his Pleas of the Crown, vol 2, p 852. He treats the subject, I think, better than any writer before or since:

> "*To forge* (a metaphorical "expression borrowed from the occupation of the smith), means, properly speaking, no more than to make or form: but in our law it is always taken in an evil sense; and therefore Forgery at common law denotes a false making (which includes every alteration of or addition to a true instrument), a making *malo animo*, of any written instrument for the purpose of fraud and deceit. This definition results from all the authorities ancient and modern taken together."

That was written in 1803, but it has been always accepted as authoritative. It seems to me to provide the key to the cases decided since it was written, as well as those before. The important thing about this definition is that it is not limited to the idea of economic loss, nor to the idea of depriving someone of something of value. It extends generally to *the purpose of fraud and deceit*. Put shortly, "with intent to defraud" means "with intent to practise a fraud" on someone or other. It need not be anyone in particular. Someone in general will suffice. If anyone may be prejudiced in any way by the fraud, that is enough.

8.53 *Forgery Act 1913*

Definition of forgery

1 (1) For the purposes of this Act, forgery is the making of a false document in order that it may be used as genuine, and in the case of the seals and dies mentioned in this Act the counterfeiting of a seal or die, and forgery with intent to

---

76 [1903] 1 Ch 728, 732.
77 *Ibid.*

defraud or deceive, as the case may be, is punishable as in this Act provided.

(2) A document is false within the meaning of this Act if the whole or any material part thereof purports to be made by or on behalf or on account of a person who did not make it nor authorise its making; or if, though made by or on behalf or on account of the person by whom or by whose authority it purports to have been made, the time or place of making, where either is material, or, in the case of a document identified by number or mark, the number or any distinguishing mark identifying the document, is falsely stated therein; and in particular a document is false:—

(a) if any material alteration, whether by addition, insertion, obliteration, erasure, removal, or otherwise, has been made therein;

(b) if the whole or some material part of it purports to be made by or on behalf of a fictitious or deceased person;

(c) if, though made in the name of an existing person, it is made by him or by his authority with the intention that it should pass as having been made by some person, real or fictitious, other than the person who made or authorised it,

(3) For the purposes of this Act—

(a) it is immaterial in what language a document is expressed or in what place within or without the King's dominions it is expressed to take effect;

(b) Forgery of a document may be complete even if the document when forged is incomplete, or is not or does not purport to be such a document as would be binding or sufficient in law;

(c) The crossing on any cheque, draft on a banker, post office money order, postal order, coupon, or other document the crossing of which is authorised or recognised by law, shall be a material part of such cheque, draft, order, coupon, or document.

Forgery of certain documents with intent to defraud

2 (1) Forgery of the following documents, if committed with intent to defraud, shall be felony and punishable with penal servitude for life:—

(a) Any will, codicil, or other testamentary document, either of a dead or of a living person, or any probate or letters of administration, whether with or without the will annexed;

(b) Any deed or bond, or any assignment at law or in equity of any deed or bond, or any attestation of the execution of any deed or bond;

(c) Any bank note, or any indorsement on or assignment of any bank note.

(2) Forgery of the following documents, if committed with intent to defraud, shall be felony and punishable with penal servitude for any term not exceeding fourteen years:—

(a) Any valuable security or assignment thereof or endorsement thereon, or, where the valuable security is a bill of exchange, any acceptance thereof;

(b) Any document of title to lands or any assignment thereof or endorsement thereon;

(c) Any document of title to goods or any assignment thereof or endorsement thereon;

(d) Any power of attorney or other authority to transfer any share or interest in any stock, annuity, or public fund of the United Kingdom or any part of His Majesty's dominions or of any foreign state or country or to transfer any share or interest in the debt of any public body, company, or society, British or foreign, or in the capital stock of any such company or society, or to receive any dividend or money payable in respect of such share or interest or any attestion of any such power of attorney or other authority;

(*e*) Any entry in any book or register which is evidence of the title of any person to any share or interest hereinbefore mentioned or to any dividend or interest payable in respect thereof;

(*f*) Any policy of insurance or any assignment thereof or endorsement thereon;

(*g*) Any charter-party or any assignment thereof;

(*h*) Any declaration, warrant, order, affidavit, affirmation, certificate, or other document required or authorised to be made by or for the purposes of the Government Annuities Act 1829, or the Government Annuities Act 1832, or by the National Debt Commissioners acting under the authority of the said Acts;

(*i*) Any certificate of the Commissioners of Inland Revenue or any other Commissioners acting in execution of the Income Tax Acts;

(*j*) Any certificate, certificate of valuation, sentence or decree of condemnation or restitution, or any copy of such sentence or decree, or any receipt required by the Slave Trade Acts.

Forgery of certain documents with intent to defraud or deceive

3 (1) Forgery of the following documents, if committed with intent to defraud or deceive, shall be felony, and punishable with penal servitude for life:—

Any document whatsoever having thereupon or affixed thereto the stamp or impression of the Great Seal of the United Kingdom. His Majesty's Privy Seal, any privy signet of His Majesty, His Majesty's Royal Sign Manual, any of His Majesty's seals appointed by the Twenty-fourth Article of the Union between England and Scotland to be kept, used, and continued in Scotland, the Great Seal of Ireland or the Privy Seal of Ireland.

(2) Forgery of the following documents, if committed with intent to defraud or deceive, shall be felony, and punishable with penal servitude for any term not exceeding fourteen years:—

(*a*) Any register or record of births, baptisms, namings, dedications, marriages, deaths, burials, or cremations, which now is, or hereafter may be, by law authorised or required to be kept in the United Kingdom, relating to any birth, baptism, naming, dedication, marriage, death, burial, or cremation, or any part of any such register, or any certified copy of any such register, or of any part thereof;

(*b*) Any copy of any register of baptisms, marriages, burials, or cremations, directed or required by law to be transmitted to any registrar or other officer;

(*c*) Any register of the birth, baptism, death, burial or cremation of any person to be appointed a nominee under the provisions of the Government Annuities Act 1829, or any copy or certificate of any such register, or the name of any witness to any such certificate;

(*d*) Any certified copy of a record purporting to be signed by an assistant keeper of the Public Records in England;

(*e*) Any wrapper or label provided by or under the authority of the Commissioners of Inland Revenue or the Commissioners of Customs and Excise.

(3) Forgery of the following documents, if committed with intent to defraud or deceive, shall be felony, and punishable with penal servitude for any term not exceeding seven years:—

(*a*) Any official document whatsoever of or belonging to any court of justice, or made or issued by any judge, magistrate, officer, or clerk of any such court;

(*b*) Any register or book kept under the provisions of any law in or under the authority of any court of justice;

547

(c) Any certificate, office copy, or certified copy of any such document, register, or book or of any part thereof;

(d) Any document which any magistrate or any master or registrar in lunacy is authorised or required by law to make or issue;

(e) Any document which any person authorised to adminster an oath under the Commissioners for Oaths Act 1889, is authorised or required by law to make or issue;

(f) Any document made or issue by an officer of state or law officer of the Crown, or any document upon which, by the law or usage at the time in force, any court of justice or any officer might act;

(g) Any document or copy of a document used or intended to be used in evidence in any Court of Record, or any document which is made evidence by law;

(h) Any certificate required by any Act for the celebration of marriage;

(i) Any licence for the celebration of marriage which may be given by law;

(j) Any certificate, declaration, or order under any enactment relating to the registration of births or deaths;

(k) Any register book, builder's certificate, surveyor's certificate, certificate of registry, declaration, bill of sale, instrument of mortgage, or certificate of mortgage or sale under Part I of the Merchant Shipping Act 1894, or any entry or endorsement required by the said Part of the said Act to be made in or on any of those documents;

(l) any permit, certificate, or similar document made or granted by or under the authority of the Commissioners of Customs and Excise.

Forgery of other documents with intent to defraud or to deceive a misdemeanour

4 (1) Forgery of any document, which is not made felony under this or any other statute for the time being in force, if committed with intent to defraud, shall be a misdemeanour and punishable with imprisonment with or without hard labour for any term not exceeding two years.

(2) Forgery of any public document which is not made felony under this or any other statute for the time being in force, if committed with intent to defraud or deceive, shall be a misdemeanour and punishable with imprisonment with or without hard labour for any term not exceeding two years.

Forgery of seals and dies

5 (1) Forgery of the following seals, if committed with intent to defraud or deceive, shall be felony and punishable with penal servitude for life:—

(a) The Great Seal of the United Kingdom, His Majesty's Privy Seal, any privy signet of His Majesty, His Majesty's Royal Sign Manual, any of His Majesty's seals appointed by the Twenty-fourth Article of the Union between England and Scotland to be kept, used, and continued in Scotland, the Great Seal of Ireland or the Privy Seal of Ireland;

(b) The seal of the Public Record Office in England;

(c) The seal of any court of record;

(d) The seal of the office of the Registrar-General of Births, Deaths, and Marriages.

(2) Forgery of the following seals, if committed with intent to defraud or deceive shall be felony, and punishable with penal servitude for any term not exceeding fourteen years:—

(a) The seal of any register office relating to births, baptisms, marriages, or deaths;

(b) The seal of any burial board or of any local authority performing the duties of a burial board;

(*c*) The seal of or belonging to any office for the registry of deeds or titles to lands.

(3) Forgery of the following seals, if committed with intent to defraud or deceive, shall be felony and punishable with penal servitude for any term not exceeding seven years:—

(*a*) The seal of any court of justice other than a court of record;
(*b*) The seal of the office of any master or registrar in lunacy.

(4) Forgery of the following dies, if committed with intent to defraud or deceive, shall be felony and punishable with penal servitude for any term not exceeding fourteen years:—

(*a*) Any die provided, made, or used by the Commissioners of Inland Revenue or the Commissioners of Customs and Excise;
(*b*) Any die which is or has been required or authorised by law to be used for the marketing or stamping of gold or silver plate, or gold or silver wares.

(5) Forgery of the following die, if committed with intent to defraud or deceive, shall be felony and punishable with penal servitude for any term not exceeding seven years:—

Any stamp or die provided, made, or used in pursuance of the Local Stamp Act 1869.

Uttering

6 (1) Every person who utters any forged document, seal, or die shall be guilty of an offence of the like degree (whether felony or misdemeanour) and on conviction thereof shall be liable to the same punishment as if he himself had forged the document, seal, or die.

(2) A person utters a forged document, seal, or die, who, knowing the same to be forged, and with either of the intents necessary to constitute the offence of forging the said document, seal, or dies, uses, offers, publishes, delivers, disposes of, tenders in payment or in exchange, exposes for sale or exchange, exchanges, tenders in evidence, or puts off the said forged document, seal, or die.

(3) It is immaterial where the document, seal, or die was forged.

Demanding property on forged documents, &c.

7 Every person shall be guilty of felony and on conviction thereof shall be liable to penal servitude for any term not exceeding fourteen years, who, with intent to defraud, demands, receives, or obtains, or causes or procures to be delivered, paid or transferred to any person, or endeavours to receive or obtain or to cause or procure to be delivered, paid or transferred to any person any money, security for money or other property, real or personal:—

(*a*) under, upon, or by virtue of any forged instrument whatsoever, knowing the same to be forged; or
(*b*) under, upon, or by virtue of any probate or letters of administration, knowing the will, testament, codicil, or testamentary writing on which such probate or letters of administration shall have been obtained to have been forged, or knowing such probate or letters of administration to have been obtained by any false oath, affirmation, or affidavit.

Possession of forged documents, seals and dies

8 (1) Every person shall be guilty of felony and on conviction thereof shall be liable to penal servitude for any term not exceeding fourteen years, who, without lawful authority or excuse, the proof whereof shall lie on the accused, purchases or receives from any person, or has in his custody or possession, a forged bank note, knowing the same to be forged.

(2) Every person shall be guilty of felony and on conviction thereof shall be liable to penal servitude for any term not exceeding fourteen years, who, without lawful authority or excuse, the proof whereof shall lie on the accused, and knowing the same to be forged, has in his custody or possession—

- (*a*) any forged die required or authorised by law to be used for the marking of gold or silver plate, or of gold or silver wares, or any ware of gold, silver, or base metal bearing the impression of any such forged die;
- (*b*) any forged stamp or die as defined by the Stamp Duties Management Act 1891;
- (*c*) any forged wrapper or label provided by or under the authority of the Commissioners of Inland Revenue or the Commissioners of Customs and Excise.

(3) Every person shall be guilty of felony and on conviction thereof shall be liable to penal servitude for any term not exceeding seven years, who, without lawful authority or excuse, the proof whereof shall lie on the accused, and knowing the same to be forged, has in his custody or possession:—

Any forged stamp or die, resembling or intended to resemble either wholly or in part any stamp or die which at any time whatever has been or may be provided, made, or used by or under the direction of the local authority for the purposes of the Local Stamp Act 1869.

Making or having in possession paper or implements for forgery

9 Every person shall be guilty of felony and on conviction thereof shall be liable to penal servitude for any term not exceeding seven years, who, without lawful authority or excuse, the proof whereof shall lie on the accused:—

- (*a*) Makes, uses, or knowingly has in his custody or possession any paper intended to resemble and pass as—
  - (i) Special paper such as is provided and used for making any bank note, Treasury bill, or London county bill;
  - (ii) Revenue paper;
- (*b*) Makes, uses, or knowingly has in his custody or possession, any frame, mould, or instrument for making such paper, or for producing in or on such paper any words, figures, letters, marks, lines, or devices peculiar to and used in or on any such paper;
- (*c*) Engraves or in anywise makes upon any plate, wood, stone, or other material, any words, figures, letters, marks, lines, or devices, the print whereof resembles in whole or in part any words, figures, letters, marks, lines or devices peculiar to and used in or on any bank note, or in or on any document entitling or evidencing the title of any person to any share or interest in any public stock, annuity, fund, or debt of any part of His Majesty's Dominions or of any foreign state, or in any stock, annuity, fund, or debt of any body corporate, company, or society, whether within or without His Majesty's dominions;
- (*d*) Uses or knowingly has in his custody or possession any plate, wood, stone, or other material, upon which any such words, figures, letters, marks, lines, or devices have been engraved or in anywise made as aforesaid;
- (*e*) Uses or knowingly has in his custody or possession any paper upon which any such words, figures, letters, marks, lines, or devices have been printed or in anywise made as aforesaid.

Purchasing or having in possession certain paper before it has been duly stamped and issued

10 Every person shall be guilty of a misdemeanour and on conviction thereof shall be liable to imprisonment, with or without hard larbour, for any term not exceeding two years, who, without lawful authority or excuse the proof whereof shall lie on the accused, purchases, receives, or knowingly has in his custody or possession—

(a) Any special paper provided and used for making Treasury bills or London county bills or any Revenue paper before such paper has been duly stamped, signed, and issued for public use;

(b) Any die peculiarly used in the manufacture of any such paper.

Accessories and abettors

11 Any person who knowingly and wilfully aids, abets, counsels, causes, procures, or commands the commission of an offence punishable under this Act shall be liable to be dealt with, indicted, tried, and punished as a principal offender.

Punishments

12 (1) Where a sentence of penal servitude may be imposed on conviction of an offence against this Act, the court may, instead thereof, impose a sentence of imprisonment, with or without hard labour, for not more than two years.

(2) (a) On conviction of a misdemeanour punishable under this Act, the court, instead of or in addition to any other punishment which may be lawfully imposed, may fine the offender:

(b) On conviction of a felony punishable under this Act, the court, in addition to imposing a sentence of penal servitude or imprisonment, may require the offender to enter into his own recognizances, with or without securities, for keeping the peace and being of good behaviour:

(c) On conviction of a misdemeanour punishable under this Act, the court, instead of or in addition to any other punishment which may lawfully be imposed for the offence, may require the offender to enter into his own recognizances, with or without sureties, for keeping the peace and being of good behaviour:

(d) No person shall be imprisoned under this section for more than one year for not finding sureties.

Jurisdiction of quarter sessions in England

13 A court of quarter sessions in England shall not have jurisdiction to try an indictment for any offence against this Act or for an offence which, under any enactment for the time being in force, is declared to be forgery or to be punishable as forgery.

Venue

14 (1) A person charged—

(a) with an offence against this Act; or

(b) with an offence indictable at common law or under any Act for the time being in force consisting in the forging or altering of any matter whatsoever, or in offering, uttering, disposing of, or putting off any matter whatsoever, knowing the same to be forged or altered;

may be proceeded against, indicted, tried, and punished in any county or place in which he was apprehended or is in custody as if the offence had been committed in that county or place; and for all purposes incidental to or consequential on the prosecution, trial, or punishment of the offence, it shall be deemed to have been committed in that county or place:

Provided that, where the offence charged relates to documents made for the purpose of any Act relating to the suppression of the slave trade, it shall, for the purposes of jurisdiction and trial, be treated as an offence against the Slave Trade Act 1873.

(2) Nothing in this section shall affect the laws relating to the government of His Majesty's naval or military forces.

Criminal possession

15 Where the having any document, seal, or die in the custody or possession of any person is in this Act expressed to be an offence, a person shall be deemed to have a document, seal or die in his custody or possession if he—

(*a*) has it in his personal custody or possession; or

(*b*) knowingly and wilfully has it in the actual custody or possession of any other person, or in any building, lodging, apartment, field, or other place, whether open or enclosed, and whether occupied by himself or not.

It is immaterial whether the document, matter, or thing is had in such custody, possession, or place for the use of such person or for the use or benefit of another person.

Search warrants

16 (1) If it shall be made to appear by information on oath before a justice of the peace that there is reasonable cause to believe that any person has in his custody or possession without lawful authority or excuse—

(*a*) any bank note; or

(*b*) any implement for making paper or imitation of the paper used for bank notes; or

(*c*) any material having thereon any words, forms, devices, or characters capable of producing or intended to produce the impression of a bank note; or

(*d*) any forged document, seal, or die; or

(*e*) any machinery, implement, utensil, or material used or intended to be used for the forgery or any document;

the justice may grant a warrant to search for the same; and if the same shall be found on search, it shall be lawful to seize it and carry it before a justice of the county or place in which the warrant was issued, to be by him disposed of according to law.

(2) Every document, seal, or die lawfully seized under such warrant shall be defaced and destroyed or otherwise disposed of—

(*a*) by order of the court before which the offender is tried; or

(*b*) if there be no trial, by order of a justice of the peace; or

(*c*) if it affects the public revenue, by the Commissioners of Inland Revenue or the Commissioners of Customs and Excise, as the case may require; or

(*d*) if it affects any of the companies of Goldsmiths or Guardians referred to in the Gold and Silver Wares Act 1844, by the said company or guardians.

Form of indictment and proof of intent

17 (1) In an indictment or information for an offence against this Act with reference to any document, seal, or die, it is sufficient to refer to the document, seal, or die by any name or designation by which it is usually known, or by its purport, without setting out any copy or facsimile of the whole or any part of the document, seal, or die.

(2) Where an intent to defraud or an intent to deceive is one of the constituent elements of an offence punishable under this Act, or under any other Act relating to forgery or any kindred offence for the time being in force, it shall not be necessary to allege in the indictment or to prove an intent to defraud or deceive any particular person; and it shall be sufficient to prove that the defendant did the act charged with intent to defraud or to deceive, as the case may require.

(3) If any person who is a member of any co-partnership, or is one of two or more beneficial owners of any property, forges any document, matter, or thing with intent to defraud the co-partnership or the other beneficial owners, he is liable to be dealt with, indicted, tried, and punished as if he had not been or was not a member of the co-partnership, nor one of such beneficial owners.

Interpretation

18 (1) In this Act unless the context otherwise requires—

The expression "bank note" includes any note or bill of exchange of the Bank of England or Bank of Ireland, or of any other person, body corporate, or company carrying on the business of banking in any part of the world, and includes "bank bill," "bank post bill," "blank bank note," "blank bank bill of exchange," and "blank bank post bill";

The expression "die" includes any plate, type, tool, or implement whatsoever, and also any part of any die plate, type, tool, or implement, and any stamp or impression thereof or any part of such stamp or impression;

The expression "document of title to goods" includes any bill of lading, India warrant, dock warrant, warehouse keepers certificate, warrant or order for the delivery or transfer of any goods or valuable thing, bought or sold note, or any other document used in the ordinary course of business as proof of the possession or control of goods, or authorising or purporting to authorise either by endorsement or by delivery the possessor of such document to transfer or receive any goods thereby represented or therein mentioned or referred to:

The expression "document of title to lands" includes any deed, map, roll, register, or instrument in writing being or containing evidence of the title or any part of the title to any land or to any interest in or arising out of any land, or any authenticated copy thereof:

The expression "revenue paper" means any paper provided by the proper authority for the purpose of being used for stamps, licences, permits, Post Office money orders, or postal orders, or for any purpose whatever connected with the public revenue:

The expression "seal" includes any stamp or impression of a seal or any stamp or impression made or apparently intended to resemble the stamp or impression of a seal, as well as the seal itself:

The expression "stamp" includes a stamp impressed by means of a die as well as an adhesive stamp:

The expression "Treasury bill," includes Exchequer bill, Exchequer bond, Exchequer debenture, and War bond:

The expression "valuable security" includes any writing entitling or evidencing the title of any person to any share or interest in any public stock, annuity, fund, or debt of any part of His Majesty's dominions or of any foreign state, or in any stock, annuity, fund, or debt of any body corporate, company, or society, whether within or without His Majesty's dominions, or to any deposit in any bank, and also includes any scrip, debenture, bill, note, warrant, order, or other security for the payment of money, or any accountable receipt, release, or discharge, or any receipt or other instrument evidencing the payment of money, or the delivery of any chattel personal.

(2) References in this Act to any Act in force at the commencement of this Act shall be held to include a reference to that Act as amended, extended, or applied by any other Act.

(3) References in this Act to any Government department shall in relation to any functions performed by that department be held to include references to any other Government department by which the same functions were previously performed.

Savings

19 (1) Where an offence against this Act also by virtue of some other Act subjects the offender to any forfeiture or disqualification, or to any penalty other than penal servitude or imprisonment or fine, the liability of the offender to punishment under this Act shall be in addition to and not in substitution for his liability under such other Act.

(2) Where an offence against this Act is by any other Act, whether passed before or after the commencement of this Act, made punishable on summary conviction, proceedings may be taken either under such other Act or under this Act: Provided that where such an offence was at the commencement of this Act punishable only on summary conviction, it shall remain only so punishable.

Repeals

20 The enactments specified in the schedule to this Act are hereby repealed as to England and Ireland to the extent specified in the third column of that schedule.

Extent

21 This Act shall not extend to Scotland.

Short title and commencement

22 This Act may be cited as the Forgery Act 1913, and shall come into operation on the first day of January one thousand nine hundred and fourteen.

False accounting

8.54 False accounting is a useful charge where the accused has the responsibility for keeping records of financial transactions effected either by him or by others, on behalf of his employer.

8.55   *Falsification of Accounts Act 1875*

Punishment for falsification of accounts, &c.

1 That if any clerk, officer, or servant, or any person employed or acting in the capacity of a clerk, officer, or servant, shall wilfully and with intent to defraud destroy, alter, mutilate, or falsify any book, paper, writing, valuable security, or account which belongs to or is in the possession of his employer, or has been received by him for or on behalf of his employer, or shall wilfully and with intent to defraud make or concur in making any false entry in, or omit or alter, or concur in omitting or altering, any material particular from or in any such book, or any document, or account, then in every such case the person so offending shall be guilty of a misdemeanour, and be liable to be kept in penal servitude for a term not exceeding seven years, or to be imprisoned with or without hard labour for any term not exceeding two years.

Intention to defraud sufficient indictment

2   It shall be sufficient in any indictment under this Act to allege a general intent to defraud without naming any particular person intended to be defrauded.

Act to be read with 24 & 25 Vict c 96

3   This Act shall be read as one with the Act of the twenty-fourth and twenty-fifth of Her Majesty, chapter ninety-six.

Short title

4   This Act may be cited as the Falsification of Accounts Act 1875.

Interpretation

8.56   The Act has generally been interpreted as applying the words "clerk, officer, or servant or any person employed or acting in the capacity of a clerk, officer, or servant" to employees only; *R v Solomons*[78]. Persons acting as independent contractors cannot therefore be charged under this section but, if at all, with some other offence of dishonesty. For example An Post employs a large number of persons as sub-postmasters around the country. These are independent contractors and are obliged, as part of their duties, to furnish weekly accounts of the outgoings of the post office on behalf of the Department of Social Welfare. If a postmaster indicates in these accounts that more money was expended by him than was in fact the case, he will seek a reimbursement for an expenditure which never occurred. While this is a false accounting the accused does not come within the Act. Clearly the scope of the legislation should be broadened to cover independent contractors whose duty it is to keep accounts on behalf of any other party.

8.57   The prosecution must prove that it was the accused who made the false entry or, if the charge is of omission, that it was he who omitted to make the entry when it was his duty to do so. The entry or omission must be false to the knowledge of the accused. This is usually proved by the prosecution referring to the details of the particular transaction to which the entry is supposed to relate. If, for example, an item is sold in a shop for £100 but the employee writes up the sale as being for £50, the prosecution will prove, through the customer, the receipt by the accused of the full amount and (usually by reference to handwriting evidence) prove that the relevant entry was made for only fifty pounds. Where a false entry is made to the knowledge of the accused, or where there is a deliberate omission to make an entry, an intention to defraud may be inferred by the jury from that fact alone. An entry may be made, within the terms of the legislation, by using another person as an innocent agent; *R v Butt*[79].

8.58   ***R v Wines***
[1954] 1 WLR 64; [1954] 2 All ER 1497; 37 Cr App R 197
Court of Criminal Appeal England, 1953

Facts: The accused was the manager of a radio department in a co-operative society. He admitted that he had made false entries in respect of sales but denied

78   [1909] 2 KB 980.
79   15 Cox 564.

that he had done so with the object of covering up thefts made by him. His evidence was that he had done so with the intention of making the gross profits from his department appear to be higher than was actually the case and that this was done in order to secure his employment. The trial judge directed the jury that, whichever of the two versions was true, there was an intent to defraud and the jury convicted.

Lord Goddard CJ: There is no ground for disturbing the verdict as to larceny; in fact the case was proved as clearly as any case could be proved. Nor is there any ground for disturbing the conviction on the count for conspiracy, and the only difficulty which has arisen in this case is in connexion with the conviction for falsification of accounts and whether the direction which the recorder gave to the jury was right.

The offence of falsification of accounts is committed if the falsification is done, not by accident or for some given reason, but with intent to defraud; and the recorder in effect directed the jury that it did not matter whether they accepted the version of the prosecution or the version of the defence as to why the appellant had falsified the accounts because, whichever version was true, it amounted to an intent to defraud. He told the jury: "Whichever version you take, that amounts to an intent to defraud."

Mr Clark has argued most clearly that that was a misdirection. If it was a misdirection, we should have to quash the convictions on the counts for falsification, although these thefts were of such a nature that it would not make any difference to the sentence because the recorder passed a sentence on each count to run concurrently. It is therefore an academic point, but one of some importance, whether this was a correct direction on a point of law. The court has come to the conclusion that the recorder's direction in these circumstances can be upheld and is correct.

Buckley J: In his well-known definition of the difference between an intent to deceive and an intent to defraud, said in *In re London and Globe Finance Corporation Ltd*[80]: In both ss 83 and 84 of the Larceny Act of 1861, and section 166 of the Companies Act 1862, the offence is that of making or publishing a false statement or account, or a false or fraudulent entry with intent to deceive or defraud." Under the Companies Acts it does not matter whether the intention is to deceive or defraud, but in dealing with accounts it does matter because it is not criminal if the intent is merely to deceive; there must be an intent to defraud. "To deceive is, I apprehend, to induce a man to believe that a thing is true which is false, and which the person practising the deceit knows or believes to be false. To defraud is to deprive by deceit:" – one observes that he does not stop there – "it is by deceit to induce a man to act to his injury. More tersely it may be put, that to deceive is by falsehood to induce a state of mind; to defraud is by deceit to induce a course of action." That is the *locus classicus* on the subject and it has been often cited with approval. What has to be considered in cases such as this is whether the deceit which has been practised had merely induced, or was intended merely to induce, a state of mind, or whether it induced a course of action.

The appellant himself said what he intended to achieve by this falsification, namely, to remain in the service of the society, or, in other words, to avoid being dismissed by them, because he feared that they would dismiss him if he did not show a proper return. If he had been dismissed because he did not show a satisficatory return, he would have lost his wages, and, therefore, assuming that his object really was what he said it was, the society by his falsification would have been induced to retain him in their service and to pay him his wages, and he would have been getting wages from the society by means of a false representation, that is to say, by falsifying these accounts.

80 [1903] 1 Ch 728, 732.

For these reasons we think that the recorder was justified, in view of what the apellant himself said, in directing the jury that whether they thought the object of the falsification was to conceal the thefts – and I should think there was very little doubt that really that was what was in his mind – or whether they thought it was merely to induce the society to keep him in their employ and pay him his wages, it did in the circumstances amount to an intent to defraud. The direction was right and, therefore, the appeal is dismissed.

Currency

8.59   *Forgery Act 1913*

See para **8.53** – see in particular ss 2(1), 7, 8 and 11.

8.60   *Central Bank Act 1942*

52   In this part of this Act the expression "bank note" has the same meaning as it has in the Forgery Act 1913, as amended or expanded by the Currency Act and by this part of this Act.

53(1) Currency notes issued by or on behalf of the Government of any country outside the State shall be deemed to be bank notes within the meaning of the Forgery Act 1913.

55(1) If any person makes, or causes to be made, or uses for any purpose whatsoever, or utters any document purporting to be or in any way resembling, or so nearly resembling as to be calculated to deceive, a bank note or part of a bank note, he shall be guilty of an offence under this subsection and shall be liable on summary conviction thereof to a fine not exceeding five pounds.

8.61   Proof of knowledge and intent is, in the absence of an admission, a matter of inference from all the circumstances proved by the prosecution. In this regard reference should be made to chapter 1. In the case of possession of forged bank notes the typical cases which have gone to trial have involved the accused possessing, or passing, a series of forged bank notes. The prosecution, from this evidence, asks the jury to infer the relevant guilty knowledge on the commonsense basis that an innocent person might possibly come into possession of one forged bank note but not a multiplicity of them. The accused may seek to defend this kind of case by giving evidence that he obtained these bank notes in an innocent manner in the course of a public transaction. That defence is likely to be successful as it is almost impossible for the prosecution to disprove the possibility that an innocent person could come into possession of forged bank notes by being given change in a shop. Clearly, however, the larger the number of bank notes the more difficult it would be to make such a defence case credible.

8.62   *Coinage Offences Act 1861*
                                   As amended

1 References to coin or any particular class of coin lawfully current by virtue of any proclamation or otherwise in any part of Her Majesty's Dominion shall be construed as indicating references to coins lawfully current in the State,
References to silver coin shall be construed as including references to nickel coin, cupro-nickel coin and coin provided under s 6 of the Act of 1950 [Coinage Act,

1950] or s 4 of the Act of 1969 and by the Second Schedule s 22 of Decimal Currency Act, 1969.

8.63 *Decimal Currency Act 1969*

14(1) Except coins issued under this Act, no piece of metal or mixed metal of any value whatsoever shall be made or issued in the State as a coin or a token for money or as purporting that the holder thereof is entitled to demand any value denoted thereon.
(3) [As amended by s 128 of the Central Bank Act 1989] Every person who makes or issues any piece of metal or mixed metal in contravention of subsection (1) of this section shall be guilty of an offence and shall be liable –

(i) on summary conviction to a fine not exceeding £1,000 or at the discretion of the court to imprisonment for a term not exceeding one year or to both such fine and such imprisonment, or
(ii) on conviction on indictment to a fine not exceeding £5,000 or at the discretion of the court to imprisonment for a term not exceeding two years or to both such fine and such imprisonment.

8.64 The provisions of four earlier statutes are effectively updated, to take account of the many changes in the State's coinage through the years, by s 22 and the Second Schedule of the Decimal Currency Act 1969. These earlier statutes are: Coinage Offences Act 1861 (see para **8.62**); Customs Consolidation Act 1876; Revenue Act 1889; Currency Act 1927.

Bribery

8.65 A typical case of bribery involves the accused seeking a favour from a public official in return for payment. For example, a Garda is paid a salary and is not entitled to take money from a motorist in order to discontinue a prosecution for drunken driving.

8.66 *Public Bodies Corrupt Practices Act 1889*
as amended by the Prevention of Corruption Acts, 1889 to 1915
Adoption Order 1928 and The Electoral Act 1963

Corruption in office a misdemeanour

1 (1) Every person who shall by himself or by or in conjunction with any other person, corruptly solicit or receive, or agree to receive, for himself, or for any other person, any gift, loan, fee, reward, or advantage whatever as an inducement to, or reward for, or otherwise on account of any member, officer, or servant of a public body as in this Act defined, doing or forbearing to do anything in respect of any matter or transaction whatsoever, actual or proposed, in which the said public body is concerned, shall be guilty of a misdemeanour.
(2) Every person who shall by himself or by or in conjunction with any other person corruptly give, promise, or offer any gift, loan, fee, reward, or advantage whatsoever to any person, whether for the benefit of that person or of another person, as an inducement to or reward for or otherwise on account of any member, officer, or servant of any public body as in this Act defined, doing or forbearing to do anything in respect of any matter or transaction whatsoever, actual or proposed, in which such public body as aforesaid is concerned, shall be guilty of a misdemeanour.

Penalty for offences

2   Any person on conviction for offending as aforesaid shall, at the discretion of the court before which he is convicted—

(*a*) be liable to be imprisoned for any period not exceeding two years, with or without hard labour, or to pay a fine not exceeding five hundred pounds, or to both such imprisonment and such fine; and

(*b*) in addition be liable to be ordered to pay to such body, and in such manner as the court directs, the amount or value of any gift, loan, fee, or reward received by him or any part thereof; and

. . .

(*e*) if such person is an officer or servant in the employ of any public body upon such conviction he shall, at the discretion of the court, be liable to forfeit his right and claim to any compensation or pension to which he would otherwise have been entitled.

Savings

3   (1) Where an offence under this Act is also publishable under any other enactment, or at common law, such offence may be prosecuted and punished either under this Act, or under the other enactment, or at common law, but so that no person shall be punished twice for the same offence.

(2) A person shall not be exempt from punishment under this Act by reason of the invalidity of the appointment or election of a person to a public office.

Restriction on prosecution

4   (1) A prosecution for an offence under this Act shall not be instituted except by or with the consent of the Attorney General.

Expenses of prosecution

5   The expenses of the prosecution of an offence against this Act shall be defrayed in like manner as in the case of a felony.

Jurisdiction of quarter sessions

6   A court of general or quarter sessions shall in England have jurisdiction to inquire of, hear, and determine an offence under this Act.

Interpretation

7   In this Act—

The expression "public body" means any council of a county or county of a city or town, any council of a municipal borough, also any board, commissioners, select vestry, or other body which has power to act under and for the purposes of any Act relating to local government, or the public health, or to poor law or otherwise to administer money raised by rates in pursuance of any public general Act, but does not include any public body as above defined existing elsewhere than in Saorstát Eireann.

The expression "public office" means any office or employment of a person as a member, officer, or servant of such public body;

The expression "person" includes a body of persons, corporate or unincorporate:

The expression "advantage" includes an office or dignity, and any forbearance to demand any money or money's worth or valuable thing, and includes any aid, vote, consent, or influence, or pretended aid, vote, consent, or influence, and also includes any promise or procurement of or agreement or endeavour to procure, or the holding out of any expectation of any gift, loan, fee, reward, or advantage, as before defined.

Application of Act to Scotland

8 In the application of this Act to Scotland the sheriff and sheriff substitute shall have jurisdiction to try any offence under this Act; and

The expression "misdemeanor" shall mean "crime and offence;" and
The expression "municipal borough" shall mean any "burgh."

50 & 51 Vict c 20 not to apply to trial under Act

9 The provisions of the Criminal Law and Procedure (Ireland) Act 1887, shall not apply to any trial under the provisions of this Act.

Short title

10 This Act may be cited as the Public Bodies Corrupt Practices Act 1889.

8.67 Two further Acts were passed in 1906 and 1916. The Prevention of Corruption Act 1906 extended the offences outlined in the Public Bodies Corrupt Practices Act 1889 to agents who are defined in the Act of 1906 at s 1(2) as "any person employed by or acting for another". Section 1(3) brought servants of the Crown or municipal councils under the Act. Under the Prevention of Corruption Order 1928[81] references to "serving under the Crown" are adapted to read "holding an office remunerated out of the central fund or monies provided by the Oireachtas or an office". The Prevention of Corruption Act 1916 increased the penalties for offences under the previous two Acts and also introduced a "presumption of corruption" in certain cases. Section 2 shifts the burden of proof on to the defendant by holding that where it is proved "that any money, gift, or other consideration has been paid or given to or received" by the accused "from a person, or agent of a person, holding or seeking to obtain a contract" from the public body who was the accused's employer, "the money, gift or consideration shall be deemed to have been paid or given and received corruptly . . . unless the contrary is proved".

Reform of the law

8.68 To keep pace with changes in technology, with particular reference to computers, the Law Reform Commission has recommended the creation of a new offence of "dishonest use of computers".

This offence would basically consist of dishonestly using or causing to be used, a computer or other machine with intent to obtain by that use, a gain or cause a loss to another. "Machine" would include those designed to be

81 SR & O 1928 no 37.

operated by means of a coin, bank note, token, disc, tape or any identifying card or article.

The Commission did not propose a definition for "computer" other than to suggest that any definition should distinguish between the computing, memory and communicating functions of computers. One reason for not defining "computer" was the publication of the Criminal Damage Bill 1990 which contained offences involving data and computers but offered no definition of a computer. The Bill subsequently passed into law to become the Criminal Damage Act 1991 which, inter alia, outlaws the unlawful use of a computer to access data either within or outside the State, usually termed "hacking" and makes it an offence to "add to, alter, corrupt, erase or move data to another storage medium or to a different location in the storage medium". The Act defines data as "information in a form in which it can be accessed by means of a computer and includes a programme"; a definition which is of limited use unless "computer" is also defined.

Protection of information

8.69 By extending the definition of property to include intellectual property protected by the equitable doctrine of confidentiality, data, trade secrets or other valuable, secret or confidential information, industrial and commercial espionage activities should be brought within the criminal law. The other difficulty in these types of offences, the lack of permanent deprivation, is addressed by providing that a person appropriating property without meaning the other permanently to lose the thing itself is nevertheless to be regarded as having the intention of permanently depriving the other of it if he does so without a claim of right and is reckless as to whether the owner be deprived permanently of the property or not or the circumstances of his withholding the property are such that the economic or utilitarian benefits of owning it or in the case of intellectual property, exclusively of knowledge or possession, are lost.

The Commission also recommended amendments to existing Acts to take account of modern technology, for example, the inclusion of records kept mechanically, electronically or otherwise in non-legible form, on film, tape or computer disc in the false accounting provisions.

In relation to fraud, the Commission did not recommend setting up a Serious Fraud Office similar to that established in the U.K. but rather recommended that additional resources be directed into the Garda Fraud Squad. It also recommended the putting in place of administrative machinery to ensure the earliest possible intervention of the Gardaí into revenue or other investigations where fraud is suspected.

The Commission recommended a number of procedural changes including:

1. The introduction of a pre-trial review similar to that introduced in the U.K.
2. Dispensing with the preliminary examination in fraud cases to be tried by jury.

3. The abolition of the peremptory challenge in jury selection and the disqualification from serving on any jury trying a fraud offence of a person convicted of any fraud offence.

Further materials

8.70 Archbold – *Criminal Pleading Evidence and Practice* (36th ed, 1966), chapter 10.

Chapter 9

SAMPLE OFFENCES

9.01 This chapter reproduces the standard form of charge used in the most important, and the commonly prosecuted, offences. In some cases the elements of these offences have already been discussed in this text. Reference should be made to the portions of the text which consider these offences. In addition, the quotation of some sections creating an offence and the definition of some of the more unusual common law offences has been given. A note is made of the more common alternatives to the form of charges quoted. Other alternatives may be seen by reading the section.

In many of the charges a multitude of different sections of Acts are referred to. Where an enactment changes the definition of an offence it must be included in the charge, or in the case of an indictment in the statement of offence. When an enactment merely increases or decreases the penalty this is not necessary. Modern practice, in the case of charges, but not in the case of indictments, has been to include a reference to enactments which merely change penalty. That practice is not incorrect it is merely unnecessary.

Homicide

9.02 Murder

You, AB, on the (date) at (place) in the (District) murdered CD.

Contrary to s 4 of the Criminal Justice Act 1964.

The section is quoted at para **5.06**. For a discussion see paras **5.12–5.45**.

You, AB, on the (date) at (place) Northern Ireland murdered CD.

Contrary to s 2(1) of the Criminal Law (Jurisdiction) Act 1976.

The section is quoted at para **7.49**. For a discussion see paras **7.48–7.50**.

You, AB, on the (date) at (place) in the (District) murdered CD a member of An Garda Síochána in the due execution of his duty.

Contrary to s 3 of the Criminal Justice Act 1990.

The section is quoted at para **5.07**. For a discussion see para **1.30** and generally chapter 5.

9.03 Manslaughter

You, AB, on the (date) at (place) in the (District) unlawfully killed CD.

Contrary to common law.

For a discussion see paras **5.25–5.64**.

You, AB, on the (date) at (place) in Northern Ireland unlawfully killed CD.

Contrary to s 2(1) of the Criminal Law (Jurisdiction) Act 1976.

The section is quoted at para **7.49**. For a discussion see paras **7.48–7.50**.

9.04 Attempted Murder

You, AB, on the (date) at (place) in the (District), administered to CD a poison called strychnine with intent to murder him.

Contrary to section 11 of the Offences Against the Person Act 1861.

The section is quoted at para **5.08**. For a discussion see paras **5.46–5.51**. Alternative charges exist pursuant to the Offences Against the Person Act 1861 of destroying a building by explosion with intent to murder (s 12), setting fire to a ship or vessel with intent to murder (s 13), attempting to administer poison or shooting at, attempting to drown, suffocate or strangle with intent to murder (s 14) and attempting by other means to commit murder (s 15). The sections are quoted at para **5.08**.

You, AB on the (date) at (place) in the (District), attempted to murder CD.

Contrary to common law.

9.05 Criminal Letters

You, AB, on the (date) at (place) in the (District), maliciously sent, knowing the contents thereof, a letter to CD threatening to kill or murder the said CD.

Contrary to s 16 of the Offences Against the Person Act 1861.

The section is quoted at para **5.08**.

9.06 Suicide

AB, on the (date) at (place) in the (District), attempted to kill himself.

Contrary to common law.

For a discussion see paras **5.37–5.40**.

9.07 Abortion

You, AB, on the (date) at (place) in the (District), with intent to procure the miscarriage of a woman named CD unlawfully administered to her a poison or other noxious thing (specify).

Contrary to s 58 of the Offences Against the Person Act 1861.

The section is quoted at para **5.30**. For a discussion see paras **5.30–5.33**.

You, AB, on the (date) at (place) in the (District), did unlawfully supply to CD a poison knowing that same was intended to be unlawfully used or employed with intent to procure the miscarriage of a woman.

Contrary to s 59 of the Offences Against the Person Act 1861.

The section is quoted at para **5.30**. For a discussion see paras **5.30–5.33**.

9.08 Infanticide

You, AB, on the (date) at (place) in the (District), unlawfully killed CD a child, then being under the age of twelve months.

Contrary to s 1 of the Infanticide Act 1949.

The section is quoted at para **5.34**.

9.09 Concealment of Birth

You, AB, on the (date) at (place) in the (District), endeavoured to conceal the birth of a child by secretly disposing of the dead body of the said child.

Contrary to s 60 of the Offences Against the Person Act 1861.

The section is quoted at para **5.30**.

Offences against the person

Assault
9.10 Less Serious Forms

You, AB, on the (date) at (place) in the (District), unlawfully assaulted CD.

Contrary to common law.

For a discussion see paras **7.35–7.44**.

You, AB, on the (date) at (place) in the (District), unlawfully assaulted CD thereby occasioning to him actual bodily harm.

Contrary to s 47 of the Offences Against the Person Act 1861.

The section is quoted at para **7.36**. For a discussion see paras **7.41–7.42**.

You, AB, on the (date) at (place) in the (District), assaulted CD with intent to commit the felony of (specify felony).

Contrary to s 30 of the Offences Against the Person Act 1861.

The section is quoted at para **7.20**.

9.11 Wounding, Grievous Bodily Harm

You, AB, on the (date) at (place) in the (District), unlawfully and maliciously wounded CD.

Contrary to s 20 of the Offences Against the Person Act 1861.

9.11 Sample offences

Alternative: inflict grievous bodily harm upon. The section is quoted at para **7.36**. For a discussion see para **7.41–7.42**.

> You, AB, on the (date) at (place) in Northern Ireland, unlawfully and maliciously wounded CD.
>
> Contrary to s 2(1) of the Criminal Law (Jurisdiction) Act 1976.

The section is quoted at para **7.49**. For a discussion see paras **7.48–7.50**.

> You, AB, on the (date) at (place) in Northern Ireland, unlawfully and maliciously inflicted grievous bodily harm upon CD.
>
> Contrary to s 2(1) of the Criminal Law (Jurisdiction) Act 1976.

The section is quoted at para **7.49**. For a discussion see paras **7.48–7.50**.

9.12 Assault with Intent

> You, AB, on the (date) at (place) in the (District), assaulted CD with intent to rob him.
>
> Contrary to s 23A of the Larceny Act 1916 as inserted by s 5 of the Criminal Law (Jurisdiction) Act 1976.

The section is quoted at para **8.35**. For a discussion see para **8.36**.

> You, AB, on the (date) at (place) in the (District), unlawfully and maliciously wounded CD with intent to do him grievous bodily harm, or to maim, disfigure or disable him, or to resist the lawful apprehension of the said AB (or EF).
>
> Contrary to s 18 of the Offences Against the Person Act 1861.

The section is quoted at para **7.36**.

> You, AB, on the (date) at (place) in the (District), unlawfully and maliciously attempted to discharge a loaded pistol at CD with intent to do him grievous bodily harm, or to main, disfigure or disable him, or to resist the lawful apprehension of the said AB (or EF).
>
> Contrary to s 18 of the Offences Against the Person Act 1861.

The section is quoted at para **7.36**.

> You, AB, on the (date) at (place) in the (District), assaulted CD with intent to steal from the person of CD (or specify other felony).
>
> Contrary to s 38 of the Offences Against the Person Act 1861.

The section is quoted at para **7.35**.

9.13 Man-Trap

> You, AB, on the (date) at (place) in the (District), caused to be placed, a man-trap, with the intent that the same might inflict grievous bodily harm upon a person coming in contact therewith.
>
> Contrary to s 31 of the Offences Against the Person Act 1861.

The section is quoted at para **7.36**.

9.14 Garda

You, AB, on the (date) at (place) in the (District), assaulted (or resisted or obstructed) Garda CD, a peace officer, in the due execution of his duty.

Contrary to s 38 of the Offences Against the Person Act 1861.

The section is quoted at para **7.36**.

You, AB, on the (date) at (place) in the (District), unlawfully assaulted CD a Garda, in the due execution of his duty.

Contrary to s 12 of the Prevention of Crimes Act 1871.

This offence is summary and does not entitle the accused to trial by jury. The section reads:

Penalty on assaults on police

12 Where any person is convicted of an assault on any constable when in the execution of his duty, such person shall be guilty of an offence against this Act, and shall, in the discretion of the court, be liable either to pay a penalty not exceeding twenty pounds, and in default of payment to be imprisoned, with or without hard labour, for a term not exceeding six months, or to be imprisoned for any term not exceeding six, or in case such person has been convicted of a similar assault within two years, nine months, with or without hard labour.

9.15 False Imprisonment

You, AB, on the (date) at (place) in the (District), falsely imprisoned CD by unlawfully detaining him against his will.

Contrary to common law and s 11 of the Criminal Law Act 1976.

Section 11 makes the offence a felony and provides the penalty. The section reads:

11 (1) The offences of kidnapping and false imprisonment and an offence under s 10 of the Criminal Law (Jurisdiction) Act, 1976, shall be felonies.

(2) A person guilty of kidnapping or guilty of false imprisonment shall be liable on conviction on indictment to imprisonment for life.

For a discussion see paras **7.45–7.47**.

9.16 Poisoning

You, AB, on the (date) at (place) in the (District), unlawfully and maliciously administered to CD a poison called (specify) with intent thereby to inflict grievous bodily harm on the said CD.

Contrary to s 23 of the Offences Against the Person Act 1861.

Alternative: or other destructive or noxious thing, so as to thereby endanger the life of such person. The section reads:

23 Whosoever shall unlawfully and maliciously administer to or cause to be administered to or taken by any other person any poison or any other destructive or noxious thing, so as thereby to endanger the life of such person, or so as thereby to inflict upon such person any grievous bodily harm, shall be guilty of felony, and being convicted thereof shall be liable to be kept in penal servitude for any term not exceeding ten years.

You, AB, on the (date) at (place) in the (District), attempted to render CD unconscious with intent to enable yourself (or EF) to commit the indictable offence of robbery.

Contrary to s 21 of the Offences Against the Person Act 1861.

The section reads:

21 Whosoever shall, by any means whatsoever, attempt to choke, suffocate, or strangle any other person, or shall by any means calculated to choke, suffocate, or strangle, attempt to render any other person insensible, unconscious, or incapable of resistance, with intent in any of such cases thereby to enable himself or any other person to commit, or with intent in any of such cases thereby to assist any other person in committing any indictable offence, shall be guilty of felony, and being convicted thereof, shall be liable to be kept in penal servitude for life.

You, AB, on the (date) at (place) in the (District), unlawfully administered to CD a stupefying drug, being (specify), with intent to enable himself (or EF) to commit the indictable offence of (specify).

Contrary to s 22 of the Offences Against the Person Act 1861.

The section reads:

22 Whosoever shall unlawfully apply or administer to or cause to be taken by, or attempt to apply or administer to, or attempt to cause to be administered to or taken by, any person, any chloroform, laudanum, or other stupefying or overpowering drug, matter, or thing, with intent in any of such cases thereby to enable himself or any other person to commit, or with intent in any of such cases thereby to assist any other person in committing any indictable offence, shall be guilty of felony, and being convicted thereof shall be liable to be kept in penal servitude for life.

9.17 Children

You, AB, on the (date) at (place) in the (District), being a person over the age of seventeen years, having the custody (charge, care) of a child (young person) CD did wilfully neglect the said CD in a manner likely to cause him unnecessary suffering or injury to health.

Contrary to s 12(1) of the Children Act 1908 as amended by s 29 of the Children Act 1941 and s 4 of the Children (Amendment) Act 1957.

Alternative: assault, neglect, abandon, expose or cause to be or procure to be. The section reads:

12 (1) If any person over the age of seventeen years, who has the custody, charge or care of any child or young person, wilfully assaults, ill-treats, neglects, abandons, or exposes such child or young person or causes or procures such child or young person to be assaulted, ill-treated, neglected, abandoned, or exposed in a manner likely to cause such child or young person unnecessary suffering or injury to his health (including injury to or loss of sight or hearing, or limb, or organ of the body, and any mental derangement), that person shall be guilty of a misdemeanour [penalty – on indictment one hundred pound fine or two years imprisonment, on summary conviction – twenty five pound fine or six months imprisonment] . . . for the purposes of this section a parent or other person legally liable to maintain a child or young person shall be deemed to have neglected him in a manner likely to cause injury to his health if he fails to provide adequate food, clothing, medical aid, or lodging for the child or young person, or if, being unable otherwise to provide such food, clothing, medical aid, or lodging, he fails to take steps to procure the same to be provided under the Acts relating to the relief of the poor. (2) A person may be convicted of an offence under this section either on indictment or by a Court of Summary Jurisdiction notwithstanding that actual suffering or injury to health, or the likelihood of such a suffering or injury to health, was obviated by the action of another person. (3) A person may be convicted of an offence under this section either on indictment or by a Court of Summary Jurisdiction notwithstanding the death of the child or young person in respect of whom the offence is committed. (4) Upon the trial of any person over the age of seventeen indicted for the manslaughter of a child or young person of whom he had the custody, charge, or care, it shall be lawful for the jury, if they are satisfied that the accused is guilty of an offence under this section in respect of such child or young person, to find the accused guilty of such offence. (5) If it is proved that a person convicted under this section was directly or indirectly interested in any sum of money accruable or payable in the event of the death of the child or young person, and had knowledge that such sum of money was accruing or becoming payable, then – (a) in the case of a conviction on indictment, the court may in its discretion either increase the amount of the fine under this section so that the fine does not exceed two hundred pounds; or, in lieu of awarding any other penalty under this section, sentence the person to penal servitude for any term not exceeding five years; and (b) in the case of a summary conviction, the court in determining the sentence to be awarded shall take into consideration the fact that the person was so interested and had such knowledge. (6) A person shall be deemed to be directly or indirectly interested in a sum of money under this section if he has any share in or any benefit from the payment of that money, though he is not a person to whom it is legally payable. (7) A copy of a policy of insurance, certified by an officer or agent of the insurance company granting the policy to be a true copy shall in any proceedings under this section be *prima facie* evidence that the child or young person therein stated to be insured has been in fact so insured, and that the person in whose favour the policy has been granted is the person to whom the money thereby insured is legally payable. (a) An offence under this section is in this part of this Act referred to as an offence of cruelty.

Section 13 reads:

13 Where it is proved that the death of an infant under three years of age was caused by suffocation (not being suffocation caused by disease or the presence of any foreign body in the throat or air-passages of the infant) whilst the infant was in bed with some other person over sixteen years of age, and that other person was at the time of going to bed under the influence of drink, that other person shall be deemed to have neglected the infant in a manner likely to cause injury to its health within the meaning of this part of the Act.

9.18   Abandoning Child

You, AB, on the (date) at (place) in the (District), unlawfully abandoned (exposed) a child CD, being under the age of two years, whereby its life was endangered (its health was permanently injured, its health was likely to be permanently injured).

Contrary to s 27 of the Offences Against the Person Act 1861.

The section is quoted at para **7.36**.

9.19 Child Stealing

You, AB, on the (date) at (place) in the (District) by fraud (force) unlawfully enticed away (took away, did lead away, decoyed, detained) CD a child being under the age of fourteen years with intent to deprive (specify parent or guardian) being the (specify whether parent, guardian, person having the lawful care or charge) of the child, of the possession of the said child.

Contrary to s 56 of the Offences Against the Person Act 1861.

The section reads:

56 Whosoever shall unlawfully, either by Force of Fraud, lead or take away, or decoy or entice away or detain, any Child under the Age of Fourteen Years, with Intent to deprive any Parent, Guardian, or other Person having the lawful Care or Charge of such Child of the Possession of such Child, or with Intent to steal any Article upon or about the Person of such Child, to whomsoever such Article may belong, and whosoever shall, with any such Intent, receive or harbour any such Child, knowing the same to have been, by Force or Fraud, led, taken, decoyed, enticed away, or detained as in this Section before mentioned, shall be guilty of Felony, and being convicted thereof shall be liable, at the Discretion of the Court, to be kept in Penal Servitude for any Term not exceeding Seven Years and not less than Three Years, – or to be imprisoned for any Term not exceeding Two Years, with or without Hard Labour, and, if a Male under the Age of Sixteen Years, with or without Whipping; Provided that no Person who shall have claimed any Right to the Possession of such Child, or shall be the Mother or shall have claimed to be the Father of an illegitimate Child, shall be liable to be prosecuted by virtue hereof on account of the getting Possession of such Child, or taking such Child out of the Possession of any Person having the lawful Charge thereof.

Sexual offences

9.20 Rape

You, AB, a male person on the (date) at (place) in the (District), had unlawful sexual intercourse with CD, a woman, who at the time of the intercourse did not consent to it or at the time knew that she did not consent to the intercourse or was reckless as to whether she did or did not consent to it.

Contrary to s 2 of the Criminal Law (Rape) Act 1981.

The section is quoted at para **6.53**. For a discussion see paras **6.45–6.69**.

You, AB, a male person, on the (date) at (place) in the (District), sexually assaulted CD, a female person, in circumstances which included the penetration of the vagina of CD by an object held or manipulated by AB (by another person).

Contrary to s 4 of the Criminal Law (Rape) (Amendment) Act 1990.

Alternative: penetration of the anus, or mouth, by the penis (the victim need not be a woman). The section is quoted at para **6.87**. For a discussion see paras **6.86–6.89**.

9.21 Buggery

You, AB, on the (date) at (place) in the (District) committed buggery with a cow.

Contrary to common law.

For a discussion see paras **6.22–6.28**.

9.22 Gross Indecency

You, AB, a male person, on the (date) at (place) in the (District), committed an act of gross indecency with CD, a male person.

Contrary to s 11 of the Criminal Law Amendment Act 1885.

The section is quoted at para **6.24**. For a discussion see para **6.25**.

9.23 Sexual Assault

You, AB, a male person, on the (date) at (place) in the (District), sexually assaulted CD, a female person (or a male person as the case may be).

Contrary to s 2 of the Criminal Law (Rape) (Amendment) Act 1990.

The section is quoted at para **6.83**. For a discussion see para **6.82**.

You, AB, a male person, on the (date) at (place) in the (District), sexually assaulted CD, a female person (or a male person as the case may be) in circumstances which involved serious violence to CD.

Contrary to s 3 of the Criminal Law (Rape) (Amendment) Act 1990.

Alternative: threat of serious violence, or was such as to cause injury, humiliation or degradation of a grave nature to the victim. The section is quoted at para **6.83**. For a discussion see para **6.84**.

9.24 Procuring

You, AB, on the (date) at (place) in the (District), by false pretences or false representations, procured CD, a female person, to have unlawful carnal connexion with him (or with EF).

Contrary to s 3 of the Criminal Law Rape Amendment Act 1885 as amended by s 8 of the Criminal Law Rape (Amendment) Act 1935.

9.25 Incest

You, AB, a male person, on the (date) at (place) in the (District), had unlawful carnal knowledge of CD, who is and was to your knowledge, your daughter.

Contrary to s 1 of the Punishment of Incest Act 1908.

The section is quoted at para **6.07**. For a discussion see paras **6.06–6.12**.

You, AB, a male person, on the (date) at (place) in the (District), had unlawful carnal knowledge of CD, who is and was to your knowledge, your daughter, and was at the time aged fourteen years.

Contrary to s 1 of the Punishment of Incest Act 1908 as amended by s 12 of the Criminal Law (Amendment) Act 1935.

This form is to be used where the victim is under fifteen, as a greater penalty is then provided by the 1935 Act. The section is quoted at para **6.07**. For a discussion see paras **6.06–6.12**.

9.26   Underage

You, AB, a male person, on the (date) at (place) in the (District), had unlawful carnal knowledge of CD, a girl under the age of fifteen years.

Contrary to s 1(1) of the Criminal Law (Amendment) Act 1935.

Attempts are charged contrary to s 1(2) of the Act. The section is quoted at para **6.31**. For a discussion see paras **6.29–6.35**.

You, AB, a male person, on the (date) at (place) in the (District), had unlawful carnal knowledge of CD, a girl over the age of fifteen years and under the age of seventeen years.

Contrary to s 2(1) of the Criminal Law (Amendment) Act 1935.

Attempts are charged contrary to s 2(2) of the Act. The section is quoted at para **6.31**. For a discussion see paras **6.29–6.35**.

9.27   Threat, Misrepresentation

You, AB, on the (date) at (place) in the (District), procured CD, a female person, to have unlawful carnal connexion with EF by threatening the said CD that (specify).

Contrary to s 3 of the Criminal Law Amendment Act 1885 as amended by s 8 of the Criminal Law (Amendment) Act 1935.

The section as amended is quoted at para **6.81**. For a discussion see para **6.80**.

You, AB, on the (date) at (place) in the (District), by falsely representing that you were a member of An Garda Síochána (specify other pretence or false representation), procured CD, a female person, to have unlawful carnal conexion with you (with EF).

Contrary to s 3 of the Criminal Law Amendment Act 1885 as amended by s 8 of the Criminal Law (Amendment) Act 1935.

The section as amended is quoted at para **6.81**. For a discussion see para **6.80**.

9.28   Mental Handicap

You, AB, a male person, on the (date) at (place) in the (District), in circumstances which did not amount to rape, had unlawful carnal knowledge of CD, a woman, who was then, to your knowledge feeble-minded.

Contrary to s 4 of the Criminal Law (Amendment) Act 1935.

Alternative: an idiot, an imbecile. The section is quoted at para **6.14**. For a discussion see paras **6.13–6.20**.

Where the offender is a nurse, etc. in a mental hospital the penalty is five years imprisonment under s 254 of the Mental Treatment Act 1945. The prosecution must be commenced within twelve months of the offence. The section is quoted at para **6.17**. For a discussion see paras **6.13–6.20**.

9.29 Possession of Obscene Article

You, AB, on the (date) at (place) in the (District) had in your possession an obscene article (specify) with intent to sell same (or otherwise gain therefrom).

Contrary to common law.

9.30 Obscene Libel

You, AB, on the (date) at (place) in the (District) published of and concerning CD an obscene libel, that is (describe the material portion).

Contrary to common law.

9.31 Managing a Brothel

You, AB, on the (date) at (place) in the (District) kept a brothel.

Contrary to s 13 of the Criminal Law (Amendment) Act 1935.

The various alternatives can be seen from the section:

Offence of keeping a brothel

13 (1) In lieu of s 3 (repealed by this Act) of the Criminal Law Amendment Act 1885, it is hereby enacted that any person who—

(*a*) keeps or manages or acts or assists in the management of a brothel, or

(*b*) being the tenant, lessee, occupier, or person in charge of any premises, knowingly permits such premises or any part thereof to be used as a brothel or for the purposes of habitual prostitution, or

(*c*) being the lessor or landlord of any premises or the agent of such lessor or landlord, lets such premises or any part thereof with the knowledge that such premises or some part thereof are or is to be used as a brothel, or is wilfully a party to the continued use of such premises or any part thereof as a brothel,

shall be guilty of a misdemeanour and shall be liable, in the case of a first conviction of such misdemeanour, to a fine not exceeding one hundred pounds or, at the discretion of the court, to imprisonment for any term not exceeding six months or to both such fine and such imprisonment and, in the case of a second or any subsequent conviction of such misdemeanour, to a fine not exceeding two hundred and fifty pounds or, at the discretion of the court, to penal servitude for any term not exceeding five years nor less than three years or imprisonment for any term not exceeding two years or to both such fine and such penal servitude or imprisonment.

(2) A Justice of the District Court shall have jurisdiction to try summarily any charge of an offence which is declared by this section to be a misdemeanour where the person so charged has not previously been convicted of any such misdemeanour and such person (inquiry having been made of him by the Justice) does not object to being so tried.

(3) Sections 5, 6, and 7 of the Disorderly Houses Act 1751, as amended by s 7 of

the Disorderly Houses Act 1818 shall apply to prosecutions for an offence which is declared by this section to be a misdemeanour.

A brothel is defined at common law as a place resorted to by persons for the purposes of prostitution. There must be at least two prostitutes for a brothel to exist but they may be of either or both sexes. A person is a prostitute if she offers her body for payment for acts which need not necessarily amount to ordinary sexual intercourse.

9.32 Living on Immoral Earnings

You, AB, a male person, on the (date) at (place) in the (District) knowingly lived in part on the earnings of prostitution.

Contrary to s 1(*a*) of the Vagrancy Act 1898 as amended by s 7 of the Criminal Law Amendment Act 1912.

Alternative: wholly. The section, as amended, reads:

1 (1) Every male person who—

(*a*) knowingly lives wholly or in part on the earnings of prostitution; or
(*b*) in any public place persistently solicits or importunes for immoral purposes,

shall be liable on summary conviction to imprisonment for a term not exceeding six months with hard labour.

(2) If it is made to appear to a court of summary jurisdiction by information on oath that there is reason to suspect that any house or any part of a house is used by a female for purposes of prostitution, and that any male person residing in or frequenting the house is living wholly or in part on the earnings of the prostitute, the court may issue a warrant authorising any constable to enter and search the house and to arrest that male person.

(3) Where a male person is proved to live with or to be habitually in the company of a prostitute or is proved to have exercised control direction or influence over the movements of a prostitute in such a manner as to show that he is aiding, abetting or compelling her prostitution with any other person or generally, he shall, unless he can satisfy the court to the contrary, be deemed to be knowingly living on the earnings of prostitution.

9.33 Prostitution

You, AB, on the (date), being a common prostitute, were found loitering at (place) in the (District), and importuning (soliciting) passers-by for the purposes of prostitution (and being offensive to passers-by).

Contrary to s 16(1) of the Criminal Law (Amendment) Act 1935.

Note the effect of the decision in *King* at para **4.146**. The section reads:

Suppression of prostitution

16 (1) Every common prostitute who is found loitering in any street, thoroughfare, or other place and importuning or soliciting passers-by for purposes of prostitution or being otherwise offensive to passers-by shall be guilty of an offence under this section and shall on summary conviction thereof be liable, in the case of a first such offence, to a fine not exceeding two pounds or, in the case of a second or any subsequent such offence, to imprisonment for any term not exceeding six months.

9.34 Indecency

You, AB, on the (date) at (place) in the (District) at or near and in sight of a place along which the public habitually pass as of right, or by permission, did (specify act of indecency) in such a way as to offend modesty (cause scandal, injure the morals of the community).

Contrary to s 18 of the Criminal Law (Amendment) Act 1935.

The section reads:

Public indecency

18 Every person who shall commit, at or near and in sight of any place along which the public habitually pass as of right or by permission, any act in such a way as to offend modesty or cause scandal or injure the morals of the community shall be guilty of an offence under this section and shall on summary conviction thereof be liable to a fine not exceeding two pounds or, at the discretion of the court, to imprisonment for any term not exceeding one month.

Criminal damage

9.35

You, AB, on the (date) at (place) in the (District), without lawful excuse, damaged the tyres of motor vehicle, registration number , the property of CD, by slashing them with a knife.

Contrary to s 2(1) of the Criminal Damage Act 1991.

The section is quoted at para **7.53**. For a discussion see paras **7.51–7.56**.

9.36 Damage with Intent

You, AB, on the (date) at (place) in the (District), without lawful excuse, damaged a motor boat, the property of CD, by rendering same liable to take on water while afloat, intending thereby to endanger the life of CD (of another) or being reckless as to whether the life of CD (of another) would be thereby endangered.

Contrary to s 2(2) of the Criminal Damage Act 1991.

The section is quoted at para **7.53**. For a discussion see paras **7.51–7.56**.

9.37 Intent to Defraud

You, AB, on the (date) at (place) in the (District) damaged a Ming vase, your own property (the property of CD) with intent to defraud the Insurance Corporation of Ireland.

Contrary to s 2(3) of the Criminal Damage Act 1991.

The section is quoted at para **7.53**. For a discussion see paras **7.51–7.56**.

9.38 Arson

You, AB, on the (date) at (place) in the (District), without lawful excuse, damaged by fire, motor vehicle, registration number , the property of CD.

Contrary to s 2(1) of the Criminal Damage Act 1991.

The statement of offence in an indictment should read: Arson, contrary to s 2(1) of the Criminal Damage Act, 1991. The section is quoted at para **7.53**. For a discussion see paras **7.51–7.56**.

You, AB, on the (date) at (place) in the (District), without lawful excuse, damaged by fire, the house premises at (specify) intending thereby to endanger the life of CD (of another) or being reckless as to whether the life of CD (of another) would be thereby endangered.

Contrary to s 2(2) of the Criminal Damage Act 1991.

The statement of offence in an indictment should read Arson, contrary to s 2(2) of the Criminal Damage Act 1991. The section is quoted at para **7.53**. For a discussion see paras **7.51–7.56**.

You, AB, on the (date) at (place) in the (District) damaged by fire your retail premises (or the property of CD) at (specify) intending thereby to defraud EF (for example an insurance company).

Contrary to s 2(3) of the Criminal Damage Act 1991.

The statement of offence in an indictment should read: Arson, contrary to s 2(3) of the Criminal Damage Act 1991. The section is quoted at para **7.53**. For a discussion see paras **7.51–7.56**.

9.39 Threat to damage

You, AB, on the (date) at (place) in the (District), without lawful excuse, threatened that you would damage the (specify property) of CD (or EF), intending that CD would fear that the said threat would be carried out.

Contrary to s 3(a) of the Criminal Damage Act 1991.

The section is quoted at para **7.53**. For a discussion see paras **7.51–7.56**.

You, AB, on the (date) at (place) in the (District), without lawful excuse, threatened CD that you would damage motor vehicle, registration number , in which you were both travelling, by driving same into a wall, knowing that such damage would be likely to endanger the life of CD (or a third person) and intending that CD would fear that the said threat would be carried out.

Contrary to s 3(b) of the Criminal Damage Act 1991.

The section is quoted at para **7.53**. For a discussion see paras **7.51–7.56**.

9.40 Possession with Intent to Damage

You, AB, on the (date) at (place) in the (District) had in your custody (or under your control) an incendiary bomb (or specify item) intending without lawful excuse to use it (or cause or permit another to use it) to damage the (specify property) belonging to CD.

Contrary to s 4(*a*) of the Criminal Damage Act 1991.

The section is quoted at para **7.53**. For a discussion see paras **7.51–7.56**.

You, AB, on the (date) at (place) in the (District) had in your custody (or under your control) a hatchet, intending without lawful excuse to use it (or cause or permit another to use it) to damage motor cycle, registration number , the property of CD, in a way which you knew was likely to endanger the life of CD (of another).

Contrary to s 4(*b*)(i) of the Criminal Damage Act 1991.

The section is quoted at para **7.53**. For a discussion see paras **7.51–7.56**.

You, AB, on the (date) at (place) in the (District) had in your custody (or under your control) a time controlled incendiary device, intending without lawful excuse to use it (or cause or permit another to use it) to damage your shop premises at (or specify the property of another) with intent to defraud the Insurance Corporation of Ireland.

Contrary to s 4(*b*)(ii) of the Criminal Damage Act 1991.

The section is quoted at para **7.53**. For a discussion see paras **7.51–7.56**.

9.41 Computer

You, AB, on the (date) at (place) in the (District), without lawful excuse, operated a computer being a (specify) with intent to access data under the control of (specify) at (specify a location within or without the State).

Contrary to s 5(1)(*a*) of the Criminal Damage Act 1991.

The section is quoted at para **7.53**. For a discussion see paras **7.51–7.56**.

You, AB, on the (date) at (place outside the State) without lawful excuse, operated a computer with intent to access data kept under the control of (specify) at (specify a location within the State).

Contrary to s 5(1)(*b*) of the Criminal Damage Act 1991.

The section is quoted at para **7.53**. For a discussion see paras **7.51–7.56**.

Dishonesty

9.42 Pawning

You, AB, on the (date) at (place) in the (District), did knowingly pawn (describe the article) which is the property of another person without the consent of that other person CD.

Contrary to s 25(1) of the Pawnbrokers Act 1964.

The section reads:

25 (1) A person who knowingly pawns any article which is the property of another person without the consent of that other person shall be guilty of an offence.

(2) Where a person is convicted of an offence under this section, the court

may, in addition to any fine imposed, order him to pay to the owner of the article by way of compensation a sum not exceeding the full value of the article as determined by the court.

You, AB, on the (date) at (place) in the (District), did offer a pawnbroker an article by way of pawn being unable (or refusing) to give a satisfactory account of the means by which you came into possession of the article.

Contrary to s 23(*a*) of the Pawnbrokers Act 1964.

The subsection reads:

23   Any person who—

    (*a*) offers to a pawnbroker any article by way of pawn being unable or refusing to give a satisfactory account of the means by which he came into possession of the article; [shall be guilty of an offence]

You, AB, on the (date) at (place) in the (District), did wilfully give false information to a pawnbroker about the ownership of an article offered by you to the pawnbroker by way of pawn.

Contrary to s 23(*b*) of the Pawnbrokers Act 1964.

Alternative: about the name and address of the owner of the article, about your name and address when offering an article. The subsection reads:

23 (*b*) wilfully gives false information to a pawnbroker about the ownership of an article offered by him to the pawnbroker by way of pawn or about his name or address or the name or address of the owner of the article; [shall be guilty of an offence]

You, AB, on the (date) at (place) in the (District), did redeem (attempt to redeem, procure another person to redeem) a pledge from a pawnbroker without being entitled to do so.

Contrary to s 23(*c*) of the Pawnbrokers Act 1964.

The subsection reads:

23 (*c*) redeems or attempts to redeem or procures another person to redeem or attempt to redeem a pledge without being entitled to do so, [shall be guilty of an offence].

9.43   Simple Larceny

You, AB, on the (date) at (place) in the (District) did steal property (specify) the property of CD.

Contrary to s 2 of the Larceny Act 1916.

Simple larceny may be charged even though it may come within one of the other specified sections of the Act; *The State (Foley) v Carroll*[1], para **8.06**. The section is quoted at para **8.18**. For a discussion see generally chapter 8.

---

1 [1980] IR 150.

9.44 Larceny of Cattle

You, AB, on the (date) at (place) in the (District) did steal five horses, the property of CD.

Contrary to s 3 of the Larceny Act 1916.

The section is quoted at para **8.18**. For a discussion generally chapter 8.

9.45 Larceny from the Person

You, AB, on the (date) at (place) in the (District) did steal from the person of CD, property being (specify).

Contrary to s 14 of the Larceny Act 1916.

The section is quoted at para **8.18**. For a discussion generally chapter 8.

9.46 Larceny by a Clerk or Servant

You, AB, on the (date) at (place) in the (District), being a clerk or servant to CD, did steal from your said employer property being (specify).

Contrary to s 17(1)(*a*) of the Larceny Act 1916.

Alternative: a person employed in the capacity of a clerk or servant. Note: Property means a chattel, money or valuable security belonging to or in the possession or power of the master or employer. The section is quoted at para **8.20**. For a discussion see paras **8.19–8.20**.

9.47 Abstracting Electricity

You, AB, on the (date) at (place) in the (District), maliciously or fraudulently abstracted a quantity of electricity to a value of £   approximately, the property of the ESB.

Contrary to s 10 of the Larceny Act 1916.

Alternative: causes to be wasted or diverted, consumes or uses. The section is quoted at para **8.18**.

9.48 Embezzlement

You, AB, on the (date) at (place) in the (District), being a clerk or servant to CD, did fraudulently embezzle (specify) delivered to you in the name of your employer CD.

Contrary to s 17(1)(*b*) of the Larceny Act 1916.

Alternative: the whole or any part of any chattel, money or valuable security; delivered or received or taken into possession by him; for or in the name of or on account of his master or employer. The section is quoted at para **8.20**. For a discussion see para **8.19**.

9.49 An Post

You, AB, on the (date) at (place) in the (District) did steal from a mailbag a postage packet addressed to (specify) the property of CD, while same was in the course of transmission by post.

Contrary to s 50(*b*) of the Post Office Act 1908 as amended by the Postal and Telecommunications Services Act 1983.

The section, as amended, reads:

50 If any person—

    (*a*) steals a mail bag; or

    (*b*) steals from a mail bag, or from a post office, or from an officer of the Post Office, or from a mail, any postal packet in course of transmission by post; or

    (*bb*) steals a postal packet from a mail box; or

    (*c*) steals any chattel or money or valuable security out of a postal packet in course of transmission by post or in a mail box; or

    (*d*) stops a mail with intent to rob or search the mail;

he shall be guilty of felony, and on conviction shall be liable, at the discretion of the court, to penal servitude for life or any term not less than three years, or to imprisonment, with or without hard labour, for any term not exceeding two years.

You, AB, on the (date) at (place) in the (District) being an officer of An Post, did steal (embezzle, secrete, destroy) a postal packet addressed to (name) the property of (specify) while same was in the course of transmission by post.

Contrary to s 55 of the Post Office Act 1908.

The section reads:

55 If any officer of the Post Office steals, or for any purposes whatever embezzles, secretes, or destroys a postal packet in course of transmission by post, he shall be guilty of felony, and shall on conviction be liable, at he discretion of the court, to imprisonment for any term not exceeding two years, with or without hard labour, or to penal servitude for a term not less than three years and not exceeding seven years, or, if the postal packet contains any chattel or money, or valuable security, to imprisonment for any term not exceeding two years with or without hard labour, or to penal servitude for life or any term not less than three years.

9.50 Demanding

You, AB, on the (date) at (place) in the (District), knowing the contents thereof, did utter a letter (or writing) demanding money (property or valuable thing) being (specify) from CD with menaces and without any reasonable or probable cause.

Contrary to s 29(1) of the Larceny Act 1916.

The section is quoted at para **8.46**. For a discussion see paras **8.45–8.47**.

You, AB, on the (date) at (place) in the (District) with menaces (by force) demanded (specify) of CD with intent to steal the said property.

Contrary to s 30 of the Larceny Act 1916.

The section is quoted at para **8.46**. For a discussion see paras **8.45–8.47**.

9.51 Fraudulent Conversion

You, AB, on the (date) at (place) in the (District), did fraudulently convert to your own use or benefit (specify sum or property) entrusted to you by (name) in order that you might (specify purpose).

Contrary to s 20(iv)(*a*) of the Larceny Act 1916.

Alternative: entrusted solely or jointly with any other person; to the use or benefit of any other person, the property or any part thereof or any proceeds thereof. The section is quoted at para **8.22**. For a discussion see paras **8.21–8.23**.

9.52   Credit by Fraud

You, AB, on the (date) at (place) in the (District), incurring a debt of £ to CD, obtained credit to the amount of £   from the said CD by means of a false pretence that (specify).

Contrary to s 13(1) of the Debtors (Ireland) Act 1872.

Alternative: debt or liability, or by means of any other fraud. The section is quoted at para **8.28**. For a discussion see paras **8.29–8.30**.

9.53   Obtaining by False Pretences

You, AB, on the (date) at (place) in the (District), with intent to defraud, did obtain from CD property being (specify) by falsely pretending that (specify precise nature of pretence).

Contrary to s 10 of the Criminal Justice Act 1951.

The section is quoted at para **8.26**. For a discussion see paras **8.24–8.30**.

You, AB, on the (date) at (place) in the (District), with intent to defraud, did obtain from CD property being (specify) by falsely pretending that (specify precise nature of pretence).

Contrary to s 32 of the Larceny Act 1916.

The section is quoted at para **8.24**. For a discussion see paras **8.24–8.30**.

9.54   Falsification of Accounts

You, AB, on the (date) at (place) in the (District), being a clerk employed by CD, with intent to defraud, destroyed an entry of (or otherwise specify) in respect of goods sold by you, on behalf of your employer in a receipts book belonging to your employer.

Contrary to s 1 of the Falsification of Accounts Act 1875.

Alternative: see the section. The section is quoted at para **8.55**. For a discussion see paras **8.54–8.58**.

9.55   Forgery, Private Documents

You, AB, on the (date) at (place) in the (District), with intent to defraud, did forge a document purporting to be (describe in the terms of the section, for example, a cheque drawn on the account of a particular person at a particular bank and purporting to be made out in favour of a particular person).

Contrary to s 2 of the Forgery Act 1913.

The section is quoted at para **8.53**. For a discussion see paras **8.48–8.53**.

9.56   Forgery, Public Documents

You, AB, on the (date) at (place) in the (District), with intent to defraud, (deceive) did forge a document purporting to be (describe the document within the terms of the section, for example, if certificate of death).

Contrary to s 3 of the Forgery Act 1913.

The section is quoted at para **8.53**. For a discussion see paras **8.48–8.53**.

9.57   Forgery, Not Otherwise Specified in the Act

You, AB, on the (date) at (place) in the (District), with intent to defraud, forged a document purporting to be (describe document within the terms of the section).

Contrary to s 4(1) of the Forgery Act 1913.

The section is quoted at para **8.53**. For a discussion see paras **8.48–8.53**.

You, AB, on the (date) at (place) in the (District), with intent to defraud, (deceived) forged a document purporting to be (describe the document within the terms of the section).

Contrary to s 4(2) of the Forgery Act 1913.

The section is quoted at para **8.53**. For a discussion see paras **8.48–8.53**.

9.58   Uttering a Forged Document

You, AB, on the (date) at (place) in the (District), uttered a certain forged document (seal, die) purporting to be (describe document) knowing it to be forged and with intent to defraud (deceive).

Contrary to s 6 of the Forgery Act 1913.

The section is quoted at para **8.53**. For a discussion see paras **8.48–8.53**.

9.59   Demanding by Forgery

You, AB, on the (date) at (place) in the (District), with intent to defraud, demanded (receive, obtain or causes or procures to be delivered, paid or transferred to any person, or endeavours to receive or obtain or to cause or to procure to be delivered, paid or transferred to any person) from CD a (describe money, security for money or other property real or personal) by virtue of (under, upon) a forged instrument purporting to be a (describe document) knowing same to be forged.

Contrary to s 7 of the Forgery Act 1913.

The section is quoted at para **8.53**. For a discussion see paras **8.48–8.53**.

9.60   Possession of Forged Bank Note

You, AB, on the (date) at (place) in the (District), without lawful authority or excuse, had in your custody (possession, purchases, or receives from any person) a forged bank note, being a (specify) knowing the same to be forged.

Contrary to s 8 of the Forgery Act 1913.

The section is quoted at para **8.53**. For a discussion see paras **8.48–8.53**.

9.61   Counterfeit Coin

You, AB, on the (date) at (place) in the (District), did utter (tender, put off) a false and counterfeit coin resembling and apparently intended to resemble or pass for (specify the coin).

Contrary to s 9 of the Coinage Offences Act 1861, as amended by the Decimal Currency Act 1969.

The section reads:

Uttering counterfeit Gold or Silver Coin

9   Whosoever shall tender, utter, or put off any false or counterfeit Coin resembling or apparently intended to resemble or pass for any of the Queen's current Gold or Silver Coin, knowing the same to be false or counterfeit, shall, in *England* and *Ireland*, be guilty of a Misdemeanour, and in *Scotland* of a Crime and Offence, and being convicted thereof shall be liable, at the Discretion of the Court, to be imprisoned for any Term not exceeding One Year, with or without Hard Labour, and with or without Solitary Confinement.

9.62   Burglary

You, AB, on the (date) at (place) in the (District), having entered as a trespasser the building known as (specify), stole therein (specify property)

Contrary to s 23A of the Larceny Act 1916, as inserted by s 6 of the Criminal Law (Jurisdiction) Act, 1976.

Alternative: building or part of a building, attempted to steal therein, inflicts or attempts to inflict grievous bodily harm or having an intent to steal, to inflict grievous bodily harm, to rape or to do unlawful damage to the building or anything therein. The section is quoted at para **8.39**. For a discussion see paras **8.38–8.44**.

You, AB, on the (date) at (place) in the (District), entered as a trespasser the building known as (describe) with intent to steal therein.

Contrary to s 23A of the Larceny Act 1916, as inserted by s 6 of the Criminal Law (Jurisdiction) Act 1976.

The section is quoted at para **8.39**. For a discussion see paras **8.38–8.44**.

9.63   Aggravated Burglary

You, AB, on the (date) at (place) in the (District), having entered as a trespasser the building known as (describe) stole therein (specify) and had with you at the time a weapon of offence (firearm, explosive, imitation firearm) being a (describe).

Contrary to s 23B of the Larceny Act 1916 as inserted by s 7 of the Criminal Law (Jurisdiction) Act 1976, as amended by the Firearms and Offensive Weapons Act 1990.

Alternative: building or part of a building, attempted to steal therein, inflicts or attempts to inflict grievous bodily harm or having an intent to steal, to inflict grievous bodily harm, to rape or to do unlawful damage to the building or anything therein. Intent can be charged in the same way as for burglary. For a discussion see paras **8.38–8.44**.

9.64 Possession of Implements for the Purpose of Stealing

You, AB, on the (date) at (place) in the (District), a place which was not your place of abode, had in your possession an article being a screwdriver (or describe) with the intention that it should be used in connection with (in the course of) burglary.

Contrary to s 28 of the Larceny Act 1916 as inserted by s 2 of the Larceny Act 1990.

Alternatives: see the section. The section which is quoted at para **8.41**. The following charge is appropriate when the accused has possession of the article in his own home. Possession is discussed in chapter 7.

You, AB, on the (date) at (place) in the (District), without lawful authority or reasonable excuse, had in your possession a barrell-popper (or describe), being an article made or adapted for use in connection with (in the course of) an offence under s 112 of the Road Traffic Act 1961, as amended by s 65 of the Road Traffic Act 1968 and by s 3(7) of the Road Traffic (Amendment) Act 1984.

Alternatives: see the section. The section, as amended, reads:

Taking vehicle without authority

112 "(1) (*a*) A person shall not use or take possession of a mechanically propelled vehicle without consent of the owner thereof or other lawful authority.
  (*b*) Where possession of a vehicle has been taken in contravention of this subsection, a person who knows of the taking shall not allow himself to be carried in or on it without the consent of the owner thereof or other lawful authority.", and

(2) A person who contravenes sub-s (1) of this section shall be guilty of an offence and shall be liable on summary conviction to a fine not exceeding £1,000 or, at the discretion of the court, to imprisonment for any term not exceeding 12 months or to both such fine and such imprisonment, and on indictment to a fine not exceeding £2,000 and/or imprisonment for any term not exceeding five years.

(3) A person shall not use or take possession of a pedal cycle without the consent of the owner thereof or other lawful authority.

(4) A person who contravenes sub-s (3) of this section shall be guilty of an offence.

(5) Where a person is charged with an offence under this section, it shall be a good defence to the charge for him to show that, when he did the act alleged to constitute the offence, he believed, and had reasonable grounds for believing, that he had lawful authority for doing that act.

(6) Where a member of the Garda Síochána has reasonable grounds for believing that a person is committing or has committed an offence under his section, he may arrest the person without warrant.

(7) Where, when a person is tried on indictment or summarily or the larceny of

a vehicle, the jury, or, in the case of a summary trial, the District Court, is of opinion that he was not guilty of the larceny of the vehicle but was guilty of an offence under this section in relation to the vehicle, the jury or court may find him guilty of that offence and he may be sentenced accordingly.

9.65   Robbery

You, AB, on the (date) at (place) in the (District), robbed CD of (specify property).

Contrary to s 23 of the Larceny Act 1916 as inserted by s 5 of the Criminal Law (Jurisdiction) Act 1976.

The section is quoted at para **8.35**. For a discussion see paras **8.34–8.37**.

9.66   Handling

You, AB, on the (date) at (place) in the (District), handled stolen property being (specify), believing same to be stolen.

Contrary to s 33(1) of the Larceny Act 1916 as inserted by s 3 of the Larceny Act 1990.

The section is quoted at para **8.32**. For a discussion see paras **8.31–8.33**.

Offences against justice

9.67   Escape from Lawful Custody

You, AB, on the (date) at (place) in the (District), being a person in lawful custody (specify jail, etc.) did escape therefrom.

Contrary to common law.

9.67   Aiding an Escape

You, AB, on the (date) at (place) in the (District), did aid CD in escaping from lawful custody at (specify jail, etc.).

Contrary to s 6 of the Criminal Law Act 1976.

Alternatives: see the section. The section reads:

6   Any person who – (*a*) aids any person in escaping or attempting to escape from lawful custody or, with intent to facilitate the escape of any person from lawful custody or enable a person after escape to remain unlawfully at large, or with intent to cause injury to persons or property in a place where a person is in lawful custody, conveys any article or thing into or out of such a place or to a person in such a place or places any article or thing inside or outside such a place, or (*b*) makes, or takes part in, any arrangement for the purpose of enabling a person to escape from lawful custody, facilitating such an escape, enabling a person after escape to remain unlawfully at large, or causing injury to persons or property in a place where a person is in lawful custody, shall be guilty of an offence and shall be liable on conviction on indictment to imprisonment for a term not exceeding 10 years.

9.69 Smuggling into Prison

You, AB, on the (date) at (place) in the (District), did, contrary to the Prison Regulations (specify) convey into the said prison a (specify forbidden article).

Contrary to s 6(2) of the Criminal Law Act 1976.

Alternatives: see the section. The section reads:

6 (2) Any person who, contrary to any rules or regulations in force in relation to a prison, conveys or attempts to convey any article or thing into or out of the prison or to a person in the prison, or places any article or thing in any place inside or outside the prison with intent that it shall come into the possession of a person in the prison, shall be guilty of an offence and shall be liable – (*a*) on summary conviction, to a fine not exceeding £500 or to imprisonment for a term not exceeding twelve months, or to both, or (*b*) on conviction on indictment, to imprisonment for a term not exceeding 5 years.

9.70 Being a Person Unlawfully at Large

You, AB, on the (date) at (place) in the (District), being a person who was lawfully imprisoned (detained) at (specify prison, etc.) and who was temporarily released under the terms of s 2 (or s 3) of the Criminal Justice Act 1960 on the (specify when released) were unlawfully at large in that the period for which you had been temporarily released had expired (you broke a condition of your release by, etc.)

Contrary to s 6(2) of the Criminal Justice Act, 1960.

The section reads:

Persons unlawfully at large

6 (1) A person who, by reason of having been temporarily released under s 2 or s 3 of this Act, is at large shall be deemed to be unlawfully at large if—

(*a*) the period for which he was temporarily released has expired, or
(*b*) a condition to which his release was made subject has been broken.

(2) A person who is unlawfully at large shall be guilty of an offence under this section and on summary conviction thereof shall be liable to imprisonment for a term not exceeding six months.
(3) Where, by reason of the breach of a condition to which his release under s 2 or s 3 of this Act was made subject, a person is deemed to be unlawfully at large and is arrested under s 7 of this Act, the period for which he was temporarily released shall thereupon be deemed to have expired.
(4) The currency of the sentence of a person who is unlawfully at large for any period shall be suspended in respect of the whole of that period.

9.71 Failing to Answer Bail

You, AB, on the (date) at (place) in the (District), having been released on bail in criminal proceedings entitled (specify) failed to appear before the (specify court) in accordance with your recognisance.

Contrary to s 13(1) of the Criminal Justice Act 1984.

The section reads:

13 (1) If a person who has been released on bail in criminal proceedings fails to appear before a court in accordance with his recognisance, he shall be guilty of an offence and shall be liable on summary conviction to a fine not exceeding £1,000 or to imprisonment for a term not exceeding twelve months or to both.

9.72 Perjury

You, AB, on the (date) at (place) in the (District), in the course of a judicial proceeding at the said Court, being the case of (specify), being a competent witness to whom an oath was administered knowingly and falsely swore that (specify perjured statement).

Contrary to common law.

For other offences see also the Tribunal of Enquiry (Evidence) Act 1920, s 1, the Commissioners for Oaths (Diplomatic and Consular) Act 1931, s 4, the Courts of Justice of the European Communities (Perjury) Act 1975, s 1 and the Tribunals of Enquiry (Evidence) (Amendment) Act 1971. The Perjury Act 1911 has never applied to Ireland leaving the law here in its usual haphazard state.

9.73 False Report

You, AB, on the (date) at (place) in the (District), knowingly made a false report tending to show that the offence of (specify) had been committed (specify date and place).

Contrary to s 12 of the Criminal Law Act, 1976.

The section reads:

12 Any person who – (a) knowingly makes a false report or statement tending to show that an offence has been committed, whether by himself or another person, or tending to give rise to apprehension for the safety of persons or property, or (b) knowingly makes a false report or statement tending to show that he has information material to any enquiries by the Garda Síochána and thereby causes the time of the Garda Síochána to be wastefully employed, shall be guilty of an offence and shall be liable – (i) on summary conviction, to a fine not exceeding £500 or to imprisonment for a term not exceeding twelve months, or to both, or (ii) on conviction on indictment, to imprisonment for a term not exceeding 5 years.

9.74 Jury Summons

You, AB, on the (date) at (place) in the (District), having been duly summonsed in accordance with the provisions of s 12 of the Juries Act 1976, as a juror and thereby being required to attend at (specify court) failed without reasonable excuse so to attend.

Contrary to s 34 of the Juries Act 1976.

The section reads:

Failure of juror to attend court etc

34 (1) Any person who, having been duly summoned as a juror, fails without reasonable excuse to attend in compliance with the summons or to attend on any day when required by the court shall be guilty of an offence and shall be liable on summary conviction to a fine not exceeding £50.

(2) A juror who, having attended in pursuance of a summons, is not available when called upon to serve as a juror, or is unfit for service by reason of drink or drugs, shall be guilty of an offence and shall be liable on summary conviction to a fine not exceeding £50.

(3) Except in a case to which s 14 applies, a person shall not be guilty of an offence under sub-s (1) in respect of failure to attend in compliance with a summons unless the summons was served at least fourteen days before the date specified therein for his first attendance.

9.75 Impersonating Garda

You, AB, on the (date) at (place) in the (District), not being a member of the Garda Síochána, for the purpose of doing (procuring to be done) an act, which you would not be by law entitled to do (to procure to be done) of your own authority, did assume the name (designation, description) of a member (other rank) of the Garda Síochána.

Contrary to s 15 of the Garda Síochána Act 1924.

The section reads:

Penalty for unlawful possession of clothing or equipment

15 (1) If any person, not being a member of the Garda Síochána, shall have in his possession any article of clothing or equipment supplied to a member of the Garda Síochána and shall not be able satisfactorily to account for his posession thereof, or shall, without the permission of the Commissioner, put on or wear the uniform of any rank or member of the Garda Síochána or any colorable imitation of such uniform, or shall, for the purpose of doing or procuring to be done any act which such person would not by law be entitled to do or procure to be done of his own authority assume the name, designation or description of any rank or of any member of the Garda Síochána, such person shall on summary conviction be liable in addition to any other punishment to a fine not excedding fifty pounds for every such offence or to imprisonment with or without hard labour for any period not exceeding six months.

(2) Every fine imposed under this section shall be paid to the Garda Síochána Reward Fund.

(3) Nothing in this section shall prevent the wearing of any uniform or dress in the course of a stage play or other dramatic representation or performance.

Public order

9.76 Official Secrets

You, AB, on the (date) at (place) in the (District), in a manner prejudicial to the safety or preservation of the State, communicated to another person information relating to the operations or projected operations of the Garda Síochána (or alternative please insert).

In contravention of s 9 of the Official Secrets Act 1963 and contrary to s 13 of the said Act.

The section is quoted at para **7.70**. For a discussion see para **7.69**.

You, AB, on the (date) at (place) in the (District), in a manner prejudicial to the safety or preservation of the State, had in your possession a document containing information relation to operations or projected operations of the Garda Síochána (or alternative please insert).

In contravention of s 9 of the Official Secrets Act 1963, and contrary to s 13 of the said Act.

The section is quoted at para **7.70**. For a discussion see para **7.69**.

You, AB, on the (date) at (place) in the (District), communicated official information to another person when not duly authorised so to do and otherwise than in the course of and in accordance with the duties of the holder of a public office and otherwise than when it was his duty in the interest of the State to communicate it.

In contravention of s 4 of the Official Secrets Act 1963, and contrary to s 13 of the said Act.

The section is quoted at para **7.70**. For a discussion see para **7.69**.

9.77   Telephone Misuse

You, AB, on the (date) at (place) in the (District), sent by means of the telecommunications system operated by Bord Telecom Eireann a message or other matter which was grossly offensive (or, of an indecent obscene or menacing character).

Contrary to s 13(1) of the Post Office Amendment Act 1951 as substituted by the Postal and Telecommunications Services Act 1983.

The section reads:

13   (1)   A person who—

    (*a*)   sends, by means of the telecommunications system operated by Bord Telecom Éireann, any message or other matter which is grossly offensive or of an indecent, obscene or menacing character, whether addressed to an operator or any other person, or

    (*b*)   sends by those means, for the purpose of causing annoyance, inconvenience or needless anxiety to another, a message which he knows to be false or persistently makes use of those means for that purpose,

shall be guilty of an offence.

9.78   Affray

You, AB, on the (date) at (place) in the (District), unlawfully fought and made an affray.

Contrary to common law.

An affray is the spectacle of fighting to the terror of reasonably courageous citizens. It can also occur by the public display of force. Whether the attack takes place in public or in private an accused, who assaults a victim in such a manner that the victim, as a person of reasonably firm character, might reasonably be expected to be terrified, is guilty of an affray. Where two persons consensually participate in a fight both will be guilty of an affray if the fight takes place in public in such a manner that a by-stander of reasonably fine character might reasonably be expected to be terrified, though the presence of such a by-stander is not required. Where a consensual fight occurs in private the by-stander is necessary.

589

9.79 Unlawful Assembly

You, AB, on the (date) at (place) in the (District), with other persons namely (specify if possible) did assemble together for the purpose of committing by open force a crime of (specify).

Contrary to common law.

Alternative: with intent to carry out any common purpose, lawful or unlawful, in such a manner as to endanger the public peace, or to give firm and courageous persons in the neighbourhood of such assembly reasonable grounds to apprehend a breach of the peace in consequence of it.

9.80 Riot

You, AB, CD, and EF, and other persons unknown, on the (date) at (place) in the (District), riotously assembled together.

Contrary to common law.

A riot is a tumultuous disturbance of the peace by three or more persons who assemble together of their own authority, with an intent mutually to assist one another against any who oppose them in the execution of an enterprise of a private nature, and afterwards actually execute the same in a violent and turbulent manner to the terror of the people.

9.81 Forceable Entry

You, AB, on the (date) at (place) in the (District), did forcibly enter land being a (specify) at (address), the property of CD.

Contrary to s 2 of the Prohibition of Forceable Entry and Occupation Act 1971.

Alternative: land or vehicle. The section reads:

Offence of forcible entry of land or a vehicle

2 A person who focibly enters land or a vehicle shall be guilty of an offence unless—

(a) he is the owner of the land or vehicle, or

(b) if he is not the owner, he does not interfere with the use and enjoyment of the land or vehicle by the owner and, if requested to leave the land or vehicle by the owner or by a member of the Garda Síochána in uniform, he does so with all reasonable speed and in a peaceable manner, or

(c) he enters in pursuance of a *bona fide* claim of right.

9.82 Forceable Occupation

You, AB, on the (date) at (place) in the (District), did remain in forceable occupation of land being (describe) situate at (address), the property of CD.

Contrary to s 3 of the Prohibition of Forceable Entry and Occupation Act 1971.

Alternative: land or a vehicle. The section reads:

Offence of remaining in forcible occupation of land or a vehicle

3 (1) A person who remains in forcible occupation of land or a vehicle shall be guilty of an offence unless he is the owner of the land or vehicle or so remains thereon in pursuance of a *bona fide* claim of right.

(2) In this section "forcible occupation of land or a vehicle" includes—

(*a*) the act of locking, obstructing or barring any window, door or other entry to or means of exit from land or a vehicle with a view to preventing or resisting a lawful attempt to enter the land or vehicle,

(*b*) the act of erecting a physical obstacle to an entry to or means of exit from land or a vehicle with a view to preventing or resisting a lawful attempt to enter the land or vehicle,

(*c*) the act of physically resisting a lawful attempt at ejection from land or a vehicle.

9.83   Entry in Contravention of Order

You, AB, on the (date) at (place) in the (District), after an under-sheriff had entered on and taken possession of the premises (specify place or premises), under an Execution Order directing him to put the owner CD into possession thereof, and having delivered the said premises to the owner pursuant to such order, did, without the consent of the owner, enter onto the said premises and take possession thereof.

Contrary to s 25 of the Enforcement of Court Orders Act 1926 to 1940, as amended by the Criminal Justice Act 1951.

9.84   Breach of the Peace

You, AB, on the (date) at (place), a public place, in the (District), did (describe behaviour), thereby causing a breach of the peace.

Contrary to common law.

You, AB, on the (date) at (place), a public place, in the (District), used threatening or abusive or insulting words or behaviour with intent to provoke a breach of the peace (whereby a breach of the peace may have been occasioned).

Contrary to s 14(13) of the Dublin Police Act 1842.

9.85   Threat of Violence

You, AB, on the (date) at (place) in the (District), did make use of threats or violence towards CD thereby putting him in fear and dread of bodily harm and injury.

In contravention of the common law, and this is to notify you to appear as accused on the hearing of the said accusation at the (specify District Court) to answer the said accusation and to show cause why you should not be bound over in solvent securities, to keep the peace and to be of good behaviour towards all citizens.

9.86   Obscene Language

You, AB, on the (date) at (place), a public place, in the (District), did use

591

profane (indecent, obscene) language to the annoyance of the inhabitants (passengers).

Contrary to s 4(13) of the Dublin Police Act 1842.

9.87 Begging

You, AB, on the (date) at (place) in the (District), having the custody (charge, care) of CD a child (young person) did allow the said child (young person) to be in the said place for the purpose of begging (receiving alms, inducing the giving of alms).

Contrary to s 14(1) of the Children Act 1908.

The section reads:

Begging

14 (1) If any person causes or procures any child or young person, or, having the custody charge or care of a child or young person, allows that child or young person, to be in any street, premises, or place for the purpose of begging or receiving alms, or of inducing the giving of alms, whether or not there is any pretence of singing, playing, performing, offering anything for sale, or otherwise, that person shall, on summary conviction, be liable to a fine not exceeding twenty-five pounds, or alternatively, or in default of payment of such fine, or in addition thereto, to imprisonment, with or without hard labour, for any term not exceeding three months.

(2) If a person having the custory charge or care of a child or young person is charged with an offence under this section, and it is proved that the child or young person was in any street, premises, or place for any such purpose as aforesaid, and that the person charged allowed the child or young person to be in the street, premises, or place, he shall be presumed to have allowed him to be in the street, premises, or place for that purpose unless the contrary is proved.

You, AB, on the (date) at (place) in the (District), did procure one CD, a child (young person) to be in the said place for the purpose of begging (receiving alms, inducing the giving of alms).

Contrary to s 14(1) of the Children Act 1908.

The section is quoted above.

9.88 Intimidation

You, AB, on the (date) at (place) in the (District), with a view to compel CD to abstain from (specify, for example, working), an act which he had a legal right to do, did wrongfully and without legal authority (specify, for example, prevent him from entering his work place).

Contrary to s 7 of the Conspiracy and Protection of Property Act 1875.

The section reads:

Penalty for intimidation or annoyance by violence or otherwise

7 Every person who, with a view to compel any other person to abstain from doing or to do any act which such other person has a legal right to do or abstain from doing, wrongfully and without legal authority,—

1. Uses violence to or intimidates such other person or his wife or children, or injures his property; or,

592

2. Persistently follows such other person about from place to place; or,
3. Hides any tools, clothes, or other property owned or used by such other person, or deprives him of or hinders him in the use thereof; or,
4. Watches or besets the house or other place where such other person resides, or works, or carries on business, or happens to be, or the approach to such house or place; or,
5. Follows such other person with two or more other persons in a disorderly manner in or though any street or road,

shall, on conviction thereof by a court of summary jurisdiction, or on indictment as herein-after mentioned, be liable either to pay a penalty not exceeding twenty pounds, or to be imprisoned for a term not exceeding three months, with or without hard labour.

Attending at or near the house or place where a person resides, or works, or carries on business, or happens to be, or the approach to such house or place, in order merely to obtain or communicate information, shall not be deemed a watching or besetting within the meaning of this section.

Democracy

9.89 Personation

You, AB, on the (date) at (place) in the (District), at an election for Dáil Eireann (or specify) applied for a ballot paper in the name of another person.

Contrary to s 3 of the Prevention of Electoral Abuses Act 1923.

The section reads:

Definition of personation

3 Every person who at an election applies for a ballot paper in the name of some other person, whether that name be the name of a living person or of a dead person or of a fictitious person, or who having voted once at an election applies at the same election for a ballot paper in his own name, shall be guilty of the offence of personation.

At a presidential election the offence is contrary to s 3 of the Prevention of Electoral Abuses Act 1923, as substituted by s 1 of the Electoral Abuses Act 1982. An election includes a referendum and the penalty is provided by s 6 of the 1923 Act, as amended by s 90 of the Electoral Act 1963.

You, AB, on the (date) at (place) in the (District), at an election for Dáil Eireann (or specify) having obtained a ballot paper once did apply at the same election for a ballot paper in your own name.

Contary to s 3 of the Prevention of Electoral Abuses Act 1923.

Unlawful organisations

9.90 Membership

You, AB, on the (date) at (place) in the (District), within the State, were a member of an unlawful organisation styling itself the Provisional IRA, otherwise the IRA, otherwise Oglaigh na hÉireann (specify other organisation).

Contrary to s 21 of the Offences Against the State Act 1939 as amended by s 2(6) of the Criminal Law Act 1976.

In distinction from all other offences the evidence on oath of a Chief Superintendent of An Garda Síochána that he believes that an accused was on the specified date a member of an unlawful organisation, is of itself sufficient evidence of the charge. A denial by the accused, on oath, may raise a reasonable doubt. The section as amended reads:

Prohibition of membership of an unlawful organisation

21 (1) It shall not be lawful for any person to be a member of an unlawful organisation.

(2) Every person who is a member of an unlawful organisation in contravention of this section shall be guilty of an offence under this section and shall—

(a) on summary conviction thereof, be liable to a fine not exceeding fifty pounds or, at the discretion of the court, to imprisonment for a term not exceeding three months or to both such fine and such imprisonment, or

(b) on conviction thereof on indictment, be liable to imprisonment for a term not exceeding 7 years.

(3) It shall be a good defence for a person charged with the offence under this section of being a member of an unlawful organisation, to show—

(a) that he did not know that such organisation was an unlawful organisation, or

(b) that, as soon as reasonably possible after he became aware of the real nature of such organisation or after the making of a suppression order in relation to such organisation, he ceased to be a member thereof and dissociated himself therefrom.

(4) Where an application has been made to the High Court for a declaration of legality in respect of an organisation no person who is, before the final determination of such application, charged with an offence under this section in relation to that organisation shall be brought to trial on such charge before such final determination, but a postponement of the said trial in pursuance of this subsection shall not prevent the detention of such person in custody during the period of such postponement.

9.91 Recruiting

You, AB, on the (date) at (place) in the (District), within the State, recruited CD for an unlawful organisation styling itself (specify).

Contrary to s 3 of the Criminal Law Act 1976.

The section reads:

3 Any person who recruits another person for an unlawful organisation or who incites or invites another person (or other persons generally) to join an unlawful organisation or to take part in, support or assist its activities shall be guilty of an offence and shall be liable on conviction on indictment to imprisonment for a term not exceeding 10 years.

The alternatives of inviting a person to join an unlawful organisation, or inciting or inviting them to join, take part in, support the activities of or assist the activities of an unlawful organisation can be seen from the section.

Drug offences

9.92 Importation

You, AB, on the (date) at (place) in the (District), unlawfully imported into the State the controlled drug (specify).

Contrary to s 21(2) of the Misuse of Drugs Act 1977 and contrary to Article 4(1)(a) of the Misuse of Drugs Regulations 1988, made under s 5 of the Misuse of Drugs Act 1977.

Alternative: export. The definition of Cannabis and Opium Poppy has been amended by s 2 of the 1984 Act. If the offence is in respect of either of these drugs then the amendment should be included in the charge. Section 21(2) is quoted at para **7.15**. Article 4(1)(*a*) is quoted at para **7.16**. For a discussion see paras **7.02–7.16**.

9.93 Possession of drugs

You, AB, on the (date) at (place) in the (District), had unlawfully in your possession the controlled drug (specify).

Contrary to s 3 of the Misuse of Drugs Act 1977.

If the offence is in respect of Cannabis or Opium Poppy then the amendment by s 2 of the 1984 Act should be included in the charge. Section 3 is quoted at para **7.15**. For a discussion see paras **7.02–7.16**.

9.94 Possession for the Purpose of Supply

You, AB, on the (date) at (place) in the (District), had in your possession the controlled drug (specify) for the purpose of unlawfully supplying same to another.

Contrary to s 15(1) of the Misuse of Drugs Act 1977 and contrary to Article 4(1)(b) of the Misuse of Drugs Regulations 1988, as made under s 5 of the Misuse of Drugs Act 1977.

If the offence is in respect of Cannabis or Opium Poppy then the amendment by s 2 of the 1984 Act should be included in the charge. Section 15(1) is quoted at para **7.15**. Article 4(1)(*b*) is quoted at para **7.16**. For a discussion see paras **7.02–7.16**.

9.95 Permitting Drug Use

You, AB, on the (date) at (place) in the (District), being a person in control of land being a (specify house, etc.), did knowingly permit CD to supply the controlled drug (specify) in contravention of Regulation 4(1)(*b*) of the Misuse of Drugs Regulations 1988.

Contrary to s 19(1) of the Misuse of Drugs Act 1977 as amended by s 11 of the Misuse of Drugs Act 1984.

If the offence is in respect of Cannabis or Opium Poppy then the amendment by s 2 of the 1984 Act should be included in the charge. Section 19(1), as amended, is quoted at para **7.31**. For a discussion see paras **7.25–7.31**.

You, AB, on the (date) at (place) in the (District), being a person in control of certain land, that is to say a greenhouse, did knowingly permit one CD to unlawfully grow Opium Poppy plants thereon in contravention of s 17 of the Misuse of Drugs Act 1977 as amended by s 11 and s 2 of the Misuse of Drugs Act 1984.

Contrary to s 19(1) of the Misuse of Drugs Act 1977 as amended by s 11 and s 2 of the Misuse of Drugs Act 1984.

You, AB, on the (date) at (place) in the (District), being the occupier of (specify place), did knowingly permit a person unknown to smoke Cannabis.

Contrary to s 19(1) of the Misuse of Drugs Act 1977 as amended by ss 11 and s 2 of the Misuse of Drugs Act 1984.

Section 19(1), as amended, is quoted at para **7.31**. For a discussion see paras **7.25–7.31**.

Animals

9.96

You, AB, on the (date) at (place) in the (District), did cruelly beat an animal, being (describe).

Contrary to s 1 of the Protection of Animals Act 1911 as amended by the Protection of Animals Act 1965 and s 20 of the Control of Dogs Act 1986.

Alternative: kick, ill-treat, over-ride, over-drive, over-load, torture, infuriate or terrify. The section, as amended, reads:

Offences of cruelty

1   (1) If any person—
    (*a*) shall cruelly beat, kick, ill-treat, over-ride, over-drive, over-load, torture, infuriate, or terrify any animal, or shall cause or procure, or, being the owner, permit any animal to be so used, or shall, by wantonly or unreasonably doing or omitting to do any act, or causing or procuring the commission or omission of any act, cause any unnecessary suffering, or, being the owner, permit any unnecessary suffering to be so caused to any animal; or
    (*b*) shall convey or carry, or cause or procure, or, being the owner, permit to be conveyed or carried, any animal in such manner or position as to cause that animal any unnecessary suffering; or
    (*c*) shall cause, procure, or assist at the fighting or baiting of any animal; or shall keep, use, manage, or act or assist in the management of, any premises or place for the purpose, or partly for the purpose, of fighting or baiting any animal, or shall permit any premises or place to be so kept, managed, or used, or shall receive, or cause or procure any person to receive, money for the admission of any person to such premises or place; or
    (*d*) shall wilfully, without any reasonable cause or excuse, administer, or cause or procure, or being the owner permit, such administration of, any poisonous or injurious drug or substance to any animal, or shall wilfully, without any reasonable cause or excuse, cause any such substance to be taken by any animal; or

(*e*) shall subject, or cause or procure, or being the owner permit, to be subjected, any animal to buy operation which is performed without due care and humanity;

(*f*) being the owner or having charge or control of any animal shall without reasonable cause or excuse abandon it, whether permanently or not, in circumstances likely to cause it unnecessary suffering, or cause or procure or, being the owner, permit it to be so abandoned;

such person shall be guilty of an offence of cruelty within the meaning of this Act and shall be liable on summary conviction thereof—

(i) in respect of a first or a second offence to a fine not exceeding £500, or to imprisonment for a term not exceeding three months, or, at the discretion of the Court, to both such fine and such imprisonment;

(ii) in respect of a third or any subsequent offence, to a fine not exceeding £500, or to imprisonment for a term not exceeding six months, or, at the discretion of the Court, to both such fine and such imprisonment.

(2) For the purposes of this section, an owner shall be deemed to have permitted cruelty within the meaning of this Act if he shall have failed to exercise reasonable care and supervision in respect of the protection of the animal therefrom:

Provided that, where an owner is convicted of permitting cruelty within the meaning of this Act by reason only of his having failed to exercise such care and supervision, he shall not be liable to imprisonment without the option of a fine.

(3) Nothing in this section shall render illegal any act lawfully done under the Cruelty to Animals Act, 1876, or shall apply—

(*a*) to the commission or omission of any act in the course of the destruction, or the preparation for destruction, of any animal as food for mankind, unless such destruction or such preparation was accompanied by the infliction of unnecessary suffering; or

(*b*) to the coursing or hunting of any captive animal, unless such animal is liberated in an injured, mutilated, or exhausted condition; but a captive animal shall not, for the purposes of this section, be deemed to be coursed or hunted before it is liberated for the purpose of being coursed or hunted, or after it has been recaptured, or if it is under control.

Bribery

9.97 Offering a Bribe

You, AB, on the (date) at (place) in the (District), did corruptly offer (give, promise) a gift (loan, fee, reward or advantage) being a (describe same) as an inducement to him (reward for him) to (describe what the official did or forbore to do as a result) while he was a servant (member, officer) of a public body being (describe public body).

Contrary to s 1(2) of the Public Bodies Corrupt Practices Act 1889.

The section is quoted at para **8.66**. For a discussion see paras **8.65–8.67**.

9.98 Accepting a Bribe

You, AB, on the (date) at (place) in the (District), corruptly received (solicit or agree to receive) for yourself (*or* for any other person) a gift (loan, fee, reward or advantage) being a (describe) as an inducement to (or reward) for doing the following (describe what the accused did) while you were a servant (member, officer) of a public body being (describe public body).

Contrary to s 1(1) of the Public Bodies Corrupt Practices Act 1889.

The section is quoted at para **8.66**. For a discussion see paras **8.65–8.67**.

Lottery

9.99 Promoting

You, AB, on the (date) at (place) in the (District), did promote an unlawful lottery.

Contrary to s 21(1) of the Gaming and Lotteries Act 1956.

Alternative: assist in promoting. The section reads:

Prohibition of lotteries

21 (1) No person shall promote or assist in promoting a lottery.

9.100 Distribution

You, AB, on the (date) at (place) in the (District), did distribute (import, print, publish) a ticket (counterfoil, coupon) for use in an unlawful lottery.

Contrary to s 21(2) of the Gaming and Lotteries Act 1956.

Alternative: have in your possession for sale or distribution, any document containing information relating to an unlawful lottery. The section reads:

21 (2) No person shall import, print, publish or distribute or sell, offer or expose for sale, invite an offer to buy or have in his possession for sale or distribution any ticket, counterfoil or coupon for use in a lottery or any document containing any information relating to a lottery.

9.101 Advertising

You, AB, on the (date) at (place) in the (District), did print (publish) in a newspaper a notice or announcement concerning an unlawful lottery.

Contrary to s 22 of the Gaming and Lotteries Act 1956.

The section reads:

Advertisement of lotteries

22 No person shall print publish in any newspaper or periodical publication, exhibit on any cinema screen or broadcast by radio any notice or announcement concerning a lottery (other than an announcement of the results of a lottery declared by any provision of this Part not to be unlawful) or cause or procure any such notice or announcement to be so printed, published, exhibited or broadcast or knowingly circulate or cause or procure to be circulated any newspaper or periodical publication containing any such notice or announcement.

9.102 Gaming

You, AB, on the (date) at (place) in the (District), did promote (assist in promoting, provide facilities for) unlawful gaming.

Contrary to s 4 of the Gaming and Lotteries Act 1956 as amended by s 1(*a*) of the Gaming and Lotteries Act 1979.

The section reads:

Unlawful gaming

4 (1) No person shall promote or assist in promoting or provide facilities for any kind of gaming—

(*a*) in which by reason of the nature of the game, the chances of all the players, including the banker, are not equal, or

(*b*) in which any portion of the stakes is retained by the promoter or is retained by the banker otherwise than as winnings on the result of the play, or

(*c*) by means of any slot-machine.

(2) Such gaming is in this Act referred to as unlawful gaming.

(3) Gaming shall not be unlawful if no stake is hazarded by the players with the promotor or banker other than a charge for the right to take part in the game, provided that—

(*a*) only one such charge is made in respect of the day on which the game is played, and

(*b*) the charge is of the same amount for all the players, and

(*c*) the promoter derives no personal profit from the promotion of the game.

9.103 Permitting

You, AB, on the (date) at (place) in the (District), did permit to be used a (describe place or premises) for the purpose of unlawful gaming.

Contrary to s 5 of the Gaming and Lotteries Act 1956.

The section is quoted at para **7.26**. For a discussion see paras **7.25–7.29**.

Betting

9.104 Under-Age

You, AB, on the (date) at (place) in the (District), being the registered proprieter of registered premises did permit a person under the age of eighteen years, and not exempted under the Betting Act 1931, to be on (to enter on) such premises.

Contrary to s 23(2) of the Betting Act 1931.

The section reads:

23 (2) No registered proprietor of registered premises shall permit any person under the age of eighteen years (other than persons ordinarily resident on such premises and officers of the Minister for Posts and Telegraphs entering such premises in the course of their duty as such officers) to enter or be on such premises.

9.104 *Sample offences*

You, AB, on the (date) at (place) in the (District), being a licensed bookmaker did make a bet (engage in a betting transaction) with CD, a person under the age of 18 years.

Contrary to s 23(1) of the Betting Act 1931.

The offence applies whether or not the person is acting on his own behalf or as agent of another person. The section reads:

Prohibition of betting with persons under the age of eighteen

23 (1) No licensed bookmaker shall make a bet or engage in a betting transaction with a person under the age of eighteen years whether such person is acting on his own behalf or as agent for another person.

Liquor licensing

9.105 Being Found on Premises During Prohibited Hours

You, AB, on the (date) at (place) in the (District), were found on the licensed premises of (name of licensee and address of premises) during the time in which the sale of intoxicating liquor on such premises is prohibited, that is to say between (specify closing time) on the (date) and (specify the following opening time) on the (date).

Contrary to s 17 of the Intoxicating Liquor Act 1927 inserted by s 12 of the Intoxicating Liquor Act 1960.

The section reads:

"**17** (1) Subject to sub-s (2) and (4) of this section, a person who is found on any licensed premises during any time in which the sale of intoxicating liquor on such premises is prohibited by this Act shall, unless he is either—

(*a*) the holder of the licence or the owner of the premises, or
(*b*) resident permanently or temporarily on the premises, or
(*c*) a person to whom intoxicating liquor may lawfully be sold or supplied on the premises at that time, or
(*d*) carrying out construction, decorative, repair, replacement or maintenance work in relation to the premises or any of the fittings or equipment thereon,
(*e*) in the employment of the holder of the licence or of the owner of the premises and is on the premises in the ordinary course of such employment, or
(*f*) an officer of customs and excise in the course of his duty as an officer,

be guilty of an offence under this subsection and shall be liable on summary conviction thereof to a fine of not less than one pound and not more than five pounds.

(2) Where any business other than the sale of intoxicating liquor (in this subsection referred to as non-licensed business) is carried on in any licensed premises and the portion of the premises in which the non-licensed business is carried on is not structurally separated from the remainder of the premises, sub-s (1) of this section shall not apply in relation to the premises during any time in which the premises are lawfully open for the carrying on of the non-licensed business.

(3) Subject to sub-s (4) of this section, a person who consumes intoxicating liquor on any licensed premises during any time in which the sale of intoxicating liquor on such premises is prohibited by this Act shall, unless he is a person as respects whom the relevant requirements of this Act for the lawful sale or supply

of intoxicating liquor on those premises at that time are satisfied, be guilty of an offence under this subsection and shall be liable on summary conviction to a fine of not less than one pound and not more than five pounds.

(4) A person shall not be convicted of an offence under both sub-s (1) and sub-s (3) of this section in respect of the same occasion."

9.106 Failing to Admit Garda

You, AB, on the (date) at your licenced premises at (premises) in the (District), did fail (refuse) to admit a member of the Garda Síochána in execution of duty, demanding entry to such license premises.

Contrary to s 16 of the Licensing (Ireland) Act 1874 as amended by s 22(3) of the Intoxicating Liquor Act 1927.

You are required to produce the above mentioned licence to the court on the hearing of this complaint. Section 16 reads:

Constable to enter on premises for enforcement of Act

16 Any constable may, for the purpose of preventing or detecting the violation of any of the provisions of the principal Act or this Act which it is his duty to enforce, at all times enter on any licensed premises, or any premises in respect of which an occasional licence is in force.

Every person who, by himself, or by any person in his employ or acting by his direction or with his consent, refuses or fails to admit any constable in the execution of his duty demanding to enter in pursuance of this section, shall be liable to a penalty not exceeding for the first offence five pounds, and not exceeding for the second and every subsequent offence ten pounds.

Section 22(3) reads:

22 (3) In the Licensing Act 1872, and in the Licensing Act (Ireland) 1874, the word "constable" shall include any member of the Garda Síochána and the said Acts be construed and have effect accordingly.

9.107 Offence on Premises

You, AB, on the (date) at the premises (describe) in the (District), being the holder of an on-licence in respect of those premises, did unlawfully permit persons to be on the said premises at a time prohibited for these purposes by the Licensing Acts 1833 to 1977, that is between (specify closing time) on (date) and (specify following opening time) on (date).

Contrary to s 2(4) of the Intoxicating Liquor Act 1927 and s 29 of the Intoxicating Liquor Act 1962.

You are required to produce the above mentioned licence to the court on the hearing of this complaint.

Alternative: sell intoxicating liquor; open the premises for the sale of intoxicating liquor; keep open the premises for the sale of intoxicating liquor; expose intoxicating liquor for sale, or permit intoxicating liquor to be consumed on the premises. Section 2(4) reads:

2 (4) Every person who shall sell or expose for sale any intoxicating liquor or open or keep open any premises for the sale of intoxicating liquor or permit any intoxicating liquor to be consumed on licensed premises in contravention of this section shall be guilty of an offence under this section and shall be liable on summary conviction thereof, in the case of a first offence, to a fine not exceeding twenty pounds or, in the case of a second or any subsequent offence, to a fine not exceeding forty pounds.

Section 29 reads:

Permitting persons to be on licensed premises during prohibited hours

29 A person who permits a person to be on licensed premises contrary to sub-s (1) of s 17 (which was inserted by the Act of 1960 and provides for certain offences in relation to prohibited hours) of the Act of 1927 shall be guilty of an offence and shall be liable on summary conviction, in the case of a first offence, to a fine not exceeding twenty pounds, or, in the case of a second or any subsequent offence, to a fine not exceeding forty pounds and the offence shall be deemed, for the purposes of Part III (which relates to the endorsement of licences) of the Act of 1927, to be an offence to which that Part of that Act applies.

Railways

9.108

You, AB, on the (date) at (place) in the (District), maliciously threw or put upon or across the (specify) railway a stone (wood or other matter or thing) with intent to endanger the safety of persons travelling or being upon the said railway.

Contrary to s 32 of the Offences Against the Person Act 1861.

The section reads:

Placing Wood, &c on a Railway, with Intent to endanger Passengers

32 Whosoever shall unlawfully and maliciously put or throw upon or across any Railway any Wood, Stone, or other Matter or Thing, or shall unlawfully and maliciously take up, remove, or displace any Rail, Sleeper, or other Matter or Thing belonging to any Railway, or shall unlawfully and maliciously turn, move, or divert any Points or other Machinery belonging to any Railway, or shall unlawfully and maliciously make or show, hide or remove, any Signal or Light, upon or near to any Railway, or shall unlawfully and maliciously do or cause to be done any other Matter or Thing, with Intent, in any of the Cases aforesaid, to endanger the Safety of any Person travelling or being upon such Railway, shall be guilty of Felony, and being convicted thereof shall be liable, at the Discretion of the Court, to be kept in Penal Servitude for Life or for any Term not less than Three Years, – or to be imprisoned for any Term not exceeding Two Years, with or without Hard Labour, and if a Male under the Age of Sixteen Years, with or without Whipping.

Explosives

9.109 Causing an Explosion

You, AB, on the (date) at (place) in the (District), unlawfully and maliciously by an explosive substance caused an explosion.

Contrary to s 2 of the Explosive Substances Act 1883 as substituted by s 4 of the Criminal Law (Jurisdiction) Act 1976.

The section as substituted reads:

2 A person who in the State or (being an Irish citizen) outside the State unlawfully and maliciously causes by an explosive substance an explosion of a nature likely to endanger life, or cause serious injury to property, shall, whether any injury to person or property is actually caused or not, be guilty of an offence and, on conviction on indictment, shall be liable to imprisonment for life.
Where the accused is an Irish citizen state that fact if the explosion took place outside the State.

9.110   Possession of an Explosive Substance

You, AB, on the (date) at (place) in the (District), had possession of an explosive substance with intent.

Contrary to s 3 of the Explosive Substances Act 1883 as substituted by s 4 of the Criminal Law (Jurisdiction) Act 1976.

The section, as substituted, reads:

3 A person who in the State or (being an Irish citizen) outside the State unlawfully and maliciously – (*a*) does any act with intent to cause, or conspires to cause, by an explosive substance an explosion of a nature likely to endanger life, or cause serious injury to property, whether in the State or elsewhere, or (*b*) makes or has in his possession or under his control an explosive substance with intent by means thereof to endanger life, or cause serious injury to property, whether in the State or elsewhere, or to enable any other person so to do, shall, whether any explosion does or does not take place, and whether any injury to person or property is actually caused or not, be guilty of an offence and, on conviction on indictment, shall be liable to imprisonment for a term not exceeding twenty years, and the explosive substance shall be forfeited.
Where the accused is an Irish citizen state that fact if the explosive took place outside the State.

9.111   Suspicious Possession

You, AB, on the (date) at (place) in the (District), had possession of an explosive substance in suspicious circumstances, that is (describe) for an unlawful object.

Contrary to s 4 of the Explosive Substances Act 1883.

The section reads:

4 (1) Any person who makes or knowingly has in his possession or under his control any explosive substance, under such circumstances as to give rise to a reasonable suspicion that he is not making it or does have it in his possession or under his control for a lawful object, shall, unless he can show that he made it or had it in his possession or under his control for a lawful object, be guilty of felony and, on conviction, shall be liable to penal servitude for a term not exceeding fourteen years, or to imprisonment for a term not exceeding two years with or without hard labour, and the explosive substance shall be forfeited. (2) In any proceeding against any person for a crime under this section, such person and his wife, or husband, as the case may be, may, if such person thinks fit, be called, sworn, examined, and cross-examined as an ordinary witness in the case.

9.112 In Northern Ireland

You, AB, on the (date) at (place) in the (District), had possession of an explosive substance, with intent, that is to endanger life or cause serious injury to property or to enable any other person so to do.

Contrary to s 2(1) of the Criminal Law (Jurisdiction) Act 1976.

The section is quoted at para **7.49**. For a discussion see paras **7.48–7.50**.

Firearms

9.113 Possession without a Firearm Certificate

You, AB, on the (date) at (place) in the (District), had unlawfully in your possession (or use or carrying) of a firearm (or ammunition) being a (specify) such possession (or use or carrying) not being authorised by a firearm certificate granted under the Firearms Acts 1925–1990 and for the time being in force.

Contrary to s 2 of the Firearms Act 1925 as amended by s 3 of the Firearms Act 1971 and s 4 of the Firearms & Offensive Weapons Act 1990.

The section as amended reads:

2 (1) Subject to the exceptions from this section hereinafter mentioned, it shall not be lawful for any person after the commencement of this Act to have in his possession, use or carry any firearm or ammunition save in so far as such possession, use, or carriage is authorised by a firearm certificate granted under this Act and for the time being in force. (2) Save in any of the cases hereinafter excepted from this section, every person who after the commencement of this Act has in his possession, uses, or carries any firearm without holding a firearm certificate therefor or otherwise than as authorised by such certificate, or purchases, uses, has in his possession, or carries any ammunition without holding a firearm certificate therefor or in quantities in excess of those authorised by such certificate, or fails to comply with any condition subject to which a firearm certificate was granted to him, shall be guilty of an offence under this section.

Section 4(2) of the 1964 Act reads:

4 (2) Where, in a prosecution for an offence under the Principal Act, possession, use or carriage of a firearm or ammunition by a person is proved, it shall not be necessary to prove that the person was not entitled to have in his possession, use or carry a firearm or ammunition.

9.114 Possession with Intent

You, AB, on the (date) at (place) in the (District), had in your possession (or control) of a firearm (or ammunition) (specify firearm or ammunition) with intent, by means thereof to endanger life or cause serious injury to property or to enable any other person so to do.

Contrary to s 15 of the Firearms Act 1925 as amended by s 4 of the Firearms Act 1971 and s 21(4) of the Criminal Law (Jurisdiction) Act 1976 and s 14(1) of the Criminal Justice Act 1984, and s 4 of the Firearms & Offensive Weapons Act 1990.

The section, as amended, reads:

15 Any person who, after the passing of this Act has in his possession or under his control any firearm or ammunition – (*a*) with intent to endanger life or cause serious injury to property, or (*b*) with intent to enable any other person by means of such firearm or ammunition to endanger life or cause serious injury to property, shall, whether any injury to person or property has or has not been caused thereby, be guilty of a felony, and on conviction thereof shall be liable to suffer imprisonment for life and the firearm or ammunition aforesaid shall be forfeited.

Section 4 of the 1971 Act reads:

4 For the removal of doubt it is hereby declared that in section 15 of the Principal Act references to life and property include references to life and property outside the area of application of the laws enacted by the Oireachtas.

9.115 Having a Firearm (or Imitation Firearm) with Intent

You, AB, on the (date) at (place) in the (District), had a firearm (or imitation firearm) with intent to commit the indictable offence of (specify) or (resist or prevent the arrest of himself, or of CD).

Contrary to s 27B of the Firearms Act 1964 as inserted by s 9 of the Criminal Law (Jurisdiction) Act 1976 and amended by s 14(5) of the Criminal Justice Act 1984, and by s 4 of the Firearms & Offensive Weapons Act 1990.

The section, as amended, reads:

27B (1) A person who has with him a firearm or an imitation firearm with intent to commit an indictable offence, or to resist or prevent the arrest of himself or another, in either case while he has the firearm or imitation firearm with him, shall be guilty of an offence and shall be liable on conviction on indictment to imprisonment for a term not exceeding fourteen years. (2) In proceedings for an offence under this section proof that the accused had a firearm or imitation firearm with him and intended to commit an indictable offence or to resist or prevent arrest is evidence that he intended to have it with him while doing so.

9.116 Using a Firearm to Resist Arrest

You, AB, on the (date) at (place) in the (District), used (or produced) a firearm (or imitation firearm) to resist arrest by Garda CD.

Contrary to s 27 of the Firearms Act 1964 as amended by s 21(6)(*b*) of the Criminal Law (Jurisdiction) Act 1976 and s 14(3) of the Criminal Justice Act 1984, and by s 4 of the Firearms & Offensive Weapons Act 1990.

The section, as amended, reads:

27 (1) A person who contravenes subsection (1) of section 112 of the Road Traffic Act 1961, and who at the time of such contravention has with him a firearm or an imitation firearm shall be guilty of an offence and shall be liable on conviction on indictment to imprisonment for a term not exceeding fourteen years. (2) Where a person is charged with an offence under this section, it shall be a good defence to the charge for him to show that he had the firearm or imitation firearm to which the charge relates with him for a lawful purpose when he did the act alleged to constitute the offence under subsection (1) of the said section 112.

9.117 Suspicious Possession

You, AB, on the (date) at (place) in the (District), had possession (or control) of a firearm (or ammunition) being (specify) giving rise to an inference that you did not have it in your possession (or under your control) for a lawful purpose.

Contrary to s 27A of the Firearms Act 1964 as substituted by s 8 of the Criminal Law (Jurisdiction) Act 1976 and amended by s 14(4) of the Criminal Justice Act 1984, and by s 4 of the Firearms & Offensive Weapons Act 1990.

The section, as amended, reads:

27A (1) A person who has a firearm or ammunition in his possession or under his control in such circumstances as to give rise to a reasonable inference that he has not got it in his possession or under his control for a lawful purpose shall, unless he has it in his possession or under his control for a lawful purpose, be guilty of an offence and shall be liable on conviction on indictment to imprisonment for a term not exceeding ten years. (2) In the application of s 2 of the Criminal Law (Jurisdiction) Act 1976, to this section, it shall be presumed, unless the contrary is shown, that a purpose that is unlawful in the State is unlawful in Northern Ireland.

9.118 In Northern Ireland

You, AB, on the (date) at (place) in the (District), produced a firearm in the course of escape from CD the person in charge of (specify person, etc.).

Contrary to s 2(1) of the Criminal Law (Jurisdiction) Act 1976.

The section is quoted at para **7.49**. For a discussion see paras **7.48–7.50**. For alternatives see s 2(1) of the Schedule to the Criminal Law (Jurisdiction) Act 1972.

You, AB, on the (date) at (place) in the (District), had in your possession a firearm with intent to endanger life.

Contrary to s 2(1) of the Criminal Law (Jurisdiction) Act 1976.

The section is quoted at para **7.49**. For a discussion see paras **7.48–7.50**. For alternatives see s 2(1) of the Schedule to the Criminal Law (Jurisdiction) Act 1976.

9.119 Reckless Discharge

You, AB, on the (date) at (place) in the (District), discharged a firearm being reckless as to whether any person would thereby be injured or not.

Contrary to s 8 and s 4 of the Firearms & Offensive Weapons Act 1990.

Section 8 reads:

8 A person who discharges a firearm being reckless as to whether any person will be injured or not, shall be guilty of an offence, whether any such injury is caused or not, and shall be liable: (*a*) on summary conviction to a fine not exceeding one thousand pounds or to imprisonment for a term not exceeding twelve months or to both, or (*b*) on conviction on indictment, to a fine or to imprisonment for a term not exceeding five years or to both.

Offensive weapons

9.120 Possession of a knife

You, AB, on the (date) at (place) in the (District), had a knife (or any other article which has a blade or which is sharply pointed) without good reason or lawful authority.

Contrary to s 9 of the Firearms & Offensive Weapons Act 1990.

The section reads:

Possession of knives and other articles

9 (1) Subject to sub-ss (2) and (3), where a person has with him in any public place any knife or any other article which has a blade or which is sharply pointed, he shall be guilty of an offence.

(2) It shall be a defence for a person charged with an offence under sub-s (1) to prove that he had good reason or lawful authority for having the article with him in a public place.

(3) Without prejudice to the generality of sub-s (2), it shall be a defence for a person charged with an offence under sub-s (1) to prove that he had the article with him for use at work or for a recreational purpose.

(4) Where a person, without lawful authority or reasonable excuse (the onus or proving which shall lie on him), has with him in any public place—

(a) any flick-knife, or

(b) any other article whatsoever made or adapted for use for causing injury to or incapacitating a person,

he shall be guilty of an offence.

(5) Where a person has with him in any public place any article intended by him unlawfully to cause injury to, incapacitate or intimidate any person either in a particular eventuality or otherwise, he shall be guilty of an offence.

(6) In a prosecution for an offence under sub-s (5), it shall not be necessary for the prosecution to allege or prove that the intent to cause injury, incapacitate or intimidate was intent to cause injury to, incapacitate or intimidate a particular person; and if, having regard to all the circumstances (including the type of the article alleged to have been intended to cause injury, incapacitate or intimidate, the time of the day or night, and the place), the court (or the jury as the case may be) thinks it reasonable to do so, it may regard possession of the article as sufficient evidence of intent in the absence of any adequate explanation by the accused.

(7) (a) A person guilty of an offence under sub-s (1) shall be liable on summary conviction to a fine not exceeding £1,000 or to imprisonment for a term not exceeding twelve months or to both.

A person guilty of an offence under sub-s (4) or (5) shall be liable—

(i) on summary conviction, to a fine not exceeding £1,000 or to imprisonment for a term not exceeding twelve months or to both, or

(ii) on conviction on indictment, to a fine or to imprisonment for a term not exceeding five years or to both.

(8) In this section "public place" includes any highway and any other premises or place to which at the material time the public have or are permitted to have access, whether on payment or otherwise, and includes any club premises and any train, vessel or vehicle used for the carriage of persons for reward.

(9) In this section "flick-knife" means a knife—

(a) which has a blade which opens when hand pressure is applied to a button, spring, lever or other device in or attached to the handle, or (*b*) which has a blade which is released from the handle or sheath by the force of gravity or the application of centrifugal force and when released is locked in an open position by means of a button, spring, lever or other device.

9.121 Possession of a Flick Knife

You, AB, on the (date) at (place), a public place, in the (District), had in your possession a flick knife (or an article made or adapted for use for causing injury to or incapacitating a person).

Contrary to s 9(4) of the Firearms & Offensive Weapons Act, 1990.

The subsection reads:

9 (4) Where a person, without lawful authority or reasonable excuse (the onus of proving which shall lie on him), has with him in any public place—

(*a*) any flick-knife, or
(*b*) any other article whatsoever made or adapted for use for causing injury to or incapacitating a person,

he shall be guilty of an offence.

9.122 Offensive Weapon

You, AB, on the (date) at (place) in the (District), had in your possession in a public place an article intended to unlawfully cause injury, incapacitate, or intimidate a person (or CD).

Contrary to s 9(5) of the Firearms & Offensive Weapons Act 1990.

The subsection reads:

9 (5) Where a person has with him in any public place any article intended by him unlawfully to cause injury to, incapacitate or intimidate any person either in a particular eventuality or otherwise, he shall be guilty of an offence.

9.123 Being an Armed Trespasser

You, AB, on the (date) at (place) in the (District), being on a building (or part of a building or land ancillary to a building) as a trespasser and possessing a knife (or any other article to which s 9(1) of the Firearms & Offensive Weapons Act 1990, applies, or weapon of offence as defined in subsection 10(2)).

Contrary to s 10(1) of the Firearms & Offensive Weapons Act 1990.

The section reads:

Trespassing with a knife, weapon of offence or other article

10 (1) Where a person is on any premises as defined in sub-s (2) as a trespasser, he shall be guilty of an offence if he has with him—

(*a*) any knife or other article to which s 9(1) applies, or
(*b*) any weapon of offence (as defined in sub-s (2)).

(2) In this section—

"premises" means any building, any part of a building and any land ancillary to a building;

"weapon of offence" means any article made or adapted for use for causing injury to or incapacitating a person, or intended by the person having it with him for such use.

(3) A person guilty of an offence under this section shall be liable—

(*a*) on summary conviction, to a fine not exceeding £1,000 or to imprisonment for a term not exceeding twelve months or to both, or

(*b*) on conviction on indictment, to a fine or to imprisonment for a term not exceeding five years or to both.

9.124 Producing a Weapon

You, AB, on the (date) at (place) in the (District), produced an article (in the course of a dispute or fight) capable of inflicting serious injury being a (specify) in such a manner as to be likely to unlawfully intimidate another person.

Contrary to s 11 of the Firearms & Offensive Weapons Act 1990.

The section reads:

Production of article capable of inflicting serious injury

11 Where a person, while committing or appearing to be about to commit an offence, or in the course of a dispute or fight, produces in a manner likely unlawfully to intimidate another person any article capable of inflicting serious injury, he shall be guilty of an offence and shall be liable—

(*a*) on summary conviction, to a fine not exceeding £1,000 or to imprisonment for a term not exceeding twelve months or to both, or

(*b*) on conviction on indictment, to a fine or to imprisonment for a term not exceeding five years or to both.

9.125 Dealing in Weapons

You, AB, on the (date) at (place) in the (District), exposed for sale or hire (or manufacturing selling or hiring or by way of business repairing or modifying) an article (specify) to which the (specify Regulations) applies.

Contrary to s 12 of the Firearms & Offensive Weapons Act 1990.

The alternatives can be seen from the section. This offence is dependent on Ministerial regulation and the articles will be specified within same in due course.

You, AB, on the (date) at (place) in the (District), gave an article (specify) on loan to which the (specify Regulations) applied.

Contrary to s 12 of the Firearms & Offensive Weapons Act 1990.

The section reads:

Power to prohibit manufacture, importation, sale, hire or loan of offensive weapons

12 (1) Any person who—

(*a*) manufactures, sells or hires, or offers or exposes for sale or hire, or by way of business repairs or modifies, or

(*b*) has in his possession for the purpose of sale or hire or for the purpose of repair or modification by way of business, or

(*c*) puts on display, or lends or gives to any other person,

609

a weapon to which this section applies shall be guilty of an offence.

(2) Where an offence under sub-s (1) is committed by a body corprate and is proved to have been so committed with the consent or connivance of or to be attributable to any neglect on the part of a director, manager, secretary or other officer of the body corporate, the director, manager, secretary or other officer or any person purporting to act in such capacity shall also be guilty of an offence.

(3) A person guilty of an offence under this section shall be liable—

(*a*) on summary conviction, to a fine not exceeding £1,000 or to imprisonment for a term not exceeding twelve months or to both, or

(*b*) on conviction on indictment, to a fine or to imprisonment for a term not exceeding five years or to both.

(4) The Minister may by order direct that this section shall apply to any description of weapon specified in the order except any firearm subject to the Firearms Acts 1925 to 1990.

(5) The Minister may by order amend or revoke an order made under this section.

(6) The importation of a weapon to which this section applies is hereby prohibited.

(7) Every order made under this section shall be laid before each House of the Oireachtas as soon as may be after it is made and, if a resolution annulling the order is passed by either such House within the next 21 days on which that House has sat after the order is laid before it, the order shall be annulled accordingly, but without prejudice to the validity of anything previously done thereunder.

Road traffic

9.126 Dangerous Driving

You, AB, on the (date) at (place), a public place, in the (District), did drive a vehicle, registration number (specify) in a manner (including speed) which having regard to all the circumstances of the case (including the condition of the vehicle, the nature, condition and use of such place and the amount of traffic which then actually was or might reasonably be expected then to be therein) was dangerous to the public.

Contrary to s 53 of the Road Traffic Act 1961, as amended by s 51 of the Road Traffic Act 1968 and by s 3 of the Road Traffic (Amendment) Act 1984.

9.127 Causing Death or Serious Bodily Harm

You, AB, on the (date) at (place), a public place, in the (District), did drive a vehicle, registration number (specify) in a manner (including speed) which having regard to all the circumstances of the case (including the condition of the vehicle, the nature, condition and use of such place and the amount of traffic which then actually was or might reasonably be expected then to be therein) was dangerous to the public thereby causing the death of (serious bodily harm to) CD.

Contrary to s 53 of the Road Traffic Act 1961, as amended by s 51 of the Road Traffic Act 1968 and by s 3 of the Road Traffic (Amendment) Act 1984.

9.128 Careless Driving

You, AB, on the (date) at (place), a public place, in the (District), did drive a vehicle, registration number (specify) without due care and attention.

Contrary to s 52(1) of the Road Traffic Act 1961, as substituted by s 50 of the Road Traffic Act 1968, and as amended by s 3 of the Road Traffic (Amendment) Act 1984.

9.129 Hit and Run – Personal Injury

You, AB, on the (date) at (place), a public place, in the (District), being the driver of a vehicle, registration number (specify), which was involved in the occurrence of an injury to CD [chose one of the following]

- (*a*) did fail to stop such vehicle, such vehicle not being stationary after such occurrence;
- (*b*) did fail to keep said vehicle at or near the place of such occurrence for a period which was reasonable in all the circumstances of the case and having regard to the provisions of s 106 of the Road Traffic Acts 1961/84;
- (*c*) did fail to give on demand the appropriate information as defined by Section 106 of the Road Traffic Acts 1961/84 to a person entitled to demand such information, there being no member of An Garda Síochána present at such occurrence;
- (*d*) did fail to report such occurrence as soon as possible to a member of An Garda Síochána, going for that purpose if necessary, to the nearest convenient Garda Síochána Station, there being no member of An Garda Síochána present at such occurrence or a person entitled to demand the appropriate information.

Contrary to s 106 of the Road Traffic Act 1961, as amended by s 6 of the Road Traffic Act 1968 and s 3 of the Road Traffic (Amendment) Act 1984.

9.130 Hit and Run – Material Damage

You, AB, on the (date) at (place), a public place, in the (District), being the driver of a vehicle, registration number (specify), which was involved in the occurrence of damage to the property of CD [chose one of the following]

- (*a*) did fail to stop such vehicle, such vehicle not being stationary after such occurrence;
- (*b*) did fail to keep said vehicle at or near the place of such occurrence for a period which was reasonable in all the circumstances of the case and having regard to the provisions of Section 106 of the Road Traffic Acts 1961/84;
- (*c*) did fail to give on demand the appropriate information as defined by Section 106 of the Road Traffic Acts 1961/84 to a person entitled to demand such information, there being no member of An Garda Síochána present at such occurrence;
- (*d*) did fail to report such occurrence as soon as possible to a member of

An Garda Síochána, going for that purpose if necessary, to the nearest convenient Garda Síochána Station, there being no member of An Garda Síochána present at such occurrence or a person entitled to demand the appropriate information.
Contrary to s 106 of the Road Traffic Act 1961, as amended by s 6 of the Road Traffic Act 1968 and s 3 of the Road Traffic (Amendment) Act 1984.

Contrary to s 106 of the Road Traffic Act 1961, as amended by s 6 of the Road Traffic Act 1968 and s 3 of the Road Traffic (Amendment) Act 1984.

9.131   Unlawful Seizure of a Vehicle

You, AB, on the (date) at (place) in the (District), by force unlawfully seized control of a motor vehicle, registration number (specify) from CD.

Contrary to s 10 of the Criminal Law (Jurisdiction) Act 1976.

The section reads:

Unlawful seizure of vehicles

10   (1) A person who unlawfully, by force or threat thereof, or by any other form of intimidation, seizes or exercises control of or otherwise interferes with the control of, or compels or induces some other person to use for an unlawful purpose, any vehicle (whether mechanically propelled or not) or any ship or hovercraft shall be guilty of an offence and shall be liable on conviction on indictment to imprisonment for a term not exceeding fifteen years.

(2) In the application of s 2 to this section, it shall be presumed, unless the contrary is shown, that a purpose that is unlawful in the State is unlawful in Northern Ireland.

(3) In this section—

"hovercraft" means a vehicle that is designed to be supported when in motion wholly or partly by air expelled from the vehicle to form a cushion of which the boundaries include the ground, water or other surface beneath the vehicle;

"ship" includes any boat or other vessel;

"vehicle" includes a railway train or any other railway vehicle.

9.132   Interference with a Mechanically Propelled Vehicle

You, AB, on the (date) at (place) in the (District), without lawful authority or reasonable cause, interfered with the mechanism of a mechanically propelled vehicle, registration number (specify) the property of CD while such vehicle was stationary in a public place.

Contrary to s 113 of the Road Traffic Act 1961, as amended by s 6 of the Road Traffic Act 1968 and by s 3(8) of the Road Traffic (Amendment) Act 1984.

Alternative: interfere or attempt to interfere with the mechanism of a mechanically propelled vehicle while it is stationary in a public place, or get on or into or attempt to get on or into the vehicle while it is so stationary. The section as amended reads:

Unauthorised interference with mechanism of vehicle

113 (1) A person shall not, without lawful authority or reasonable cause, interfere or attempt to interfere with the mechanism of a mechanically propelled vehicle while it is stationary in a public place, or get on or into or attempt to get on or into the vehicle while it is so stationary.

(2) A person who contravenes sub-s (1) of this section shall be guilty of an offence.

(3) Where a member of the Garda Síochána has reasonable grounds for believing that a person is committing or has committed an offence under this section, he may arrest the person without warrant.

(4) This section shall not apply to a person taking, in relation to a mechanically propelled vehicle which is obstructing his lawful ingress or egress to or from any place, such steps as are reasonably necessary to move the vehicle by human propulsion for a distance sufficient to terminate the obstruction.

(5) Where a person is charged with an offence under this section, it shall be a good defence to the charge for him to show that, when he did the act alleged to constitute the offence, he believed, and had reasonable grounds for believing, that he had lawful authority for doing that act.

9.133 Unauthorised Use

You, AB, on the (date) at (place) in the (District), did unlawfully use (take possession of) a mechanically propelled vehicle, registration number (specify), the property of CD, without the consent of the owner thereof, or other lawful authority.

Contrary to s 112 of the Road Traffic Act 1961, as amended by s 65 of the Road Traffic Act 1968, and by s 3(7) of the Road Traffic (Amendment) Act 1984.

Alternative: use or take possession of, or if possession of a vehicle has been taken in contravention of this subsection, a person who knows of the taking shall not allow himself to be carried in or on it without the consent of the owner thereof or other lawful authority. The section is quoted at para **9.64**.

9.134 Unlawful Carriage

You, AB, on the (date) at (place) in the (District), being a person who knew that a mechanically propelled vehicle, registration number (specify), was taken possession of or used without the consent of the owner thereof CD, or other lawful authority, did allow yourself to be carried in (on) that vehicle, without the consent of the owner or other lawful authority.

Contrary to s 112 of the Road Traffic Act 1961, as amended by s 65 of the Road Traffic Act 1968, and by s 3(7) of the Road Traffic (Amendment) Act 1984.

The section, as amended, reads:

112 (1)(*a*) A person shall not use or take possession of a mechanically propelled vehicle without the consent of the owner thereof or other lawful authority. (*b*) Where possession of a vehicle has been taken in contravention of this subsection, a person who knows of the taking shall not allow himself to be carried in or on it without the consent of the owner thereof or other lawful authority.

(2) A person who contravenes subsection (1) of this section shall be guilty of an offence and shall be liable – (*a*) on summary conviction, to a fine not exceeding £1,000 or, at the discretion of the court, to imprisonment for a term not exceeding 12 months, or to both such fine and such imprisonment; (*b*) on conviction on indictment, to a fine not exceeding £2,000 or, at the discretion of the court, to imprisonment for a term not exceeding five years or to both such fine and such imprisonment.

(3) A person shall not use or take possession of a pedal cycle without the consent of the owner thereof or other lawful authority.

(4) A person who contravenes subsection (3) of this section shall be guilty of an offence.

(5) Where a person is charged with an offence under this section, it shall be a good defence to the charge for him to show that, when he did the act alleged to constitute the offence, he believed, and had reasonable grounds for believing, that he had lawful authority for doing that act.

(6) Where a member of the Garda Síochána has reasonable grounds for believing that a person is committing or has committed an offence under this section, he may arrest the person without warrant.

(7) Where, when a person is tried on indictment or summarily for the larceny of a vehicle, the jury, or, in the case of a summary trial, the District Court, is of opinion that he was not guilty of the larceny of the vehicle but was guilty of an offence under this section in relation to the vehicle, the jury or court may find him guilty of that offence and he may be sentenced accordingly.

9.135 Having a Firearm while Taking a Vehicle

You, AB, on the (date) at (place) in the (District), had a firearm (or imitation firearm), such possession not being authorised by a firearm certificate granted under the Firearms Acts 1925–1971 and for the time being in force, whilst committing an offence under s 112 of the Road Traffic Act 1961, as amended.

Contrary to s 26 of the Firearms Act 1964 as amended by s 21(6)(*b*) of the Criminal Law (Jurisdiction) Act 1976 and s 14(2) of the Criminal Justice Act 1984, and by s 4 of the Firearms & Offensive Weapons Act 1990.

The section as amended reads:

26 (1) A person who contravenes subsection (1) of section 112 of the Road Traffic Act 1961, and who at the time of such contravention has with him a firearm or an imitation firearm shall be guilty of an offence and shall be liable on conviction on indictment to imprisonment for a term not exceeding fourteen years.

(2) Where a person is charged with an offence under this section, it shall be a good defence to the charge for him to show that he had the firearm or imitation firearm to which the charge relates with him for a lawful purpose when he did the act alleged to constitute the offence under subsection (1) of the said section 112.

Attempts are charged contrary to the same section.

Inchoate offences

9.136 Attempt

You, AB, on the (date) at (place) in the (District), attempted to rob CD of her handbag (or specify whatever other offence the accused attempted).

Contrary to common law.

For a discussion see paras **2.02–2.36**.

9.137   Incitement

You, AB, on the (date) at (place) in the (District), incited CD to commit the crime of (specify crime).

Contrary to common law.

For a discussion see paras **2.56–2.62**.

9.138   Conspiracy

You, AB, did between the (date) and (date) within the (District), did conspire, confederate and agree with CD to (specify crime or other unlawful wrong).

Contrary to common law.

The above wording is standard but is unnecessary. A modern form would read as follows:

You, AB, between the (date) and (date) within the Dublin Metropolitan District, did conspire with a person or persons unknown to commit fraud being (specify).

Contrary to common law.

For a discussion see paras **2.37–2.55**.

9.139   Aiding and Abetting

You, AB, on the (date) at (place) in the (District), did aid (abet, counsel, procure) the commission of an offence by CD by (for example, supplying him with a gun) whereby he (indicate the offence committed by the principal offender).

Contrary to common law.

For summary offences charge contrary to s 22 of the Petty Sessions (Ireland) Act 1851, as amended by s 43(7) of the Criminal Justice (Administration) Act 1914. For a discussion see generally chapter 3.

Companies offences

9.140   Fraudulent Trading

AB, between the (date) and (day) at (place) in the (District), were knowingly a party to the carrying on of the business of X Company Limited with intent to defraud the Revenue Commissioners, as creditors of the said company, by falsely pretending that the said company during the tax year ended April 6, 1993 had a turnover of £   and had made no profit when, in fact, the turnover of the said company exceeded that figure and rendered it liable to pay corporation tax.

9.140 *Sample offences*

Contrary to s 297 of the Companies Act 1963 as inserted by s 137 of the Companies Act 1990.

The fraudulent purpose should be stated in terms of the actual pretence which the accused proposed to perpetrate. The section as amended is quoted at para **7.59**. For a discussion see paras **7.58–7.62**.

9.141 Insider Dealing

You, AB, on the (date) at (place) in the (District), being a person connected with the X Company Limited, in that you were a director of that company, sold 5,000 ordinary shares in the aforesaid company at £ each on the Dublin Stock Exchange while you were in possession of information, that is to say, that the said company was insolvent and about to cease trading, which information was not generally available but, if it were, would have been likely materially to affect the price of the said shares.

Contrary to Part V of the Companies Act 1990 and contrary to s 114 thereof.

The section is quoted at para **7.67**. For a discussion see paras **7.63–7.68**.

9.142 Common Offences

You, AB, (or insert name of company) on the (date) at (place) in the (District) (specify), recklessly made a false statement as to the nature of the service provided by such trade or business, that is (specify).

Contrary to s 6 of the Consumer Information Act 1978.

You, AB, (or insert name of company) on the (date) at (place) in the (District), while offering to supply goods namely (specify) gave a misleading indication of the price of such goods in a sign at your premises.

Contrary to s 7 of the Consumer Information Act 1978.

You, AB, (or insert name of company) on the (date) at (place) in the (District), caused to be published in the (specify) an advertisement, in relation to the supply of goods, which was likely to mislead and thereby cause loss, damage or injury to members of the public in a material degree.

Contrary to s 8 of the Consumer Information Act 1978.

The relevant sections read:

2 (1) Section 3(1) of the Principal Act (the Merchandise Marks Acts, 1887 to 1970) is hereby amended by the substitution for the definition of "trade description" of the following definition:

"'trade description' means any description, statement or other indication, direct or indirect—

    (a) as to the number, quantity, measure, gauge, capacity or weight of any goods, or

    (b) as to the place or country in which any goods were manufactured, produced, processed, reconditioned, repaired, packed or prepared for sale, or

(c) as to the mode of manufacturing, producing, processing, reconditioning, repairing, packing or preparing for sale of any goods, or

(d) as to the person by whom and the time at which any goods were manufactured, produced, processed, reconditioned, repaired, packed or prepared for sale, or

(e) as to the material of which any goods are composed, or

(f) as to any goods being the subject of an existing patent, privilege or copyright, or

(g) as to the fitness for any purpose, strength, performance, behaviour or accuracy of any goods, or

(h) as to any physical characteristic of any goods not referred to in the preceding paragraphs of this definition, or

(i) as to the conformity of any goods with any standard or their passing of any test or their commendation by any person, or

(j) as to the identity of the supplier or distributor, or the standing, commercial importance, competence or capabilities of, the manufacturer, producer, supplier or distributor, of any goods, or

(k) as to the contents of books or as to their authors, as to the contents of cinematograph films (within the meaning of the Performers' Protection Act, 1968) or as to their producers or as to the contents of recordings (within the meaning of the Performers' Protection Act, 1968) or as to the performers on such recordings, or

(l) as to any history of any goods not referred to in the preceding paragraphs of this definition, including their previous ownership,

and the use of any figure, word or mark which, according to the custom of the trade is commonly taken to be an indication of any of the above matters shall be deemed to be a trade description within the meaning of this Act;"

(2) (a) The definition of "false trade description" in the said section 3(1) shall be construed as if the references to false in a material respect were references to false to a material degree and included references to misleading to a material degree.

(b) In paragraph (a) of this subsection "misleading to a material degree" means likely to be taken for such an indication of any of the matters specified in the definition of "trade description" in the said section 3(1) of the Principal Act as would be false to a material degree.

(c) Anything which, though not a trade description, is likely to be taken for an indication of any of the matters specified in the definition of "trade description" in the said section 3(1) and, as such an indication, would be false in a material respect, shall be deemed to be a false trade description.

(d) A false indication or anything likely to be taken as an indication which would be false that any goods comply with a standard specified or recognised by any person or implied by the approval of any person shall be deemed to be a false trade description, if there is no such person or no standard so specified, recognised or implied.

3 (1) In a prosecution of a person for an offence under section 2(1) of the Principal Act as amended by this Act in relation to the application to goods of a false trade description or the causing of such an application to be made, it shall not be a defence for the person to prove that he acted without intent to defraud.

(2) In a prosecution of a person for an offence under section 2(2) of the Principal Act as amended by this Act in relation to the sale, exposure for sale or having in possession for sale in the course of any trade, business or profession of goods or things to which a false trade description is applied, it shall not be a defence for the person to prove the matters specified in paragraphs (a), (b) and (c) of the said section 2(2).

(3) This section is without prejudice to section 22 of this Act.

617

4 (1) Section 2(1) of the Principal Act is hereby amended by the substitution for paragraph (*d*) of the following paragraph:

"(*d*) in the course of any trade, business or profession, applies any false trade description to goods, or".

(2) Section 2(2) of the Principal Act is hereby amended insofar as it relates to trades descriptions, by the substitution of "in the course of any trade, business or profession" for "or any purpose of trade or manufacture".

(3) Section 5 of the Principal Act is hereby amended, insofar as it relates to trade descriptions, by the substitution for subsection (1) of the following subsection:

"(1) (*a*) A person shall be deemed to apply a trade description to goods if—
      (i) he affixes or annexes it to them or in any manner marks it on or incorporates it with—
         (I) the goods themselves, or
         (II) anything in, on or with which the goods are sold,"

6 (1) If a person, in the course or for the purposes of a trade, business or profession—

(*a*) makes a statement which he knows to be false, or
(*b*) recklessly makes a statement which is false

as to any of the following matters, that is to say—

    (i) the provision in the course of the trade, business or profession of any services, accommodation or facilities,
    (ii) the nature, effect or fitness for purpose of any services, accommodation or facilities provided in the course of the trade, business or profession,
    (iii) the time at which, manner in which or persons by whom any services, accommodation or facilities are so provided,
    (iv) the examination, approval, use or evaluation by any person of any services, accommodation or facilities so provided, or
    (v) the place where any service, facility or accommodation is so provided or the amenities of any such accommodation,

he shall be guilty of an offence.

(2) For the purposes of this section—

(*a*) anything (whether or not a statement as to any of the matters specified in the preceding subsection) likely to be taken for such a statement as to any of those matters as would be false shall be deemed to be a false statement as to that matter; and
(*b*) a statement made regardless of whether it is true or false shall be deemed to be made recklessly, unless the person making it had adequate reasons for believing that it was true.

(3) In relation to any services consisting of or including the application of any treatment or process or the carrying out of any repair, the matters specified in subsection (1) of this section shall be taken to include the effect of the treatment, process or repair.

(4) In this section "false" means false to a material degree.

7 (1) If a person offering to supply goods of any description or provide any services or accommodation gives by any means a false or misleading indication of—

(*a*) the price or charge for the goods, services or accommodation,
(*b*) the price or charge at or for which the goods or goods of the same description or the services or accommodation were or was previously offered,
(*c*) a recommended price for the goods, or
(*d*) any charge for installation of or servicing of the goods or any price for ancillary equipment reasonably required for the purpose of the use or enjoyment of the goods,

he shall be guilty of an offence.
(2) For the purposes of this section—

(*a*) an indication that goods, services or accommodation were or was previously offered at a different price or charge or at a particular price or charge shall be treated, unless the contrary is expressed, as an indication that they were so offered openly at the same place within the preceding 3 months for not less than 28 successive days;
(*b*) an indication as to a recommended price—
   (i) shall be treated, unless the contrary is expressed, as an indication that it is a price recommended by the manufacturer, producer or other supplier, and
   (ii) shall be treated, unless the contrary is expressed, as an indication that it is a price recommended generally for supply by retail in the area where the goods are offered;
(*c*) anything likely to be taken as an indication as to a recommended price or as to the price or charge at or for which goods, services or accommodation were or was previously offered shall be treated as such an indication;
(*d*) a person advertising goods, services or accommodation as available for supply or provision shall be taken as offering to supply or provide them or it; and
(*e*) an indication of the price or charge at or for which any goods, services or accommodation are or is offered by a person shall be treated, unless the contrary is expressed, as an indication that those goods, services or accommodation are or is offered at or for that price or charge in every place in the State where those goods, services or accommodation are or is offered by the person:
   Provided that, where such an indication is given at the place where the goods, services or accommodation are offered, the indication shall be treated, unless the contrary is expressed, as relating only to the goods, services or accommodation offered at that place.

8 (1) A person shall not publish, or cause to be published, an advertisement in relation to the supply or provision in the course or for the purposes of a trade, business or profession, of goods, services or facilities if it is likely to mislead, and thereby cause loss, damage or injury to members of the public to a material degree.
(2) Any person who contravenes subsection (1) of this section shall, subject to the provisions of this Act, be guilty of an offence.
(3) The Director may, upon giving notice of the application to any person against whom the order the subject of the application is sought, apply to the High Court for, and may, at the discretion of that Court, be granted, an order prohibiting the publication, or the further publication, of an advertisement the publication of which is or would be a contravention of subsection (1) of this section.

11 (1) Where it appears to the Minister to be necessary or expedient in the interest of persons to whom goods, services, accommodation or facilities, of any description are to be supplied or provided that advertisements or any class of advertisements of the goods, services, accommodation or facilities should contain or refer to any information (whether or not amounting to or including a trade description or the name and address of the publisher of an advertisement or his agent) relating to the goods, services, accommodation or facilities, the Minister may, subject to the provisions of this Act, by order impose requirements as to the inclusion of that information, or of an indication of the means by which it may be obtained, in advertisements, or in such classes of advertisements as may be specified in the order, of the goods, services, accommodation or facilities, of that description.

(2) An order under this section may specify the form and manner in which any such information or indication as is specified in subsection (1) of this section is to be included in advertisements or in advertisements of any class specified in the order and may make different provision for different circumstances and different classes of advertisements.

(3) Where an advertisement fails to comply with any requirement imposed under this section, any person who publishes the advertisement shall, subject to the provisions of this Act, be guilty of an offence.

12 Where it appears to the Minister to be necessary or expedient in the interest of persons to whom goods, services, accommodation or facilities, of any description are supplied or provided that any words or expressions used in relation to the goods, services, accommodation or facilities should be understood as having definite meanings, the Minister may by order assign meanings either—

(*a*) to those words or expressions when used in the course of a trade or business, as, or as part of, a trade description applied to goods, services, accommodation or facilities, of that description, or

(*b*) to those words or expressions when so used in such circumstances as may be specified in the order,

and where such a meaning stands so assigned to a word or expression, it shall be deemed for the purposes of this Act to have that meaning when used in the manner mentioned in paragraph (*a*) or (*b*), as the case may be, of this section.

13 (1) Where an advertisement in relation to the supply or provision of any goods, services, accommodation or facilities is published and does not include the name and address of the person who procured such publication or his agent, the publisher of the advertisement shall, if the Director or an officer of the Minister or an officer of a council of a county or corporation of a county or other borough in whose functional area the publisher has a place of business so requests within 12 months of the publication of the advertisement, give to the Director or officer, the name and address of such person or his agent.

(2) A person to whom information is given pursuant to a request under subsection (1) of this section shall not give the information to another person other than for the purposes of this Act.

(3) A person who contravenes subsection (1) or (2) of this section shall be guilty of an offence.

14 (1) A person who offers food for sale by retail by weight (other than food packed for such sale by its manufacturer or producer or by the person who supplied it for such sale) in any place in the course of any trade or business shall provide in a prominent position in a part of the place to which, for the purpose of such sales, the public have access, a weighing scales or weighing machine, and shall permit any person to weight or observe the weighing of any food sold by retail or for sale by retail at the place (being food which that person has bought or is buying or about to buy) on the scales or machine.

(2) A weighing scales or weighing machine provided pursuant to this section shall be deemed, for the purposes of the Weights and Measures Acts, 1878 to 1961, to be being used for trade.

(3) A person who contravenes subsection (1) of this section shall be guilty of an offence.

15 (1) A person shall not, without reasonable cause, prevent another person from, or interfere with or obstruct another person who is—

(*a*) entering a place where goods are offered for sale in the course of any trade or business for the purpose of reading any prices displayed on, with or in relation to the goods, or

(*b*) reading any prices displayed as aforesaid, if the prices of the goods are not displayed (whether outside the place or elsewhere) so as to be capable of being read by the person while at or near the place without entering the place.

(2) A person who contravenes subsection (1) of this section shall be guilty of an offence.

17 (1) A person guilty of an offence under the Acts involving a trade description or under this Act shall, in lieu of any other fine or term of imprisonment, be liable—

(*a*) on summary conviction, to a fine not exceeding £500 or, at the discretion of the court, to imprisonment for a term not exceeding 6 months or to both the fine and the imprisonment, or

(*b*) on conviction on indictment, to a fine not exceeding £10,000 or, at the discretion of the court, to imprisonment for a term not exceeding 2 years or to both the fine and the imprisonment.

(2) When considering what penalty (if any) under subsection (1) of this section is appropriate to an offence, the Court may take into consideration any advertisement published by or on behalf of the person convicted of the offence and correcting any misleading advertising, or any false or misleading description, statement or indication to which the offence relates.

(3) (*a*) Where a court imposes a fine or affirms or varies a fine imposed by another court for an offence referred to in subsection (1) of this section of which a person was convicted summarily, it may, at its discretion, on the application (made before the time of such imposition of affirmation) of any person who was summoned as a witness on behalf of the prosecution in the proceedings in which the fine was imposed and who suffered personal injury, loss or damage resulting, wholly or partly, from the offence provide by order for the payment of the amount of the fine or of a specified part of it as compensation in respect of the injury, loss or damage to the person making the application.

(*b*) An application shall not lie under paragraph (*a*) of this subsection in respect of any personal injury, loss or damage if proceedings claiming damages for the injury, loss or damage have been instituted in any court.

(*c*) Where the whole or part of a fine imposed under this section is paid to a person pursuant to this subsection and the person is awarded damages by a court in respect of the personal injury, loss or damage to which the payment relates, the payment shall be deemed to be in satisfaction of so much of the damages as is equal to the amount of the payment.

18 (1) Proceedings in relation to an offence under the Acts involving a trade description or under this Act may be brought and prosecuted by the Minister or by the council of the county or the corporation of the county or other borough in which the offence is alleged to have been committed.

(2) Notwithstanding section 10(4) of the Petty Sessions (Ireland) Act, 1851, summary proceedings for an offence under this Act may be instituted within 12 months from the date of the offence.

(3) Any expenses incurred by a council of a county, or the corporation of a

county or other borough under this section shall be defrayed in the same manner as expenses incurred under section 19 of the Merchandise Marks Act, 1931, by a local authority specified in that section.

19 Where an offence under this Act which is committed by a body corporate or an unincorporated body of persons is proved to have been committed with the consent or connivance of, or to be attributable to any neglect on the part of, any person (or any person acting on his behalf) being a director, manager, secretary, member of the committee of management or other controlling authority of any such body or being any other similar officer of any such body, that person or the person so acting as the case may be shall also be guilty of that offence and shall be liable to be proceeded against and punished accordingly.

20 Where, in any proceedings under the Acts involving a trade description or under this Act, the truth of any indication, direct or indirect and by whatever means given—

(*a*) by a manufacturer, producer or other supplier thereof with respect to goods or the price of goods, or

(*b*) by a person providing services, accommodation or facilities with respect to the services, accommodation or facilities, or the charges for the services, accommodation or facilities,

is an issue, and the person who gave the indication does not establish that on the balance of probabilities the indication is true, it shall be presumed to be untrue.

21 Where the commission by any person of an offence under the Acts involving a false trade description, or an offence under this Act is due to the act or default of some other person, that other person shall be guilty of the offence, and a person may be charged with and convicted of the offence by virtue of this section whether or not proceedings are taken against the first-mentioned person.

22 (1) In any proceedings for an offence under section 2 of the Principal Act involving a false trade description or an offence under this Act it shall, subject to subsection (2) of this section, be a defence for the person charged to prove—

(*a*) that the commission of the offence was due to a mistake or the reliance on information supplied to him or to the act or default of another person, an accident or some other cause beyond his control; and

(*b*) that he took all reasonable precautions and exercised all due diligence to avoid the commission of such an offence by himself or any other person under his control.

(2) If in any case the defence provided by subsection (1) of this section involves the allegation that the commission of the offence was due to the act or default of another person or to reliance on information supplied by another person, the person charged shall not, without leave of the court, be entitled to rely on that defence unless, not less than 7 clear days before the hearing, he has served on the prosecutor a notice in writing giving such information identifying or assisting in the identification of that other person as was then in his possession.

(3) In any proceedings for an offence under section 2(2) of the Principal Act in relation to goods to which a false trade description is applied it shall be a defence for the person charged to prove that he did not know, and could not with reasonable diligence have ascertained, that the goods did not conform to the description or that the description had been applied to the goods.

(4) In proceedings for an offence under section 2 of the Principal Act involving a false trade description or an offence under this Act committed by the publication of an advertisement it shall be a defence for the person charged to prove that he is a

person whose business it is to publish or arrange for the publication of advertisements and that he received the advertisement for publication in the ordinary course of business and did not know and had no reason to suspect that its publication would amount to an offence under the Principal Act or this Act.

You, AB, (or insert name of company) on the (date) at (place) in the (District), applied a false trade description to your goods that is to say (specify false description).

Contrary to s 2 of the Merchandise Marks Act 1887 as amended by s 2 of the Consumer Information Act 1978.

Sections 2 and 3 of the Merchandise Marks Act read:

2 (1) Every person who—

(*a*) forges any trade mark; or
(*b*) falsely applies to goods any trade mark or any mark so nearly resembling a trade mark as to be calculated to deceive; or
(*c*) makes any die, block, machine, or other instrument for the purpose of forging, or of being used for forging, a trade mark; or
(*d*) applies any false trade description to goods; or
(*e*) disposes of or has in his possession any die, block, machine, or other instrument for the purpose of forging a trade mark; or
(*f*) causes any of the things above in this section mentioned to be done,

shall, subject to the provisions of this Act, and unless he proves that he acted without intent to defraud, be guilty of an offence against this Act.

(2) Every person who sells, or exposes for, or has in his possession for, sale, or any purpose of trade or manufacture, any goods or things to which any forged trade mark or false trade description is applied, or to which any trade mark or mark so nearly resembling a trade mark as to be calculated to deceive is falsely applied, as the case may be, shall, unless he proves—

(*a*) That having taken all reasonable precautions against committing an offence against this Act, he had at the time of the commission of the alleged offence no reason to suspect the genuineness of the trade mark, mark, or trade description; and
(*b*) That on demand made by or on behalf of the prosecutor, he gave all the information in his power with respect to the persons from whom he obtained such goods or things; or
(*c*) That otherwise he had acted innocently;

be guilty of an offence against this Act.

(3) Every person guilty of an offence against this Act shall be liable—

(i) on conviction on indictment, to imprisonment, with or without hard labour, for a term not exceeding two years, or to fine, or to both imprisonment and fine; and
(ii) on summary conviction to imprisonment, with or without hard labour, for a term not exceeding four months, or to a fine not exceeding twenty pounds, and in the case of a second or subsequent conviction to imprisonment, with or without hard labour, for a term not exceeding six months, or to a fine not exceeding fifty pounds; and
(iii) in any case, to forfeit to Her Majesty every chattel, article, instrument, or thing by means of or in relation to which the offence has been committed.

(4) The court before whom any person is convicted under this section may order any forfeited articles to be destroyed or otherwise disposed of as the court thinks fit.

623

(5) If any person feels aggrieved by any conviction made by a court of summary jurisdiction, he may appeal therefrom to a court of quarter sessions.

(6) Any offence for which a person is under this Act liable to punishment on summary conviction may be prosecuted, and any articles liable to be forfeited under this Act by a court of summary jurisdiction may be forfeited, in manner provided by the Summary Jurisdiction Acts: Provided that a person charged with an offence under this section before a court of summary jurisdiction shall, on appearing before the court, and before the charge is gone into, be informed of his right to be tried on indictment, and if he requires be so tried accordingly.

3 (1) For the purposes of this Act—

The expression "trade mark" means a trade mark registered in the register of trade marks kept under the Patents, Designs, and Trade Marks Act, 1883, and includes any trade mark which, either with or without registration, is protected by law in any British possession or foreign State to which the provisions of the one hundred and third section of the Patents, Designs, and Trade Marks Act, 1883, are, under Order in Council, for the time being applicable:

The expression "trade description" means any description, statement, or other indication, direct or indirect,

- (*a*) as to the number, quantity, measure, gauge, or weight of any goods, or
- (*b*) as to the place or country in which any goods were made or produced, or
- (*c*) as to the mode of manufacturing or producing any goods, or
- (*d*) as to the material of which any goods are composed, or
- (*e*) as to any goods being the subject of an existing patent, privilege, or copyright,

and the use of any figure, word, or mark which, according to the custom of the trade, is commonly taken to be an indication of any of the above matters, shall be deemed to be a trade description within the meaning of this Act:

The expression "false trade description" means a trade description which is false in a material respect as regards the goods to which it is applied, and includes every alteration of a trade description, whether by way of addition, effacement, or otherwise, where that alteration makes the description false in a material respect, and the fact that a trade description is a trade mark, or part of a trade mark, shall not prevent such trade description being a false trade description within the meaning of this Act:

The expression "goods" means anything which is the subject of trade, manufacture, or merchandise:

The expressions "person," "manufacturer, dealer, or trader," and "proprietor" include any body of persons corporate or unincorporate:

The expression "name" includes any abbreviation of a name.

(2) The provisions of this Act respecting the application of a false trade description to goods shall extend to the application to goods of any such figures, words, or marks, or arrangement or combination thereof, whether including a trade mark or not, as are reasonably calculated to lead persons to believe that the goods are the manufacture or merchandise of some person other than the person whose manufacture or merchandise they really are.

(3) The provisions of this Act respecting the application of a false trade description to goods, or respecting goods to which a false trade description is applied, shall extend to the application to goods of any false name or initials of a person, and to goods with the false name or initials of a person applied, in like manner as if such name or initials were a trade description, and for the purpose of this

enactment the expression false name or initials means as applied to any goods, any name or initials of a person which—

(a) are not a trade mark, or part of a trade mark, and

(b) are identical with, or a colourable imitation of the name or initials of a person carrying on business in connexion with goods of the same description, and not having authorised the use of such name or initials, and

(c) are either those of a fictitious person or of some person not bonâ fide carrying on business in connexion with such goods.

INDEX